FORENSIC HUMAN IDENTIFICATION

An Introduction

FORENSIC HUMAN IDENTIFICATION

An Introduction

Edited by

Tim Thompson and Sue Black

BAHID

British Association for Human Identification

CRC Press
Taylor & Francis Group
Boca Raton   London   New York

CRC Press is an imprint of the
Taylor & Francis Group, an informa business

CRC Press
Taylor & Francis Group
6000 Broken Sound Parkway NW, Suite 300
Boca Raton, FL 33487-2742

© 2007 by Taylor & Francis Group, LLC
CRC Press is an imprint of Taylor & Francis Group, an Informa business

International Standard Book Number-10: 0-8493-3954-5 (Hardcover)
International Standard Book Number-13: 978-0-8493-3954-7 (Hardcover)

Library of Congress Cataloging-in-Publication Data

Forensic human identification / [edited by] Timothy Thompson, Susan Black.
    p. cm.
  Includes bibliographical references and index.
  ISBN 0-8493-3954-5 (alk. paper)
  1. Identification. 2. Dead--Identification. 3. Forensic pathology. I. Thompson, Timothy (Timothy J. U.) II. Black, Sue M.

RA1055.F67 2006
614'.1--dc22
                                               2006048966

Visit the Taylor & Francis Web site at
http://www.taylorandfrancis.com

and the CRC Press Web site at
http://www.crcpress.com

Foreword

The British Association for Human Identification (BAHID) held its first scientific meeting at Glasgow University in October of 2001. As it now approaches its fifth birthday, it has grown to more than 500 members with a respected and recognized academic profile. The individual interests of the membership encompass a wide variety of disciplines within this multifaceted area, and one of the strengths of the association has been the introduction of members to each other's areas of expertise at the scientific sessions. It was believed that an introductory textbook would be pertinent, especially as more than 20 percent of the members are undergraduate or postgraduate students.

The text does not claim to be a definitive reference on identification but rather seeks to introduce the reader to a number of the different specialties that operate under the umbrella of human identification. It does not cover every single aspect of the subject but draws upon the specific expertise within the association and aims to provide an introduction — primarily to the student, but also to others interested in unfamiliar areas.

The text has been separated into two parts. The first considers biological indicators and methods of determination in 21 chapters broken down into wider headings including biomolecular information, identification from prints and tissues, facial reconstruction, and personal effects. The second part considers the context and significance of biological human identification. It culminates in three case studies that exemplify the value of the identification process in criminal and humanitarian arenas.

In recent years, the headlines have been dominated by disasters such as the Asian tsunami and the London tube bombings, so that never before has biological human identification been more relevant. It is a pleasure, as president of BAHID, to highly recommend this book as an introduction and to thank the participants who have willingly contributed so much of their time and energies to this project.

Louise Scheuer
President, British Association for Human Identification

Editors

Tim Thompson is a lecturer in forensic anthropology at the University of Dundee, Scotland. He holds a Bachelor of Science (Honors) degree in archaeological science and geography, a Master of Science degree in forensic anthropology, a postgraduate certificate in higher education and a Doctor of Philosophy degree in forensic anthropology. He has been a practicing forensic anthropologist since 2000 in both the U.K. and abroad for the Foreign and Commonwealth Office (FCO), British police forces, and private clients. He is membership secretary for the British Association for Human Identification, a registered practitioner with the Council for the Registration of Forensic Practitioners, an accredited member of the Forensic Science Society, and a listed expert on the National Centre for Policing Excellence database.

Currently Dr. Thompson's main research interests include the examination of heat-induced changes in bone; improving methods of human identification; the legal, ethical, and social ramifications of forensic anthropology; forensic anthropology and education; and the management of mass fatality incidents. He has published many papers on these topics, and peer reviews articles for several leading forensic journals.

Sue Black, head of anatomy and forensic anthropology at the University of Dundee, is a founding director of the Centre for International Forensic Assistance. She holds a Bachelor of Science (Honors) degree and a doctorate in Human Anatomy. She also holds an honorary Doctor of Science degree in recognition of services to forensic anthropology and is a Fellow of the Royal Society of Edinburgh. Prof. Black has more than 20 years of experience in the national and international field of forensic anthropology and human identification, and has given evidence in criminal and coroner's courts in the U.K., Europe, and U.S. In her professional capacity as a forensic anthropologist, she has assisted the British government, various European and foreign governments, national and international police forces, military investigators, the U.N., and the FBI. She is lead assessor for forensic anthropology and a registered practitioner for the Council for the Registration of Forensic Practitioners, founder member for the British Association for Human Identification, and a registered expert with the National Centre for Policing Excellence. She was awarded the Order of the British Empire in February of 2002 for services to forensic anthropology in Kosovo.

Professor Black has published many academic papers and is coauthor of the award-winning text *Developmental Juvenile Osteology.*

Contributors

Sue Black
Anatomy and Forensic Anthropology
College of Life Sciences
University of Dundee
Dundee, U.K.

Teri Blythe
Identification and Reconstruction Department
National Missing Persons Helpline
London, U.K.

Dave Charlton
Scientific Support Unit
Leicestershire Constabulary
St John's, Enderby
Leicester, U.K.

James Clarkson
Ninewells Hospital
Dundee, U.K.

John Daugman
Computer Laboratory
University of Cambridge
Cambridge, U.K.

Vivianne Galloway
Scientific Support Unit
Leicestershire Constabulary
St John's, Enderby
Leicester, U.K.

M. Thomas P. Gilbert
Center for Ancient Genetics
Niels Bohr Institute
University of Copenhagen
Copenhagen, Denmark

William Goodwin
Department of Forensic and Investigative Science
University of Central Lancashire
Preston, U.K.

Michael G. Grant
Plymouth Marine Laboratory
Plymouth, U.K.

Sibte Hadi
Department of Forensic and Investigative Science
University of Central Lancashire
Preston, U.K.

James H. Hardy
Dental Centre, Minley
Gibraltar Barracks, Blackwater
Camberley, U.K.

Ian Hill
Department of Aviation Pathology
RAF Centre of Aviation Medicine
Henlow, U.K.

Emily Hines
Association of Forensic Radiographers
London, U.K.

George J.R. Maat
Barge's Anthropologica
Department of Anatomy
Leiden University Medical Center
Leiden, The Netherlands

Gaille MacKinnon
Independent Forensic Anthropologist
Banffshire, U.K.

Wolfram Meier-Augenstein
Environment and Engineering Research Centre
School of Civil Engineering
Queens University Belfast
Belfast, U.K.

Lynn Meijerman
Department of Anatomy and Embryology
Leiden University Medical Center
Leiden, The Netherlands

Christopher Milroy
Department of Forensic Pathology
University of Sheffield
The Medico-Legal Centre
Sheffield, U.K.

Amy Z. Mundorff
Department of Archaeology
Simon Fraser University
Burnaby, British Columbia

Terry Napier
Napier Associates
York, U.K.

Will O'Reilly
Operation Minstead
Kent, U.K.

Geoffrey Oxlee
Kalagate Imagery Bureau
Cambridgeshire, U.K.

Alan Puxley
Kenyon International Emergency Services
Bracknell, U.K.

Helena Ranta
Department of Forensic Medicine
Helsinki, Finland

Catherine Rock
Association of Forensic Radiographers
London, U.K.

Guy N. Rutty
Department of Cancer Studies and
   Molecular Medicine
Leicester Royal Infirmary
Leicester, U.K.

Maureen Schaefer
Anatomy and Forensic Anthropology
College of Life Sciences
University of Dundee
Dundee, U.K.

Louise Scheuer
Anatomy and Forensic Anthropology
College of Life Sciences
University of Dundee
Dundee, U.K.

Natasha Semmens
Department of Law
University of Sheffield
Sheffield, U.K.

Philip Sincock
Devon and Cornwall Police
Dorchester, U.K.

Iain Henry Stewart
LGC-Questioned Documents Section
Teddington, U.K.

Kari Takamaa
Department of Forensic Medicine
Helsinki, Finland

Andrew Thean
Institute of Applied Physics
Netherlands Organisation for Applied Research
The Netherlands

Tim Thompson
Anatomy and Forensic Anthropology
College of Life Sciences
University of Dundee
Dundee, U.K.

Cornelis van der Lugt
Politieacademie
Apeldoorn, The Netherlands

Wesley Vernon
Sheffield Podiatry Service
Sheffield, U.K.

Mark Viner
Association of Forensic Radiographers and
   St. Bartholomew's and the Royal London Hospitals
London, U.K.

Caroline Wilkinson
Anatomy and Forensic Anthropology
College of Life Sciences
University of Dundee
Dundee, U.K.

Andrew S. Wilson
Department of Archaeological Sciences
University of Bradford
Bradford, Yorkshire, U.K.

Sophie Woodforde
Identification and Reconstruction Department
National Missing Persons Helpline
London, U.K.

Introduction

Identity

In philosophy, "identity" is whatever makes an entity definable and recognizable, in terms of possessing a set of qualities or characteristics that distinguish it from entities of a different type. "Identification," therefore, is the act of establishing that identity. In the 17th century, John Locke proposed his *tabula rasa* (blank slate) philosophy, which concluded that the newborn child is without identity and that it is entirely defined by society and circumstances after birth. While this may have some basis for discussion in the worlds of metaphysics, psychology, and social anthropology it has restricted relevance in the worlds of disaster-victim identification, biometrics, and forensic science. It is, however, true to say that, although many of our parameters of biological identity may be acquired after birth (tattoos, trauma, disease, dental intervention, etc.), many are biologically inherent and established in the period between conception and birth (DNA profile, sex, fingerprints, blood group, etc.).

The United Nations Convention on the Rights of the Child is the only international convention that addresses the subject of identity as a fundamental human right by proclaiming that childhood is entitled to special care and assistance. There is no equivalent international article relating to the adult and therefore these rights pertain only until the age of 18 years or when the child is deemed to have attained majority. Articles 7 and 8 of the Convention explicitly refer to the child's right to an identity. Article 7 of the Convention establishes that, from birth, every child has the right to a name and to have that individuality recognized. Article 8 emphasizes the preservation of that identity and the fundamental importance of preserving that name, nationality, and family belonging.

The right to an identity is largely defined as the "existential interest of each person in not seeing the external or social projection of his or her personality upset, denaturalized, or denied." Yet the notion of human "identity" is a somewhat abstract and ephemeral concept that relies upon philosophy and psychology for its interpretation and implies the existence of a private space or lebensraum for each person regarding attitudes, actions, and beliefs. As such, we live under the somewhat misguided conception that each and every one of us is unique, although identical twins and doppelgangers highlight some obvious inconsistencies in this approach.

Further, the conundrum of mistaken identity and identity theft has fascinated humanity and formed the cornerstone of many aspects of literature, film, television, and criminal reality. Shakespeare, Gilbert and Sullivan, and Dumas are among the many literary masters who have entertained audiences with the well tried formula of identity deception, investigation, and ultimate moral satisfaction achieved through exposure and justice. Yet, by its very nature, misappropriation of identity is a crime that may require forensic assistance to reach a resolution and, in such a situation, scientific verification generally assumes central relevance.

Human Identification

We live in a society where personal and national security is ever more prominent on our agendas, and so we require more stringent and reliable measures to verify and secure our identities. Although, in Dumas' world of Martin Guerre, identity was finally established through trickery and confession, in today's world a simple DNA comparison with his son (Sanxi) would have solved the problem beyond all reasonable doubt. Biological indicators of identity harness the composite "uniqueness" of our bodies to provide signatures that can confirm our legitimacy with reasonable certainty and, by natural extension, confirm the provenance of our physical remains in the event of death. Maintaining and protecting the integrity of our identity has reached levels of unprecedented importance and has led to international legislation designed to protect our human rights. However, we rather confusingly also retain the rights to multiple identities (e.g., as performers do) and to change our identity (e.g., security personnel) and so the concept of assigning one single identity to one single physiological being is inherently flawed.

Equally flawed is the utilization of the word "identity." It originates from the Latin "idem" which means "the same," i.e., identical. This causes a rather conspicuous problem for identification in relation to biological organisms such as humans, as by their inherent nature they are not static, but grow and alter with the passage of time or the introduction of different environments or stimuli. The German philosopher Gottfried Leibniz proposed a law that states:

> X is the same as Y if, and only if, X and Y have all the same properties and relations. Thus, whatever is true of X is also true of Y, and vice versa.

For this argument to hold true, then change in any property would imply that the original form no longer exists and has been replaced by an entirely new form. Every little change in every little property would mean the whole original is destroyed. Leibniz's Law can be salvaged for the real world, however, when the statement is time-index-linked by allowing properties to be described as occurring at particular times and therefore accepting and recognizing the importance and effects of a time-related continuum.

The Greek philosopher Heraclitus upheld the metaphysical approach to identity and change by stating that "No man can cross the same river twice, because neither the man nor the river can remain the same." This is a fundamental problem in the confirmation of identity of a biological form as it does not remain "identical" at any two points in time. Philosophers have long tackled the thorny question of just how much change an identity can tolerate.

The quandary of change or replacement in relation to identity is typified by the "Theseus paradox." In classical Greek mythology, the ship that brought Theseus home from Crete (after the Minotaur incident) was faithfully preserved for generations. The old planks were removed as the wood decayed, putting in new and stronger timber in their place, insomuch that this ship became a standing example among philosophers for the debate over the constancy of identity in relation to change. One side held that the ship remained the same, while the other contended that it was not identical and therefore not the same.

But how much replacement is required, or can be tolerated, before that point of common identity is lost? The composition of the baby has been completely replaced, yet she retains the same identity as the teenager whose biological components will again be completely replaced by the time she becomes an old woman. Yet, in terms of identity of the individual, they are all considered to be one and the same person who has metamorphosed yet maintains a continuity of person through a traceable history and the retention of verifiable facts. But, does this still hold when the woman develops Alzheimer's disease and she can either no longer prove or recognize her own identity? This implies that identity can operate independent of the individual and is therefore a much wider social concept rather than solely restricted to appreciation of "self." Identity can of course be traced through reasonable channels of change but some specific characteristics are independent of extraneous change and therefore have the ability to operate on an isolated level. These verifiable biological parameters of identity exist independent of the internal psychological "self" (e.g. DNA, fingerprints, and blood grouping) and tend to be those inherent characteristics that develop between the period of conception and birth. Even in the world of identical twins and doppelgangers, these factors can retain the discriminatory capability to identify the individual beyond reasonable doubt.

Humans do not have the inherent capability exhibited by some life forms to display complete body transformation (e.g., the caterpillar into the butterfly). Yet there is some speculation that the rise in cosmetic surgery, organ and bone marrow transplants, blood transfusion, genetic engineering, and even cloning may be the human biological equivalent of the paradox displayed by the ship of Theseus.

Identification requires the comparison of two data sets to establish their likelihood of belonging to one and the same individual. Aristotle's law of identity states that for two objects to be identical then the predicate must equal (not approximate) the subject (i.e., A=A). Yet the concept of biological change requires greater flexibility in this law so that it is perhaps more appropriate to refer to it as A=A* (reflecting Leibniz's time-indexed law) where the asterisk introduces the possibility of accountable change. In the field of biological human identity it is essential that the value attributed to that asterisk be as small as possible. The distance between the two data sets, in terms of statistical probability, must be low if the two are to be linked with confidence and forensic credibility. It is vital that one of these data sets must be grounded in the certainty of verifiable identity. For example, the DNA sample retrieved from the toothbrush of the missing person must be shown to be indigenous and not a contaminant. Once verified, this information forms the baseline upon which other DNA samples will be compared until a match is confirmed — bringing together two data sets of identity information. A mistake in the verifiable data set will never lead to a confirmation of identity. This approach is central to the premise of DVI (disaster victim identification) rationale but is equally applicable to the suspect/perpetrator scenario or to the abductee/missing-person concept, all of which concentrate on issues of identification.

Therefore, in biological identity, we can accept that with regard to the definition of "change," an object changes with respect to a property, providing that object has that property at one time, and, at a later time, the object does not. What changes is the fact that the object has a particular property. The only way that property can change is if the object remains in existence. One can therefore think of a continuing object as the axis for change, or indeed the arena where change occurs. The confirmation of identity of the biological form therefore accepts change, and judicially we interpret that change through the realms of statistics, probability, and rationality. The formulation of the approach is therefore: How likely is it that "x" can equate to "y" knowing or assuming the potential for realistic change between the two points?

Forensic Human Identification

Human "identification" and, more specifically, the biological aspects of human identity, are grounded in the well defined and statistically verifiable sciences of biology, chemistry, and physics. The ability to evaluate the probability of biological identity is particularly pertinent to medico-legal investigations concerning the deceased. The requirement to establish the identity of the deceased tends to fall into three wide categories:

1. Criminal investigations resulting from an unexplained natural death, homicide, or suicide. It is virtually impossible to satisfactorily investigate a situation where one is confronted with a corpse to which no identity can be assigned. The investigating authority can carry the inquiries no further, as they cannot know whom to interview — family, friends, or colleagues. Most unidentified deceased in this situation result in an open case investigation with no resolution until identity can be secured.

2. Accidents and mass disaster incidents, whether as a result of forces of nature or human intervention, either accidental or intentional. The Interpol resolution on DVI recommended to all 184 member countries that they should adopt a common recording format and establish, where possible, a DVI team, thereby facilitating international cooperation and information sharing. The ultimate aim of all DVI operations must invariably be to establish the identity of every victim by comparing and matching accurate antemortem (AM) and postmortem (PM) data. It has been recognized that the inability to identify human remains has important economic and moral consequences for the families of the deceased and ultimately for the state. As this book is written in 2006, we have seen an unprecedented demand for human-identification capabilities both at home and overseas. The 2005 hurricane season will go down in meteorological history books as having the most named tropical cyclones, from Hurricanes Arlene, Katrina, and Rita through Hurricane Wilma, and on to inclusion of additional usage of the Greek alphabet for storms designated as alpha, beta, gamma, delta, epsilon, and zeta. Never before have there been 22 named tropical cyclones in any one-year period. In addition to this, we have witnessed the devastation of the Asian tsunami, the earthquakes in Iran, Pakistan, and Sumatra, terrorist attacks in London, Iraq, and Sharm-el-Sheikh, as well as plane crashes in Iran, Nigeria, and Cyprus, to name but a few. *terremoto*

3. War crimes and genocide. The Geneva Conventions of 1949 served to commit to international law the protection and amelioration of the wounded and sick involved in armed conflicts, prisoners of war, and civilians in times of war. Article 17 of Convention 1 states:

> Parties to the conflict shall ensure that burial or cremation of the dead, carried out individually as far as circumstances permit, is preceded by a careful examination, if possible by a medical examination, of the bodies, with a view to confirming death, establishing identity and enabling a report to be made. ... For this purpose, they shall organize at the commencement of hostilities an Official Graves Registration Service, to allow subsequent exhumations and to ensure the identification of bodies, whatever the site of the graves, and the possible transportation to the home country.

Interpol categorizes identity into two broad groupings: (1) circumstantial evidence includes information pertaining to personal effects (e.g., clothing, jewelry, and pocket contents) and also visual confirmation of identity by a relative, friend, or colleague; (2) physical evidence of identity is generally provided either by external examination of features, e.g., skin color, sex, tattoos, scars, or specific features such as fingerprints. Internal examination of the physical evidence of identity is achieved from medical/scientific information (e.g., healed fractures, pathological conditions, blood groups, DNA, or from dental evidence). It is generally accepted that the order of credibility for confirmation or establishing identity increases as the investigator passes from circumstantial evidence into physical evidence and particularly through to internal indicators.

It is not always possible to achieve a confirmed identity and Jensen (1999, p. xiv) described three categories of identity:

1. Positive or confirmed identity, which occurs when two sets of information are compared and enough specific unique data markers match to conclude that the records were, with all likelihood, created from the same individual. Furthermore, no irreconcilable differences are established. Unique data markers may include fingerprints, DNA, dentition, and even previously diagnosed medical conditions.

2. Possible or presumptive identity (BTB: believed to be) occurs when several individual factors are considered and, although no single factor alone justifies the establishment of identification, taken together the factors are sufficient for a possible or presumptive identification (ID). Factors may include identifiable personal effects, visual recognition, racial characteristics, age, sex, stature, anomalies, or individualizing skeletal traits.

3. Finally, Jensen proposed that exclusion occurs when all deceased in a definable category such as male or female have been identified and all surviving victims have been accounted for. BTB have all been confirmed and only one remaining deceased could not be someone else. No factors exclude identification.

There is an addition to this exclusion category that is particularly important. While it is impossible to confirm identity with "absolute" certainty, it is possible to exclude identity with absolute certainty. For example, when a skull washed up onto the beach on the west coast of Scotland recently, police thought it likely to be the remains of a known missing person in the area — a female of 42 years of age. The skull showed the presence of an active metaphyseal surface at the spheno-occipital synchondrosis indicating an age at death in excess of 18 years. This skull could not have been that of a 42-year-old. This capability to exclude with certainty is important and is a powerful tool in the identification process.

The recognition of a self identity may be a basic tenet of humanity and therefore, by extension, the scientific ability to confirm that identity is a natural progressive step. In a world where our physical security has never been less certain and our identity has never been so under siege, it is inevitable that the demands placed on the multidisciplinary subject of biological human identification will be challenging. The determination of biological identity of the living or the deceased is undertaken by forensic practitioners to fulfill our obligations to international humanitarian law, to uphold human rights, and to assist those who survive.

Sue Black

Further Reading

Bonasso, A. (2001). The Right to an Identity. http://iin.oea.org/default_ingles.htm.

Christen, H.T. and Maniscalco, P.M., *EMS Incident Management System: Operations for Mass Casualty and High Impact Incidents*, Prentice Hall, London, 2004.

Convention on the Rights of the Child (1990). http://www.unhchr.ch/html/menu3/b/k2crc.htm.

Dumas, A. (original publication 1839). *Martin Guerre*. Rogue Publishing. http://www.roguepublishing.com/cgi-bin/viewbook.cgi?value=g004.

Hamadi, R., *Identity Theft: What It Is, How to Prevent It and What to Do If It Happens to You*, Vision Paperbacks, London, 2004.

International Commission on Missing Persons. http://www.ic-mp.org. Last accessed 02.01.06.

International Committee of the Red Cross — Geneva conventions and Protocols. http://www.icrc.org/ihl.nsf/CONVPRES?OpenView.

International Covenant Civil and Political Rights (1976). http://www.unhchr.ch/html/menu3/b/a_ccpr.htm.

Interpol DVI. http://www.interpol.int/Public/Disastervictim/guide/default.asp. Last accessed 02.01.06.

Interpol resolution on Disaster Victim Identification (1996). http://www.interpol.int/Public/DisasterVictim/Guide/appendices.asp#d.

Jensen, R.A., *Mass Fatality and Casualty Incidents*, CRC Press, Boca Raton, FL, 1999.

National Aeronautics and Space Administration (NASA). http://www.nasa.gov/vision/earth/lookingatearth/record_breaker.html.

NHS Emergency Planning Guidance 2005. http://www.dh.gov.uk/PublicationsAndStatistics/Publications/PublicationsPolicyAndGuidance/PublicationsPAmpGBrowsableDocument/fs/en?CONTENT_ID=4121195&MULTIPAGE_ID=5441373&chk=/VR9qr.

PAHO (2004). Management of Dead Bodies in Disaster Situations. Disaster manuals and guidelines, Series No. 5, Washington, DC. http://www.paho.org/English/DD/PED/ManejoCadaveres.htm.

Universal Declaration of Human Rights (1948). http://www.un.org/Overview/rights.html.

Table of Contents

Part A

**BIOLOGICAL INDICATORS AND
METHODS OF DETERMINATION**.. 1

Section 1

**IDENTIFICATION FROM
BIOMOLECULAR EVIDENCE**... 3

1   DNA   5

William Goodwin
Sibte Hadi

**2   Stable Isotope Fingerprinting —
Chemical Element "DNA"?**   29

Wolfram Meier-Augenstein

Section 2

IDENTIFICATION FROM LATENT PRINTS 55

3   Fingerprints   57

Vivianne Galloway
Dave Charlton

4   Earprints   73

Lynn Meijerman
Andrew Thean
Cornelis van der Lugt
George J.R. Maat

Section 3

IDENTIFICATION FROM THE SOFT TISSUES 85

5   Physical Appearance   87
Ian Hill

6   Soft Tissue Pathology   99
Christopher Milroy

7   Soft Tissue Trauma   113
Guy N. Rutty

8   Surgical Intervention   127
James Clarkson
Maureen Schaefer

9   Hair and Nail   147
Andrew S. Wilson
M. Thomas P. Gilbert

Section 4

IDENTIFICATION FROM THE HARD TISSUES 175

10   Odontology   177
James H. Hardy

11   Osteology   199
Louise Scheuer
Sue Black

12   Radiography   221
Emily Hines
Catherine Rock
Mark Viner

Section 5

FACIAL IDENTIFICATION 229

13 Facial Anthropology and Reconstruction   231

Caroline Wilkinson

14 Facial Recognition and Imagery Analysis   257

Geoffrey Oxlee

15 Identifying Persons by Their Iris Patterns   271

John Daugman

Section 6

IDENTIFICATION FROM METHODS OF COMMUNICATION 287

16 Handwriting   289

Iain Henry Stewart

Section 7

IDENTIFICATION FROM PODIATRY AND WALKING 301

17 The Foot   303

Wesley Vernon

18 Footwear Marks   321

Terry Napier

19 Gait   343

Michael G. Grant

Section 8

IDENTIFICATION FROM PERSONAL EFFECTS 363

20   Personal Effects   365

Tim Thompson
Alan Puxley

21   Body Modification   379

Sue Black
Tim Thompson

Part B

THE CONTEXT AND SIGNIFICANCE OF FORENSIC HUMAN IDENTIFICATION.....................................401

Section 9

THE CONTEXT OF FORENSIC HUMAN IDENTIFICATION 403

22   Identity Fraud and Theft   405

Natasha Semmens

23   Biometric Identity Cards   415

Tim Thompson

24   Missing Persons in the United Kingdom   425

Teri Blythe
Sophie Woodforde

25   Crimes against Humanity and Other War Crimes   445

Helena Ranta
Kari T. Takamaa

Section 10

FORENSIC HUMAN IDENTIFICATION

CASE STUDIES 457

26 **The Rolex Murder, Southwest England** **459**

Philip Sincock

27 **The "Adam" Case, London** **473**

Will O'Reilly

28 **The World Trade Center — September 11, 2001** **485**

Gaille MacKinnon
Amy Z. Mundorff

Index **501**

Part A

Biological Indicators and Methods of Determination

Section 1

Identification from Biomolecular Evidence

DNA

1

WILLIAM GOODWIN
SIBTE HADI

Contents

1.1   Introduction 5
1.2   The Role of the Forensic Geneticist 6
1.3   DNA Structure 7
1.4   The Human Genome...7
1.5   DNA Polymorphisms Used in Forensic Genetics.....................8
1.6   Analysis of Short Tandem Repeats 10
      1.6.1   Collection of Biological Evidence....................................10
      1.6.2   Extraction of DNA 11
      1.6.3   Quantification of DNA 12
      1.6.4   Amplification of DNA — The Polymerase Chain Reaction (PCR) 12
      1.6.5   The Development of STR Systems.....................................14
      1.6.6   Detection of Amplified PCR Products...............................15
      1.6.7   Statistical Analysis of STR Profiles 16
              1.6.7.1   Allelic Frequencies, Hardy Weinberg Equilibrium,
                        and the Product Rule..17
1.7   Presentation of DNA Evidence 18
      1.7.1   Two Fallacies 19
              1.7.1.1   Prosecutor's Fallacy...19
              1.7.1.2   The Defendant's Fallacy 19
1.8   DNA Databases 19
      1.10.1   The U.K. National DNA Database 19
1.9   SNPs and Lineage Markers 21
1.10 Single Nucleotide Polymorphisms (SNPs)................................21
1.11 Lineage Markers..22
      1.11.1   Mitochondrial DNA 22
              1.11.1.1   Inheritance of the mtDNA Genome 22
              1.11.1.2   Polymorphisms in mtDNA 22
              1.11.1.3   Interpretation and Evaluation of mtDNA Profiles.........23
      1.11.2   The Y Chromosome 23
1.12 Future Developments 23
Further Reading...24
References 24

1.1   Introduction

The concept of DNA profiling was introduced in 1985 by Alex Jeffreys when he found that certain regions of DNA were highly variable between individuals (Gill et al. 1985, Jeffreys and Wilson 1985, Jeffreys et al. 1985b). Analysis of these polymorphic regions of DNA produced a "DNA fingerprint" — more commonly referred to now as a DNA "profile."

The DNA profiling technique was initially applied to paternity testing in the U.K., when in 1985 at the request of the Home Office, it was used to resolve an immigration case (Jeffreys et al. 1985a). Following this, it was applied to criminal cases. The first successful prosecution in the U.K. where DNA evidence played a central role was on January 22, 1988, when DNA profiling was successfully used to identify Colin Pitchfork as the person who had raped and murdered two girls in Leicestershire, England. It was soon applied to the problem of human identification, and in 1992 was used to confirm the identity of a set of skeletal remains from Argentina as those of Josef Mengele (Jeffreys et al. 1992).

Following these early successes, forensic genetics has become a key tool in forensic science and, 20 years after the first DNA profile was reported, all developed countries routinely use DNA analysis. Many countries also have national DNA databases that contain large numbers of DNA profiles.

The aim of this chapter is to provide an overview of the types of DNA profiling that are possible. The methodology involved with detecting polymorphisms will be briefly covered and, finally, one of the most important aspects of DNA profiling, the evaluation of the results, will be discussed.

1.2   The Role of the Forensic Geneticist

The forensic geneticist can be involved in cases ranging from the identification of material recovered from a crime scene to the identification of human remains and to paternity testing. In virtually all scenarios the role is the same: to extract DNA from biological material and generate a DNA profile from both unidentified and reference samples. Once the DNA profiles have been compared, it is then necessary to provide a statistical evaluation of the data. This is ultimately presented in the form of a report that will feed into an investigation and may ultimately be submitted to a court. The relationship of the forensic geneticist to other parts of the forensic process is illustrated in Figure 1.1.

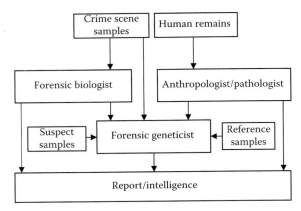

Figure 1.1   The role of the forensic geneticist.

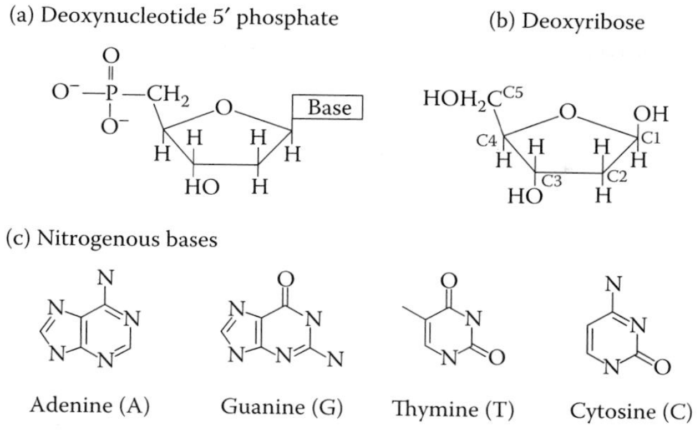

Figure 1.2 The components of the DNA molecule. The DNA molecule is made up of deoxynucleotides (a): the deoxyribose sugar (b) contains five carbon atoms (labeled C1 to C5); one of the four different types of nitrogenous bases (c) is attached to the C1 carbon, a hydroxyl group is attached to the C3 carbon, and a phosphate group is attached to the C5 carbon.

Before dealing with the technical aspects of DNA profiling the essential details of DNA structure and genome organization are briefly addressed.

1.3 DNA Structure

DNA is commonly referred to as "the blueprint of life" and carries hereditary information that an organism requires to function. The molecule that carries out such a fundamental biological role is relatively simple. The basic building block of DNA is the nucleotide (Figure 1.2a) which is composed of three different chemical groups: a sugar (deoxyribose) (Figure 1.2b), a phosphate group, and a nitrogenous base. There are four different types of nitrogenous bases in DNA: adenine, guanine, thymine, and cytosine (Figure 1.2c).

Throughout the DNA molecule, the sugar and the phosphate groups polymerize to form the sugar–phosphate backbone of the DNA molecule. This is invariant along the length of the molecule. The information within the "blueprint" is carried by the DNA molecule in the order that the four different nitrogenous bases are attached to the sugar–phosphate backbone (Figure 1.3a).

DNA normally exists as a double-stranded molecule. The two strands of DNA are held together by hydrogen bonds between complementary bases: adenine always pairs with thymine, and cytosine always pairs with guanine. The paired strands of DNA are therefore complementary (Figure 1.3b). A base pair (bp) is the basic unit of measurement for the size of a fragment of DNA.

1.4 The Human Genome

The genome can be defined as the genetic complement of a living organism. The human genome contains approximately 3,200,000,000 bp of information which is organized onto 23 chromosomes (Lander et al. 2001, Venter et al. 2001). Humans contain two sets of chromosomes. One version of each chromosome is inherited from each parent, giving a total of 46 chromosomes. Twenty-two pairs of chromosomes are autosomes and the

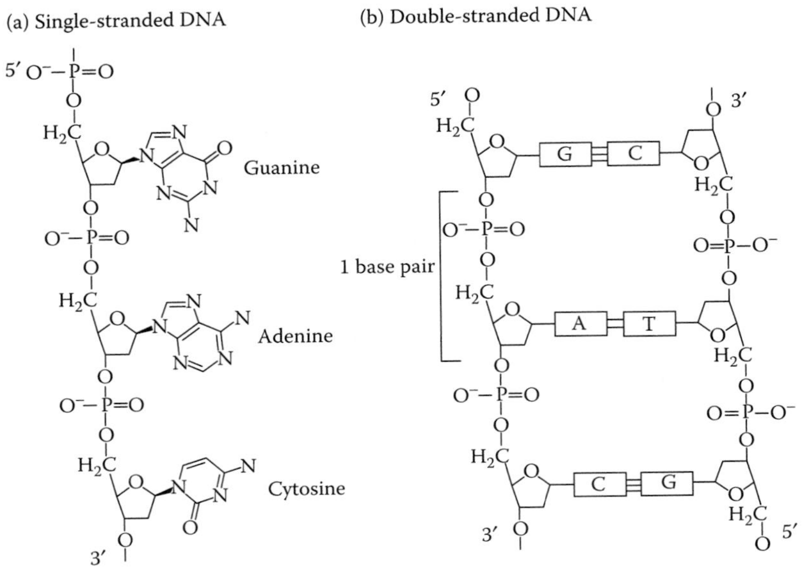

Figure 1.3 The DNA molecule: the nucleotides are joined together to form a single-stranded molecule (a) which is held together by covalent bonds. The DNA molecule is normally double stranded (b) with two complementary single-stranded molecules held together by hydrogen bonds; the double-stranded molecule adopts a helical structure.

23rd pair are the X and Y sex chromosomes. Females have two X chromosomes, whereas males have one X and one Y chromosome.

The regions of DNA that encode and direct the synthesis of proteins are called *genes*. These are the most extensively studied regions of the chromosome because they play a vital role in the structure and function of all cells. Some of the proteins that are encoded for by genes are polymorphic (occurring in more than one state), and these have been used extensively in forensic science. The best known system is the ABO blood typing system.

The development of molecular techniques has made the characterization of polymorphisms possible at the DNA level without having to analyze the protein directly. This has increased the amount of information available as less than 2% of the genome encodes for proteins (Figure 1.4). The analysis of DNA directly has also expanded the types of sample that can be successfully analyzed. DNA is found in nearly all cell types (red blood cells being an exception), whereas many of the polymorphisms protein are specific to particular cell types.

1.5   DNA Polymorphisms Used in Forensic Genetics

The vast majority of DNA, around 99.5%, is identical between individuals. The aim of forensic genetics is to differentiate between people, and it is therefore important to focus on the regions of the genome that are commonly different between individuals; these regions are polymorphic.

A large number of different types of DNA polymorphisms are found throughout the genome. To be an effective tool in forensic applications a polymorphism should be:

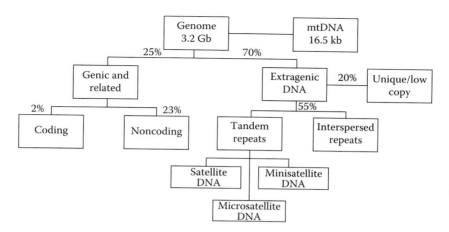

Figure 1.4 The genome can be classified into different types of DNA based on its structure and function. The DNA that encodes for proteins accounts for only around 3% of the genome; molecular techniques have made it possible to analyze all polymorphic sites in the genome. (based on Jasinska and Krzyzosiak et al. 2004.)

- Highly polymorphic (varying widely between individuals)
- Easy and cheap to characterize
- Simple to interpret
- Should have a low mutation rate
- Results should be easy to compare between laboratories

The class of polymorphism that has been widely adopted by the forensic community is the tandem repeat. Variable number tandem repeats (VNTRs) were the first class of polymorphism to be used for DNA profiling. Their use was however limited by the types of samples that could be profiled because a large amount of good quality DNA was required. Their use in forensic genetics has now been superseded by the use of short tandem repeats (STRs). The structure of a typical STR with a 4 bp core repeat unit is shown in Figure 1.5. STRs range in size between 100 and 350 bp and are highly polymorphic, with STR loci typically having between 5 and 15 alleles; the small size of STR loci make them highly amenable to profiling poor quality DNA samples that are often all that is available for forensic casework.

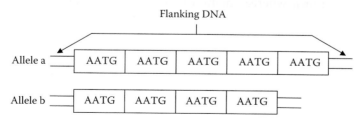

Figure 1.5 An example of the structure of a short tandem repeat DNA polymorphism. The two alleles differ by one repeat unit, and the amplified alleles will differ in length by 4 bp. The repeats are all orientated in the same direction. The DNA on either side of the core repeats is called a *flanking* DNA and is a nonrepetitive sequence.

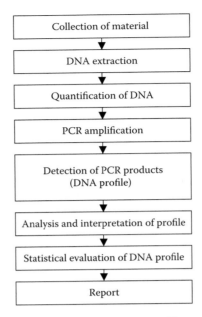

Figure 1.6 Processes involved in generating a DNA profile.

Another class of polymorphism, single nucleotide polymorphisms (SNPs), are used in specialist applications and are discussed later.

1.6   Analysis of Short Tandem Repeats

A large variety of sample types are amenable to DNA profiling. The exact procedures involved in the collection, storage of the samples, and the extraction of the DNA do vary between different types of samples, but the general steps that are involved in producing a profile are the same (Figure 1.6).

1.6.1   Collection of Biological Evidence

The potential sources of DNA are very diverse and include blood, buccal swabs, semen, and saliva (see Table 1.1). The integrity of the sample is of utmost importance in forensic casework. Contamination of evidence by biological material from another source is a very real possibility, especially when dealing with trace evidence. It is therefore vital that appropriate care, such as officers at a crime scene wearing full protective suits and face masks, is taken when collecting samples from a crime scene (Rutty et al. 2003). The method of collection will vary depending on the type of sample: bloodstains and contact marks can be swabbed initially using a sterile cotton swab that has been moistened with sterile water and then by using a dry cotton swab (Sweet et al. 1997). Liquid blood can also be collected using a swab. Evidence can also be taken from a person's body; for example, a vaginal swab would be taken following a rape. Other sources of evidence such as clothing are normally analyzed in the forensic biology laboratory where bloodstains and contact areas can be recorded before being submitted for analysis. Several types of evidence including semen, blood, and saliva can be tested chemically to facilitate locating the evidence or confirm the identification of a type of material present (Ballantyne et al. 2000, Anslinger et al. 2004).

Table 1.1   The Types of Biological Material That Can Be Used for DNA Profiling

Crime Scene Samples	Human Remains
Blood	Teeth
Semen	Bones
Hair	Muscle
Feces	Skin
Epithelial cells — shed skin cells:	Hair
Saliva	
Dandruff	*Reference Samples*
Clothing	Buccal swabs/venous blood from:
Cigarette butts	Parents
Touch DNA	Children
	Siblings
Suspect Samples	Maternal relations
Buccal swabs	Paternal relations
Pulled hairs (containing roots)	
Venous blood	Artifacts:
	Hair brushes
	Toothbrushes
	Razors, etc.

Reference samples have to be taken to compare with the unidentified sample. Reference material is routinely collected from suspects and in some cases, such as rape, from the victim of a crime. This may help the interpretation of the profiles, especially when mixtures are detected. The material is normally collected by swabbing the inside of the cheek (buccal swab) or taking a venous blood sample.

When using DNA profiling for the identification of human remains, the type of material that is used depends on what is available and also the state of degradation. If there is a significant time between death and the recovery of the body, then decomposing muscle, skin, and hair will be of limited use, and bone and teeth samples will be the material most likely to provide a DNA profile. Reference samples can be from a relative or an artifact that belonged to a missing person (see Chapter 20 for further discussion of this latter source).

1.6.2   Extraction of DNA

A diverse range of material can be submitted for DNA profiling, and several methods are available for extracting DNA. Some of the methods have restricted uses while others can be applied to most types of evidence. Methods that have proven to be popular for forensic samples are the Chelex extraction (Walsh et al. 1991), resin-based extraction (for example, Qiagen) (Scherczinger et al. 1997, Greenspoon et al. 1998, Johnson et al. 2005), and the organic (phenol-based) extraction (Sambrook et al. 1989). The different methods all work on similar principles. The first stage of any extraction involves breaking the cell membranes to release the contents of the cell into solution. Following this, the cellular protein is then denatured, and the DNA can then be separated from the bulk of the cellular material. The extraction from calcified material is more difficult and involves the mechanical disruption of the material to produce a powder before the cellular material can be dissolved in an aqueous solution. The process after this is similar to DNA from other types of samples.

1.6.3   Quantification of DNA

After extracting DNA, measuring the amount of DNA in the extract enables the appropriate amount of DNA to be added to the PCR reaction (see below). The amounts of DNA that are recovered from forensic samples can be extremely low and difficult to quantify and adding too much or not enough DNA will result in a profile that is difficult to interpret.

The simplest methods for detecting and quantifying DNA involve using dyes that bind to double-stranded DNA and fluoresce when exposed to light of specific wavelengths. Ethidium bromide is commonly used in molecular biology to detect and quantify DNA. Picogreen is also used and has the advantage that it is more sensitive. Another widely used method of quantification involves placing a small amount of DNA extract onto a nylon membrane and then challenging the membrane with a labeled human-specific probe that binds to human DNA. The label on the probe can then be detected chemically, and the amount of signal is proportional to the amount of DNA. This quantification method provides a useful estimate and is specific to human DNA, but it is limited by its sensitivity. Real-time PCR, which is based on the amplification of a defined fragment of DNA, is becoming a common method for quantification. The amount of PCR product (see below) is measured as the cycling reaction proceeds. The major advantages of this methodology is that it is very sensitive, relatively rapid, and also human specific (von Wurmb-Schwark et al. 2002).

1.6.4   Amplification of DNA — The Polymerase Chain Reaction (PCR)

At the same time that the first DNA fingerprint was reported in 1985, a new method that has been described as being a molecular "photocopier" was being developed (Mullis et al. 1986). The polymerase chain reaction (PCR) can amplify a specific region of DNA billions of times over, and the technique has revolutionized all areas of molecular biology, including forensic genetics. The power of the technique is illustrated in Table 1.2; in theory, a single molecule can be amplified one billion fold by 32 cycles of amplification.

Table 1.2   The Polymerase Chain Reaction[a]

PCR Cycle	Number of PCR products	Comments
1	0	
2	0	
3	2	
4	4	
5	8	
6	16	
7	32	
8	64	
9	128	
10	256	
20	262,144	
28	67,108,864	Standard number of cycles using SGM Plus® and Identifiler™ kits
30	268,435,456	
32	1,073,741,824	Standard number of cycles using the PowerPlex 16® kit
34	4,294,967,296	Maximum number of cycles normally used in forensic analysis

[a] Theoretically, it can multiply DNA over 1 billionfold after 32 cycles. In reality, it is not 100% efficient but is still extremely powerful.

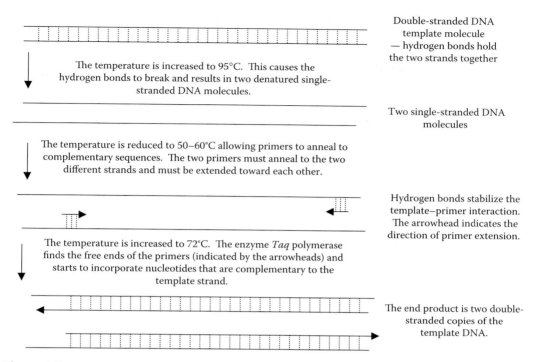

The temperature is increased to 95°C. This causes the hydrogen bonds to break and results in two denatured single-stranded DNA molecules.

Double-stranded DNA template molecule — hydrogen bonds hold the two strands together

Two single-stranded DNA molecules

The temperature is reduced to 50–60°C allowing primers to anneal to complementary sequences. The two primers must anneal to the two different strands and must be extended toward each other.

Hydrogen bonds stabilize the template–primer interaction. The arrowhead indicates the direction of primer extension.

The temperature is increased to 72°C. The enzyme *Taq* polymerase finds the free ends of the primers (indicated by the arrowheads) and starts to incorporate nucleotides that are complementary to the template strand.

The end product is two double-stranded copies of the template DNA.

Figure 1.7 The PCR reaction. Each PCR cycle consists of denaturation, annealing, and extension.

The increased sensitivity of DNA profiling using PCR has had a dramatic effect on the types of sample that can yield a DNA profile; it is now possible to successfully profile trace evidence and highly degraded samples — albeit with less than 100% success.

All that is required to carry out PCR is target DNA (isolated from an evidential sample), two primers, a thermo-stable enzyme (*Taq* polymerase), and nucleotides. The primers are short pieces of synthesized single-stranded DNA, which bind to specific regions of the target DNA and define the region that is to be amplified. Once the components of the reaction have been combined in a single tube (the reaction volumes are routinely between 5 and 50 μl) the temperature is changed in a tightly controlled cycle. The most common cycles contain three phases (Figure 1.7), each one lasting approximately 60 seconds:

Denaturation: The reaction is heated to 95°C. This causes the double-stranded DNA molecule to "melt" forming two single-stranded molecules. DNA melts at this temperature because the hydrogen bonds that hold the two strands of the DNA molecule together are relatively weak.

Annealing: The temperature is reduced to between 50 and 60°C. At this temperature the DNA will begin to renature, the primers are in a high concentration, and so these find and anneal to "melted" single-stranded DNA before the DNA template molecule can renature.

Extension: Once the primers have been given the opportunity to anneal, then the temperature is increased to 72°C, which is the optimum temperature for the *Taq* polymerase. This enzyme adds nucleotides to the 3′ ends of the primers using the original DNA strand as a template. The end product is an exact copy of the part of the original DNA molecule that was defined by the two primers.

The normal range of cycles for a PCR reaction is between 28 and 32. In extreme cases, where the amount of target DNA is very low, the cycle number can be increased to up to

Table 1.3   STR Systems That Have Been Widely Used in the U.K.

QUAD	SGM	SGM Plus	CODIS
	Amelogenin	Amelogenin	Amelogenin
vWA	vWA	vWA	vWA
THO1	THO1	THO1	THO1
F13A1	D8S1179	D8S1179	D8S1179
FES	D21S11	D21S11	D21S11
	D18S51	D18S51	D18S51
	FGA	FGA	FGA
		D3S1358	D3S1358
		D16S359	D16S359
		D2S1338	TPOX CSF1PO D5S818
		D19S433	D13S317
			D7S820

Note: The QUAD was introduced in 1993, the SGM in 1995, and the SGM Plus in 1998. The CODIS loci were selected in 1998. Two commercial kits, the Identifiler™ (Applied Biosystems USA) and Powerplex 16 (Promega® USA), incorporate the CODIS loci.

34 cycles. It has been demonstrated that going above this cycle number does not increase the likelihood of obtaining a profile but does increase the probability of artifacts forming during the PCR (Gill 2001a). Using 34 cycles is known as low copy number (LCN) PCR, and it is used sparingly as extreme precautions have to be taken to reduce the chance of contamination; the more cycles, the higher the chance of detecting contaminating DNA. In addition to the problems associated with contamination other artifacts can appear when using LCN. Because of the small number of template molecules, it is sometimes not possible to produce an accurate profile. Some alleles may not be detected ("drop out"), whereas some that are not part of the profile may appear ("drop in"). To help the interpretation, LCN is always carried out twice, and alleles are only called when they appear in each analysis.

1.6.5   The Development of STR Systems

Short tandem repeat loci suitable for forensic applications were first well characterized in 1991 (Edwards et al. 1991) and thousands have now been described. Individually STRs are not highly discriminating, but with the development of fluorescent-based detection of DNA, it is possible to simultaneously analyze several loci. This is termed *multiplexing*. The first multiplex introduced to casework in the U.K. was the QUAD (Table 1.3), which analyzed four loci (Kimpton et al. 1993, Lygo et al. 1994). This was successful but was limited by the power of discrimination, especially when the analysis of one or more locus failed, as was relatively common with the QUAD.

The QUAD was replaced by the SGM (Second Generation Multiplex) where two of the less successful loci were replaced by four different loci, and the amelogenin locus was added (Kimpton et al. 1996, Sparkes et al. 1996a; Sparkes et al. 1996b). The amelogenin locus is a region of DNA that can be amplified from both the X and Y chromosome. A 6 bp deletion on the X chromosome allows the X and Y chromosomes to be differentiated (Sullivan et al. 1993). The power of discrimination and the success rate of the profiling

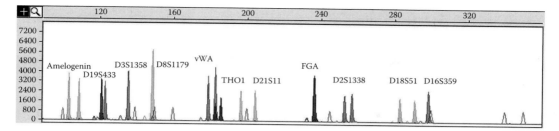

Figure 1.8 A full SGM Plus profile contains the amelogenin and 10 STR loci. The four different color labels allow loci that contain alleles with overlapping size ranges to be differentiated from each other and from the size standard. For example, D3S1358 and D19S433 are very close together but can be easily differentiated because D3S1358 is labeled with a blue dye, whereas D19S433 is labeled with a black dye (the dye is actually yellow but shown as black for visual clarity). In the above profile four loci (D19S433, D8S1179, FGA, and D16S359) are homozygous, containing two copies of the same allele; the other loci are heterozygous and have two different alleles. The nine smaller peaks that are not shaded are the size standard.

led to the SGM replacing the QUAD in 1995. The SGM was deemed to be powerful enough to justify the start of the national DNA database, and all entries into the U.K. database were made using the SGM technology until the SGM Plus was introduced. Four more loci were added to the SGM to make the total number of STR loci analyzed 10, plus the amelogenin. This system is currently used for standard analysis in the U.K. and many other countries (Cotton et al. 2000; Gill et al. 2003). The SGM Plus is very robust with a very high success rate for all of the loci, and its power of discrimination is extremely high. An example of a SGM Plus profile is shown in Figure 1.8.

In the U.S. the FBI selected 13 STR loci that would form the basis of their STR analysis. These are called the CODIS loci (Combined DNA Index System) (Budowle et al. 1999). Commercially available multiplexes have been developed that analyze 15 and 16 loci (including all the CODIS loci). These have extremely high powers of discrimination and are used widely for paternity testing.

1.6.6 Detection of Amplified PCR Products

After the PCR reaction the lengths of the different PCR products have to be measured. Polyacrylamide gel electrophoresis is used to separate DNA molecules by their size. An electrical current is passed across the gel, and this causes the DNA to migrate through the gel towards the positive electrode (the DNA is negatively charged). The smaller molecules pass through the gel at a faster rate than the larger molecules. The resolution of the gel system has to be very high as some STR alleles only differ in size by one base pair. Electrophoresis of the PCR products through polyacrylamide allows this level of resolution with DNA molecules that are between 20 and 600 bp.

The PCR products are labeled using a fluorescent dye that is attached to one of the two primers, and as the PCR products migrate through the gel a laser excites the fluorescent label. The PCR product can then be detected. Different fluorescent dyes that emit different wavelengths of light enable the detection system to differentiate between PCR products from different loci.

Different formats exist for polyacrylamide gel electrophoresis. The most commonly used systems are based on capillary electrophoresis. The polymer gel is injected into a

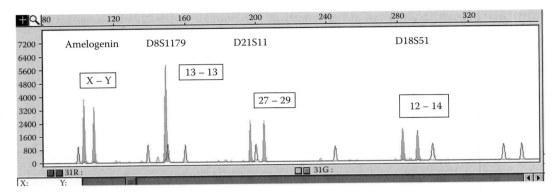

Figure 1.9 The green loci from the SGM Plus kit. The identity of the alleles is shown in the boxes. The amelogenin loci allows the sex of the sample to be determined; this profile is a male, X–X would be a female. The D8S1179 locus is homozygous whereas the D21S11 and D18S51 loci are heterozygous. The nine smaller peaks that are not shaded are the size standard.

capillary, and the PCR products are electrokinetically injected into the capillary, then migrate through the polymer. At a point along the capillary, a laser shines through a glass window and excites the fluorescent dyes that have been integrated into the PCR products. The fluorescence is detected and recorded.

A labeled PCR product appears as a peak on the computer output (the results are displayed on an electropherogram (Figure 1.8). Each peak on the profile represents an allele at a particular locus. If a person is heterozygous at a particular locus, two peaks will be detected. If only one peak is detected, the locus is homozygous. The combination of all the allelic peaks is called a *profile*.

To be able to interpret the results, the computer software has to calculate the size of the peaks. To do this, a size standard that contains a series of DNA fragments of known size (the internal size standard) is added to the PCR products before they are subjected to electrophoresis. The computer software calculates the sizes of the unknown fragments by comparison with the size standard. In Figure 1.9, an electropherogram displays the results from three loci: D8S1179, D21S11, and D18S51 (the green loci of the SGM Plus Kit). By measuring the size of the allele it is possible to assign each allele a number. This number represents the number of repeats that are present in the allele; the D8S1179 locus contains two alleles that both contain 13 repeats of the core unit; the D21S11 locus has two alleles, one with 27 repeats and one with 29 repeats; and the D18S51 also has two alleles, one with 12 repeats and one with 14 repeats. The complete profile is decoded in this way.

1.6.7 Statistical Analysis of STR Profiles

Generating a profile is only the first part of the analysis. Profiles then have to be compared. So, for example, if a profile has been generated from evidence collected from the scene of a crime, and it is compared to a suspect, there are two possible outcomes of the comparison: the profiles will be the same, or they will be different. If they are different the interpretation is simple: the evidence collected at the scene of crime is not from the suspect — this is an exclusion. If the profiles are the same, then it is an inclusion and the significance of the match has to be estimated. To illustrate the process the simple profile shown in Figure 1.9 will be analyzed.

Table 1.4   The Allele Frequencies in a Caucasian Population of the D8S1179, D21S11, and D18S51 Loci

Locus	Allele	Frequency (%)	Locus	Allele	Frequency (%)	Locus	Allele	Frequency (%)
	8	1.75		24.2	0.50		10	0.50
D	9	1.00	D	27	3.75	D	11	2.00
8	10	8.00	2	28	16.25	1	12	14.25
S	11	6.25	1	29	20.75	8	13	15.00
1	12	14.25	S	29.2	0.50	S	14	16.75
1	13	34.75	1	30	26.25	5	15	14.25
7	14	18.75	1	30.2	2.50	1	16	14.00
9	15	13.00		31	5.50		17	10.50
	16	2.00		31.2	10.50		18	6.00
	17	0.25		32	1.25		19	3.75
				32.2	7.25		20	1.50
				33	0.25		21	1.00
				33.2	4.00		22	0.25
				34.2	0.75		23	0.25

Source: SGM Plus User's Manual, Applied Biosystems.

1.6.7.1   Allelic Frequencies, Hardy Weinberg Equilibrium, and the Product Rule

The first step is to estimate the frequency of each of the matching alleles. This is done by profiling a sample of the relevant population. Normally at least 100 individuals are profiled and the frequency of each of the alleles is calculated. Table 1.4 shows the allelic frequencies of the alleles found in the D8S1179, D21S11 and D18S51 loci in a Caucasian sample.

With this information the genotype frequencies (referred to as genotype proportions) can be calculated; in other words, the frequencies of D8S1179: 13–13, D21S11: 27–29 and D18S51: 12–14 in the population. If we had a big enough database we could do this in the same way that we calculate allele frequencies. The problem with this approach is that the occurrence of many genotypes is low and it would be difficult to make accurate estimates.

Instead of direct counting, the Hardy Weinberg equilibrium model is used to predict genotype proportions. This is a model, published in 1908, that describes how alleles or genes behave in an "ideal" population. Like all models, the aim is to simplify the problems associated with complex systems. This entails imposing some assumptions that cannot be met. The assumptions of Hardy Weinberg equilibrium are: an infinite population size, completely random mating, no mutation, no selection, and no migration into and out of the gene pool. The important feature of a population from the point of view of a forensic scientist is whether a population behaves as if it is in Hardy Weinberg equilibrium, even though all of the five above assumptions are violated. In practice the departures from the Hardy Weinberg equilibrium are normally too small to have a large effect.

Using the Hardy Weinberg model a homozygote genotype is calculated using p^2 (where p is the frequency of the allele) and the frequency of a heterozygote genotype is $2pq$ (p and q are the frequencies of the two alleles; the letters p and q have been traditionally used to represent alleles). By using the allele frequency data (Table 1.4) it is possible to calculate the genotype proportions; the workings are shown in Table 1.5.

The final step is to calculate the combined frequency of all the loci. Assuming that there is no linkage between the different markers, this is done by simply applying the product rule and multiplying the individual genotype proportions together. The STRs that

Table 1.5 Application of the Hardy Weinberg Equilibrium Model to the Calculation of a DNA Profile Frequency

Locus	Genotype (allele frequency)	Equation	Genotype Proportion
D8	13–13 (0.3475–0.3475)	p^2	0.1208
D21	27–29: (0.0375–0.2075)	$2pq$	0.0156
D18	12–14: (0.1425–0.1675)	$2pq$	0.0478
Combined profile frequency			0.00009

Note: Based on the frequency data in Table 1.4, the D8–D21–D18 profile has an estimated frequency of 0.00009 in the U.S. Caucasian population.

are commonly used in forensic analysis are all on different chromosomes, and they are not linked. (The second law of Mendelian genetics states that the assortment of chromosomes during meiosis is independent.)

When dealing with profiles that contain more loci, the process is the same, with all the genotype proportions multiplied together. In the case of the SGM Plus, the probability of two profiles from unrelated individuals being identical is extremely small; the probability of two profiles drawn from the Caucasian population being identical is 2.99×10^{-13}. (This number can also be represented as 1 in 3,344,481,605,000).

Because there are limitations in the ability to predict profile frequencies and to allow for populations containing subpopulations, some correction factors are commonly used in casework that attempt to avoid overstating the strength of the evidence (see Further Reading).

This section has not covered the statistical analysis involved with kinship testing, which is an important component of criminal paternity testing and the identification of human remains. These areas are covered in depth in Buckleton et al. 2005; Butler et al. 2005 and Evett and Weir 1998 (see Further Reading).

1.7 Presentation of DNA Evidence

There are essentially three different ways to present the results of DNA profiling: these are the frequentist approach, the likelihood ratio, and Bayesian analysis. Bayesian analysis is commonly used in statistics but has not found widespread use for reporting DNA evidence to the courts, and so will not be considered further here.

The first two approaches are represented as follows, assuming that the profile shown in Figure 1.9 with a calculated frequency of 0.00009 [or 1 in 11,1111] was from a bloodstain found at a crime scene and also matched a suspect:

A frequentist approach (also called the *conditional match probability*) states the frequency of the profile seen in the evidence sample, given that it is also seen in the suspect. It would be worded as: "The DNA profile from the bloodstain found at the scene of crime matched the DNA profile of the suspect. The probability of finding a matching DNA profile if another unrelated male left the material at the scene of crime is approximately 1 in 11,000."

A likelihood ratio is the ratio of two probabilities of competing hypotheses, stated:
1. That the suspect left the material at the crime scene. The probability of the profiles being identical if they are from the same person is 1 (100%).
2. That somebody other than the suspect left the material at the scene of crime. (This value is the same as the frequency of the profile occurring in the given population.)

The likelihood ratio in this case would be $1/0.00009 = 11,111$, and this could be presented as: "The results of the DNA analysis are approximately 11,000 times more likely if the bloodstain was left by the suspect than if the bloodstain was left by a person unrelated to the suspect."

The actual match probabilities/likelihood ratios from SGM Plus profiles are routinely 10s or 100s of billions. In many laboratories a figure of 1 in 1 billion is routinely cited; this is believed to be sufficiently strong evidentially and removes the need to calculate individual profiles (the most common profile that is possible being greater than one in several billion).

1.7.1 Two Fallacies

Since the introduction of DNA evidence into legal proceedings, two common misrepresentations of the results have occurred. These are the prosecutor's and defendant's fallacies.

1.7.1.1 *Prosecutor's Fallacy*

This has been committed when representing the results of DNA profiling as a likelihood ratio. If the above likelihood ratio is rephrased to commit the prosecutor's fallacy, it may not be immediately obvious why the statement is incorrect. A fallacy could be worded:

"It is approximately 11,000 times more likely that the suspect left the bloodstain at the scene, given the results of the DNA evidence, than another unrelated person left the blood."

This is called *transposing the conditional*, and the effect is demonstrated by this example: An animal, if it is a horse, has four legs, therefore an animal, if it has four legs, is a horse.

1.7.1.2 *The Defendant's Fallacy*

Keeping to the same example, the defendant's fallacy would accept that the frequency of, on average, the profile is approximately correct and that it is likely to occur once in every 11,000 individuals. Based on the offense occurring in England, with its more than 50 million individuals, the argument would be that there are around 4550 people in England with the same profile and, therefore, the probability that the defendant left the blood at the crime scene is 1 in 4550. This is incorrect because not all individuals are equally likely to have left the blood; in most cases there are additional reasons to believe that the suspect left the blood or he would not have been arrested. The possible exception to this could be when the suspect is identified through searching a database.

1.8 DNA Databases

In 1995 the first national DNA database was established in the U.K. This national DNA database (NDNAD) was made possible by changes in legislation and advances in DNA profiling technology. The U.K. NDNAD currently contains approximately 3 million profiles.

When scene of crime officers find and recover biological evidence from a scene of crime (SOC), it can be submitted for DNA analysis. If a good quality profile is obtained then it is searched against the profiles that are present on the database, and any positive hits are reported. The SOC profiles are compared to the profiles that have been loaded from individuals. Figure 1.10 shows the number of profiles generated from criminal justice (CJ) swabs and scene of crime (SOC) samples that have been loaded into the U.K. NDNAD, along with the resulting number of matches between CJ swabs and SOC samples.

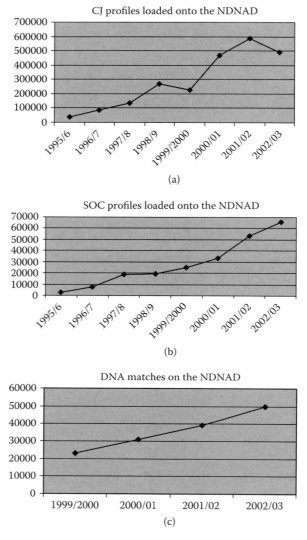

Figure 1.10 The number of samples loaded onto the U.K. NDNAD from criminal justice (CJ) swabs (10a), scene of crime (SOC) samples (10b), and matches between CJ samples and SOC (10c). Figures based on Williams et al. 2004.

In addition to matching scene of crime evidence directly to CJ profiles, it is also possible to search for people who may be in the database and are related to an individual that has left evidential material at the scene of crime; this is called *familial searching*.

Following the success of the U.K. NDNAD, many other countries have now established their own national databases. Many differences exist between the different databases; the sample that can be loaded onto the database varies widely as does the length of time the profiles remain on the database. The U.K. NDNAD is governed by relatively liberal laws that regulate what samples can be placed onto the database and also when profiles are removed. In England and Wales, any person who is arrested as a result of a crime having being committed can have his DNA profile loaded into the NDNAD; it will remain there indefinitely, even if the charges are dropped or the person is acquitted. This position contrasts strongly with several European countries, including the Netherlands, Sweden, Belgium, and France. In these countries, under current legislation, a profile is not placed into the NDNAD unless suspects receive a prison sentence, and the profile will be removed between 5–40 years after conviction (Schneider and Martin 2001).

1.9   SNPs and Lineage Markers

This chapter has focused on the application of STRs. These are by far the most commonly used forensic markers, and the vast majority of casework draw on STRs as a tool. There are, however, a number of cases where alternative DNA markers can be valuable.

1.10   Single Nucleotide Polymorphisms (SNPs)

The simplest types of polymorphism are single-base differences in the sequence of the DNA. These are called *single nucleotide polymorphisms* and are found every 1–2 kb (kb: 1000 bp) throughout the genome. Some regions are richer in SNPs than others; for example, chromosome 1 contains a SNP on average every 1.45 kb compared with chromosome 19 where SNPs occur on average every 2.18 kb (Thorisson and Stein 2003). SNPs are formed when errors (mutations) occur as the cell undergoes DNA replication during meiosis (cell division leading to the formation of sperm and ova). The mutations happen at a very low frequency at any given position, and the frequency is so low that most SNPs are considered to be unique events.

SNPs typically have only two variants; the different states are called *alleles* (Figure 1.11). This lack of diversity does not fit in with the ideal properties of DNA polymorphisms for forensic analysis. However, SNPs are so abundant that it is possible in theory to type hundreds of them, which will make the power of discrimination very high. To achieve the same discriminatory power that is achieved by the SGM Plus kit, approximately 50–80 SNPs would have to be analyzed (Krawczak 1999, Gill 2001b).

With the exception of the analysis of mitochondrial DNA, which will be discussed later, SNPs have not been widely used in forensic science to date, and the dominance of tandemly repeated DNA will continue for the foreseeable future (Gill et al. 2004). SNPs are, however, finding a number of niche applications including the analysis of highly degraded DNA samples. Profiling of the World Trade Center victims has acted as a catalyst for this application. Another application is the inference of ethnic/geographical origin of unknown crime scene samples and unidentified individuals (Frudakis et al. 2003, Wetton et al. 2005). The frequency of different SNP alleles characteristically varies between broad ethnic groups, lending themselves to this specialist application.

Allele 1   5′—GATGGCA—3′

*

Allele 2   5′—GATAGCA—3′

Figure 1.11   A single nucleotide polymorphism (SNP). Two alleles are shown which differ at one position indicated by the star: the fourth position in allele 1 is a G (guanine) while in allele 2 it is an A (adenine). In most cases, the mutation event at the specific locus which creates a SNP is a unique event and only two different alleles are normally found.

1.11   Lineage Markers

The Y chromosome and the mitochondrial (mtDNA) genome are passed down the male and female lineages, respectively, and both have properties that make them valuable in some circumstances.

1.11.1   Mitochondrial DNA

Mitochondria are energy producing organelle that contain their own genome; this is a circular genome which, in humans, is 16,569 bp long and encodes for 37 genes. Mitochondrial DNA analysis is a valuable tool in cases where the analysis of nuclear STR markers is impossible or impractical. There are three features of the mtDNA genome that make it a valuable forensic marker: there are 1000s of copies of the mtDNA genome in each somatic cell, the genome is polymorphic, and mtDNA is maternally inherited.

Crime scene material that is commonly profiled using mtDNA include hair shafts (Melton and Nelson 2001; Melton et al. 2005) and fecal samples (Hopwood et al. 1996). mtDNA analysis is also useful for the analysis of human remains that are highly degraded and not amenable to standard STR typing (Holland et al. 1993; Goodwin et al. 1999). Some human remains contain large amounts of DNA that are suitable for nuclear DNA profiling; however, there may be no close relative with which to compare the profile. In these cases, the maternal inheritance of mtDNA can prove to be a valuable trait (Gill et al. 1994).

1.11.1.1   Inheritance of the mtDNA Genome

The mtDNA genome is inherited through the maternal lineage. During fertilization of an ovum only the sperm head penetrates, the sperm head does contain a few mitochondria but these are not retained after fertilization (AnkelSimons and Cummins 1996).

The maternal inheritance is a useful feature in some circumstances, particularly when identifying human remains, as any maternal relative can be used as a reference. The maternal inheritance is also one of the weak points of mtDNA in a forensic context; all members of a maternal lineage, in the absence of any mutation event, will contain identical mtDNA genomes.

1.11.1.2   Polymorphisms in mtDNA

The mtDNA genome accumulates mutations relatively rapidly when compared to the nuclear genome (Brown et al. 1979). In most forensic cases the aim of the DNA profiling is to differentiate between individuals; therefore areas of DNA that display the highest levels of polymorphisms are analyzed.

Following the sequencing of the human mtDNA genome it was apparent that the D-loop was not under the same functional constraints as the rest of the genome. Some blocks within the control region are highly conserved but large parts are not. Two main regions are the focus of most forensic studies; these are known as *hypervariable regions* I and II, and contain the highest levels of variation within the mtDNA genome. Both of the hypervariable blocks are approximately 350 bp long, the level of mutation is not constant throughout the hypervariable regions, and some sites are hotspots for mutation, whereas others show much lower levels of alteration (Tamura and Nei 1993, Excoffier and Yang 1999, Meyer et al. 1999).

1.11.1.3   *Interpretation and Evaluation of mtDNA Profiles*

Either one or both hypervariable regions are sequenced. This allows the sequence of bases within the hypervariable region(s) to be determined. The sequence is compared to the Cambridge Reference Sequence (Anderson et al. 1981, Andrews et al. 1999), which was the first complete sequence of the mtDNA genome, published in 1981.

After the interpretation of the sequence data and the comparison of the questioned and reference samples, the forensic scientist has to assess, firstly, whether definitive matches or exclusions can be declared.

Whereas declaring a match is straightforward, declaring an exclusion can be more problematic. When a questioned sample and a reference sample differ at only one position, the likelihood of that difference occurring through a mutation has to be assessed, and the results are usually classified as inconclusive. When there are two or more differences between a questioned and known sample it is normally classified as an exclusion (Carracedo et al. 2000).

If a match is declared, the statistical significance of the match has to be assessed. The mtDNA genome is inherited as a single locus; this limits the evidential value of the marker in forensic cases. The sequence of the hypervariable regions (this can be the sequence in one or both regions) is called the *haplotype*. Haplotype frequencies have to be measured directly by counting the occurrence of a particular haplotype in a database. When databases are relatively small — for example, 100 — many of the less common haplotypes that are within a population will not be represented. The results are often expressed as a frequency, e.g., the mtDNA profile of the reference sample and the unknown sample are identical. This profile has been seen once in a database of 500 samples; matches can also be expressed as a conditional match probability or a likelihood ratio.

1.11.2   The Y Chromosome

The Y chromosome is one of the sex chromosomes. It contains the SRY gene that causes the developing fetus to become a male (Sinclair et al. 1990). As with all the autosomal chromosomes, the Y chromosome contains a large number of short tandem repeats (STRs) and single nucleotide polymorphisms (SNPs), which can be used to differentiate between different Y chromosomes (Prinz et al. 1997; Miller et al. 2005). The paternal inheritance of the Y chromosome has made it a useful tool for paternity testing, especially when the alleged father is not available for testing. In these cases, other males in the paternal lineage can be used as a reference (Foster et al. 1998). This feature of the Y chromosome can also be useful when identifying human remains. The other common application is the analysis of the male component of a mixed sample, particularly following a sexual assault (Corach et al. 2001, Sibille et al. 2002). When assessing the evidentiary value of a match, as with mtDNA, the profiles are not unique, and there may be hundreds of males in a given population with the same Y chromosome. Reporting the significance of a match using Y chromosome markers is done in the same way as for mtDNA.

1.12   Future Developments

In twenty years DNA profiling has become a central tool within forensic science, and its use will continue to expand. The technology used to analyze STRs for the purposes of matching samples from the scene of crime to suspects and paternity testing is well established and is unlikely to change fundamentally over the next ten to twenty years. Rather, the equipment and methodology along with the interpretation of the data will be refined. Portable testing facilities may play a limited role in the foreseeable future.

The use of DNA databases will also increase. Many countries are following the British model (although many are governed by legislation that provides its citizens with more rights) and some smaller countries are planning to profile the entire resident population; an idea mooted by senior police officers in the U.K.

More types of analysis will also become more commonplace, for example, using single nucleotide polymorphisms to infer the geographical origins of either scene of crime material or human remains. The analysis of compromised samples is also likely to develop further; the World Trade Center identifications acted as a primer for the development of SNPs for typing highly degraded remains that could not be analyzed using conventional methodologies.

Further Reading

Buckleton, J., Triggs, C.M., and Walsh, S.J., Eds., *Forensic DNA Evidence Interpretation*, CRC Press, Boca Raton, FL, 2005.

Butler, J., *Forensic DNA Typing: Biology and Technology behind STR Markers*, Academic Press, London, 2001.

Butler, J., *Forensic DNA Typing: Biology and Technology behind STR Markers*, 2nd ed., Elsevier Academic Press, London, 2005.

Evett, I.W. and Weir, B.S., *Interpreting DNA Evidence*, Sinauer Associates, Inc., Sunderland, MA, 1998.

Inman, K. and Rudin, N., *An introduction to Forensic DNA analysis*, 2nd ed., CRC Press, Boca Raton, FL, 2001.

Klug, W.S. and Cummings, M.R., *Concepts of Genetics* (International Edition), Prentice Hall International, Upper Saddle River, NJ, 2005.

Kobilinsky, L., Liotti, T.F., and Oeser-Sweat, J., *DNA Forensic and Legal Applications*, John Wiley & Sons, Hoboken, NJ, 2005.

Lincoln, P.J. and Thomson, J., Eds., *Forensic DNA Profiling Protocols*, Humana Press Inc., Totowa, NJ, 1998.

National Research Council, *The Evaluation of Forensic DNA Evidence*, National Academy Press, Washington, DC, 1996.

References

Anderson, S., Bankier, A.T., Barrell, B.G., Debruijn, M.H.L., Coulson, A.R., Drouin, J., Eperon, I.C., Nierlich, D.P., Roe, B.A., Sanger, F., Schreier, P.H., Smith, A.J.H., Staden, R., and Young, I.G., Sequence and organization of the human mitochondrial genome, *Nature* 290, 457–465, 1981.

Andrews, R.M., Kubacka, I., Chinnery, P.F., Lightowlers, R.N., Turnbull, D.M., and Howell, N., Reanalysis and revision of the Cambridge reference sequence for human mitochondrial DNA, *Nat Genet* 23, 147–147, 1999.

AnkelSimons, F. and Cummins, J.M., Misconceptions about mitochondria and mammalian fertilization: Implications for theories on human evolution, *Proc Natl Acad Sci USA* 93, 13859–13863, 1996.

Anslinger, K., Selbertinger, U., Bayer, B., Rolf, B., and Eisenmenger, W., Ninhydrin treatment as a screening method for the suitability of swabs taken from contact stains for DNA analysis, *Int J Legal Med* 118, 122–124, 2004.

Ballantyne, J., Serology, in Siegel, J.A., Saukko, P.J., and Knupfer, G.C., Eds., *Encyclopedia of Forensic Sciences*. Academic Press, San Diego, 2000, pp. 1322–1331.

Brown, W.M., George, M., and Wilson, A.C., Rapid evolution of animal mitochondrial-DNA, *Proc Natl Acad Sci USA* 76, 1967–1971, 1979.

Budowle, B., Moretti, T.R., Baumstark, A.L., Defenbaugh, D.A., and Keys, K.M., Population data on the thirteen CODIS core short tandem repeat loci in African Americans, U.S. Caucasians, Hispanics, Bahamians, Jamaicans, and Trinidadians, *J Forensic Sci* 44, 1277–1286, 1999.

Carracedo, A., Bar, W., Lincoln, P., Mayr, W., Morling, N., Olaisen, B., Schneider, P., Budowle, B., Brinkmann, B., Gill, P., Holland, M., Tully, G., and Wilson, M., DNA commission of the international society for forensic genetics: guidelines for mitochondrial DNA typing, *Forensic Sci Int* 110, 79–85, 2000.

Corach, D., Risso, L.F., Marino, M., Penacino, G., and Sala, A., Routine Y-STR typing in forensic casework, *Forensic Sci Int* 118, 131–135, 2001.

Cotton, E.A., Allsop, R.F., Guest, J.L., Frazier, R.R.E., Koumi, P., Callow, I.P., Seager, A., and Sparkes, R.L., Validation of the AMPFlSTR (R) SGM Plus (TM) system for use in forensic casework, *Forensic Sci Int* 112, 151–161, 2000.

Edwards, A., Civitello, A., Hammond, H.A., Caskey, C.T., DNA typing and genetic-mapping with trimeric and tetrameric tandem repeats, *Am J Hum Genet* 49, 746–756, 1991.

Excoffier, L. and Yang, Z.H., Substitution rate variation among sites in mitochondrial hypervariable region I of humans and chimpanzees, *Mol Biol Evol* 16, 1357–1368, 1999.

Foster, E.A., Jobling, M.A., Taylor, P.G., Donnelly, P., de Knijff, P., Mieremet, R., Zerjal, T., and Tyler-Smith, C., Jefferson fathered slave's last child, *Nature* 396, 27–28, 1998.

Frudakis, T., Venkateswarlu, K., Thomas, M.J., Gaskin, Z., Ginjupalli, S., Gunturi, S., Ponnuswamy, V., Natarajan, S., and Nachimuthu, P.K., A classifier for the SNP-based inference of ancestry, *J Forensic Sci* 48, 771–782, 2003.

Gill, P., Application of low copy number DNA profiling, *Croatian Med J* 42, 229–232, 2001a.

Gill, P., An assessment of the utility of single nucleotide polymorphisms (SNPs) for forensic purposes, *Int J Legal Med* 114, 204–210, 2001b.

Gill, P., Foreman, L., Buckleton, J.S., Triggs, C.M., and Allen, H., A comparison of adjustment methods to test the robustness of an STR DNA database comprised of 24 European populations, *Forensic Sci Int* 131, 184–196, 2003.

Gill, P., Ivanov, P.L., Kimpton, C., Piercy, R., Benson, N., Tully, G., Evett, I., Hagelberg, E., and Sullivan, K., Identification of the remains of the Romanov family by DNA analysis, *Nat Genet* 6, 130–135, 1994.

Gill, P., Jeffreys, A.J., and Werrett, D.J., Forensic application of DNA fingerprints, *Nature* 318, 577–579, 1985.

Gill, P., Werrett, D.J., Budowle, B., and Guerrieri, R., An assessment of whether SNPs will replace STRs in national DNA databases, *Sci Justice* 44, 51–53, 2004.

Goodwin, W., Linacre, A., and Vanezis, P., The use of mitochondrial DNA and short tandem repeat typing in the identification of air crash victims, *Electrophoresis* 20, 1707–1711, 1999.

Greenspoon, S.A., Scarpetta, M.A., Drayton, M.L., and Turek, S.A., QIAamp spin columns as a method of DNA isolation for forensic casework, *J Forensic Sci* 43, 1024–1030, 1998.

Holland, M.M., Fisher, D.L., Mitchell, L.G., Rodriguez, W.C., Canik, J.J., Merril, C.R., and Weedn, V.W., Mitochondrial-DNA sequence-analysis of human skeletal remains — identification of remains from the Vietnam War, *J Forensic Sci* 38, 542–553, 1993.

Hopwood, A.J., Mannucci, A., and Sullivan, K.M., DNA typing from human feces, *Int J Legal Med* 108, 237–243, 1996.

Jasinska, A., Krzyzosiak, W.J., Repetitive sequences that shape the human transcriptome. *Febs Letters* 567, 136–141, 2004.

Jeffreys, A.J., Allen, M.J., Hagelberg, E., and Sonnberg, A., Identification of the skeletal remains of Mengele, Josef by DNA analysis, *Forensic Sci Int* 56, 65–76, 1992.

Jeffreys, A.J., Brookfield, J.F.Y., and Semenoff, R., Positive identification of an immigration test-case using human DNA fingerprints, *Nature* 317, 818–819, 1985a.

Jeffreys, A.J., Wilson, V., and Thein, S.L., Hypervariable minisatellite regions in human DNA, *Nature* 316, 67–73, 1985.

Johnson, D.J., Martin, L.R., and Roberts, K.A., STR-typing of human DNA from human fecal matter using the QIAGEN QIAamp (R) stool mini kit, *J Forensic Sci* 50, 802–808, 2005.

Kimpton, C.P., Gill, P., Walton, A., Urquhart, A., Millican, E.S., and Adams, M., Automated DNA profiling employing multiplex amplification of short tandem repeat loci, *PCR-Methods Appl* 3, 13–22, 1993.

Kimpton, C.P., Oldroyd, N.J., Watson, S.K., Frazier, R.R.E., Johnson, P.E., Millican, E.S., Urquhart, A., Sparkes, B.L., and Gill, P., Validation of highly discriminating multiplex short tandem repeat amplification systems for individual identification, *Electrophoresis* 17, 1283–1293, 1996.

Krawczak, M., Informativity assessment for biallelic single nucleotide polymorphisms, *Electrophoresis* 20, 1676–1681, 1999.

Lander, E.S., Linton, L.M., Birren, B., Nusbaum, C., Zody, M.C., Baldwin, J., Devon, K. et al., Initial sequencing and analysis of the human genome, *Nature* 409, 860–921, 2001.

Lygo, J.E., Johnson, P.E., Holdaway, D.J., Woodroffe, S., Whitaker, J.P., Clayton, T.M., Kimpton, C.P., and Gill, P., The validation of short tandem repeat (STR) loci for use in forensic casework, *Int J Legal Med* 107, 77–89, 1994.

Melton, T., Dimick, G., Higgins, B., Lindstrom, L., and Nelson, K., Forensic mitochondrial DNA analysis of 691 casework hairs, *J Forensic Sci* 50, 73–80, 2005.

Melton, T. and Nelson, K., Forensic mitochondrial DNA analysis: two years of commercial casework experience in the U.S., *Croatian Med J* 42, 298–303, 2001.

Meyer, S., Weiss, G., and von Haeseler, A., Pattern of nucleotide substitution and rate heterogeneity in the hypervariable regions I and II of human mtDNA, *Genetics* 152, 1103–1110, 1999.

Miller, R.D., Phillips, M.S., Jo, I., Donaldson, M.A., Studebaker, J.F., Addleman, N., Alfisi, S.V. et al., High-density single-nucleotide polymorphism maps of the human genome, *Genomics* 86, 117–126, 2005.

Mullis, K., Faloona, F., Scharf, S., Saiki, R., Horn, G., and Erlich, H., Specific enzymatic amplification of DNA in vitro: the polymerase chain-reaction, *Cold Spring Harbor Symp Quant Biol* 51, 263–273, 1986.

Prinz, M., Boll, K., Baum, H., and Shaler, B., Multiplexing of Y chromosome specific STRs and performance for mixed samples, *Forensic Sci Int* 85, 209–218, 1997.

Rutty, G.N., Hopwood, A., and Tucker, V., The effectiveness of protective clothing in the reduction of potential DNA contamination of the scene of crime, *Int J Legal Med* 117, 170–174, 2003.

Sambrook, J., Fritsch, E.F., and Maniatis, T., *Molecular Cloning: A Laboratory Manual*, Cold Spring Harbor Laboratory Press, Cold Spring Harbor, NY, 1989.

Scherczinger, C.A., Bourke, M.T., Ladd, C., and Lee, H.C., DNA extraction from liquid blood using QIAamp, *J Forensic Sci* 42, 893–896, 1997.

Schneider, P.M. and Martin, P.D., Criminal DNA databases: the European situation, *Forensic Sci Int* 119, 232–238, 2001.

Sibille, I., Duverneuil, C., de la Grandmaison, G.L., Guerrouache, K., Teissiere, F., Durigon, M., and de Mazancourt, P., Y-STR DNA amplification as biological evidence in sexually assaulted female victims with no cytological detection of spermatozoa, *Forensic Sci Int* 125, 212–216, 2002.

Sinclair, A.H., Berta, P., Palmer, M.S., Hawkins, J.R., Griffiths, B.L., Smith, M.J., Foster, J.W., Frischauf, A.M., Lovellbadge, R., and Goodfellow, P.N., A gene from the human sex-determining region encodes a protein with homology to a conserved DNA-binding motif, *Nature* 346, 240–244, 1990.

Sparkes, R., Kimpton, C., Watson, S., Oldroyd, N., Clayton, T., Barnett, L., Arnold, J., Thompson, C., Hale, R., Chapman, J., Urquhart, A. and Gill, P., The validation of a 7-locus multiplex STR Test for Use in Forensic Casework (I), *Int. J. Legal Med.* 109, 186–194, 1996b.

Sparkes, R., Kimpton, C., Gilbard, S., Carne, P., Andersen, J., Oldroyd, N., Thomas, D., Urquhart, A. and Gill., P., The validation of a 7-locus multiplex STR Test for Use in Forensic casework (II), *Int. J. Legal Med.* 109, 195–204, 1996a.

Sullivan, K.M., Mannucci, A., Kimpton, C.P., and Gill, P., A rapid and quantitative DNA sex test: fluorescence-based PCR analysis of X–Y homologous gene amelogenin, *Biotechniques* 15, 636–638, 1993.

Sweet, D., Lorente, M., Lorente, J.A., Valenzuela, A., and Villanueva, E., An improved method to recover saliva from human skin: the double swab technique, *J Forensic Sci* 42, 320–322, 1997.

Tamura, K. and Nei, M., Estimation of the number of nucleotide substitutions in the control region of mitochondrial-DNA in humans and chimpanzees, *Mol Biol Evol* 10, 512–526, 1993.

Thorisson, G.A. and Stein, L.D., The SNP consortium web site: past, present and future, *Nucl Acids Res* 31, 124–127, 2003.

Venter, J.C., Adams, M.D., Myers, E.W., Li, P.W., Mural, R.J., Sutton, G.G., Smith, H.O. et al., The sequence of the human genome, *Science* 291, 1304–1351, 2001.

von Wurmb-Schwark, N., Higuchi, R., Fenech, A.P., Elfstroem, C., Meissner, C., Oehmichen, M., and Cortopassi, G.A., Quantification of human mitochondrial DNA in a real-time PCR, *Forensic Sci Int* 126, 34–39, 2002.

Walsh, P.S., Metzger, D.A., and Higuchi, R., Chelex-100 as a medium for simple extraction of DNA for PCR-based typing from forensic material, *Biotechniques* 10, 506–513, 1991.

Wetton, J.H., Tsang, K.W., and Khan, H., Inferring the population of origin of DNA evidence within the U.K. by allele-specific hybridization of Y-SNPs, *Forensic Sci Int* 152, 45–53, 2005.

Williams, R., Johnson, P., Martin, P., Genetic Information and Crime Investigation, reported by Wellcome Trust, 2004.

Stable Isotope Fingerprinting — Chemical Element "DNA"?

2

WOLFRAM MEIER-AUGENSTEIN

Contents

2.1 Introduction 29
2.2 Background on Stable Isotopes 30
   2.2.1 Natural Abundance of Stable Isotopes.....................................30
2.3 Isotope Effects, Mass Discrimination, and Isotopic Fractionation.......31
   2.3.1 Isotopic Fractionation of ^{13}C in Nature....................................32
2.4 Stable Isotope Analysis at Natural Abundance Level 33
   2.4.1 Principal Considerations 33
   2.4.2 Instrumentation 34
      2.4.2.1 Bulk Material Stable Isotope Analysis (BSIA) 34
      2.4.2.2 Isotopic Calibration and Quality Control in EA-IRMS.....35
      2.4.2.3 Compound Specific Stable Isotope Analysis (CSIA).....36
2.5 Forensic Applications of Stable Isotope Profiling (SIP) 37
   2.5.1 Stable Isotopes and Physical Evidence 37
      2.5.1.1 Drugs 37
      2.5.1.2 Other Physical Evidence 38
         2.5.1.2.1 Paint...38
         2.5.1.2.2 Adhesive Tape...39
         2.5.1.2.3 Safety Matches..39
         2.5.1.2.4 Soil 41
   2.5.2 Stable Isotopes and Human Identification 41
      2.5.2.1 Light Element Isotopes in Human Tissue 42
         2.5.2.1.1 Stable Isotope Profiling of Murder Victims..................43
      2.5.2.2 Radiogenic Trace Element Isotopes in Human Tissue 47
2.6 Conclusions and Caveats..48
2.7 Acknowledgments...49
References 49

2.1 Introduction

The seemingly provocative title of this chapter was chosen deliberately, not to stir up controversy but to draw the reader's attention to the remarkable similarities between the organic, life-defining material DNA and the more basic, lifeless on their own, chemical elements in their various isotopic forms when examined in the context of forensic sciences in general and human identification in particular. Generally speaking, DNA evidence is at its most powerful when it can be matched against a comparative sample or a database entry, and the same is true for the information locked into the isotopic composition of a given material. Similarly, the specificity of a DNA match based on 6 loci and the theoretical specificity of a multi-isotope signature are equally matched. Consider two materials such as bone mineral and bone collagen and assume they may exist naturally in 10 different isotopic states per element. Analyzing the bone mineral for its isotopic composition with regards to oxygen (O), strontium (Sr), lead (Pb), and yttrium (Y), while analyzing the bone collagen's isotopic composition with regards to hydrogen (H), carbon (C), nitrogen (N), oxygen (O), and sulphur (S) would theoretically yield a combined specificity of $1/(10^4 \times 10^5)$ or $1/10^9$, i.e., 1 in 1 billion.

In the following chapter the background, theory, instrumentation, as well as application of stable isotopes in an identification context are discussed. In the main, this discussion will focus on stable isotopes of light elements of which all organic material is comprised. Given the limited number of cases in which stable isotope profiling (SIP) has been used to aid in the identification of victims of serious crime, examples of forensic applications of SIP other than human identification are also presented to illustrate the potential of this technique as a forensic tool.

2.2 Background on Stable Isotopes

2.2.1 Natural Abundance of Stable Isotopes

Of the 92 natural chemical elements, almost all occur in more than one isotopic form with the vast majority being stable isotopes, which do not decay, unlike radioisotopes, which are not stable and, hence, undergo radioactive decay. The word *isotope* borrows its origin from the two Greek words, *isos* meaning "same" and *topos* meaning "place or position." Hence, isotope means "in the same position." This refers to the fact that isotopes of a given chemical element occupy the same position in the Periodic Table of Elements, as they share the same number of protons and electrons but have a different number of neutrons. So, their chemical character is the same; they only differ in atomic weight.

Isotope abundances of all elements were fixed when the Earth was formed and, on a global scale, have not changed since. Figures usually quoted for isotope abundance refer to these global values, i.e., when considering the entire carbon mass of the earth system, the natural abundance of carbon-12 (^{12}C) and the one neutron heavier isotope carbon-13 (^{13}C) is 98.88 and 1.11 atom percent, respectively. However, compartmental isotope abundance of light elements is not fixed but is in a continuous state of flux due to mass discriminatory effects of biological, biochemical, chemical, and physical processes. For instance, when looking at individual carbon pools one finds some with a higher abundance of ^{13}C, such as marine carbonate sediments, whereas others are more depleted in ^{13}C, such as hydrocarbons found in crude oil.

Expressed in units of atom% and staying with the example of ^{13}C, these differences are very small, amounting to less than 0.1 atom%. To express these minute variations, the δ-notation in units of per mil [‰] has been adopted to report changes in isotopic abundance as a per mil deviation compared to a designated isotopic standard (Equation 1).

Various isotope standards are used for reporting isotopic compositions. By virtue of Equation 1, the δ-values of each of the standards have been defined as 0‰. Carbon stable isotope ratios are reported relative to the Pee Dee Belemnite (PDB) or the equivalent Vienna PDB (VPDB) standard. The oxygen stable isotope ratios of carbonates are commonly reported relative to PDB or VPDB also. Stable oxygen and hydrogen isotopic ratios are normally reported relative to the Standard Mean Ocean Water (SMOW) standard or Vienna-SMOW (VSMOW), as it is now called. Sulphur and nitrogen isotopes are reported relative to Cañon Diablo troilite (CDT) and atmospheric air (AIR), respectively.

Use of VSMOW and VPDB as standard reference points is preferred (and in some journals is now required) because their use implies that measurements have been normalized according to IAEA (International Atomic Energy Agency) guidelines for expression of δ-values relative to available reference materials on internationally agreed per mil scales (Coplen 1994, Coplen 1996).

$$\delta_s = ([R_s - R_{std}] / R_{std}) \times 1000 \ [\text{\textperthousand}] \tag{1}$$

In this equation, R_s is the measured isotope ratio of the heavier isotope over the lighter (e.g., $^{13}C/^{12}C$ or $^{2}H/^{1}H$) for the sample, and R_{std} is the measured isotope ratio for the standard (e.g., VPDB or VSMOW). To give a convenient rule-of-thumb approximation, in the δ-notation, a difference in ^{13}C-abundance of 0.011 atom% corresponds to a change in $\delta^{13}C$-value of 10 ‰. In other words, a change in ^{13}C abundance from 1.0893 atom% to 1.0783 atom% corresponds to a change in $\delta^{13}C$-value from −20‰ to −30‰ on the VPDB scale, respectively.

2.3 Isotope Effects, Mass Discrimination, and Isotopic Fractionation

If, for a given compound, a nonquantitative chemical reaction or a physicochemical process such as vaporization has taken place, this will be subject to mass discrimination (or associated with an isotope effect), which will cause a change in isotope abundance and, hence, isotopic fractionation. In principle, two different types of isotope effects can cause isotopic fractionation: kinetic isotope effects and thermodynamic isotope effects. In general, mass discrimination is caused by differences in vibration energy levels of bonds involving heavier isotopes as compared to bonds involving lighter isotopes. This difference in bond strength can lead to different reaction rates for a bond when different isotopes of the same element are involved (Melander and Saunders 1980). The most significant kinetic isotope effect is the primary isotope effect, whereby a bond containing the atom or its isotope in consideration is broken or formed in the rate-determining step of the reaction (Rieley 1994), e.g., the reaction between two amino acids leading to the formation of the peptide bond R-CO-NH-R′.

The second type of isotope effect is associated with differences in physicochemical properties such as infrared absorption, molar volume, vapor pressure, boiling point, and melting point. Of course, these properties are all linked to the same parameters as those mentioned for the kinetic isotope effect, i.e., bond strength, reduced mass and, hence, vibration energy levels. However, to set it apart from the kinetic isotope effect, this effect is referred to as the *thermodynamic isotope effect* (Meier-Augenstein 1999a), because it manifests itself in processes where chemical bonds are neither broken nor formed. Typical examples for such processes in which the results of thermodynamic isotope effects can be observed are infrared spectroscopy, distillation, and any kind of two-phase partitioning (e.g., liquid/liquid extraction). The thermodynamic isotope effect, or physicochemical isotope effect, is the reason for the higher infrared absorption of $^{13}CO_2$ as compared to

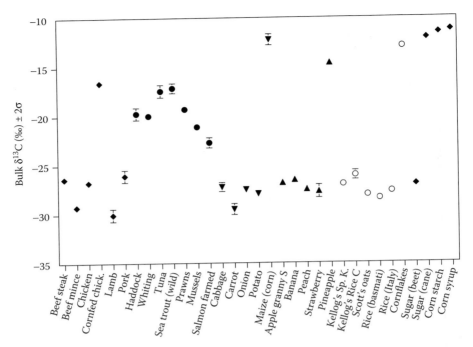

Figure 2.1 Bulk ¹³C isotope composition of different foodstuffs as measured by EA-IRMS. Error bars are ± 2σ but are not always visible due to scaling of the Y-axis. Purely for illustrative purposes, different symbols have been chosen to divide foods into meat, seafood, vegetables, fruit, and processed food.

$^{12}CO_2$, for the vaporization of ocean surface water resulting in clouds (water vapor) being depleted in both ^2H and ^{18}O, compared to ocean surface water, and for the isotopic fractionation observed during chromatographic separations.

2.3.1 Isotopic Fractionation of ¹³C in Nature

Going from the simplest organic compounds comprising only one carbon atom (C_1 bodies) such as methane or vegetation-derived methyl chloride to sediments or marine carbonate, the variation in natural abundance of ¹³C covers approximately 0.1 atom% or 90‰. This wide range reflects the varying degree of mass discrimination associated with the different photosynthetic pathways used by plants for carbon assimilation and fixation. To give an example, in terms of ¹³C isotopic abundance, beet sugar is not the same as cane sugar. In sugar beet, carbon dioxide (CO_2) fixation results in the formation of a C_3 body, 3-phosphoglycerate (3-PGA). This photosynthetic pathway of CO_2 fixation is known as the Calvin cycle. Plants using the 3-PGA pathway for CO_2 fixation such as sugar beet are commonly called C_3-plants. However, some plants make use of a different pathway. Here, CO_2 fixation yields a C_4-dicarboxylic acid, oxalo acetate, hence the term C_4-plants (the C_4-dicarboxylic acid pathway is also known as the Hatch-Slack cycle). The most important C_4-plants in terms of impact on dietary intake of ¹³C by domestic animals and (directly or indirectly) by humans are sugarcane, maize/corn (Figure 2.1), sorghum, and millet. The products of these two pathways are characterized by their different ¹³C abundance. Glucose derived from C_3-plants has a δ¹³C-value of about 25‰ whereas glucose derived from C_4-plants exhibits a more positive δ^{13}C-value of about 11‰ indicating a mass discriminatory bias towards $^{13}CO_2$ of the Hatch-Slack cycle.

Differences in ^{13}C-abundance due to different carbon fixation pathways are found in every compartment when analyzing total leaf tissue, total surface lipid extracts, or individual n-alkanes isolated from plants utilizing either C_3, C_4, and crassulacean acid metabolism (CAM) pathways (Collister et al. 1994; Rieley et al. 1993). The average δ^{13}C-values obtained from C_3 plant material are usually between 10 and 15‰ lower compared to the corresponding δ^{13}C-values obtained from C_4 and CAM plant material.

Although the vast majority of plants belong to the C_3 group (> 300,000) with bulk δ^{13}C-values of < 24‰, differences in the rate of photosynthesis (mainly caused by differences in climate and geographical location) and in enzyme kinetics of biochemical pathways result in subtle variations of $^{13}C/^{12}C$ ratios that can be detected by IRMS. Thanks to the sensitivity of modern IRMS instrumentation, inter- and intra-specific differences in δ^{13}C-values could be determined for n-alkanes and alcohols in sun and shade leaves from oak and beech ranging from 0.7 to 3.0‰ (Lockheart, vanBergen, and Evershed 1997). These subtle differences in δ^{13}C-values can be used to determine the origin of an organic compound and, thus, for example, authenticity of a particular plant product such as high quality single-seed vegetable oils (Angerosa et al. 1999; Angerosa et al. 1997; Kelly et al. 1997; Kelly and Rhodes 2002; Royer et al. 1999; Spangenberg, Macko, and Hunziker 1998; Spangenberg and Ogrinc 2001; Woodbury et al. 1995; Woodbury, Evershed, and Rossell 1998b; Woodbury, Evershed, and Rossell 1998a).

2.4 Stable Isotope Analysis at Natural Abundance Level

2.4.1 Principal Considerations

Scanning mass spectrometers (MS) use a single detector and therefore cannot continuously detect any particular isotopomeric ion pair of M^+ and $(M+1)^+$ simultaneously. To make isotope ratio measurement by MS at all possible, a conventional MS has to be operated in selected ion monitoring mode (SIM) to optimize sensitivity to selected masses, and mass analyzer conditions have to be changed rapidly to and fro for either mass to be detected half of the time. Therefore 50% of the detectable ion of either mass are lost to the data integration process, and the resulting limited accuracy and precision of such isotope ratio measurements in SIM mode permit only the detection of isotopically enriched compounds with a minimum working enrichment for ^{13}C and ^{15}N of at least 0.5 atom% excess (APE) (Preston and Slater 1994; Rennie et al. 1996). In other words, scanning MS cannot provide reliable quantitative information on differences in isotopic composition at natural abundance level caused by the kinetic or thermodynamic isotope effects mentioned above. For this reason, isotope ratio mass spectrometers (IRMS) have become the method of choice to determine the origin of a given organic compound by measuring its characteristic isotope "fingerprint."

IRMS instruments achieve highly accurate and precise measurement of isotopic abundance at the expense of the flexibility of scanning MS. IRMS systems have been designed to measure isotopic composition at low enrichment and natural abundance level. To this end, any complex material or compound subject to stable isotope analysis has to be converted into a permanent gas such as CO_2 or nitrogen (N_2) that must be isotopically representative of the parent material. The sample gas is subsequently introduced into the ion source of the IRMS. Once inside the IRMS, molecular ions emerge from the ion source and are separated by a magnetic sector set to a particular field strength throughout the experiment. Mass-filtered ions are focused onto dedicated Faraday cup (FC) detectors positioned specifically for the masses of interest. For example, IRMS instruments equipped to determine CO_2 for ^{13}C abundance analysis have three FCs for measurement of masses m/z 44, 45, and 46, positioned so that the ion beam of each mass falls simultaneously into the appropriate cup. The masses m/z 44, 45, and 46 correspond to the CO_2 isotopomers $^{12}C^{16}O_2$, $^{13}C^{16}O_2$, and $^{12}C^{18}O^{16}O$, respectively.

High-precision stable isotope analysis (SIA) of ^{13}C isotopic abundance at both natural abundance and low enrichment levels can yield measurements of $\delta^{13}C$-values with a precision of 0.12‰ on average. Thanks to this high precision, even minute changes in ^{13}C isotopic abundance of 0.5‰ can be reliably detected, irrespective of whether these minute changes have been caused by kinetic isotope effects associated with enzyme mediated biochemical reactions or batch-to-batch variations of reaction conditions during its chemical synthesis.

2.4.2 Instrumentation

Since the inception of the first continuous-flow (CF) interface to couple an elemental analyzer to a multicollector IRMS in 1983 (Preston and Owens 1983), CF-IRMS instruments have become an indispensable tool for stable isotope analysis (SIA). In a CF-IRMS system, a helium (He) carrier gas stream passes continuously into the ion source and sweeps bands or peaks of analyte gas into the source for analysis. This approach overcomes the sample size requirements for viscous gas flow because the He carrier gas stream maintains viscous gas flow conditions independent of sample size (Brenna 1994). Another benefit of the continuous flow set-up is that an isotope reference gas can be introduced into the ion source at virtually any time during an analysis, thus bracketing the sample peak between multiple reference gas peaks of known isotopic composition (MeierAugenstein 1997, Werner and Brand 2001).

2.4.2.1 *Bulk Material Stable Isotope Analysis (BSIA)*

Modern commercially available elemental analyzers (EA) provide an automated means for on-line high-precision stable isotope analysis of bulk or single component materials. Samples are placed in a capsule, typically silver or tin, and loaded into a carousel for automated analysis. From there, the sample is dropped into a heated reactor that contains an oxidant, such as copper and chromium oxide for C or S analysis, where combustion takes place in a He atmosphere with an excess of oxygen. Combustion products such as N_2, NO_x, CO_2, and water are transported in a carrier gas stream of He through a reduction furnace for removal of excess oxygen and conversion of nitrous oxides into N_2. A drying tube is used to remove all traces of water in the system. The gas-phase products are separated on a gas chromatographic (GC) column under isothermal conditions and detected nondestructively before introduction to the IRMS. Precision of measurement are typically SD($\delta^{13}C$) < 0.15‰ and SD($\delta^{15}N$) < 0.3‰ (Brand 1996; Hofmann and Brand 1996).

Oxygen and hydrogen are the two most recent elements for which EA-IRMS data of bulk or individual compounds have been reported. Oxygen-containing samples are converted on-line to carbon monoxide (CO) by pyrolytic reaction with carbon (the "Unterzaucher reaction") (Brand, Tegtmeyer, and Hilkert 1994). Several other reports using this principle subsequently appeared, showing elemental analyzer (Werner et al. 1996) or direct injection analysis (Begley and Scrimgeour 1997). In the case of nitrogen-containing compounds, CO is separated from N_2 using a GC column packed with molecular sieve 5Å. Precision of measurement for samples such as water and organic compounds are typically $SD(\delta^2H) < 2‰$ and $SD(\delta^{18}O) < 0.3‰$.

Nowadays, thanks to advances in electronics and instrument design, dual isotope analysis of ^{15}N and ^{13}C is possible from the same sample in one analytical run on a modern combustion/reduction EA-IRMS system. Provided good chromatographic separation of the N_2 peak from the CO_2 peak can be achieved, a high-precision magnetic field or accelerating voltage jump from ^{15}N to ^{13}C mode can be performed resulting in a total analysis time of 7 minutes per sample. Similarly, dual isotope analysis for ^2H and ^{18}O from the same sample can be carried out using a high-temperature thermal conversion EA (TC/EA). Here, high-temperature conversion of the sample on glassy carbon at 1400–1450°C is used to generate H_2 and CO. Both solid and liquid samples, the latter by means of a special liquid injector, can be analyzed for ^2H and ^{18}O simultaneously with total analysis time being as fast as 6 minutes per sample. In conclusion, EA-IRMS and TC/EA-IRMS would appear to be the method of choice for many forensic applications (drugs, explosives, hair, fingernails, etc.), either as a quickly performed initial measurement helping to focus efforts and resources or as a means to provide additional intelligence on samples for which conventional analytical methods do not yield sufficient information on similarity and provenance.

2.4.2.2 *Isotopic Calibration and Quality Control in EA-IRMS*

Stable isotope data are reported in the literature against an international standard (δ-values; see above). All modern CF-IRMS systems come equipped with an inlet permitting mass discrimination-free introduction of a suitable reference gas into the ion source. This approach safeguards against day-to-day variation in IRMS performance but does not address important issues such as "identical" treatment of sample and reference material (MeierAugenstein 1997; MeierAugenstein, Watt, and Langhans 1996) or quality control of results (Werner and Brand 2001). Since the nature of stable isotope analysis by EA-IRMS forbids mixing of the sample with a standard, good practice demands bracketing a batch of samples by a set of 2 certified standards of known yet different isotopic composition. In addition, system performance should be cross-checked at regular intervals by running an international reference material as sample. Typically, a batch analysis may comprise four or five actual samples run in triplicate with a standard in triplicate on either side acting as quality controls (QC). In addition, a batch should be preceded and followed by a set of triplicates of a second standard. Finally, two empty tin or silver capsules should be placed at either end of a complete sample set to act as blanks. An example of such a QC procedure is illustrated in Table 2.1, which shows a typical autosampler run comprising two sets of samples between two brackets; only the $\delta^{13}C$-values for the QC standards are shown. Raw data can thus be blank corrected and calibrated against the reference gas peaks by the proprietary instrument software. If necessary, $\delta^{13}C$-values can be drift-corrected according to the deviation of measured, reference gas calibrated $\delta^{13}C$-values from known $\delta^{13}C$-values of the standards acting as quality controls.

Table 2.1 Typical Setup of a Batch Run for ^{13}C Stable Isotope Analysis by EA-IRMS Together with Typical Results

Sample ID	δ^{13}C [‰]		
	Measured	Mean ± S.D.	Expected
QC1	30.62		
QC1	30.56	30.56 ± 0.14	30.52
QC1	30.46		
QC2	45.79	45.74 ± 0.07	45.54
QC2	45.69		
	Samples		
QC2	45.35		
QC2	45.79	45.57 ± 0.10	45.54
QC1	30.47		
QC1	30.57	30.52 ± 0.07	30.52
IS	10.51		10.40
QC1	30.58		30.52
IS	10.50		10.40
QC1	30.81	30.69 ± 0.16	30.52
QC2	46.23		
QC2	46.24	46.23 ± 0.01	45.54
	Samples		
QC2	46.24		
QC2	46.04	46.14 ± 0.14	45.54
QC1	30.70		
QC1	30.46	30.58 ± 0.16	30.52
QC1	30.58		

Note: QCn = quality control standard, IS = International Standard.

2.4.2.3 Compound Specific Stable Isotope Analysis (CSIA)

Accurate and precise stable isotope analysis depends on careful sample manipulation from sampling through to final sample preparation. In addition, in the case of on-line compound specific isotope analysis (CSIA) of individual constituents of a complex sample, high-precision CSIA also depends on high-resolution capillary gas chromatography (HRcGC) (Meier-Augenstein 1999a, Meier-Augenstein 2002). Demands on sample size, sample derivatization, quality of GC separation, interface design, and isotopic calibration have been discussed in a number of reviews (Brand 1996, Brenna 1994, Ellis and Fincannon 1998, Meier-Augenstein 1999b, Metges and Petzke 1999).

The need for sample conversion into simple analyte gases has prompted the design of a special interface adapted to the particular sample size and carrier gas flow requirements of capillary gas chromatography (cGC). In a set-up for either ^{13}C or ^{15}N CISA, the GC effluent is fed into a combustion reactor (C), either a quartz glass or ceramic tube, filled with copper oxide/platinum (CuO/Pt) or copper oxide/nickel oxide/platinum (CuO/NiO/Pt) wires, and maintained at a temperature of approximately 820 or 940°C, respectively (Merritt et al. 1995; Rautenschlein, Habfast, and Brand 1990). Users of this technique need to be aware of the influence of combustion tube packing on analytical performance of GC/C-IRMS (Eakin, Fallick, and Gerc 1992). Similar to the set-up discussed for BSIA above, for conversion of NO_x generated alongside N_2 during the combustion, a reduction tube, filled with copper (Cu) and held at 600°C, is positioned behind the combustion reactor. Next in line is a water trap to remove water vapor generated during combustion and most instrument manufacturers employ a Nafion™ tube for this purpose that acts as a semipermeable membrane through which water passes freely while all the other combustion products are retained in the carrier gas stream. Quantitative water removal prior to admitting the combustion gases into the ion source is essential because any water residue would lead to protonation of, e.g., CO_2, to produce HCO_2^+ (*m/z* 45), which interferes with the isotopic analysis of $^{13}CO_2$ (isobaric interference) (Leckrone and Hayes 1998).

Even more important, especially from a forensic point of view, is the following problem. Since organic compounds have to be converted into simple analyte gases, isotopically representative of the parent material, naturally all structural information that could otherwise be used to confirm the identity of the organic compound whose isotopic signature has been measured is lost. One potential "solution" to overcome this dilemma is to split the sample and analyze another aliquot of the same sample on a scanning GC-MS system employing the same, but not identical, chromatographic conditions that were used for CSIA on the GC/C-IRMS system. This approach relies ultimately on a mere comparison of gas chromatographic properties of a given organic compound such as its retention index or retention time, a *modus operandi* that could cause severe problems if such results were put forward as evidence in a court of law. This problem was recognized by the author, who, in collaboration with an instrument manufacturer, developed a hyphenated mass spectrometric hybrid system that enables CSIA, while at the same time recording a conventional mass spectrum of the target organic compound to aid its unambiguous identification (Meier-Augenstein et al. 1994). To this end, a GC/C-IRMS system was interfaced with an ion trap mass spectrometer to facilitate splitting of the GC effluent to the conversion interface with simultaneous admission to the ion source of the organic MS without incurring isotopic fractionation (Meier-Augenstein 1995, MeierAugenstein et al. 1995).

2.5 Forensic Applications of Stable Isotope Profiling (SIP)

Analytical methods currently applied in forensic science laboratories establish a degree of identity between one substance and another by identifying its constituent elements, functional groups, and by elucidating its chemical structure. Should the spectroscopic data of two compounds correspond, it may be concluded that they are chemically indistinguishable. Whereas it could be argued that although two substances in question are chemically indistinguishable, they may not be the same isotopically if they do not share the same origin or are derived from a different source. Stable isotope profiling (SIP) using IRMS enables one to establish as to whether two compounds or substances share a common trait or characteristic. With the help of SIP, forensic scientists will be able to link a person to an event, a crime scene, or a criminal organization (such as a drug cartel or terrorist group) based on a unique characteristic of physical evidence (Meier-Augenstein and Liu 2004).

As SIP has only been applied to aid human identification in five cases thus far, in addition to describing two of these cases, the following section also gives examples of other types of forensic evidence to which SIP can be and has been applied successfully.

2.5.1 Stable Isotopes and Physical Evidence

2.5.1.1 *Drugs*

Research carried out on cocaine has confirmed the potential probative power of isotope data by analyzing the ^{13}C and ^{15}N isotopic composition of trimethoxycocaine and truxilline extracted from coca leaves sampled at different geographic locations in South America (Ehleringer et al. 2000). Measured $\delta^{13}C$ and $\delta^{15}N$ values for whole coca leaves from Bolivia, Colombia, and Peru ranged from 32.4‰ to 25.3‰ and +0.1 to +13.0‰, respectively. Differences in light and humidity levels, the length of the rainy season, and soil fertility are thought to affect processes such as CO_2 fixation and cause the observed subtle variations in ^{13}C and ^{15}N composition. In conjunction with the variations in content of trace alkaloids (truxilline and trimethoxycocaine) found in cocaine, researchers were able to correctly identify 96% of 200 cocaine samples originating from the regions studied. This work confirmed that the stable isotope make-up of a substance is a function of its origin. In other words, two substances that are chemically the same may have different stable isotope compositions if either their origin/geo-location and/or (bio-) chemical history differ (Ehleringer et al. 1999). The ability to demonstrate the origin of a natural compound or material due to its specific nature of isotope markers removes the defense that substances that are chemically indistinguishable may not necessarily originate from identical sources. SIP has therefore the potential to provide a significant advance to forensic science, intelligence gathering, and crime detection and reduction.

Of equal, if not more interest is the question as to whether SIP will be able to determine origin of semisynthetic and even fully synthetic drugs such as 3,4-(methyldioxy)-methylamphetamin (MDMA, known as "ecstasy"), thus implicating and identifying the "cook" or the clandestine lab where they were made, in much the same way in which SIP can provide information on geo-location or geographic origin of cocaine. A preliminary study to trace the origin of different batches of confiscated MDMA tablets by GC/C-IRMS allowed the discrimination of four different groups of MDMA tablets based on variations in their natural abundance $\delta^{13}C$-values. The same study showed that further discrimination could be obtained when using $\delta^{15}N$-values of MDMA (Mas et al. 1995). More recently, it was shown that observed variations in the $\delta^{13}C$ and $\delta^{15}N$ content of amphetamines can be attributed to kinetic isotope effects during synthesis and that isotopic characterization provides a means to identify the synthetic origins of illicit MDMA and other amphetamines (Carter et al. 2002a; Carter et al. 2002b). By combining δ^2H-, $\delta^{13}C$-, and $\delta^{15}N$-values from stable isotope analysis of seized "ecstasy" tablets, preliminary work carried out in the author's lab has given an indication of how BSIA of ground tablet material might be used as a fast screening tool to determine whether tablets from separate seizures are linked to a common batch (Figure 2.2).

2.5.1.2   Other Physical Evidence

SIP, especially when combined with other independent spectroscopic data, will significantly increase the probative power of analytical results for physical evidence such as fuel, explosives, fibers, textiles, paints, varnishes, wood, paper, plastics, adhesives including adhesive tape, and even soil — indeed, any nonbiological physical evidence in general.

2.5.1.2.1   Paint.   Paint is commonly encountered as forensic trace evidence and subjected to a variety of tests. The presence of paint on a foreign surface is regarded as being evidentially significant because it indicates contact with a surface as the result of trace evidence transfer.

A preliminary study carried out in the author's lab on 28 different architectural paints provided by a government agency showed that $\delta^{13}C$-values need to be different by at least 1.09‰, so two paint samples of unknown history can be discriminated on the basis of ^{13}C isotopic composition alone (Reidy, Meier-Augenstein, and Kalin 2005). In other words,

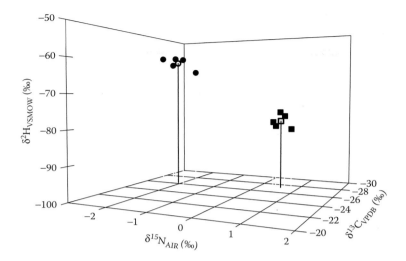

Figure 2.2 Three-dimensional isotope abundance plot of two different seizures of Ecstasy tablets. Five tablets from each seizure were analysed; ● = seizure A, ■ = seizure B, open symbols indicate corresponding mean values of 5 tablets.

should two paint samples exhibit $\delta^{13}C$-values within ± 1.09‰ of each other, these two samples would be indistinguishable by ^{13}C isotope analysis. This finding emphasizes the need for multidimensional data, including either more isotope markers such as ^{2}H and ^{18}O or the combination of single isotope analysis with data from other analytical techniques such as pyrolysis-GC/MS, inductively coupled plasma–mass spectrometry (ICP-MS), Fourier transformed infrared spectroscopy (FTIR), and FT Raman spectroscopy.

2.5.1.2.2 Adhesive Tape. Adhesive tape such as brown parcel tape is a commonly used tool by criminals for a variety of purposes such as the restraint of individuals during robbery and offenses against the person, the enclosure of explosive devices, and the packaging and concealment of controlled drugs. Packaging materials are ubiquitous in modern society and are mass produced, thus making it increasingly difficult to distinguish between different products or to link materials to a common source. However, stable isotope signatures hold the potential to characterize parcel tapes based on a number of properties. An initial study indicated the bulk ^{13}C signature of the entire tape, i.e., comprised of substrate polymer, associated additives, and adhesive to be seemingly highly characteristic of a particular tape, thus permitting samples from different sources to be readily distinguished. Analysis for ^{2}H and ^{18}O isotopic composition, as well as analysis of the isolated backing polymer, yielded even further discrimination (Carter et al. 2004).

2.5.1.2.3 Safety Matches. As part of a crime investigation, the author's laboratory has undertaken probably the first-ever attempt of a comparative analysis of wooden safety matches between matches retrieved from a crime scene and matches seized during a search of a suspect's premises. Match heads were removed using a scalpel, and the remaining matchsticks were prepared for stable isotope analysis by grinding them into a fine flour-like powder using a SPEX CertiPrep 6850 Freezer Mill (Glen Creston LTD). Milled samples were placed in labeled glass vials and stored in a desiccator over phosphorus pentoxide to remove residual traces of moisture. Bulk ^{13}C isotope analysis of matchsticks from a variety of brands

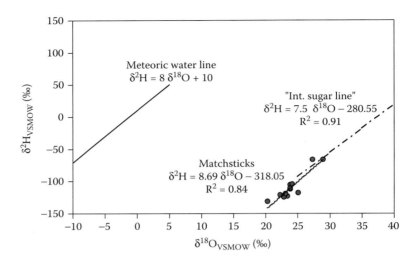

Figure 2.3 Plot of δ^2H vs. $\delta^{18}O$ values for wooden matchsticks with linear regression line. Both the meteoric water line and the trend line for plant sugars are shown for comparison.

and different batches of the same brand showed a potential variability in ^{13}C isotopic composition between matches from the same brand and box of up to 6‰. Given the limited range of ^{13}C isotopic abundance in whole wood of −30 to −20‰, it was clear that a mass-produced product such as matchsticks could not be differentiated on the basis of bulk ^{13}C isotope analysis alone (Farmer, Meier-Augenstein, and Kalin 2005).

In much the same way atmospheric CO_2 constitutes the only source of carbon for plants, water constitutes the only source of hydrogen. We therefore analyzed the samples for ^2H isotopic abundance and, at the same time, for ^{18}O isotopic abundance. As hydroxyl-bound H atoms in cellulose and lignin have the potential to exchange with H atoms in ambient moisture, all samples were exposed to the same ambient environment after collection so labile H-atoms prone to exchange would all reflect the same ^2H level, i.e., that of the ambient humidity in our laboratory. In other words, samples were analyzed in accordance with the "principle of identical treatment" (PIT) (Bowen et al. 2005), as under controlled conditions, any given offset will affect each sample the same way, so differences between samples will remain the same no matter where they are analyzed. After the equilibration period and subsequent grinding, samples were placed in labeled glass vials and stored in a desiccator containing phosphorus pentoxide to remove residual water from the sample prior to isotope abundance analysis. Entering the resulting data in an XY scatter plot showed the matchstick δ^2H and $\delta^{18}O$ values to be well correlated ($R^2 = 0.84$), falling on a line more or less parallel to the meteoric water line of precipitation (Figure 2.3). The reason for a correlation with an $R^2 < 0.9$ and the vast off-set of −318.05 is, of course, the fact that water is not the only source of oxygen available to the plant as oxygen present in cellulose and lignin is also derived from CO_2 and atmospheric O_2 (Fronza et al. 2002; Werner et al. 2004).

However, combining the results of the bulk ^2H and ^{18}O isotope analysis with that of the bulk ^{13}C analysis yielded a 3-dimensional plot, which quite clearly demonstrated that the matches retrieved from the crime scene and those seized at the suspect's premises were distinctly different (Figure 2.4). Whereas crime scene matches and our controls showed δ^2H-values of between −100‰ and −130‰, consistent with wood grown in Northern

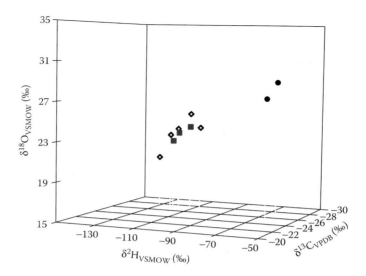

Figure 2.4   Three-dimensional isotope abundance plot of wooden matchsticks; ● = seized samples, ■ = crime scene samples. The open diamonds represent samples from five different brands of safety matches, which were analysed for control purposes.

European countries such as Scandinavia, matches seized at the suspect's premises were found to have δ^2H-values of around –65‰.

2.5.1.2.4   Soil.   Comparative analysis of soil samples has a long-standing tradition in forensic science. Routine comparisons usually involve several techniques in combination such as spectro-photometric color determination, laser diffraction particle size analysis, and chemical element analysis, with choice being dependent on several factors including sample size and character, time constraints, and cost limitations. In recent years, the potential use of continuous-flow isotope-ratio mass spectrometry (CF-IRMS) as an additional tool has attracted some attention and ^{13}C and ^{15}N isotope analyses have been carried out in situations that have arisen from forensic casework. The usefulness of $\delta^{13}C$- and $\delta^{15}N$-values has been demonstrated for discriminating between soil types and sample locations, even when sampling occurred at a different time. In cases of primary transfer, the combination of $\delta^{13}C$- and $\delta^{15}N$-values appears to be a valuable tool in discriminating between sites and in showing the relationship of the transferred samples to the relevant source soils (Croft and Pye 2004; Croft and Pye 2003).

2.5.2   Stable Isotopes and Human Identification

It is clear that SIP of human tissues cannot be used for the identification of human remains or living people in the same way that DNA profiling can. However, SIP can be used to reconstruct a geographic profile or geographic life history of an individual, alive or deceased, thus narrowing the potentially large number of possibilities to a small ascertainable figure. In this respect, SIP gained from soft and hard tissues can complement the biological profile provided by other identification scientists through examination of skeletal remains and interpreting skeletal markers with regards to age, sex, height, and race of the deceased. Information on geographic origin and geographic life history is particularly useful in cases where a body has been compromised too much for identification by

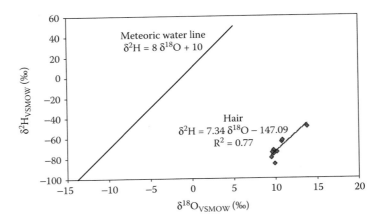

Figure 2.5 Plot of δ^2H vs. $\delta^{18}O$ values for human hair with linear regression line. The meteoric water line is shown for comparison.

distinguishing features (scars, tattoos, fingerprints, dental records) or by methods such as facial reconstruction. In addition to murder inquiries where bodies have been deliberately dismembered and mutilated to prevent identification, SIP can also been used in cases of extremely young victims of serious crime such as infants and neonates where the lack of distinguishing features hampers identification. Other potential applications for SIP of human tissues are disaster victim identification, people trafficking (people smuggling), and antiterrorism contexts.

2.5.2.1 Light Element Isotopes in Human Tissue

Variations in the isotopic abundance of ^2H, ^{13}C, ^{14}N, ^{18}O, and ^{34}S (Richards et al. 2003; Richards, Fuller, and Hedges 2001) in compounds forming the human body reflect the isotopic make-up of food and water consumed and as such reflect lifestyle and geographic origin of a person. In other words, diet and geo-location influence the isotopic signature of body tissues such as hair, nail, teeth, and bone, and can hence be used to aid human identification in cases where no material is available for DNA comparison or where no DNA match can be found. The basic principle behind establishing lifestyle and geographic life history using SIP is the fact that the body's only source of carbon and nitrogen is a person's staple diet. Similarly, the body's major source of hydrogen is water (H_2O), either from directly consumed water as liquid intake or from water indirectly consumed in foods such as fruit and vegetables. Based on a tracer experiment, there is evidence suggesting that at least 31% of hydrogen preserved in human hair is directly derived from ingested water with the remainder derived from hydrogen present in diet be it as water or be it organically bound (Sharp et al. 2003). For this reason, ^2H and to a degree ^{18}O isotopic composition of human hair is highly correlated to the isotopic composition of drinking water and virtually all the water we drink is ultimately derived from rain and snow fall (Figure 2.5). In much the same way that water is the major source of hydrogen for bio-organic compounds in the human body, drinking water is the major source of the oxygen for the formation of dental enamel and bone bio-apatite.

Mass discrimination associated with evaporation, condensation, and precipitation ultimately results in drinking water having different isotopic composition depending on geo-location. Depending upon temperature and distance to the open seas, δ^2H-values of meteoric water (precipitation) and, hence drinking water can range from 20 to −230‰ across the world with the "heavier" or less negative δ^2H-values typical of coastal / near equatorial regions and the "lighter" or more negative δ^2H-values typical of inland / high altitude / high latitude regions. Geographical information system (GIS) maps and contour maps of meteoric ^2H and ^{18}O isotope abundance are in the public domain (http://www.waterisotopes.org, the hydrogeology section of the IAEA at http://isohis.iaea.org/userupate/waterloo/index.html, and NASA at http://www.giss.nasa.gov/data/o18data).

Differences in dietary composition between Europe and North America lead to differences chiefly in ^{13}C and ^{15}N isotope abundances in body tissues of people living in either region. The main reason for this is the pervasion in the North American diet of sugarcane and sweet corn (both C_4-plants; see section titled "Isotopic Fractionation of ^{13}C in Nature") whether directly in the form of sugarcane-derived sugar or corn syrup–sweetened beverages (Brooks et al. 2002), or indirectly due to the use of sweet corn as animal feed for pigs and chickens (Figure 2.1). It should be noted that, though ^{15}N isotope abundance in body tissues is more indicative of a person's dietary habit, i.e., carnivore vs. omnivore vs. vegetarian, it must be treated with caution since factors such as health status, including pregnancy, influence the body's overall nitrogen balance (Fuller et al. 2004).

While hair and nail can provide a record of both diet and water through ^2H, ^{13}C, ^{15}N, and ^{34}S ranging from 10 days up to 6 months (Cerling et al. 2003; O'Connell et al. 2001; Sharp, Atudorei, Panarello, Fernandez, and Douthitt 2003), mineral material in bones and teeth reflect geographic environment by recording isotope signatures of elements present in drinking water, namely ^{18}O. The main component of tooth enamel is carbonate-hydroxyapatite, the mineral that gives bones their rigidity. Permanent teeth, and in particular tooth enamel, provide an ideal window into an unidentified body's geographic past. Enamel from adult teeth can provide an ^{18}O record of the drinking water and the region where a person has lived during childhood and adolescence, because tooth enamel does not remodel once formed. On the other hand, isotope signatures from bone apatite can yield information on a person's origin and life history because different bones and different types of bone grow and remodel at different rates. Broadly speaking, cortical bone has a slower turnover rate than trabecular bone (Teitelbaum 2000). Accordingly, long bones such as the femur remodel over a period of 20+ years, while predominantly trabecular bones such a ribs remodel approximately every 10 years (Hill 1998; Simmons, Pritzker, and Grynpas 1991).

2.5.2.1.1 Stable Isotope Profiling of Murder Victims.

Case A. In a murder case under investigation by the Police Service Northern Ireland (PSNI), the body of a young Caucasian female was found dumped in a ditch. Due to circumstances of the case and nature of the local area, 1200 DNA samples were collected from potential next of kin but no match for a relative was found, prompting the question by the senior investigating officer as to whether the person was actually of local origin.

Samples of scalp hair and bone (femur) were analyzed in our laboratory and cross-checked by another for isotopic composition of ^2H, ^{13}C, ^{15}N, and ^{18}O. Results of the ^{18}O analysis from bone apatite showed clearly that the deceased did not come from Northern Ireland, the Republic of Ireland, or mainland U.K. (Figure 2.6) but pointed toward either eastern Europe or the northern part of the U.S. as potential points of origin when comparing $\delta^{18}O$-values for drinking water calculated from measured $\delta^{18}O$-values of femur apatite (Longinelli 1984; Luz, Kolodny, and Horowitz 1984) with global $\delta^{18}O$ contour plots. Analysis of the hair samples for ^{13}C and ^{15}N isotopic abundance ruled out North America

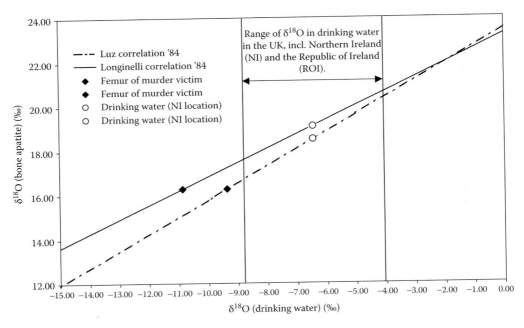

Figure 2.6 Correlation plot for $\delta^{18}O$ values from drinking water versus bone apatite. Irrespective of which regression line is used, both place the murder victim (◆) outside the range for drinking water in the U.K. and Ireland. The open circle represents a drinking water sample collected in Northern Ireland in the vicinity of where the victim was found.

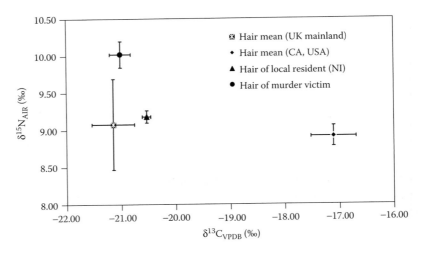

Figure 2.7 Two-dimensional isotope abundance plot for ^{13}C and ^{15}N composition from hair samples; error bars are ±1σ; values for U.K. mean and California mean are pooled means from 20 and 5 individuals, respectively.

as geographical origin (Figure 2.7). Even though an exact point of origin could not be determined due to compounding factors relating to the exact nature of the body, isotope signatures could clearly demonstrate the deceased did not originally come from the British Isles but most likely from eastern Europe or northern Scandinavia, thus providing valuable intelligence that helped to refocus the investigation.

Case B. In a murder case under investigation by the Garda (An Garda Síochána, Republic of Ireland), our lab was asked if we could provide intelligence on geographic and life history of a headless body of a male, aged between 35 and 40 years old and of African, Afro-American or Afro-Caribbean ethnicity. A complete set of fingernails from one hand, several strands of pubic hair, and a section of femur were received for SIP. For comparison purposes, fingernail clippings and a hair sample from a male control person whose geographic origin and life history were known had also been submitted for SIP.

Comparison of SIPs obtained from hair and nail for ^2H, ^{13}C, ^{15}N, and ^{18}O from both the victim and the control showed no significant differences. Assuming the control to be a good representative of the population in and around the region where the victim was found in terms of lifestyle and staple diet, we could only deduce that in all probability the murder victim lived in that part of Ireland for at least the last 9 months, possibly 1 year prior to death. This time line was based on known growth rates for pubic hair (Africoid) and nails of approximately 5 mm/month and 3 mm/month, respectively.

To see if differential ^{18}O-SIPs of bone apatite would provide more information about the victim's life history, a segment cut from the slice of femur was subdivided into an inner part (I) and an outer part (O) and bio-apatite from these subsections were analyzed separately for ^{18}O composition.

Due to the various chemical processes involved during bone formation and bone mineralization, $\delta^{18}O$-values obtained from bone apatite have to be translated into corresponding $\delta^{18}O$-values for drinking water. At present, the best two models (Luz 1985; Longinelli 1984) we have for determining ^{18}O isotope signatures of water taken up by a human body and used for bone mineralization come from studies in bio-archaeology and paleo-ecology. We used both equations to ensure we would not exclude potential geographic areas of origin (Figure 2.8).

The inner, and hence more recently formed, part of the bone yielded an ^{18}O signature of 21.03‰, which corresponds to an average oxygen signature for drinking water of −3.31‰ (95% CL range of −2.83 to −3.78‰). Since the femur remodels relatively slowly, this signature is a composite of the ^{18}O-signature of the drinking water consumed by the victim in recent times and prior to his arrival in the Republic of Ireland.

In contrast, the outer, and hence "older" part of the bone, yielded an ^{18}O signature of 22.13‰. The corresponding drinking water would have to have an ^{18}O signature of the order of −1.73‰, with a 95% CL range of −2.20 to −1.27‰. This isotopic signature is very unique. Broadly speaking, it is indicative of a coastal region near the equator. However, based on the latest data released by the IAEA from its Global Network for Isotopes in Precipitation (GNIP) for observations up to December 2001, there are only five regions worldwide with a matching signature. These are part of the east coast of Brazil (Salvador to Recife), the Windward Islands (Lesser Antilles), the Horn of Africa, the United Arab Emirates and part of Oman, and on the West coast of India the area between the Gulf of Kachchh and the Gulf of Khambat.

The above findings clearly suggest that the victim lived in Dublin for a prolonged period of time prior to death but ultimately came from one of those five regions. Based on suggested remodeling times for femoral bone of 25 years, the victim could have come to Ireland any time between 6 to 8 years before he was murdered. Taking this time frame into consideration, we looked to interpret our findings in the context of ^{18}O data in meteoric precipitation prior to 1999 or a data set that was not merely based on estimated

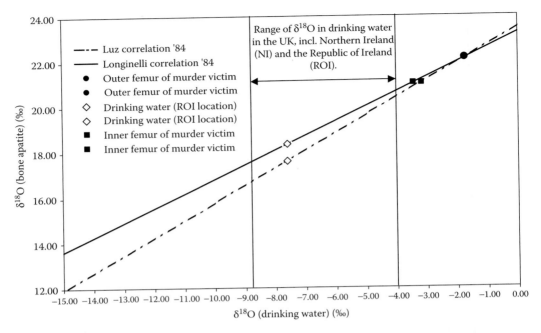

Figure 2.8 Correlation plot for δ¹⁸O values from drinking water versus bone apatite. Irrespective of which regression line is used, both place the murder victim (closed symbols) outside the range for drinking water in the U.K. and Ireland. While bioapatite obtained from the outer segment of the femur (●) provides an indication where the victim originally came from, the bioapatite from the inner part of the femur (■) in conjunction with remodelling rates gives an indication how longe the victim lived in Ireland prior to death. The open diamond represents a drinking water sample collected in the region of the Republic of Ireland where the victim was presumed to have lived prior to death.

$\delta^{18}O$-values for precipitation ($\delta^{18}O_{ppt}$) derived from interpolation between GNIP stations. We found the desired information from a best-fit model map derived from $\delta^{18}O$-values for precipitation published by the IAEA in 1998. This map, generated by Bowen and Wilkinson, accounts for the effect of local topography on $\delta^{18}O_{ppt}$, such as geographic parameters that control temperature (latitude and altitude). Their map depicts modern, globally averaged relationships between $\delta^{18}O_{ppt}$ and a number of explicit (latitude, altitude) and more obscure (vapor sources, storm tracks) geographic variables (Bowen and Wilkinson 2002).

Interpreting the ¹⁸O-SIP of the victim's femur in conjunction with his complexion, the nature or characteristics of his pubic hair and the data published by Bowen and Wilkinson, we narrowed down the aforementioned five possible points of origin to just one, namely the Horn of Africa, i.e., countries such as Ethiopia, Somalia, Kenya, Eritrea, Uganda, and the eastern part of Sudan.

Based on the Stable Isotope Profiles (SIP) obtained from different tissues of the victim (bone, hair, and nails) and a local control (hair and nails), on how much is known about growth and remodeling rates of these tissues and on the ethnicity of the victim, we concluded the victim had definitely lived in the eastern part of the Republic of Ireland for the last 9 to 12 months of his life. However, he did not live there all his life. In all probability, he originally came from the region called the "Horn of Africa" and he left his country of origin and came to Ireland between 6.8 to 13.7 years prior to death.

These conclusions were confirmed by independent police enquiries that showed the victim came from an area along the border between Kenya and Somalia. He entered the Republic of Ireland in or before 1998 and lived there until his death.

2.5.2.2 Radiogenic Trace Element Isotopes in Human Tissue

In addition to stable isotope of light elements, radiogenic isotopes of trace elements such as strontium present in drinking water and bulk diet are incorporated into body tissues, predominantly into bone and teeth (Pye 2004). Tooth enamel stores a chemical record of their owner's childhood living environment, such as local climate and geology. Each tooth therefore opens a window of information covering the short time of tooth enamel formation. Apart from being a source of oxygen derived from water, apatite also contains trace amounts of other elements such as strontium, neodymium, and lead, which are of special interest to forensic archaeologists and anthropologists since their relative isotopic abundance is not subject to isotopic fractionation as a result of biochemical processes. These elements therefore offer themselves as strong independent indicators for linking bone and teeth to a person's local environment or geo-location. However, because trace elements can enter the body as inhaled dust and, more importantly from a bioavailability point of view as soil leachate incorporated into food and drink, these elements reflect rock and sediment sources from a wider geographical area rather than a discrete location. Despite this drawback, valuable information can be obtained by comparing sample values with values of matrix-matched samples from candidate source areas, so-called "geographic proxy data," having eliminated potential source areas on the basis of sample data vs. geochemical data first.

In common with the approach discussed above for stable light element isotopes, discriminatory power of data, and hence robustness of information, increases when isotope ratios of more than one element are employed. In addition, if one isotope used for isotope ratio measurement derives exclusively from the decay of a radioactive isotope of another element, trace element isotope ratios can only be compared if samples are of the same age. To compensate for age difference, some scientists use the epsilon notation (Equation 2) that relates the sample isotope ratio to the isotope ratio of a modern-day standard or a known, universally agreed value (Beard and Johnson 2000).

$$\varepsilon = ([R_s \ / \ R_{std}] - 1) \times 10^4 \tag{2}$$

In the case of strontium, opinion is divided as to whether use of the ε_{Sr}-notation is appropriate since the standard $^{87}Sr/^{86}Sr$ ratio used ($[^{87}Sr/^{86}Sr]_{bulk\ Earth}$: 0.7045) is not precisely known, with the opponents of this approach preferring to publish measured $^{87}Sr/^{86}Sr$ ratios only albeit normalized to a recognized standard. However, as long as data are reported in a consistent fashion, and if data are generated and compared on a like-for-like basis, trace element isotope ratios of bone can provide very useful intelligence in cases of decomposed and accidentally or deliberately mutilated bodies by eliminating potential source areas which on the basis of anthropological markers alone could not be excluded. Up-to-date and in-depth information on the contributions of forensic geoscience to human identification can be found in a book published by The Geological Society of London (2004).

2.6   Conclusions and Caveats

On the basis of our current knowledge and understanding of stable isotope chemistry and biochemistry, it is fair to say that Stable Isotope Profiling already makes an important contribution to criminal investigations, especially those also involving forensic anthropology and forensic chemistry. Stable isotope analyses of human tissues with medium to long-term survival rates such as hair and nail, and bone and teeth, respectively, hold the potential to yield intelligence on lifestyle and geographic life history providing a window into a person's past and point of origin.

At present, the application of this technique is restricted by the limited availability of appropriate regional and global databases. It must also be pointed out that conclusions drawn from isotope signatures of bone and teeth toward potential country and region of origin are largely based on proxy data from archaeological and palaeo-environmental research (Dangela and Longinelli 1990; Longinelli 1984; Longinelli 1996; Luz and Kolodny 1985; Luz, Kolodny, and Horowitz 1984). The link between the isotopic signal of food and drink and the corresponding body tissue isotopic values are generally known but need to be better defined so SIPs derived from materials such as hair, nails, teeth and bone of modern people can be used with greater confidence in a forensic context (Hedges, Stevens, and Richards 2004; O'Connell and Hedges 1999; Richards, Fuller, and Hedges 2001; Sponheimer et al. 2003). A particularly important point is the determination of the duration between consumption of food and water, the appearance of the isotopic signature in different body tissues, and the corresponding fractionation and correlation factors. Equally important is precise knowledge of the level of intra- and inter-individual variability of SIPs in various human tissues so meaningful uncertainty intervals and cut-off points can be defined with a view toward robustness of SIPs and SIP-derived conclusions when it comes to these being challenged in a court of law.

There is a clear need for further research and longitudinal studies to generate SIP databases and to determine natural variability of SIPs because it is the extent of the natural or biological "noise" that will determine the usefulness of this technique to human identification rather than the uncertainty of the actual isotope ratio measurement. That said, SIP can already be exploited fully in cases where it is possible to compare case samples with authentic, matrix-matched materials of known history and provenance on a like-for-like basis.

Practitioners and would-be practitioners of this technique must be aware of the fact that drawing conclusions on the basis of the abundance of one isotope alone is rarely possible. To obtain robust and meaningful intelligence, the abundance of several independent isotopes should be measured and considered in combination, and these data should ideally be cross-referenced with data from independent analytical techniques probing different sample properties or characteristics. This approach must be complemented by further basic research aimed at quantifying, or at least capturing, the influence of compounding factors such as the globalization of food and drink as well as freedom of travel. Yet, despite these potential drawbacks and pitfalls, recent studies and casework have shown encouraging evidence that a person's staple diet is still dominated by locally or regionally sourced food and drink, which should ultimately enable us to determine factors or off-sets to correct for the contribution "foreign" or "alien" food and drink might make to the record of isotope signatures preserved in human tissues.

2.7   Acknowledgments

The author gratefully acknowledges financial support through a Platform Grant on Environmental Forensics received from the EPSRC. I would like to thank my Ph.D. students N. Farmer, I. Fraser, and L.J. Reidy, who produced some of the data presented here. Thanks are also due to C. Chenery (NIGL, Keyworth, U.K.) and V. Grimes (University of Bradford, U.K.) for their assistance and advice regarding ^{18}O analysis of bio-apatite. I am indebted to R.M Kalin for access to analytical facilities of the Environmental Engineering Research Centre and last but not least to my research fellow H.F. Kemp for unwavering support during the last 6 years and for her critical reading of the manuscript.

References

Angerosa, F., Breas, O., Contento, S., Guillou, C., Reniero, F., and Sada, E., Application of stable isotope ratio analysis to the characterization of the geographical origin of olive oils, *J Agric Food Chem* 47(3), 1013–1017, 1999.

Angerosa, F., Camera, L., Cumitini, S., Gleixner, G., and Reniero, F., Carbon stable isotopes and olive oil adulteration with pomace oil, *J Agric Food Chem* 45, 3044–3048, 1997.

Beard, B.L. and Johnson, C.M., Strontium isotope composition of skeletal material can determine the birth place and geographic mobility of humans and animals, *J Forensic Sci* 45(5), 1049–1061, 2000.

Begley, I.S. and Scrimgeour, C.M., High-precision delta H-2 and delta O-18 measurement for water and volatile organic compounds by continuous-flow pyrolysis isotope ratio mass spectrometry, *Anal Chem* 69, 1530–1535, 1997.

Bowen, G.J., Chesson, L., Nielson, K., Cerling, T.E., and Ehleringer, J.R., Treatment methods for the determination of delta H-2 and delta O-18 of hair keratin by continuous-flow isotope-ratio mass spectrometry, *Rapid Commun Mass Spectrom* 19(17), 2371–2378, 2005.

Bowen, G.J. and Wilkinson, B., Spatial distribution of delta O-18 in meteoric precipitation, *Geology* 30(4), 315–318, 2002.

Brand, W.A., High precision isotope ratio monitoring techniques in mass spectrometry, *J Mass Spectrom* 31, 225–235, 1996.

Brand, W.A., Tegtmeyer, A.R., and Hilkert, A., Compound-specific isotope analysis — extending toward n-15 n-14 and o-18 o-16, *Org Geochem* 21, 585–594, 1994.

Brenna, J.T., High-precision gas isotope ratio mass-spectrometry — recent advances in instrumentation and biomedical applications, *Acc Chem Res* 27, 340–346, 1994.

Brooks, J.R., Buchmann, N., Phillips, S., Ehleringer, B., Evans, R.D., Lott, M., Martinelli, L.A., Pockman, W.T., Sandquist, D., Sparks, J.P., Sperry, L., Williams, D., and Ehleringer, J.R., Heavy and light beer: A carbon isotope approach to detect C-4 carbon in beers of different origins, styles, and prices, *J Agric Food Chem* 50(22), 6413–6418, 2002.

Carter, J.F., Grundy, P.L., Hill, J.C., Ronan, N.C., Titterton, E.L., and Sleeman, R., Forensic isotope ratio mass spectrometry of packaging tapes, *Analyst* 129(12), 1206–1210, 2004.

Carter, J.F., Titterton, E.L., Grant, H., and Sleeman, R., Isotopic changes during the synthesis of amphetamines, *Chem Commun* (21), 2590–2591, 2002a.

Carter, J.F., Titterton, E.L., Murray, M., and Sleeman, R., Isotopic characterisation of 3,4-methylenedioxyamphetamine and 3,4-methylenedioxymethylamphetamine (ecstasy), *Analyst* 127(6), 830–833, 2002b.

Cerling, T.E., Ehleringer, J.R., West, A., Stange, E., and Dorigan, J., Forensic applications of stable isotopes in hair, *Forensic Sci Int* 136, 172, 2003.

Collister, J.W., Rieley, G., Stern, B., Eglinton, G., and Fry, B., Compound-specific delta-c-13 analyses of leaf lipids from plants with differing carbon-dioxide metabolisms, *Org Geochem* 21, 619–627, 1994.

Coplen, T.B., Reporting of stable hydrogen, carbon, and oxygen isotopic abundances, *Pure Appl Chem* 66(2), 273–276, 1994.

Coplen, T.B., More uncertainty than necessary, *Paleoceanography* 11(4), 369–370, 1996.

Croft, D.J. and Pye, K., Multi-technique comparison of source and primary transfer soil samples: an experimental investigation, *Sci Justice* 44(1), 21–28, 2004.

Croft, D.J. and Pye, K., The potential use of continuous-flow isotope-ratio mass spectrometry as a tool in forensic soil analysis: a preliminary report, *Rapid Commun Mass Spectrom* 17(23), 2581–2584, 2003.

Dangela, D. and Longinelli, A., Oxygen isotopes in living mammals bone phosphate — further results, *Chem Geol* 86(1), 75–82, 1990.

Eakin, P.A., Fallick, A.E., and Gerc, J., Some instrumental effects in the determination of stable carbon isotope ratios by gas-chromatography isotope ratio mass-spectrometry, *Chem Geol* 101, 71–79, 1992.

Ehleringer, J.R., Casale, J.F., Lott, M.J., and Ford, V.L., Tracing the geographical origin of cocaine, *Nature* 408(6810), 311–312, 2000.

Ehleringer, J.R., Cooper, D.A., Lott, M.J., and Cook, C.S., Geo-location of heroin and cocaine by stable isotope ratios, *Forensic Sci Int* 106(1), 27–35, 1999.

Ellis, L. and Fincannon, A.L., Analytical improvements in irm-GC/MS analyses: Advanced techniques in tube furnace design and sample preparation, *Org Geochem* 29, 1101–1117, 1998.

Farmer, N., Meier-Augenstein, W., and Kalin, R.M., Stable isotope analysis of safety matches using IRMS — a forensic case study, *Rapid Commun Mass Spectrom* 19, 3182–3186, 2005.

Fronza, G., Fuganti, C., Schmidt, H.L., and Werner, R.A., The delta O-18-value of the p-OH group of L-tyrosine permits the assignment of its origin to plant or animal sources, *Eur Food Res Technol* 215(1), 55–58, 2002.

Fuller, B.T., Fuller, J.L., Sage, N.E., Harris, D.A., O'Connell, T.C., and Hedges, R.E.M., Nitrogen balance and delta N-15: why you're not what you eat during pregnancy, *Rapid Commun Mass Spectrom* 18(23), 2889–2896, 2004.

Hedges, R.E.M., Stevens, R.E., and Richards, M.P., Bone as a stable isotope archive for local climatic information, *Quaternary Sci Rev* 23(7–8), 959–965, 2004.

Hill, P.A., Bone remodelling, *Br J Orthopaed* 25, 101–107, 1998.

Hofmann, D. and Brand, W.A., Microcombustion of ng amounts of carbon in non-volatile materials for isotope ratio evaluation, *Isotopes Environ Health Stud* 32, 255–262, 1996.

Kelly, S., Parker, I., Sharman, M., Dennis, J., and Goodall, I., Assessing the authenticity of single seed vegetable oils using fatty acid stable carbon isotope ratios (C-13/C-12), *Food Chem* 59, 181–186, 1997.

Kelly, S.D. and Rhodes, C., Emerging techniques in vegetable oil analysis using stable isotope ratio mass spectrometry, *Grasas y Aceites* 53(1), 34–44, 2002.

Leckrone, K.J. and Hayes, J.M., Water-induced errors in continuous-flow carbon isotope ratio mass spectrometry, *Anal Chem* 70, 2737–2744, 1998.

Lockheart, M.J., vanBergen, P.F., and Evershed, R.P., Variations in the stable carbon isotope compositions of individual lipids from the leaves of modern angiosperms: Implications for the study of higher land plant-derived sedimentary organic matter, *Org Geochem* 26, 137–153, 1997.

Longinelli, A., Oxygen isotopes in mammal bone phosphate — a new tool for paleohydrological and paleoclimatological research, *Geochim Cosmochim Acta* 48(2), 385–390, 1984.

Longinelli, A., Special issue — biogenic phosphates as palaeoenvironmental indicators: introduction, *Palaeogeogr Palaeoclimatol Palaeoecol* 126(1–2), R7–R8, 1996.

Luz, B. and Kolodny, Y., Oxygen isotope variations in phosphate of biogenic apatites: 4. mammal teeth and bones, *Earth Planetary Sci Lett* 75(1), 29–36, 1985.

Luz, B., Kolodny, Y., and Horowitz, M., Fractionation of oxygen isotopes between mammalian bone phosphate and environmental drinking-water, *Geochim Cosmochim Acta* 48(8), 1689–1693, 1984.

Mas, F., Beemsterboer, B., Veltkamp, A.C., and Verweij, A.M.A., Determination of common-batch members in a set of confiscated 3,4-(Methylendioxy)Methylamphetamine samples by measuring the natural isotope abundances — a preliminary study, *Forensic Sci Int* 71, 225–231, 1995.

Meier-Augenstein, W., Stable isotope analysis of fatty acids by gas chromatography-isotope ratio mass spectrometry, *Anal Chim Acta* 465, 63–79, 2002.

Meier-Augenstein, W., Applied gas chromatography coupled to isotope ratio mass spectrometry, *J Chromatogr A* 842(1–2), 351–371, 1999a.

Meier-Augenstein, W., Use of gas chromatography-combustion-isotope ratio mass spectrometry in nutrition and metabolic research, *Curr Opin Clin Nutr Metab Care* 2(6), 465–470, 1999b.

Meier-Augenstein, W., Online recording of C-13/C-12 ratios and mass-spectra in one gas-chromatographic analysis, *HRC-J.High Resol. Chromatogr* 18, 28–32, 1995.

Meier-Augenstein, W., Brand, W., Hoffmann, G.F., and Rating, D., Bridging the information gap between isotope ratio mass-spectrometry and conventional mass-spectrometry, *Biol Mass Spectrom* 23, 376–378, 1994.

Meier-Augenstein, W. and Liu, R.H., Forensic applications of isotope ratio mass spectrometry, in *Advances in Forensic Applications of Mass Spectrometry*, Yinon, J., Ed., CRC Press, Boca Raton, FL, 2004, pp. 149–180.

MeierAugenstein, W., A reference gas inlet module for internal isotopic calibration in high precision gas chromatography combustion-isotope ratio mass spectrometry, *Rapid Commun Mass Spectrom* 11, 1775–1780, 1997.

MeierAugenstein, W., Rating, D., Hoffmann, G.F., Wendel, U., Matthiesen, U., and Schadewaldt, P., Determination of 13C enrichment by conventional GC-MS and GC-(MS)-C-IRMS, *Isotopes in Environmental and Health Studies* 31, 261–266, 1995.

MeierAugenstein, W., Watt, P.W., and Langhans, C.D., Influence of gas-chromatographic parameters on measurement of C-13/C-12 isotope ratios by gas-liquid-chromatography combustion isotope ratio mass-spectrometry. I, *J Chromatogr A* 752, 233–241, 1996.

Melander, L. and Saunders, W.H., *Reaction Rates of Isotopic Molecules*, John Wiley & Sons, New York, 1980.

Merritt, D.A., Freeman, K.H., Ricci, M.P., Studley, S.A., and Hayes, J.M., Performance and optimization of a combustion interface for isotope ratio monitoring gas-chromatography mass-spectrometry, *Anal Chem* 67, 2461–2473, 1995.

Metges, C.C. and Petzke, K.J., The use of GC-C-IRMS for the analysis of stable isotope enrichment in nitrogenous compounds, in *Methods of Investigation of Amino Acid and Protein Metabolism*, El-Khoury, A.E., Ed., CRC Press, Boca Raton, FL, 1999, pp. 121–134.

O'Connell, T.C. and Hedges, R.E.M., Investigations into the effect of diet on modern human hair isotopic values, *Am J Phys Anthropol* 108(4), 409–425, 1999.

O'Connell, T.C., Hedges, R.E.M., Healey, M.A., and Simpson, A.H.R., Isotopic comparison of hair, nail and bone: Modern analyses, *J Archaeol Sci* 28(11), 1247–1255, 2001.

Preston, T. and Owens, N.J.P., Interfacing an automatic elemental analyser with an isotope ratio mass spectrometer: the potential for fully automated total nitrogen and nitrogen-15 analysis, *Analyst* 108, 971–977, 1983.

Preston, T. and Slater, C., Mass-spectrometric analysis of stable-isotope-labeled amino-acid tracers, *Proc Nutr Soc* 53, 363–372, 1994.

Pye, K., Isotope and trace element analysis of human teeth and bones for forensic purposes, in *Forensic Geoscience: Principles, Techniques and Applications*, Vol. 232, Pye, K. and Croft, D.J., Eds., Geology Society, London, 2004, pp. 215–216.

Pye, K. and Croft, D.J., Eds., *Forensic Geoscience: Principles, Techniques and Applications*, Geological Society, London, 2004.

Rautenschlein, M., Habfast, K., and Brand, W.A., High-precision measurement of 13C/12C ratios by on-line combustion of GC eluates and isotope ratio mass spectrometry, in *Stable Isotopes in Paediatric, Nutritional and Metabolic Research*, Chapman, T.E. et al., Eds., Intercept Ltd., Andover, 1990, pp. 133–148.

Reidy, L.J., Meier-Augenstein, W., and Kalin, R.M., C-13-isotope ratio mass spectrometry as a potential tool for the forensic analysis of white architectural paint: a preliminary study, *Rapid Commun Mass Spectrom* 19(13), 1899–1905, 2005.

Rennie, M.J., MeierAugenstein, W., Watt, P.W., Patel, A., Begley, I.S., and Scrimgeour, C.M., Use of continuous-flow combustion MS in studies of human metabolism, *Biochem Soc Trans* 24, 927–932, 1996.

Richards, M.P., Fuller, B.T., and Hedges, R.E.M., Sulphur isotopic variation in ancient bone collagen from Europe: implications for human palaeodiet, residence mobility, and modern pollutant studies, *Earth Planetary Sci Lett* 191(3–4), 185–190, 2001.

Richards, M.P., Fuller, B.T., Sponheimer, M., Robinson, T., and Ayliffe, L., Sulphur isotopes in palaeodietary studies: a review and results from a controlled feeding experiment, *Int J Osteoarchaeol* 13(1–2), 37–45, 2003.

Rieley, G., Derivatization of organic-compounds prior to gas-chromatographic combustion-isotope ratio mass-spectrometric analysis — identification of isotope fractionation processes, *Analyst* 119, 915–919, 1994.

Rieley, G., Collister, J.W., Stern, B., and Eglinton, G., Gas-chromatography isotope ratio mass-spectrometry of leaf wax n-alkanes from plants of differing carbon-dioxide metabolisms, *Rapid Commun Mass Spectrom* 7, 488–491, 1993.

Royer, A., Gerard, C., Naulet, N., Lees, M., and Martin, G.J., Stable isotope characterization of olive oils. I — compositional and carbon-13 profiles of fatty acids, *J Am Oil Chem Soc* 76(3), 357–363, 1999.

Sharp, Z.D., Atudorei, V., Panarello, H.O., Fernandez, J., and Douthitt, C., Hydrogen isotope systematics of hair: archaeological and forensic applications, *Journal of Archaeol Sci* 30(12), 1709–1716, 2003.

Simmons, E.D., Pritzker, K.P.H., and Grynpas, M.D., Age-related changes in the human femoral cortex, *J Orthopaed Res* 9(2), 155–167, 1991.

Spangenberg, C.E., Macko, S.A., and Hunziker, J., Characterization of olive oil by carbon isotope analysis of individual fatty acids: Implications for authentication, *J Agric Food Chem* 46(10), 4179–4184, 1998.

Spangenberg, J.E. and Ogrinc, N., Authentication of vegetable oils by bulk and molecular carbon isotope analyses with emphasis on olive oil and pumpkin seed oil, *J Agric Food Chem* 49(3), 1534–1540, 2001.

Sponheimer, M., Robinson, T., Ayliffe, L., Roeder, B., Hammer, J., Passey, B., West, A., Cerling, T., Dearing, D., and Ehleringer, J., Nitrogen isotopes in mammalian herbivores: Hair delta N-15 values from a controlled feeding study, *Int J Osteoarchaeol* 13(1–2), 80–87, 2003.

Teitelbaum, S.L., Bone resorption by osteoclasts, *Science*, 289(5484), 1504–1508, 2000.

Werner, R.A. and Brand, W.A., Referencing strategies and techniques in stable isotope ratio analysis, *Rapid Commun Mass Spectrom* 15(7), 501–519, 2001.

Werner, R.A., Kornexl, B.E., Rossmann, A., and Schmidt, H.L., Online determination of delta-O-18 values of organic-substances, *Anal Chim Acta* 319, 159–164, 1996.

Werner, R.A., Rossmann, A., Schwarz, C., Bacher, A., Schmidt, H.L., and Eisenreich, W., Biosynthesis of gallic acid in Rhus typhina: discrimination between alternative pathways from natural oxygen isotope abundance, *Phytochemistry* 65(20), 2809–2813, 2004.

Woodbury, S.E., Evershed, R.P., and Rossell, J.B., Delta C-13 analyses of vegetable oil fatty acid components, determined by gas chromatography combustion isotope ratio mass spectrometry, after saponification or regiospecific hydrolysis, *J Chromatogr A* 805, 249–257, 1998a.

Woodbury, S.E., Evershed, R.P., and Rossell, J.B., Purity assessments of major vegetable oils based on delta C-13 values of individual fatty acids, *J Am Oil Chem Soc* 75, 371–379, 1998b.

Woodbury, S.E., Evershed, R.P., Rossell, J.B., Griffith, R.E., and Farnell, P., Detection of vegetable oil adulteration using gas-chromatography combustion isotope ratio mass-spectrometry, *Anal Chem* 67, 2685–2690, 1995.

Section 2

Identification from Latent Prints

Fingerprints

3

VIVIANNE GALLOWAY
DAVE CHARLTON

Contents

3.1 Early Beginnings 57
3.2 Founders of Modern Fingerprinting...58
    3.2.1 Herschel and Faulds 58
    3.2.2 Galton and Bertillon..59
    3.2.3 Henry and Vucetich 60
3.3 The Age of Modern Fingerprinting..61
3.4 The Fingerprint Standard..62
3.5 The Identification Process..62
3.6 Fingerprint Patterns...63
3.7 Ridge Characteristics 64
    3.7.1 Analysis...65
    3.7.2 Comparison...65
    3.7.3 Evaluation...65
    3.7.4 Verification 65
3.8 Fingerprints and Modern Biometric Identification 66
3.9 Fingerprints and Major Disasters..70
3.10 Acknowledgments..71
Further Reading...72

3.1 Early Beginnings

When humans began taking an interest in the strange patterns on their hands and fingers will never be known, but the presence of fingerprints on cave walls and on ancient artifacts has led some historians to believe that the individuality of fingerprints has been recognized for many centuries. In Gavrinis near Brittany, the Belgian scientist Stockis discovered Neolithic carvings on the walls of caves that resembled friction ridge detail. On the surfaces of granite slabs, circles similar to fingerprint patterns have been observed; similar patterns have been found in another Neolithic site in County Meath, Ireland. The origins of the markings are unknown but claims that the slabs reflect ancient observations of finger and palm impressions are not convincing. It is more than likely that the carvings merely depict patterns found in the natural world. The oldest acceptable representation of a hand and the strange patterns on the friction ridge skin is an aboriginal carving found on a slate discovered at the edge of Kejimkujik Lake, Nova Scotia. While the carving does not support evidence that the aboriginal carver had any knowledge of the individuality of fingerprints, it does show an awareness of the patterns on the fingers.

Archaeological expeditions in the Middle East and Egypt uncovered numerous artifacts bearing fingerprints, some believed to be accidental markings, others seen as intentional marking of property. The earliest evidence of intentional use of fingerprinting is recorded on legal documents in Japan and China, dating back hundreds of years.

The practice of signing with a fingerprint on legal documents spread to India, but as there is no evidence to suggest that the marks could have been individualized, it is most likely that the marks were little more than a symbolic gesture.

Prior to 1900 the study and examination of fingerprints was carried out by medical practitioners. The earliest European writing on fingerprints is accredited to the 17th-century English botanist Neremiah Grew, fellow of the College of Physicians and the Royal Society. In 1684 he presented a paper to the Royal Society, later to be published in *Philosophical Transactions,* on his observations of patterns on the fingers and palm. Grew wrote about ridge formation and about the pores on the ridges, likening them to "little fountains."

Italian anatomist Professor Marcello Malpighi wrote about ridge formations. He discussed skin friction and described various patterns on the fingertips, recognizing that sweat was discharged from the lower stratum of the epidermis, later to be termed the *Malpighian layer.* However, it was not until 1823 when Joannes Evangilist Purkinje described the ridges on the finger in his thesis "Commentatio de Examine Physiological Organi Visus et Systematis Cuteanei" that modern day fingerprinting began to develop. Purkinje described each ridge pattern, dividing them into nine groups and formulating rules for classification. His work evoked little interest after publication; nevertheless, it has made a significant contribution to modern fingerprinting.

3.2 Founders of Modern Fingerprinting

3.2.1 Herschel and Faulds

Modern fingerprinting began to develop in the last two decades of the 19th century. The individuality of fingerprints was first realized by Sir William Herschel while working for the East India Company, where as an administrator in Hooghly District, he started the practice of recording handprints on contracts. The first such marked contract was that of Radyadhar Konai to prevent repudiation of his signature. Herschel admitted that the idea of taking the handprint was totally unrelated to the modern concept of fingerprint identification. Illustrations of the Konai contract shows that the hand friction ridge detail is clearly visible but that there is very little detail on the fingers. Herschel continued his interest in fingerprints but did not publish anything about his activities until Dr. Henry Faulds published a letter in the scientific journal *Nature* in October 1880.

Faulds' interest in fingerprints had developed during his time in India and Japan while observing the intricate designs of human finger imprints on prehistoric pottery. The letter to the editor of *Nature* was a culmination of Faulds' studies, commenting on how fingerprints could be classified, how the friction ridge detail never changed, and advocating a method of apprehending criminals by locating fingerprints at crime scenes.

The letter in *Nature* prompted lively correspondence between Faulds and Herschel, each claiming to be the originator of modern fingerprinting. However, both men contributed to the science of friction ridge identification. Faulds offered to set up a bureau at Scotland Yard to test the practicality of his methods at his own expense, but a report that was unfavorable to Faulds recommended the adoption of the Bertillon anthropometric system,

p dependence

relying on body measurement. The contents of Faulds' and Herschel's letters spread far and wide, and their early contributions led more people to take an interest in this new concept.

3.2.2 Galton and Bertillon

The studies of Sir Francis Galton had a far greater impact. Believed to be one of the greatest scientists of the 19th century, he was the author of nine books and over 200 papers on many diverse interests ranging from foreign travel to psychometric experiments. An astronomer, geographer-explorer, inventor, and relative of Charles Darwin, his principal scientific obsession was anthropology.

In 1888 Alphonse Bertillon invited Galton to Paris. The purpose of the visit was in preparation for Galton's lecture to the Royal Institution on "Bertillonage," a system he had devised for identifying people by their bodily dimensions. The system had been introduced in Paris on an experimental basis. Less than 2 weeks before the experiment was due to finish, Bertillon had his first identification. With the lack of any successful alternative identification method, the anthropometric system spread worldwide.

Bertillon ignored the possibility of identifying individuals by means of fingerprints due to the lack of a robust classification system, but Galton's interest grew. He recalled that fingerprints had been written about in *Nature* and started correspondence with Herschel. Galton began adding his own observations to that of Herschel and other information he had collected on fingerprints. He presented his research together with an appraisal of the "Bertillonage" system to the Royal Institution under the heading of "Personal Identification and Description." At this meeting Galton gave the first public demonstration of the persistence of ridge characteristics by producing a print of the right forefinger and right middle finger of Herschel taken in 1860 and of the same finger taken 28 years later in 1888.

The interest in fingerprints was gaining momentum, and as time went by, Bertillon included fingerprints on the reverse of his anthropometric cards as a final check of identification. Little did he know that his system was soon to be replaced with this new method of identification called *fingerprinting*. After the presentation to the Royal Institution, Galton, using Herschel's findings and his own research, published a book in 1892 entitled *Fingerprints*. In this book Galton discussed the anatomy of fingerprint patterns, outlined practical methods for recording them, and described techniques for classifying them that he divided into three groups: arches, loops, and whorls. By this time Galton had amassed a large collection of fingerprints not only from Englishmen but also from those of other ethnic origins. The book was a masterpiece of analysis, and later the following year he published a supplement entitled *Deciphering of Blurred Finger Tips*.

In 1893 the Home Secretary in England appointed a committee under Charles Troop to review the identification procedures and the effectiveness of the Habitual Criminal Registry. The Troop Committee was assigned to investigate the current methods of registering and identifying habitual criminals in England, the use of the anthropometric Bertillonage System, and the suggested system of identifying individuals by means of fingerprints. The committee was to evaluate and report on which system should be used and how it would be implemented.

Following extensive enquiries, including visits to Galton's laboratory, where he demonstrated his ability to classify a collection of 2,645 cards using Galton's three pattern types, the committee settled on a compromise. They decided that the anthropometric system would remain the primary method of identification and that they would employ Galton's fingerprint system for the subdivisions. The committee further recommended that

Scotland Yard would maintain an anthropometric register and that prison officers should take the measurements and fingerprints of prisoners. Thereafter, the fingerprints should be classified and used for identification through a central registry for the whole of England.

3.2.3   Henry and Vucetich

The practicality and success of fingerprints soon overshadowed the anthropometric system. Following in Galton's footsteps were the developers of a classification system that would revolutionize fingerprint identification. Sir Edward Henry had been working in India for many years and had developed an interest in fingerprints as a means of registration for Indian workers. He started experimenting with the anthropometric system, using ten measurements and noting eye color. Later, he refined the system to only six measurements but included a left thumbprint on the anthropometric record card. Henry began to have strong doubts about the accuracy of identification by measurement and became convinced that a record system based solely on fingerprints would solve many of their difficulties. To increase his knowledge, Henry wrote to Galton, and in 1894 he returned to England, where he visited Galton at his laboratory. Galton gave Henry access to all that he had learned, including the work of Herschel and Faulds. On his return to India, Henry was determined to find a formula that could enable a fingerprint collection of several thousands to be classified, filed, and retrieved. His first task was to record all ten fingers of each prisoner in a study, in addition to continuing to use the anthropometric system. He assigned two Bengali police officers, Azizul Hacque and Chandra Bose, to study the classification problem. Their hard work was rewarded, and a classification system that allowed 1,024 primary positions, with secondary and tertiary divisions, was devised.

In 1897, Henry applied to the Indian government for an independent evaluation of his classification system. As a result of this evaluation, a resolution signed by the governor-general directed that the official method for identifying criminals in British India should be fingerprints. The anthropometric system continued alongside the Henry system until anthropometric cards were gradually phased out and replaced by Henry classified fingerprint cards.

At the same time as Henry was experimenting with his system, Juan Vucetich, who was employed as a statistician in the police department at La Planta, Argentina, was developing a fingerprint classification system. In 1891 Vucetich was appointed head of the Argentine Bureau of Anthropometric Identification. It did not take long for Vucetich to start experimenting with fingerprints and setting up his own equipment for taking prisoners' fingerprints. Using Galton's basic material he formulated a ten-finger classification system.

In 1892 Vucetich played an important role in the first murder case solved by the identification of fingerprints found at the crime scene. Two children were murdered in the town of Necochea on the coast of Argentina. The mother, Francesca Rojas, accused a neighbor of the murder; the neighbor was arrested but protested his innocence. Fortunately, Inspector Alvarez, one of the officers examining the crime scene, found what appeared to be fingerprints in blood on a door adjacent to the place where the bodies had been found. The marks were sent to the La Planta Identification Bureau, together with the fingerprints of both the accused and Rojas. The fingerprints were compared, and it was quickly confirmed that, in fact, Rojas had made the marks. Confronted with the evidence, Rojas broke down and confessed to the murder of her sons and was sent to prison. Many more identifications followed, but in spite of this, Vucetich was not officially recognized for his work on fingerprints until many years later.

In 1896 Argentina became the first country to abolish anthropometry and file criminal records by fingerprint classification.

3.3 The Age of Modern Fingerprinting

In 1899 Henry was invited by the Association for the Advancement of Science to present a paper entitled "Fingerprints and the Detection of Crime in India." Giving due credit to Galton, the paper recalled the historical aspects of fingerprints and compared the anthropometric system with the fingerprint system. Henry's paper was well received.

At about the same time, concern was being expressed once again about the ineffectiveness of the combined measurement and fingerprint system. The Home Secretary appointed a five-man committee under the chairmanship of Lord Belper. They were directed to investigate the workings of the methods of identification of criminals by measurement and fingerprints and also the administrative arrangements for maintaining the system. The committee found that very little had changed since the recommendations of the Troop Committee and that some methods of identification in use before 1894 were still being employed.

In 1900 Henry presented evidence to the Belper Committee, wherein he gave an account of his system together with a practical demonstration using a fingerprint collection of about 7,000 persons. Shortly after Henry's presentation, his book entitled *Classification and Uses of Fingerprint* was published. The Belper Committee finalized its report in December 1900 and recommended that the fingerprints of criminals should be taken and classified using the system that had been introduced in India.

In 1901 the Belper recommendations were implemented. In May of the same year Henry was appointed assistant commissioner of police in charge of criminal identification at Scotland Yard. He selected three officers from the Anthropometric Office, Detective Inspector Charles H. Steadman, Detective Sergeant Charles Stockley Collins, and Detective Constable Frederick Hunt, to form the Fingerprint Branch. The officers soon mastered the new techniques and set about converting the fingerprints recorded on the anthropometric cards to the new classification system. So successful were they that police forces from all over the world sent their officers to Scotland Yard for instruction in this new technique.

Detective Sergeant Collins' enthusiasm to extend the use of fingerprints led to his looking at the possibility of linking criminals not only to their past criminal records but also to their present and undetected crimes. He also studied photography so that when an opportunity arose he would be able to record fingerprints inadvertently left at a crime scene. This chance came in 1902 when a detective investigating the scene of a burglary at a house in Denmark Hill noticed a number of dirty fingerprints on a newly painted windowsill at the point where the burglar had entered the house. The information was passed to the Fingerprint Branch at Scotland Yard, whereupon Sergeant Collins visited the scene to examine the marks. He photographed the clearest mark and after checking that it had not been left by a member of the household, returned to the Yard. Even though he knew there were thousands of comparisons to be made, he set about with the assistance of his colleagues to identify the mark. His efforts were rewarded when he identified a 41-year-old laborer named Harry Jackson who had several previous convictions. Fortunately, when Jackson was arrested, he was found to be dealing in property from another burglary.

The identification was the easier part of the forensic process. It was more difficult to get a court to accept the identification of a mark left inadvertently at the scene as the sole means of proving that Jackson had committed the crime. After some discussion between Henry and the director of public prosecutions, it was arranged for the prosecution case to be conducted by Richard Muir, a well-established Treasury counsel. Detective Inspector Collins was called as a witness to explain in simple terms the basic principles of fingerprint identification, producing an enlargement of the left thumb mark on the windowsill and the left thumb print of Jackson. He produced tracings of the ridges on both prints and indicated ten ridge characteristics, which were present in both prints and in the same coincident sequence. There was no attack by the defense on the fingerprint evidence. Jackson was subsequently found guilty, and a precedent for fingerprint evidence was set.

The first case in the U.K. of using fingerprints evidence in a murder conviction took place in 1905. Two brothers, Alfred and Albert Stratton, were charged with the murder of Thomas Farrow, who was found dead in his paint shop in Deptford. During an examination of the premises, a thumb mark was found on an empty cash box. Elimination fingerprints were taken from the deceased, staff, and other persons who had access to the shop, but the marks were not identified. On information received from a witness, the Stratton brothers were arrested and fingerprinted by D.I. Collins, who later identified the thumbprint on the cash box tray as the right thumb of Alfred Stratton. The two brothers were eventually charged with murder. The fingerprint identification became the vital evidence of the trial. Once again, Collins described the method of identification by fingerprints and produced a comparison chart to illustrate how the identification had been made and the 12 characteristics he found that agreed in both prints. It is not known what effect the thumbprint had on the jury, but it accepted the mark as positive evidence of identification and, after deliberating for only 2 hours, returned a guilty verdict. Both brothers were sentenced to death by hanging.

3.4   The Fingerprint Standard

In the early days of fingerprint identification, there was no strict numerical standard for the number of characteristics in agreement. In the Stratton case, D.I. Collins presented his fingerprint identification with 12. In 1924 the Fingerprint Department at Scotland Yard introduced the 16-point standard, but it was not until 1953 that this became a national standard. Due to the varying standards used throughout the country, fingerprint standards were reexamined at a meeting on September 29, 1953 among representatives from the Home Office, the deputy director of public prosecutions, and five major police fingerprint bureaus. It was agreed that it would be advantageous to have a national standard for officers giving fingerprint identification evidence in court, that the standard should be a minimum of 16 points in agreement, and that any other mark from the same scene with a minimum of 10 characteristics could be mentioned. In 1983, the use of fewer than 16 characteristics was accepted with the caveat that the evidence must be crucial, of dire importance, and that the evidence should be given only by an expert of long experience and standing in the profession.

3.5   The Identification Process

Fingerprints have been used for identification purposes for over 100 years, but what makes them unique? Prints are created during fetal development by the formation of friction skin on the fingers, palms, toes, and feet. The friction skin development is random, and this gives each finger, toe, palm, and foot its unique qualities. They are not genetically determined and therefore are unique even in identical twins, unlike DNA.

Friction skin consists of two main layers: the epidermis or outer skin (also known as the stratum Malpighi) and the dermis or inner skin. The dermis acts as a template for the epidermal development. In this way fingerprints remain the same even after small cuts or abrasions affect the surface because the skin's regeneration is based on the original dermis pattern. Only deep cuts that damage the dermis will result in a permanent scar.

The skin on the inner parts of the hand and the soles of the feet differs from the skin on the rest of the body. This hornier type of skin is made up of minute skin ridges that run roughly parallel to each other, but frequently change direction forming clearly defined patterns, particularly on the end pads of the fingers and thumbs. Identifying a fingerprint consists of looking at several layers of information within each print. This is done by comparing the similarities of details between fingermarks found at a crime scene or fingerprints taken from an unidentified person against a set of fingerprints held on record.

3.6 Fingerprint Patterns

The first layer is the actual pattern of the print itself of which there are four basic groups of patterns now recognized: arch, loop, whorl, and composite (Figure 3.1).

1. Arch: The arch is the simplest of all fingerprint patterns; the ridges run from one side to the other without making a backward turn.
2. Loop: In loops, the ridges about the center of the print appear to form a hairpin. The ends have a downward trend towards the left or the right. There are two fixed points in all prints of the loop type: the delta and the core.
3. Whorl: In whorls the ridges form a more intricate pattern. In some patterns, the ridges present well-defined spiral formations, whereas others possess more or less elongated cores. There are two deltas in all whorls.
4. Composite: As the word indicates, the composite pattern comprises a combination of two or more of the preceding patterns. There are at least two deltas, but sometimes there are three.

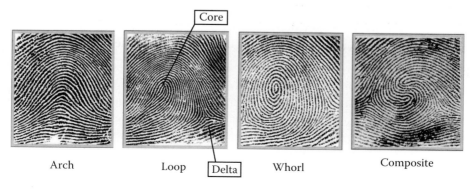

Arch   Loop   Whorl   Composite

Figure 3.1 Basic fingerprint patterns.

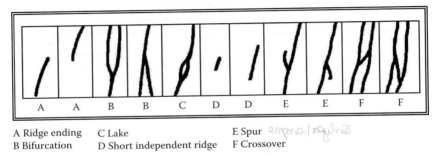

Figure 3.2   Ridge characteristic chart.

3.7   Ridge Characteristics

The second layer of information is unique and forms the most common method used for fingerprint identification. Examining the ridge structure of the fingerprint shows that the ridges are not continuous and that there are frequents breaks and interruptions in the ridge flow. For example, a ridge may end suddenly or a single ridge may divide into two ridges; these are known as ridge characteristics (Figure 3.2) or sometimes Galton details (after the man who researched them and gave them their name). Identity by means of fingerprints is conclusively established by comparing the ridge detail in two impressions and taking into account the position, direction, and orientation of each ridge characteristic in relation to another (coincident sequence) and by the sequence of ridge characteristics appearing in the same order and position to each other with none in disagreement.

Along the summit of the ridges are microscopic pores that discharge sweat from the body. When an article or surface capable of retaining a latent (invisible) impression of the ridges is touched, the ridges can be made visible by the application of a suitable developing agent, usually aluminum powder. The resulting developed finger mark is lifted from the surface by a low-adhesive tape and mounted onto a piece of clear plastic, where the fingermark is preserved. Similarly, ink is applied to the fingers, which are then pressed lightly on paper, and a permanent record is made. Those articles or surfaces that require specialized treatments are recovered from the crime scene. Any porous items such as paper, cardboard, or untreated wood or articles bearing marks in blood, dirt, or grease are such examples.

The ridge characteristics are present on the hand at birth and persist throughout life. They are one of the last recognizable features to disappear after death.

The third layer of information comprises the pore structure. This involves comparing the edges of the ridges (edgeoscopy) and the position and shape of the pores (poroscopy). The use of edgeoscopy and poroscopy is limited, as many latent prints and a high proportion of fingerprints held in the U.K.'s national collection do not show pore detail. However, if the pore structure is visible in both the latent print and the fingerprint record, together with an amalgamation of all the other information, it can enhance the comparison and the ability of the fingerprint examiner to articulate on how fingerprint identification is made.

In 1997 The National Fingerprint Evidence Standard Project Board was formed with a mandate from the Association of Chief Police Officers (ACPO) to replace the 16-point standard with a nonnumerical standard. On June 11, 2001, the police forces of England and Wales adopted a nonnumeric standard, and fingerprint identification became firmly

Table 3.1   The Principles of Analysis, Comparison, Evaluation, and Verification (ACE-V) of Friction Ridge Skin

Analysis	Comparison	Evaluation
Collect intelligence	*Use intelligence*	*Form an opinion*
Unknown surface effect	Unknown to known	Elimination
Substance effect	Overall pattern	Agreement
Development medium	Specific ridge path	Individualize
Deposition pressure	Specific ridge shape	
Pressure distortion	Relative pore position	
Anatomical aspects		
Clarity		
Verification		
Peer review		

established on the principles of analysis, comparison, evaluation, and verification (ACE-V) of friction ridge skin, as shown in Table 3.1.

3.7.1   Analysis

The first stage of the ACE-V process is an in-depth analysis of the latent friction ridges (fingermark from a crime scene). This is an intelligence-gathering exercise to establish the level of detail available for comparison. In the majority of friction ridge comparisons there is more than ample detail to individualize, and identification is straightforward. However, there are times when analysis can be extremely difficult, particularly in situations where the friction ridges lack clarity or when varying amounts of distortion are present. All deposited fingermarks suffer from some form of distortion; some of the most common factors are distortion of the development medium, pressure distortion, and deposition distortion. The analysis of clarity establishes the level of detail available to compare and the level of tolerance for minor differences.

3.7.2   Comparison

The comparison stage is where the visual comparison is made between an unknown area of friction ridges (from a crime scene) against a known area of friction ridge detail.

3.7.3   Evaluation

The evaluation stage can often take place at the same time as the comparison, especially when the crime scene mark is clear, needs little analysis, and has enough unique details to individualize or eliminate. The fingerprint examiner has to determine (1) if there is agreement between the unknown friction ridge detail and the known friction ridge detail and (2) if there is sufficient detail in agreement to eliminate all other possible donors. If the answer to both questions is yes, then an opinion of individualization or identification has been established.

3.7.4   Verification

The final stage, verification, is not part of the identification process but is the scientific basis of a peer review. The peer review is a form of quality assurance to ensure that high standards of accuracy are maintained. Fingerprint examiners are human and thus fallible.

Therefore, verification is the most critical stage of the ACE-V process. Each verifier repeats all of the steps taken by the initial fingerprint examiner to establish individualization. It is possible that all known identification mistakes have arisen through the failure to properly apply this stage of the process.

3.8 Fingerprints and Modern Biometric Identification

By the beginning of the 21st century, fingerprints had been used as a means of identifying individuals within a law enforcement context for over 100 years. Today, automated systems are used to store, match, and compare latent fingerprints found at crime scenes with those held on record. This process is both efficient and accurate. Automated systems can achieve such accuracy in processing 10 rolled fingerprints (tenprints) that what is known as "lights out" processing (where there is no human component in the identification process) is being introduced worldwide. When systems search latent crime scene marks against a database of tenprints, it is now commonplace to see accuracy levels well above 75 to 80%. This by far exceeds what would have been possible in the days when fingerprint experts searched databases manually using an eyeglass and a "thumb stool." Searches against the database that might have taken weeks and months in the past can now be carried out in minutes. Automated image retrieval systems have transformed the processes of fingerprint examination and searching. The Automated Fingerprint Identification System (AFIS) can deliver candidate lists from which an identification may result, but any positive result must still be verified by a minimum of three fingerprint experts.

AFIS is a storage, search, and retrieval system for finger- and palm-print electronic images and demographic data. AFIS enhances the ability of the fingerprint examiner to search and identify crime scene evidence in an accurate and timely manner. AFIS systems have replaced outdated manual methods of fingerprint classification employed by law enforcement agencies over the past century. The Henry classification method is now largely redundant and is not taught as a standard prerequisite in many training establishments — a practice that many fingerprint experts around the world regret. Many examiners feel that the very process of learning the Henry classification enhances their knowledge and understanding of fingerprint patterns, friction ridge skin structure, and elasticity. All facets of the skill of latent print examiners that aid in the apportioning of finger choice during the comparison process also help in the correct orientation of fingerprint images on AFIS systems, which is still very important to AFIS accuracy, even today. AFIS systems utilize specialized software to create unique "mathematical maps" or algorithms that are based upon the relationships between characteristics present within the finger or palm friction ridge skin structures. The use of such mathematical algorithms enables a fingerprint to be compared with millions of file prints in a matter of seconds. Despite the progress made in computer hardware and software, AFIS technology has not yet eliminated the need for human verification of AFIS match results. Indeed, even if such technological advances were to facilitate such a thing in the future, it is doubtful whether there would be the political will to undertake such a radical course of action. After all, the preparation of evidence and the presentation of such evidence in the courtroom will always be the role of a human expert in fingerprint examination.

Fingerprint forms from arrested suspects can be searched against a tenprint database to establish whether a criminal history is present. Latent fingermarks can also be captured from crime scenes and can be searched against a database of tenprints from offenders. In addition, tenprints from an individual held in custody can be compared against the database of crime scene marks to establish whether there is a possible match. Crime scene marks can also be taken from a location and can be searched against the database of other crime scene marks to help link crimes.

The power and speed of automated identification systems has led to innovative uses of such technology within police forces. A Serious Crime Cache (SCC) of marks from crime scenes can now be established. It is possible for all submitted tenprint cards to be compared automatically against a central database of high-profile marks from serious crimes. This has become a central tool in the linking of crimes to the individual. Many high-profile serial murderers and rapists have been linked to multiple crime scenes using global databases.

An Operational Response Database (ORD) allows each fingerprint bureau to carry out tenprint and mark searches against tenprint and mark databases the bureau has created for special events, for example, a serious crime or sets of crimes.

All around the world, automated fingerprint identification systems (AFIS) are becoming standard tools in all major crime-fighting laboratories. Vendors and systems integrators are developing applications that possess fingerprint search engines with ever-increasing accuracy thresholds. Many algorithms developed for the task are now so accurate that "lights out" processing is considered appropriate for tenprint-to-tenprint verification without the need for human intervention. With most, if not all, of the top eight global economies now operating criminal AFIS, we are seeing its increased use among developing nations for criminal applications, too.

Today, digital technology is the driver toward making fingerprints core to the emerging marketplace associated with biometric identification and verification. Post-9/11, both governments and the private sector are turning to fingerprints as a method of controlling access to sensitive data and property, employing access verification software that utilize the uniqueness of friction ridge skin.

Fingerprint scanning is the acquisition and recognition of a person's fingerprint characteristics for identification purposes. This allows for the recognition of a person through quantifiable physiological characteristics that verify the identity of an individual. Fingerprint recognition is the core identifier for mass-market biometric-ID systems as fingerprint-based systems have a high accuracy rate. Fingerprints are also considered to be "safe." Many users of biometrics devices, when questioned, are suspicious of the safety of using iris and retinal scanning techniques, for example, fearing that such devices will damage human eyesight over time. On balance, this may be a totally unfounded fear, but human concerns can be disproportionate to the actual risk of using such technology, a fact that a vendor must consider when designing and implementing systems.

Without doubt, fingerprints continue to play a huge role in the fight against crime, but fingerprints are becoming increasingly popular as a means of identification and verification in non-law enforcement domains as well. Today, fingerprints are being considered as important biometrics identifiers in worldwide civil applications, such as with federal ID cards, passports, bank cards, and library cards, as well as other less obvious applications, such as school access verification and as a substitute for money in the school cafeteria line.

In Nigeria, the driver's license application form includes questions regarding the applicant's blood type, facial marks, height, use of glasses, and date of birth; it also requires a set of the applicant's fingerprints. Singapore's Changi Airport has introduced immigration kiosks that read fingerprints and facial features and doubles an as automated check-in counter in a bid to cut flight check-in times. The project, known as Fully Automated Seamless Travel (FAST), cuts the time needed for passengers to register for flights. The system, which began trials at Changi, Asia's sixth-busiest airport, requires users to lodge facial details and thumbprints as biometric data on a credit card-sized identification card. Passengers insert their card into a kiosk, look into a camera, and press their thumb onto a plate to check their details. Hong Kong is preparing to introduce one of the world's most advanced identity cards in an attempt to curb illegal immigration. An embedded computer chip on the card will hold personal details such as name and date of birth, as well as a digital copy of both thumbprints.

Within Europe, fears of global terrorism and illegal immigration are also driving the development of biometrics technology, and here, too, fingerprints are playing a huge part in the successful deployment and acceptance of such systems. In the U.K., fingerprints could be added to travel documents within the next 3 years. The European Visa System (E-VIS) is to adopt fingerprints to counter fraud and terrorism. Fingerprint use is still predominantly to be found on government applications, and this trend is likely to continue for at least the next 5 years. However, there is an increasing uptake of fingerprint-based security (supported by the emergence of international standards) in the nongovernment arena. Microsoft and IBM are recognizing the advantages of biometrics identifiers and are supporting their introduction, particularly as security applications. Many different USB-drive solutions incorporating fingerprint sensors and applications are now available.

Access control using biometrics is just starting to reach critical mass but is still sluggish. There are misconceptions as to public attitude and marketing, and when there are biometric measures, they almost always focus on security, rather than convenience. For example, a retail store will always highlight the security advantages of scanning a fingerprint in verifying bankcard details when paying for items. However, it could also be argued that a fingerprint scan could drastically reduce checkout times for shoppers and increase customer throughput at the point of sale, saving shoppers' time and enabling a more convenient shopping experience. At present, biometric systems are being developed and marketed as tools to counter the fear of terror and criminality, but could also be marketed as tools of convenience and enhanced service.

Almost all of the nongovernment applications employ nonstandard AFIS capture protocols and algorithms. The move is toward low-cost silicon-based solutions, such as ultrasound, capacitive, and thermal analysis. All fingerprint sensors try to generate a digital picture of the finger surface. Optical sensors use high-resolution optics (cameras and prisms) to capture the fingerprint image. Capacitive sensors use electrodes to measure the conductivity of existing pixels. Acoustic (ultrasound) sensors record the fingerprint surface with very high frequency ultrasound (e.g., 50 MHz). Thermal line sensors register temperature differences over time between the ridges and valleys on the fingerprint. There are two main fingerprint recognition algorithms: pattern and minutiae. Pattern recognition will predominate in the 1:1 verification arena, but minutiae will continue to lead in the 1:n scenarios.

There is a major trend toward placing user profile templates on "tokens," mainly smartcards, and not keeping them in databases except where the application requires it. A template is a binary file created from distinctive information from a biometric sample, created during enrollment and verification. Authentication and verification techniques secure network access by replacing the log-on password with fingerprint authentication.

Fingerprint templates created during the enrollment process are stored as an attribute of a user account, or on a smart card or similar personal storage device. A live fingerprint capture is authenticated against a user's stored fingerprint template during the log-on process, and access to the network is either granted or denied depending on the result of this authentication process. One potential stumbling block to all biometric systems using fingerprints is the enrollment process in which users place their fingerprints on a sensor to either submit their biometric information in order to register or when confirming such data to gain access to buildings or files. For example, many construction workers have worn-down fingerprints because of the wear and tear experienced in using building materials and tools. It is debatable whether access verification systems for entry to building sites using fingerprints would be viable, as many users would not be able to register, and the failure rate on confirmation would be prohibitive. Fingerprint matching "on the card" is now the preferred option, as it is self-contained and secure. There are already smartcards that also have a fingerprint sensor on them, which makes them even more secure.

The major private sector biometrics markets are likely to be financial (particularly point-of-sale), private healthcare, and company access control, but we are already seeing large volumes of consumables, such as laptop computers, coming onto the market with incorporated fingerprint sensors for access security. The major uptake and use of biometrics identification is still in government and law enforcement, and this will continue. However, there is a shift toward private sector use, although the current uptake of such devices is comparatively slow.

The public is constantly bombarded with misleading reports about privacy and accuracy of biometrics devices. The U.K. government is currently pushing through the countrywide use of ID cards containing biometrics data to positively identify the holder. The main biometric identifier suggested is fingerprints. This is relatively easy to read and verify, as the technology is already available. Some argue that this would be premature and dangerous. The enrollment processes for biometric systems must be easy enough to use, yet robust enough to provide solid data. As mentioned earlier in this chapter, there are inherent problems in using fingerprints as not everyone can reliably enroll in systems using their fingerprints because they may not have well-defined fingerprints. Thus, their enrollment failure rate will be high. This would be both inefficient and inconvenient to both authorities and the public alike.

It is suggested that the manufacturers of fingerprint equipment have not solved the live detection problem (i.e., detect the difference between a live finger and a dummy). It is argued that biometric fingerprint sensors should not be used in combination with identity cards or in medium- to high-security applications. Many even believe that identity cards with fingerprint biometrics are in fact weaker than cards without it. Let us suppose, because of the fingerprint check, that there is no longer visual identification by an official or a controller. When the fingerprint matches with the template in the card, access is granted if it is a valid card. An individual whose own card is blacklisted could buy a valid identity card with a matching dummy fingerprint and still get access without anyone's noticing. Or, we can suppose that there is still visual identification and, where there is doubt, the fingerprint could be checked for additional verification. Should the photo on the identity card and the person not match and the official asks for fingerprint verification, most likely the positive result of the fingerprint scan will prevail. That is, the confirmation from the technical fingerprint system would remove any doubt that may have legitimately arisen.

Figure 3.3   The wall of remembrance in Phuket, Thailand.

By the middle of 2007, the British passport could be quite different from the document currently waved at immigration. As a result of growing concerns about national and global security, the official U.K. travel document will not only carry a photograph but also a microchip. The chip will hold biometric data — unique physiological or behavioral characteristics — and will be mandatory in passports.

In May 2003, the International Civil Aviation Organization (ICAO) approved facial recognition as the global standard for biometric data, with the option of including secondary biometrics, such as a fingerprint or iris image. Iris pattern or fingerprints will be stored on the chip, and trials are under way in the U.K. to decide which one is to be used.

3.9   Fingerprints and Major Disasters

On December 26, 2004, a tsunami devastated Southeast Asia (see Figure 3.3). Many thousands were killed. The disaster had no respect for wealth, status, or nationality. All peoples of the world succumbed to the terrible power of the ocean. Properties were taken away; hotels were leveled. Countries were ravaged.

Police agencies from around the world joined an international effort to use automated fingerprint recognition systems to try to identify the victims of the tsunami by comparing the fingerprints of the deceased with antemortem fingerprints from a victim's property, house, or identification documents (Figure 3.4).

Biometric data was being used, probably for the first time on this scale, in a civil application to identify victims, rather than to catch criminals, as is usually the case. It is clear that had many people not enrolled in biometric systems during their lives, many of the victims of the tsunami might still remain unidentified. Many of the victims were found in an advanced state of decomposition, so, in many cases, only fingerprints and dental

Figure 3.4 Fingerprints being compared in Phuket, Thailand, as part of the victim identification effort.

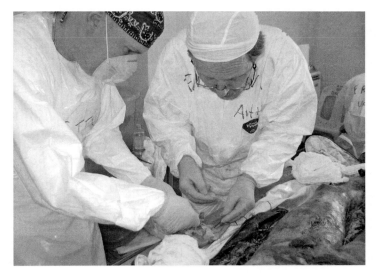

Figure 3.5 U.K. forensic specialists retrieving fingerprints from a tsunami victim in Phuket, Thailand.

records provided sufficient information to individualize them (Figure 3.5). This is the power of biometric science. The persistence of fingerprints, even after death, greatly aided the identification task set before the authorities in Southeast Asia.

It is clear that we as individuals and citizens will have to get used to the surveillance culture in the domain of the biometric identifier. What is unclear at this time is how such technology can be effective and appropriate. When will the needs and desire to travel and generally go about our daily business outweigh the need for personal safety and security? Only the future will reveal the real price of freedom. But whatever the future may hold, fingerprints will be core to biological human identification for both civil and law enforcement applications.

3.10   Acknowledgments

Special thanks to Clive Reedman of Emerging Technology Services, chairman of the International Association for Biometrics.

Further Reading

A Ridge Too Far, http://www.david.charlton97.btinternet.co.uk/.

Association for Biometrics, http://www.afb.org.uk/docs/objectives.htm.

CLPEX, http://www.clpex.com/.

Fingerprint Whorld, http://www.fpsociety.org.uk/.

Maltoni, D., Maio, D., Jain, A., and Prabhakar, S., Eds., *A Handbook of Fingerprint Recognition*, Springer-Verlag, New York, 2003.

PITO, http://www.pito.org.uk/.

Ratha, N. and Bolle, R., Eds., *Automatic Fingerprint Recognition Systems*, Springer-Verlag, New York, 2003.

Shen, M., A Guide to Biometric Fingerprint Sensors: Major Manufacturers and Technical Specifications, http://www.biometritech.com/features/shen0902.htm.

The Thin Blue Line Web Resource, http://www.policensw.com/info/fingerprints/finger15.html.

Earprints

4

LYNN MEIJERMAN
ANDREW THEAN
CORNELIS VAN DER LUGT
GEORGE J.R. MAAT

Contents

4.1   Earprints as an Identification Tool..73
4.2   Intra-Individual Variation...75
4.3   Automatic Classification and Matching...78
4.4   Acknowledgments...82
References 82

4.1   Earprints as an Identification Tool

When a burglar listens at, for instance, a door or window before breaking and entering, oils and waxes on the ear leave a print that can be made visible using techniques similar to those used when lifting fingerprints. This print is characteristic of the ear that made it. Hirschi (1970) was among the first to recognize the value of earprints for personal identification. In the years to follow, several reports of personal identification using earprints recovered at crime scenes were made (Dubois 1988; Hammer 1986; Kennerley 1998; van der Lugt 1998; Pasescu and Tanislav 1997; Scaillet 1971). Earprints offer useful leads during forensic investigations. Scene-of-crime officers emphasize the practical utility of earprints for interlinking various cases (Meijerman et al. 2005b) and use the location of the print to estimate the height of the perpetrator (van der Lugt 2001; van der Lugt et al. 2005). Judges in the Netherlands have even used them as a tool to pry confessions from a defendant (Egan 1999). Kennerley (1998) reported many successful prosecutions based on earprint evidence in the U.K. Indeed, earprints were becoming steadily more important in the U.K., where, according to Champod et al. (2001), they had gained a status as identification evidence that was becoming as reliable as that of fingerprints. There was, however, increasing criticism of the use of earprints as evidence in court on the grounds that the process of individualization was considered to be subjective (e.g., Champod et al. 2001; Egan 1999; Moenssens 1999). Indeed, formal protocols for collecting earprints have not yet been implemented, and there are no methods for analyzing earprints that have been generally accepted by the scientific community. The use of earprints became more controversial when, in January of 2004 in the U.K., charges against Mark Dallagher, accused of murdering an elderly woman and convicted in 1998 on the basis of earprint evidence, were formally dropped when it was found that his DNA did not match the DNA that was later recovered from the original earmark. Moenssens (2004) referred to these events to illustrate "the superiority of DNA analysis over most other forensic methods of individualization" and argued that the DNA evidence proved that Mark Dallagher could not have made the recovered earmark. However, the possibility that the DNA evidence was contaminated should also be considered as the print was lifted by officers not intending to perform a DNA analysis — therefore, not taking precautions to prevent contamination — and using equipment that could have been contaminated from previous cases. In addition, Kieckhoefer et al. (2005b) pointed out that the original mark had been stored for years on a nonsterile surface.

It is important to distinguish between the legal and the scientific conclusions that may be drawn from the Dallagher case. It is also important to distinguish between specific conclusions about this case and general conclusions about advantages and limitations of earprint and DNA or other types of biometric evidence. Nowadays, there is less chance that DNA evidence will be contaminated than in 1998, when the murder for which Dallagher was initially convicted took place, because scene-of-crime officers will take greater care to prevent contamination when collecting DNA evidence. Obviously, DNA evidence is very reliable in cases where sufficient quantities of bodily substances can be recovered and linked to a perpetrator. However, the strengths of DNA evidence can be overemphasized. In the Netherlands it was suggested that scene-of-crime officers should only collect DNA and fingerprint evidence (Vermaas 2003), but we would argue that it is best to keep all options open toward solving a crime. Not all types of evidence will be equally valuable — or present — in all cases of crime. DNA, for instance, has the disadvantage that it may be relatively easily planted at the crime scene to frame an innocent person. In contrast, earprints are almost tamperproof. A print is usually created when someone is intentionally listening at a door or window. This may decisively place the listener at the crime scene. Planting earprints from innocent people at a crime scene is relatively difficult as they are difficult to obtain without the consent of the donor for the purpose of creating duplicates. They are, furthermore, not so easily left by an innocent passer-by.

Earprints, however, have various limitations. Firstly, the study of earprints as a quantitative and rigorous discipline is immature, and standard tools and methods for analyzing earprints are only now becoming available. Secondly, an earmark is usually left in a publicly-accessible area before the crime itself is committed (e.g., on the outside of a building before a break-in). Furthermore, no accurate indication of the time of its formation may usually be inferred. In the case of Mark Dallagher, it was reported that the window from which the earmarks were recovered had been cleaned three or four weeks before the murder took place (Crown 2002). Thus, all that the presence of his earprint could have proved was that Dallagher listened at the house of the murdered woman within the three- to four-week period leading up to the murder. This may be considered suspicious but without additional evidence, the sole presence of his earprint would not be sufficient grounds for a murder conviction. Bearing in mind the limitations of earprint evidence, let us now consider what is needed for earprints to be accepted as evidence in court. What fundamental questions need to be addressed before we can confidently use earprints for individualization? A frequently quoted definition for the process of individualization was provided by Tuthill (1994):

> The individualisation of an impression is established by finding agreement of corresponding individual characteristics of such number and significance as to preclude the possibility (or probability) of their having occurred by mere coincidence, and establishing that there are no differences that cannot be accounted for.

But when can corresponding individual characteristics be said to agree? Not even characteristics in two prints from the same ear will ever be identical. Judging agreement in practice means judging the degree of similarity between the various characteristics, and because degrees of similarity usually vary continuously, the term *agreement* is difficult to define objectively.

Next, when is the degree of similarity of such significance as to preclude the possibility (or probability) of it having occurred by mere coincidence? We may even ask whether it is ever possible to preclude the possibility that agreements occur by coincidence: the mere concept of precluding a probability is unusual. We may further ask whether ruling out coincidence is relevant to individualization. It is known, for example, that the earprints of monozygotic (identical) twins usually share numerous characteristics that are valuable for individualization (Meijerman et al. 2006d). The reason for this is genetic, and one may safely rule out the role of coincidence in causing the agreement without coming any closer to addressing issues of individual identity. And, finally, when are differences sufficiently small or insignificant as to claim that we can account for them, or — rephrased — when are differences too great to pass off as intraindividual variation? Evidently, when subjected to closer scrutiny, the definition provided by Tuthill (1994) is flawed and has limited use in practice where unbiased, standardized methods are required. There is now a growing consensus that expressing opinions on individualization in absolute terms should be avoided in favor of using probabilistic statements (Champod and Evett 2001; Broeders 2003). Progress is being made in developing quantitative methods for comparing large samples of earprints. The statistics of these samples could be used to put lower limits on the degree of genetic randomness that characterizes earprints and to estimate the likelihood that two earprints were created by the same ear.

4.2 Intra-Individual Variation

For an earprint to have evidential value in a forensic or identification setting, it needs to possess a feature, or set of features, for which the intra-individual rate of occurrence is high and the inter-individual rate of occurrence is low. To strengthen the scientific basis for earprint individualization, we must understand more about how to select and use earprint features and know more about the factors that determine the range of intra-individual variation. Ideally, we would then be able to determine the limits to intra-individual variation.

What are the factors that may generate variation in different prints from a single ear? Figure 4.1 shows the entire procedure leading up to the realization of earprint evidence, from the moment the ear is in contact with the listening surface, via lifting and securing the latent print, to scanning and storing the digitized print for the purpose of automated matching. This process of creating earprint evidence can be described in terms of a flow of information. The ear, as well as areas of the head that may get imprinted, contains a full set of information that is assumed to be donor-specific. As information is passed from the ear to an earprint it is transformed, censored, and augmented by various processes. If individualization is to be possible, enough donor-specific information must survive the entire process to arrive at the stored earprint.

The aim is to use donor-specific information that is contained in the earprint to map the print back to the ear from which it originated. This cannot be done directly, and the only practical option is to compare a print of unknown origin to a print of known origin

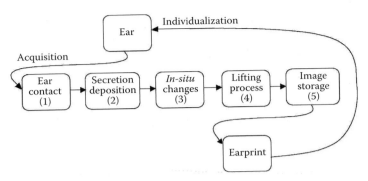

Figure 4.1   A schematic overview of the procedure leading up to the realization of earprint evidence. Steps 1 to 5 transform, censor, and augment the information contained in an ear as an earprint is formed and collected. The goal of individualization is to uniquely associate an earprint with a real ear.

(i.e., a suspect's earprint or an identified print in a database). Herein lies one of the biggest challenges for using earprints for individualization. It is impossible to repeat exactly the process outlined in Figure 4.1, even under controlled conditions. Some degree of natural intra-individual variation in earprint appearance is therefore unavoidable. In the worst circumstances, any of the steps in the process can prevent donor-specific information reaching the (stored) earprint, making it impossible to trace the print back to an ear with confidence. In the following sections we explore potential sources of variation at the various stages of the process. The sources of variation identified should be considered when determining the effects of intra-individual variation, i.e., when compiling a reference or research database.

A potentially important source of intra-individual variation in earprints appeared to be variation in the force that is applied by the ear to the surface during listening (Hammer and Neubert 1989; Neubert 1985; Saddler 1996). During various studies into applied force while listening, we noted that intra-individual variation in applied force was comparatively small compared with the inter-individual variation (Meijerman et al. 2005a; Meijerman et al. 2006c). This was confirmed by Kieckhoefer et al. (2005b). We hypothesized that applied force may possibly reflect a balance between the aim of creating an airtight seal between the ear and the listening surface to optimize hearing, and the inclination to minimize discomfort to the ear or cheek. The individual anatomy of one's ear would then play a key part in determining both the amount of force needed to create a reasonable seal and the amount of force that would cause discomfort to the listener. Force applied by the ear to the surface during multiple attempts of listening would thus fall within certain individual limits. We would therefore advise that, if possible, reference prints of suspects are "functional earprints," i.e., taken after actual efforts at listening. To explore the limits of a person's functional force range, i.e., the force that is applied by the ear during the act of listening, we have tried to predict possible grounds for changes in applied force. We experimented by varying the level of ambient noise while recording the force that was applied during listening. No significant effect from the level of ambient noise on applied force was observed (Meijerman et al. 2006c). Listening to either sound or silence did also not appear to significantly affect applied force (Meijerman et al. 2005a). We did, however, notice a significant effect from changes in the level of the target sound. When the sound level was reduced between listening efforts, it caused the listeners to apply more force

(Meijerman et al. 2006c). In addition, we observed that listeners generally applied less force during their first listening effort. We assumed that — unfamiliar with the procedure — our subjects were more cautious during their first listening efforts.

How long a donor listens at a surface also affects the appearance of the retrieved earprint. We have explored the effect of the listening duration on earprints by using the size and the intensity (i.e., gray values of pixels) of the imprinted area to calculate a print-mass. We found that print-mass significantly increased with length of listening (Meijerman et al. 2006a). Kieckhoefer et al. (2005b) showed that "fidgeting" of the ear during listening increased the amount of imprinted surface. Another effect of increased listening time may be a higher chance of smudging due to a sliding of the ear across the surface. During a preliminary study into the effect of listening time on earprints it was observed that some blurring of features generally occurred after 20 to 25 seconds of listening, although it was usually not so marked as to distort minutiae to the extent that it was expected to affect individualization (De Conti et al. 2003). Smudging in earprints may, however, occur, and it may be easily recognized. If smudging is too severe, one might consider dismissing the print.

Not only differences in the act of listening between various listening efforts cause intra-individual variation in earprints. The amount of oils and waxes that are naturally present on the ear may vary, depending on outside temperature and whether the ear was recently cleaned or not. More or less secretion available for printing could, in theory, influence the dimensions or intensity of the imprinted area. In turn, this might affect the area in which characteristics can be found or the visibility of such details. We therefore continued our explorations into intra-individual variation by comparing the print-mass retrieved from prints collected before and after an ear was cleaned but found no evidence for a significant decrease in the mass of prints created by cleaned ears (Meijerman et al. 2006b). This, however, provides no guarantee that the imprinted details are of equal quality. Investigations into the stability of characteristic features (i.e., valuable for individualization) in prints of recently cleaned ears are ongoing. The level of donor-specific detail to be retrieved in a print — hence, its evidential value — may further be influenced by the quality of the surface from which prints are recovered. Saddler (1996) observed that, for instance, brush-strokes on the paint greatly reduced skin detail in a mark that was lifted from a painted wooden door. In our experience, smooth, nonporous surfaces such as glass and metal offer the greatest potential for the recovery of prints that are rich in detail. Varnished wood may also provide good-quality prints, particularly when the paint is not old and porous. Prints recovered from synthetic materials appeared to be of lesser quality. In situ changes may also affect the extent to which details may be recovered. In cases of burglary, even daytime burglary, a search for evidence will usually not start until the following day. In between deposition and securing, weathering or — less likely — cleansing may affect the latent print. It may, furthermore, be possible that secondary imprints of ears, cheeks, palms, or fingers are superimposed on the principal print.

Discrepancies between different prints of a single ear may further occur as a result of variation in the quality of the material that was used to lift and secure the latent prints. The Forensic Ear Identification (FearID) research team found that black gel lifters were particularly good for preserving details. These prints offered more clues for individualization than prints secured using adhesive and acetate sheets (De Conti et al. 2002). The inkless impression kit (IIK), which makes use of chemically treated paper that reacts with a coater, which has to be applied to the ear in advance, was also tested. IIK initially promised to offer a cheap and quick method to create reference prints of suspects as IIK prints offered a good recovery of details. IIK was, however, dismissed when it was found that, mostly due to variation in the distribution of the applied coater, obtained prints sometimes deviated greatly from natural "functional" earprints (Meijerman 2002).

Finally, when the physical medium onto which a print has been lifted is digitized in order to perform, for instance, a quantitative analysis using image processing techniques, we need to consider the effect of digitization parameters on the ability to recover details from the print. The digitization of a print involves sampling the information contained on the lifting medium, which results in the loss of some information. Therefore, digitization parameters, such as the spatial resolution and the color depth, need to be taken into account when comparing prints. Digital image formats that involve image compression are not appropriate because they can introduce spurious image details. A spatial resolution of 600 dots per inch and a color depth of 8 bits per pixel were found to give acceptable image quality for the FearID project.

When exploring the limits of intra-individual variation, all mentioned sources of variation have to be taken into account. Unfortunately, no golden rule can be provided here to distinguish between inter- and intra-individual variation. With respect to applied force, for instance, it was found that equal variation in applied force did not necessarily lead to equal intra-individual variation in the prints. For some ears, small changes in force appeared to have a relatively large effect on the prints, whereas for other ears, relatively large changes in force seemed to have little effect on the appearance of the prints (Meijerman et al. 2004; Meijerman et al. 2006c). Prints of the same ear may further be affected by a change in pressure distribution (Kieckhoefer et al. 2005b; Meijerman et al. 2004; Meijerman et al. 2006c).

Describing and documenting the characteristics of intra-individual variation can provide useful information for assessing the evidential value of earprints or designing robust algorithms. However, at present, there is no practical substitute for a specialist who has studied a large number of prints. In the future, statistical techniques for modeling variations in images may help encapsulate and transfer knowledge about inter- and intra-individual variation, but these methods are not yet properly tested. A start in this direction has been made by using active appearance models (Cootes et al. 1998) to model inter-individual variations in the gross anatomical appearance of a sample of earprints during the FearID project. For an expert, or an algorithm, to learn about inter- and intra-individual variations, a suitable sample is required. Such a sample needs to incorporate multiple prints from each of the included ears. If required, it would be possible to influence the amount of intra-individual variation in a sample by exploiting the experience gained about the factors that affect the appearance of a print. For example, applied listening force appears to be generally lower during a first-listening effort. A loud target source during this attempt, or a relatively short duration of ear-surface contact, will increase the chance of yielding a print with a relatively low print-mass.

4.3 Automatic Classification and Matching

An important issue that can diminish the evidential value of earprints is that of subjectivity. Even when automatic systems are used to analyze forensic data, human experts are required to make the final judgment about individualization. On the issue of subjectivity in fingerprint individualization, Stoney (1991) commented: "The modern image processing techniques used to classify fingerprints may provide an illusion of complete objectivity, yet only a list of most likely matches from a database are provided, and the expert will have to compare and make conclusions." This would also be the case for earprint individualization, and some level of subjectivity must be accepted. If the option to calculate the match probability for any combination of two prints was provided, the expert would, however, have an objective means to support his opinion. Seemingly "perfect matches" containing few individualizing features might then be presented in the context of their reduced evidential value.

A number of initiatives toward a (semi-) automated classification or matching of earprints have been undertaken. Valvoda (1999, cited in Champod et al., 2001) presented image-processing algorithms to extract features from the anthelix area. More recently, Rutty et al. (2005) presented their concept of a computerized earprint identification system. Rutty et al. made use of a database containing 800 prints of 800 different ears. Their research, therefore, did not allow the possibility to verify if selected parameters offered, besides a high interindividual variability, also a sufficiently small intra-individual variability. In line with Ingleby et al. (2000), Rutty et al. (2005) proposed to calculate centroids of imprinted areas, the pattern formed by these centroids offering clues for individualization. In both studies, it was assumed that the effect of pressure would be overcome by the use of centroids. However, as we pointed out in Meijerman et al. (2004), the imprints of morphological structures do not only narrow or widen due to a change in applied force. Features may change position in relation to each other as well. Still, the proof-of-concept paper by Rutty et al. may serve as a useful starting point for further investigations.

The FearID team has also striven to design a (semi-) automatic matching system for earprints, and a number of approaches have been explored, e.g., vector template matching, active appearance modeling, and a calculation of the width, relative intensity, and curvature of the imprinted gross anatomical features (weighted width comparison; angular comparison) (Alberink and Ruifrok 2005b; Van Munster et al. 2005 and Kieckhoefer et al. 2005a). To facilitate the (automatic) detection of the various imprinted anatomical structures for analyses, the imprinted ear surface in each analyzed print was captured into a spiral shape (Figure 4.2). To obtain this shape, an operator points out the location of the imprinted ear by adding an indicator line, i.e., a spiral-shaped poly-line starting at the apex of the anthelix and ending in the lowest point of the imprinted earlobe. This line does not need to be extremely accurate, and when parts of the ear are not imprinted, their position can be estimated, as only the imprinted surface is used for classification.

The computer uses the spiral line to calculate the contours of the imprinted ear surface. This data is then used to calculate the width and curvature of the various parts in the spiral shape, which can be compared among prints (weighted width and angular comparisons). Differences in relative intensity along the spiral shape may provide further information for classification. The operator may further annotate minutiae, landmarks, and other characteristics in the earprints, and indicate transitions between the imprinted gross anatomical features in the spiral shape. This provides additional data for comparison that is analyzed through a method called *vector template matching*. It was found that the performance of the weighted-width comparison of earprints was operator independent (Alberink and Ruifrok 2005a; Alberink and Ruifrok 2005b). Achieving interoperator objectivity for the method of vector template matching based on manual annotations appeared more problematic. Performance of the method

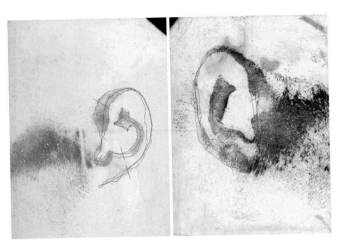

Figure 4.2 Imprinted earprint features captured in a spiral-shape. The longitudinal center line is the indicator line; transverse lines indicate transitions between gross anatomical feature zones.

appeared significantly worse when prints had been annotated by different operators (Alberink et al. 2006).

In addition to these semiautomated approaches, we have applied a method to automatically match earprints (Meijerman et al. 2006d). The fact that the method requires no human input confers two main advantages. First, it allows objective and repeatable earprint comparisons that are free from observer bias. Second, it has the potential to handle tasks that are too time-consuming for a human expert to consider. In this method, called *keypoint matching*, algorithms automatically detect and describe salient regions (keypoints) in an earprint. In the current implementation, keypoints are detected and described using methods described by Lowe (2004a) and implemented using his executable code (2004b).

The appearance and constellation of the described keypoints in an earprint can be compared with that in all other prints of a collection. The number of matching keypoints can be used to express the level of similarity between any two prints. The result is a ranking list, or "hit list," for potential matches and could provide a tool for recovering matching earprints from a large database. Figure 4.3 illustrates the method. The top two prints show all keypoints that are described for two different prints of the same ear; the middle two prints show shared keypoints in a similar constellation that are used for matching. The bottom three prints show the same for two prints that are not of the same ear. Note that there are fewer shared keypoints in prints in the bottom print combination as compared to the middle.

Another potential application of keypoint matching is to assess the evidential value of a given earprint comparison. Champod et al. (2001) have highlighted the need for methods to describe the weight of evidence offered by an earprint comparison as a likelihood ratio. They consider the case of an earmark being recovered at the scene of a crime and compare it with earprints taken from Suspect X under controlled conditions. The proposed likelihood ratio is the ratio between two probabilities. The numerator is the probability of obtaining a piece of evidence, given that the earmark was made by Suspect X. The denominator is the probability of obtaining a piece of evidence, given that the earmark was made by some unknown person. Keypoint matching represents a step toward the goal of calculating such

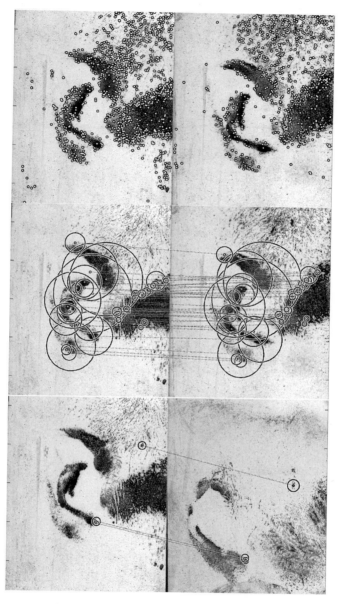

Figure 4.3 Keypoint matching illustrated. For each pair of illustrations, the print on the left is the same. The upper pair shows all detected keypoints in two different prints of the same ear. For the middle pair, dotted lines join matching keypoints. In the lower pair, three keypoint matches to a print from a different ear are shown. Note that prints do not need to be aligned. (From Meijerman, L. et al., *Forensic Science, Medicine and Pathology* 2(1), 2006. With permission.)

likelihood ratios. In the equations given by Champod et al. (2001) the nature of the "evidence" is unspecified. However, if we were to take the evidence for two prints being made by the same ear as the number of keypoint matches, we can make statistical estimates of the numerator and denominator in the likelihood ratio. For the method described, the likelihood ratio increases as the number of keypoint matches increases. So far, the method was tested using 36 prints from 6 identical twin pairs (Meijerman et al. 2006d). It should be emphasized that the data studied in this paper is very challenging for automated methods because the earprints from twins show strong similarities. Still, as the used sample is small, we are at this point able to make only loose and biased estimates on the proposed likelihood ratios. Making more reliable estimates will require a large, well-defined sample. For the first time, such a large sample is now available as a result of the FearID project. In the future, work on this sample will offer the promise of a solid scientific basis for the use of earprints in forensic investigations and as evidence in court.

4.4   Acknowledgments

The text of this chapter was chiefly compiled using Meijerman et al., 2005b and 2006d, both published in *Forensic Science, Medicine and Pathology*. The research was carried out within the framework of the FearID project. This shared-cost Research and Technological Development project was funded under the 5th Framework Programme of the European Community (Competitive and Sustainable Growth Programme, Measurements and Testing Activity, Contract G6RD-CT-2001-00618).

References

Alberink, I.B. and Ruifrok, A.C.C., Inter-Operator Test for the Clicking of Polylines in Earprints, Internal FearID report, Netherlands Forensic Institute, The Hague, submitted for publication, November 2005a.

Alberink, I.B. and Ruifrok, A.C.C., Performance of the FearID Earprint Identification System, Internal FearID report, Netherlands Forensic Institute, The Hague, submitted for publication, July 2005b.

Alberink, I.B., Ruifrok, A.C.C., and Kieckhoefer, H., Inter-operator test for anatomical annotation of earprints, *J Forensic Sci*, accepted for publication February 2006.

Broeders, A.P.A., *Op zoek naar de bron, Over de grondslagen van de criminalistiek en de waardering van het forensisch bewijs*, Kluwer, Deventer, The Netherlands, 2003.

Champod, C. and Evett, I.W., A probabilistic approach to fingerprint evidence, *J Forensic Identification* 51(2), 101, 2001.

Champod, C., Evett, I.W., and Kuchler, B., Earmarks as evidence: a critical review, *J Forensic Sci* 46(6), 1275, 2001.

Cootes, T.F., Edwards, G.J., and Taylor, C.J., Active Appearance Models, in *Proc. European Conference on Computer Vision*, Vol. 2, Burkhardt, H. and Neumann, B., Eds., Springer-Verlag, Berlin, 1998, p. 484.

Crown, Rv Mark Anthony Dallagher, In the Supreme Court of Judicature — Court of Appeal (Criminal Division), Neutral Citation No. (2002) EWCA Crim 1903, Case No. 2000/5024/Z2, London, 2002.

De Conti, F. et al., Cross Media Study Report, Internal FearID report, University of Padova, Padova, Italy, 2002.

De Conti, F. et al., Effect of Sound File Length on the Quality of Earprint Images, Internal FearID report, University of Padova, Padova, Italy, 2003.

Dubois, N., Oren naar hebben, *Technisch Informatie Bulletin* 1, 7, 1988.

Egan, T., Are Dutch ears different from American ears? A comparison of evidence standards, Forensic-Evidence.com/UMKC School of Law, Kansas City, 1999, http://www.forensic-evidence.com/site/ID/ID00004_1.html.

Hammer, H.J., The identification of earprints secured at the scene of the crime, *Fingerprint Whorld* 12, 49, 1986.

Hammer, H.J. and Neubert, F., Experimentelle Untersuchungen zur Auswertung von Ohrabdrückspuren, *Kriminalistik und Forensische Wissenschaften* 73–74, 136, 1989.

Hirschi, F., Cambrioleurs internationaux convaincus à l'aide de preuves peu communes, *Revue Internationale de Police Criminelle* 239, 184, 1970.

Ingleby, M. et al., Ear-Prints: A Neglected Forensic Resource? Internal report, School of Computing and Engineering, University of Huddersfield, Huddersfield, UK, 2000.

Kennerley, J., Ear Print Identification, presented at National Conference on Craniofacial Identification, Windsor, UK, September 4–6, 1998.

Kieckhoefer, H., Ingleby, M., and Alberink, I., Vector Template Matching of Earprints, Research Report series (RR05 13d), School of Computing and Engineering, University of Huddersfield, Huddersfield, UK, 2005a.

Kieckhoefer, H., Ingleby, M., and Lucas, G., Monitoring the physical formation of earprints: Optical and pressure mapping evidence, *Measurement*, accepted for publication December 2005b.

Lowe, D., Distinctive image features from scale-invariant keypoint, *Int J Comp Vision* 60(2), 91, 2004a.

Lowe, D., Demo Software, SIFT Keypoint Detector (version 3), 2004b, http://www.cs.ubc.ca/~lowe/keypoints.

Lugt, van der, C., Ear identification — state of the art, *Info. Bull. SP/TM Examiners* 4, 69, 1998.

Lugt, van der, C., *Earprint Identification*, Elsevier Bedrijfsinformatie, The Hague, The Netherlands, 2001.

Lugt, van der C., Nagelkerke, N., and Maat, G.J.R., Study of the relationship between a person's stature and height of an ear imprint from the floor, *Med. Sci. Law* 45, 135, 2005.

Meijerman, L., Appendix to Cross Media Study Report, Internal FearID report, Leiden University Medical Center, Leiden, The Netherlands, 2002.

Meijerman, L. et al., Exploratory study on classification and individualization of earprints, *Forensic Sci Int* 140, 91, 2004.

Meijerman, L. et al., Exploring the effect of occurrence of sound on force applied by the ear when listening at a surface, *Forensic Sci Med Pathol* 1(3), 187, 2005a.

Meijerman, L., Thean, A., and Maat, G.J.R., Earprints in forensic investigations, *Forensic Sci Med Pathol* 1(4), 247, 2005b.

Meijerman, L. et al., Exploring the effect of duration of listening on earprints, in *Inter- and Intra-Individual Variation in Earprints*, Meijerman, L., Barge's Anthropologica, Leiden, The Netherlands, 2006a, chap. 6.

Meijerman, L. et al., Preliminary comparison of earprints that were made before and after cleaning the ear, in *Inter- and Intra-individual Variation in Earprints*, Meijerman, L., Barge's Anthropologica, Leiden, The Netherlands, 2006b, chap. 7.

Meijerman, L. et al., Inter- and intra-individual variation in applied force when listening at a surface, and resulting variation in earprints, *Med Sci Law* 46(2), 46(2), 141, 2006.

Meijerman, L. et al., Individualization of earprints: variation in earprints of monozygotic twins, *Forensic Sci Med Pathol* 2(1), 2(1), 39, 2006.

Moenssens, A.A., Identifying individuals by ear photographs, and earprints — is this process reliable enough to justify expert opinion of identity in court? *Proc. First International Conference on Forensic Human Identification in the Next Millennium,* London, October 24–26, 1999.

Moenssens, A.A., DNA Evidence Proves Ear ID Wrong, Forensic-Evidence.com/UMKC, School of Law, Kansas City, MO, 2004, http://www.forensic-evidence.com/site/ID/DNAdisputesEarlID.html.

Munster, van R.J., van Antwerpen, G., and Thean, A., FearID Image Processing for Earprint Analysis: Final report TNO contribution to WP5, Internal FearID report, Netherlands Organization for Applied Scientific Research, Delft, 2005.

Neubert, F., Die Bedeutung der Täteridentifizierung durch Ohrabdrücke, M.Sc. thesis, Karl-Marx University, Leipzig, 1985.

Pasescu, G. and Tanislav, E., Person identification on the basis of earprints in the activity of Bucharest Police Department, *Info. Bull. SP/TM Examiners* 3, 10, 1997.

Rutty, G.N., Abbas, A., and Crossling, D., Could earprint identification be computerized?: an illustrated proof of concept paper, *Int J Legal Med* 119(6), 335, 2005.

Saddler, K., The Establishment and Evaluation of an Ear-Print Database at the National Training Centre for Scientific Support to Crime Investigation, M.Sc. thesis, University of Strathclyde, Glasgow, 1996.

Scaillet, M., Une identification originale, *Revue Internationale de Police Criminelle* 245, 41, 1971.

Stoney, D.A., What made us ever think we could individualize using statistics? *J Forensic Sci Soc* 31(2), 197, 1991.

Tuthill, H., *Individualization: Principles and Procedures in Criminalistics,* Lightning Powder Company, Salem, OR, 1994.

Valvoda, J.T., Otolobe — Earprint Recognition, Ecole poytechnique fédérale de Lausanne (EPFL), Semester project report, 1999.

Vermaas, P., Concentreer je op DNA en dacty: Plaatsvervangend korpschef Hans Visser wil een omslag in het werk van de TR, *Algemeen Politieblad van het Koninkrijk der Nederlanden* 152, 12, 2003.

Section 3

Identification from the Soft Tissues

Physical Appearance

5

IAN HILL

Contents

5.1 Introduction 87
5.2 Nature of Physical Appearances 87
5.3 Collecting the Information 89
5.4 Making an Identification...90
5.5 Postmortem Changes...92
5.6 Discussion...93
5.7 Conclusion 96
Further Reading..97

5.1 Introduction

Identification is a multidisciplinary exercise in which disparate observations are matched with information culled from a variety of sources. In this way a comprehensive picture is created that allows us to ascribe its identity to an individual. The physical appearances of someone are one part of the process, at least in ideal circumstances, but on occasion they may be our only method of identification. However, there are instances in which the disruptive nature of events may mar someone's appearance to such an extent that the method is of doubtful value. In other circumstances, physical appearance may be the only method of identification that is available, and this can create problems, because a large question mark may hover over the validity of the diagnosis. The lack of specificity of physical appearances makes differentiation between people surprisingly difficult. Identification using physical appearance is, of course, used routinely in situations where someone has died suddenly and relatives or friends are asked to view the body. Even in good circumstances, this is not an error-free process. Nevertheless, it is one that enjoys routine use by coroners and procurators fiscal (U.K.), also known as a public prosecutor in the U.S.

5.2 Nature of Physical Appearances

The types of information that fall into the category of physical appearances are listed in Table 5.1. To a large extent, these are obvious and self-explanatory. It has to be remembered, though, that people's conceptions of some of these features are subjective; moreover, they may be altered as is discussed in Chapter 21. At its simplest level, hair color may have been changed recently, either by design or, for example, because the body was immersed in water containing chemicals that dye the hair. Relatives and friends who provide antemortem

Table 5.1   Physical Appearance

Hair
Color
Natural
Dyed
Length
Wavy
Straight

Build
Height
Weight
Lean
Medium
Muscular
Obese

Skin
Complexion
Color
Birthmarks
Makeup

Eyes
Color

Ears
Pierced
Large
Small

Arms
Long
Short

Hands
Long fingers
Short fingers

Nose
Shape
Size
Pierced

Lips
Thin
Full
Pierced

Clothing
Sizes
Items

Congenital defects
Birthmarks

Note: Medical/surgical factors such as skin diseases/scars have been omitted. These features have to be considered in relation to other methods of identification.

descriptions may be unaware of the change. A haircut may have the same effect. What this tells us about physical appearances is that they are changeable features that can mislead.

In Table 5.1 we can see how many elements compose the physical appearance by which others recognize us. Although they are what nature has provided, they have been adapted by lifestyle and health, and perhaps even by artificial modification. Insofar as the latter is concerned, this may be a result of medical intervention, cosmetic procedures, or the manner of death and postmortem change, all of which can contrive to make identification more difficult. Moreover, these may be altered by clothing and makeup, and by other means, which are discussed elsewhere. The reason for stressing this here, at the outset, is that all these contribute to the concept we have about what a person looks like and, thus, may be misleading. The features that we recognize, and are recognized by, are a complex mixture of characteristics that are almost certainly asymmetrical. They will change with age, in accordance with the normal developmental processes, and whereas the nature of these alterations is predictable, the degree is not. Ill health, diet, and other factors may alter the process. Thus, removal of all of the teeth may alter the height of the lower third of the face and eventually produce a "Mr. Punch"-like appearance. Replacement of the teeth by dentures may restore some of the shape and height but not all and, of course, only if they are being worn. Consequently, descriptions of physical appearances are, to a degree, a changeable phenomenon. Suffice it to say here that the easily changeable nature of physical appearances presents potent challenges to any attempts to use them as a means of identification, even in ideal circumstances when there has been little or no postmortem degradation.

5.3   Collecting the Information

There are two phases to this procedure. Initially, details about a person are collected by interviewing relatives and friends. Obviously, this has to be done cautiously and with great tact to avoid exacerbating their distress as much as possible. Photographs can be very helpful because these show what the person looked like, but some caution has to be exercised. Families and friends may want to present their loved ones in a good light, and this may not be accurate. Posed pictures or those that do not show distinctive and perhaps physically detracting features such as facial asymmetry or birthmarks may not be most useful. Also, the photographs should be as recent as possible. However, any demands designed to acquire anatomically correct pictures must be tempered with sympathy. Moreover, a photograph of a broadly smiling individual may help the forensic odontologist by showing an uneven dentition, but it may not be so helpful when looking at other features. In other words, do not reject any picture or, indeed, any information, no matter how irrelevant it may seem initially. It may prove to be more helpful than expected.

Because physical appearances are more than the sum of facial features, size of clothing is important. There can be some coyness about relating the believed heights and weights of relatives and friends, especially at either extreme. While it is reasonable in this context to ask if there have been any recent changes, especially in weight, this must not be pursued too rigorously in case it causes distress. It may be that this information can be supplied by the individual's doctor.

The first phase will usually be done by a separate team from those working in the mortuary. Normally, they will have been specially trained so that they can get as much information as possible without increasing any distress. These people usually work within a casualty unit. They may either contact relatives and friends themselves, or they may be telephoned by the latter seeking information about their loved ones. Usually this is done by telephone, but sometimes a personal visit may be necessary. It may often be necessary to revisit people, allowing them to compose themselves in the meantime. Experience has shown in a number of disasters in the U.K. that great sensitivity is needed. Calling at a relative's home late at night when people are at a low ebb can be very upsetting.

Postmortem information or observation is gathered in the mortuary. The pathologist must record as much detail as it is possible to glean from the body. Information about each of the items listed in Table 5.1 must, wherever possible, be obtained and recorded. Occasions will arise when postmortem depredation has been so extensive that this can only be effectively done with the help of forensic odontologists and anthropologists. The techniques they use are discussed in Section 4 of this book. The autopsy procedures are the same whether the pathologist is dealing with intact bodies or body parts. However, the value and detail of the information will depend upon the circumstances and the condition of the remains. This is discussed further below.

5.4 Making an Identification

Making an identification using physical appearances falls into two categories, each of which is divisible into two parts. It may be a visual process by someone who knows the person, such as a family member, a friend, or work colleague. Another way of doing this is by what may be called a *paper exercise*, that is, by comparing autopsy records with the antemortem information gathered by teams from the casualty unit. In either case, the identification made may be used as the primary source or as a secondary or confirmatory method.

Visual identification may be done by relatives or friends visiting the mortuary and viewing a body or bodies to see if they can recognize their relative or friend. Usually the body is prepared by cleaning it up, covering injuries, and then laying it out in a "chapel of rest" (U.K.). It is not unknown in some jurisdictions for the relative or friend to be taken into a room containing a number of bodies either in coffins or in body bags. They are led from one to another or are left to wander among the bodies to see if they recognize someone. Once they have done so, they report the fact to those in charge of the process. This may be done before the autopsy and before the bodies have been cleaned up, or after the postmortem. It is not recommended.

The photographic method is arguably a little more sophisticated and perhaps sympathetic, in that it can be done away from the mortuary. A photograph of a cleaned-up corpse with the face visible or perhaps a distinctive physical feature can be shown to a relative or friend to see if there is any recognition. Alternatively, if the family and or friends have provided photographs or if there is an identity card or driver's license with a photograph, those working in the mortuary may be able to confirm a likeness.

One other aspect of visual identification that deserves mention is its use as a confirmatory process. When someone has been identified by other means or it is believed that they may have been identified, someone who knows that person can be asked to look at the body or a photograph. If the body has to be viewed, then this should be done in a specially prepared area, preferably a room set aside for that purpose. Sometimes it may be necessary to use the mortuary or part of it. If that is the case, then all work should cease, telephones should be silenced, and the viewing area cordoned off. It is vital that those doing the viewing should be able to do so in a peaceful, quiet way, free from any stimuli that may exacerbate their grief. Mortuary premises that are temporarily set up to deal with violent incidents are not ideal for this purpose because of their associations. They are a last resort.

The so-called paper exercise is a comparison of the antemortem information with the postmortem record. Dividing these cases into males and females, then adults and children, is psychologically helpful because it reduces the number of records each worker has to analyze and thus may speed up the process. Insofar as physical appearances are concerned, further divisions of the records should be made. Here, those people with outstanding physical features can be separated from the remainder. Thus, tall people, the very small, obese, those with long hair, and those who are bald can be differentiated from the rest. In fact, any of the features we normally consider identification points in recognizing someone can be separated out. This is, of course, a crude grouping. Just because someone is very tall or short does not necessarily differentiate them from the rest. Normally, this process will yield a range of possibilities that have to be cross-checked against other information about a person's physical appearance. It may be helpful to list these so that they can be compared against the remainder in the group. Each attribute is checked until no more are left; when this has been completed, and only if there is sufficient information to differentiate one person from the remainder, an identity may be ascribed. Thus, if there were two men who were 6 feet, 3 inches tall, both of whom were of average build, it would be dangerous to identify either on this basis. However, if one had a full head of hair and the other was bald, and there were no other men of similar height and build in the population being studied, then these distinctions might be satisfactory to identify them. It would, though, be better if other physical features could be added to the list. In that way, the identification achieves greater credibility. Thus, it may be possible to add items of information such as eye color, the presence or absence of nasal hair, and factors like the lengths of the legs and arms. In women, breast size and other gender-specific body features may help to differentiate.

This process is continued until all of the bodies have been identified. Inevitably, the range of distinguishing features and their diagnostic value will vary greatly, depending upon the circumstances. Also, the capacity to single out groups of people from the remainder will decrease as the investigation progresses, because there is a limit to the diversity of features; consequently, the task will get progressively harder — which may seem to be a paradox. It has to be remembered, though, that we are trying to differentiate one person from another, and recourse to tenuous evidence may not be acceptable. In recent years, computerization has been able to help, but in a surprisingly limited way. Such is the diversity of mankind that all physical appearances show huge variation. Consequently, computers will give only broad groupings, in much the same way as manual methods. Their problem is that computers are highly specific, and most available programs do not seem to be adaptable. That is, they will discard something that does not meet the exact criteria, which may cause delays. They cannot make allowances for variations and deficiencies in human descriptions.

One further feature of this aspect of identification by physical appearance that needs discussion in the present context is the process of exclusion. Although this has marked similarities to the method already described, there is a very important difference: a lack of information. This may be because no one has been traced who can or will assist; alternatively, it may be because of the effects of the accident itself, possibly coupled with the depredation

Table 5.2   Identification by Exclusion

Missing People				Features		
Body Number	A	B	C	Hair	Height	Build
1011				Dark	190	Average
1020				Blonde	185	Average
1050				Dark	190	Muscular
Hair	Dark	Dark	Blonde			
Height	190	190	185			
Build	Average	Muscular	Average			

Note: This shows the method and its problems, especially when used in isolation. It must be used with extreme caution.

wrought by postmortem change. The latter is discussed later in the text; here, we are concerned primarily with the techniques involved.

Identification by exclusion, when considered as a method itself, is predicated on the fact that all other avenues have been exhausted, and there is firm evidence that no one else is involved. Consequently, it is a last resort that is only reluctantly employed. Here, though, there is a subtle difference because we are looking at physical appearances and thus ignoring all other avenues.

Assuming that the whole of the population has been studied, all of the available features that can be used in the identification process have been carefully compared and contrasted, and that a number of unidentified bodies remain, there still have to be further attempts made to resolve the problem. In the first instance, all of those believed to have been identified must be cross-checked against one another. If this proves satisfactory and there are still a small number of unidentified bodies, it is wise to recheck the bodies to see if anything has been missed. Unfortunately, it often proves necessary to do this, not just because there are unidentified bodies but also because something may have been missed at autopsy or, for one reason or another, the antemortem information was wanting. Sadly, this may mean talking to the relatives and friends again, thus heightening their anxiety and exacerbating their grief. If there is no further information to help in the process, then, and only then, the process of identification by exclusion using physical appearances can begin. In essence, this is just another form of the main process of identification in which competing features are contrasted with one another. The difference here, though, is that we are working in what can be termed an *information vacuum*, both postmortem and antemortem. The method is shown in Table 5.2.

5.5   Postmortem Changes

After death, the body may undergo a range of changes that will alter its physical appearances to a greater or lesser degree. To a large extent, these are time-related. In the early hours, the patchy blotches of hypostasis (the settling of blood in the lower part of an organ or the body as a result of decreased blood flow) appear, which may coalesce as gravity pulls the stagnant blood downwards. As it cannot penetrate compressed tissues, the pressure areas are relieved. This should not have any effect upon identification by physical appearances, despite altering the complexion.

Decomposition is a process in which the tissues undergo destruction by internal chemical breakdown and animal predation, which may be by maggots or other animals. It is a variable process, with mummification coexisting with liquefying putrefaction. Eventually, the body will become skeletonized. The time scale and the diversity of changes is variable and dependent upon the circumstances. It can be very rapid in warm, moist environments but prolonged in the cold. It is faster in air and water than it is in buried bodies.

Adipocere is a waxy change that occurs in body fat. It may affect a part of the body or its entirety. Initially, it is greasy, but after years it becomes brittle. Although most cases are associated with immersion in water, there are examples of its occurring after incarceration in vaults and crypts. Unlike other forms of postmortem decomposition, adipocere formation may maintain the bodily features, albeit in an altered form, but nevertheless potentially recognizable. There will be loss of detail and distortion; thus, the eyes may be lost, but nevertheless an element of preservation exists. As with other aspects of identification by physical appearances, caution has to be exercised.

Mummification is arguably a little like adipocere formation in that some details of physical appearance may be maintained. It can occur only in a dry environment and is often associated with degeneration by mold or animal predation or both.

All these changes — the bloating, marbling, tissue-destroying autolysis, and the waxy alteration of adipocere, together with the drying of mummification — distort the tissues. Appearances can be markedly altered, making recognition impossible although some of the features may remain. There are no rules about what will happen and when. Consequently, a cautious approach to identification has to be adopted. Animal predation is a compounding feature in which even more of the tissues, and thus the features, are devoured. In essence, where the postmortem changes are advanced, a very cautious approach to identification by physical appearances has to be maintained. The observations are not always as reliable as would be hoped, and it is generally best to decline to make such an identification but to use any information gained as an addition to other processes.

5.6   Discussion

We are all supremely confident that we can recognize someone we know, but it becomes more difficult when asked to describe that person. Equally, not everyone can recognize someone whom they have only met briefly and with whom they became reacquainted in different circumstances. To some extent, the difficulties encountered are a function of the capacity to recall an accurate picture of someone and to convert this to a word picture that will be useful to a third party who has never met the person concerned. Added to this is the effect of circumstances. Victims of crimes and witnesses may be asked to describe those involved, so that pictures of the wanted person can be prepared and published. They are in a similar situation of heightened emotions to those whose family member or friend may have been killed in an accident. Being asked to provide accurate descriptions in such a situation must be extremely unpleasant. Not surprisingly, the details may not always be as accurate as might be desired. Thus, there is considerable potential, which is often realized, for the information about the physical appearances of people in whatever circumstances to be sparse and not always accurate. To this must be added the capacity of the observer to understand and translate the information provided into an identification.

The term *physical appearance* is in some respects artificial as a distinction, because it excludes body mutilation, surgery, and decoration, but there are good reasons for this. It is essentially a wider and in some ways more nebulous criterion. Our object is to try to create a comprehensive picture of an individual. Thus, if someone's having only one leg were the sole physical feature considered for identification, in some circumstances this may be all that we need to know. However, in the context of a major accident, it might not be distinctive enough. In attempting to create a comprehensive word picture of someone, we are faced with a range of problems. The capacity to describe a feature, the relevance paid to it, and the highly charged emotional conditions mean that descriptions may be flawed. In an accident or situation where bodies are not recovered for some time, bodily features may be altered to a greater or lesser degree. Added to this is the need to relate what is seen in the mortuary to the terms used in antemortem descriptions, as well as the problems created by translations from other languages, cultures, and customs.

Major incidents and accidents come in a variety of guises, but there are essentially two broad categories: they are either open or closed events. The differences between the two have a profound effect upon how they are handled. Essentially, an open disaster is one in which at the outset we have no firm idea of who was involved, and, indeed, like the Kings Cross Underground (subway) fire in London, it may be many years before the casualty list is finalized. This makes identification much more difficult, because there is a wider range of inputs. People may, for whatever reason, suggest that a relative or friend may have been involved, when in reality he or she was not. A closed disaster is one in which the names of those involved are known. Even so, in an age when identity fraud is known to occur, and when stowaways and those with criminal intent may, for example, hide themselves aboard an aircraft, caution has to be exercised. Nevertheless, the process in closed disasters is generally not so problematical. Whereas this may make identification easier, it should not imbue investigators with complacency.

Hitherto, our discussion has centered on incidents in which there are a number of casualties. It must be remembered, though, that identifications have to be made in other circumstances. The need for identification following criminal acts has been referred to previously. In addition to crimes should be added missing persons, whom we may be asked to recognize from pictures in the media and handbills. From time to time, people lose their memory and photographs are published to see if they can be helped to remember their identity. In all of these cases and any related events, the process is, in principle, the same: their physical characteristics are compared with a memory, a photograph, or a description.

Despite the fact that recognizing people is an integral part of our daily lives that we unconsciously do many times a day, it is a technique fraught with difficulty. No one can have escaped the embarrassment of recognizing the wrong person. A back view or a glimpse, perhaps in crowded circumstances, convinces us that someone we know is nearby or in pictures of a street scene on television, or in a photograph of a crowd. It is this type of inaccuracy that is so easily transferred to the identification of casualties unless great care is exercised. Even then, caution has to be attached to the results.

Visual identification of bodies in mortuaries is particularly problematical. People may want to help or others may want a body, any body, to grieve over. There are many recorded instances of misidentification in this context. In one air disaster some years ago, a man positively identified three mutilated bodies as being that of his daughter; two were men.

In another, an acquaintance identified a man by his feet, ignoring the fact that he was looking at three feet. There can be little, if any, excuse for exposing people to this kind of gross psychological trauma, the more so because the results are questionable. As is stated above, relatives or friends may be asked to go to a mortuary or chapel to identify someone who has died suddenly. It is not a method that is error-free. In one instance, parents who had last seen their son only hours before identified a body they thought was his in the mortuary. He actually was alive and well, and arrived home shortly after they did. These errors are not, so far as we know, as commonplace in a widely used procedure. Nevertheless, they are an indication of the frailty of the method.

Greater reliability occurs when a member of the investigating team compares a body with a photograph or when a body has been identified and a relative or friend confirms the fact visually. In either case, identification by physical appearance is acting in a confirmatory manner rather than being the prime factor. In this context, the family or friends are confirming what the identification team has done.

Because physical appearances have a rather nebulous quality, being open to considerable individual interpretation, they lack the finiteness of other methods, such as dental or medical, and have to be treated with great caution. For the most part, their value lies in the fact that they help to build up a picture of someone. Obviously, there will be cases where an identity is obtained by these alone, which may perhaps be later confirmed by techniques such as DNA. Mostly, though, they are a link in a chain of evidence. In one aircraft accident in which there was an intense postcrash fire, two grossly incinerated female bodies remained to be identified. The only distinguishing feature was a strip of material giving the brassiere size of one of them. Although this may more strictly be classified as clothing, it did indicate something about the woman's physical appearance and allowed a distinction to be made between the two. Subsequently, other evidence became available that confirmed the identification. This also is an example of physical appearance being used to exclude an individual. For the most part, physical appearance is an adjunct to identification and not the primary source. It is a cautious guide and in most circumstances should be treated as such.

Exclusion is a very tenuous method because it relies upon flimsy data, and thus it can only be used in very restricted circumstances. In the case cited above, the population was closed, and there was little or no chance that anyone else could have been involved. Nevertheless, great caution was needed. For the most part, exclusion using physical appearances is a device that acts as a pointer. It allows further approaches to be made to other sources of information that may help. In the present climate, the availability of DNA arguably makes the method redundant.

This case is an example of the problems that can occur because of postmortem change. It is, though, wrong to assume that this is restricted to decomposition or mummification. The kind of force found in accidents may cause fragmentation of the body or obliterate facial features. In these instances, especially the former, physical appearances have very little, if any, part to play in the identification process. Similarly, in instances in which there are true postmortem, rather than cummortem, changes, the value of physical appearances in the identification is very limited. Bodies remaining in water may be affected by fish. Fresh-water shrimp, for example, are active feeders capable of destroying features on human remains, especially when the effects of immersion are considerable. The combination of distortion and loss of tissue can make bodies unrecognizable. Even so, it is usually possible to glean some useful evidence. Hair color may be preserved, as opposed to what happens to hair exposed to fire, which, if it does not burn the hair off, may change its color. Pubic and axillary hair tend to retain their color longer, provided that the body is not exposed to chemical action while in the water. Skin color will change; this may be to a pale gray or brown in Caucasians. Much depends upon the length of time the body is immersed and the temperature. The colder it is, the slower will be the changes; the longer the body is in water, the greater will be the changes and the chances of postmortem depredation. Adipocere formation is a change in which there is saporification of the fat to form a crumbly matter. It is accompanied by distortion of the features. Clearly, under these circumstances there may be little to aid the identification process.

A similar situation occurs in postmortem change occurring outdoors on land and when the body has been buried. Animal depredation, decomposition, and mummification may so alter the body's appearance that little, if any, help can be given. It may be possible to assess height, but that is an anthropological exercise dealt with in Chapter 11.

5.7   Conclusion

Identification is a multidisciplinary process in which a variety of different types of evidence are used to create a picture of an individual. In ideal circumstances, the picture should be so detailed and descriptive that the person concerned would be recognizable to someone else. For most people that means that the description of physical appearance is sufficiently accurate for them to make the recognition. In ideal circumstances, this ought not to be too difficult, but frequently the situation is blighted because of the effects of the accident or postmortem changes. This has a markedly deleterious effect upon the identification process, materially weakening the position of physical appearance as a means of establishing identity. Moreover, the ability of families and friends to give an accurate word picture that can be translated into a visual idea is limited, if not because of their capacity to describe the features, then certainly because of the nature of the circumstances.

It is only natural that people will want to present their loved ones in as favorable a light as possible. Consequently, their descriptions may lack accuracy; a deformity may be glossed over or weight may be underestimated. These and other similar glosses may have a marked effect upon the capacity to achieve a match. Also, it must be remembered that people do alter their appearance. Dyeing the hair, for example, is commonplace and may have been done while the individual was away, so that family and friends are not aware of the change. Thus, even without the effects of cum- and postmortem changes, physical appearance tends to be a weak form of evidence. It is best used as an adjunct to the process, providing verification overall. Viewed in this light, it is a more powerful test than it might seem to be, given all of its inherent problems. It is only rarely that physical appearance alone should be used as the sole means of identification. Having said that, it has to be remembered that visual identification by a relative or friend, who is using the person's physical appearance to recognize him or her, is probably the most popular method used by the police on behalf of the coroner or procurator fiscal. Identification by physical appearances alone is a rather special situation for identification specialists, because usually it is done as a confirmation process, other methods having been used beforehand.

Further Reading

Clarke, L.J., Public Inquiry into the Identification of Victims following Major Transport Accidents, HMSO, London, 2001.

Hill, I.R. et al., Identification in the Manchester air disaster, *Br Dent J* 165(12), 445–446, 1986.

Knight, B., *Forensic Pathology*, 2nd ed., Arnold, London, 1996.

Soft Tissue Pathology

6

CHRISTOPHER MILROY

Contents

6.1   Introduction 99
6.2   The Usefulness of Soft Tissue Pathology in Biological Human Identification 100
6.3   Age-Related Changes and Soft Tissue Pathology 101
    6.3.1   Skin 101
    6.3.2   Central Nervous System 101
    6.3.3   Cardiovascular System 102
    6.3.4   Respiratory System 104
    6.3.5   Gastrointestinal System 105
    6.3.6   Biliary System..105
    6.3.7   Genitourinary System..106
    6.3.8   Lymphoreticular System..107
    6.3.9   Endocrine System 107
    6.3.10 Musculoskeletal System 107
6.4   Occupational Disorders...108
    6.4.1   The Pathology of Industrial Disease 108
    6.4.2   Drug Misuse..109
    6.4.3   Toxicology 110
    6.4.4   Sex Identity and Soft Tissue Pathology.......................................111
6.5   Conclusions...111
Further Reading...111

6.1   Introduction

Following a mass disaster in the U.K. that resulted in the need to identify over 30 bodies, one individual's identity remained unknown, despite the person's having undergone very distinctive surgery. The presence of natural disease processes had led to the conclusion that the body was between 40 and 60 years of age. Search parameters were therefore set but failed to identify the victim. A decade later, a review of the findings led to the identification of the victim, who was in his 70s. This illustrates the difficulties of confirming specific age ranges from soft tissue pathology and the importance of not setting search identification parameters too narrowly.

Soft tissue pathology can provide useful information for identification purposes as well as being fundamental in determining cause and manner of death. Even where there has been considerable damage to the body, residual soft tissue may indicate preinjury pathology. Furthermore, decomposition does not necessarily preclude pathological diagnosis.

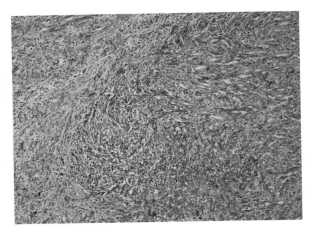

Figure 6.1   Kaposi's sarcoma of the skin. (See color insert following page 362.)

6.2   The Usefulness of Soft Tissue Pathology in Biological Human Identification

Pathological processes vary with age and can therefore be used to give some guidance as to the age of a victim. For example, different types of tumors show different age distributions. Testicular teratomas are seen in men in their 20s and 30s. Sarcomas typically occur in younger age groups, whereas carcinomas develop in the 50s and 60s. The various organs react in different ways and have different responses to injury. The brain cannot regenerate itself, and cardiac muscle responds to damage with fibrous tissue deposition. However, the liver has considerable powers of regeneration, as does the mucosa of the gastrointestinal tract. Acute infections of the soft tissues are unlikely to aid identification, but chronic infections can have distinctive pathology often associated with a recorded clinical history. Such infections include tuberculosis, histoplasmosis, and AIDS. An obvious visual effect of HIV infection is Kaposi's sarcoma (Figure 6.1), which may appear in the skin as well as internal organs. Many occupations have been associated with distinct pathology, whereas social behavior such as drug misuse may leave characteristic stigmata. Different organs decompose at different rates. Those organs that have a high concentration of fibrous tissue are more resilient to decomposition. Therefore, the prostate gland and uterus are typically the last organs to remain recognizable in a decomposed body. The kidneys and lungs also resist decomposition, whereas the brain undergoes liquefaction quickly. The liver and heart will start to decompose after the brain.

It is standard practice to take sections of organs for histology in all autopsies. Even in decomposed bodies it is worth taking organ histology. Although tissue will inevitably undergo postmortem change, known as autolysis, useful findings may be revealed. Taking histological sections is a simple procedure, and failure to take material removes a possible means of identification. Stored histological material has also been used for DNA analysis.

As the age of the childhood and teenage victim can usually be identified by other means and soft tissue pathology is not usually present, this chapter concentrates on soft tissue pathology in the adult, where pathological processes can help in providing information on the age range of an unidentified person.

6.3 Age-Related Changes and Soft Tissue Pathology

6.3.1 Skin

The skin may be affected by local and systemic disorders, and these may have a genetic background. These disorders may significantly affect appearance. Genetic disorders such as epidermolysis bullosa and icthyosis (which may be acquired) are rare but distressing diseases to the sufferer and very evident when present. Neurofibromatosis causes significant changes to the appearance as well as affecting other areas of the body. The changes worsen with age as the neurofibromata develop. Rheumatoid nodules may be seen in patients with rheumatoid arthritis.

Acne vulgaris is a common disorder of skin that develops after puberty and can be very disfiguring. Acne rosacea tends to occur at a later age. One of its most characteristic features is rhinophyma — an enlargement of the nose. It is more common in women and is rare below the age of 30 years. Psoriasis is a common skin disorder affecting all age groups and so is less useful. There may be joint and fingernail involvement. It most commonly affects the elbows, knees, scalp, and lower back. Vitiligo is a depigmentation of skin that may affect the face as well as the trunk and wrists. Melasma is a disorder resulting in tan to brown patches in the face area. Benign and malignant tumors of the skin are common. Basal cell carcinoma (rodent ulcer) and squamous cell carcinoma typically affect the face. There may be associated solar damage in adjacent skin. Seborrhoeic keratosis is a common warty-appearing benign tumor in middle-aged and elderly people. Benign vascular lesions such as port wine stains and strawberry naevi (benign moles) may result in an obvious appearance. Whereas strawberry naevi may regress, port wine stains characteristically persist through life. Pigmented lesions such as naevi are common. Malignant melanoma tends to be diagnosed in the 40–60 age group. Slow-growing variants such as lentigo maligna melanoma may persist on the skin of the face for years.

Sebaceous cysts can grow to a considerable size, as may lipomata. Tumors of underlying tissues may result in a distortion of facial features. For example, parotid gland tumors may be slow growing and manifest as an obvious lump protruding from the face.

Because skin disorders affecting the face are so visible, they may alter appearances, allowing identification on CCTV and similar images. Other systemic disorders such as acromegaly and Paget's disease of bone may also alter the facial skeleton, whereas skin loses its pigment-bearing layer in decomposition and heavily pigmented skin may appear white. (Figure 6.2).

6.3.2 Central Nervous System

The most common age-replaced changes seen in the brain are cerebrovascular disease and dementia. Atheromatous change may be seen in the cerebral arteries of the circle of Willis. It is unusual to see significant atheroma in those under 50 years of age. Cerebral artery atheroma may not have caused any clinical symptoms. Where cerebrovascular disease has led to cerebral infarction or hemorrhage, this will be reflected in long-term damage, typically as large areas of cystic infarction or smaller lacunae. Alzheimer's disease, the commonest type of senile dementia, is associated with the presence of senile plaques and other changes. Such plaques are seen in the aging brain. The determination of dementia requires a formal neuropathological analysis. However, if present, they are a good indicator of age, as they increase with age even if dementia is not present.

Figure 6.2 Depigmented skin of an Afro-Caribbean female whose partially decomposed body was found 3 months after she disappeared. (See color insert following page 362.)

Past neurotrauma may be reflected in long-standing damage. Cortical contusions heal by the laying down of hemosiderin. This can be demonstrated histologically using stains for iron such as Perls' stain. Hemosiderin staining of the meninges may be seen where there has been a previous subdural hematoma. Previous subarcahnoid hemorrhage may also be associated with hemosiderin staining, as well as previous surgery to clip a berry aneurysm.

6.3.3 Cardiovascular System

The commonest disease of the arteries in Western society is atherosclerosis (atheroma). The first changes of atherosclerosis, fatty streaks, can be seen in people in their twenties or even late teens. As the disease progresses there is increased build-up of fatty plaques, with ulceration and calcification. In the aorta the most significant disease is seen in the infrarenal abdominal aorta (Figure 6.3a and Figure 6.3b). Where there is calcified ulcerated plaques, sometimes called *complex atheroma*, the likelihood is that the person is over 50 years of age. This may lead to the development of aortic aneurysm formation. Of these, 90% are in the infrarenal aorta. Accelerated atherosclerosis is seen most commonly in patients with diabetes mellitus or hyperlipidemias, when advanced atherosclerosis may occur in patients less than 40 years of age.

The most significant consequence of atherosclerosis is the development of coronary artery atheroma. Heavily calcified atheromatous coronary arteries usually indicate someone over 50 years of age and often much older. Noncalcified atheroma may be seen in younger patients. Coronary artery atheromatous disease is the most common cause of myocardial infarction. It is the commonest cause of sudden death in Western society. Survival of a myocardial infarct (a "heart attack") leads to the development of a characteristic area of

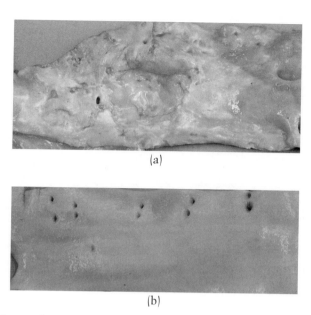

(a)

(b)

Figure 6.3 (a) Abdominal aorta of a 70-year-old male with extensive atheroma; (b) normal aorta of a 20-year-old male.

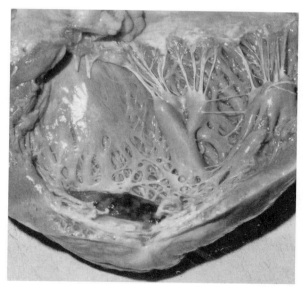

Figure 6.4 Old fibrosis in the apex of the heart of a 53-year-old male from a previous myocardial infarction.

fibrosis (Figure 6.4). Although myocardial infarction may occur in the younger age group, it is typically associated with the over-40s. In women, myocardial infarction is unusual before menopause. Myocardial infarction may be clinically silent. It is therefore not uncommon to find evidence of previous infarction where no history exists. Other disorders of the myocardium may be seen. Among the more common chronic conditions are hypertrophic and dilated cardiomyopathy. Hypertrophic obstructive cardiomyopathy (HOCM)

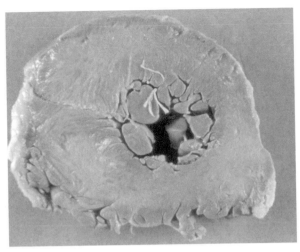

Figure 6.5 Hypertrophic obstructive cardiomyopathy (HOCM) in a 27-year-old male with asymmetrical hypertrophy.

is a genetic disorder of muscle, resulting in abnormal muscle fibers producing a thickened, often asymmetrical left ventricle (Figure 6.5).

Valvular heart disease has a number of causes. Rheumatic heart disease most commonly results in damage to the mitral and aortic valves. This can occur at a young age. Aortic stenosis may result from rheumatic heart disease, and in congenitally bicuspid valves at a younger age. In normal triscupid valves, senile calcification may occur, leading to aortic stenosis and myocardial hypertrophy. Calcification of the mitral valve ring is a frequent finding at autopsy in older people.

In the myocardium the pigment lipofuschin accumulates with age. The heart can also atrophy with age, leading to the condition of "brown" atrophy.

6.3.4 Respiratory System

The laryngeal cartilages undergo ossification with age. The young adult has a pliant, cartilaginous larynx. By the 30s, ossification is present. The elastic cartilaginous structures in the larynx do not normally calcify. Chronic obstructive pulmonary disease, also called chronic bronchitis and emphysema, is typically a disease of the older person, especially smokers. Emphysema may be seen in the younger patient — for example, in patients with α-1-antitrypsin deficiency. The presence of anthracosis may reflect smoking or city dwelling. It increases with age, but its absence does not necessarily indicate a younger person.

Tuberculosis is a worldwide infection that is increasing in the U.K. Previous infection is most characteristically associated with apical fibrosis. Other chronic infections seen in the lung such as histoplasmosis may be identified if the person has been exposed in the appropriate geographical area. This may give an indication of geographical migration during life and therefore could contribute to identification. Asthma is a chronic disorder causing reversible bronchospasm. Status asthmaticus may result in sudden death, with evidence of mucus plugs in the airway and acute eosinophilia. Even without evidence of an acute asthmatic attack, changes of asthma may be seen on histology, with hypertrophy of smooth muscle around bronchi, and tissue eosinophilia (Figure 6.6).

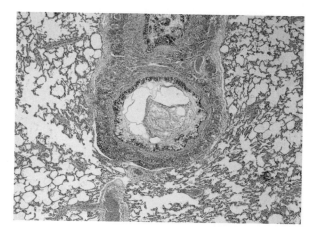

Figure 6.6 Asthmatic changes in a bronchus with thickening of the smooth muscle and plugging with mucus.

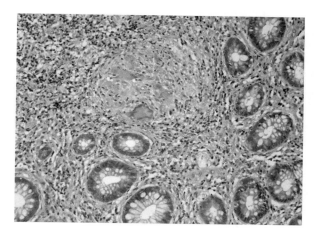

Figure 6.7 Granulomatous inflammation in Crohn's disease

6.3.5 Gastrointestinal System

Many diseases in the gastrointestinal tract can occur throughout adulthood. Therefore, peptic ulcer disease, if present, does not provide significant age differentiation. It can also be present without a clinical history.

Inflammatory bowel disease may occur throughout adulthood, but carcinoma of the large bowel is typically a disease of the older age group. Ulcerative colitis affects the large bowel, whereas Crohn's disease may affect any part of the gastrointestinal tract. Microscopically, Crohn's disease is characterized by granulomatous inflammation (Figure 6.7). Diverticular disease is a common disease of Western society and therefore a frequent finding at autopsy in those over 50 years of age.

6.3.6 Biliary System

The liver may be damaged by a number of external agents, the most common being alcohol (ethanol). Excess consumption of alcohol may result in fatty change (Figure 6.8) and cirrhosis. Most alcoholics do not develop cirrhosis, and its presence does not necessarily

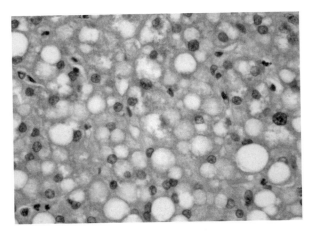

Figure 6.8   Fatty change in the liver due to excess alcohol consumption.

mean that alcohol was the cause, as many other causes exist — for example, viral hepatitis. In alcoholics it takes time to develop. Alcoholic liver cirrhosis may be seen in the 30s, but typically occurs in older patients.

Gallstones are a common incidental finding at autopsy. They are more common in females and may develop in the young adult. In the famous case of the "Acid Bath Murderer" (John George Haigh) in 1949, a Dr. Simpson identified three faceted gallstones among material left following the attempted disposal of an elderly female victim by dissolving her in sulfuric acid. Parts of human bones were also still present. The dentures also survived this process, allowing identification.

The pancreas is the first organ to undergo autolysis and therefore often provides no useful information at autopsy. Where there has been previous pancreatitis, there may be fibrosis. Pancreatitis is most commonly associated with biliary disease and alcohol. It may lead to diabetes mellitus.

6.3.7   Genitourinary System

The kidney may be subject to many diseases that are not too age-specific. Renal carcinoma may develop in the young adult. One change that is seen with age is known as benign nephrosclerosis, which is associated with a granular external surface and histological changes of thinning of the cortex with sclerosis of some glomeruli and changes in vessels. The kidney shows specific changes in diabetes mellitus, particularly in insulin-dependent diabetes, and these changes may be visible on routine microscopy. Renal stones are typically calcified and therefore identifiable on plain radiographs. The bladder may also contain calculi.

The prostate undergoes nodular hyperplasia with age. Similarly, prostatic carcinoma can be a feature of people over 50. The bladder may reflect changes in the prostate. With obstruction there may even be chronic distension and trabeculation.

In the female, the adult uterus becomes more bulky. Postmenopause, it atrophies. There are frequently fibroids in the menstruating female. Postmenopause, they atrophy and may calcify (womb stones). The endometrium can be examined to determine whether the woman was menstruating or postmenopausal. The uterus should be opened to see if an intrauterine contraceptive device is *in situ* or if she was pregnant. Similarly, there may be clips or surgical division associated with the fallopian tubes.

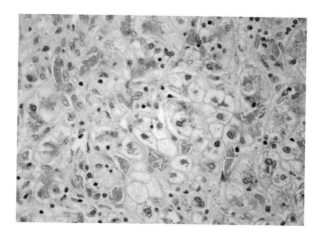

Figure 6.9 Section of liver with the red cells elongated by sickling (sickle cells).

6.3.8 Lymphoreticular System

The spleen tends to get smaller with age. A small atrophic spleen is suggestive of an elderly victim. The spleen may be enlarged by disease. The tonsils and adenoids also atrophy with age, but this occurs at a younger age. The thymus involutes in the teenage years and in adulthood is not normally identified on dissection of the chest. Enlargement of lymph nodes may occur in disease, including malignant disease (primary and secondary) and infection. The vertebral bone marrow may provide evidence of hematological disorders. Some tumors are particularly recognized to spread to bone. These tumors include breast, kidney, lung, prostate, and thyroid. An examination of the red blood cells may identify the presence of sickle cell disease or sickle cell trait appearing as the red blood cells sickle postmortem that occurs in men of sub-Saharan African origin (Figure 6.9).

6.3.9 Endocrine System

Changes in the endocrine organs can have dramatic effects on the individual's appearance, and this may be significant in visual identification. The pituitary gland tumors can be associated with acromegaly and Cushing's disease. Adrenal gland tumors may also be associated with the Cushingoid appearance affecting someone with long-term steroid use. Examination of the thyroid may show a goiter, which is more common in women. Nodules hyperplasia in the adrenal gland is not uncommon but is characteristically not associated with any clinical disease.

6.3.10 Musculoskeletal System

Skeletal changes are common and may be able to be related to medical records or other history. The musculature does not often provide useful information on age-related changes. Primary muscle disorders are rare and require specialist muscle pathology examination that is not routinely performed in medicolegal autopsies. Muscle wasting secondary to central nervous system disease may be identified. Such conditions as multiple sclerosis may occur throughout adulthood. A common cause of unilateral muscle wasting is previous cerebral infarction, which has been discussed above.

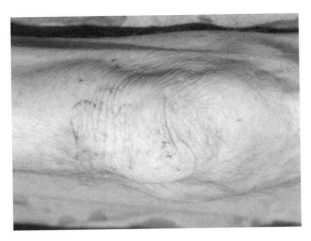

Figure 6.10   Coal dust tattoos on the knee of an ex-miner.

6.4   Occupational Disorders

Since, in 1775, Sir Percival Potts identified the association between scrotal carcinoma and working as a chimney sweep, many other occupations have been associated with disease and other stigmata. These soft tissue pathologies may go some way to building an identification profile of an individual.

At autopsy, a consideration of findings associated with occupation should begin with the external examination. For example, in coal miners, there may be characteristic coal dust tattoos, which are scars on the skin that become impregnated with coal, giving a characteristic appearance (Figure 6.10). Internally, the results of occupation may be seen as disease in many organs. A vast number of occupational diseases, and occupational medicine, together with its pathology, represent a distinct branch of pathology. This section will concentrate on the more common soft tissue pathological findings. It should be pointed out that occupational disease is often geographically weighted, and in a mining disaster, for example, the presence of changes associated with coal mining is unlikely to be very discriminatory. However, the finding of occupational disease in the solitary unidentified body may provide the key to identity.

6.4.1   The Pathology of Industrial Disease

Although coal mining has been cleaned up in many countries, thereby reducing exposure to coal dust, the changes in coal miners are essentially irreversible and therefore are still regularly encountered. The presence of coal dust tattoos has already been mentioned. These can occur in the absence of significant pneumoconiosis. Internally, there may be degrees of change associated with the inhalation of coal dust. Typically, the lungs in miners who have spent years at the coal face appear very black. Hilar lymph nodes contain heavy carbon deposits. Many miners have a degree of chronic obstructive pulmonary disease. Where complicated pneumoconiosis, also known as massive pulmonary fibrosis, is present, there are large areas of blackened fibrotic nodules called anthrosilicotic nodules.

Many workers have been exposed to asbestos. This may be evident as asbestos bodies seen on microscopy of the lungs (Figure 6.11). Although crocidilite, the main type of

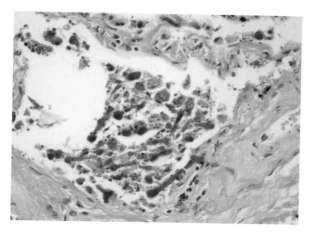

Figure 6.11   Asbestos bodies in the lung.

asbestos fiber associated with the development of asbestos-related disease, is no longer used in industry, it is still very prevalent in buildings and other structures from the 1970s. Like changes in coal miners, asbestos-related disease is irreversible and longstanding. The most common finding at autopsy is pleural plaques. These are often found at autopsy, but past exposure may not have been appreciated. Asbestosis, lung fibrosis caused by asbestos exposure, is a relatively nonspecific change, as fibrosis may occur in a variety of conditions, including exposure to other fibrosing agents such as silica, causing silicosis and "cotton," which in turn causes bysinossis. Lung fibrosis may occur due to other nonoccupational related disorders. Asbestos exposure is associated with the development of lung carcinoma, whereas pleural and peritoneal malignant mesothelioma are tumors highly associated with asbestos exposure. Whereas industrial exposure may be known, many patients with mesothelioma have had a short exposure that was not appreciated at the time. Survival from diagnosis is typically a matter of months.

6.4.2   Drug Misuse

The use of recreational drugs, both legal and illicit, is very frequent in modern society. Changes due to alcohol have already been discussed above. Smoking tobacco is associated with many disorders, particularly of the respiratory and cardiovascular systems. However, the most specific change associated with cigarette smoking is the presence of nicotine staining of the fingers. Cannabis smoking is associated with brown pigment macrophages in the alveoli and is a common finding as cannabis smoking is widespread.

Other patterns of drug use may be associated with more specific changes. With intravenous drug misuse there is often external stigmata, due to the action of injecting. Repeat injection into the arms can give rise to tracking (Figure 6.12). When the veins become thrombosed, the femoral veins may be used, resulting in sinus tracks in the groin. Internally, the habit may be associated with infectious complications. Hepatitis and HIV infection may be present. Endocarditis of the right side of the heart is highly associated with intravenous drug misuse. Microscopic examination of the lungs may reveal intravascular granulomata caused by foreign material in the injected drugs. This is particularly seen in those addicts who crush and inject tablets (Figure 6.13). Cocaine is typically smoked or snorted. Snorting cocaine can result in changes to the nasal septum. Smoking

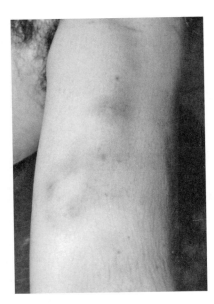

Figure 6.12   Bruises in the arm due to repeated injection of drugs ("tracking").

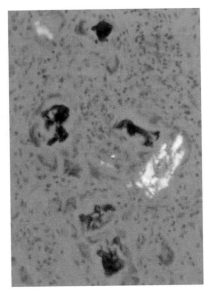

Figure 6.13   Foreign-body granulomata in the lung due to intravenous drug misuse.

crack cocaine may be associated with a number of external stigmata including burns to the hand ("crack thumb") and the eyes ("crack keratitis"). On microscopy of the lungs there may be prominent carbon pigmented intra-alveolar macrophages. These chronic changes will be present even in the absence of recent drug use.

6.4.3   Toxicology

Toxicological examination will clearly provide information on the state of drug use. Positive toxicology may provide information about both prescribed medication, which can give further indication of medical conditions, though some medications, particularly some psychiatric drugs, are not easily detectable in postmortem samples. As most pharmaceutical agents, by law, have to be prescribed by medical practitioners, the presence of a therapeutic agent can be checked against medical records. Where blood and urine samples are not available, soft tissues from various organs can be used to perform toxicological analysis. Muscle is proving a particularly useful tissue for toxicology. Where significant entomological activity is present, maggots may be submitted for toxicology (entomotoxicology).

6.4.4 Sex Identity and Soft Tissue Pathology

Obvious ways of determining the sex of a person from soft tissue is by identification of the generative organs at autopsy. Diseases may have a sex bias, and occupations may be predominantly practiced by one sex. Coal-face workers in the U.K. have been exclusively male, for example. Ischemic heart disease is unusual in the premenopausal woman. Endocrine disorders such as thyroid disease are more common in women. However, the frequency of a disorder in one sex does not usually exclude it in the other, unless it has a sex-linked genetic inheritance, such as hemophilia.

6.5 Conclusions

Many jurisdictions do require full postmortem examinations when a medicolegal investigation is launched. Whether an investigation involves a single victim or multiple victims, the soft tissue pathology can provide useful information for identification purposes, as well as for fulfilling the other requirements of the investigation. Whereas modern identification techniques such as DNA profiling will play the significant role where the victim's identity is likely to be known, when an unknown victim is found and no data exits to compare past and present, the soft tissue pathology may provide useful information to give a profile of the age, physical condition, and occupational and social habits.

Further Reading

Brunning, R.D., Desmet, V.J., Ordonez, N.G., Rosenblum, M.K., Ang, L.C., Bibao, J.M., and Rosai, J., *Rosai and Ackerman's Surgical Pathology,* 9th ed., Mosby, New York, 2004.

Kumar, V., *Robbins and Cotran's Pathologic Basis of Disease,* 7th ed., Saunders, Philadelphia, 2004.

Saukko, P. and Knight, B. *Knight's Forensic Pathology,* 3rd ed., Arnold, London, 2004.

Underwood, J.C.E., Ed., *General and Systemic Pathology,* 4th ed., Churchill Livingstone, New York, 2004.

Soft Tissue Trauma

7

GUY N. RUTTY

Contents

7.1   Introduction 113
7.2   Role of the Pathologist in Identification..114
7.3   Types of Trauma 116
    7.3.1   The Abrasion..116
    7.3.2   The Bruise 117
    7.3.3   The Laceration 117
    7.3.4   The Incised Wound 118
    7.3.5   The Burn 118
7.4   Identification Criteria and Documentation..118
7.5   Trauma as an Aid to Identification 120
    7.5.1   Occupational Trauma...120
    7.5.2   Posture 121
    7.5.3   Hobbies and Leisure Activities 122
    7.5.4   Body Modifications 122
    7.5.5   Self-Inflicted Injury 122
    7.5.6   Accidents and Assaults 122
    7.5.7   Medical Intervention 122
7.6   Trauma as a Hindrance to Identification..123
    7.6.1   Blunt Trauma 124
    7.6.2   Firearms..124
    7.6.3   Explosives 124
    7.6.4   Transportation 124
    7.6.5   Burns...125
    7.6.6   Dismemberment 125
7.7   Conclusion 125
References 126

7.1   Introduction

The identification of a body that has been subjected to disfiguring or disruptive trauma may at first appear to be a daunting task. A single-occupancy air crash may yield thousands of tiny body parts, which may lead to problems related to body recovery, storage, packaging and identification. The use of standardized body identification paperwork may be rendered useless. The processes involved may stretch the skills of the investigators to the very limits of their ability and at the same time place significant pressure upon their personal and work environments due to the necessity to try and identify the deceased, often within unrealistic time limits, or place psychological stress upon themselves and their families in dealing with the task and sights before them. Just because police officers are trained exhibits officers and have been to autopsies before does not mean that they will cope with working in a temporary mortuary set up to deal with the burned and disrupted remains of the aftermath of a school bus accident. This scenario applies equally to the pathologist as it does to any member of an identification team. Thus, all team members, no matter who they are, must have appropriate before and after medical and psychological support for the sights, sounds, and smells that they may endure, as well as the physical and environmental strains placed upon them while undertaking identification work. That is, assuming that the remains can be recovered in the first place which, in this age of global terrorism and the threat of chemical, biological, or radiological attack, may not be possible. This, then, raises the moral question as to how to deal with such an event and whether the welfare of the body recovery and identification teams outweighs the necessity to recover and identify the dead.

Thus, trauma by itself should not be a reason not to identify the deceased. Although, at times, trauma can hinder the process of identification, its characteristics can work to an investigator's advantage. Historical trauma, its treatment, and its complications can all assist in the process of identification.

This chapter will explore how trauma can be used or can hinder the process of human identification. It will cover the role of the pathologist in the identification of the deceased, the definition of different types of trauma, and the role of trauma in the identification process. The emphasis of this chapter is upon the identification of the victim of trauma, not the causation of the trauma itself, although this will be touched upon briefly within the text.

7.2   Role of the Pathologist in Identification

In dealing with the dead, the pathologist should have a central and often pivotal role in the identification of a body or body parts, both at the scene to advise on body recovery and at the mortuary. Although it is possible to use and apply identification protocols without the involvement of a pathologist, the application of their medical training and obsession with detailing minutiae makes them an often indispensable member of an identification team. Although one does not have to have a medical degree to identify and document professional multichromic tattoos on the body, the nonmedical members of the disaster victim identification (DVI) team may miss the accessory nipple, the significance of the small dot tattoos on the chest of a person who has received radiotherapy for a malignancy and who will thus have extensive antemortem medical records, or the fine pitting of the toenails or sole of the dismembered foot of an individual who suffers from psoriasis (Figure 7.1).

In the case of mass fatalities, pathologists will be key members of the identification commission, and they will be expected to be up-to-date with all forms of identification parameters that can be applied to, or obtained from, the body. They will advise the investigating authorities — for example, the coroner — on the most appropriate methods of identification considering the circumstances of the case and later, using the data made available to the commission, agree that the body has been identified prior to release for repatriation and disposal.

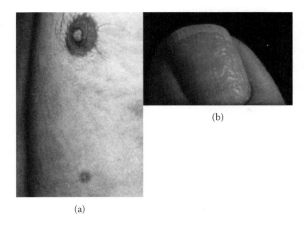

(b)

(a)

Figure 7.1   (a) Accessory nipple; (b) nail pitting caused by psoriasis.

The pathologist, as with the entire identification team, should be objective, scientific, and independent to any criminal or civil proceedings that surround the incident. For example, within England and Wales, the pathologist works for Her Majesty's Coroner, not the police, who may have a different agenda in relation to the identification of the dead. Their work must fall within the legislation governing the country where they are working, especially if they have traveled from their native country to another and must respect current opinion, culture, and religious attitudes regarding the handling of the dead. Although, at times, by adhering to such strict requirements this may appear to hinder the process of identification, with the application of modern identification techniques there is no need to undertake mutilating procedures (for example, the removal of digits or hands or the use of incisions to exposed body surfaces such as on the face) unless these are measures of last resort when all other techniques have failed. Having said this, when working in multicultural teams in global disasters, procedures that are alien and uncomfortable to you may be routine practice to others.

Even the taking of biological samples such as DNA must be undertaken under strict adherence to the law, with provision being made for appropriate handling, storage, disposal, or return of the retained biological material. The pathologist should not only be able to advise on which samples can be used for what purpose but should also be able to advise on these other issues. They can be a medical guide so that the most appropriate test is undertaken on the most appropriate samples. They should also be able to advise on any health and safety issues of potentially contaminated samples and be prepared to advise on more basic health and safety issues related to their working environment.

It should be remembered that not all pathologists are trained in identification techniques. Again, if we consider England and Wales as an example, the majority of autopsy examinations are undertaken by hospital-based histopathologists or their trainees. They have little, if any, formal training in techniques that can be used to identify the deceased, as the autopsies that they undertake are performed on those already identified, and there is no need for this training. Thus, when considering who should be a member of a DVI team, one must ensure that the pathologist is trained and even accredited in what is being undertaken. Often, due to a shortage of personnel, nonforensic pathologists or trainees may be brought in to assist, but they should never be in a situation were they are unsupervised, as critical information may be missed by the untrained eye.

The pathologist must be aware of standardized international protocols involved in identification — for example, the Interpol DVI forms (Interpol 2006) or the U.K. ACPO (Association of Chief Police Officers) forms — and if possible they should have rehearsed the use of these protocols on real cadavers with other members of their team. Unfamiliarity with the paperwork that they are supplied with often leads to long delays and mistakes in the identification process.

When considering the dead, there are four basic questions that apply to all cadavers: who the people were, where they died, when they died, and how they came to their deaths. In the vast majority of cases the answer to the first three questions will be known, and it is how they came to their deaths that occupies the majority of the pathologist's time. However, in the case of an unidentified body, body part, or in mass fatalities, the emphasis is now placed upon who the person was. Temporary mortuaries for mass fatalities are designed around the process of identification of the dead; the other questions are secondary and may already be answered. Invasive autopsy examination is often not required unless part of the identification process. This is particularly so with an open incident, such as an environmental disaster, where one starts with not knowing how many have died, let alone who they were, as opposed to a closed incident such as a plane crash where, assuming that those on the passenger list are who they are supposed to be (which can never be presumed), then it is a case of confirming their known identification. The pathologist must be familiar with the workflow processes of the mortuary and their role within the process of identification. This, again, comes down to regular training and updating one's understanding of current identification practice.

7.3 Types of Trauma

Before considering how trauma may affect the identification of an individual, one must be acquainted with the principal types of injuries and how they affect the body. Fresh trauma may hinder the examination, but healed trauma will aid identification. It is also critical that one use the correct terminology when describing injuries. Unfortunately, mistakes are made in this area by medical and nonmedical personnel alike (Milroy and Rutty 1997). Again, this is due to a lack of training and the failure to realize the importance of the meaning of the terminology used during body examination and the identification process. This is especially pertinent in the context of international incidents.

Following are descriptions of the five basic types of injury groups (Saukko and Knight 2004). These in turn may cause soft tissue, visceral, or skeletal trauma or any combination thereof. An injury in the living, be it to the skin, an organ, or bone, will cause an inflammatory reaction, the course of which is in part predictable and the outcome of which will result in healing. It is the consequence of this healing process, possibly supplemented by medical intervention, which results in the long-lasting identification tools that result from trauma. The resulting mark may be semipermanent — for example, a callus on the hand or foot — or permanent, such as an area of scarring or bone deformity.

7.3.1 The Abrasion

The abrasion or graze is the most superficial of the blunt trauma injuries. It is caused by a force being applied to the skin, either in a perpendicular manner (the *crush* abrasion) or tangentially (the *brush* abrasion). The injury results to the epidermis only, and thus the injury is associated with minimal, if any, bleeding or bruising (only if the papillary dermal blood vessels are also injured). Although the examination at the time of occurrence may assist in the identification of, for example, the direction of travel of the person relative to the object (for example, a brush abrasion caused as the person traveled along a road following impact by a vehicle) or the identification of an object that has been crushed onto a person (for example, a person crushed between a wall and a vehicle), there will be no long-lasting mark remaining to assist in the future identification of an individual, as the abrasion will heal without the formation of scar tissue.

7.3.2 The Bruise

A bruise is a blunt trauma injury that results when a force is applied to the skin (or an organ, in which case it is referred to as a *contusion*) such that blood escapes out of the vessels into the surrounding supporting tissues (Vanezis 2001). A bruise will develop in size, site, and appearance over the following days to weeks, again yielding information as to potential causes for the trauma, e.g., the oblong bruises of a slap mark or the complex wavy pattern of a shoe or tire tread. However, as with the abrasion, the bruise will resolve in time with the blood being broken down into its basic constituents. Thus, although it is possible to seek the site of a historic bruise by staining for iron, one would have to know where it may have been, and one or more injuries at the same site caused by different trauma cannot be distinguished. Thus, again, as with the abrasion, the bruise holds no long-term use in the identification of the deceased.

One other use for the bruise and the abrasion — for example, a fingernail mark or constituent of a bite mark — is that the trauma may identify one or more individuals who caused the trauma. By swabbing the mark (single- or double-swabbing technique) one can look for secondary genomic DNA transference (see Chapter 1) and attempt to identify the assailant using standard STR-based identification protocols. The problem will be the interpretation, especially due to the affect of tertiary contamination (Rutty 2002, Rutty et al. 2000, Rutty et al. 2003).

7.3.3 The Laceration

The laceration is a blunt trauma injury, often mistaken by medical and laypeople alike as, in fact, a sharp injury (see below). The laceration is caused by tearing and splitting of the skin or organ. The edges are irregular, often abraded and bruised with strands of tissue seen to bridge the injury. This injury group includes blunt trauma assaults in the form of kicks and stamps, weapon injuries such as hammers or pool cues, and also projectile injuries such as gunshot and shotgun injuries, explosives, crossbows, etc. In the ballistic group, the projectile enters the body by tearing the skin and soft tissues and dispersing its energy along its passage through the body.

Unlike the abrasion and the bruise, the laceration can be used for future identification. The injury will heal with the formation of scar tissue. This can be in the shape of an entrance wound of a bullet or a scar across a bony prominence. Internal organ tears may require surgical intervention, repair, or removal. Bone trauma may require prosthesis or metal repair.

In Negroid people the scar formation may be exaggerated with the formation of keloid. This may be at the site of an accidental or nonintentional injury or an injury may be self-inflicted as part of a rite of passage or tribal tradition, resulting in potentially distinctive markings (Byard and Simpson 2005).

7.3.4   The Incised Wound

The incised wound is a sharp trauma injury inflicted by objects ranging from the edge of paper to knives, pottery, and glass (Davison 2003). It can affect the full depth of the skin from the epidermis to the underlying subcutaneous fat, as well as bone or viscera. The incised wound can be further categorized by the cut where the width is greater than the depth, and the stab wound where the depth is greater than the width. At the time of infliction the characteristics of the external wound and internal tract can be used to identify the causative weapon, although it cannot identify the wielder of the weapon.

The wound will heal by first intention, resulting in a neat, often linear scar, depending upon the original wound shape and any supporting treatment and healing environment. Thus, as with the laceration, this type of injury may yield identification information. Suturing of the wound may result in symmetrical small marks with a resulting scar resembling something out of comic book pictures. Groups of incised wounds — for example, to the forearms of a person — may yield more identification information than single scars. Thus, although the causation of the wound/scar may not be able to be determined by the appearance of the healed injury, important medical history (for example, the mental state of an individual) may be discerned from the scar.

7.3.5   The Burn

The burn can be caused by cold or hot temperature and from a dry or wet source (Cooper 2006). It predominately affects the external surface of the body but can affect internal parts, depending upon the nature of the substance causing a burn (for example, hot gases of a house fire can affect the air passages and esophagus) or depending on how long the body is exposed to the source (for example, a body in a fire will be consumed from the outside inward). Depending upon the nature and depth of the burn, there may be no residual mark left to assist in identification, or there may be extensive scaring, deformity and, if medical intervention has been necessary, skin grafting sites. One observation that may be seen in burns is that the site of healing may show marked skin pigmentation due to an excess amount of melanin produced during the healing process. Equally, skin depigmentation may be seen with these injuries. Permanent hair loss, possibly to all areas of the body, may be another feature of extensive burns. Hair loss can also result — for example, from natural disease, the use of therapeutic medications, radiotherapy, or trauma (for example, in the form of hair pulling in child abuse).

7.4   Identification Criteria and Documentation

One should approach the identification of the deceased in a logical, systematic approach; in that way, although a methodology should always be adaptable, no important step should be missed. One method to try to ensure the identification of the deceased is to use standardized criteria. These can be divided into primary, secondary, and accessory identification criteria, some of which are pathological but all of which require the knowledge of the pathologist in how to gain maximum information. These criteria are illustrated in Table 7.1. As forensic practice expands, other personnel such as odontologists or anthropologists may play a more significant role within the identification process, although ultimately all forms of human personnel identification may be replaced by

Table 7.1   Criteria for Use in Identification of the Dead

Criteria		
Primary	Fingerprints	
	Odontology	
	DNA	
	Unique characteristics (prosthesis)	
Secondary	Jewelry	X-rays
	Personal effects	Physical disease
	Distinctive marks	Blood grouping
	Distinctive scars	Tissue identification
Accessory	Photographs	
	Body location	
	Clothing	
	Descriptions	

laboratory or mortuary-based DNA technologies — for example, lab-on-a-chip technology (Graham 2005). However, modern disasters such as the Asian tsunami or the World Trade Center (see Chapter 28) attacks have reiterated the importance of a team approach and the pros and cons of DNA-based identification (Rutty et al. 2005, Gill 2006).

Primary identification criteria are those that can be used on their own to confirm the identification of the deceased. Two secondary criteria are required to make an identification, and in the case of accessory parameters, these can be used on their own as a last resort or in combination with the other two types. From Table 7.1 we can see that the long-term effect of trauma can assist under two different sections. Within the primary criteria, unique marks resulting as a consequence of trauma can be used on their own for identification purposes. This will include prostheses and amputations. Scars, deformities, and visceral effects of trauma all fall under the criteria of distinguishing marks that are considered a secondary criteria. Of interest, those parameters that form the bulk of DVI forms — for example, clothing and descriptions, and that take so long to record during cadavic DVI work — in fact form part of the accessory group, i.e., the least reliable form of information used in human identification.

When considering the effect of trauma and its role in identification, one must take great care to document findings, whether in writing, tape recording, drawing, or photographs. These will ultimately be compared with antemortem data — for example, an antemortem Interpol DVI form on which subjective information collected from surviving relatives or friends is collected, or information gathered from medical and dental records, which may contain x-rays, clinical information, or the serial number of a unique prosthesis. Examples of body diagrams can be found in standard texts (Rutty and Burton 2001). These documents will be disclosable if there are subsequent court proceedings related to the event. It is advisable to have all observations documented in writing, preferably on standardized proforma and body diagrams, if the environment in which one is working is conducive to writing and seeing notes. An assistant who could make these notes would be helpful, assuming that what you are talking about is understood and the person's writing is legible. Do not use abbreviations; avoid later interpretative mistakes unless you use standardized systems — for example, dental charting (although even here you must agree which dental system to use to avoid international misinterpretation). Wet contaminated environments will cause significant difficulties in these procedures and — for example, in a chemical, biological, radiological, or nuclear (CBRN) event — may even mean that written documents cannot leave the identification area. Remote dictation or Bluetooth technology could be used to overcome these difficulties, although to date these systems remain experimental. In addition to this, observations should be photographed and, in the case of bone trauma or prosthesis, x-ray examination should be undertaken. Again, photographs are disclosable, and thus storage and use of images must follow standardized evidence protocols. Finally, always remember that those who transcribe your spoken word may not be inured to the traumas of a mass disaster and should be counseled before and after to ensure their well being.

7.5   Trauma as an Aid to Identification

Any incident that occurs to the body that results in a change to the body, be it external or internal, may prove useful as an aid to the identification of the deceased. However, as a prerequisite in all methods employed in identification, someone must first know that a person is missing: the identification of the missing person must be known to someone and the result of the identification parameter to be used must also be known. There is no point in trying to identify someone from dentition if there are no antemortem records for comparison or even if there are records, no one knows the person is missing because those who knew him or her have also perished (for example, in the Asian tsunami). Also, the most expensive high technology method may yield no better result than traditional pathological, dental, or anthropological examination and, in fact, may lead to longer delays and false expectations for the final results.

The identification process related to body modification due to trauma will start with the external examination of the front and back of the body. A systematic approach is required to consider general morphological characteristics, medical intervention, historical marks, and fresh marks and injuries. The state of decomposition and/or consumption of the body (for example, by animals or fire) will be documented in writing, drawings, and photographic records. Following this, an internal examination may be undertaken (depending upon the circumstances of the case) to consider disease processes and trauma, be they old or new, to the viscera and skeleton of the body. Example areas where long-lasting changes can arise due to the effect of trauma are considered to illustrate some of the changes that can assist with identification.

7.5.1   Occupational Trauma

Injuries may occur due to two mechanisms: unforeseen single incidents that result in trauma occurring while the person was in the work environment (as a worker at the site or a visitor to the area) and those that occur over time due to repetitive strain/injury in specific anatomical locations. Few injuries in the first group are specific to a specific occupation, and thus several causes could account for the same result. The clinical history of the missing person needs to be known and whether there are antemortem records that could associate the autopsy observations with antemortem data. Repetitive strain injuries may be more occupationally oriented, and thus, on observing such a change, the investigator should recognize the significance of the observation and potentially be directed down a specific line of enquiry.

An example of a single catastrophic occupational injury would be the loss of a digit or limb (Figure 7.2). Prior to the introduction of safety guards, machinery operators could

Figure 7.2 The loss of part of a finger of the left hand can be identified despite advanced decomposition of the body.

suffer such injuries. Although the absence of a digit could be congenital, the examination of the site would reveal changes related to surgical intervention which might have been recorded in the medical notes of the deceased. This could then lead to the discovery of other identifying tools such as x-rays, therapeutic drugs, or blood grouping results.

Those who worked within the coal industry at the coal face were prone to small injuries that healed with scar formation. Often these scars incorporated the coal dust of the work face. Coal miners' tattoos can thus be seen on the face and limbs of such individuals. These people will also have internal diseases in their respiratory systems, either to their pleura or lungs. Exposure to asbestos or working within the wood industry can also result in respiratory disease processes.

Spot welders are exposed to a continuous spray of fine hot metal, which may not only cause distinctive burn patterns to their clothing but may result in large numbers of fine scars to the arm and leg area. Similar fine linear scars may be seen on those who work in agricultural or horse-breeding occupations due to injuries caused by the handling of bales of straw. These scars should be distinguished from other causes of small scarring to the body (for example, blistering skin diseases or intravenous drugs).

A more extreme example of an occupational injury would be compression of the spine in airmen who have ejected from planes. Carpenters may suffer injuries to their hands from the action of wood and tools, and morticians may suffer injuries from the use of sharp knives or from muscle loss due to bacterial infections acquired from the bodies of the deceased.

Repetitive strain injuries may occur to the ligaments and tendons of the body or the bones. Soccer players get cartilage injuries to the knee, and ballet dancers can acquire thickening of the Achilles' tendons and bony spurs of the talus bones of the feet.

7.5.2 Posture

If a person adopts a particular posture for long periods of time and that posture places an abnormal load on the bones and joints, then deformities may occur over time that can be used to consider the identification of an individual. Examples of this would be motorcyclists, who can develop bony deformities of the elbow and knee joints, or the aborigines of Australia who squat in a manner that causes bony abnormalities of their lower limbs (Byard and Simpson 2005).

7.5.3 Hobbies and Leisure Activities

A number of hobbies and leisure activities can result in localized abnormalities, mainly to the hands. Examples of this would be the callus seen on the palmar aspect of the digits of campanologists (bell ringers) or rowers. Those who practice archery may develop lesions to the draw hand. Boxers can develop deformities of the nose and ears as well as the knuckles of their hands. More significant trauma can occur during sporting activity — for example, bony injuries from skiing and the major trauma of motor sports. Even the pastime of cheese rolling is associated with injuries that could later be used to identify a person (Carter 1999).

7.5.4 Body Modifications

Body modifications are a separate area of identification characteristics beyond the scope of this chapter. The reader should consider such texts as those written by Swift, who covers this area in detail (Swift 2003). Having said this, piercings may be altered by traumatic avulsion, especially to the ear lobes, with resulting lobar deformities. Branding and scarification are other traumatic procedures that result in permanent marks to the body. See Chapter 21 for a fuller discussion of this area.

7.5.5 Self-Inflicted Injury

Anywhere that you can physically touch your own body, you can inflict an injury. Although it could be one of any of the five main types of injuries, most are caused by incised wounds, usually to the limbs, although they can be seen to the chest, abdomen, and face. Typically, the scars occur in groups, often parallel to each other, and have a linear appearance. Persistent self-harm can result in significant deformities or loss of muscle bulk from medical intervention or superimposed infection. Foreign objects inserted into the body — for example, parts of pens into the abdominal musculature wall — may be recovered at autopsy examination. Although interesting from a medical perspective, they may have little identification evidential value.

7.5.6 Accidents and Assaults

Accidents and assaults may result in scar formation, deformities, and avulsions. An example would be the loss of teeth caused by blows to the mouth. Examination of the absent teeth sockets may reveal the possible etiology for tooth loss.

Pedestrian road traffic incidents may result in lower-limb fractures. These may be unilateral or bilateral. Examination of the bones would reveal healing injuries. They could show marks left by medical intervention. Comparison of the healed injury with antemortem x-rays may prove successful.

7.5.7 Medical Intervention

It is, of course, impossible to consider in this chapter all forms of medical procedures that can be done on a person's body. Medical or surgical intervention may result in external scarring and internal findings. The removal of an organ — for example, the spleen, following blunt abdominal trauma or a more common procedure such as the removal of the appendix — may be used to eliminate a number of people from one's inquiry, but by

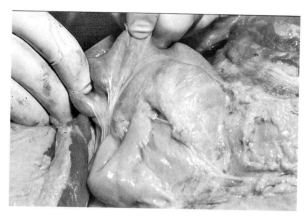

Figure 7.3   The appendix is absent.

Figure 7.4   Metal prosthesis on a limb bone, bearing a unique serial number.

itself is not unique enough to make a positive identification (Figure 7.3). The undertaking of a specific surgical procedure — for example, the fusing of the cervical vertebrae after trauma — can be sought although the site and nature of the procedure may be technically difficult to examine and be technically difficult to name or identify especially after a long time period or if the original surgeon modified a standard approach.

Surgical prostheses can be used to make unique identification by their presence alone. The name of the manufacturer as well as a unique serial number may be found on a variety of surgical prosthesis from orthopedic prosthesis to pacemakers to breast implants (Figure 7.4). Although a surgical procedure — for example, a pin and plate to the mandible — may not have a unique number, it will be the starting point to further enquiries that can be used in conjunction with other parameters in the identification process.

7.6   Trauma as a Hindrance to Identification

The results of different types of trauma may at first appear to hinder the process of identification. This will be dependent upon the type of trauma and the anatomical site affected on the body. However, as shown in Table 7.1 for example, although visual identification may be impossible at times due to the aftermath of trauma, one does not depend upon this to identify the body. Thus, significant trauma to the body does not preclude identification. The following will consider a number of examples of trauma that can occur to a body and show how these may slow down, but not necessarily stop, the process of identification.

7.6.1 Blunt Trauma

At times the result of a blunt trauma assault in the form of punches, blows by shod feet (i.e., kicks and stamps), or an assault by a blunt weapon can lead to significant facial distortion, swelling, and bruising. Broken facial bones and disruption of the teeth may further hinder the identification process. Although this may preclude direct visual identification by a relative as this type of assault is focused on the head and face, it will not affect the primary identification tools of fingerprints, DNA, unique characteristics or, in the hands of a skilled forensic odontologist, dental identification.

7.6.2 Firearms

Shotguns can cause marked localized skin, soft tissue, and bony disruption. Again, in the case of a complete body, the main problem will be direct visual identification of a person with a shotgun injury to the head. When shotguns are discharged within the mouth or against the skin of forehead there will be marked tissue expansion and disruption. Although the pathological team is likely to reconstruct this disruption, this is primarily to assess the nature of the entrance wound, not for the purpose of identification which will be undertaken using other primary parameters.

In the case of gunshot injuries, revolvers and pistols usually do not cause the extensive disruption seen with shotguns. High-velocity weapons can cause severe tissue disruption, especially to the exit wound, but, again, this will be an effect to a localized anatomical area, and thus the identification process will turn to the rest of the body.

7.6.3 Explosives

The effect of an explosion on a body depends on the nature of the explosive, which part of the body was exposed to it, and how close the body was to the explosive substance at the time of the explosion. Thus, the effect can range from complete disruption to localized trauma. The more disrupted a body, the greater the challenge for identification. The first question will be how many individuals are involved, especially with many commingled body parts. Detailed pathological and anthropological examination is required. A question that may arise in extreme cases is how far one goes to not only identify all the parts but to reassociate them with each other. With modern DNA technology one could theoretically undertake DNA examination of all pieces but this may prove prohibitively expensive and time consuming (regarding the pressures to release the remains), and may still result in the failure to identify some parts.

7.6.4 Transportation

The bodies of victims of car, rail, boat, and plane incidents may, like explosive cases, receive a range of disruption from trivial trauma to complete body disruption. The approach and considerations are shown in 7.6.3.

7.6.5 Burns

The victim may receive burns as part of the primary trauma — for example, in a house fire — or as part of the complications of an event — for example, a plane crash followed by a fire. The problems related to identification again depend on the nature of the burns and the extent of consumption of the body. It is remarkable at times how extensive the effects of fire can be to a body and yet one can still retrieve fingerprints. As the body is consumed by the fire the muscles dehydrate and contract. The fingers curl up into a fist, often protecting the skin of the fingertips, thus allowing for the process of fingerprinting. The teeth may become exposed to heat, and care must be taken to preserve them at autopsy examination. This can be achieved by the use of nail varnish or tape that is applied to stop the teeth from disintegrating. DNA, although affected by heat, can, of course, still be sourced from hair, teeth, bone, and deep muscle. Even in burned bodies, blood can often be obtained from the popliteal vessels at the back of the knees. Finally, if the body is virtually consumed by fire, as in the case of legal cremation, unique identifying features such as hip prostheses may still survive, allowing for identification.

7.6.6 Dismemberment

The process of dismemberment by itself causes difficulties in identifying the location of the body parts and the tools used to dismember the body, but usually does not pose a problem in relation to primary identification techniques. Even in cases where the body is extensively defleshed and unique features are removed by the assailant, identification is usually still achievable by anthropological, dental, and DNA examination. Finally, even when extreme lengths are undertaken to dispose of the victim, a careful search of the scene may find identifiable remains — for example, hair or cellular material in the drain of the U-bend of the bath or sinks. Again, these should be examined by a pathologist, who will be trained in the histopathological examination of cellular material. The presence of squamous cells and hair is expected, as these are shed all the time from the external surface of the body, but the presence of the components of organs or supporting internal tissues is another matter.

7.7 Conclusion

This introductory chapter gives an overview of the pathologist's role in the identification of a cadaver, whether it is a single fatality or part of a mass-disaster DVI team. It does not explore all the techniques and methodology employed by the pathologist, as these will be covered elsewhere within this book. Rather, it concentrates on the pathologist's role, the classification of injuries, and the documentation used. It gives brief examples of areas where trauma can both assist and hinder identification processes, but trauma by itself does not preclude the identification of the deceased. As trauma can occur under a vast spectrum of circumstances, it is not possible to consider every example known to man, so generalized examples have been used to illustrate key points. The reader is advised to consider specific texts concerning the results of trauma to the body or is encouraged to work alongside a skilled forensic pathologist to gain an insight into the systematic approach used to identify a body.

References

Byard, R.W. and Simpson, E., Characteristic acquired features of indigenous Australians that may be observed in forensic practice, *Forensic Sci Med Pathol* 1(3), 207–213, 2005.

Carter, N., in *The Pathology of Trauma*, Purdue, B.N., and Mason, J.K., Eds., Arnold, London, 1999.

Cooper, P.N., Burn injury, in *Essentials of Autopsy Practice: Current Methods and Modern Trends*, Vol. 3, Rutty, G.N., Ed., Springer-Verlag, London, 2006, pp. 215–232.

Davison, A.M., The incised wound, in *Essentials of Autopsy Practice: Recent Advances, Topics and Developments*, Vol. 2, Rutty, G.N., Ed., Springer-Verlag, London, 2003, pp. 187–220.

Gill, J.R., 9/11 and the New York Office of Chief Medical Examiner, *Forensic Sci Med Pathol* 2(1), 27–30, 2006.

Graham, E.A.M., Lab-on-a-chip technology, *Forensic Sci Med Pathol* 1(3), 221–224, 2005.

Interpol, http://www.interpol.int/Public/DisasterVictim/default.asp. 2006.

Milroy, C.M. and Rutty, G.N., If a wound is neatly incised it is not a laceration, *Br Med J* 315, 1312, 1997.

Rutty, G.N., An investigation into the transference and survivability of human DNA following simulated manual strangulation with consideration of the problem of third party contamination, *Int J Legal Med* 116, 170–173, 2002.

Rutty, G.N. and Burton, J.L., The external examination, in *The Hospital Autopsy*, Burton, J. and Rutty, G.N., Eds., Arnold, London, 2001, p. 43.

Rutty, G.N., Byard, R.W., and Tsokos, M., The Tsunami: an environmental mass disaster, *Forensic Sci Med Pathol* 1(1), 3–7, 2005.

Rutty, G.N., Hopwood, A., and Tucker, V., The effectiveness of protective clothing in the reduction of potential DNA contamination of the scene of crime, *Int J Legal Med* 117, 170–174, 2003.

Rutty, G.N., Watson, S., and Davison, J., Contamination of mortuary instruments and work surfaces by human DNA: a significant problem in forensic practice? *Int J Legal Med* 114, 56–60, 2000.

Saukko, P. and Knight, B., Eds., *Forensic Pathology*, Arnold, London, 2004.

Swift, B., Body art and modification, in *Essentials of Autopsy Practice: Recent Advances, Topics and Developments*, Vol. 2, Rutty, G.N., Ed., Springer-Verlag, London, 2003, pp. 159–186.

Vanezis, P., Bruising: concepts of aging and interpretation, in *Essentials of Autopsy Practice*, Vol. 1, Rutty, G.N. Ed., Springer-Verlag, London, 2001, pp. 221–240.

Surgical Intervention

JAMES CLARKSON
MAUREEN SCHAEFER

Contents

8.1   Outline of Surgical Specialties 128
    8.1.1   Cardiothoracic Surgery 128
    8.1.2   Ear, Nose, and Throat Surgery (Otolaryngology) 128
    8.1.3   General Surgery 131
    8.1.4   Neurosurgery..132
    8.1.5   Pediatric Surgery...132
    8.1.6   Obstetrics and Gynecology 132
    8.1.7   Ophthalmology...133
    8.1.8   Orthopedic Surgery..133
    8.1.9   Plastic Surgery and Maxillofacial Surgery 134
        8.1.9.1   Plastic Surgical Reconstruction 134
        8.1.9.2   Hand Surgery...134
        8.1.9.3   Breast Reconstructive Surgery 136
        8.1.9.4   Burns Surgery..136
        8.1.9.5   Cosmetic Surgery...137
        8.1.9.6   Rhinoplasty 137
        8.1.9.7   Breast Augmentation 137
        8.1.9.8   Liposuction..137
        8.1.9.9   Eyelid Surgery 138
        8.1.9.10 Face Lift 138
        8.1.9.11 Orthognathic Surgery....................................138
        8.1.9.12 Facial Implants 138
        8.1.9.13 General Maxillofacial Surgery.......................138
    8.1.10 Urology..138
    8.1.11 Nonsurgical Specialties that Operate 139
8.2   Implant Material (Artifacts) 139
    8.2.1   Evolution of the Breast Implant.......................................141
8.3   Biological Changes...143
8.4   Conclusion 144
References 145

Although the field of surgery is broad, evidence that surgery has taken place is often obvious and should point the investigator toward the most likely surgical specialist who will be able to advise them. The effect of surgery is to produce a controlled injury to the soft and hard tissues, and this is often done in response to traumatic injury. As such, this chapter links well with the previous chapter on trauma. Surgery produces scarring and may leave behind artifacts such as implants, in addition to altering normal anatomy. We will provide the reader with a broad outline of the effect of surgical interventions on the human body, along with a guide to scar placement to help decide which surgical specialty has performed the operation. The reader should bear in mind that surgery, like all technologies, changes with time and differs in its practice between countries. This alone may provide useful information for the investigator. In addition, the reason for surgery may be deduced. For example, the discovery of a metal plate will indicate a previous fracture, or a pacemaker will indicate serious underlying heart disease. Finally, the effect of wound healing on the soft tissues is to produce scarring. Although this phenomenon is highly variable, careful observation based on the maturation of this process will provide a rough estimation of time from surgery or injury within the first year or two. The site and position of scars will inform the investigator much about the nature of the surgery (Figure 8.1 to Figure 8.6 and Figure 8.8).

To get a balanced view of a case, we advise that more than one surgeon is approached, ideally from differing specialties. The lead author of this chapter is a plastic surgeon, and the content will therefore lean in this direction.

This chapter is split into three sections:

1. Outline of surgical specialties related to scar maps
2. Implant materials (artifacts)
3. Biological changes with time

8.1   Outline of Surgical Specialties

Within the U.K. surgeons are trained at the Royal College of Surgeons in Scotland, Ireland, and England. Surgeons from these colleges are titled "Mr.," to traditionally differentiate them from hospital physicians. Although the vast majority of operations are performed by surgeons (Table 8.1), any physician with the required experience may operate in his area of specialty (Table 8.2). There is considerable overlap, and in many cases more than one surgical specialty will do the same or similar operations.

8.1.1   Cardiothoracic Surgery

This specialty is responsible for operations on organs within the chest wall including the rib cage. The classic access scars are given in Figure 8.1. Commonly implanted material includes mechanical or pig heart valves. Rib implants and thoracic contouring silicone implants are also used, as well as metal work. They commonly harvest the great saphenous vein as a vein graft from the medial aspect of the calf and connect it (anastomosis) between the internal thoracic arteries and the coronary arteries to provide more blood to the heart (Figure 8.1, incision 5).

8.1.2   Ear, Nose, and Throat Surgery (Otolaryngology)

With the exception of head and neck cancer surgery, ENT surgeons try to make use of scopes or incisions within the mouth and throat for much of their surgery and avoid skin incision wherever possible. Frequent exceptions include: (1) postauricular scars that provide access to the ear drum and mastoid cavity (Figure 8.2, incision 7), (2) preauricular scars to

Table 8.1 Surgical Specialties and Subspecialties

Main Specialty	Subspecialty
Cardiothoracic surgery	Cardiac
	Thoracic
	Transplant
	Pediatric
Ear nose and throat surgery	Cosmetic
	Rhinology
	Head and Neck
	Laryngology
	Nose
General surgery	Breast
	Colorectal
	Endocrine
	Transplant
	Upper GI
	Vascular surgery
Maxillofacial surgery	Cleft
	Cosmetic
	General
	Head and Neck
	Orthognathic
Neurosurgery	General
	Pediatric
	Spinal
Obstetrics and Gynecology	Obstetrics
	Gynecology
	Oncological
Ophthalmic surgery	Anterior chamber
	General
	Oculoplastic
	Retinal
	Vitreus
Orthopedic surgery	General
	Hand
	Shoulder
	Spinal
	Specialist
Pediatric surgery	General
Plastic and reconstructive surgery	Breast
	Burns
	Cleft
	Cosmetic
	Craniofacial
	General
	Hand
	Head and Neck
	Hypospadias
	Oculoplastic
Urology	

Table 8.2   Nonsurgical Specialties that Operate

Cardiology
Dermatology
General practitioners
Radiology

1. **Sternotomy**
   - Access to heart and mediastinum
2. **Anterolateral thoracotomy**
   - Access to lung
3. **Posterolateral thoracotomy**
   - Access to aorta and lungs
4. **Transverse bilateral thoracotomy**
   - Heart, lungs, great vessels
5. **Great saphenous vein donor site**
6. **Pacemaker position**

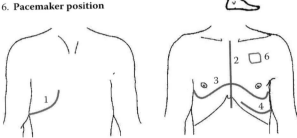

Figure 8.1   Scars on the human body associated with surgical intervention.

1. **Parietal neurosurgical incision**
2. **Neck dissection**
   - Access to lymph nodes
3. **Bi-coronal neurosurgical incision**
   - Craniofacial surgery
   - Neurosurgery
4. **Tracheostomy, thyroid, and parathyroid surgery**
5. **Anterior neurosurgical incision**
6. **Parotid and submandibular salivary gland surgery**
7. **Mastoid or tympanum surgery**

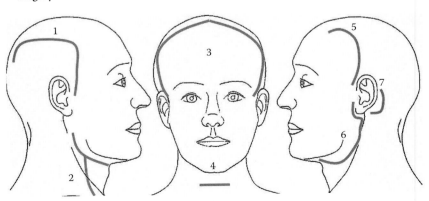

Figure 8.2   Scars on the human body associated with surgical intervention.

1. **Subcostal/kocher's**
   - Choleocystectomy
2. **Right paramedian**
   - Laparotomy
3. **Gridiron**
   - Appendectomy
4. **Midline laparotomy**
   - Emergency access
   - All organs
5. **Laparoscopic**
   - Choleocystectomy
   - Appendectomy
   - Colectomies
6. **Suprapubic/Pfannenstiel**
   - Gynecological surgery
   - Hysterectomy
   - Other pelvic surgery
7. **Left paramedian**
   - Anterior rectal resection
8. **Inguinal hernia**
   - Hernia repair
9. **Femoral incision**
   - Groin dissection
   - Vascular access
10. **Nephrectomy/loin**
    - Renal surgery
    - Adrenal gland surgery
11. **Common pediatric incision**

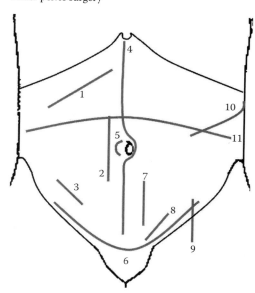

Figure 8.3   Scars on the human body associated with surgical intervention.

gain access to the parotid salivary gland (Figure 8.2, incision 6), and (3) neck scars, usually running parallel to the mandible and including a vertical component (Figure 8.2, incision 2). This procedure provides access to the lymph nodes and is commonly performed to remove cancer. Tracheostomy scars are found just below the thyroid cartilage ("Adam's apple") (Figure 8.2, incision 4). ENT surgeons often perform this operation, but plastic and maxillo-facial surgeons may also perform this surgery, along with other intensive care doctors. A tracheostomy scar indicates that the individual is likely to have required prolonged venti-lation on intensive care during his lifetime.

8.1.3   General Surgery

Despite its title, general surgery has with time become centralized to the abdomen, although specialists within this area will also focus on vascular, transplant, and endocrine surgery. Figure 8.3 shows the common abdominal incisions used by this specialty, along with the type of operation that requires the incision. Foreign material introduced during surgery frequently includes abdominal wall synthetic meshes, such as polypropylene used to repair hernias. Increasingly over the last 15 years, minimal access surgery is being offered that simply utilizes small incisions to introduce telescopes and thin instruments into the abdomen, often near the umbilicus (Figure 8.3, incision 5). Gall bladder surgery is most frequently performed this way. Vascular reconstruction of the great vessels, including the abdominal aorta, popliteal, femoral, and axillary arteries, may be undertaken with a variety of materials, the most common being Dacron. Vascular surgeons also perform arterio-venous anastomoses (connections) in the cubital fossa of the elbow or at the wrist for patients undergoing long-term renal dialysis. Endocrine surgeons may operate on the thyroid and parathyroid gland through an incision just below the thyroid cartilage on the front of the neck (Figure 8.2, incision 4). They also operate on the adrenal gland through a similar incision below the ribs on the flank for kidney surgery (Figure 8.3, incision 10), and for the pancreas, usually through a midline abdominal incision (Figure 8.3, incision 4). Transplant surgery is most commonly done for liver, heart, and kidney. The National Transplant Database has existed in the U.K. since 1972. With correct ethical and legal approval, patients may be identified from this.

8.1.4   Neurosurgery

During surgery of the brain and the spinal cord, access incisions are made to the skull and spine as shown in Figure 8.2 and Figure 8.4, incision 6. The bi-coronal flap is used for elective surgery and is formed by making an incision from ear to ear (Figure 8.2 incision 3). The same incision is also used by plastic and maxillofacial surgeons to gain access to the facial skeleton. For emergency burr holes (trephination), used to decompress the brain after head injuries, a more parietal scar may be created along the length of the scalp (Figure 8.2, incisions 1 and 5). Neurosurgeons use implants including cerebrospinal fluid shunts for hydrocephalus. They may also implant cranial plates and leave behind metallic vascular clips placed during brain surgery.

8.1.5   Pediatric Surgery

Pediatric surgeons have to address the functional problems of congenital deformity often involving the digestive tract and bowel. They may also be involved in some plastic surgical procedures such as cleft surgery and urogenital deformity. Surgery performed by pediatric surgeons is most often on very young children under 5 years of age; the other specialties will often operate on children for problems within their own field. One important characteristic of pediatric abdominal scars is that they tend to be horizontal if surgery was performed on a child under 5 years old (Figure 8.3, incision 11). Therefore, if an individual bears a horizontal mid-abdominal scar then it is likely he or she was operated on as a young child. Pediatric surgeons occasionally manage burns in children.

8.1.6   Obstetrics and Gynecology

These doctors manage the female genital and reproductive system. The most common scar will run just above the pubic hairline used for Caesarean sections and pelvic operations (Figure 8.3, incision 6). They frequently perform groin dissections to remove cancerous lymph nodes, either by vertical groin incisions (Figure 8.3, incision 9) or groin crease incisions. Implants include the uterine contraceptive coil and fallopian tube ligation clips.

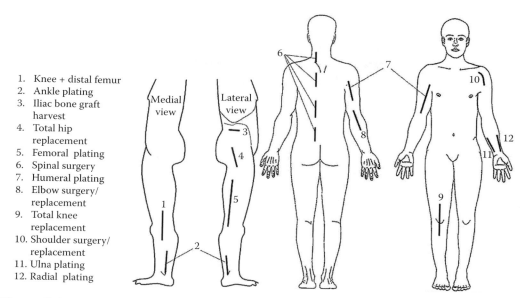

Figure 8.4 Scars on the human body associated with surgical intervention.

1. Knee + distal femur
2. Ankle plating
3. Iliac bone graft harvest
4. Total hip replacement
5. Femoral plating
6. Spinal surgery
7. Humeral plating
8. Elbow surgery/ replacement
9. Total knee replacement
10. Shoulder surgery/ replacement
11. Ulna plating
12. Radial plating

8.1.7 Ophthalmology

Ophthalmology, or eye surgery, leaves behind very little evidence for the investigator as their incisions are nearly all within the eye globe or conjunctiva. Implanted materials that may be found include artificial lenses or prosthetic globes. Ophthalmic as well as plastic surgeons may operate on the eyelids (Figure 8.8, incision 6).

8.1.8 Orthopedic Surgery

Orthopedic surgery is responsible for the management of fractured limb bones, joint replacements due to arthritis, and some hand surgery. It may also be used on the spine. Orthopedic surgeons leave behind more implanted material than any other surgical specialty. Orthopedics began using steel plates and screws to stabilize bone fractures in the early 20th century (Lane 1914). Orthopedic implants have evolved over time to include many metallic alloys and other more inert metals. The invention of the Charnley Hip prosthesis in the early '60s marked the beginning of the era of total joint replacement. With the population aging, orthopedics is growing quickly as a specialty. The most common joint replacement being performed today is the hip, followed closely by the knee and then shoulder. It is estimated that the British National Health Service (NHS) performs over 40,000 hip replacements every year making it a very useful tool in determining identity. Common scars that indicate that joint replacement has taken place are shown in Figure 8.4 (incisions 4, 9, and 10), along with common access scars for fracture fixation.

In addition to fracture fixation and joint replacement, orthopedic surgery can also be used to lengthen bones, a process known as Ilizarov bone distraction. This may be performed on any bone that requires lengthening due to bone loss or growth failure as a result of pathology such as osteomyelitis or achondroplasia. The procedure may also be performed on individuals who wish to be taller for cosmetic or social reasons. One indication that this has taken place will be longitudinal "tracking" scars on either side of a long bone, marked by the pins dragging against the skin. Orthopedic surgeons, along with plastic surgeons, may perform bone grafting, either with cancellous bone harvested most commonly from the iliac crest (Figure 8.4 incision 3) or with bone substitutes, such as hydroxyapatite, a ceramic cement that allows bone in-growth. They are usually used about metal implants to strengthen the surrounding bone.

8.1.9 Plastic Surgery and Maxillofacial Surgery

Although both were originally the same specialty, in the U.K., maxillofacial surgery became an independent specialty in the early '60s in order to recognize the dental training that was required for their work. Plastic surgery is the last truly general specialty covering both adults and children from head to foot. As such, plastic surgeons are involved in multidisciplinary teams with other specialties on a frequent basis. In tandem with this, maxillofacial surgery will be discussed, especially regarding orthognathic surgery (the rearrangement of maxillofacial bone alignment), which in combination with plastic surgery may produce very striking changes in appearance.

First, we shall concentrate on the most common areas that plastic surgeons are involved with.

8.1.9.1 *Plastic Surgical Reconstruction*

Plastic surgeons reconstruct many soft- and hard-tissue defects whether from injury or surgery involving the head and neck, limbs, and trunk. One good example is extensive cancer resection about the head and neck. The wide removal of throat or mouth cancers results in a substantial tissue defects that can be both functionally debilitating and highly disfiguring. Plastic surgery has developed techniques of transferring large volumes of bone and soft tissue, while maintaining their blood supply, in order to reconstruct the defect. These *flaps* of soft tissue may be left attached to their origin, thereby preserving their blood supply, or may be completely removed from the donor location. If completely removed, the severed vessels within the flap must then be sewn into a recipient site under a microscope. Two examples of this are the free radial forearm flap and the free fibular flap (Figure 8.5, incision 1 and 9). Tissue may also be *grafted* from one site to another, and this tissue does not require a blood supply. Examples include split skin grafting, taken from the thigh (Figure 8.5, incision 8) or cancellous bone grafting taken from the iliac crest (Figure 8.4 incision 3).

The above techniques will all produce a *donor site* at the location where the tissue has been harvested; Figure 8.5 shows some common donor sites. The recognition of a donor site should raise awareness that extensive reconstruction has taken place somewhere in the body. Recent application of transplant technology to the face and hands will add further complexity to the interpretation of soft tissue surgery. To date, however, these transplants are still rarely performed.

8.1.9.2 *Hand Surgery*

In the U.K. most hand operations are performed by plastic surgeons, however, orthopedic surgeons may also perform this surgery. Hand injuries are most commonly a consequence of trauma and in the adult can be associated with risk-taking behavior. Links between risk taking and criminality have been made (Dahlbäck 1990). While no prospective studies link hand injury with criminality, it is certainly the subjective experience of many hand surgeons that criminality may be more prevalent in their patient population.

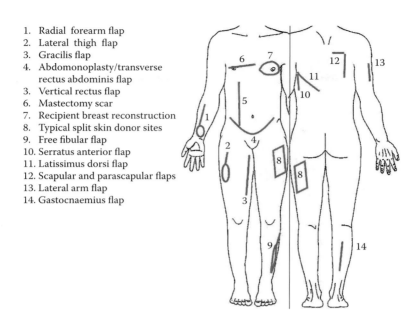

1. Radial forearm flap
2. Lateral thigh flap
3. Gracilis flap
4. Abdomonoplasty/transverse rectus abdominis flap
3. Vertical rectus flap
6. Mastectomy scar
7. Recipient breast reconstruction
8. Typical split skin donor sites
9. Free fibular flap
10. Serratus anterior flap
11. Latissimus dorsi flap
12. Scapular and parascapular flaps
13. Lateral arm flap
14. Gastocnaemius flap

Figure 8.5   Scars on the human body associated with surgical intervention.

1. Common surgical exploration incisions
2. Swanson's arthroplasty
3. Carpel tunnel release
4. Self harm

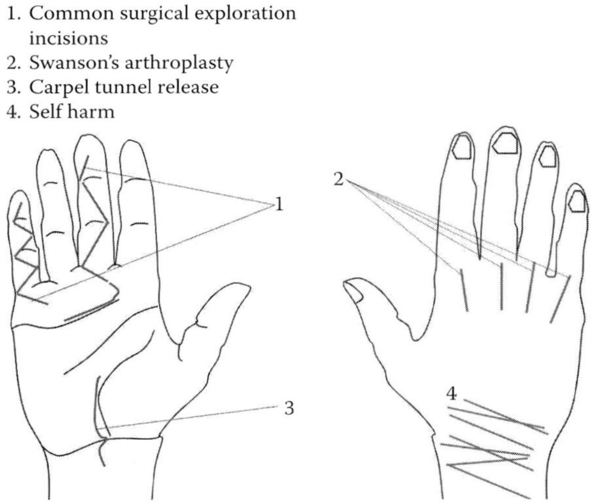

Figure 8.6   Scars on the human body associated with surgical intervention.

Nonemergency hand surgery is largely concerned with degenerative conditions such as median nerve compression and arthritis, in addition to dealing with long-term complications after hand trauma. Figure 8.6 shows common incisions used in hand surgery. Implants are often used in the form of wires, screws, and plates for bone fractures and in the form of silastic silicone for joint replacements (e.g., Swanson's arthroplasty Figure 8.6, incision 2). Note that Swanson's arthroplasty implants do not carry a serial number.

The reattachment of hands and arms are also covered under this specialty. In the case of amputated fingers, toes may be used as substitute fingers. Hand and arm transplantation from one individual to another is now possible, and this produces obvious implications for fingerprint analysis, though this remains a vanishingly rare operation.

Figure 8.7   Scars on the human body associated with surgical intervention following a burn.

An important scar to be aware of occurs as a result of deliberate self-harm (Figure 8.6, incision 4), which is strongly associated with personality and psychiatric disorders (Morgan et al. 1975) and criminality (Fotiadou et al. 2006). These are often found on the nondominant forearm and take the form of multiple parallel scars, from repeated episodes of self-inflicted lacerations. These patients will have received multiple operations at their local plastic surgical department and are likely to be frequent accident and emergency attendees.

8.1.9.3   *Breast Reconstructive Surgery*

Breast reconstruction is increasingly being performed after mastectomy (removal of the breast) by both general and plastic surgeons. Implants with expanding characteristics have been most commonly used to recreate the breast mound. However, as these implants were not found to be very breast-like, more complex reconstructive options are increasingly being utilized in which a soft tissue envelope is imported by means of a flap to create a more realistic, natural breast. The standard mastectomy scar is shown along with the most common locations of donor sites (Figure 8.5, incisions 4, 6, 7, 11). Flap reconstruction usually involves fat and skin from either the abdomen or back. Muscles lying deep to the fat are moved with it to maintain the blood supply to the overlying skin. For example, fat on the back is transported along with the latissimus dorsi muscle, and abdominal fat is moved in conjunction with the rectus abdominis muscle. Implants may also be inserted under these flaps once inserted onto the chest wall to give greater volume to the breast. Nipples and areolae are recreated by means of tattooing in some cases.

8.1.9.4   *Burns Surgery*

Within the U.K., burns tend to afflict people from lower socioeconomic backgrounds (Hippisley-Cox et al. 2002) and are frequently associated with alcoholism, drug abuse, and psychiatric illness (Anwar et al. 2005). Worldwide, burn injuries are seen more frequently in developing countries where health and safety standards are low and poverty levels are high. Burns are managed with either dressings alone or may require excision and grafting. Scars created from burns are highly disfiguring due to their large size and the possibility of joint contracture. A characteristic of burn surgery is the presence of a donor site where fresh skin was removed to be applied to the burn, which leaves behind a graze containing squared edges, most commonly occurring on the thigh (Figure 8.5, incision 8). The skin is then meshed into a net pattern, to spread the skin over a wider area (Figure 8.7). The meshed skin then scars into the recognizable stippled cross hatched pattern where the skin was grafted into the recipient site. Burn scars are recognizable and to some degree will inform the investigator of an approximate time from injury (see Section 8.3). It is important to realize that a patient with large burns, especially a child, will be likely to undergo multiple operations to release scar contractures and increase the cosmesis for the patient. Most severely burnt patients are well known to those who are involved in their treatment, which lasts many years.

8.1.9.5   Cosmetic Surgery

Plastic surgery developed as a discipline during World War 1 as a means to reconstruct severely deforming injuries sustained while fighting. After the war, however, these freshly developed reconstructive skills found new peacetime application in the form of cosmetic surgery. Within the past decade, cosmetic surgery has undergone considerable growth in both public awareness and popularity. Cosmetic surgery involves the realignment of soft and hard tissues with or without the aid of implanted prosthetic materials. As the body ages, the skin loses its elastic tone and tends to pull downward as the result of gravity. This process is known as *ptosis*. Many of the most common cosmetic procedures are designed to reverse the effect of aging and recreate a more youthful appearance. The five most common operations, including (1) rhinoplasty, (2) breast augmentation, (3) liposuction, (4) eyelid surgery, and (5) face lift, will be discussed along with other cosmetic operations that can radically change appearance, including: orthognathic surgery and facial implants.

8.1.9.6   Rhinoplasty

Rhinoplasty (popularly known as a "nose job") has the ability to change the bony skeleton of the face, which, along with orthognathic surgery and facial implants, can make striking changes to appearance. Scars for this are small and tend to be within the nasal rim or just across the skin in front of the septum, known as the collumella (Figure 8.8, incision 1). The nasal hump is often rasped off and the nasal bones fractured inward to reduce the nasal bridge.

8.1.9.7   Breast Augmentation

This popular operation involves an outer silicone shell filled with either a silicone gel or saline solution, and is placed either over or beneath the pectoralis major muscle. In the U.K. and Europe they are most commonly silicone filled; however, in the U.S. the majority are saline filled. Incisions are most commonly made in the breast fold or around the nipple, although other routes of insertion do exist (Figure 8.8, incisions 2–5).

8.1.9.8   Liposuction

As people age, they may also develop excess fat as a by-product of their lifestyle. Liposuction is used to reshape the body contours to be more cosmetically pleasing. A suction cannula is introduced via short incisions of no more than 1 cm long, often around the umbilicus, costal margin and suprapubic regions. Liposuction may be performed in many areas including the chin, buttocks, thighs, and arms.

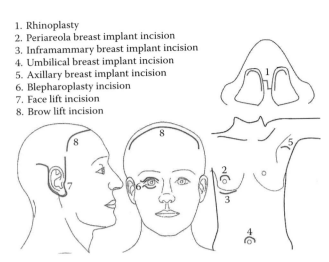

1. Rhinoplasty
2. Periareola breast implant incision
3. Inframammary breast implant incision
4. Umbilical breast implant incision
5. Axillary breast implant incision
6. Blepharoplasty incision
7. Face lift incision
8. Brow lift incision

Figure 8.8   Scars on the human body associated with surgical intervention.

8.1.9.9   Eyelid Surgery
Blepharoplasty is also called *eyelid reduction*. Scars here are hard to see, due to the nature of eyelid skin (Figure 8.8, incision 6). Brow lift is often done in tandem with eyelid surgery and the incision is shown (Figure 8.8, incision 8).

8.1.9.10   Face Lift
Evidence of a face lift may be seen as a scar running in between the "sideburns" and front of the ear and continuing down to wrap around the back of the ear (Figure 8.8, incision 7).

8.1.9.11   Orthognathic Surgery
This can produce profound alterations to facial appearance by fracturing and realigning the facial skeleton and is performed by maxillofacial surgeons. This type of surgery is usually reserved for correction of deformities and is relatively rarely used in cosmetic surgical practice.

8.1.9.12   Facial Implants
Facial implants produce contour changes in the underlying facial skeleton with less surgical risk and complexity than orthognathic surgery. Due to their relative simplicity, they are the favorite choice of the cosmetic surgeon over orthognathic surgery.

8.1.9.13   General Maxillofacial Surgery
Maxillofacial surgeons manage functional, cancer, and traumatic conditions of the facial skeleton, jaws, throat, and mouth. This specialty overlaps extensively with head surgery performed by ENT surgeons and plastic surgeons. From a trauma perspective, artifacts left behind will include wires, screws, and plates. Like ENT, many of their incisions are inside the oral cavity.

8.1.10   Urology
This specialty focuses on the kidney, ureter, bladder, prostate gland, penis, and testicles. There is often little superficial evidence of this type of surgery due to the use of scopes, as with

ENT surgery. Lower abdominal scars may be produced by open bladder and prostate surgery (Figure 8.3, incision 7). Upper flank scars just below the ribs indicate kidney operations (Figure 8.3, incision 10). Prosthetic material includes synthetic silicone testicular implants.

8.1.11   Nonsurgical Specialties that Operate

Of these specialties, interventional cardiology and radiology are the most likely to leave behind implanted material. These implants may be inserted via vascular cannulas and include intravascular stents and cardiac implants. Both of these are placed within the lumen of the vascular system and may be absorbed or become incorporated into the vessel wall as nonabsorbable metallic or nonmetallic implants. Most vascular access is achieved by a small incision over the femoral artery in the groin crease, often too small to notice (Figure 8.3, incision 9). Pacemakers are inserted by interventional cardiologists (Figure 8.1, incision 6) and usually sit under the skin of the left upper anterior chest wall. General practitioners often do minor operations on the skin, such as mole and wart removal, and infrequently maintain a surgical interest in other areas such as cosmetic surgery or orthopedics. Dermatologists perform similar minor surgery, but their scars have not been covered in the scar map. The most common areas to require surgery are those regions directly exposed to sunlight, as they are most prone to developing cancer. These regions commonly include the head, face, and neck region, the back in males and in females, the calves and shins.

8.2   Implant Material (Artifacts)

Artificial devices associated with many of the various medical disciplines are frequently implanted into the body during surgical intervention. Materials used in the construction of implants can be broken down into three basic categories consisting of metals, polymer/fabrics, and ceramics (Flood 2000). Metal components are usually constructed from titanium, a cobalt/chromium alloy, or stainless steel. Implanted items categorized as polymers and fabrics include substances such as silicone, Gore-Tex, and Teflon. Ceramics include the bone cement hydroxyapatite. Prosthetic devices may contain multiple components constructed from any of the three categories.

The usefulness of an implanted device in determining identity depends on the ability to associate that item to an individual. The placement of logos and serial numbers on devices has greatly simplified this assignment (Ubelaker and Jacobs 1995, Wilson et al. 2006). Unfortunately, while many devices include serial numbers, many others do not. Devices associated with plastic surgery, for example, frequently do not carry any identifying number. This includes many facial, breast, or other contour-enhancing implants. Orthopedic devices, on the other hand, will generally carry a serial number if the implant is sufficiently large. Smaller items such as screws or wires do not generally have individual numbers associated with them and therefore cannot be easily tracked back to either the manufacturer or the type of implant. Fortunately for identification purposes, national and regional registries of implanted products within the U.K. are becoming increasingly popular due to European working standards. Many of the registries now in existence were implemented to achieve postmarket surveillance so that devices that did not tend to have good results could be taken off the market or changed. Information collected in the registry generally includes patient information such as name and address, and the serial number of the product (regardless

Table 8.3 National and Regional Registries for Implanted Device

Registry	Acronym	Start Date
National Pacemaker Database	NPBD	January 1977
U.K. Heart Valve Registry	UKHVR	January 1986
Implantable Cardiac Defibrillator Database	ICD	January 1989
North West Arthroplasty Register	NWAR	1991
National Breast Implant Registry	NBIR	July 1993
U.K. Hydrocephalus Shunt Registry	SHUNT	May 1995
National Joint Registry	NJR	January 2004

of whether it is actually illustrated on the product itself), among additional information regarding clinical outcome. While these databases did not originate for the sake of identification purposes, their utility in the identification process is obvious. If human remains are found with an implanted device that bears a serial number, the national registry for that device in the U.K. can be contacted, which can then provide information on the recipient. The registry can, therefore, act as a centralized database by which an implant can be directly linked to an individual. The databases are strictly confidential and open access is not automatically granted. Specific information can be given under certain circumstances, and this request frequently must come from the police. Some of the more useful registries are listed in Table 8.3.

Unfortunately, a national database does not exist in the U.K. for all implanted products, and many of those that are in existence have only been recently established. Information on patients receiving implants prior to the starting date of the registry will not be included. In addition, not all individuals who should be included in the database are registered, leaving gaps in the documentation (due to either patient refusal or reasons within the hospital). Where a patient does not give consent, their information may still be collected using a hospital identifier (a unique number within each hospital). The hospital itself can then be contacted for further information regarding the recipient. In the event that a national database does not exist for a recovered implant, the presence of a corporate logo can guide an investigator to the correct manufacturer for information on the purchasing hospital or health authority. With this information, the operating theater log book held locally by the hospital may be able to match serial numbers with a patient ID. Again, patient confidentiality will prevent access without the correct legal and ethical authority.

The ability to contact the correct manufacturer relies on the investigator's being able to recognize company logos placed on the implants (Ubelaker and Jacobs 1995, Wilson et al. 2006). This is easier said than done, as many logos do not necessarily bear any resemblance to the name of the company. A list of some of the more popular orthopedic manufacturers within the U.K. is provided in Table 8.4, along with their Web addresses and telephone numbers. Figure 8.9 also provides logos associated with various companies. Some companies may have more than one logo associated with their products, as company buyouts and takeovers have been numerous, but the products will retain their original trademarks. This is by no means an exhaustive account due to the large numbers of orthopedic manufacturers. If the investigator has no knowledge of company logos or is simply unfamiliar with a pertinent logo, their local orthopedic or other surgical specialist can be contacted for assistance. It is also important to realize that a serial number or logo may be present but not easily viewable. For instance, the identifying mark may be covered as a result of osseous integration, or the device itself may be located within the bone, i.e., an intramedullary nail.

Table 8.4 Common Orthopedic Manufacturers in the U.K.

Company	Phone	Web Address	Identifying Marks
Amdale	(0)2392 660726	www.amdale.co.uk	Stylized A
Biomet Europe		www.biomet.co.uk	B; BIOMET; BMT
Corin	(0)1285 659866	www.corin.co.uk	Stylized C
DePuy Ace		see Johnson and Johnson	Dot
Forth Medical	(0)1635 550100	www.forthmedical.co.uk	Hexagon forming edge of diamond
Johnson and Johnson		www.jnjgateway.com	J&J
Global Orthopaedics	(0)2392 383366	www.globalorthopaedics.co.uk	Globe
McKenna Group	(0)1909 541414	www.mckennagroup.co.uk	Three arrows; pointing right, down, and left
NorthStar	(0)1635 275380	www.northstar-ortho.co.uk/	Star within diamond
Orthofix	(0)1628 594500	www.orthofix.it	F encircled by an O
Osteonics	(0)1635 262400	see Stryker Howmedica Osteonics	Stylized femur
Smith and Nephew	(0)1926 482400	www.ortho.smith-nephew.com/uk/home.asp	Flower
Stryker Howmedica Osteonics	(0)1635 262400	www.stryker.co.uk	Stryker
Synthes	(0)1707 332212	www.synthesis.com/html	Stylized pelvis
Tornier	(0)1635 275380	see NorthStar	T in hexagon
Zimmer	(0)17935 84500	www.zimmer.com	Bold Z in a circle

Lastly, if the device does not carry a serial number, recognition of styles and trends can be used to age the implants. It can also give indication as to whether you might be dealing with a foreigner or someone who has lived abroad as styles and materials vary from one country to another. By way of an example we shall discuss the evolution of the silicone breast implant.

8.2.1 Evolution of the Breast Implant

About 1% of women within the U.S. have had artificial breast implantation, and its popularity is fast growing in Europe and the U.K. Over 240 styles, including 8300 models of both inflatable and noninflatable varieties, are now available. Prior to the early 1960s breast augmentation was accomplished through direct injection of either liquid silicone or paraffin, or the implantation of sponges made from varying synthetic compounds including silicone-based polymers. The era of modern breast implants commenced in 1963, when prostheses made of silicone gel contained within a silicone shell were first introduced into the market (Cronin and Gerow 1964). These implants had a dacron mesh attached to the back surface to enhance adhesion to the chest wall. Over the past four decades several modifications have been introduced to address specific complications that arose as a result of these implants.

The first of these problems was the high rate of capsular development that caused the breast to become hard and painful. In an attempt to address this issue, a light brown colored polyurethane foam coating was introduced onto the shell but was discontinued in 1990 due to fears of toxicity. After further trials, the foam coating was remarketed in the U.K. from 2005 onward.

In 1974 a second generation of implants was designed to make the implant less palpable and firm. Implants designed with a thinner softer shell were subsequently produced. It is unlikely that any of these have survived until today due to their very high rupture and

Figure 8.9 Logos for various orthopedic companies. (U.K. logos revised from Wilson, R.J., Bethard, J.D., and DiGangi, E.A., Orthopedic devices and the William M. Bass collection: Implications for forensic anthropological identification, poster presented at the Annual Meeting of the American Academy of Forensic Sciences, Seattle, WA, 2006 and Ubelaker, D.H. and Jacobs, C.H., Identification of orthopedic device manufacturer, *J Forensic Sci* 40(2), 168, 1995.) (See color insert following page 362.)

leakage rates. They were replaced in the mid-1980s by a third generation of implant, which once again had a thicker shell in addition to a more cohesive and thicker gel filling. In the U.S., silicone gel implants have been banned since 1994 following media and legal hysteria leading to multimillion-dollar lawsuits. They have been replaced with silicone shell implants that are saline filled, with only a small minority of patients being given silicone gel filled implants. This trend was not followed within Europe and the U.K. where most implants are still silicone gel filled. Subsequent large-scale studies have not been able to prove claims of ill health from the use of breast silicone-filled implants. By the late 1980s new technology allowed the silicone shell surface to be given a fine texturing that helped to reduce the rate of capsule contracture. As a result, it is now rare to find clear implants in use and most, since this time, have a frosted glass appearance. Starting in 2002 a fourth generation of implant was developed that is very similar to the third but has a more profiled shape and varying degrees of gel cohesiveness.

Table 8.5   Vancouver Scale

Pigmentation
0 Normal
1 Hypopigmented
2 Hyperpigmented
Vascularity
0 Normal
1 Pink
2 Red
3 Purple
Pliability
0 Normal
1 Supple
2 Yielding
3 Firm
4 Banding, blanching, ropey
5 Contracture
Height
0 flat
1 < 2mm
2 <5mm
3 >5mm

Source: From Sullivan, T., Smith, J., Kermode, J., McIver, E., and Courtemanche, D., Rating the burn scar, *J Burn Care Rehabil* 11, 256, 1990.

8.3   Biological Changes

Biological changes occur after surgery and continue to change for months and years. This feature may provide the forensic investigator with a means of estimating the length of time that has passed since a surgical procedure or injury has occurred. There is little research directed to standardize the answer to the question of time since surgery, and we therefore must relay on medical observation of this process. Scars take up to 24 months to mature and during this period experienced clinicians can often make fairly accurate estimates of the age of the scar. Few, if any, long-term studies exist on the relationship between scar maturation and the number of years since surgery, beyond the first 24 months; this represents an interesting potential avenue of research. Scar assessment is prone to subjectivity, and to avoid this, various methods have been employed. One example is the Vancouver Scale (Table 8.5), which has been designed to produce a validated and repeatable scar assessment based on scoring 4 main variables. One of these variables, scar height, shows an early peak with a slow decline, as illustrated in Figure 8.10. Naturally, color features related to the degree of vascularity will not be present postmortem. Other parameters that vary with time will require laboratory analysis (Table 8.6). Once again, long-term results for these variables have not been studied.

Implants interact with their biological environment and produce secondary effects, the two most obvious being capsular formation with silicone implants and bone remodeling around orthopedic implants. Variability between individuals hinders the accuracy to which the time since implantation can be estimated. The authors of this chapter are not aware of any forensic studies attempting to standardize for this variation, despite the

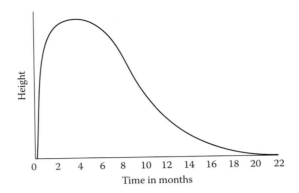

Figure 8.10 Idealized graph showing scar height from time of injury or surgery.

Table 8.6 Potential Laboratory-Based Scar Variables that Will Vary with Time

Variable	Rise or fall with time	Reference
Nerve in-growth	↑	Stella, M. et al.
Blood vessels	↑	Ueda, K. et al.
Abnormal blood vessels	↓	Ueda, K. et al.
Endothelium	↓	Ueda, K. et al.
Lactate	↓	Ueda, K. et al.
Collagen fibril diameter	↑	Linares, H.A. et al.
Melanocyte numbers	↑	Velangi, S.S. and Rees, J.
Elastin	↑	Roten, S.V.
Hyaluronan	↑	Bertheim, U. and Hellstrom, S.

Note: Arrows indicate rising or falling variables.

obvious usefulness of such information for investigators. Medical observations have provided some minimal information regarding biological reactions with time. Remodeling of the proximal femur occurs to some degree in all hip replacements and is likely to be more evident the older the implant. One change includes diaphyseal cortical hypertrophy occurring at the distal end of the implant stem (Reitman et al. 2003). Other bony effects include the gradual increase of "osseous integration," or bone growth, at a microscopic level into the crystalline surface of the implant or hydroxyapatite cement surrounding it (Ayers et al. 1998).

All breast implants produce some form of capsular formation; however, considerable variation is displayed between individuals. Shanklin and Smalley provide a profile of capsule formation thickness that peaks at 6 years and then attenuates (Shanklin and Smalley 1999). Baker classifies findings on clinical examination for breast capsule formation into four stages of increasing severity (Spear and Baker 1995) (Table 8.7), which has since been shown to be proportional to capsule thickness (Siggelkow et al. 2003).

8.4 Conclusion

The discovery of surgical intervention can aid in the identification of both living and deceased persons. Scar location can indicate the type of surgery an individual may have

Table 8.7 Baker Classification of Breast Capsule Formation

1. Grade I:
   Feels as soft as an unoperated breast.
2. Grade II:
   The implant can be palpated but is not visible.
3. Grade III:
   Implant can be palpated easily and may be distorted or visible.
4. Grade IV:
   Hard, tender, and painful with significant distortion present.

undergone and guide the investigator to the appropriate surgical specialist for consultation. Implants may be used to lead identification efforts if a device can be directly linked to an individual. If direct linkage is not possible (the implant contains no unique identifier), the implant can still provide evidence to support a presumptive ID. Biological changes such as scar maturation may also provide evidence to support identifications by providing more accurate information as to the time from surgery. This chapter cannot provide an exhaustive account of the scope of surgical intervention, but we hope that a broad view of the possibilities has been provided.

References

Anwar, M.U., Majumder, S., Austin, O., and Phipps, A., Smoking, substance abuse, psychiatric history, and burns: trends in adult patients, *J Burn Care Rehabil* 26(6), 493–501, 2005.

Ayers, R.A., Simske, S.J., Nunes, C.R., Wolford, L.M., and Holmes, R.E., Long-term bone ingrowth and residual microhardness of porous block hydroxyapatite implants in humans, *J Oral Maxillofacial Surg* 56(11 Suppl. 5), 1297–1302, 1998.

Bertheim, U. and Hellström, S., The distribution of hyaluronan in human skin and mature, hypertrophic and keloid scars, *Br J Plast Surg* 47, 483, 1994.

Cronin, T.D. and Gerow, F.J., Augmentation mammaplasty: a new "natural feel" prosthesis, in *Transactions of the Third International Congress of Plastic and Reconstructive Surgery,* Excerpta Medica, Amsterdam, 1964.

Dahlbäck, O., Criminality and risk-taking, *Pers Indiv Differ* 11(3), 265, 1990.

Flood, J., Implantation: bone, cartilage, and alloplasts, *Select Read Plast Surg* 9(8), 1, 2000.

Fotiadou, M., Livaditis, M., Manou, I., Kaniotou, E., and Xenitidis, K., Prevalence of mental disorders and deliberate self-harm in Greek male prisoners, *Int J Law Psychiatry* 29(1), 68, 2006.

Hippisley-Cox, J., Groom, L., Kendrick, D., Coupland, C., Webber, E., and Savelyich, B., Cross sectional survey of socioeconomic variations in severity and mechanism of childhood injuries in Trent 1992–7, *Br Med J* 324, 1132–1138, 2002.

Lane, W.A., *Operative Treatment of Fractures,* Medical Publishing Company Ltd., London, 1914.

Linares, H.A., Kischer, C.W., Dobrkovsky, M., and Larson, D., The histiotypic organization of the hypertrophic scar in humans, *J Invest Dermatol* 59(4), 323, 1972.

Morgan, H.G, Burns-Cox, C.J., Pocock, H., and Pottle, S., Deliberate self-harm: clinical and socio-economic characteristics of 368 patients, *Br J Psychiatry* 127, 564, 1975.

Reitman, R.D., Emerson, R., Higgins, L., and Head W., Thirteen year results of total hip arthroplasty using a tapered titanium femoral component inserted without cement in patients with type C bone, *J Arthroplasty* 18(7 Suppl. 1), 116, 2003.

Roten, S.V., Bhat, S., and Bhawan, J., Elastic fibers in scar tissue, *J Cutan Pathol* 23, 37, 1996.

Shanklin, D.R. and Smalley, D.L., Dynamics of wound healing after silicone device implantation, *Exp Mol Pathol* 67, 26–39, 1999.

Siggelkow, W., Faridi, A., Spiritus, K., Klinge, U., Rath, W., and Klosterhalfen, B., Histological analysis of silicone breast implant capsules and correlation with capsular contracture, *Biomaterials* 24(6), 1101–1109, 2003.

Spear, S.L. and Baker, J.L., Jr., Classification of capsular contracture after prosthetic breast reconstruction, *Plast Reconstr Surg* 96(5), 1119–1123, October 1995.

Stella, M., Calcagni, M., Teich-Alasia, S., Ramieri, G., Cellino, G., and Panzica, G., Sensory endings in skin grafts and scars after extensive burns, *Burns* 20(6), 491, 1994.

Sullivan, T., Smith, J., Kermode, J., McIver, E., and Courtemanche, D., Rating the burn scar, *J Burn Care Rehabil* 11, 256, 1990.

Ueda, K., Yasuda, Y., Furuya, E., and Oba, S., Inadequate blood supply persists in keloids, *Scand J Plast Reconstr Surg Hand Surg* 38, 267, 2004.

Ubelaker, D.H. and Jacobs, C.H., Identification of orthopedic device manufacturer, *J Forensic Sci* 40(2), 168, 1995.

Velangi, S.S. and Rees, J., Why are scars pale? An immunohistochemical study indicating preservation of melanocyte number and function in surgical scars, *Acta Dermato Venereol* 81, 326, 2001.

Wilson, R.J., Bethard, J.D., and DiGangi, E.A., Orthopedic devices and the William M. Bass collection: implications for forensic anthropological identification, poster presented at the Annual Meeting of the American Academy of Forensic Sciences, Seattle, WA, 2006.

Hair and Nail

ANDREW S. WILSON
M. THOMAS P. GILBERT

Contents

9.1 Introduction: Hair and Nail — Increasingly Important Resources to the Identification Scientist..147
9.2 Structure of Hair and Nail..148
9.3 Physical and Chemical Evidence..150
    9.3.1 Hair and Nail Form, Style, Color, and Other Traits 150
    9.3.2 Hair and Nails as a Source of Residual Information........................151
    9.3.3 Shampoos, Conditioners, and Other Cosmetic Products................152
    9.3.4 Environmental Evidence (Pollen, Soil, Skin, Semen, etc.)................152
    9.3.5 Explosives and Gunshot Residues 153
9.4 Biomolecular Evidence from Hair and Nail 153
    9.4.1 What Can DNA Do?...153
    9.4.2 DNA from Hair...154
    9.4.3 Heteroplasmy and Allelic Dropout..155
    9.4.4 DNA from Nail...155
    9.4.5 Nonhost Sources of DNA from Nail..156
9.5 Hair and Nail Growth as a Record of Recent Life History 156
    9.5.1 Time-Resolved Information for Diet and Location — Isotopic Evidence....157
    9.5.2 A Record of Drug Use or Exposure to Pollutants............................159
9.6 Integrity of Tissue Samples — Taphonomy, Contamination, and Methods for Sample Preparation and Storage 160
9.7 Conclusion 161
9.8 Acknowledgments...162
References 163

9.1 Introduction: Hair and Nail — Increasingly Important Resources to the Identification Scientist

Hair and nail are important tissues for human identification, employing morphological traits as well as biomolecular information for individualization/direct comparison. The nature of hair and nail growth also provides unique chronological information along the length of the nail or fiber that is of utility in identification, biomonitoring, and in reconstructing recent life history.[1] One of the major advantages of utilizing hair and nail is that, in comparison with other tissues, sample size and sampling process can be considered relatively noninvasive and nondestructive,[2] and yet each fiber or nail retains a discrete record of detailed information on genetic inheritance, drug use, pathology, diet, and location history, as well as exposure to explosives residues or other pollutants.[2–5]

Identifications based on hair morphological comparisons are among the first recorded uses of hair in forensic work.[6,7] The average human scalp has roughly 100,000 hair follicles, a higher density of hair follicles per area than other primates. Today hair is seen as important trace evidence, because adults shed on average about 100 hairs each day.[8] Hair is important contact evidence because of the potential for transfer of hair between individuals during assault and sexual intercourse[9–12] and because of the persistence of hair on clothing, hair brushes, etc.[13] Specialized hair combing kits are used to retrieve such evidence from the hair of crime victims.[14]

Whereas this chapter is largely concerned with human identification, it is important to note that animal hair, particularly from dogs or cats,[15,16] may also prove an important means of identification. For example, dog hair[17] was used to help to convict the killer of teenager Leanne Tiernan, whose body was found in a woodland wrapped in plastic and concealed beneath a duvet cover with adherent dog hair.

There is a far greater literature concerning forensic identification using hair than there is for nail. Whereas much of the forensic literature is concerned with analysis of drugs from hair, the purpose of this chapter is to broaden the view to consider hair and nail as part of the larger picture of human identification.[18]

9.2   Structure of Hair and Nail

The main biological functions of hair and nail are as protection for the underlying tissue of the nail bed, cranium, and pubic regions. Hair has the additional functions of serving as insulation, for sexual display and to carry scent as sensory organs, and as a possible waste sink for toxic substances. Humans have three main types of hair: *lanugo*, which is generally shed about 30 weeks *in utero*; *terminal* hair, which includes scalp, pubic, axillary, beard, eyebrow, eyelash, and nasal hair; and *vellus* hair, which is the fine downy hair covering the body, having little or no pigment. For the purposes of this chapter we will focus on terminal hair, alongside nail. The anatomy and physiology of hair has been summarized previously.[19–22] Briefly, the hair shaft (see Figure 9.1) comprises outer cuticle cells built up in layers, up to 10 cells thick, which have a protective function and influence the optical characteristics of the fiber. The outer surface of each cuticle cell is hydrophobic. The underlying cortex, comprising the main bulk of the hair fiber, is composed of elongate cortical cells. These impart strength and flexibility and are responsible for physical and mechanical properties such as tensile strength. The central medulla, which may or may not be present, is either air- or fluid-filled and may be discontinuous along the fiber length.

Hair grows by active mitosis in the hair follicle, and each follicle may grow 20–30 new hairs in a lifetime. Hair undergoes a cyclic mosaic pattern of growth, with 90% of the follicles on a normal scalp in *anagen*, the growth phase, lasting 6–10 years. Anagen is followed by *catagen*, the regression phase, lasting 14–21 days (with ~2% of the follicles on normal scalp in this phase). *Telogen* is the mature phase during which hair is shed, and it lasts 30–90 days.

The anatomy of the nail and nail bed (see Figure 9.2) is summarized in detail elsewhere.[23] Basically, the nail plate grows from the matrix, hidden by the proximal nail fold, eponychium, and true cuticle. The white proximal region to the nail, known as the

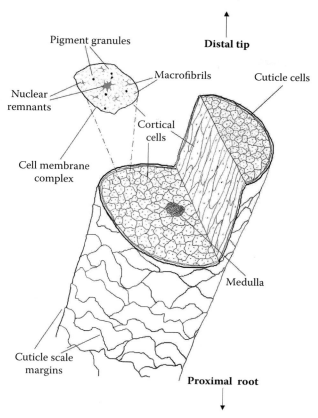

Figure 9.1   Anatomy of the hair shaft. (Adapted from Swift, J.A., in *Formation and Structure of Human Hair*, Jolles, P., Zahn, H., and Hocker, H., Eds., Birkhauser Verlag, Basel, 1997, pp. 149–175. With permission.)

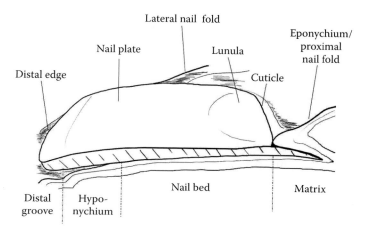

Figure 9.2   Anatomy of the nail plate and nail bed. (From Baden, H.P. and Fewkes, J., in *Biochemistry and Physiology of the Skin*, Goldsmith, L.A., Ed., Oxford University Press, Oxford, 1983, pp. 553–566. With permission.)

lunula, is most prominent on the thumb and results from keratin that has not been completely flattened in the nail bed.

Hair and nails share a common structural chemistry; the bulk of each is comprised of hard alpha keratin. There are roughly 65–95% keratin proteins by weight in hair. It is the disulphide bonds in keratin that impart strength to these tissues. The water content will affect the flexibility of hair and nails and in both tissue types can vary from 10% to 30%. Whereas melanin pigment granules may be found in the hair cortex and occasionally in the cuticle,[24] they are absent from nails.

9.3 Physical and Chemical Evidence

9.3.1 Hair and Nail Form, Style, Color, and Other Traits

The majority of identification work from hair, until relatively recently, involved the use of light microscopy and comparison microscopy,[25–27] and occasionally electron microscopy,[28] to examine morphological characteristics of the hair shaft such as color and pigmentation (e.g., density, granule size, distribution); shape; length; fiber diameter; number of cuticle layers; shape, size and condition of the cuticle scale pattern; shapes of transverse sections; the shape and form of the medulla (e.g., continuity or whether it is air- or fluid-filled), and the root and hair tip, etc.[4,29–34] Traditionally, hair has been classified[33,35] using these morphological traits, according to three broad racial categories — Caucasoid, Africoid,[36] and Mongoloid. Mongoloid-type hair, for instance, is generally rounded in cross section, in comparison with the more ovoid Caucasoid-type hair, and Africoid-type hair is usually woolly, black, and with high twist. Some specific population subgroups have also been discussed in more recent literature,[37] e.g., Australoid-type hair, Afro-Caribbean hair,[38] and Polynesian hair.[39] Similarly, morphological traits are used to discriminate human from animal hair, largely on the basis of hair cross section and diameter, cuticle scale pattern, and medulla.[40–44]

In contrast to hair, few physical traits have been discussed in relation to human nail for the purposes of identification, other than the condition of the margins (which may be used to determine wear) and the longitudinal striae of the lower concave surface of finger and toenails in postmortem remains.[45]

For hair, basic light and comparison microscopy is often augmented by the use of hair casts[46,47] to examine cuticle scale pattern. However, technological advances in electron microscopy (in particular, the advent of variable pressure SEM which allows for examination of hair or nail in its native, uncoated state) and atomic force microscopy,[48] the use of image analysis tools,[49] and the development of cross-section techniques[50] now provide a more comprehensive suite of techniques available to the hair and nail examiner.

The accuracy of forensic hair comparisons based on morphological traits has been evaluated in a number of studies,[51–54] and debate continues as to the efficacy of hair morphological comparison[51,55] as there remain no accepted probability standards for human hair identification.[56] However, it has recently been argued that hair microscopic examination is a useful first-screening step, ahead of DNA analysis.[57]

Hair color may be a difficult trait to quantify because of the use of cosmetic hair dyes and highlights and inherent variability with natural hair color.[58] However, microspectrophotometry may be used to aid the characterization of hair fiber color in relation to other fiber types. Different chemicals can induce color change; of particular note is the condition known as "green hair," frequently due to exogenous copper deposition.[59] It is also important to note that various environmental conditions such as extremely anoxic or desiccating environments may result in alteration to hair color.[60] Similarly, under extremes of heating, hair may change color prior to charring; gray hair has turned "brassy blonde" at about 120°C, whereas brown hair may take on a reddish hue at about 200°C.[61]

Although much of the literature is concerned with the hair shaft, the morphology and variation of the hair root[62] may also be examined for evidence of forcible pulling of hair pre- or postmortem.[63] During putrefaction, hair and nails may be shed, particularly in aqueous environments, and it is important, for instance, to understand the extent to which the hair root is affected by postmortem alteration.[64] However, it is not possible to use this to provide accurate predictions of time since death.[65]

Identification may be aided by cultural practices and current fashion trends which influence the outward appearance of hair style,[66] e.g., removal of curl from hair in people of black ancestry to give it a straight or slight wavy appearance.[67] Modifications to hair include extensions using either synthetic or real hair, either woven or braided into the hair, or glued to the hair or scalp. Hair clip-ins, also known as *wefts*, provide a cheaper alternative. Nail extensions have a similar variety of types (e.g., acrylic, UV gel, fiberglass, and silk wraps). In addition, different types of nail polish, artwork, and jewelry are also now used on nails.

Despite its robust form, hair may be subject to alteration due to physical damage or biological damage.[68,69] It is important to note that these changes not only aid, but they can also hinder identification. The surface characteristics of the hair[70] and physical strength of hair fibers[71] may be damaged by grooming practice, e.g., combing with different types of combs, the use of heat tongs, and as a result of "permanent" curling.[72] Progressive change along the length of the hair shaft, known as "weathering," is particularly evident in long hair and refers to the damage done to the cuticle scales.[73]

Nail and hair shaft abnormalities[74–76] are also important in forensic identification.[77,78] These patterns of irregular growth include the following in hair: rare, largely congenital and inherited disorders[79–81] where there is increased hair fragility such as trichorrhexis nodosa, monilethrix,[82] trichothiodystrophy,[83] and pili torti.[84] In contrast, conditions such as pili annulati[85] and "spun-glass" hair do not result in increased hair fragility.[22,25] Common disorders in nail can involve alteration to the nail plate, nail bed, and periungual tissue.[86] Fungal infection of hair[87,88] and nail (termed *onychomycosis*[89])[90] are caused largely by dermatophytes,[91,92] a specific group of fungi that can exploit keratin as a direct nutrient source. They result in clinical conditions such as tinea capitis caused predominantly by *trichophyton* or *microsporum* species.[93]

9.3.2   Hair and Nails as a Source of Residual Information

The hair shaft is naturally imbued with oils derived from the sebaceous and eccrine sweat glands on the scalp and the apocrine sweat glands present in the pubic, axillary, and perianal regions. These secretions are a source of endogenous information and an important trap for exogenous materials. Similarly, nails may also be a useful source of residues trapped in the distal groove beneath the nail plate or around the cuticle.

There are major difficulties in the use of multielemental comparisons because of the potential for both endogenous and exogenous contaminants, and the difficulty in establishing reference values.[94] However, targeted elemental analysis does have a place in the identification of poisoning or exposure to pollutants.[95]

Table 9.1   Typical Additives to Modern Shampoos

Category of Additive	Use and Type
Primary surfactant	Cleaning and foaming
Secondary surfactant	Foam/viscosity enhancement
Viscosity builders	Gums, salt, amide
Solvents	Clarifying the product
Conditioning agents	Oily or waxy substances, etc.
Opacifier	Visual effect
Acid or alkali	pH balance
Colors	
Fragrance	
Preservative	
UV absorber	
Miscellaneous	Antidandruff agents, etc.

Source: Nelson, D. and De Forest, P., in *Forensic Examination of Hair*, Robertson, J., Ed., Taylor and Francis, London, 1999, pp. 229–242.

9.3.3   Shampoos, Conditioners, and Other Cosmetic Products

There are a diverse range of cosmetic products designed specifically for use with hair or nails that may leave evidence of their use.[96] Analysis of organic material on the surface of human hair may indicate various subject characteristics that will provide pointers as to age, sex, and race.

Sensitive extraction protocols and separation techniques, such as supercritical fluid extraction and pyrolysis-gas chromatography (PyGC), can yield evidence of natural residues such as amino acids, free fatty acids, squalene, cholesterol, and various wax esters.[97–99] These surface-extractable components from hair have been studied to assess whether or not they yield consistent chemical profiles and to investigate if the profiles are sufficiently different to distinguish them from those of other individuals.[100]

An enormous range of hair care products are commercially available, and these may potentially leave evidence that is of use in identification. These include different brands of shampoo,[101–104] hair dyes,[105] hair oils,[106] bleach,[96,107] hair sprays, and hair growth promoters.[108] Each cosmetic will contain a vast array of additives that may provide the potential to discriminate between different residues on hair or nail (see Table 9.1). Different formulations of nail polish and lacquer may be visually similar but have markedly different chemical compositions and formulations.[109]

9.3.4   Environmental Evidence (Pollen, Soil, Skin, Semen, etc.)

Textile fibers and other fibrous debris are frequently found trapped in scalp hair.[110,111] Also hair may trap traces of semen in cases of sexual assault,[112] and skin may be recovered from beneath the nail margin in instances where there has been contact with an assailant. Furthermore, scalp hair and hair from within the nasal cavity are known to trap debris such as pollen or soil that may have forensic relevance in aiding determination of recent location histories using ecological approaches.[113] Similarly, diatoms may be recovered from victims of drowning that, again, may aid in the reconstruction of location histories.[114] The presence of flakes of scalp, ectoparasites, or nit cases may also provide information that relates to the antemortem health status of the individual.

9.3.5   Explosives and Gunshot Residues

The presence of explosives and gunshot residues in hair or beneath fingernails can be used to identify individuals, link them to a crime, and provide source information — of particular importance with increasing terror attacks. Both inorganic and organic powder additives[115] may provide characteristic signatures for sourcing explosive and gunshot residues. Hair can concentrate chemicals from the ambient vapor of a variety of military explosives.[116] As little as a 1 hour vapor exposure can result in measurable traces of explosives.[117] Collection of explosive and gunshot residues using adhesive tapings[118] and hair combing[115] are now common practice. It is important to note that because both the inorganic and organic fractions may be of relevance, a number of different analytical procedures may be required, and these will have different sensitivities.[119]

9.4   Biomolecular Evidence from Hair and Nail

Prior to the development of DNA technologies for forensic identification,[120] gel electrophoresis was used to determine individual differences in hair proteins for forensic individualization.[121–123] However, with the development of the polymerase chain reaction (PCR) in the late 1980s, DNA sequences have become the tool of choice in discriminatory and identification assays. DNA sequences can, in theory, be recovered from almost all biological tissues, including hair and nail, and as both often survive relatively better than other tissues in the postmortem context, both have obvious appeal for human identification. As such, their use has been explicitly tested in the forensic context, with studies validating the use of DNA from hair, published in 1995[124,125] and from nail in 1999.[126]

9.4.1   What Can DNA Do?

DNA is often described as "the building block of life." Present within every living organism, it provides the means by which information is encoded and inherited between generations. As in most animals, human DNA is predominantly found within the nucleus of each cell as nuclear DNA (nuDNA), structurally distributed among the 23 pairs of chromosomes, and as the multiple circular plasmids found within the mitochondria (mitochondrial DNA [mtDNA]). With the exception of identical twins, genetic differences exist between every individual and, as such, these differences convey on every individual a discriminatory genetic fingerprint that can provide a powerful means to both discriminate between and match different samples. Furthermore, the fact that DNA encodes the genome also means that it can be used to investigate other questions of interest, such as a genetic predisposition of the specimen to diseases.[127]

Although genetic differences exist between all individuals, the degree of difference varies across the human genome. Whereas some areas (for example, within the nuclear major histocompatibility complex) vary between individual humans, others are conserved within a species but vary between species (such as the nuclear gene PECAM-1, which is very similar among humans but differs in human–chimpanzee comparisons). Others (e.g., the nuclear CENP-B gene) can remain very conserved even when quite distantly related species (for example, human and mouse) are compared. As such, the particular markers used in any analysis must be chosen from the genome with a particular question in mind. For example, if the aim of an assay is to discriminate between two individuals, a fast-evolving marker (or group of markers) that are known to differ between individuals should be used. However, if the aim of an assay is to identify members of one population and discriminate them from others, more conserved markers will need to be chosen. It may be that the more quickly evolving markers used to discriminate between any two individuals do not retain the degree of conservation necessary to identify individuals to each population. Should even greater resolution be required, for example, to discriminate species, even more conserved markers can be chosen. The choice of what genetic marker to use is an art that takes practice and experience, but with such analyses becoming routine, it is not difficult to quickly identify a target.

9.4.2 DNA from Hair

Although DNA can be successfully recovered from both fresh and degraded hair sources,[128] success is limited by several important factors. Chief among these are the biology of hair itself and the effects of DNA degradation, although other factors are also important.[129]

During keratinization, the nuDNA content of hair cells is rapidly degraded; thus, it is difficult to recover nuDNA from hair shafts and, when possible, often large amounts of hair are required. For example, one study[130] reports that successful HLA-DQ1 typing required over 10 cm of fresh hair shaft. As such, most studies that report the recovery of nuDNA from hairs have utilized hair root. In contrast, mitochondrial DNA appears to survive the keratinization process well, and both hair roots and hair shafts (including axillary, pubic, scalp, and eyebrow hair shafts[131,132]) are an excellent source of mtDNA.[133–135] However, it is important to note that DNA yields and recovery success are known to vary between different hair types, individual donors, and between hairs from different organisms. For example, Pfeiffer et al. report that while 75% of head hairs tested for DNA yielded positive results, pubic and axillary hairs only yielded success rates of 66% and 52%, respectively[131] (these authors also note, however, that no statistically significant correlation exists between morphological parameters or sex and the success rate).

In addition to the limitations placed by the biology of the hair, however, DNA analyses are further complicated by postmortem degradation of the DNA molecules. DNA is not a structurally stable molecule, and *in vivo* a host of DNA repair mechanisms exist to help counter this problem. Their absence postmortem results in the accumulative degradation of a sample's DNA, ultimately to levels beyond which no successful DNA analyses can be performed. Although some have argued that the rate of degradation simply correlates with time,[136] and it may be possible that the geochemistry of the direct burial or exposure environment is important, the close relationship of thermal energy with nucleic acid degradation kinetics[137] suggests that the most important factor is the storage temperature of the sample. As such, one must expect that the older and warmer a specimen is, the less likely successful retrieval of analyzable DNA will be. Furthermore, a recent study has demonstrated that the structural integrity of the hair shaft is an important indicator of mtDNA survival.[138]

The degradation of DNA does not affect mtDNA and nuDNA equally. Most cells contain 2 copies of each locus within the nuDNA (gametes contain only a single copy) but can contain up to 10,000 mtDNA genomes. Therefore, with all else being equal, it is to be expected that at similar rates of DNA, degradation nuDNA will survive for less time than the more numerous mtDNA, and thus samples that do not yield nuDNA may successfully yield mtDNA. Similarly, those that yield mtDNA cannot be guaranteed to yield nuDNA. Despite these problems of degradation, however, both nuDNA[136] and mtDNA[132,138–141] have been successfully recovered from a number of old specimens, some of which date back over 100 years.[132,139,140]

Despite the reported successes, the recovery of DNA from hair is not void of technical challenges. Since the earliest studies were made, it has been known that the hair pigment melanin is an inhibitor of the PCR reaction, the predominant tool used to recover DNA sequences,[142,143] and, as such, DNA extracts from heavily pigmented hairs may erroneously indicate a lack of amplifiable DNA. Furthermore, various reports indicate that some artificial hair treatments (e.g., peroxide bleaching) reduce DNA yields.[124,125,132,144] More serious, however, are problems that are commonly associated with DNA studies on samples (such as hair) that contain low levels of endogenous DNA. These include the risk of sample contamination with other sources of external DNA, plus the mtDNA-related phenomena of *heteroplasmy*, and the nuDNA phenomena known as *allelic dropout*.

9.4.3   Heteroplasmy and Allelic Dropout

MtDNA heteroplasmy is the natural occurrence of multiple mitochondrial DNA sequences in individual cells or tissues, phenomena that can provide misleading results to genetic analyses. Although, in general, rare in mammalian tissue, heteroplasmy has recently been recorded in both hair shafts[134,145,146] and roots[147] at frequencies of up to 11.4% of samples investigated. Furthermore, in some cases, heteroplasmy has been recorded as both differences between independent hairs from one individual and as phenomena apparent even within the length of a single human hair shaft.[146] The underlying cause of heteroplasmy in hairs remains unknown, although one possible explanation is that heteroplasmy arises as a result of mitochondrial donation to keratinocytes from melanocytes during hair shaft sythesis.[64] Heteroplasmy itself may potentially arise as replication errors associated with the rapid rate of mitochondrial replication in the hair root or simply as an effect of the large mitochondrial population. Therefore, due to its putative link to metabolic rate, melanocytes, and pigment production, heteroplasmy may be associated with hair from areas of the body where hair growth rate is the fastest (i.e., the scalp in humans).

Allelic dropout is a problem related to data authenticity that has also been reported with nuclear DNA analyses from fresh hair roots — in particular, with the phenomena known as "allelic dropout."[148] In essence, due to the low levels of nuclear DNA found even in fresh hair roots, microsatellite studies on chimpanzee hairs have noted that results can be inconsistent, particularly with the frequent loss of different markers during sequential replicates of a study on a particular sample. Thus, it is possible that repeated analyses on one sample will yield inconsistent microsatellite genotypes, solely through the stochasticity of the PCR. Naturally, if this is found to be a problem for freshly sampled hairs, older degraded samples are likely to suffer worse problems.

9.4.4   DNA from Nail

In many respects the recovery of DNA from nail is similar to that from hair. Both fresh[126,149–153] and old or degraded[126,135,136,154–156] nail has been used as a source of both nuDNA and mtDNA. Unlike hair, however, it seems that the DNA content of fresh nail does not appear to vary significantly between individuals or by individual finger.[151] Furthermore, DNA from nail is subject to the similar problems of degradation, contamination, and probably allelic dropout. Whether heteroplasmy is an issue as yet remains unstudied, although the biological similarities between the nail and hair cells suggest that this may be the case. Studies into the degradation of DNA in old nail suggest that, as with hair, age, environmental conditions, and thermal energy (often as identified through exposure environment) are important in DNA survival,[154,157] as is the structural integrity[136] of the nail itself.

9.4.5 Nonhost Sources of DNA from Nail

In addition to host DNA, nails can also often be used to recover nonhost sources of DNA. For example, in a small number of cases, nail has been shown to hold traces of pathogen DNA, presumably which had been incorporated into the cells during nail synthesis. For example, hepatitis B viral DNA has been reported detectable in DNA preparations from nail clippings of hepatitis B antigen positive patients.[158] Of probably greater interest in the forensic context, however, is the use of DNA recovered from fingernail debris. For example, a number of studies have reported the successful identification of assailants and rapists using DNA extracted from epithelial cells trapped below, and subsequently recovered, from fingernails of the victim.[155,159–161]

9.5 Hair and Nail Growth as a Record of Recent Life History

Because hair and nail do not remodel, detailed chemical information (i.e., both isotopic information on food and water ingestion and molecular information on alcohol and other drugs) is locked into the hair and nail as they form. This type of information can be used to build up a detailed picture of individual diet, recent location history, and exposure to pollutants or drugs, of particular relevance to (1) the identification of unidentified remains, (2) tracking the recent movement of people, and (3) exposure history or drug use. The resolution of this chemical data (particularly from serial measurements along the hair) is governed by the growth rates of these tissues (see Table 9.2) and the precision of the instrumentation used to analyze them. Hair and nail growth rates are generally assumed to be more or less constant. However, there are seasonal,[162,163] racial, and sex- and age-related[164–166] differences, with growth rate slightly increased during spring and summer (an evolutionary relic), during pregnancy, and in adolescents, and with some growth differences between pigmented and nonpigmented hair. As such, a limiting factor worthy of mention is that natural intra- and interindividual variability of such data remains to be fully understood before the advance of widespread application of this kind of testing to forensic investigation.

The information provided by hair and nails can be considered unique because other tissues provide contrasting information. Bone remodels throughout the lifetime of an individual, hence isotopic evidence from bone collagen represents an averaged signal of diet and residence. The rate of remodeling means that this averaged signal may represent an average signal over several decades, depending on the bone in question. Although tooth enamel does not remodel once formed, it does show growth over the timeframe that the tooth was forming, representing childhood to early adulthood, depending on the tooth in question. These differences in tissue formation times and rates can be exploited to build up a more detailed picture of lifetime history by intertissue comparison.

Table 9.2 Hair and Nail Growth Rates

Tissue	Daily Growth Rate (mm)	Monthly Growth Rate (mm)
Scalp hair (Caucasoid)	0.33–0.35	9.9–10.5
Scalp hair (Africoid)	0.26	7.7
Beard hair	0.38	11.4
Axillary	0.3	9
Pubic/thigh	0.2	6
Eyebrow	0.16	4.8
Fingernail	0.1	3
Toenail	0.03	1

Source: From Baden, H.P. and Fewkes, J., in *Biochemistry and Physiology of the Skin*, Goldsmith, L.A., Ed., Oxford University Press, Oxford, 1983, pp. 553–566; Loussouarn, G., African hair growth parameters, *Br J Dermatol* 145, 294–297, 2001; Gaudette, B.D., in *Encyclopedia of Forensic Sciences*, Siegel, J.A., Saukko, P.J., and Knupfer, G.C., Eds., Academic Press, London, 2000, pp. 999–1002.

9.5.1 Time-Resolved Information for Diet and Location — Isotopic Evidence

The principles of stable isotope evidence have been summarized in Chapter 2. Essentially, hair and nails, like other body tissues, are formed from chemical elements derived from ingested food and water. Each element has different forms (isotopes) — varying according to the number of neutrons present in the nucleus of the atom but with the same number of protons. This means that isotopes have different atomic weights relative to the regular element. When measured relative to international standards, the resultant value (cited in ‰) for the isotopes of interest can be considered to be a chemical signature reflecting information on diet and location history. These tools have been used for a number of years with archaeological material[167,168] and are now beginning to be exploited in forensic science.[169]

The light stable isotopes of carbon, nitrogen, sulfur, oxygen, and hydrogen are most useful in this approach. Carbon isotopes can be exploited to tell us if dietary protein was derived from largely marine or terrestrial sources, or from C_3- or C_4-type plants[170] such as maize. In North America, for example, much of the livestock is corn-fed, and this produces distinct isotopic differences compared with a European diet.[171] In this context, it should be mentioned that corn (maize) is a C_4 plant that discriminates toward ^{13}C. Nitrogen isotopes tell us if a diet consisted of plant or animal components with, on average, a 3‰ increase in consumer nitrogen over dietary protein. Importantly, nitrogen values can be affected by climate and physiology.[172,173] Used in conjunction with carbon isotopes, nitrogen isotopes can help to identify breastfeeding and weaning in infants.[174] Sulfur isotopes reflect geological values at inland sites and marine values in coastal locations and can therefore be used to identify geolocation and movement.[175,176] Oxygen and hydrogen isotopes[177] reflect local drinking water and can show a gradation, as precipitation results in loss of the heavier isotope fractions with distance from the coast. Similarly, the reactions of these isotopes are temperature dependent and will therefore be affected by latitude and seasonal effects. Importantly, keratin substrates are subject to rapid exchange with atmospheric moisture, which has been shown to have a substantial effect on measured ^2H and ^{18}O values, unless preparation methods are standardized.[178]

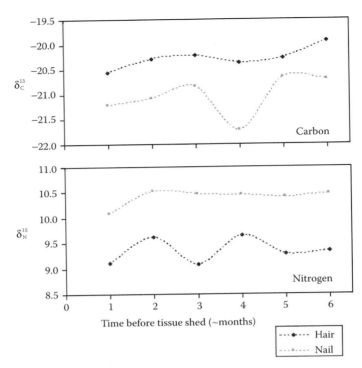

Figure 9.3 Loss of a fingernail due to injury provided the opportunity for direct isotopic comparison of hair and nail from an individual resident in the Netherlands. Hair was sampled close to the scalp at the same time as the nail was shed. The hair was cut into 1 cm serial sections (hence, the data from the first serial section is represented at 1 month on the chart). The nail was also cut into serial sections each ~3 mm, equivalent to 1 month's growth, representing roughly 6 month's growth in total. Nail was enriched in ^{15}N relative to scalp hair by on average just over 1‰. Similarly, the nail was depleted in ^{13}C relative to scalp hair by on average just over 0.75‰.

The power of these isotopic tools comes with use of a multi-isotope approach. In forensic terms these chemical signatures have potential application in the identification of people from arid and warm climates or from areas where people have very different diets. This could be used as part of intelligence-led policing to identify recent entries to the U.K. (as in asylum seekers or terrorist suspects) or to provide background information on the life history of unidentified human remains. Much baseline work has been obtained using archaeological proxies and animal models as well as some limited work on modern humans;[179–185] however, some isotopes and some geographic regions have been better studied than others.

Importantly, the rapid formation rates of hair and nails provide detailed diachronic information,[184,186,187] enabling a picture of recent activity such as dietary variation and movement to be obtained. Although hair and nails may provide related isotopic information, they are not directly comparable in absolute terms[188] (see Figure 9.3).

As well as stable isotopes, radiogenic isotopes have also been used as part of human identification to date recent hair samples using "bomb spike" carbon as a marker,[189–191] although this work remains developmental.

9.5.2 A Record of Drug Use or Exposure to Pollutants

There has been considerable interest in hair analysis for information on drug use and history,[192,193–198] following judicial acceptance of hair tests in the U.S. courts for evidence of substance abuse,[199] with more than 100 documented pharmaceuticals now detectable as evidence in hair.[200]

Drugs and metabolites are incorporated into hair during formation of the hair shaft (via diffusion from blood to the actively-growing follicle), after formation (via secretions of the apocrine and sebaceous glands), and after hair has emerged from the skin (from the external environment). Furthermore, drugs can be transferred to hair from multiple body compartments or pools located in tissues surrounding the hair follicle, although these mechanisms can also be drug-specific.[201] Scalp, pubic, and axillary hair may yield different drug concentrations, due both to the different hair growth rates and different potential for exposure to exogenous drug concentrations.[202] Hair and nail are useful substrates to use when other tissues are in advanced stages of decomposition, and there is a need to identify drugs of abuse in exhumed or unidentified human remains.[203,204]

Technical advances in (1) procedures, such as use of solid phase extraction which has advantages of high sensitivity, small sample volume, simplicity and rapidity, high purity of the extract, avoidance of organic solvents, and simple technical manipulation;[205,206] (2) instrumentation of high sensitivity such tandem mass spectrometry;[207] and (3) the use of standard reference materials (SRM) for drugs of abuse in human hair[208] now result in high-resolution data from small sample sizes.

Nails have been found to be a powerful alternative to hair for the detection of past drug use. Methamphetamine, amphetamine,[209] cocaine, and opiates have been detected[210–212] in forensic cases, although, so far, developing the potential of drug monitoring in nails has been held back by lack of harmonization and validation of analytical methodologies, and better comprehension is needed of the possible correlation between drug concentrations in the matrix and period of exposure.[213]

The presence of therapeutic drugs in hair and nail (such as antidepressant and anti-psychotic drugs) may be useful in identifying postmortem remains. Sectional or "segmental" analysis provides a high-resolution chronology for the last few months prior to death, which, together with postmortem examination, can distinguish deadly chronic abuse from single acute drug overdosage.[214–216,217] Additionally, sectional analysis of hair or nail may be used to indicate dosage history and the state of addiction or the compliance of patients under long-term treatment.[215,218–219] Hair may also be used to document exposure, even in the case of single exposure, to date-rape drugs such as GHB[220] that are rapidly cleared from the body.[221] There are now also a number of markers for alcohol consumption.[222–225]

Nails also provide a substrate for sectional analysis; however, drugs are incorporated into nails by both deposition at the root end of the growing nail (via the blood flow in the nail matrix) and via the nail bed during growth from the lunula to the beginning of the free margin.[213]

Interpretation of parent drug and/or metabolites in hair and nail is not straightforward.[226] Certain drugs remain difficult to analyze in routine clinical and forensic toxicology because of their thermal instability and low therapeutic range (0.5–5 ng/ml).[227] Natural hair color may be an important factor involved in the uptake of drug metabolites into hair.[228,229] There is still a degree of debate as to the contribution of biophysical attributes such as hair color to bias in the analysis of drugs in hair or nails.[230] Similarly, cosmetic treatment and grooming practice are considered potential factors influencing drug uptake in hair and the nail.[231]

In the case of exposure to pollutants, several elements, including arsenic, cadmium, cobalt, germanium, lead, lithium, manganese, mercury, nickel, and thallium, show a relationship between body burden, dosage, and exposure or toxicity,[232] as with arsenic poisoning.[233–236] Two different techniques — neutron activation analysis (NAA) and graphite furnace atomic absorption spectroscopy (AAS) — have both been used for segmental analysis for the presence of arsenic, and the results were found to be comparable.[237] Periodic ingestion of arsenic can manifest in tissues with correspondent formation of Mee's lines on the nails, characterized by white streaks.[2] The nail has also been used to track heavy metal exposure as with uptake of high levels of tungsten traced in nails of a patient exposed during drinking.[238]

9.6 Integrity of Tissue Samples — Taphonomy, Contamination, and Methods for Sample Preparation and Storage

Forensic evidence requires rigorous controls during sampling, packaging, and storage to ensure best preservation and to avoid problems of contamination.[239] Although there is a certain degree of parity between different analytical techniques,[240] it is important to take account of possible variation, particularly when dealing with small sample concentrations as with hair or nail evidence, and also when this evidence may already be degraded.[241] It is important to remember that use of one type of packaging material suited to one type of analysis may not benefit another, e.g., plastic packaging may affect chromatography because of the presence of labile plasticizers, which can mask characteristic peaks on the spectra.

In any scenario where low levels of DNA are present there is a risk that levels of external sources of DNA may be high enough to bias, mask, or modify results of genetic analyses. As such it is important to ensure that potential sources of contamination, which may include foreign fluids such as blood, semen, or saliva, or even the cellular debris left on a hair or nail, posthandling with bare hands, are removed prior to any genetic analysis. A number of studies have, therefore, been focused on the efficiency of potential cleaning methods in removing foreign DNA,[124,141,242] and, in general, all conclude that even when degraded,[141] hairs can be easily decontaminated using simple methods such as washes in dilute bleach[141] or detergent with ultrasonication.[124] The similarities between the structure of hair cells and nail also lend themselves to choosing nail decontamination protocols — most of which are similar to those used on hair shafts. These include more elaborate protocols such as cleaning the nail through ultrasonication and treatment with boiling water, acetone, bleach, ethanol, and detergents,[126,152] and to simpler, yet apparently efficient methods such as a direct soak for 1 hour in a detergent (e.g., SDS) plus proteinase K solution.[155]

Despite the suggestion that external contamination of hair with drugs is not widespread,[243] diffusion of substances into hair can occur,[244,245] and a number of potential problems with hair analysis do exist.[246] Decontamination procedures can be used where samples become contaminated but may be insufficient in certain circumstances.[247] Soil burial can produce ultrastructural alteration[241] (see Figure 9.4), which has been shown to affect drug analysis.[248] Furthermore, natural photo-oxidative change (see Figure 9.5) and use of chemicals such as

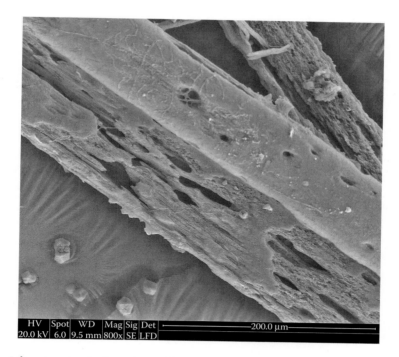

HV | Spot | WD | Mag | Sig | Det | ————200.0 μm————
20.0 kV | 6.0 | 9.5 mm | 800x | SE | LFD

Figure 9.4 Ultrastructural alteration of hair as evidenced by loss of hair cuticle and characteristic holes caused by fungi in this scanning electron micrograph.

hydrogen peroxide bleach [249] and oxidative hair dyes [250] can result in damage to the hair fiber. Consequently, the integrity of information from hair, such as the stability of opiates after exposure to cosmetic treatment[251] or environmental exposure,[248] can be affected.

9.7   Conclusion

Hair and nail are uniquely important trace evidence with a key use in human identification. Each nail or fiber may yield discrete information. Furthermore, the unique growth of these tissues (with rapid formation rates and no further biogenic change once formed) introduces the potential for gaining important time-series data of high chronological resolution. This may be used to follow patterns of drug use or to track recent location history.

In contrast to soft tissues, hair and nails survive relatively well in the decomposition environment. Furthermore, in contrast to other long-lasting tissues (such as bone and teeth) hair and nails are easy to decontaminate from external sources of DNA.[114,115] In addition, as the DNA within such samples is essentially mummified prior to sampling, hair and nail samples are both easy to acquire and store without further degradation. Therefore, hair and nails represent a useful source of genetic information. However, it is important for anyone undertaking such analyses to recognize that despite these benefits, the innately low levels of DNA found in both samples does predispose them toward risks not associated with fresh nonkeratinized tissues. As such, it is important that any genetic analyses on such samples be performed in suitably controlled environments — for example, those provided by specialist forensic or ancient DNA laboratories.

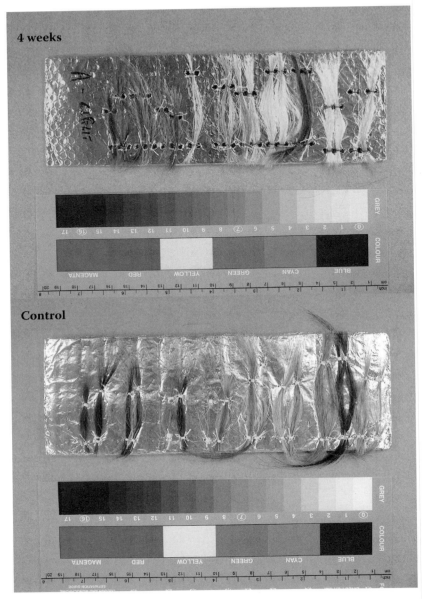

Figure 9.5 Fading of hair color is evidenced by different Caucasoid hair samples subject to photodegradation for 4 weeks using a Heraeus CPS Suntester light source, with emission spectra that is similar to that of natural sunlight. The degraded samples are arranged in the same order as undegraded controls on similar mounts. (See color insert following page 362.)

9.8 Acknowledgments

The authors would like to thank the Wellcome Trust for funding (grants 024661, 053966) and to acknowledge the support of the following colleagues: Andy Gledhill, Jean Siddall, Rob Janaway, Des Tobin, Hilary Dodson, Carl Akeroyd, Mark Pollard, Howell Edwards, Vincent Van Vilsteren, and Michael Worobey.

References

1. Wilson, A.S., in *Hair in Toxicology: An Important Biomonitor* Tobin, D.J., Ed., Royal Society of Chemistry, Cambridge, 2005, pp. 321–345.

2. Daniel, C.R., III, Piraccini, B.M., and Tosti, A., The nail and hair in forensic science, *J Am Acad Dermatol* 50, 258–261, 2004.

3. Seta, S., Sato, H., and Miyake, B., in *Forensic Science Progress*, Maehly, A. and Williams, R.L., Eds., Springer-Verlag, Berlin, 1988, 47–166.

4. Robertson, J., *Forensic Examination of Hair*, Taylor & Francis, London, 1999.

5. Berg, S., Identification value of the human hair, *Arch Kriminol* 159, 65–73, 1977.

6. Bisbing, R.E., in *Forensic Science Handbook* Saferstein, R., Ed., Prentice Hall, Englewood Cliffs, NJ, 1982, pp. 184–221.

7. Sachs, H., History of hair analysis, *Forensic Sci Int* 84, 7–16, 1997.

8. Linch, C.A., Smith, S.L., and Prahlow, J.A., Evaluation of the human hair root for DNA typing subsequent to microscopic comparison, *J Forensic Sci* 43, 305–314, 1998.

9. Cwiklik, C., An evaluation of the significance of transfers of debris: criteria for association and exclusion, *J Forensic Sci* 44, 1136–1150, 1999.

10. Gaudette, B.C., in *Encyclopedia of Forensic Sciences*, Siegel, J.A., Saukko, P.J., and Knupfer, G.C., Eds., Academic Press, London, 2000, pp. 1032–1034.

11. Exline, D.L., Smith, F.P., and Drexler, S.G., Frequency of pubic hair transfer during sexual intercourse, *J Forensic Sci* 43, 505–508, 1998.

12. Taupin, J.M., Hair and fiber transfer in an abduction case — evidence from different levels of trace evidence transfer, *J Forensic Sci* 41, 697–699, 1996.

13. Dachs, J., McNaught, I.J., and Robertson, J., The persistence of human scalp hair on clothing fabrics, *Forensic Sci Int* 138, 27–36, 2003.

14. Griffin, R.M.E. and Crawford, C., An improved method for the preparation of combs for use in hair combing kits, *Sci Justice* 37, 109–111, 1997.

15. D'Andrea, F., Fridez, F., and Coquoz, R., Preliminary experiments on the transfer of animal hair during simulated criminal behavior, *J Forensic Sci* 43, 1257–1258, 1998.

16. Wetton, J.H. et al., Mitochondrial profiling of dog hairs, *Forensic Sci Int* 133, 235–241, 2003.

17. Boda, S.-J., *Real Crime*, London, Granada, 2003.

18. Buchner, A., The identification of human remains, *Int Dent J* 35, 307–311, 1985.

19. Harkey, M.R., Anatomy and physiology of hair, *Forensic Sci Int* 63, 9–18, 1993.

20. Harding, H. and Rogers, G., in *Forensic Examination of Hair*, Robertson, J., Ed., Taylor and Francis, London, 1999, pp. 1–77.

21. Swift, J.A., in *Formation and Structure of Human Hair*, Jolles, P., Zahn, H., and Hocker, H., Eds., Birkhauser Verlag, Basel, 1997, pp. 149–175.

22. Tobin, D.J., in *Hair in Toxicology: An Important Biomonitor*, Tobin, D.J., Ed., Royal Society of Chemistry, Cambridge, 2005, pp. 34–56.

23. Baden, H.P. and Fewkes, J., in *Biochemistry and Physiology of the Skin*, Goldsmith, L.A., Ed., Oxford University Press, Oxford, 1983, pp. 553–566.

24. Tobin, D.J., in *Hair in Toxicology: an Important Biomonitor*, Tobin, D.J., Ed., Royal Society of Chemistry, Cambridge, 2005, pp. 57–86.

25. Robertson, J., in *Forensic Examination of Hair*, Robertson, J., Ed., Taylor & Francis, London, 1999, pp. 79–154.

26. Barnett, P.D. and Ogle, R.R., Probabilities and human hair comparison, *J Forensic Sci* 27, 272–278, 1982.

27. Gaudette, B.C., in *Encyclopedia of Forensic Sciences*, Siegel, J.A., Saukko, P.J., and Knupfer, G.C., Ed., Academic Press, London, 2000, 1018–1024.

28. Clement, J.L., Hagege, R., Le Pareux, A., Connet, J., and Gastaldi, G., New concepts about hair identification revealed by electron microscope studies, *J Forensic Sci* 26, 447–458, 1981.

29. Gaudette, B.C., Probabilities and human pubic hair comparisons, *J Forensic Sci* 21, 514–517, 1976.

30. Bisbing, R.E., in *Encyclopedia of Forensic Sciences*, Siegel, J.A., Saukko, P.J., and Knupfer, G.C., Eds., Academic Press, London, 2000, pp. 1002–1016.

31. Robertson, J., An appraisal of the use of microscopic data in the examination of human head hair, *J Forensic Sci Soc* 22, 390–395, 1982.

32. Ogle, R.R. and Fox, M.J., *Atlas of Human Hair Microscopic Characteristics*, CRC Press, Boca Raton, FL, 1999.

33. Hicks, J.W., *Microscopy of Hairs, A Practical Guide and Manual*, Federal Bureau of Investigation (FBI) Laboratory, Washington, DC, 1977.

34. Clement, J.L., Le Pareux, A., and Ceccaldi, P.F., The specificity of the ultrastructure of human hair medulla, *J Forensic Sci Soc* 22, 396–398, 1981.

35. Trotter, M., A review of the classifications of hair, *Am J Phys Anthropol* XXIV, 105–126, 1938.

36. Pavlov, Iu.V., Morphology of hairs on the head and other parts of the body in the residents of Africa, *Sud Med Ekspert* 43, 18–21, 2000.

37. Hrdy, D., Quantitative hair form variation in seven populations, *Am J Phys Anthropol* 39, 7–18, 1973.

38. Lamb, P. and Tucker, L.G., A study of the probative value of Afro-Caribbean hair comparisons, *J Forensic Sci Soc* 34, 177–179, 1994.

39. Kerley, E.R. and Rosen, S.I., The identification of Polynesian head hair, *J Forensic Sci* 18, 351–355, 1973.

40. Appleyard, H.M., *Guide to the Identification of Animal Fibres*, British Textile Technology Group, Leeds, 1978.

41. Meyer, W., Seger, H., Hulmann, G., and Neurand, K., Species determination of mammals based on the hair cuticle pattern: a comparison of domestic mammals and their wild ancestors from the forensic viewpoint, *Arch Kriminol* 200, 45–55, 1997.

42. Teerink, B.J., *Hair of West European Mammals*, Cambridge University Press, Cambridge, 2004.

43. Goodway, M., Fiber identification in practice, *J Am Inst Conserv* 26, 27–44, 1987.

44. Gaudette, B.C., in *Encyclopedia of Forensic Sciences*, Siegel, J.A., Saukko, P.J., and Knupfer, G.C., Eds., Academic Press, London, 2000, pp. 1034–1041.

45. Endris, R. and Poetsch-Schneider, L., Value of human lip lines and nail striations in identification, *Arch Kriminol* 175, 13–20, 1985.

46. Ogle, R.R. and Mitosinka, G.T., A rapid technique for preparing hair cuticular scale casts, *J Forensic Sci* 18, 82–83, 1973.

47. Greaves, P.H. and Saville, B.P., *Microscopy of Textile Fibres*, BIOS Scientific Publishers Ltd./Royal Microscopical Society, Oxford, 1995.

48. Gurden, S.P., Monteiro, V.F., Longo, E., and Ferreira, M.M.C., Quantitative analysis and classification of AFM images of human hair, *J Microscopy-Oxford* 215, 13–23, 2004.

49. Sato, H., Preliminary study of hair form of Japanese head hairs using image analysis, *Forensic Sci Int* 131, 202–208, 2003.

50. Rosen, S.I. and Kerley, E.R., An epoxy method of embedding hair for histologic sectioning, *J Forensic Sci* 16, 236–240, 1971.

51. Wickenheiser, R.A. and Hepworth, D.G., Further evaluation of probabilities in human scalp hair comparisons, *J Forensic Sci* 35, 1323–1329, 1990.

52. Aitken, C.G.G. and Robertson, J., The value of microscopic features in the examination of human head hairs: statistical analysis of questionnaire returns, *J Forensic Sci* 31, 546–562, 1986.

53. Robertson, J. and Aitken, C.G.G., The value of microscopic features in the examination of human head hairs: analysis of comments contained in questionnaire returns, *J Forensic Sci* 31, 563–573, 1986.

54. Gaudette, B.D., in *Forensic Examination of Hair*, Robertson, J., Ed., Taylor & Francis, London, 1999, pp. 243–260.

55. Taupin, J.M., Forensic hair morphology comparison — a dying art or junk science? *Sci Justice* 44, 95–100, 2004.

56. Smith, S.L. and Linch, C.A., A review of major factors contributing to errors in human hair association by microscopy, *Am J Forensic Med Pathol* 20, 269–273, 1999.

57. Kolowski, J.C., Petraco, N., Wallace, M.M., De Forest, P.R., and Prinz, M., A comparison study of hair examination methodologies, *J Forensic Sci* 49, 1253–1255, 2004.

58. Trotter, M., Classifications of hair color, *Am J Phys Anthropol* XXV, 237–260, 1939.

59. Fisher, A.A., Green hair: causes and management, *Cutis* 63, 317–318, 1999.

60. Wilson, A.S. et al., Yesterday's hair — human hair in archaeology, *Biologist* 48, 213–217, 2001.

61. Spitz, W.U., Ed., *Medicolegal Investigation of Death*, Charles C Thomas, Springfield, IL, 1993.

62. Petraco, N., Fraas, C., Callery, F.X., De Forest, P.R., and Crim, D., The morphology and evidential significance of human hair roots, *J Forensic Sci* 33, 68–76, 1988.

63. Tafaro, J.T., The use of microscopic postmortem changes in anagen hair roots to associate questioned hairs with known hairs and reconstruct events in two murder cases, *J Forensic Sci* 45, 495–499, 2000.

64. Linch, C.A. and Prahlow, J.A., Postmortem microscopic changes observed at the human head hair proximal end, *J Forensic Sci* 46, 15–20, 2001.

65. Hobischak, N.R. and Anderson, G.S., Time of submergence using aquatic invertebrate succession and decompositional changes, *J Forensic Sci* 47, 142–151, 2002.

66. Gummer, C.L., Hair shaft effects from cosmetics and styling, *Exp Dermatol* 8, 317, 1999.

67. Byers, S.A., *Introduction to Forensic Anthropology*, Allyn & Bacon, London, 2002.

68. Appleyard, H.M., Identification of biological damage to fibres, *Wira Report* 164, 1–10, 1972.

69. Appleyard, H.M., The possibility of identifying fibre damage by microscopy, *Wira Report* 128, 1–8, 1971.

70. Schick, M.J., Ed., *Surface Characteristics of Fibers and Textiles*, Part 1, Marcel Dekker, New York, 1975.

71. Feughelman, M., *Mechanical Properties and Structure of Alpha-Keratin Fibres: Wool, Human Hair and Related Fibres*, University of New South Wales Press, Sydney, 1997.

72. Pavlov, Iu.V., Study of microinjuries to hair cuticle of human head by scanning electron microscopy, *Sud Med Ekspert* 43, 39–41, 2000.

73. Bottoms, E., Wyatt, E., and Comaish, S., Progressive changes in cuticular pattern along the shafts of human hair as seen by scanning electron microscopy *Br J Dermatol* 86, 379–384, 1972.

74. Whiting, D.A., Structural abnormalities of the hair shaft, *J Am Acad Dermatol* 16, 1–25, 1987.

75. Dawber, R. and Comaish, S., Scanning electron microscopy of normal and abnormal hair shafts, *Arch Dermatol* 101, 316–322, 1970.

76. Dawber, R.P., An update of hair shaft disorders, *Dermatol Clin* 14, 753–772, 1996.

77. Niyogi, S.K., Abnormality of hair shaft due to disease: its forensic importance, *J Forensic Med* 15, 148–151, 1968.

78. Archer, M.S., Bassed, R.B., Briggs, C.A., and Lynch, M.J., Social isolation and delayed discovery of bodies in houses: the value of forensic pathology, anthropology, odontology and entomology in the medico-legal investigation, *Forensic Sci Int* 151, 259–265, 2005.

79. Dawber, R., Congenital and hereditary hair abnormalities, *Exp Dermatol* 8, 296–297, 1999.

80. Rogers, M., Hair shaft abnormalities: part II, *Australasian J Dermatol* 37, 1–11, 1996.

81. Rogers, M., Hair shaft abnormalities: part I, *Australasian J Dermatol* 36, 179–184, quiz 185-6, 1995.

82. Gummer, C.L., Dawber, R.P., and Swift, J.A., Monilethrix: an electron microscopic and electron histochemical study, *Br J Dermatol* 105, 529–541, 1981.

83. Gummer, C.L., Dawber, R.P., and Price, V.H., Trichothiodystrophy: an electron-histochemical study of the hair shaft, *Br J Dermatol* 110, 439–449, 1984.

84. Dawber, R.P., Weathering of hair in monilethrix and pili torti, *Clin Exp Dermatol* 2, 271–277, 1977.

85. Gummer, C.L. and Dawber, R.P., Pili annulati: electron histochemical studies on affected hairs, *Br J Dermatol* 105, 303–309, 1981.

86. Mainusch, O.M., Common disorders and diseases of the nails: anatomy, physiology, disorders, clarification and therapy, *Hautarzt* 55, 567–579; quiz 580–581, 2004.

87. Suhonen, R.E., Dawber, R.P.R., and Ellis, D.H., *Fungal Infections of the Skin, Hair and Nails*, Martin Dunitz, London, 1999.

88. Baran, R., Hay, R.J., Tosti, A., and Haneke, E., A new classification of onychomycosis, *Br J Dermatol* 139, 567–571, 1998.

89. Torres-Rodriguez, J.M. and Lopez-Jodra, O., in *Biology of Dermatophytes and Other Keratinophilic Fungi*, Kushwaha, R.K.S. and Guarro, J., Eds., Revista Iberoamericana de Micologia, Bilbao, Spain, 2000, pp. 122–135.

90. Midgley, G. and Moore, M.K., Nail infections, *Dermatol Clin* 14, 41–49, 1996.

91. Hainer, B.L., Dermatophyte infections, *Am Fam Physician* 67, 101–108, 2003.

92. Sinski, J.T., *Dermatophytes in Human Skin, Hair and Nails*, Charles C. Thomas, Springfield, IL, 1974.

93. Gupta, A.K. and Summerbell, R.C., Tinea capitis, *Med Mycol* 38, 255–287, 2000.

94. Miekeley, N., Dias Carneiro, M.T., and da Silveira, C.L., How reliable are human hair reference intervals for trace elements? *Sci Tot Environ* 218, 9–17, 1998.

95. Goulding, J., in *Forensic Examination of Hair*, Robertson, J., Ed., Taylor and Francis, London, 1999, pp. 175–205.

96. Nelson, D. and De Forest, P., in *Forensic Examination of Hair*, Ed., Robertson, J., Taylor and Francis, London, 1999, pp. 229–242.

97. Goodpaster, J.V., Drumheller, B.C., and Benner, B.A., Evaluation of extraction techniques for the forensic analysis of human scalp hair using gas chromatography/mass spectrometry (GC/MS), *J Forensic Sci* 48, 299–306, 2003.

98. Goodpaster, J.V., Bishop, J.J., and Benner, B.A., Forensic analysis of hair surface components using off-line supercritical fluid extraction and large volume injection, *J Sep Sci* 26, 137–141, 2003.

99. Ishizawa, F. and Misawa, S., Capillary column pyrolysis-gas chromatography of hair: a short study in personal identification, *J Forensic Sci Soc* 30, 201–209, 1990.

100. Benner, B.A., Goodpaster, J.V., DeGrasse, J.A., Tully, L.A., and Levin, B.C., Characterization of surface organic components of human hair by on-line supercritical fluid extraction-gas chromatography/mass spectrometry: A feasibility study and comparison with human identification using mitochondrial DNA sequences, *J Forensic Sci* 48, 554–563, 2003.

101. Andrasko, J. and Stocklassa, B., Shampoo residue profiles in human head hair, *J Forensic Sci* 35, 569–579, 1990.

102. Tatarenko, V.A., Manzhela, V.I., Dlikman, I.B., and Cherniavskaia, M.V., Possibility of detecting hair treatment with shampoos, *Sud Med Ekspert* 21, 34–36, 1978.

103. Fujita, Y. et al., Forensic chemical study on human hair 1: identification of brand of hair care products by components remaining on human hairs, *Eisei Kagaku: Jpn J Toxicol Environ Health* 33, 321–327, 1987.

104. Fujita, Y. et al., Forensic chemical study on human hair 2: identification of brand of women's hair care products by remaining components on human hair, *Eisei Kagaku: Jpn J Toxicol Environ Health* 35, 37–48, 1989.

105. Fujita, Y. et al., Forensic chemical study on human hair 3: identification of oxidative dyes and presumption of the brands from remaining components on human hair, *Eisei Kagaku: Jpn J Toxicol Environ Health* 35, 444–453, 1989.

106. Saini, H.K., Sharma, R., and Sidhu, K.S., A forensic examination of hair oils through pyrolysis-gas chromatography, *J Forensic Sci Soc* 24, p. 417, 1984.

107. Robbins, C.R., *Chemical and Physical Behavior of Human Hair*, 3rd ed., Springer-Verlag, New York, 2004.

108. Fujita, Y., Mitsuo, N., and Satoh, T., Forensic chemical study on human hair 4: identification of brand of hair sprays and hair-growth promoters by components remaining on human hair, and example of forensic hair examination, *Eisei Kagaku: Jpn J Toxicol Environ Health* 36, 211–218, 1990.

109. Gresham, G.L., Groenewold, G.S., Bauer, W.F., and Ingram, J.C., Secondary ion mass spectrometric characterization of nail polishes and paint surfaces, *J Forensic Sci* 45, 310–323, 2000.

110. Cook, R., Webb-Salter, M.T., and Marshall, L., The significance of fibers found in head hair, *Forensic Sci Int* 87, 155–160, 1997.

111. Palmer, R. and Oliver, S., The population of colored fibers in human head hair, *Sci Justice* 44, 83–88, 2004.

112. Enos, W.F. and Beyer, J.C., The importance of examining skin and hair for semen in sexual assault cases, *J Forensic Sci* 26, 605–607, 1981.

113. Coyle, H.M., *Forensic Botany: Principles and Applications to Criminal Casework*, CRC Press, Boca Raton, FL, 2005.

114. Krstic, S. et al., Diatoms in forensic expertise of drowning: a Macedonian experience, *Forensic Sci Int* 127, 198–203, 2002.

115. MacCrehan, W.A., Layman, M.J., and Secl, J.D., Hair combing to collect organic gunshot residues (OGSR), *Forensic Sci Int* 135, 167–173, 2003.

116. Oxley, J.C., Smith, J.L., Kirschenbaum, L J., Shinde, K.P., Marimganti, S., Accumulation of explosives in hair, *J Forensic Sci* 50, 826–31, 2005.

117. Sanders, K.P., Marshall, M., Oxley, J.C, Smith, J.L., and Egee, L. Preliminary investigation into the recovery of explosives from hair, *Sci Justice* 42, 137–142, 2002.

118. Zeichner, A. and Levin, N., Collection efficiency of gunshot residue (GSR) particles from hair and hands using double-side adhesive tape, *J Forensic Sci* 38, 571–584, 1993.

119. Tagliaro, F., Bortolotti, F., Manetto, G., Pascali, V.L., and Marigo, M., Dermal nitrate: an old marker of firearm discharge revisited with capillary electrophoresis, *Electrophoresis* 23, 278–282, 2002.

120. Yoshino, M., Sato, H., and Seta, S., in *Encyclopedia of Forensic Sciences,* Siegel, J.A., Saukko, P.J., and Knupfer, G.C., Eds., Academic Press, London, 2000, pp. 1025–1032.

121. Wittig, M., Protein patterns of keratins: the probable role in forensic hair examination, *J Forensic Sci Soc* 22, 387–389, 1982.

122. Marshall, R.C., Gillespie, J.M., and Klement, V., Methods and future prospects for forensic identification of hairs by electrophoresis, *J Forensic Sci Soc* 25, 57–66, 1985.

123. Lee, L.D., Ludwig, K., and Baden, H.P., Matrix proteins of human hair as a tool for identification of individuals, *Forensic Sci* 11, 115–121, 1978.

124. Wilson, M.R., DiZinno, J.A., Polanskey, D., Replogle, J., and Budowle, B., Validation of mitochondrial DNA sequencing for forensic casework analysis, *Int J Legal Med* 108, 68–74, 1995.

125. Wilson, M.R. et al., Extraction, PCR amplification and sequencing of mitochondrial DNA from human hair shafts, *Biotechniques* 18, 662–669, 1995.

126. Anderson, T.D., Ross, J.P., Roby, R.K., Lee, D.A., and Holland, M.M., A validation study for the extraction and analysis of DNA from human nail material and its application to forensic casework, *J Forensic Sci* 44, 1053–1056, 1999.

127. Chang, H.W., Yen, C.Y., Liu, S.Y., Singer, G., and Shih, I.M., Genotype analysis using human hair shaft, *Cancer Epidemiol Biomarkers Prev* 11, 925–929, 2002.

128. Dizinno, J.A., Wilson, M.R., and Budowle, B., in *Forensic Examination of Hair,* Robertson, J., Ed., Taylor and Francis, London, 1999, pp. 155–173.

129. Gilbert, M.T.P., Tobin, D.J., and Wilson, A.S., in *Molecular Markers, PCR, Bioinformatics and Ancient DNA — Technology, Troubleshooting and Applications,* Dorado, G., Ed., Science Publishers, New York, in press.

130. Nozawa, H. et al., Purification of nuclear DNA from single hair shafts for DNA analysis in forensic sciences, *Legal Med* 1, 61–67, 1999.

131. Pfeiffer, H., Huhne, J., Ortmann, C., Waterkamp, K., and Brinkmann, B., Mitochondrial DNA typing from human axillary, pubic and head hair shafts — success rates and sequence comparisons, *Int J Legal Med* 112, 287–290, 1999.

132. Baker, L.E., McCormick, W.F., and Matteson, K.J., A silica-based mitochondrial DNA extraction method applied to forensic hair shafts and teeth, *J Forensic Sci* 46, 126–130, 2001.

133. Budowle, B., Allard, M.W., Wilson, M.R., and Chakraborty, R., Forensics and mitochondrial DNA: applications, debates, and foundations, *Annu Rev Genomics Hum Genet* 4, 119–141, 2003.

134. Melton, T., Dimick, G., Higgins, B., Lindstrom, L., and Nelson, K., Forensic mitochondrial DNA analysis of 691 casework hairs, *J Forensic Sci* 50, 73–80, 2005.

135. Foran, D.R. and Starrs, J.E., In search of the Boston Strangler: genetic evidence from the exhumation of Mary Sullivan, *Med Sci Law* 44, 47–54, 2004.

136. Ishida, K. et al., Significance of DNA analysis for determination of ABO blood groups from hair and nail of decomposed human remains: a comparison with phenotyping by the absorption-elution method, *Leg Med (Tokyo)* 2, 212–215, 2000.

137. Smith, C.I. et al., Neanderthal DNA. Not just old but old and cold? *Nature* 410, 771–772, 2001.

138. Gilbert, M.T.P., Janaway, R.C., Tobin, D.J., Cooper, A., and Wilson, A.S., Histological correlates of post-mortem DNA damage in degraded hair, *Forensic Sci Int* 156, 201–207, 2006.

139. Thangaraj, K. et al., Genetic affinities of the Andaman islanders, a vanishing human population, *Curr Biol* 13, 86–93, 2003.

140. Gilbert, M.T. et al., Ancient mitochondrial DNA from hair, *Curr Biol* 14, R463-4, R1-7, 2004.

141. Gilbert, M.T.P. et al., Resistance of degraded hair shafts to contaminant DNA, *Forensic Sci Int* 2005.

142. Wilson, M.R. and Budowle, B., in *45th Annual Meeting of the American Academy of Forensic Sciences*, Williams Printing, Colorado Springs, 1993.

143. Uchihi, R., Tamaki, K., Kojima, T., Yamamoto, T., and Katsumata, Y., Deoxyribonucleic acid (DNA) typing of human leukocyte antigen (HLA)-DQA1 from single hairs in Japanese, *J Forensic Sci* 37, 853–859, 1992.

144. Yoshii, T., Tamura, K., and Ishiyama, I., Presence of a PCR-inhibitor in hairs, *Nippon Hoigaku Zasshi — Jpn J Legal Med* 46, 313–316, 1992.

145. Sekiguchi, K., Sato, H., and Kasai, K., Mitochondrial DNA heteroplasmy among hairs from single individuals, *J Forensic Sci* 49, 986–991, 2004.

146. Tully, G. et al., Results of a collaborative study of the EDNAP group regarding mitochondrial DNA heteroplasmy and segregation in hair shafts, *Forensic Sci Int* 140, 1–11, 2004.

147. Grzybowski, T., Extremely high levels of human mitochondrial DNA heteroplasmy in single hair roots, *Electrophoresis* 21, 548–553, 2000.

148. Gagneux, P., Boesch, C., and Woodruff, D.S., Microsatellite scoring errors associated with noninvasive genotyping based on nuclear DNA amplified from shed hair, *Mol Ecol* 6, 861–868, 1997.

149. Kaneshige, T. et al., Genetic analysis using fingernail DNA, *Nucl Acids Res* 20, 5489–5490, 1992.

150. Michino, J. et al., Demonstration of A antigen and A allele of ABO histo-blood group in nail in a case with the absence of A antigen and anti-A antibody in blood, *Leg Med (Tokyo)* 7, 194–197, 2005.

151. Cervantes, J., HLA class II allele typing using DNA obtained from human fingernail clipping material, *Rev Invest Clin* 56, 341–344, 2004.

152. Tahir, M.A. and Watson, N., Typing of DNA Hla-Dq-Alpha alleles extracted from human nail material using polymerase chain-reaction, *J Forensic Sci* 40, 634–636, 1995.

153. Nishiyori, A., Fukuda, K., Ogimoto, I., and Kato, H., Detection of ADH2(1) and ADH2(2) alleles in fingernails from Japanese, *Clin Chem* 44, 675–676, 1998.

154. Fujita, Y. et al., Influence of post-mortem changes on DNA typing (D1S80, TH01, HLA DQA 1, and PM typing system): case studies for personal identification, *Leg Med (Tokyo)* 6, 143–150, 2004.

155. Cline, R.E., Laurent, N.M., and Foran, D.R., The fingernails of Mary Sullivan: developing reliable methods for selectively isolating endogenous and exogenous DNA from evidence, *J Forensic Sci* 48, 328–333, 2003.

156. Tahir, M.A. et al., DNA typing of samples for polymarker, DQA1, and nine STR loci from a human body exhumed after 27 years, *J Forensic Sci* 45, 902–907, 2000.

157. Nakanishi, A., Moriya, F., and Hashimoto, Y., Effects of environmental conditions to which nails are exposed on DNA analysis of them, *Leg Med* 5, S194–S197, 2003.

158. Nishiyori, A., Fukuda, K., Sata, M., and Tanikawa, K., HBV DNA can be detected from nail clippings of HBs Ag positive patients, *Kurume Med J* 47, 95–96, 2000.

159. Gangitano, D.A., Garofalo, M.G., Juvenal, G.J., Budowle, B., and Padula, R.A., Typing of the locus DYS19 from DNA derived from fingernail clippings using PCR Concert rapid purification system, *J Forensic Sci* 47, 175–177, 2002.

160. Oz, C. and Zamir, A., An evaluation of the relevance of routine DNA typing of fingernail clippings for forensic casework, *J Forensic Sci* 45, 158–160, 2000.

161. Allen, M., Saldeen, T., and Gyllensten, U., Allele-Specific Hla-Drb1 amplification of forensic evidence samples with mixed genotypes, *Biotechniques* 19, 454–463, 1995.

162. Courtois, M., Loussouarn, G., Hourseau, S., and Grollier, J.F., Periodicity in the growth and shedding of hair, *Br J Dermatol* 134, 47–54, 1996.

163. Randall, V.A. and Ebling, F.J., Seasonal changes in human hair growth, *Br J Dermatol* 124, 146–152, 1991.

164. Duggins, O.H. and Trotter, M., Age changes in head hair from birth to maturity II: medullation in hair of children, *Am J Phys Anthropol* 8, 399–415, 1950.

165. Duggins, O.H. and Trotter, M., Changes in morphology of hair during childhood, *Ann N Y Acad Sci* 53, 569–575, 1951.

166. Trotter, M. and Duggins, O.H., Age changes in head hair from birth to maturity, *Am J Phys Anthropol* 8, 467–484, 1950.

167. White, C.D., Isotopic determination of seasonality in diet and death from Nubian mummy hair, *J Archaeol Sci* 20, 657–666, 1993.

168. O'Connell, T.C. and Hedges, R.E.M., Isotopic comparison of hair and bone: archaeological analyses, *J Archaeol Sci* 26, 661–665, 1999.

169. Cerling, T.E., Ehleringer, J.R., West, A., Stange, E., and Dorigan, J., Forensic applications of stable isotopes in hair, *Forensic Sci Int* 136, p. 172, 2003.

170. Hobbie, E.A. and Werner, R.A., Intramolecular, compound-specific and bulk carbon isotope patterns in C3 and C4 plants: a review and synthesis, *New Phytol* 161, 371–385, 2004.

171. McCullagh, J.S., Tripp, J.A., and Hedges, R.E., Carbon isotope analysis of bulk keratin and single amino acids from British and North American hair, *Rapid Commun Mass Spectrom* 19, 3227–3231, 2005.

172. Sponheimer, M. et al., Nitrogen isotopes in mammalian herbivores: hair d 15N values from a controlled-feeding study, *Int J Osteoarchaeol* 13, 80–87, 2003.

173. Fuller, B.T. et al., Nitrogen balance and delta N-15: why you're not what you eat during pregnancy, *Rapid Commun Mass Spectrom* 18, 2889–2896, 2004.

174. Fuller, B.T., Fuller, J.L., Harris, D.A., and Hedges, R.E., Detection of breastfeeding and weaning in modern human infants with carbon and nitrogen stable isotope ratios, *Am J Phys Anthropol*, 129, 279–293, 2006.

175. Richards, M.P., Fuller, B.T., Sponheimer, M., Robinson, T., and Ayliffe, L., Sulphur isotopes in palaeodietary studies: a review and results from a controlled feeding experiment, *Int J Osteoarchaeol* 13, 37–45, 2003.

176. Katzenberg, M.A. and Krouse, H.R., Application of stable isotope variation in human tissues to problems of identification, *Can Soc Forensic Sci J* 22, 7–19, 1989.

177. Sharp, Z.D., Atudorei, V., Panarello, H.O., Fernandez, J., and Douthitt, C., Hydrogen isotope systematics of hair: archeological and forensic applications, *J Archaeol Sci* 30, 1709–1716, 2003.

178. Bowen, G.J., Chesson, L., Nielson, K., Cerling, T.E., and Ehleringer, J.R., Treatment methods for the determination of delta2H and delta18O of hair keratin by continuous-flow isotope-ratio mass spectrometry, *Rapid Commun Mass Spectrom* 19, 2371–2378, 2005.

179. O'Connell, T.C. and Hedges, R.E., Investigations into the effect of diet on modern human hair isotopic values, *Am J Phys Anthropol* 108, 409–425, 1999.

180. Petzke, K.J., Boeing, H., and Metges, C.C., Choice of dietary protein of vegetarians and omnivores is reflected in their hair protein 13C and 15N abundance, *Rapid Commun Mass Spectrom* 19, 1392–1400, 2005.

181. Petzke, K.J., Boeing, H., Klaus, S., and Metges, C.C., Carbon and nitrogen stable isotopic composition of hair protein and amino acids can be used as biomarkers for animal-derived dietary protein intake in humans, *J Nutr* 135, 1515–1520, 2005.

182. Minagawa, M., Reconstruction of human diet from delta-C-13 and delta-N-15 in contemporary Japanese hair — a stochastic method for estimating multisource contribution by double isotopic tracers, *Appl Geochem* 7, 145–158, 1992.

183. Yoshinaga, J. et al., Stable carbon and nitrogen isotopic composition of diet and hair of Gidra-speaking Papuans, *Am J Phys Anthropol* 100, 23–34, 1996.

184. Fraser, I., Meier-Augenstein, W., and Kalin, R., The role of stable isotopes in human identification: a longitudinal study into the variability of isotopic signals in human hair and nails, *Rapid Commun Mass Spectrom*, in press.

185. Macko, S.A. et al., Documenting the diet in ancient human populations through stable isotope analysis of hair, *Philos Trans R Soc London Ser B: Biol Sci* 354, 65–75, 1999.

186. Bol, R. and Pflieger, C., Stable isotope (13C, 15N and 34S) analysis of the hair of modern humans and their domestic animals, *Rapid Commun Mass Spectrom* 16, 2195–2200, 2002.

187. Schwertl, M., Auerswald, K., and Schnyder, H., Reconstruction of the isotopic history of animal diets by hair segmental analysis, *Rapid Commun Mass Spectrom* 17, 1312–1318, 2003.

188. O'Connell, T.C., Hedges, R.E.M., Healey, M.A., and Simpson, A.H.R.W., Isotopic comparison of hair, nail and bone: modern analyses, *J Archaeol Sci* 28, 1247–1255, 2001.

189. Geyh, M.A., Bomb radiocarbon dating of animal tissues and hair, *Radiocarbon* 43, 723–730, 2001.

190. Wild, E.M. et al., C-14 dating with the bomb peak: an application to forensic medicine, *Nuclear Instruments and Methods in Physics Research Section B: Beam Interactions with Materials and Atoms* 172, 944–950, 2000.

191. Wild, E. et al., First C-14 results from archaeological and forensic studies at the Vienna Environmental Research Accelerator, *Radiocarbon* 40, 273–281, 1998.

192. Arnold, W., The determination of drugs and their substitutes in human hairs, *Forensic Sci Int* 46, 17–18, 1990.

193. Tagliaro, F., Smith, F.P., De Battisti, Z., Manetto, G., and Marigo, M., Hair analysis, a novel tool in forensic and biomedical sciences: new chromatographic and electrophoretic/electrokinetic analytical strategies, *J Chromatogr B* 261–271, 1997.

194. Baumgartner, W.A. et al., in *Forensic Applications of Mass Spectrometry*, Yinon, J., Ed., CRC Press, London, 1995, pp. 61–94.

195. Spiehler, V., Hair analysis by immunological methods from the beginning to 2000, *Forensic Sci Int* 107, 249–259, 2000.

196. Maurer, H.H., Liquid chromatography-mass spectrometry in forensic and clinical toxicology, *J Chromatogr B Biomed Sci Appl* 713, 3–25, 1998.

197. Tebbett, I.R., in *Forensic Examination of Hair*, Robertson, J., Ed., Taylor & Francis, London, 1999, pp. 207–227.

198. Kintz, P., *Drug Testing in Hair*, CRC Press, New York, 1996.

199. Huestis, M.A., Judicial acceptance of hair tests for substances of abuse in the U.S. courts: scientific, forensic, and ethical aspects, *Ther Drug Monit* 18, 456–459, 1996.

200. Gaillard, Y. and Pepin, G., Testing hair for pharmaceuticals, *J Chromatogr B Biomed Sci Appl* 733, 231–246, 1999.

201. Henderson, G.L., Mechanisms of drug incorporation into hair, *Forensic Sci Int* 63, 19–29, 1993.

202. Kintz, P. and Mangin, P., Opiate concentrations in human head, axillary, and pubic hair, *J Forensic Sci* 38, 657–662, 1993.

203. Arado, M.G., Garrote, I.V., Laborde, L., Bosch, A., and Ferrari, L.A. in *Proceedings of the 2001 TIAFT conference — poster abstracts*, http://www.tiaft.org/tiaft2001/posters/p75.doc, 2001.

204. Mari, F. and Bertol, E., in *Proceedings of XXXV TIAFT annual meeting — poster abstracts*, http://www.tiaft.org/tiaft97/proceedings/abstract/posters/113.html, 1997.

205. Sporkert, F. and Pragst, F., Use of headspace solid-phase microextraction (HS-SPME) in hair analysis for organic compounds, *Forensic Sci Int* 107, 129–148, 2000.

206. Liu, J.T., Cheng, P., and Suzuki, O., Solid-phase microextraction (SPME) of drugs and poisons from biological samples, *Forensic Sci Int* 97, 93–100, 1998.

207. Miki, A., Katagi, M., and Tsuchihashi, H., Recent improvements in forensic hair analysis for illicit drugs, *J Health Sci* 49, 325–332, 2003.

208. Welch, M.J., Sniegoski, L.T., and Tai, S., Two new standard reference materials for the determination of drugs of abuse in human hair, *Anal Bioanal Chem* 376, 1205–1211, 2003.

209. Suzuki, O., Hattori, H., and Asano, M., Nails as useful materials for detection of methamphetamine or amphetamine abuse, *Forensic Sci Int* 24, 9–16, 1984.

210. Garside, D., Ropero-Miller, J.D., Goldberger, B.A., Hamilton, W.F., and Maples, W.R., Identification of cocaine analytes in fingernail and toenail specimens, *J Forensic Sci* 43, 974–979, 1998.

211. Engelhart, D.A. and Jenkins, A.J., Detection of cocaine analytes and opiates in nails from postmortem cases, *J Anal Toxicol* 26, 489–492, 2002.

212. Lemos, N.P., Anderson, R.A., Valentini, R., Tagliaro, F., and Scott, R.T., Analysis of morphine by RIA and HPLC in fingernail clippings obtained from heroin users, *J Forensic Sci* 45, 407–412, 2000.

213. Palmeri, A., Pichini, S., Pacifici, R., Zuccaro, P., and Lopez, A., Drugs in nails — physiology, pharmacokinetics, and forensic toxicology, *Clin Pharmacokinet* 38, 95–110, 2000.

214. Clauwaert, K.M., Van Bocxlaer, J.F., Lambert, W.E., and De Leenheer, A.P., Segmental analysis for cocaine and metabolites by HPLC in hair of suspected drug overdose cases, *Forensic Sci Int* 110, 157–166, 2000.

215. Tsatsakis, A.M. and Tzatzarakis, M., Sectional hair testing: judicial and clinical applications, *Pure Appl Chem* 72, 1057–1066, 2000.

216. Tsatsakis, A.M., Tzatzarakis, M.N., Psaroulis, D., Levkidis, C., and Michalodimitrakis, M., Evaluation of the addiction history of a dead woman after exhumation and sectional hair testing, *Am J Forensic Med Pathol* 22, 73–77, 2001.

217. Kintz, P., Value of hair analysis in postmortem toxicology, *Forensic Sci Int* 142, 127–134, 2004.

218. Couper, F.J., McIntyre, I.M., and Drummer, O.H., Detection of antidepressant and antipsychotic drugs in postmortem human scalp hair, *J Forensic Sci* 40, 87–90, 1995.

219. Wainhaus, S.B., Tzanani, N., Dagan, S., Miller, M.L., and Amirav, A., Fast analysis of drugs in a single hair, *J Am Soc Mass Spectrom* 9, 1311–1320, 1998.

220. Kintz, P., Cirimele, V., Jamey, C., and Ludes, B., Testing for GHB in hair by GC/MS/MS after a single exposure: application to document sexual assault, *J Forensic Sci* 48, 195–200, 2003.

221. Kintz, P., Villain, M., and Ludes, B., Testing for the undetectable in drug-facilitated sexual assault using hair analyzed by tandem mass spectrometry as evidence, *Ther Drug Monit* 26, 211–214, 2004.

222. Hartwig, S., Auwarter, V., and Pragst, F., Effect of hair care and hair cosmetics on the concentrations of fatty acid ethyl esters in hair as markers of chronically elevated alcohol consumption, *Forensic Sci Int* 131, 90–97, 2003.

223. Pragst, F., Auwaerter, V., Sporkert, F., and Spiegel, K., Analysis of fatty acid ethyl esters in hair as possible markers of chronically elevated alcohol consumption by headspace solid-phase microextraction (HS-SPME) and gas chromatography-mass spectrometry (GC-MS), *Forensic Sci Int* 121, 76–88, 2001.

224. Wurst, F.M., Kempter, C., Seidl, S., and Alt, A., Ethyl glucuronide — a marker of alcohol consumption and a relapse marker with clinical and forensic implications, *Alcohol Alcohol* 34, 71–77, 1999.

225. Seidl, S., Wurst, F.M., and Alt, A., Ethyl glucuronide — a biological marker for recent alcohol consumption, *Addict Biol* 6, 205–212, 2001.

226. Wennig, R., Potential problems with the interpretation of hair analysis results, *Forensic Sci Int* 107, 5–12, 2000.

227. Audinot, J.N. et al., Detection and quantification of benzodiazepines in hair by ToF-SIMS: preliminary results, *Appl Surf Sci* 203, 718–721, 2003.

228. Rothe, M., Pragst, F., Thor, S., and Hunger, J., Effect of pigmentation on the drug deposition in hair of grey-haired subjects, *Forensic Sci Int* 84, 53–60, 1997.

229. Mieczkowski, T. and Newel, R., Statistical examination of hair color as a potential biasing factor in hair analysis, *Forensic Sci Int* 107, 13–38, 2000.

230. Kelly, R.C., Mieczkowski, T., Sweeney, S.A., and Bourland, J.A., Hair analysis for drugs of abuse. Hair color and race differentials or systematic differences in drug preferences? *Forensic Sci Int* 107, 63–86, 2000.

231. Kidwell, D.A., Lee, E.H., and DeLauder, S.F., Evidence for bias in hair testing and procedures to correct bias, *Forensic Sci Int* 107, 39–61, 2000.

232. Shamberger, R.J., Validity of hair mineral testing, *Biol Trace Elem Res* 87, 1–28, 2002.

233. Pirl, J.N., Townsend, G.F., Valaitis, A.K., Grohlich, D., and Spikes, J.J., Death by arsenic: a comparative evaluation of exhumed body tissues in the presence of external contamination, *J Anal Toxicol* 7, 216–219, 1983.

234. Shapiro, H.A., Arsenic content of human hair and nails: its interpretation, *J Forensic Med* 14, 65–71, 1967.

235. Lander, H., Hodge, P.R., and Crisp, C.S., Arsenic in the hair and nails: its significance in acute arsenical poisoning, *J Forensic Med* 12, 52–67, 1965.

236. Curry, A.S. and Pounds, C.A., Arsenic in hair, *J Forensic Sci Soc* 17, 37–44, 1977.

237. Koons, R.D. and Peters, C.A., Axial distribution of arsenic in individual human hairs by solid sampling graphite furnace AAS, *J Anal Toxicol* 18, 36–40, 1994.

238. Marquet, P. et al., Tungsten determination in biological fluids, hair and nails by plasma emission spectrometry in a case of severe acute intoxication in man, *J Forensic Sci* 42, 527–530, 1997.

239. Keating, S.M. and Allard, J.E., What's in a name? — Medical samples and scientific evidence in sexual assaults, *Med Sci Law* 34, 187–201, 1994.

240. Sachs, H. and Arnold, W., Results of comparative determination of morphine in human hair using RIA and GC/MS, *J Clin Chem Clin Biochem* 27, 873–877, 1989.

241. Wilson, A.S., in *Principles of Forensic Taphonomy: Applications of Decomposition Processes in Recent Gravesoils*, Tibbett, M. and Carter, D.O., Eds., Humana Press, Totowa, NJ, in press.

242. Jehaes, E., Gilissen, A., Cassiman, J.J., and Decorte, R., Evaluation of a decontamination protocol for hair shafts before mtDNA sequencing, *Forensic Sci Int* 94, 65–71, 1998.

243. Miller, M.L., Donnelly, B., and Martz, R.M., The forensic application of testing hair for drugs of abuse, *NIDA Res Monogr* 167, 146–160, 1997.

244. Skopp, G., Potsch, L., and Aderjan, R., Experimental investigations on hair fibers as diffusion bridges and opiates as solutes in solution, *J Forensic Sci* 41, 117–120, 1996.

245. Potsch, L. and Moeller, M.R., On pathways for small molecules into and out of human hair fibers, *J Forensic Sci* 41, 121–125, 1996.

246. Wennig, R., Potential problems with the interpretation of hair analysis results, *Forensic Sci Int* 107, 5–12, 2000.

247. Blank, D.L. and Kidwell, D.A., Decontamination procedures for drugs of abuse in hair: are they sufficient? *Forensic Sci Int* 70, 13–38, 1995.

248. Potsch, L., Skopp, G., and Becker, J., Ultrastructural alterations and environmental exposure influence the opiate concentrations in hair of drug addicts, *Int J Legal Med* 107, 301–305, 1995.

249. Tanaka, S., Iio, R., Chinaka, S., Takayama, N., and Hayakawa, K., Analysis of reaction products of morphine and codeine with hydrogen peroxide by high-performance liquid chromatography/mass spectrometry, *Anal Sci* 19, 163–165, 2003.

250. Tanada, N., Kashimura, S., Kageura, M., and Hara, K., Practical GC/MS analysis of oxidation dye components in hair fiber as a forensic investigative procedure, *J Forensic Sci* 44, 292–296, 1999.

251. Potsch, L. and Skopp, G., Stability of opiates in hair fibers after exposure to cosmetic treatment, *Forensic Sci Int* 81, 95–102, 1996.

252. Loussouarn, G., African hair growth parameters, *Br J Dermatol* 145, 294–297, 2001.

253. Gaudette, B.D., in *Encyclopedia of Forensic Sciences*, Siegel, J.A., Saukko, P.J., and Knupfer, G.C., Eds., Academic Press, London, 2000, pp. 999–1002.

Section 4

Identification from the Hard Tissues

Odontology

10

JAMES H. HARDY

Contents

10.1 Introduction 177
10.2 Problems Encountered When Using Teeth for Postmortem
Identification Purposes..179
10.3 Dental Charts and Charting Systems 184
10.4 Some Other Problems Encountered with Dental Identification 185
10.5 An Example of Best Practice...185
10.6 Dental Radiographs 187
10.7 Use of Study Casts to Aid Postmortem Identification..........................190
10.8 Use of DNA in Forensic Dentistry 190
10.9 Age Assessment Using Teeth 191
10.10 Dentures and Denture Marking...192
10.11 Surface Marking Techniques..193
10.12 Inclusion Marking Technique 194
10.13 Dental Profiling...195
10.14 Conclusion...196
10.15 Acknowledgments 197
References 197

10.1 Introduction

Forensic dentistry, or forensic odontology, was defined by Keiser-Neilson in 1970 as "that branch of forensic medicine which in the interest of justice deals with the proper handling and examination of dental evidence and with the proper evaluation and presentation of the dental findings." His definition remains as true today as it was when originally proposed, representing the overlap between the dental and the legal professions. There are three major areas of activity embracing current forensic odontology namely:

1. The examination and evaluation of injuries to teeth, jaws, and oral tissues resulting from various causes
2. The examination of marks with a view to the subsequent elimination or possible identification of a suspect as the perpetrator
3. The examination of dental remains (whether fragmentary or complete, and including all types of dental restorations) from unknown persons or bodies with a view to the possible identification of the latter (Keiser-Neilsen 1968)

This chapter deals exclusively with the identification of unknown bodies of deceased persons by dental means, i.e., postmortem dental identification. It should be mentioned, however, that dental identification is used, on occasions, to help confirm the identification of living persons, e.g., illegal immigrants into a country and persons suffering from memory loss or Alzheimer's disease.

Identification by dental means is not a new technique. It has been said that Nero's mistress, Sabina, in 66 A.D., satisfied herself that the head presented to her on a platter was Nero's wife as she was able to recognize a black anterior tooth (Furness 1970). Paul Revere, a patriot and a dentist, identified a General Warren who was killed at the battle of Bunker Hill through a silver-and-ivory bridge that he had constructed for the general some time previously (Forebes 1967). In November 1849, Dr. George Parkman disappeared in Boston. One week later some incinerated bone fragments, part of a mandible, one human tooth, small lumps of melted gold, and some porcelain block teeth were found in a furnace belonging to a Dr. Webster (a professor of chemistry and mineralogy at Harvard University). Dr. Keep, who had been Dr. Packman's dentist, was able to identify the denture he had made for him. Dr. Webster was subsequently charged with murder and found guilty as a result of the dental evidence (Rehfuss 1892). In the Haigh acid bath murders in Britain in 1949, remains of complete upper and lower dentures were found in a bath of sulfuric acid. These were subsequently identified by a London dentist as belonging to one of Haigh's victims (Gustafson 1966).

Dental identification is an important method of postmortem identification. Sometimes, it may prove to be the only method that can be used to make or disprove identification. As a method used in the identification process, it has a very important part to play in assisting with the postmortem identification of victims in mass disasters, because there is such a great variation in identifiable dental features. Most recently dental identification has proved its worth in helping to identify victims from the Bali bombing and the Southeast Asia tsunami disaster of 2004. As other means of identification become less effective, so the importance of dental identification increases. The dental structures and dental restorations (fillings, etc.) may be the only parts of the body not destroyed, and they can be used even though they may be scattered over a wide area, such as occurs in aircraft accidents, terrorist attacks, partial incineration, fragmentation, and severe decomposition (Levine 1977).

Statistically, it has been calculated that there are over two billion possibilities in the charting of adult dentition. However, this complex "fingerprint" is only as helpful as it is accurate. Identification is only as reliable as the antemortem records permit. Good quality, comprehensive, accurate, and legible antemortem dental records must be available for comparison purposes with good quality postmortem dental records in order that a postmortem identification can be proved or disproved. Unfortunately, this is not always the case; the quality and accuracy of antemortem dental records varies considerably. It is interesting to note that, as with fingerprints, even identical twins are not necessarily dentally identical. This fact would therefore rule out the possibility of two adults having exactly the same mouths, and it is on this fact that the science of forensic dentistry is based (Furness 1970). The mouth has fittingly been identified as the organ system "where it all begins." Yet when all is said and done, the mouth — and especially the teeth — may also turn out to be where it all ends. For in the final forensic analysis it is the human dentition — or the postmortem remains thereof — that, in legal terms, may have "the last word" (Sognnaes 1976).

THE THEILMAN (FÉDÉRATION DENTAIRE INTERNATIONAL) (FDI)
TOOTH NOTATION (Permanent Dentition)

18 17 16 15 14 13 12 11 21 22 23 24 25 26 27 28
48 47 46 45 44 43 42 41 31 32 33 34 35 36 37 38

THE FÉDÉRATION DENTAIRE INTERNATIONAL (FDI) TOOTH NOTATION
(Deciduous Dentition)

55 54 53 52 51 61 62 63 64 65
85 84 83 82 81 71 72 73 74 75

PALMER ZSIGMONDY TOOTH NOTATION (Permanent Dentition)

8 7 6 5 4 3 2 1 1 2 3 4 5 6 7 8
8 7 6 5 4 3 2 1 1 2 3 4 5 6 7 8

PALMER ZSIGMONDY TOOTH NOTATION (Deciduous Dentition)

E D C B A A B C D E
E D C B A A B C D E

THE HADERUP TOOTH NOTATION

8+ 7+ 6+ 5+ 4+ 3+ 2+ 1+ +1 +2 +3 +4 +5 +6 +7 +8
8− 7− 6− 5− 4− 3− 2− 1− −1 −2 −3 −4 −5 −6 −7 −8

CUNNINGHAM'S TOOTH (UNIVERSAL SYSTEM 1)

1 2 3 4 5 6 7 8 9 10 11 12 13 14 15 16
32 31 30 29 28 27 26 25 24 23 22 21 20 19 18 17

UNIVERSAL TOOTH NOTATION (UNIVERSAL SYSTEM 2)

1 2 3 4 5 6 7 8 9 10 11 12 13 14 15 16
17 18 19 20 21 22 23 24 25 26 27 28 29 30 31 32

Some of the different ways that may be used to identify the upper-left first premolar tooth:

*24, *12, *5, *+4, */ 4, *G4, *UL4

Figure 10.1 Some of the different charting and tooth notations in use around the world.

10.2 Problems Encountered When Using Teeth for Postmortem Identification Purposes

As already mentioned, for a postmortem identification to be made by dental means there need to be good quality, comprehensive, accurate, and legible antemortem dental records available for comparison purposes. The major problem for the forensic dentist in dental identification is having to compare postmortem chartings and radiographs with incomplete and/or inaccurate antemortem dental records. These may include:

1. A lack of adequate recording of the dental status at a fixed point in time
2. A lack of uniformity in charting and tooth numbering systems (see Figure 10.1)
3. Inadequate dental radiographs
4. Illegible dental records
5. The dynamic state of the dentition (Kessler 1995)

Human error is to blame for all of these.

A study by Platt and Yewe-Dyer in 1970 (Platt and Yewe-Dyer 1995) examined the accuracy of dental chartings among general dental practitioners working in Scotland. Disappointingly, they found that only 48% of the chartings were correct, 38% were incorrect, and 14% of patient records examined had no charting recorded at all. It is highly unlikely that a person could be successfully identified by dental means simply from examination of a body without any antemortem dental records. Antemortem dental records ideally should include:

1. A comprehensive antemortem dental chart and comprehensive written notes
2. Antemortem dental radiographs, e.g., bitewing, periapical, occlusal, and ortho-pantomogram. Additional antemortem records that may be available would be study casts, orthodontic models, and intraoral and extraoral photographs. Individuals with numerous and complex dental treatments are often easier to identify than those who have had little or no restorative treatment carried out. Pretty and Sweet (Pretty and Sweet 2001) provide a useful table of features that may be available for examination during comparative dental identification, and this is reproduced in Table 10.1.

Antemortem dental records will only be available if the decedent has at some time in their life attended a dental practitioner for a dental check and if any subsequent dental treatment that has been carried out has been accurately recorded. In some parts of the world, dental treatment is carried out by unqualified "tooth doctors" who are unlikely to record or retain any records of treatment, and there remain parts of the world today where people do not visit or have access to a dental practitioner. These people will be difficult to identify postmortem on account of the lack of any antemortem records for comparison purposes. Sometimes a family member may possess a photograph of a smiling face clearly showing the anterior teeth. In these cases it may be possible, with the aid of magnification, to identify certain features of the anterior teeth from the photograph, such as a mid-line diastema, spaces between the teeth, crowns, bridges, or an unusual feature which may help to exclude or help positively to identify the deceased.

As populations become more educated about methods available to prevent dental disease, the incidence of dental caries will hopefully lessen, and the number of teeth requiring restorative treatment will also decrease. This will result in less iatrogenic antemortem dental information being available for direct comparison. Such identification cases with few or no unrestored teeth are likely to become more common, and therefore dental practitioners will need to record many more of the naturally occurring anomalies and anatomical details than perhaps they have in the past. Antemortem dental records will need to include details of teeth rotations, naturally occurring spaces between teeth, tooth displacements (buccal, lingual, or palatal), small fractures or chipped teeth, areas of hypoplasia, fluorosis, intrinsic staining, tooth mutilations, tooth jewelry, and any other features that might help when comparing the antemortem and postmortem dental records (see Figure 10.2 to Figure 10.9). However, cosmetic dentistry and advanced restorative procedures involving greater use of implants, etc., in the more affluent populations will continue to provide a great deal of useful postmortem material — providing it is well documented in the antemortem records!

Another worrying problem which will have an impact on postmortem identification from dental records is the one affecting the U.K. at present (2005) due to a serious under-funding

Table 10.1   Features Examined during Comparative Dental Identification

Teeth

Teeth present
  a. Erupted
  b. Unerupted
  c. Impacted
Missing teeth
  a. Congenitally
  b. Lost antemortem
  c. Lost postmortem
Tooth type
  a. Permanent
  b. Deciduous
  c. Mixed
  d. Retained Primary
  e. Supernumerary
Tooth position
  a. Malposition
Crown morphology
  a. Size and shape
  b. Enamel thickness
  c. Contact points
  d. Racial variations
Crown pathology
  a. Caries
  b. Attrition, abrasion, erosion
  c. Atypical variations enamel pearls, peg laterals, etc.
  d. Dentigerous cyst
Root morphology
  a. Size
  b. Shape
  c. Number
  d. Divergence of roots
Root pathology
  a. Dilaceration
  b. Root fracture
  c. Hypercementosis
  d. Root resorption
  e. Root hemisections

Pulp chamber/root canal morphology
  a. Size, shape and number
  b. Secondary dentine
Pulp chamber/root canal pathology
  a. Pulp stones, dystrophic calcification
  b. Root canal therapy
  c. Retrofills
  d. Apicectomy
Periapical pathology
  a. Abscess, granuloma, or cysts
  b. Cementomas
  c. Condensing osteitis
Dental restorations
1. Metallic
  a. Nonfull coverage
  b. Full coverage
2. Nonmetallic
  a. Nonfull coverage
  b. Laminates
  c. Full coverage
3. Dental implants
4. Bridges
5. Partial and full removable prosthesis

Periodontal Tissues

Gingival morphology and pathology
  a. Contour, recession, focal/diffuse enlargements, interproximal Craters
  b. Color — inflammatory changes physiological (racial) or pathological pigmentations
  c. Plaque and calculus deposits
Periodontal ligament morphology and pathology
  a. Thickness
  b. Widening
  c. Lateral periodontal cysts and similar

Alveolar process and lamina dura
  a. Height, contour, density of crestal bone
  b. Thickness of interradicular bone
  c. Exostoses, tori
  d. Pattern of lamina dura
  e. Bone loss (horizontal/vertical)
  f. Trabecular bone pattern and bone islands
  g. Residual root fragments

Anatomical Features

Maxillary sinus
  a. Size, shape, cysts
  b. Foreign bodies, fistula
  c. Relationship to teeth
Anterior nasal spine
  a. Incisive canal (size, shape, cyst)
  b. Median palatal suture
Mandibular canal
  a. Mental foramen
  b. Diameter, anomolous
  c. Relationship to adjacent structures
Coronoid and condylar processes
  a. Size and shape
  b. Pathology
Temporomandibular joint
  a. Size, shape
  b. Hypertrophy/atrophy
  c. Ankylosis, fracture
  d. Arthritic changes
Other pathologies
  a. Developmental cysts
  b. Salivary gland pathology
  c. Reactive/neoplastic
  d. Metabolic bone disease
  e. Focal or diffuse radiopacities
  f. Evidence of surgery
  g. Trauma — wires, pins, etc.

Note: This extensive list represents the complexity of these cases, particularly in those instances in which restorative treatment is absent or minimal.

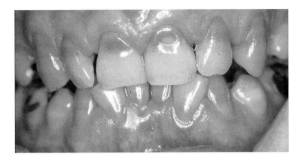

Figure 10.2   Tetracycline staining of teeth.

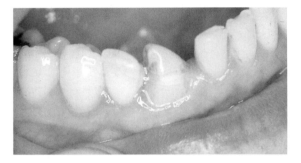

Figure 10.3   Rotated lower incisor tooth.

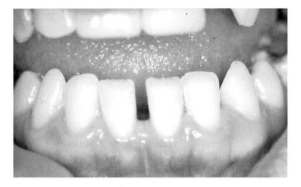

Figure 10.4   Spacing between lower anterior incisor teeth.

Figure 10.5   Supernumerary tooth in the palate.

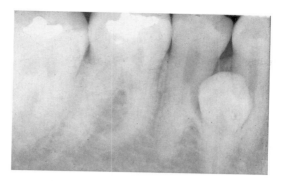

Figure 10.6   Unerupted supernumerary premolar tooth (radiograph).

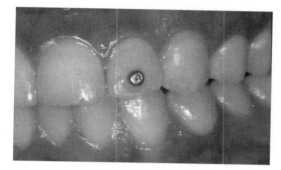

Figure 10.7   Tooth jewelry ("twinkie") on upper lateral incisor tooth.

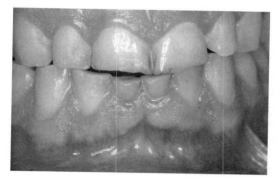

Figure 10.8   Marked tooth surface loss (TSL).

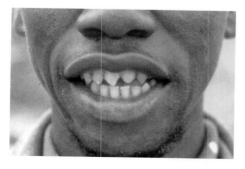

Figure 10.9   Ritual tooth mutilation (photo provided by Alan Jones).

of National Health Service (NHS) dentistry between 1990 and 2004, compounded by a shortage of dental practitioners. These problems have led to a decrease of about 8 million patients being registered with an NHS dentist. Some of these patients now have dental treatment privately, but about four or five million do not now see a dentist at all and therefore are unlikely to have any antemortem dental records or at least ones that are recent and up-to-date (Hall 2005). Dental identification — although a very important and, sometimes, the only method that can be used in the identification process — does have its limitations because in any population there will always be individuals who never visit a dental practitioner and therefore will never have any antemortem dental records. It is very important to be aware of this fact.

Comparison of an antemortem dental record with a postmortem one will allow the forensic odontologist to draw conclusions. The American Board of Forensic Odontology (ABFO) recommends that these are limited to the following four conclusions (ABFO 1994):

1. *Positive identification:* The antemortem and postmortem data match in sufficient detail, with no unexplainable discrepancies, to establish that they are from the same individual.
2. *Possible identification:* The antemortem and postmortem data have consistent features but, because of the quality of either the postmortem remains or the antemortem evidence, it is not possible to establish identity positively.
3. *Insufficient evidence:* The available information is insufficient to form the basis for a conclusion.
4. *Exclusion:* The antemortem and postmortem data are clearly inconsistent.

For many years forensic odontologists were concerned with the necessity to have a minimum of 12 concordant points in order to satisfy the criteria for a positive identification. A minimum of 16 concordant points had been the minimum required for fingerprint matching, but this is no longer so (see Chapter 3). Matching is now reliant on pattern matching between a known individual's prints and those found at an incident scene or via postmortem identification. Three independent fingerprint experts are, however, required to agree on the pattern match in order to confirm a positive identification (Summers 2005).

Similarly, there is now no longer a minimum number of concordant points or features that are required for a positive dental identification. A single tooth can be used for identification if it contains sufficient unique features. Equally, a full-mouth series of radiographs may not reveal sufficient detail to allow a comparison to be made (ABFO 1994). The forensic odontologist must be the final arbiter following the comparison of antemortem and postmortem data. He must be prepared to justify his conclusions in court if so required.

10.3 Dental Charts and Charting Systems

Dental practitioners record the dental status of a patient's mouth by transferring details of what they observe in the mouth onto a chart and/or record card. The chart provides the diagrammatic representation of the mouth, but the amount of information transcribed onto the chart varies very much from practitioner to practitioner. Some charts are very comprehensive and supported by good quality radiographs and notes in the record card, whereas others have much less detail and may not be supported by good quality radiographs or any radiographs at all. Many have notes which are lacking in detail or that are illegible.

The forensic odontologist involved with postmortem identification of victims from a mass disaster must be familiar with the great variety of different dental charts and charting systems that abound and are in use throughout the various countries of the world. Exactly how many different types of dental charts are in use worldwide is probably not known with any great degree of certainty. It has been stated that more than 150 different types of records are currently in regular use in the U.S. alone (Cottone and Standish 1982). To confuse matters more, there are many different charting systems that are used to record the position of the dentition in the oral cavity, e.g., Palmer-Zsigmondy, Haderup, Universal, and FDI, to name but a few. There are also different methods used in different countries to identify different surfaces of the teeth.

Efforts have been made by various forensic organizations to try to introduce a common dental "charting language" worldwide. The preferred "language" among most forensic odontologists is the Fédération Dentaire International (FDI) system. Unfortunately, there is at present no one antemortem charting system used worldwide, and it would probably prove impossible to enforce. Interpol uses the FDI tooth notation on their antemortem and postmortem victim identification forms (Figure 10.10).

The standard of dental data recording varies not only between different dentists but also between different countries and is largely dependent on the legislation governing dental record keeping and the standard of dentistry in a particular country (Clark 1992).

10.4   Some Other Problems Encountered with Dental Identification

Unfortunately, errors are common in dental charting and may be due to a number of different causes ranging from clerical errors by the assistant responsible for transcribing to misidentification of teeth by the dental practitioner. Teeth with similar morphologies can easily be confused if one of the teeth is missing, i.e., first and second premolars, and maxillary first and second and sometimes third molars which can be mischarted when one of the series is missing or has been extracted and teeth have then drifted mesially or distally. Lower incisor teeth can also easily be confused if one of them is missing. Cases of fraud have also been reported, in which a dental practitioner has inserted details onto a record card for work that has not actually been carried out on the patient. The fraudulent practitioner then claims for this "phantom" work in an attempt to defraud such schemes as the U.K. National Health Service. Such malpractices obviously cause serious problems when trying to match fraudulent antemortem records with accurate postmortem ones.

10.5   An Example of Best Practice

The U.K. Defence Dental Services have an excellent system for the recording of antemortem dental data on all service personnel. It is a model that could be adopted by many other organizations. Within one week of enlistment, new recruits are given a mandatory dental inspection. Details of all previous dental treatment, restorative work already completed and work required, missing teeth, details of fixed and removable appliances etc., are recorded. Charting is made using the FDI notation. This initial chart, written in red pen, records the dental status of the individual at time of enlistment and has no further additions made to it. A set of posterior bitewing radiographs are also made at time of the initial inspection, mounted, dated, and recorded as an insert to the dental record. The radiographs

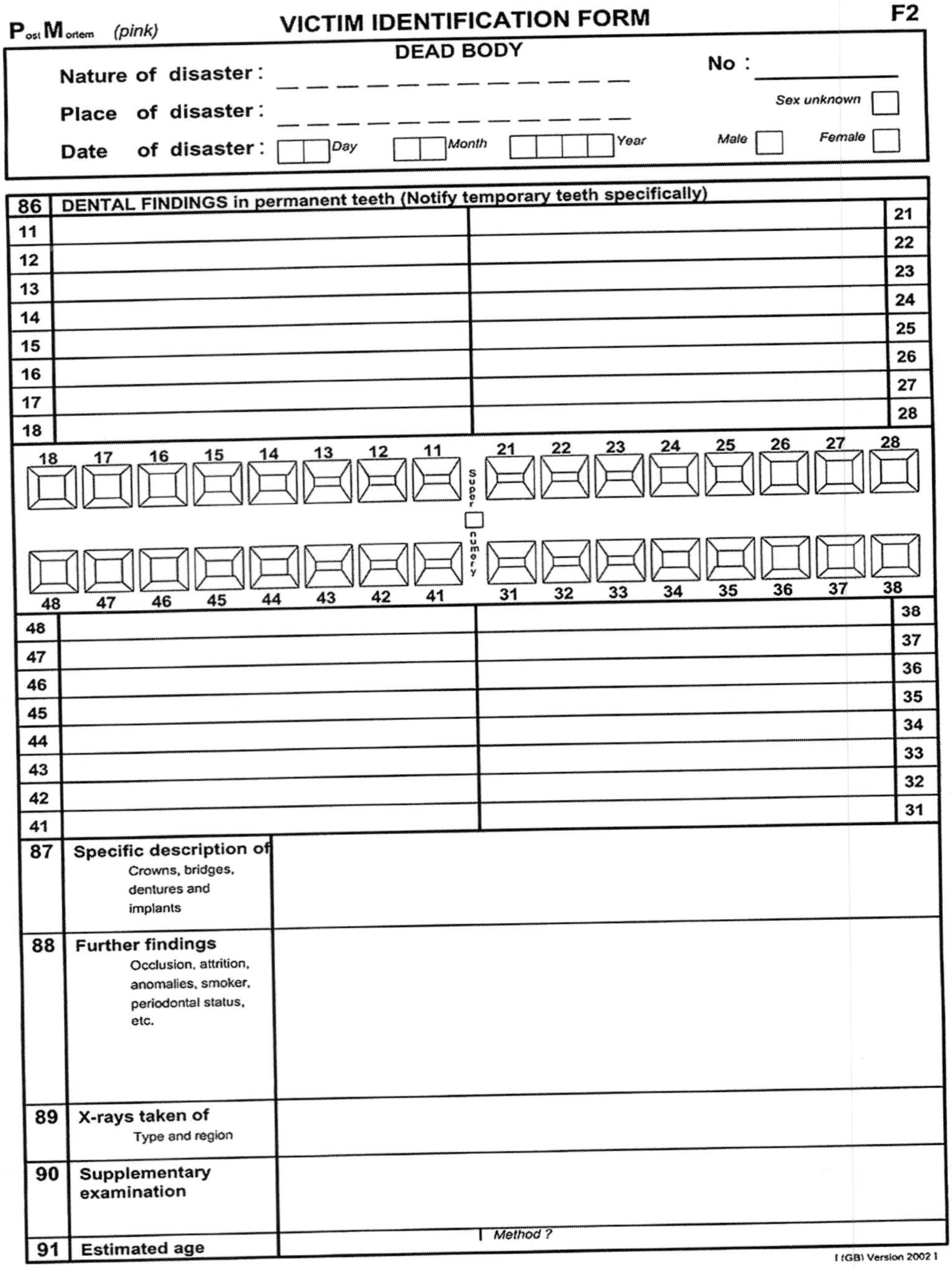
PostMortem (pink) **VICTIM IDENTIFICATION FORM** F2

DEAD BODY

Nature of disaster : ______________ No : ________

Place of disaster : ______________ Sex unknown ☐

Date of disaster : ☐☐ Day ☐☐ Month ☐☐☐☐ Year Male ☐ Female ☐

BINDING HOLES

86	DENTAL FINDINGS in permanent teeth (Notify temporary teeth specifically)		
11			21
12			22
13			23
14			24
15			25
16			26
17			27
18			28

18 17 16 15 14 13 12 11 Super numery 21 22 23 24 25 26 27 28

48 47 46 45 44 43 42 41 31 32 33 34 35 36 37 38

48			38
47			37
46			36
45			35
44			34
43			33
42			32
41			31

BINDING HOLES

87	**Specific description of** Crowns, bridges, dentures and implants	
88	**Further findings** Occlusion, attrition, anomalies, smoker, periodontal status, etc.	
89	**X-rays taken of** Type and region	
90	**Supplementary examination**	
91	**Estimated age**	Method ?

I (GB) Version 2002 1

Figure 10.10 Form used by Interpol disaster victim identification (DVI) odontologists for recording postmortem dental charting details in FDI notation.

are carefully examined and any further details obtained from them such as root-filled teeth, partially erupted teeth, supernumerary teeth, etc. are added to the dental chart. Details of any dental anomalies or peculiarities are also recorded. Occasionally intraoral tattoos, tongue studs, and tooth jewelry are found, and these additional details are also noted. A basic periodontal examination (BPE) is recorded as are details of any tooth substance loss

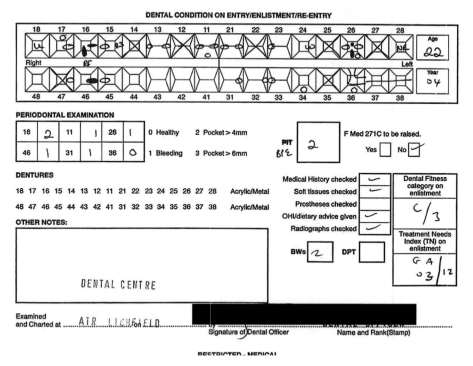

Figure 10.11 Dental chart used by U.K. armed forces dental service to record the dental status on entry of all new personnel.

(tooth wear) and occlusal or temporomandibular joint problems (Figure 10.11). The initial charting is then reproduced on a separate insert to the dental record and as treatment is carried out, details are entered on the chart using a different colored marker. Dental inspections are repeated on each individual annually. A new insert is used for each inspection, and the same notation is used for recording the charting and any subsequent treatment. Bitewing radiographs are repeated when they are considered clinically necessary by the inspecting dental practitioner. A service person completing a full career will build up, during their service, a very comprehensive and detailed dental history dossier. All U.K. armed forces dental practitioners have a number of their patients and dental record cards audited annually as part of a total quality (TQ) assurance process. This routine ensures that the dental records of all U.K. service personnel are of a very high standard. When these records are required for postmortem purposes, the forensic odontologist knows that he will have high quality data that will allow postmortem identification to be made rapidly. When a member of the U.K. armed forces leaves active service their dental records are archived and stored but always remain available should they be required.

10.6   Dental Radiographs

Dental radiographs are the most positive aid in identification. They provide the most reliable and important element of the antemortem data upon which to base a postmortem identification (Fischman 1985). They provide detail of tissues and restorations far beyond that available from written notes (Clark 1992). Conventional radiography provides accurate antemortem detail at a fixed point in time. The old adage that "the camera never lies" is as true for conventional as opposed to digital radiography as it is for conventional as opposed to digital photography, i.e., the conventional image cannot be manipulated. As few as one unusually shaped restoration or one endodontic filling may be all that is needed to make a positive identification (Brannon 1983).

Probably the most common antemortem dental radiograph is the posterior bitewing. Bitewing radiographs, when correctly positioned using some form of aiming device, will provide detail of the crowns of the upper and lower molar and premolar teeth. They also provide detail of the interdental area, levels of crestal bone, crown morphology, size and shape of pulp chambers, shape of dental restorations, overhanging margins of restorations, lining material, caries, and supra- and subgingival calculus deposits. All of these features can be compared with a postmortem image. However, it is very important for this comparison that the forensic odontologist tries to reproduce as accurately as possible the angulation and the positioning of the x-ray tube in the same way as that used for the antemortem radiograph. It may require repeated postmortem radiography to achieve this. Deviation in horizontal angulations between the antemortem and postmortem radiographs by as little as 5° can make identification comparison difficult. Changes in vertical angulations or focal film distance have no effect. Bitewing radiographs have a high degree of accuracy for general use in dental identifications. However, in some specific cases, such as identification of children or when long time lapses occur between the antemortem and postmortem radiograph, the sensitivity and accuracy falls off somewhat (Kogon 1996). Bitewing radiographs can also be taken without too much difficulty postmortem. There should be a reduction of kilovolts (kv) and milliamperes and/or exposure time of the order of 25% in order to compensate for the absence of soft tissue when working with skeletal remains (Mertz 1977).

Comparison of minute radiographic details may allow positive identification on the basis of a single tooth, a single uniquely shaped restoration, a dental prosthetic attachment, or even the pattern of roots and surrounding alveolar bony trabecular detail (Clark 1992). In a study comparing antemortem with postmortem radiographs, participants believed that root morphology and alignment provided the greatest aid to matching, rather than crown morphology (Fischman 2002).

The quality of antemortem dental radiographs varies quite considerably. Dental practitioners should routinely use some form of aiming device for all intraoral radiography. Unfortunately, this practice is still too often the exception rather than the rule. If aiming devices are not used there is always a danger of "cone cutting" the radiograph so that only part of the image is reproduced on the x-ray film, which produces an x-ray of limited value for comparison purposes with a postmortem radiograph.

It is not uncommon to find antemortem radiographs that have been either overexposed and are, therefore, too dark or underexposed and, therefore, too light and are of limited diagnostic value.

Another area of dental practice that is often poorly controlled and monitored is the processing of conventional radiographs. Poor quality radiographs result from using chemicals that are too old and that are at an incorrect temperature, or can result when films have been washed for too short a period after developing and fixing, or have been damaged during the processing. After processing, dental radiographs should be correctly mounted, labeled with the patient's name, and dated. It is essential that some form of

As oral health improves worldwide, the incidence of postmortem victims identified who are denture wearers will probably decrease. However, national surveys on the prevalence of edentulousness in selected age groups during 1970–1990 in the Scandanavian countries indicate that it will remain an oral health status issue well into the future (Ainamo and Osterberg, 1992). In Sweden during the period 1975–1995, the number of individuals with dentures in the age group 65–74 years decreased from 52% to less than 39%. But in one study it was found that 54% of persons older than 79 years had complete dentures (Hellden et al. 1989). The incidence of denture wearers in general appears to be greater in males than females. The percentage of a population who are denture wearers does vary from country to country. In the U.S., about 42% of persons between the ages of 65 and 74 years are edentulous (Redford et al. 1996). Projections of the population of senior citizens aged 65+ years and 85+ years are both expected to increase by the year 2050, but some authors have suggested that by that time (2050) less than 5% of the population will be edentulous (Weintraub and Burt 1985).

The importance of teeth for identification purposes of deceased victims whose remains have been severely mutilated or badly damaged by, for example, fire, water, or traffic accidents is a well-known fact. If dentures are included they are often retained in the mouth and remain intact or are only slightly damaged, even in the most violent accidents. In one study (Maibaum and Pousada 1990) it was found that about 30% of patients that were examined wore their dentures in bed at night. Dentures, therefore, can prove to be a useful aid in postmortem identification, especially when they have some form of identification marking incorporated into them at time of manufacture. The value of ID marking of dentures cannot be overemphasized. A survey from the Nordic countries (Andersen et al., 1995) showed that when denture marking was in general use, the contribution to identification by forensic odontology in fire cases increased by about 10% (Borrman et al. 1999).

In the U.K. there has been resistance to the marking of dentures for identification purposes. Denture marking is not a mandatory requirement in the U.K. except in the armed forces. The reason most commonly given for not marking dentures is that the denture wearer would not like it and would feel it was an infringement of personal liberty. Perhaps it is time the dental profession in the U.K. became more persuasive about the importance of denture marking and explained the beneficial reasons more fully to their patients. Undoubtedly, another reason for this failure is the fact that dentures that are made for NHS patients remunerate the dental practitioner so poorly that the added cost of denture marking tends not to be considered.

There are many different methods available for the marking of dentures. They fall into two distinct categories: (1) surface marking techniques and (2) inclusion marking techniques.

10.11 Surface Marking Techniques

This technique includes:

1. Engraving either patient or laboratory details on the casts upon which the denture is made with a dental bur or sharp instrument, which creates a corresponding positive mark on the fit surface of the denture.
2. Inscribing or engraving an identifying mark directly onto the fit surface of the denture (Dorion 1972). The fit surface of the denture can be given an identifying mark by use of a dental bur or other sharp object.

3. Writing on the denture surface with a penetrating permanent marker pen or by writing on the denture surface and sealing the surface with a clear varnish or resin. This method has the disadvantage of wearing off after quite a short period of time or becoming illegible.

10.12 Inclusion Marking Technique

This method of denture marking involves the processing of a metallic or nonmetallic strip containing patient or laboratory references into the fit surface of the denture. Although more time consuming, it is the better technique as it is likely to be more durable (Figure 10.15 and Figure 10.16).

In some countries dentures are marked with the individual's Social Security number or reference, a unique identifier which is easily traceable. Using the patient's name or a laboratory reference mark can be confusing and difficult to trace if required as part of a postmortem identification. This was well demonstrated by difficulty in identifying one of the 27 victims from the King's Cross Underground fire on November 18, 1987. One of the victims had complete dentures, which he was still wearing at time of the postmortem.

Figure 10.15   Dentures may be marked to assist in the identification process in a variety of different ways.

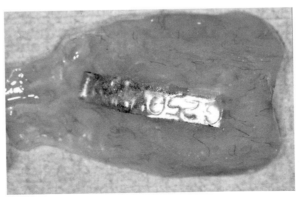

Figure 10.16   The fit surface of a partial upper denture has been marked with a soft metallic strip incorporated into the denture.

The dentures did contain an identifying mark — probably one used by the processing laboratory and which unfortunately did not assist in this case in the identification process. Different methods for marking dentures have been tried but as yet no one method has been adopted universally. A system using bar codes has been described. A small photograph can be processed into the fit surface of the denture, and this could be a useful aid in postmortem identification providing one could be certain that the photograph was of the deceased and not their favorite pop idol.

It is very important that dental practitioners and dental technicians are aware of the best position for placement of the denture identification marker at time of processing of the denture(s). In an upper denture, the marker should be incorporated as close to the back edge or postdam area of the denture and parallel to it. In denture-wearing victims who are badly burnt, there may only be a small portion of the denture remaining for examination at the time of postmortem examination, and this is likely to be near the rear of the denture. If the marker is incorporated near the front, it is less likely to survive fire damage.

Deciding on where to place the marker in a lower denture presents more of a problem to the practitioner and technician due to the smaller surface area available. In partial lower dentures, the dental technician will have to place the marker in the most appropriate position commensurate with available space.

10.13   Dental Profiling

There are occasions when the investigating authorities are unable to obtain any antemortem dental records. As has been previously pointed out, it may be that the deceased never visited the dentist and therefore did not have any records or that the authorities were unable to trace the deceased's dental records. In these situations the forensic odontologist may be able to provide the investigating authorities with useful information. Although the information may not positively identify the individual, it may help to build up a picture of some of the deceased's habits and ethnicity. This technique is known as *dental profiling*.

As already stated it is possible to make a rough age estimation of an individual by examining various features of teeth (See the section on Age Assessment Using Teeth).

An indication of socioeconomic status may be gained from examination of the quality and type of dental restorative work present in the mouth and the type of materials used. Use of amalgam or composite, precious metals, implants, acrylic resin, or cobalt chromium dentures may all be useful pointers of socioeconomic background. Habits, both social and occupation-related, can provide useful information, for instance, as to whether or not the deceased was a smoker or nonsmoker, pipe smoker, betel nut chewer, or a tea, coffee, red wine, or port drinker.

Evidence of tooth surface loss due to erosion may be an indicator of dietary habits or psychological problems, e.g., bulimia, anorexia nervosa, or alcoholism. Medical problems such as a hiatus hernia resulting in gastroesophageal reflux (GOR) can cause erosion of the teeth. Attrition may indicate some form of stress-related parafunctional habit. Dress makers and seamstresses used to wear a notch in the incisal edge of their central incisor teeth from constant biting of the thread they were using. Electricians who use their anterior teeth to strip the plastic casing from electric wire may produce a similar appearance. Carpenters and roof tilers who hold nails between their teeth may produce grooving in their anterior incisor teeth.

Teeth can be indicators of previous illnesses and diseases that have affected people at some stage in their life and while the teeth were developing. Tetracycline used to be prescribed in the U.K. for many childhood illnesses until it was realized that tetracycline is absorbed into developing mineralizing tissues such as teeth and bones. Tetracycline absorbed into developing teeth produces an unsightly brownish or yellow intrinsic staining of the enamel — "tetracycline staining." It is possible to examine the stained teeth and to make an estimation of the approximate age at which the drug had been prescribed. If good medical records are available, the prescribing of the antibiotic for a certain condition can be confirmed, which is directly related to the age of that individual, and additional evidence will be provided for the identification process.

A disturbance of the regular pattern of incremental developmental lines in dentine and cementum can be observed in ground sections of teeth, and these can be related to some specific lifetime event of the individual. Hutchinson's incisors and Mulberry molars are specific and recognizable developmental anomalies affecting the normal morphology of specific teeth of the permanent dentition and is associated with congenital syphilis.

Areas of enamel hypoplasia may indicate some previous lifetime event or illness that may be possible to confirm from medical records and that would help in the identification process.

Fluorosis of the teeth produces an unsightly intrinsic staining of the teeth known as "mottling of the enamel." The amount and depth of staining varies and may be mild to severe. Children who routinely swallow fluoride toothpaste during the development stage of their permanent teeth may cause mild but unsightly mottling of the enamel of some of their teeth. Individuals who have lived all their lives in an area where they have been subjected to excessive amounts of fluoride in their diet will often have generalized, severe, dark, unsightly, intrinsic staining of their teeth, and it is sometimes possible to relate this to the country of origin of the individual. By grinding up teeth and analyzing trace elements found in the mineralized tissue, it is possible to associate these with a country of origin or where that individual has lived while their teeth were developing. (See Chapter 2).

Size of teeth can sometimes help to provide an indication of the sex of an individual but must never be considered a reliable indicator. Larger teeth are often associated with the male and smaller with the female. This indicator should only be considered when dealing with a closed incident such as an aircraft accident and then only when all of the individuals are known to be from the same ethnic background and when used in conjunction with other anatomical and more reliable features.

Atypical morphology of teeth demonstrates specific identifiable features which tend to occur more regularly and specifically in certain ethnic races. Examples are shovel-shaped incisor teeth and three-rooted lower first molar teeth; these, therefore, can help in profiling an individual.

10.14   Conclusion

Society's need to identify conclusively a body or bodies postmortem, or, on occasion, a living person unable to self-express adequately, will always be among its highest priorities. Close relatives and friends are unable to bring to closure the grieving of the loss of a loved one until the deceased has been identified. Legal disputes and matters relating to inheritance, the conduct of funeral arrangements, and sometimes forensic investigations are all hampered if the identity of the deceased is unknown. This chapter has attempted to look at the various ways in which teeth are used in the forensic identification process and at some of the problems that may arise. The forensic odontologist is just one member of the forensic identification team, and teeth are just one small part of the identification jigsaw puzzle. It is important to remember that dental identification should never be considered in isolation from all the other methods that will be used in an attempt to identify a deceased person.

On occasion, though, an important positive identification may only be made by dental identification, and it is for this reason that dental practitioners must always be aware of just how important comprehensive, accurate, and legible records are for the forensic odontologist.

10.15   Acknowledgments

I acknowledge with gratitude the helpful advice given to me by Jane Reece and Roger Summers following their proofreading of the original draft of this chapter. I also acknowledge the help and advice given to me by my wife. I am very grateful to her for the encouragement and support she has given me and for her proofreading and correcting of the final draft. I am also grateful to Stephen Hancocks, editor of the *British Dental Journal*, for his permission to reproduce the table from the article by Pretty and Sweet from the *BDJ*, Volume 190 (7), April 14, 2001, on page 361.

References

Ainamo, A. and Österberg, T., Changing demographic and oral disease patterns and treatment needs in the Scandinavian populations of old people, *Int Dent J* 42, 31–32, 1992.

American Board of Forensic Odontology, Body identification guidelines, *J Am Dent Assoc* 125, 1244–1254, 1994.

Andersen, L., Juhl, M., Solheim, T., and Borrman, H., Odontological Identification of fire victims — potentialities and limitations, *Int J Legal Med* 107, 229–234, 1995.

Borrman, H.I.M., DiZinno, J., Wasén, J., and René, N., On denture marking, *J Forensic Odontostomatol* 17(1), 20–26, 1999.

Brannon, L.S., Forensic odontology: an application for the army dentist, *Mil Med* 148, 655–659, 1983.

Cassiman, J.J., DNA profiling in forensics, *Proceedings of the European IOFOS Millenium Meeting*, Leuven University Press, Leuven (Belgium), 2000.

Ciapperelli, L., *Practical Forensic Odontology*, John Wright & Sons, Bristol, 1992, pp. 22–42, Chap 3.

Clark, D.H., *Practical Forensic Odontology*, John Wright & Sons, Bristol, 1992, pp. 101–110, Chap. 8.

Cottone, J. and Standish, S., *Outline of Forensic Dentistry*, Year Book Medical Publishers, Chicago, 1982.

Dorion, R.B.J., Marking of dentures — follow up, *J Can Dent Assoc* 38, 14, 1972.

Fischman, S.L., The use of medical and dental radiographs in identification, *Int Dent J* 35, 301–306, 1985.

Fischman, S.L., The identification process, *Alpha Omegan* 95(4), 13–16, 2002.

Forebes, E., cited in Dental radiography and photography in identification, by Lunz, L.L., *Dent Radiogr Photogr* 40(4), 78–90, 1967.

Furness, J., cited in Forensic Odontology, Report of BDA Winter Scientific Meeting, *Br Dent J* 130(4), 161–162, 1970.

Gustafson, G., *Forensic Odontology*, Staples Press, London, 1966.

Hall, C., *Daily Telegraph Newspaper* (U.K.), Saturday, April 30, 2005 edition, p. 8.

Helldén, L., Salonen, L., and Gustafson, I., Oral health in an adult Swedish population: prevalence of teeth, removable dentures and occlusal supporting zones, *Swed Dent J* 12, 45–60, 1989.

Keiser-Neilsen, S., Forensic odontology, *Int Dent J* 18(3), 668–681, 1968.

Keiser-Neilsen, S., *Person Identification by Means of Teeth*, John Wright & Sons, Bristol, 1980.

Kessler, H.J., An Overview of Forensic Dentistry, lecture at Armed Forces Institute of Pathology 31st Annual Course of Forensic Dentistry, Rockville, MD, 13–17, 1995.

Kogon, S.L., A review of validation studies of dental bitewing radiographs for forensic identification, *J Can Soc Forensic Sci* 29(3), 113–117, 1996.

Levine, S., Forensic odontology — identification by dental means, *Aust Dent J* 22(6), 481–487, 1977.

Maibaum, W.W. and Pousada, L., Dental labeling for geriatric patients, *Dent Manage* 30, 44–45, 1990.

Mertz, C.A., Dental identification, *Dent Clin North Am* 21(1), 47–67, 1977.

Platt, M. and Yewe-Dyer, M., How accurate is your charting? *Dent Update* 22(9), 374, 1995.

Pretty, I.A. and Sweet, D., A look at forensic dentistry: part 1: the role of teeth in the determination of human identity, *Br Dent J* 190(7), 359–366, 2001.

Redford, M., Drury, T.F., Kingman, A., and Brown, L.J., Denture use and the technical quality of dental prosthesis among persons 18–74 years of age: U.S., 1988–1991, *J Dent Res* 75, 714–725, 1996.

Rehfuss, W.F., A Treatise on Dental Jurisprudence for Dentists and Lawyers, The Wilmington Dental Mfg. Co., Philadelphia, 22–23, 1892.

Sognnaes, R.F., Talking teeth, *Am Sci* 64, 369–373, 1976.

Solheim, T. and Kvaal, S., Age estimation in adults, *Forensic Odontology — Proceedings of the European IOFOS Millenium Meeting*, Leuven University Press, Leuven, Belgium, 2000.

Summers, R., Personal communication on DNA analysis, 2005.

Sweet, D. and DiZinno, J.A., Personal identification through dental evidence — tooth fragments to DNA, *J Calif Dent Assoc* 24, 35–42, 1996.

Thomas, C.J., The role of the denture in identification: a review, *J Forensic Odontostomatol* 2, 13–16, 1984.

Weintraub, J.A. and Burt, B.A., Oral health status in the U.S.: tooth loss and edentulism, *J Dent Educ* 49, 368–378, 1985.

Whittaker, D.K., The principles of forensic dentistry: 1. identification procedures, *Dent Update* 17(8), 315–321, 1990.

Whittaker, D.K. and MacDonald, D.G., *A Colour Atlas of Forensic Dentistry*, Wolfe Medical Publications Ltd., London, 1989, pp. 9–13, Chap. 1.

Osteology

11

LOUISE SCHEUER
SUE BLACK

Contents

11.1 Introduction 199
11.2 Biological Identity...202
11.3 Determination of Sex 203
    11.3.1 Adults..203
    11.3.2 Juveniles...205
11.4 Age at Death..205
    11.4.1 Juveniles...207
    11.4.2 Young Adults 210
    11.4.3 Adults...210
11.5 Stature..212
11.6 Ethnic Identity 213
11.7 Positive Identification of Personal Identity...214
References 216

11.1 Introduction

Forensic osteology is a subdiscipline within forensic anthropology and principally concerns the analysis of the human skeleton for medicolegal purposes. A need for this most frequently arises following an investigation of human remains resulting from an unexplained natural death, homicide, suicide, or mass disaster, or following allegations of war crimes or genocide. However, with increasing frequency, the forensic osteologist may be asked to provide assistance to the forensic medical examiner regarding the confirmation of age of living subjects for the purposes of both judicial accountability and appropriate immigration status.

Within the U.K. there are no formal qualifications or licensing agreements that recognize the competence of a forensic osteologist to practice, but in 2002 the register held by the Council for the Registration of Forensic Practitioners (CRFP) was opened to the discipline through its Medicine and Healthcare sector panel (Black 2003). The aims of CRFP are:

- To publish a register of competent forensic practitioners
- To ensure through periodic revalidation that forensic practitioners keep up to date and maintain competence
- To address registered practitioners who fail to meet standards of competency

Figure 11.1 The bone to the left is a human neonatal tibia, while the two to the right are from a chicken.

Registration is voluntary, and although courts retain the right to hear evidence from whomsoever they choose, registration is regarded as an indicator of professional competence (www.crfp.org.uk). The initiative is supported and recognized by many authorities including the Home Office, Association of Chief Police Officers, Association of Chief Police Officers of Scotland, Police Service of Northern Ireland, Her Majesty's Inspector of Constabulary, and the Forensic Science Service.

Whereas the tasks performed by a forensic osteologist can be extremely varied, only the more traditional role will be discussed here from the perspective of the analysis of human skeletal remains. Upon the discovery of a skeleton, the investigating authority (police, military, coroner, or procurator fiscal in the U.K.) requires confirmation that the remains are indeed human. Frequently, nonhuman bone is presented for identification (Figure 11.1) and, occasionally, what appears to be human may not in fact even be bone as it is not uncommon for investigators to encounter the inappropriate disposal of polymer anatomical replicas.

The successful macroscopic identification of human bone will depend heavily not only on the experience of the forensic osteologist but also on which elements of the skeleton are present. Small, relatively featureless sections from the shafts of long bones or fragments of rib are difficult to distinguish from animal remains, particularly those of pig or sheep. Understandably, animals that are significantly smaller or indeed larger than a human being are often more readily differentiated (Figure 11.2). Although it is not essential for forensic osteologists to be skilled in comparative vertebrate osteology, they must be sufficiently familiar with each and every aspect of the adult and juvenile human skeleton to be competent at eliminating nonhuman material. It is an expensive mistake if a police investigation is initiated on the misidentification of animal bone.

It is important to establish the temporal deposition of the remains to allow a classification of either forensic or archaeological provenance. It is generally recognized that a somewhat artificial and arbitrary cut-off point of 70 years before the present date (BP) is accepted

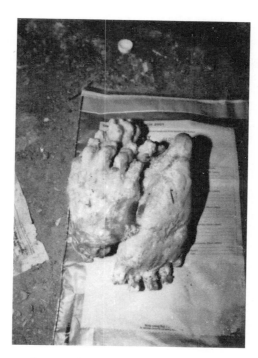

Figure 11.2 Bear paws are often confused with human appendages, but the "stepped" appearance of the digits (specimen on left) and the massive heel projection (specimen on right) are indicative of nonhuman quadrupedal locomotion.

as the dividing line that fundamentally represents the three score and ten years of a hypothetical average lifespan. This protracted time period ensures that it is highly unlikely the perpetrator of a crime committed more than 70 years BP will still be alive to be brought to justice. However, there are some notorious cases, such as the "Moor's Murders," that will retain a forensic relevance regardless of the passage of time. Also, in many jurisdictions there is no statute of limitation on the investigation of war crimes.

Evaluation of the time since death interval (TDI) is one of the most difficult questions to answer as many different factors may alter the composition of the remains. After burial, the decomposition of the body and the subsequent skeletonization and preservation of the bones are affected by both the physical conditions and the activities of humans, animals, and microbial activity (Haglund and Sorg 2002). These can include temperature, level of the water table, pH of soil, the growth and metabolism of bacteria, fungi and vegetation, disturbance by animals, and many other factors. In hot, dry conditions, decomposition and full skeletonization can take place in as little as two weeks yet the environment or the way in which the body is treated prior to its death may result in extraordinary preservation as exemplified by bog burials (e.g., Lindow man), glacial deposits (e.g., Ötzi), or mummification (e.g., the Incan Capacocha). Taphonomy, the study of the way in which elements of a dead body are degraded or dispersed, has been investigated mainly by animal bone specialists in the U.K. as there is no equivalent to the Tennessee "body farm" facility. Therefore, the reliable determination of the TDI in the U.K. requires assistance from other areas of discipline outside forensic osteology.

There are numerous potential long-term chemical and isotope indicators of TDI including ^{14}C and ^{90}Sr levels, the equilibrium between ^{210}Po and ^{210}Pb levels, nitrogen content, and ultraviolet fluorescence (see Chapter 2). Most of these methods are time consuming, complex, and require a specialist laboratory (Saukko and Knight 2004). There is increasing reliance on the use of botanical and entomological evidence as forensic environmental profiling has proved to be invaluable and remarkably accurate in its prediction of the events surrounding death, particularly with regards to recent incidents and TDI estimation (Byrd and Castner 2000, Coyle 2004).

One of the first steps in the analysis and description of human remains is to establish the biological identity of the deceased. This is then followed by an assessment of indicators of personal identity, and it is from the amalgamation of the two sets of information that a positive identification is most likely to arise. A confirmation of identity requires that both the biological and the personal indicators be in concordance, and this is equally true for adult as it is for juvenile skeletal remains. This chapter will consider biological identity in greater depth as many of the issues pertaining to personal identity are discussed elsewhere in this text.

11.2 Biological Identity

There are four basic categories associated with biological identity: sex, age-at-death, stature, and ethnic origin. Each of these, taken either in isolation or collectively, allow a preliminary picture to be built regarding the possible identity of the deceased and permits targeting of specific aspects of a missing persons register. The accuracy with which each factor will be determined will depend heavily upon which skeletal elements are available and also on their state of preservation. As a general rule, the more fragmented the remains and the less complete the skeleton, the more difficult it will be to realize full identification of the deceased. Therefore, it is essential that the remains are recovered by forensic archaeologists or appropriately trained recovery personnel to ensure maximal retrieval of potential evidence.

If there is a multiple burial of commingled remains or, indeed, a fragmentation perhaps through explosive disruption, the first stage is to attempt to reconstruct the body of the individual through assignation of skeletal elements. This serves to establish a minimum number of individuals (MNI) represented. At this point it becomes important to assign a bone confidently to the correct side of the body and also identify its correct position within a skeletal sequence. For instance, if two left capitates are found, there must be at least two individuals present, which is equally true if two left third ribs are encountered. Therefore, it is essential that every element presented is identified and seriated where appropriate.

Other factors that may assist in separating bones of specific individuals are the relative sizes of the bones, discernible pathological conditions, and their color or preservation status (although the latter two can vary within the same skeleton if the elements become separated and exposed to different physical environmental conditions). The state of skeletal development can be used to separate adult and juvenile individuals with relative ease, but the ability to separate commingled juveniles depends on a detailed knowledge of the osteology of immature bones. For example, the presence of a separate pars lateralis of the occipital bone together with a distal ulnar epiphysis and a distinct iliac crest will identify the presence of at least three subadults as these elements cannot coexist (Scheuer and Black 2000).

11.3   Determination of Sex

11.3.1   Adults

Because methods for age and stature estimation are sex-dependent, sex determination is usually the first step of the biological identification process. Reliability of sex determination depends on the completeness of the remains and the degree of sexual dimorphism inherent in the population from which the individual originates. In general, there are two main morphological differences between male and female skeletons. Male bones are generally larger and more robust than female bones due to the attachment of a larger and thus more powerful muscle mass, larger body size, and a period of delayed pubertal growth compared to the female. Second, the male pelvis is primarily adapted to a bipedal striding gait, whereas the size and shape differences of the female reflect the biomechanical compromise between efficient walking and the modifications necessary for the passage of a large fetal head through the pelvic canal (Schultz 1949). It is generally accepted that the two most sexually dimorphic elements of the skeleton are the pelvis and the skull. Many workers claim an accuracy of sex prediction in the region of 90% from the pelvis alone and 80% from the skull alone (Mays and Cox 2000). However, these values are optimal, and they will be lower if the bones are damaged or, indeed, if the individual originates from a population with low levels of sexual dimorphism.

Generally, the shape of the male pelvis is high and narrow whereas that of the female is wider and shallower with relatively, and often absolutely, larger inlet and outlet dimensions. These differences are most obviously reflected posteriorly in the shape of the greater sciatic notch (Figure 11.3) and the relative proportions of the body and alae of the sacrum and anteriorly in the subpubic angle, and shape of the pubic bone. A wide, shallow greater sciatic notch is considered to be a female characteristic as is the greater width of the ala of the sacrum compared to the width of its body. Probably the element of the skeleton that can offer the most reliable indication of sex is the pubic bone (Figure 11.4). Owing to its thin covering of compact bone and its ventral position in many burials, it is unfortunately one of the parts of the skeleton to survive inhumation least successfully.

Although the morphological determination of sex is the preferred method of analysis by the expert, as it permits a multifaceted accumulation of information, it is not sufficiently statistically robust to satisfy judicial requirements (see the concept of Daubert 1993).

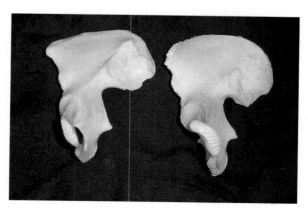

Figure 11.3   The wider female greater sciatic notch is on the left, and the narrower and more hooked male morphology is on the right.

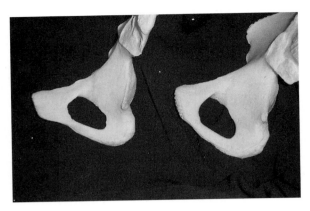

Figure 11.4 The more square shaped female pubic bone resulting in a wider sub pubic angle is on the left, and the more triangular male pubic bone is on the right.

A variety of single and multivariate measurements have been derived for the determination of sex. These display varying degrees of reliability and concentrate on measurements of bone length and bone width in an attempt to maximize the developmental and functional dimorphism of the pelvis (Krogman and Iscan 1986).

The differences between male and female skulls become discernible at puberty when the male skull develops features that reflect sites of increased muscle attachment, whereas the female skull tends to retain its more pedomorphic features. In the male, the glabella, supraorbital ridges, mastoid process, and the nuchal and malar areas become more prominent (Figure 11.5), in contrast to the female where all these features are smaller and the forehead remains vertical with more pronounced frontal and parietal eminences. The orbits are more rounded in the female, have sharper margins, and are larger relative to the upper facial skeleton. The male mandible generally has a more prominent chin region, a more robust lower border, a greater body height, and more prominent muscle markings. The angle formed between the body and ramus is more acute in the male than in the female (Krogman and Iscan 1986, Ferembach et al. 1980).

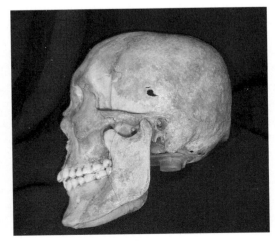

Figure 11.5 This male skull shows well-developed supraorbital ridging, mastoid process, and external occipital protuberance. The mandible is robust and the chin region is pronounced.

In the rest of the postcranial skeleton, sex differences generally reflect the larger size and larger muscular development of the male, especially in relation to overall joint size (Pons 1955). In general, a joint that transmits greater body weight (i.e., in the male) will be larger than the corresponding joint in the female. The difficulty in this concept is the extensive interethnic variation that occurs in relation to body robusticity. It is likely that the joints of a robust and heavy female of rural Russian origin will be significantly larger than those from a gracile urban Thai male. Therefore, the use and value of such indicators of sex must be tempered by an appreciation of inherent ethnic and even occupational variation.

There are other areas of the skeleton that can assist in the determination of sex. For example, in mature human remains where some soft tissue is retained, a radiograph of the chest plate showing the costal cartilages can provide useful additional information (Sanders 1966, Navani et al. 1970). It has long been established that there is a distinct difference in the sexual pattern of costal cartilage calcification although the etiology is poorly understood (Figure 11.6).

11.3.2 Juveniles

As in the adult, observations on sexual dimorphism have tended to concentrate on the pelvis and skull. Some researchers claim an accuracy of between 70–80% for certain measurements of the ilium and femur, but these figures have failed to be confirmed on retesting (Schutkowski 1987). Claims that the morphological differences in the surface of the sacro-iliac joint could separate males from females have proved to be of limited use in sexing (Hunt 1990, Mittler and Sheridan 1992). Some traits of the orbit and mandible show dimorphism if used under carefully controlled conditions but remain to be tested further on a population of known sex (Molleson et al. 1998). At the present time, however, it has to be concluded that the juvenile skeleton cannot be sexed with any degree of reliability from morphological observations alone. Although some slight sexual dimorphism may exist from an early age, it does not reach a high enough level to permit accurate sexing until pubertal modifications have taken place (Scheuer and Black 2000).

Some of the issues pertaining to sex determination from both adult and juvenile skeletal remains have been addressed with some success following technological advances that facilitate the isolation and amplification of DNA from bones and teeth (see Chapter 1). The amelogenin gene, responsible for the production of one of the organic components of the enamel of teeth, has sequence differences on the X and Y chromosomes, and a method utilizing molecular genetic techniques correctly identified 19 out of 20 skeletons of a known sex (Stone et al. 1996). At the present time there are still problems with contamination and degradation of DNA obtained from both bone and teeth, especially in certain burial conditions (Brown 2000). However, with the improvement of current techniques and the development of new methods, sex-typing from genetic material could in the future become routine in forensic cases.

11.4 Age at Death

It is useful to divide age-related changes in the skeleton into three different phases of an individual's lifespan: growth and development, equilibrium, and senescence. The first phase is largely under genetic and environmental influences and includes children and

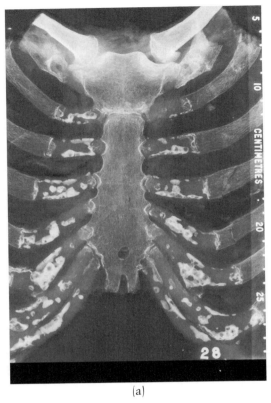

(a)

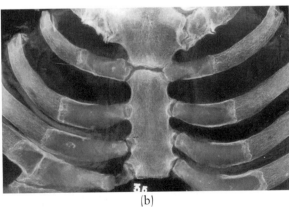

(b)

Figure 11.6 (a) Female pattern costal cartilage calcification. Note that the deposits are sclerotic in appearance and tend to be located more centrally within the cartilage. (b) Male pattern costal cartilage calcification. Note the more trabecular appearance and its peripheral (superior and inferior) positioning.

young adults who undergo changes that proceed in a relatively well-documented pattern at a moderately predictable rate. The multiplicity of the composition of the juvenile skeleton offers an extensive array of growth-related parameters from which to estimate age, and accuracy is, therefore, reasonably high (Scheuer and Black 2000). Once maturity is reached, the age-related changes in the adult skeleton vary quite significantly and are more individual and population specific, especially at the stage when maturity proceeds towards senescence and subsequent degeneration. In this phase, factors such as health status, occupation, nutrition, and endocrine function are principal determinants of degenerative status. In addition most of the methods in use for adult aging rely on studies developed from large archaeological samples of unknown sex and age. Bocquet-Appel and Masset (1982, 1985) argued that aging methods developed on such samples have reflected misconceptions about longevity in past populations and, in turn, have resulted in the replication of the original sample's mortality profile. When tested against samples of known age this has resulted in systematic errors, the most important of which has been the tendency to under-age individuals of over 40 years. In more recent work on documented material, particularly following the Balkan conflict (Schaefer and Black 2005), this principle is changing, although the genetic homogeneity of that material must be borne in mind before attempting to utilize the data on material of different origin.

11.4.1 Juveniles

For best use of the information in this section, the reader is directed to the poster included with this book.

In the juvenile age range, before cessation of growth in height, age may be estimated from numerous markers from the teeth and skeleton so that estimated age bands are usually narrower than those for adults. Dental age estimates may be derived from the eruption or mineralization of the teeth (Figure 11.7) and are closer to actual chronological age than those of skeletal age, but the basis for this is not fully understood. A possible reason is that the development of all the deciduous dentition and part of the permanent dentition takes place before birth in a protected environment, whereas skeletal growth and development, although having a strong genetic basis, is exposed for a longer time to external factors such as nutrition, socioeconomic status, and even climate.

Eruption is a continuous process by which teeth move from their crypts in the alveolar bone of the jaws to full occlusion in the mouth (Figure 11.8), but many studies are confined to their emergence into the mouth, often wrongly referred to as *eruption*. The presence of emerged teeth may be observed easily by the osteologist to give a rapid estimate of age, but increased accuracy can be obtained from evaluation of the calcification of the teeth

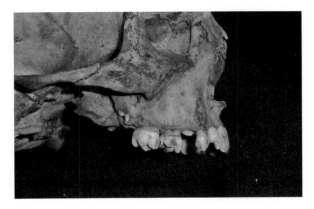

Figure 11.7 This is the skull of a child of approximately 10 years of age. The permanent incisors are in occlusion, the deciduous canine is retained, the first premolar is erupting, the second deciduous molar is retained, the first permanent molar is in occlusion, and the second permanent molar can be seen in its alveolar crypt.

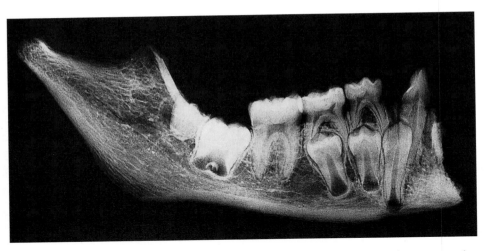

Figure 11.8 Radiograph of a hemimandible from a child of approximately 9 years of age.

(Smith, 1991). However, this necessitates radiographic analysis and comparison with defined stages of mineralization of both crowns and roots. This is a complex process that requires a considerable degree of experience and should be undertaken in conjunction with a forensic odontologist (see Chapter 10).

Studies of dental microstructure such as the counting of perikymata, the incremental lines on the surface of enamel, can provide an absolute method of age determination, independent of the growth standards of a comparative population (Fitzgerald 1998). One particular incremental line, the neonatal line, can be of special medicolegal significance in determining if an infant was live born or stillborn. It is formed in all teeth that start to mineralize before birth, i.e., the whole deciduous dentition and the first permanent molars. In practice, it may be visualized by light microscopy if a child has survived for about three weeks after birth or by electron microscopy within a day or two of birth (Whittaker and MacDonald 1989). It has been suggested that further observations of the relationship of the neonatal line to other enamel striae could provide information about certain birth defects and sudden infant death syndrome (Skinner and Dupras 1993). All these factors could prove important in individual forensic casework, but it should be appreciated that the methods require the facilities of a hard-tissue laboratory and experience in the technique, and, in addition, are time consuming and expensive.

Skeletal age can also be estimated from the size and length of the long bones and the developmental state of centers of ossification (Scheuer and Black 2000). When using the lengths of long bone shafts, accuracy will vary with the period of life. Lengths in the fetus are closely related to gestational age, and there are large amounts of clinical ultrasound data available for reference. Postnatally, accuracy of age estimation decreases with increasing age as external factors start to affect growth, and there is individual and sex variation in height, especially during the adolescent growth spurt. Data also becomes a problem as the tables for comparison are based on systematic, nonrepeatable cross-sectional, and longitudinal radiological surveys of children from at least two generations ago (Maresh 1970, Tanner et al. 1983). The majority of these surveys were drawn from white, middle-class people of European origin, but there are many populations for whom there is no adequate sample for comparison.

It is also possible to age a juvenile skeleton from the developmental state of the primary and secondary centers of ossification. Most centers of the skull, vertebrae, and primary

Figure 11.9 Ossification in the neonatal sternum. At this stage, the nodules that will go on to form the manubrium and the body of the sternum are relatively featureless. (Courtesy of A. Christie.)

centers of the long bones and their girdles commence ossification in the embryonic and fetal periods, whereas the majority of secondary centers develop within cartilaginous templates throughout postnatal life (Scheuer and Black 2000). With a few exceptions, ossification centers commence as nondescript spherical or ovoid nodules of bone and would not be identifiable in isolation in skeletonized or commingled remains (Figure 11.9). Therefore, their use in aging in a forensic context would be limited to the examination of a body where sufficient soft tissue remained to hold them in an anatomically identifiable position. It may be of legal importance in some forensic situations to recognize if a fetus has reached full term, and the presence of secondary centers of the distal femur, proximal tibia, calcaneus, and talus is usually taken to signify this stage (see poster included with this book).

When a primary or secondary center has reached a recognizably distinctive morphology it may be used to advantage in aging. This critical point varies with each bone, so that accuracy will depend on which skeletal elements are available. Most of the bones of the skull, vertebrae, ribs, and major long bones of the limbs and girdles are recognizable from midfetal life onwards, but others do not reach a recognizable stage until later childhood. Age estimation will naturally be determined with greater accuracy using those bone elements which undergo distinct changes within a relatively short period of time. For instance, the fusion of the ischium and pubis at their rami takes place between three and ten years so it is of limited value, whereas the changes in shape and fusion between the main epiphysis and the tuberosity of the upper tibia take place in a shorter time and are therefore more informative.

Perhaps the most useful phase of bone development is when fusion occurs between one or more primary centers or between a primary and its secondary center (Figure 11.10). This stage covers a wide age range, partly in response to the function of the soft tissues with which the bones are associated. The primary centers of the skull and vertebral column are normally fused by the age of 6 years reflecting the precocious development of the human nervous system, whereas the fusion of secondary epiphyses of the long bones cover the adolescent and early adult periods (Scheuer and Black 2000). The difficulties of sexing juveniles complicate the use of fusion times in the adolescent period (see above). Details of fusion times for all the bones of the skeleton can be found in the chart at the end of this text.

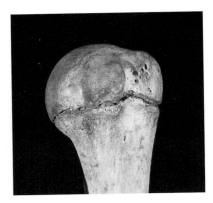

Figure 11.10 Fusion of the proximal humeral epiphysis with the diaphysis.

Figure 11.11 The medial epiphysis of the clavicle where fusion has just begun. (Courtesy of A. Christie.)

11.4.2 Young Adults

Several areas of the skeleton do not complete their growth until the second and third decades of life and are consequently valuable for estimating age at death in young adulthood. This period extends from the cessation of growth in height, signaled by the fusion of all the long bone epiphyses, until final fusion of all other epiphyses (Scheuer and Black 2000). These include the jugular growth plate of the skull and postcranially, the sacral vertebral bodies, the iliac and ischial epiphyses, the ring epiphyses of the vertebral bodies, epiphyses of the scapula, costal notches of the sternum, and medial epiphysis of the clavicle (Figure 11.11). A summary of the closure times for these epiphyses are also given in the chart included at the end of this text.

11.4.3 Adults

Aging in the mature adult has traditionally utilized four areas of the skeleton: the state of fusion of the cranial sutures, morphological changes in the pubic symphysis, sacroiliac joint, and ventral aspect of the ribs (Ferembach et al. 1980, Meindl and Lovejoy 1985, Saunders et al. 1992). Closure of the ecto- and endocranial aspects of the vault sutures have proved very unreliable as age markers in spite of much work attempting to test and refine original methods (Key et al. 1994). This is unfortunate as the cranial vault survives inhumation

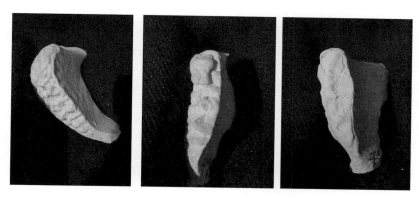

Figure 11.12 Morphological changes in the pubic symphyseal face. The youngest is on the left, and the oldest is on the right.

probably better than any other skeletal element. Related to this, recent observations stated that the pits on the endocranial surface of the frontal and parietal bones that accommodate arachnoid granulations — granular foveolae — increase in number with age (Barber et al. 1995). Early results showed a high correlation with age but the method still needs to be tested for reliability on a large sample of age-documented individuals.

It has long been accepted that the epiphyseal morphology of the ventral demiface of the pubic symphysis undergoes a prolonged period of age-related change up to 35–40 years (Figure 11.12). This has been used for age estimation using component phase analysis, with each age range displaying its own distinct morphology (McKern and Stewart 1957, Gilbert and McKern 1973). The original methods, based on archaeological samples, have been subjected to extensive study, testing, and modification but are not really accurate enough for forensic identification as they produced large age ranges with enormous overlaps. More recent studies on forensic samples have proved to be more encouraging (Suchey 1979, Katz and Suchey 1986, Brooks and Suchey 1990).

The changes in the appearance of the sacroiliac joint have also been used to estimate age at death as part of a multifactorial method but, again, it was found that age ranges were too large for forensic application (Lovejoy et al. 1985, Waldron and Rogers 1990, Murray and Murray 1991, Buckberry and Chamberlain 2002, Mulhern and Jones 2005). This approach has the advantage of the sacroiliac joint's being more resistant to decay than the pubic symphysis, but the surface of the joint may not be visible after the age of 50 years as it frequently undergoes ankylosis, particularly in males.

Methods for aging from the sternal end of the fourth rib also employ a phase-analysis system, which is claimed to display an accuracy similar to that obtained for the pubic symphysis and better than aging from cranial sutures (Iscan, 1985, Iscan et al. 1984, 1985; Loth 1995). However, further testing showed that it was more accurate at determining age in males than in females and tended to under-age individuals over 60 years (Cox 2000). Apart from the wide estimates of age, the disadvantages are that it uses one of the least well-preserved parts of the skeleton and also requires the identification of the fourth rib which can prove difficult in a disarticulated, fragmented, or disrupted skeleton. The method has been reported to display a high degree of interobserver error, which makes it more than usually reliant on the previous experience of the observer. Used together with a histological technique on a documented sample, it showed a poor correlation with chronological age (Saunders et al. 1992).

The examination of areas of hyaline cartilage ossification has proved to have some corroborative value in the prediction of age. The partially calcified tissue that may occur at these sites, even if recognized, is often not recovered and is easily damaged, but ossification can arise at a surprisingly young age. Costal cartilage calcification does not usually appear until the middle of the fourth decade and in the upper four ribs until after the age of 50 years although it has been reported occasionally in the later teenage years (McCormick 1983). Laryngeal cartilage ossification has been much studied and it appears to be accepted, contrary to the evidence that increasing ossification is positively correlated with age. Most studies have demonstrated a recognizable progressive pattern which increases with age, but timing is highly variable, and the correlation between actual age and the degree of ossification involves a wide margin of error (Scheuer 2002). Ossification of the tracheal rings can also be detected, and it is likely that they follow the same age profile for calcification as is witnessed in the laryngeal structures.

The appearance of degenerative joint disease as signaled by lipping of vertebral bodies and osteophytes surrounding other joints and muscle attachments does not normally appear until after the age of 40 years. However, the onset of these features is again very variable and dependent on such factors as genetics, nutrition, and lifestyle so that the later decades of life are difficult to estimate with any degree of accuracy. Sclerotic fusion of the manubriosternal joint, seen predominantly in females, increases with advancing years (Scheuer and Black 2000). The primary cartilaginous joints between the manubrium and costal cartilages of the first ribs may also synostose in older individuals but have never been reported in an individual where prior manubriosternal fusion has occurred. Paget's disease of bone, although only seen in 2–3% of adults, is rarely diagnosed in individuals less than 50 years old. The synostosis of the sacroiliac joint (see above) seen after the age of about 50 years is reported to be about 4 times more common in males so it could be used as corroboration of sex (Waldron and Rogers 1990).

Remodeling of bone takes place throughout adult life and has been used in various ways to provide estimates of age at death. Histomorphometric methods are based on quantifiable patterns of intact and fragmentary osteons viewed in bone sections taken from specified sites in the body (Stout 1989, 1992, Stout and Paine 1992). Some authors claim that these methods are accurate to within 5.5 years, but this has not been confirmed by others. Other methods are based on trabecular bone loss reflected in radiographs of either whole bones or cross sections of the midshaft, but the patterns of trabecular bone loss showed marked variation among individuals of the same age in both sexes (Macchiarelli and Bondioli 1994, Feik et al. 1997). Again, the variation with sex and age between individuals precludes this method from being used as a predictor of age in forensic cases.

There is a large literature on aging from individual teeth, using changes that occur in root dentine translucency and in the number of annulations of the cementum (Whittaker 2000). These methods need specialized laboratory facilities and an experienced observer for the interpretation of results and readers are directed to Chapter 10.

11.5   Stature

The establishment of the height of an individual from skeletal remains can be, with certain exceptions, one of the most straightforward parameters to be established. The calculation of stature is based on the relative proportions of different body parts, both in relation to

**Table 11.1   Relative Height of Parts of the Body at
Different Ages, in Approximate Percentages**

Age	Head and Neck	Trunk	Lower Limb
Birth	24	35	41
2 years	22	31	47
6 years	18	33	49
Adult	15	35	50

each other and in relation to the overall height of the individual. The relative sizes of some parts of the body at different ages are shown in Table 11.1. Stature can be estimated with considerable ease and quite some accuracy from the long bones of a disarticulated adult skeleton. The greatest accuracy will be obtained when undamaged bones of known sex and ethnic identity are utilized, as the height of the individual is both sex and race dependent. Most standard forensic texts contain regression equations from which adult male and female stature can be calculated, and recourse to these is recommended (Trotter and Gleser 1958, 1977, Krogman and Iscan 1986). Those formulae that use the femur and tibia have the lowest standard error of the estimate as these bones form an integral part of an individual's height. However, when the preferred skeletal elements are not available, an attempt at stature estimation may be made from a metacarpal, metatarsal, clavicle, or even fragmentary long bones, but accuracy will decline rapidly with the use of incomplete bones (Scheuer 2002). Again, it must be stated that there are many populations for which no data are available.

11.6   Ethnic Identity

The determination of race or ethnic origin is the most difficult and unreliable attribute that the forensic osteologist must attempt to establish. The differences between the various "races" of man are small, and the consequent variation exhibited in the skeleton is difficult to assess with any degree of accuracy (St. Hoyme and Iscan, 1987). It follows that as the most obvious ethnic differences in the living are either displayed in the face or the integumentary system, so the skull is the most studied skeletal element in this regard. Although the history of anthropology is littered with explorers who have returned home with the skulls of various tribes to study, much of the early work concentrated on variation rather than discrimination. More recently, two computer-based multivariate approaches have been developed on large database samples with the specific purpose of analyzing ancestry and therefore ethnic origin. The CRANID program developed by Richard Wright in Australia was derived on measurements from nearly 3,000 museum skulls around the world. The FORDISC2.0 system developed by Ousley and Jantz (2005) was derived from over 1,400 forensic cases.

Ethnic identity from the limb bones utilizes variation in the intermembral indices. For the upper limb, the brachial index is radial length × 100/humeral length and for the lower limb, the crural index is the tibial length × 100/femoral length. Tables in standard texts show that the ranges for Black, White, and Asian categories are wide with considerable overlap, so that identification of race by this method should only be used as corroborative rather than diagnostic evidence (Krogman and Iscan 1986). Both artificial dental work and innate dental traits can be useful for assigning ethnicity. Population studies of nonmetrical tooth variation are summarized by Hillson (1996). Ethnic variation in gene frequency and expression is gaining credibility in the determination of ethnicity, and readers are directed to Chapter 1.

11.7 Positive Identification of Personal Identity

Once biological identity has been established, the forensic osteologist must attempt to personalize the information available so that individual identity is achieved. Many of the ways in which this can occur have been outlined in other chapters of this text and, therefore, only a very cursory discussion takes place here for the sake of completeness.

During the Asian tsunami, the three principal means of personal identity were achieved through dental records, fingerprints, and DNA analysis. All of these require that a pre-existing antemortem dataset be available for comparison. When it is known that a person is missing or deceased, then these records, should they exist, are passed to the investigating authority. However, when an unidentified set of remains are found, then dental records are of no value until a possible identity has been achieved, and it is common that no match is forthcoming from either the national DNA or fingerprint databases. Under these circumstances, the forensic osteologist must look to other possible evidence within the remains that may assist with the identification process.

Identification of a pre-existing medical condition (Figure 11.13) or the presence of surgical hardware (Figure 11.14) may prove of value in establishing a productive line of enquiry. Equally, the forensic osteologist has a prominent role to play in the identification and reconstruction of trauma to the skeleton (Black 2005). This may include healed trauma that has occurred some considerable time before death (Figure 11.15) or damage that could indicate the likely cause of death (Figure 11.16). Imaging techniques such as facial reconstruction, facial superimposition, or facial art can be attempted with varying levels of success (see Chapter 13). These are specialized areas that tend to lie outside the capabilities of most forensic osteologists, and therefore it is essential that a good working relationship is developed between discipline-specific experts. If the osteologist provides a flawed set of information pertaining to biological identity, then the chances of achieving a personal identification are slim.

Figure 11.13 Gall stones.

Figure 11.14 Pacemaker.

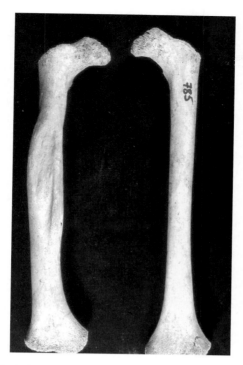

Figure 11.15 Femoral shaft fracture in a child of approximately 10 years of age.

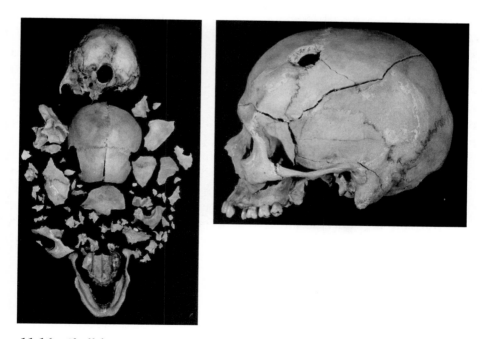

Figure 11.16 Skull fragmentation as a result of gunshot trauma with subsequent reconstruction. (Courtesy of M. Warren.)

The forensic osteologist may feel pressured, by investigating authorities anxious to solve a case, to make a positive identification of an individual. However, this is a serious responsibility, and it is essential to be absolutely sure that the remains are those of the missing person and that the identification process rests on secure and verifiable evidence. The consequences could mean the end of distressing uncertainty and eventual closure for the family of a deceased individual with the acceptance of death and the beginning of the process of grieving. In the case of a possible crime, it could also mean the arraignment and trial of a suspect.

Throughout the forensic examination of skeletal remains, there are various legal, and sometimes political, issues and procedures such as confidentiality and continuity of evidence that must be carefully followed. These usually involve cooperation with other personnel such as forensic pathologists, archaeologists, odontologists, and forensic examiners. The value of interdisciplinary discussion and consultation cannot be over-emphasized, and the forensic anthropologist must work as part of an active team rather than as an isolated adjunct.

Most of a forensic osteologist's written skeletal reports will be accepted as evidence and written testimony by a pathologist, coroner, procurator fiscal (U.K.), or senior investigative officer, but sometimes a personal appearance at an inquest or other court is required. Legal proceedings may occur many months, or even several years, after the initial investigation when recall of a case can be difficult, especially under the harassing conditions of a courtroom. Care must be taken not to be drawn outside the area of expertise if harangued by a lawyer determined to prove the expert's incompetence. The osteologist is the expert witness on bones, and it is essential that this can be endorsed by a report that is as detailed, accurate, and free from jargon as possible. It must be borne in mind that the testimony can result in evidence that incarcerates the defendant or in the case of international investigations, it can carry sufficient weight to invoke a death penalty. All aspects of forensic investigation have potentially serious consequences and, therefore, it is essential that the expert has appropriate training and expertise in the subject matter. Should the case be unsolved, then it is likely that the report by the anthropologist, pathologist, and odontologist will be all that is available for the cold-case review team. A detailed analysis may well prevent the unnecessary exhumation of remains.

Forensic osteology is not something that can be learned from a textbook in a single year. It is a subject that relies heavily on practical experience that must be gained over time and, therefore, it is essential that rigorous accreditation procedures be in place. As was stated boldly in the House of Lords Select Committee Report on Science and Technology (HMSO 2000): " … the field is wide open for the plausible quack … science for the defence has a regrettable history of incompetence and charlatans." It is essential that the science of forensic osteology does not descend into a subject which provides advice that is unhelpful at best and positively misleading as worst but continues to serve within the confines of its capabilities with caution, diligence, and propriety.

References

Barber, G., Shepstone, L., and Rogers, J., A methodology for estimating age at death using arachnoid granulation counts, *Am J Phys Anthropol* Suppl. 20, 61, 1995.

Black, S.M., Forensic anthropology — regulation in the U.K., *Sci Justice* 43, 187–192, 2003.

Black, S.M., Bone pathology and ante-mortem trauma in forensic cases, in *Encyclopedia of Forensic and Legal Medicine*, Payne-James, J., Ed., Elsevier, London, 2005, pp. 105–113.

Bocquet-Appel, J.-P. and Masset, C., Farewell to palaeodemography, *J Hum Evol* 11, 321–323. 1982.

Bocquet-Appel, J.-P. and Masset, C., Matters of moment, *J Hum Evol* 14, 107–111, 1985.

Brooks, S. and Suchey, J.M., Skeletal age determination based on the *Os pubis*: comparison of the Acsádi–Nemeskéri and Suchey–Brooks methods, *Hum Evol* 5, 227–238, 1990.

Brown, K., Ancient DNA applications in human osteoarchaeology, in *Human Osteology in Archaeology and Forensic Science*, Cox, M. and Mays, S., Eds., Greenwich Medical Media Ltd., London, 2000, pp. 455–473.

Buckberry, J. and Chamberlain, A., Age estimation from the auricular surface of the ilium: a revised method, *Am J Phys Anthropol* 119, 231–239, 2002.

Byrd, J.H. and Castner, J.L., *Forensic Entomology: The Utility of Arthropods in Legal Investigations*, CRC Press, Boca Raton, FL, 2000.

Cox, M., Ageing adults from the skeleton, in *Human Osteology in Archaeology and Forensic Science*, Cox, M. and Mays, S., Eds., Greenwich Medical Media Ltd., London, 2000, pp. 61–81.

Coyle, H.M., *Forensic Botany: Principles and Applications to Criminal Casework*, CRC Press, Boca Raton, FL, 2004.

Daubert v Merrell Dow Pharmaceuticals, U.S. Supreme Court Collection 92–102, 509 US 579, 1993.

Feik, S.A., Thomas, C.D.L., and Clement, J.G., Age-related changes in the cortical porosity of the midshaft of the human femur, *J Anat* 191, 407–416, 1997.

Ferembach, D., Schwidetsky, I., and Stloukal, M., Recommendations for age and sex diagnoses of skeletons. report of the workshop of European anthropologists (WEA), *J Hum Evol* 9, 517–549, 1980.

Fitzgerald, C.M., Do dental microstructures have a regular time dependency? Conclusions from the literature and a large-scale survey, *J Hum Evol* 35, 371–386, 1998.

Gilbert, B.M. and McKern, T.W., A method for aging the female *Os pubis*, *Am J Phys Anthropol* 38, 31–38, 1973.

Haglund, W.D. and Sorg, M.H., *Advances in Forensic Taphonomy*, CRC Press, Boca Raton, FL, 2002.

Hillson, S., *Dental Anthropology*, Cambridge University Press, Cambridge, 1996, pp. 101–102.

HMSO, House of Lords Select Committee on Science and Technology — Report 6, HMSO, London, 2000.

Hunt, D.R., Sex determination in the subadult ilia: an indirect test of weaver's non-metric sexing method, *J Forensic Sci* 35, 881–885, 1990.

Iscan, M.Y., Osteometric analysis of sexual dimorphism in the sternal end of the rib, *J Forensic Sci* 30, 1090–1099, 1985.

Iscan, M.Y., Loth, S.R., and Wright, R.K., Age estimation from the rib by phase analysis: white males, *J Forensic Sci* 29, 1094–1104, 1984.

Iscan, M.Y., Loth, S.R., and Wright, R.K., Age estimation from the rib by phase analysis: white females, *J Forensic Sci* 30, 853–863, 1985.

Katz, D. and Suchey, J.M., Age determination of the male *Os pubis*, *Am J Phys Anthropol* 69, 435–436, 1986.

Key, C.A., Aiello, L.C., and Molleson, T.I., Cranial suture closure and its implications for age estimation, *Int J Osteoarchaeol* 4, 193–207, 1994.

Krogman,, W.M. and Iscan, M.Y., *The Human Skeleton in Forensic Medicine*, 2nd ed., C.C. Thomas, Springfield, IL, 1986.

Loth, S.R., Age assessment of the Spitalfields cemetery population by rib phase analysis, *Am J Hum Biol* 7, 465–471, 1995.

Lovejoy, C.O., Meindl, R.S., Mensforth, R.P., and Barton, T.J., Multifactorial determination of age at death: a method and blind tests of its accuracy, *Am J Phys Anthropol* 68, 1–14, 1985.

Macchiarelli, R. and Bondioli, L., Linear densitometry and digital image processing of proximal femur radiographs: implications for archaeological and forensic anthropology, *Am J Phys Anthropol* 93, 109–122, 1994.

Maresh, M.M., Measurements from roentgenograms, in *Human Growth and Development*, McCammon, R.W., Ed., C.C. Thomas, Springfield, IL, 1970.

Mays, S. and Cox, M., Sex determination in skeletal remains, in *Human Osteology in Archaeology and Forensic Science*, Cox, M. and Mays, S., Eds., Greenwich Medical Media Ltd., London, 2000, pp. 117–130.

McCormick, W.F., Ossification patterns of costal cartilages as an indicator of sex, *Arch Patholol Lab Med* 107, 206–210, 1983.

McKern, T.W. and Stewart, T.D., Skeletal Age Changes in Young American Males Analysed from the Standpoint of Age Identification, HQ Quartermaster Research and Development Command Technical Report EP-45, Natick, MA, 1957.

Meindl, R.S. and Lovejoy, C.O., Ectocranial suture closure: a revised method for the determination of skeletal age at death based on the lateral-anterior sutures, *Am J Phys Anthropol* 68, 57–66, 1985.

Mittler, D.M. and Sheridan, S.G., Sex determination in subadults using auricular surface morphology: a forensic science perspective, *J Forensic Sci* 37, 1068–1075, 1992.

Molleson, T., Cruse, K., and Mays, S., Some sexually dimorphic features of the human juvenile skull and their value in sex determination in immature juvenile remains, *J Archaeol Sci* 25, 719–728, 1998.

Mulhern, D.M. and Jones, E.B., Test of revised method of age estimation from the auricular surface of the ilium, *Am J Phys Anthropol* 126, 61–65, 2005.

Murray, K.A. and Murray, T., A test of auricular surface ageing techniques, *J Forensic Sci* 36, 1162–1169, 1991.

Navani, S., Shah, J.R., and Levy, P.S., Determination of sex by costal cartilages, *Am J Radiol* 108, 771–774, 1970.

Ousley, S.D. and Jantz, R.L., FORDISC3, University of Tennessee, 2005, http://web.dii.utk.edu/fordisc.

Pons, J., The sexual diagnosis of isolated bones of the skeleton, *Hum Biol* 27, 12–22, 1955.

Sanders, C.F., Sexing by costal cartilage calcification, *Br J Radiol* 39, 233, 1966.

Saukko, P. and Knight, B., *Knight's Forensic Pathology*, 3rd ed., Hodder Arnold, London, 2004.

Saunders, S.R., Fitzgerald, C., Rogers, T., Dudar, C., and McKillop, H., A test of several methods of age estimation using a documented archaeological sample, *Can Soc Forensic Sci J* 25, 97–117, 1992.

Schaefer, M. and Black, S.M., Comparison of ages of epiphyseal union in North American and Bosnian skeletal material, *J Forensic Sci* 50, 777–784, 2005.

Scheuer, L., Application of osteology to forensic medicine, *Clin Anat* 15, 297–312, 2002.

Scheuer, L. and Black, S., *Developmental Juvenile Osteology*, Academic Press, London, 2000.

Schultz, A.H., Sex differences in the pelves of primates, *Am J Phys Anthropol* 7, 401–423, 1949.

Schutkowski, H., Sex determination of fetal and neonatal skeletons by means of discriminant analysis, *Int J Anthropol* 2, 347–352, 1987.

Skinner, M. and Dupras, T., Variation in birth timing and location of the neonatal line in human enamel, *J Forensic Sci* 38, 1383–1390, 1993.

Smith, B.H., Standards of tooth formation and dental age assessment, in *Advances in Dental Anthropology*, Kelley, M.A. and Larsen, C.S., Eds., Wiley-Liss, New York, 1991.

St. Hoyme, L.E. and Iscan, M.Y., Determination of sex and race: accuracy and assumptions, in *Reconstruction of Life from the Skeleton*, Iscan, M.Y. and Kennedy, K.A.R., Eds., Alan R. Liss Inc., New York, 1989, pp. 53–93.

Stone, A.C., Milner, G.R., Pääbo, S., and Stoneking, M., Sex determination of ancient human skeletons using DNA, *Am J Phys Anthropol* 99, 231–238, 1996.

Stout, S.D., The use of cortical histology to estimate age at death, in *Age Markers in the Human Skeleton*, Iscan, M.Y., Ed., C.C. Thomas, Springfield, IL, 1989, pp. 195–207.

Stout, S.D., Methods of determining age at death using bone microstructure, in *Skeletal Biology of Past Peoples*, Saunders, S.R. and Katzenberg, M.A., Eds., John Wiley & Sons, New York, 1992, pp. 21–35.

Stout, S.D. and Paine, R.R., Brief communication: histological age estimation using rib and clavicle, *Am J Phys Anthropol* 87, 111–115, 1992.

Suchey, J.M., Problems in the aging of females using the *Os pubis, Am J Phys Anthropol* 51, 467–471, 1979.

Tanner, J.M., Whitehouse, R.H., Cameron, N., Marshall, W.A., Healy, M.J.R., and Goldstein, H., *Assessment of Skeletal Maturity and Prediction of Adult Height (TW2 Method)*, 2nd ed., Academic Press, London, 1983.

Trotter, M. and Gleser, G.C., A re-evaluation of estimation of stature based on measurements of stature taken during life and of long bones after death, *Am J Phys Anthropol* 16, 79–123, 1958.

Trotter, M. and Gleser, G.C., Corrigenda to estimation of stature from long bones of American Whites and Negroes, *Am J Phys Anthropol* (1952), *Am J Phys Anthropol* 47, 355–356, 1977.

Waldron, T. and Rogers, J., An epidemiologic study of sacro-iliac fusion in some human skeletal remains, *Am J Phys Anthropol* 83, 123–127, 1990.

Whittaker, D., Ageing from the dentition, in *Human Osteology in Archaeology and Forensic Science*, Cox, M. and Mays, S., Eds., Greenwich Medical Media Ltd., London, 2000, pp. 83–99.

Whittaker, D.K. and MacDonald, D.G., *A Colour Atlas of Forensic Dentistry*, Wolfe Medical Publications Ltd., London, 1989, p. 61.

Radiography

12

EMILY HINES
CATHERINE ROCK
MARK VINER

Contents

12.1 Introduction 221
12.2 Radiography Procedures in the Identification of Human Remains 222
12.3 Human Profiling and Radiography 224
12.4 Role of the Radiographer in the Identification of Human Remains...................224
12.5 Conclusion 225
References 226
Bibliography/Further Reading..228

12.1 Introduction

Radiography has been utilized extensively in forensic, archaeological, and humanitarian investigation since "a new kind of ray" was described by William Roentgen in 1895.[1] X-ray imaging utilizes the principles of the absorption of x-ray photons to demonstrate differentiations in atomic structure (or density) of the subject under examination. Minimally invasive, objective, permanent, and comparatively cost effective imaging techniques are now commonplace in the capture of physical evidence in the forensic investigation.

In May 1896, Bordas suggested that x-rays be used "… for identification through the visualization of old fractures, bullets, or other known peculiarities … "[2] This was echoed by others. Angerer suggested that wrist bone development could be used to measure bone age in 1896,[3] Levinsohn[4] recognized that x-ray images could produce more accurate measurements of the skeleton than the then-popular method of anthropological classification developed in 1883 by Alphonse Bertillon. Through painstaking research of anthropological features, Bertillon identified five areas of human anatomy that remain consistent in the adult skeletal frame. These were length and breadth of the head, length of the middle finger, left foot, and distance between elbow and distal end of middle finger. When these measurements were taken and recorded systematically, individuals could be distinguishable from each other. This system was first adopted in criminal investigation in 1894, together with the fingerprinting method, as a means of identification.

The specific use of radiographic imaging for identifying human remains is also widely recognized and well documented.[5,6,7] Radiology is used extensively in anthropological and odontological assessment of postmortem radiographs (x-ray images) and antemortem radiographs, records, or other images for concordance. Radiographs and associated records are an excellent source of data for comparison of anatomical features: clinical images in the U.K. are normally retained for 8 years (in pediatrics, until patients reach their 25th year) and for 3 years following death,[8] and are, on the whole, fairly accessible. Image records are usually stored with a general dental practitioner and hospital premises, and copies can be acquired for investigative purposes by contacting them directly. However, clinical imaging can also play a role in the objective capture of a biological profile of the deceased including race, sex, age, height, congenital anomalies, skeletal trauma, or other pathology.

Numerous specific cases have been reported where radiography has had a significant role in postmortem identification of human remains.[9,10,11,12] Kahana and Hiss (2002) even report on suprapelvic and pelvic phleboliths or calcified vessels as a reliable marker for positive identification.[13] In 1927, Culbert and Law[14] made the first identification of human remains by comparison of antemortem and postmortem radiographs of the frontal air sinuses. The degree of human variation in sinus patterns based on size, asymmetry, outline, partial septia, and supraorbital cells makes effective comparison for identification, providing antemortem data is available and of adequate quality.[15,16,17,18] In fact, the availability of adequate antemortem images and/or records is a key determinant of the value of radiography in identification of remains.

The most commonly used methods of identification (such as fingerprints, DNA analysis, etc.) depend, to a greater or lesser extent, upon the integrity of the soft tissues of remains.[19] In some cases involving skeletonization, fragmentation, decomposition, incineration, mutilation, or other disfigurement, identification by means of the skeleton and highly resilient dentition assume a greater importance; it is here that x-ray imaging comes into its own.

12.2   Radiography Procedures in the Identification of Human Remains

A wide range of imaging modalities have been reported to be of value in mass fatality incidents. Fluoroscopy (real time "live" scanning) provides an effective anatomical overview, together with health and safety assurance, by demonstrating foreign artifacts such as explosives and clinical sharps (needles, scalpel, etc.); plain film (x-ray "photography") and dental radiography demonstrate skeletal and dental detail to complement the pathological, anthropological, and odontological examination of the deceased (see Figure 12.1).

The Association of Forensic Radiographers (2004) recommends that initial radiography examination should commence prior to or concomitant with the provisional external examination of the body and before autopsy.[20] Fluoroscopy is the imaging modality of choice at this point, providing real-time imaging for the demonstration of skeletal material, commingling, personal artifacts, or clothing, ballistic material, and other forensic evidence. Comprehensive, full-body examinations can be completed in less than 10 minutes with the rapid acquisition of a permanent (digital or hard-copy) record of physical evidence. Experience in pattern recognition equips the radiography practitioner to guide

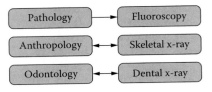

Figure 12.1   Radiography imaging provision in the mass fatality investigation (recommended work flow).

the pathologist in the interpretation of the images produced and their significance in the autopsy examination. It has been accepted as good practice that these interpretations are documented at the time of the examination to be used as reference and are included in the investigation documentation.[20]

Plain film radiography plays an important role in the provision of highly detailed anthropological images for assessment and comparison.[21-23] Timeframes for examinations of this nature are dependent on image acquisition methodologies and can be up to approximately 90 minutes in duration. However, the advent of digital x-ray imaging equipment allows superior, rapid visualization using a broad spectrum of imaging parameters to allow optimal demonstration of soft and hard tissue on the same image, with greatly reduced examination times.[24]

Dental radiography is also extensively used in conjunction with the odontological examination to assist and, in some cases, confirm postmortem identifications. Most recently dental radiography was imperative in the postmortem identification of victims of the Asian tsunami of 2004 and London terrorist bombings in 2005. These three modalities, though frequently used extensively in the temporary mortuary for mass fatality investigations, are also of significant value in the establishment of routine postmortem identification of unknown and archaeological remains.

Other modalities of use include computed tomography (CT) and magnetic resonance imaging (MRI), which allow effective representation of three-dimensional structures. Though antemortem CT scans assisted in identifying an individual by comparison with postmortem lateral skull radiographs in 1993,[25] the first reported confirmation of identification using CT was in 1995.[26] Similarly, comparison of cranial CT images led to the positive identification of an unknown individual in 2002.[27] With the volume of cranial CT scans in the U.K. increasing,[28] there is the potential for a much larger database of antemortem cranial CT images, but there is also a need for a comparison tool to allow accurate matching of postmortem data; this presents difficulties because of the various different software packages used by CT scanner manufacturers. In addition, lumbar spine CT images were compared, and demonstrated identically placed Schmorl's nodes, ileal lucency, and disc herniation alongside similarities in vertebral structure.[29] Cost and availability implications of computed tomography examinations result in the restriction of these procedures to specialist service providers. The extent of digital data that requires retention for individual scanning equipment will determine the length of time this information will be retained, with the average CT scanning department keeping full examinations for 3–5 years.

Recent publications by Thali have supported the use of MRI as a virtual autopsy tool.[30] These found MRI and CT techniques to be "superior to autopsy in revealing certain cases of cranial, skeletal, or tissue trauma" and stated that "radiological imaging techniques are particularly beneficial for reconstruction and visualization of forensic cases." A 4-year study in 2002 established confident diagnoses in 87% of cases examined by MRI. Bisset suggests that MRI can, in some situations, be an effective alternative to necropsy.[31] Although MRI has been used to establish cause of death and injury patterns,[32,33] little has been published regarding its use in the identification process due to its restricted availability in routine postmortem examinations. However, changing cultural, religious, and society values, coupled with controversies over organ removal and retention, have seen a significant increase in the use of this modality in postmortem examination.

12.3 Human Profiling and Radiography

There are a number of radiological standards for determination of bone age, although the range of standard deviations for skeletal maturation of various ages is quite broad. The majority of the current radiological standards are based on Caucasian populations, and greater standard deviations may be found in different ancestries, which need to be used with reservation as bone age in late childhood and adolescents for certain populations may exceed the chronological age by up to 11.5 months.[34] However, radiography of the hand and wrist is still used as a rapid, cost-effective, and comparatively accurate method of the age estimation of children. Although calcification of the costal cartilages may be visualized in younger subjects, it is rarely seen under the age of 30 and more readily seen in the over-50s.[35] Research has demonstrated that, although chest radiography demonstrates this calcification, its specificity can be reduced due to similar amounts of mineralization throughout adulthood,[36] but it was recognized that this was a quick, inexpensive method to obtain a general age estimate in the absence of a forensic anthropologist.

Various other profile markers, including gender, stature, height, etc., can accurately be represented using radiographic imaging to provide a permanent record for review and future referral if necessary.

12.4 Role of the Radiographer in the Identification of Human Remains

As stated by the College of Radiographers (1999), only persons trained specifically in medical imaging are appropriate to practice forensic radiography and should receive regular training as part of continuing professional development.[37] It is therefore reasonable to expect the radiographer to be competent in a wide range of imaging modalities and comprehensive service provision, both in the temporary and in the hospital mortuary within the U.K. However, due to the *ad hoc* responses to national and international mass fatality incidents in the past, a need was established to develop a response team to provide forensic radiography services in such situations without draining the local resources. The recently established Association of Forensic Radiographers (AFR) was launched in 2005 as the specialist interest group in forensic radiography and is professionally recognized for its development and promotion of best practices in forensic radiography and the provision of training and education in this field. This organization is also frequently called upon to conduct risk assessments and provide expertise with particular regard to radiation protection, manual handling, and health and safety issues in the radiography service provision within the hospital or emergency temporary mortuary. A coordinated U.K. response team of radiography practitioners specifically trained in forensic radiography provides a new approach to delivering a comprehensive imaging service on a national level and is now included in the temporary mortuary plans of local authorities of the U.K.

Radiography practice in the U.K. falls under the Ionising Radiation (Medical Exposure) Regulations 2000[38] and the Ionisation Radiations Regulations (1999).[39] As such, responsibility for x-ray exposure justification and minimization of radiation risk to staff working in the proximity of the examination falls within the professional duty of the radiography practitioner.

12.5   Conclusion

During the first 50 years following Roentgen's announcement of the discovery of x-rays, radiography rapidly developed as an essential tool in many fields of scientific investigation including those of forensic medicine, pathology, and human investigation. In recent years, however, developments in these fields have increasingly lagged behind developments in medical investigation. New technologies such as ultrasound, CT scanning, and magnetic resonance imaging have become essential tools for the physician, offering noninvasive methods of diagnosis and three-dimensional reconstruction with impressive image quality. Older techniques such as angiography and fluoroscopy have been coupled with advances in medical instrumentation to allow previously complex and highly invasive operations to be performed quickly and simply using radiologically controlled "keyhole surgery" referred to as "interventional radiology."

The field of forensic medicine pathology and human identification has struggled to keep pace with the speed of these changes, and the high price of such technology has prohibited its use for examination of the deceased in all but the most complex of cases. However, Cordner and McKelvie recognize differences in "national standards" in the identification of missing persons and recommend international standards.[40] To this means, radiography has a significant role to play in the objective, permanent capture of physical evidence to assist and, in some cases, confirm postmortem identification.

Increasingly, in the U.K. and elsewhere, the invasive nature of autopsy and post-mortem methods of data collection for identification are coming under closer scrutiny. The greater awareness of cultural and humanitarian issues are forcing society to reexamine some of the methods traditionally employed and look for alternate, less invasive methods of data collection.

It has previously been (and still is, in many countries) standard practice to resect mandible and maxillae from a cadaver to allow them to be taken to a dental center for examination and radiography. However, on-site access to intraoral radiography and odontology is now recognized as an essential requirement for the management of such cases. Some centers are now investigating the use of postmortem CT scanning as a method of dental imaging, obtaining by multiplanar reconstruction similar results to those obtained from an antemortem pan-oral radiograph, thus permitting accurate comparison and identification.

The rapid decline in the use of skull radiographs for diagnosis of antemortem pathologies in hospitals as a result of the introduction of CT scanning is beginning to render the technique of comparing antemortem and postmortem radiographs of the paranasal sinuses obsolete as an identification technique. The CT and MRI scan are now the imaging techniques of choice for examination of the skull and brain in the living subject and identification via comparison of antemortem and postmortem scans has been shown to be an effective substitute for comparison of plain film radiographs. It is not, however, a widely used technique due to the unavailability of CT scanners for examination of the deceased.

The forensic community must grasp the challenge posed by the pace of change in radiological techniques. Within a few years, most medical imaging will be undertaken by digital methods — from CT and MRI to "simple" radiographs taken using direct digital or computed radiography techniques. Such technology has enormous potential for the investigator. Highly accurate measurements can be taken from living subjects of known demographic data, allowing population specific anthropological data to be obtained and updated for postmortem evaluation of the deceased. The wide dynamic range offered by digital radiography permits both soft tissue and bone detail to be visualized from the same image.

Images can be superimposed digitally to prove a positive identification, and can be transmitted electronically to permit evaluation by a remote specialist or with antemortem data in a different location.

The decreasing cost of image storage is leading many hospitals to question the need to delete data after a set period of time, and many are keeping such information for much longer periods than was usual. This may lead to the collation of a large reservoir of antemortem material, forming a valuable resource for the investigator.

The speed and image quality of modern digital fluoroscopy images permits rapid evaluation of the victims of mass fatality incidents, allowing pathological features and dental or surgical intervention to be recorded for later evaluation, location, and retrieval of personal effects and small body parts, as well as items of forensic evidence. It has already established itself as an essential tool in the investigation of mass fatality incidents and large-scale human rights abuses.

The portability and ease of use of such equipment lends itself to application in both the mortuary and field situations, thus increasing its availability and offering greater opportunities for the investigator.

The scope of radiology, therefore, has opened the door to a range of future possibilities for the use of radiographic imaging in multidisciplinary human identification.

Further Reading

Asnaes, S. and Paakes, F., Uncertainty of determining mode of death in medicolegal material without autopsy: a systematic autopsy study, *Forensic Sci Int* 15, 3–17, 1980.

Atkins, L. and Potsaid, M., Roentgenographic identification of human remains, *JAMA* 240, 2307–2308, 1978.

Baker, M. and Hughes, N., The Provision of Forensic Radiography: A Research Survey Report, unpublished report, University of Central England, Birmingham, 1997.

Christensen, A.M., Assessing the variation in individual frontal sinus outlines, *Am J Phys Anthropol* 127, 3, 291–295, 2004

Fischman, L., The use of medical and dental radiographs in identification, *Int Dent J* 35, 301–306, 1985.

Greulich, W., Skeletal features visible on the Roentgenogram of the hand and wrist which can be used for establishing identity, *Am J Roentgenol* 83, 756–764, 1960.

Kahana, T. and Hiss, J., Forensic radiology, *Br J Radiol* 72, 129–133, 1999.

Mora, S. et al., Skeletal age determinations in children of European and African descent: Applicability of the Greulich and Pyle Standards, *Pediatric Research*, 50, 5, 624–628, 2001.

Murphy, W.A., Sprull, F.G., and Ganther, G.E., Radiographic identification of unknown human remains, *J Forensic Sci* 24(4), 727–735, 1980.

Rhine, S. and Sperry, K., Radiographic identification by mastoid sinus and arterial pattern, *J Forensic Sci* 36, 272–279, 1991.

References

1. Roentgen, W.C., A new kind of ray. Sitzungsberichte der Würzburger, *Phys-Med Ges* 137, 132–141, 1895 [German].

2. Brogdon, B.G. and Lichtenstein, J.E., Forensic radiology in historical perspective, in *Forensic Radiology*, Brogdon, B.G., Ed., CRC Press, Boca Raton, FL, 1998, p. 25, chap.2.

3. Goodman, P.C., The new light: discovery and introduction of the x-ray, *Am J Roentgenol* 165, 1041, 1995.

4. Levinsohn, Beitraz zur feststellung der identitat, *Arch Krim-Anthrop Leipzig* 2, 221, 1899.

5. Fischman, S.L., The use of medical and dental radiographs in identification, *Int Dent J* 35, 301–306, 1985.

6. Kahana, T. and Hiss, J., Identification of human remains: forensic radiology, *J Forensic Med* 4, 7–15, 1997.

7. Scwartz, S. and Woolridge, E.D., The use of panoramic radiographs for comparison in cases of identification, *J Forensic Sci* 31, 145–146, 1976.

8. Dimond, B., *Legal Aspects of Radiography and Radiology*, Blackwell Science, Oxford, 2002.

9. Culbert, W.C. and Law, F.M., Identification by comparison of roentgenograms of nasal accessory sinuses and mastoid process, *J Am Med Assoc* 88(4), 1634–1636, 1927.

10. Kahana, T. and Hiss, J., Positive identification by means of trabecular bone pattern comparison, *J Forensic Sci* 39(5), 1325–1330, 1994.

11. Kullman, L., Eklund, B., and Grundin, R., The value of the frontal sinus in identification of unknown persons, *J Forensic Odontostomatol* 8(1), 3–10, 1990.

12. Messmer J.M. and Fierro M.F., Personal identification by radiographic comparison of vascular groove patterns of the calverium, *Am J Forensic Med Pathol* 7(2), 159–162, 1986.

13. Kahana, T. and Hiss, J., Suprapelvic and pelvic phleboliths — a reliable radiographic marker for positive identification, *J Clin Forensic Med* 9, 115–118, 2002.

14. Culbert, W.L. and Law, F.M., Identification by comparison of roentgenograms of nasal accessory sinuses and mastoid processes, *JAMA* 88, 1632–1636, 1927.

15. Reichs, K and Dorion, R.B.J., The use of computed tomography (CT) scans in the analysis of frontal sinus configuration, *Can Soc Forensic Sci J* 25, 1, 1992.

16. Nambiar, P., Naidu, M.D., and Subramaniam, K., Anatomical variability of the frontal sinuses and their application in forensic identification, *Clin Anat* 12, 16–19, 1999.

17. Marlin, D.C., Clark, M.A., and Standish, S.M., Identification of human remains by comparison of frontal sinus radiographs: a series of four cases, *J Forensic Sci* 36, 1765–1772, 1991.

18. Kirk, N.J., Wood, R.E., and Goldstein, M., Skeletal identification using the frontal sinus region: a retrospective study of 39 cases, *J Forensic Sci* 47, 318–323, 2002.

19. Brogdon, B.G., Vogel, H., and McDowell, J., *A Radiologic Atlas of Abuse, Torture and Inflicted Trauma*, CRC Press, Boca Raton, FL, 2003, p. 246, chap. 22.

20. Radiography facilities for temporary emergency mortuaries in the event of a mass fatality incident (unpublished paper), The Association of Forensic Radiographers, London, 2004.

21. Martel, W., Wicks, J.D., Hendrix, R.C., The accuracy of radiological identification of humans using skeletal landmarks: a contribution to forensic pathology, *Radiology* 124, 681–684, 1977.

22. Leichtenstein, J., Fitpatrick, J., and Madewell, J., The role of radiology in fatality investigations, *Am J Roentgenol* 150, 751–755, 1998.

23. Buchner, A., The identification of human remains, *Int Dent J* 35, 307–311, 1985.

24. Association of Forensic Radiographers, The Role of Radiography in the London Bombings, 2005 (unpublished).

25. Haglund, W.D., Fligner, C.L., Ulmeke, D., Ogbuihi, S., and Schweden, F., Confirmation of human identification using computerized tomography (CT), *J Forensic Sci* 38, 708–712, 1993.

26. Riepert, T. et al., Identification of an unknown corpse by means of computed tomography (CT) of the lumbar spine, *J Forensic Sci* 40, 126–127, 1995.

27. Smith, D.R., Limbird, K.G., and Hoffman, J.M., Identification of human skeletal remains by comparison of bony details of the cranium using computerised tomography (CT) scans, *J. Forensic Sci* 47, 937–939, 2002.

28. National Institute for Clinical Excellence, Clinical Guideline 4: Head injury: triage, assessment, investigation and early management of head injury in infants, children and adults, Oaktree Press, London, 2003.

29. Riepert, T. and Rittner, C. et al., Identification of an unknown corpse by means of computed tomography of the lumbar spine, *J Forensic Sci* 40(1), 126–127, 1995.

30. Thali, M.J. et al., Virtopsy, a new imaging horizon in forensic pathology: virtual autopsy by post-mortem multislice computed tomography (MSCT) and magnetic resonance imaging (MRI) — a feasibility study, *J Forensic Sci* 48, 386–403, 2003.

31. Bisset R.A.L, Thomas N.B, Turnbull, I.W, and Lee S., Post-mortem examinations magnetic resonance imaging: four year review of a working service, *Br Med J* 324, 1423–1424, 2002.

32. Thali, M.J. et al., Charred body: virtual autopsy with multi-slice computed tomography and magnetic resonance imaging, *J Forensic Sci* 47, 1326–1331, 2002.

33. Plattner, T. et al., Virtopsy: post-mortem multislice computed tomography (MSCT) and magnetic resonance imaging (MRI) in a fatal scuba diving incident, *J Forensic Sci* 48, 1347–1355, 2003.

34. Ontell, F.K., et al., Bone age in children of diverse ethnicity, *Am J Roentgenol*, 167, 1395, 1997.

35. Mora, S. et al., Applicability of the Greulich and Pyle standards, *Pediatr Res* 50, 624–812, 2001.

36. McCormick, W.F., Mineralization of the costal cartilages as an indicator of age: preliminary observations, *J Forensic Sci* 25, 736–741, 1980.

37. Guidance for the Provision of Forensic Radiography Services, The College of Radiographers, London, 1999.

38. Ionising Radiation (Medical Exposure) Regulations, Statutory Instrument No. 1059, Crown Copyright ISBN 0717617467, 2000.

39. Ionising Radiations Regulations, Statutory Instrument 1999 No. 3232, Crown Copyright ISBN0110856147, 1999.

40. Cordner S. and McKelvie H., Developing standards in international forensic work to identify missing persons, *Int Rev Red Cross* 84, 867–884, 2002.

Section 5

Facial Identification

Facial Anthropology and Reconstruction

13

CAROLINE WILKINSON

Contents

13.1 Skeletal Remains 233
   13.1.1 Access to Original Specimen...235
   13.1.2 Three-Dimensional Skull Models from Clinical Imaging 237
   13.1.3 Three-Dimensional Skull Models from Limited Two-Dimensional Data...240
   13.1.4 Two-Dimensional Images...240
13.2 Soft Tissue Remains..242
13.3 Methods of Facial Reconstruction..245
   13.3.1 Two-Dimensional Facial Reconstruction 245
   13.3.2 Three-Dimensional Facial Reconstruction 246
13.4 Presentation of the Facial Reconstruction to the General Public.......248
References 251

In some forensic investigations the usual methods utilized for human identification can be unsuccessful, and the police may have few clues as to the identity of an individual. The majority of identification techniques require a known individual with whom to compare data, such as DNA, fingerprints, or dental records, and where there are no suspects for identification, it is practically impossible to compare data with records from an entire population. In these circumstances the police may employ less definitive methods in an attempt to focus on a population from which the individual may be identified. Facial reconstruction is one of the methods that is frequently employed in such investigations.

Facial reconstruction (otherwise known as *facial approximation*) is the process utilized to reproduce the facial appearance of an individual and includes a number of different procedures. Traditionally, facial reconstruction has involved the analysis of skeletal detail to determine facial morphology. However, facial soft tissues may be present as partially decomposed, damaged, distorted, or preserved remains. In these cases it may not be appropriate to present images of the remains to the public, and facial reconstruction is utilized to visualize facial appearance. In these circumstances the practitioner will analyze the soft tissues rather than skeletal detail, although it may be possible to analyze both soft and hard tissues where clinical imaging or dissection are employed.

Facial reconstruction practitioners have evolved from a variety of backgrounds, which include forensic anthropology, anatomy, medical art, and computer science. Different approaches in this field have created some confusion with regard to the reliability and presentation of a facial reconstruction within a forensic scenario. Some practitioners attempt to reproduce a facial "type," an approximation of the facial proportions and morphology that relies on sets of average tissue data and facial templates relating to the sex, age, and ethnic group of the individual (Evison et al. 1999, Vanezis et al. 2000, Stephan 2004). These practitioners believe that current methods are inexact and can merely suggest a facial type that may apply to many other skulls or faces. Therefore, many facial variations from the same skull may be produced in an attempt to narrow the field for identification and inspire recognition from the public. These practitioners prefer the term *facial approximation* to describe the procedure. Other practitioners believe that the face and the skull directly affect one another and that it is possible to determine facial morphology from skeletal detail with enough reliability to produce a recognizable depiction of the individual (Gerasimov 1971, Prag and Neave 1997, Wilkinson 2004). These practitioners attempt to characterize the individual by determining idiosyncratic facial detail, and only one face will be produced from each skull. These practitioners prefer the term *facial reconstruction* to describe the procedure, as this is their ultimate aim.

Facial reconstruction practitioners have carried out studies that suggest good levels of accuracy for their methods (Snow et al. 1970, Prag and Neave 1997, Wilkinson and Whittaker 2002), whereas facial approximation practitioners produce results that suggest estimation alone is possible (Helmer et al. 1989, Van Rensburg 1993, Stephan and Henneberg 2001). Facial reconstructors argue that approximators are inexperienced and do not analyze all the available skeletal information, therefore miss vital clues to facial morphology (Gerasimov 1971) and rely too heavily upon preexisting faces, either as computer-generated templates (Vanezis et al. 2000) or references for ethnic stereotypes (Evison 2002). Approximators respond that reconstruction relies heavily upon anecdotal standards and intuition (Stephan 2004) and that success in forensic investigations may be related to publicity and media interest rather than any resemblance to the target individual (Evison 1996). All these views hold some truth.

Without question, facial reconstruction or approximation has been a valuable tool for forensic investigations, and many individuals have been successfully identified as a direct result of a publicity campaign employing a facial reconstruction or approximation. In the U.K., practitioners report success rates of 70%[*] and 64%,[**] whereas in the U.S. 50% (Caldwell 1981) and 75% (Haglund and Raey 1991). To what degree the facial reconstructions were directly responsible for recognition, and thus identification, is unclear from these success rates. Success rates may be determined a number of ways, but perhaps the most useful calculation is to show the number of forensic cases where the facial reconstruction generated recognition leading to identification as a percentage of the total number of cases employing facial reconstruction work. It must be noted that this will inevitably lead to changing success rates in different publications, as annual variation in the numbers of cases and successes will produce fluctuations. It must also be noted that facial reconstruction is not a method of identification, rather a tool for recognition to produce a list of names from which the individual may be identified by DNA assessment, dental record analysis, or other accepted methods of identification.

This chapter will attempt to summarize the different circumstances where facial reconstruction may be utilized for human identification and will describe the techniques available. As the analysis and study of the skull and face can be described as facial anthropology, I will hereafter describe both reconstruction and approximation practitioners as facial anthropologists.

---

[*] Reported success rate from the University of Manchester, 1982–2005. Number of forensic cases = 23, number of successful cases = 16, success rate = 70%.
[**] Current success rate for Caroline Wilkinson, 1997–2005: number of forensic cases = 11, number of successful cases = 7, success rate = 64%.

13.1 Skeletal Remains

Where skeletal remains alone are available, the facial anthropologist will usually have access to the skull for assessment. Skeletal remains are the commonest presentation, as identification will be limited by the amount of forensic evidence. It is rare that the facial anthropologist will have been involved in the investigation from its onset and often prior analysis of the remains will have been invasive (i.e., postmortem or dental assessment). Photographs from the scene and/or postmortem may be invaluable, and where destructive analysis is utilized by the coroner or odontologist, photographs should be taken prior to any procedures.

However the skull is visualized, the facial anthropologist will carry out a skull assessment prior to the facial reconstruction or approximation procedure. Facial anthropologists should be able to carry out a detailed skull assessment, including determination of sex, age, ancestry, and facial morphology. Ideally, a team of experts, including a forensic anthropologist, pathologist, and odontologist, will be employed to provide the maximum amount of information prior to the facial reconstruction or approximation. Skull assessment guidelines with regard to facial feature determination from skeletal morphology have been presented in several publications (Gerasimov 1955, Krogman and Iscan 1986, Fedosyutkin and Nainys 1993, Taylor 2001, Stephan 2002, Wilkinson and Mautner 2003, Wilkinson et al. 2003, Stephan 2003a, Stephan 2003b, Wilkinson 2004).

The skull is made up of approximately 22 bones (excluding Wormian bones and ear ossicles), consisting of 14 facial bones and 8 vault bones:

The *skull* is the entire skeletal framework of the head.
The *mandible* is the lower jaw.
The *cranium* is the skull without the mandible.
The *calvaria* is the cranium without the face.
The *Frankfurt Horizontal Plane* is reached when a horizontal line passes through the inferior border of the orbit (*orbitale*) and the anterior margin of the external auditory meatus (*porion*).

Figure 13.1 and Figure 13.2 illustrate the position and name of each of the bones of the skull and describe common cranial terms.

Most methods of facial reconstruction or approximation utilize soft tissue data, and these tissue depth measurements should be chosen from the most appropriate data set, dependant upon the ethnic group, sex, and age of the individual. There are a large number of datasets from all over the world including White European (Helmer 1984); Indian (Sahni 2002); North American Black, White, and Hispanic (Manhein et al. 2000); South African mixed race (Phillips and Smuts 1996); Japanese (Suzuki 1948); Egyptian (El-Mehallawi and Soliman 2001); Zulu (Auslebrook et al. 1996) Korean; Buryat; Kazakh; Bashhir; Uzbek; Armenian; Abkhazian; Russian; Lithuanian (Lebedinskaya et al. 1993); and Southwestern Indian (Rhine, 1983) for adults, and White European (Wilkinson 2002) and North American White, Black, and Hispanic (Manhein et al. 2000) for juveniles. Figure 13.3 describes common cranial landmarks employed in tissue depth analysis and facial reconstruction.

Methods of skull visualization and analysis will vary, dependent upon the circumstances of the investigation, given as follows.

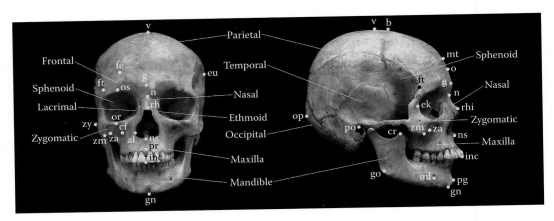

Figure 13.1   Bones of the skull and common cranial terms.

al	Alare	The most lateral point on the margin of the nasal aperture
b	Bregma	Cranial point where the coronal and sagittal sutures intersect
cf	Canine fossa	The deepest point at the canine fossa. Also known as maxillary point
cr	Coronion	Point at the tip of the coronoid process of the mandible
ek	Ectoconchion	The most lateral point on the orbital margin
eu	Euryon	Cranial point where the cranial breadth is greatest
fe	Frontal eminence	A point between the metopion and the ophryon on the lateral frontal bone, directly above the midpoint of the eyebrow
ft	Frontotemporale	Lateral point from the elevation of the linea temporalis, or the terminal points of the tail of the eyebrow
g	Glabella	The most anterior midline point on the frontal bone above the frontonasal suture
gn	Gnathion	The most inferior midline point on the mandible
go	Gonion	Point at the center of the mandibular angle
inc	Incision	Point where the central incisors meet on the occlusal line
l	Lambda	Cranial midline point where the sagittal and lambdoidal sutures intersect
mt	Metopion	Cranial midline point on the frontal bone where the elevation of the curve is greatest
ml	Mentale	The most inferior point on the margin of the mental foramen
n	Nasion	Point in the midline where the nasal bones and the frontal bone intersect
ns	Nasospinale	Midline point of a tangent between the most inferior points of the nasal aperture
o	Ophryon	The most anterior midline point of the forehead
op	Opisthocranion	Midline cranial point on the occipital bone that is most distant from the glabella
or	Infraorbital	The most inferior point on the orbital margin. Also known as orbitale
os	Supraorbital	The most superior point on the orbital margin
pg	Pogonion	The most anterior midline point on the chin
po	Porion	The uppermost point on the margin of the external auditory meatus
pr	Prosthion	The most anterior midline point on the alveolar process of the maxilla
rhi	Rhinion	The midline point at the inferior end of the internasal suture
v	Vertex	The highest midline cranial point on the skull, in the Frankfurt plane
za	Zygomatic	Point of the zygomatic muscle attachments on the cheek bone. Also known as malare
zm	Zygomaxillare	The most inferior point on the zygomaticomaxillary suture
zy	Zygion	The most lateral point on the lateral surface of the zygomatic arch

13.1.1 Access to Original Specimen

The skull may be fragile in parts and should be handled above a soft surface, such as a foam sheet or padded layer, and stabilized to prevent rolling. Care should be taken when handling the skull, and both hands should always be used. The orbital bones, nasal bones, sinus bones, and zygomatic arches may be damaged easily and should not be used to grip the skull.

Frequently, the skull is presented incomplete and fragmented, when deliberate or accidental trauma, burial distortion, or bone demineralization has occurred. In these cases the skull must be reassembled before the facial reconstruction procedure can continue (see Figure 13.1). Dental wax (Wilkinson and Neave 2001) or vinyl acetate (Knott 2002) can be used to glue the skull fragments together (Figure 13.4), and these materials are optimal for reassembly as reshuffling of the fragments can be achieved by loosening the adherence.

Manual skull reassembly can be very time consuming and painstaking, but must be carried out with the maximum degree of accuracy as a small error in alignment will be greatly magnified throughout the whole skull. The advice of a pathologist or forensic anthropologist as to the cause of any distortion will be invaluable. Dental wax can be removed with warm water or steam application, and vinyl acetate can be removed using dental tools, but even experienced manual reassembly will include some risk of material impregnation. The surface of the bone may be removed through handling and removal of glue materials, and heat and water application may cause irreversible skeletal damage. Although these risks are low with experienced facial anthropologists, they must be considered as they may have an effect upon any further analysis.

Any missing areas are modeled in wax onto the skull (see Figure 13.3). Unilateral missing areas can be modeled from the available area on the other side of the skull, so that a mirror image is created. Very few skulls are symmetrical. This modeling technique does create some errors, as the resulting skull will have false symmetry. Where the missing areas of the skull are from unilateral features, or where both sides of the skull have absent areas, they are estimated using the surrounding bones as guides. Research has shown that most areas of the skull can be estimated with reasonable accuracy, apart from the mandible (Colledge 1996). A mandible that has been estimated from the cranium alone may have a large detrimental effect upon the accuracy of any resultant facial reconstruction.

Some facial anthropologists will mount the original specimen and work directly on the bone during the facial reconstruction/approximation procedure (Taylor 2001). The risk of damage to the specimen with this method must be considered, as the weight of modeling clay, the armature mounts and the pressure applied to the skull by the facial anthropologist may cause fracture, fragmentation, or even destruction of the skeletal material. In addition, the modeling clay may permanently adhere to the surface of the bone or impregnate the internal skeletal structure, and thorough cleaning may not be possible, leading to irreversible material impregnation. This may have implications for future biological analysis in forensic or archaeological investigations. It is also worth noting that when the modeling material is applied directly to the original specimen, the skull becomes more and more obscured. This does not allow reference to skeletal morphology during the procedure.

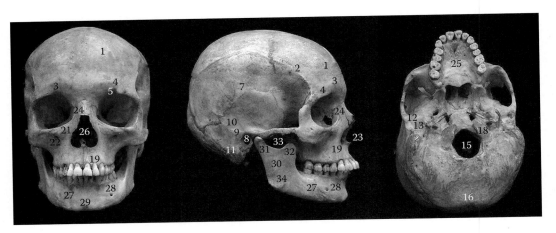

Figure 13.2 Common cranial landmarks.

1	*Frontal eminences*	Paired frontal bossing
2	*Temporal lines*	Mark the attachment of the temporalis muscles on the lateral cranial surfaces of the frontal and parietal bones
3	*Superciliary arches and brow ridges*	Bony prominences above the orbits
4	*Supraorbital margins*	The upper orbital edges
5	*Supraorbital notches* or *foramina*	Holes that pierce the supraorbital margin to transmit the supraorbital nerve
6	*Metopic suture*	Vertical suture between the right and left halves of the frontal bone (not shown on image). Usually obliterates by adulthood
7	*Parietal striae*	Striations or rays that pass posterosuperiorly on the cranial surface of the parietal bone from its bevelled squamosal edge
8	*External auditory* meatus	External opening of the ear canal
9	*Suprameatal crest*	Raised edge that runs horizontally above the external auditory meatus
10	*Supramastoid crest*	Raised edge that marks the inferior limit of the temporalis attachment
11	*Mastoid process*	Lump on the temporal bone where the sternocleidomastoid, splenius capitis and longissimus capitis muscles attach
12	*Articular eminence*	Anterior portion of the temperomandibular articular surface
13	*Mandibular fossa (glenoid fossa)*	Hole lying posterosuperior to the anterior eminence
14	*Styloid process*	Thin, pointed, bony rod from the base of the temporal bone (not shown on image)
15	*Foramen magnum*	Large hole in the occipital bone through which the brain stem passes into the vertebral canal
16	*External occipital protruberance*	Lies on the midline where the occipital and nuchal planes meet
17	*External occipital crest*	Highly variable median line that passes between left and right nuchal musculature (not shown on image)
18	*Occipital condyles*	Raised oval structures on either side of the foramen magnum
19	*Alveolar process*	Horizontal portion of the maxilla that holds the tooth roots
20	*Alveoli*	Holes for the tooth roots (not shown on image)
21	*Infraorbital foramen*	Located below the infraorbital margin and transmits the infraorbital nerve
22	*Canine fossa*	Hollow of variable depth located on the facial surface below the infraorbital foramen
23	*Anterior nasal spine*	Thin projection of bone on the midline of the inferior surface of the nasal aperture
24	*Anterior lacrimal crest*	Vertical crest located on the lateral aspect of the nasal bones

Figure 13.2 (continued) Common cranial landmarks.

25	*Incisive foramen*	Hole that perforates the anterior hard palate at the midline
26	*Vomer*	Small, thin, midline bone that divides the nasal cavity
27	*Corpus of the mandible*	Body of the mandible that anchors the teeth
28	*Mental foramen*	Large hole on the lateral corpus surface below the premolar region of the mandible, to transmit the mental vessels
29	*Mental eminence*	Triangular bony chin at the base of the corpus
30	*Ramus of the mandible*	Vertical part of the mandible that articulates with the cranial base
31	*Mandibular condyle*	Large, rounded, articular prominence on end of ramus, which articulates the temperomandibular joint
32	*Coronoid process*	Thin, triangular part of ramus where the temporalis muscle inserts
33	*Mandibular notch*	Depression between the condyle and the coronoid process
34	*Gonial angle*	Rounded posteroinferior corner of the mandible

Many facial anthropologists will produce a copy of the original specimen on which to carry out the facial reconstruction/approximation (Prag and Neave 1997, Wilkinson 2004). Such copies are usually plaster or acrylic casts made from alginate or silicone molds (see Figure 13.5). There are detailed published descriptions of manual skull replication (Taylor and Angel 1998). Mold-making is a complicated and time-consuming craft, and a great deal of specialized experience is necessary for skull replication. It is not recommended that inexperienced practitioners carry out skull replication on human remains involved in forensic or archaeological investigations, as irreparable damage may occur that may preclude further forensic analysis or historical documentation. Any risks to the original specimen can be minimized by foil protection of the skull and scrupulous preparation, and the experienced mold maker will not cause any damage to the original specimen.

13.1.2 Three-Dimensional Skull Models from Clinical Imaging

Where soft tissues are present, access to the original specimen is restricted or computer-based facial reconstruction or approximation is planned. Cross-sectional data created by x-ray computed tomography (CT) or surface scans can be employed to produce a three-dimensional digital model of the skull (Spoor et al. 2000). Sometimes replica skulls may be produced from digital data using stereolithography (Hjalgrim et al. 1995) or another form of three-dimensional model manufacture (Seitz et al. 2005) (see Figure 13.6).

Where digital data from surface scans and CT scans are employed the limitations of the data must be taken into account. With CT data, the slice thickness, scan plane, spatial resolution, filters, and angle of rotation will all affect the resulting three-dimensional model. In addition, dental filling and appliances will cause artifacts and may require some manual intervention.

A variety of software packages render the surface cross-sectional CT data by extracting selected tissues and visualizing the tissues as three-dimensional models for use in computer-based facial reconstruction or approximation systems, or for production of a physical replica. Surface rendering involves segmentation (isolation of the tissue by thresholding), interpolation between the slices to create a smooth surface, and illumination of the surface. Spoor and his colleagues (2000) state that "However, improved visual representation [is, this]does not imply that the image is more accurate as well. The extent to which the reconstruction reflects reality primarily depends upon limitations inherent to CT or MRI."

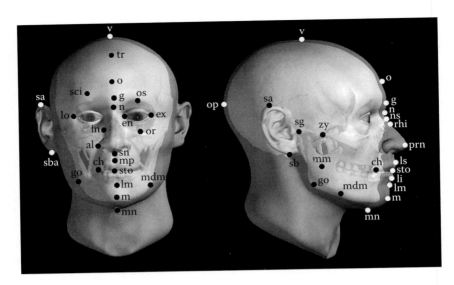

Figure 13.3 Common facial anthropometry points.

al	Alare	The most lateral point on each alar contour. Also known as supracanine
ch	Chelion	The corner of the mouth fissure
en	Endocanthion	Inner corner of the eye
ex	Exocanthion	Outer corner of the eye
g	Glabella	The most prominent midline point between the eyebrows
go	Gonion	The most lateral point on the mandibular angle, close to the bony gonion
li	Lower lip border	The midpoint of the lower vermilion line
lm	Labiomental	The midpoint of the labiomental groove. Also known as the sublabiale or supramentale point
ln	Lateral nasal	A point on the lateral nasal bone that is on the Frankfurt plane
lo	Lateral orbit	A point on the lateral orbital margin on a line with the eye fissure
ls	Upper lip border	The midpoint of the upper vermilion line
m	Mental	The most anterior midpoint of the chin, on the surface above the bony landmark
mdm	Midmandible	A point on the mandibular border inferior to the premolar region
mm	Midmasseter	A point on the occlusal line at the centre of the ramus of the mandible. Also known as the occlusal line
mn	Menton	The lowest medial landmark beneath the chin
mp	Midphiltrum	The midpoint of the philtral column
n	Nasion	The midline point of the nasal root, identical to the bony landmark
ns	Midnasal	The midpoint of the nasal bones
prn	Pronasale	The most protruding point at the tip of the nose
rhi	Rhinion	The end of the nasal bones at the cartilagebone junction
sa	Superaurale	The most superior point on the helix of the ear
sba	Subaurale	The most inferior point on the helix of the ear
sci	Superciliary	The highest midpoint of the eyebrow
sg	Supraglenoid	The point anterior to the tragus at the root of the zygoma. Also known as the pretragal point or the root of the zygoma
sn	Subnasale	The midpoint of the columella base below the nasal spine
sto	Stomion	The midpoint of the incisive line of the lips
tr	Trichion	Midpoint of the hairline
v	Vertex	The highest point on the head
zy	Zygomatic arch	Most lateral point over the zygomatic arch, identical to the bony landmark. Also known as the zygion

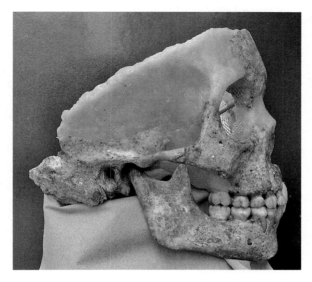

Figure 13.4   Skull fragments partially reassembled using dental wax, metal mesh, and wooden props.

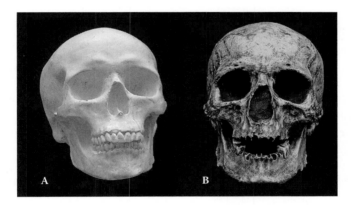

Figure 13.5   Plaster (A) and acrylic (B) skull replicas produced from silicone or alginate molds.

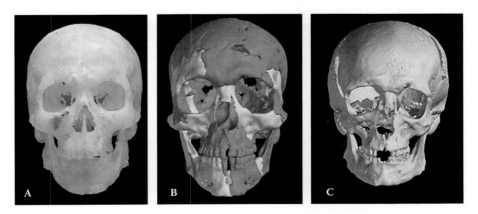

Figure 13.6   Replica skull (A) produced from (B) reassembled CT data or (C) laser scans.

With surface scan data morphology, details may also be lost due to discrepancies at apertures, fossae, and holes where the scanning mechanism cannot visualize the surface. In addition, hair on the face and the head may cause surface artifacts. As surface scanners produce a series of profiles from a number of viewpoints, which then require computational reconstruction of the object and subsequent manual editing to ascertain clean, raw data sets, there may be inconsistencies to the original specimen. Where possible, attention should be given to the original specimen, so that errors are not perpetuated to the facial reconstruction. There are many surface scanners currently available, including laser (Kau et al. 2005, Moss et al. 1989, Bush and Antonyshyn 1996), photographic projection (Yamada et al. 1999, Motoyoshi et al. 1992, Techalertpaisarn and Kuroda 1998, Curry et al. 2001, Siebert and Marshall 2000), or holographic (Bongartz et al. 2000, Giel et al. 2004), and three-dimensional models will be created that can be imported into computer-based facial reconstruction or approximation systems or employed to produce a three-dimensional replica.

Where the skull is fragmented and each piece has been scanned, reassembly can take place using some computer-based systems (see Figure 13.6). There are computer-based systems (Wilkinson 2003, Sanghera et al. 2002, Bibb et al. 2000) that allow manual reassembly on the computer in three dimensions. Computerized skull reassembly is much more efficient and rapid as no support mechanisms are necessary. Computerized remodeling of missing fragments is also easier and less time-consuming with the computer-based systems and perhaps involve a few hours of work rather than days or weeks. Some fragment-edge detail may be lost on the digital models, but access to the original specimens will avoid any resolution problems.

When replica skulls are produced from digital models using stereolithography (Hjalgrim et al. 1995) or three-dimensional printing (Seitz et al. 2005), the models will suffer from the same limitations as the original digital data. In addition, problems relating to the replication procedure may also occur, such as material fragility (susceptibility to water damage or crumbling), material resistance (difficulties with drilling or inability to bond with glues), or smoothing of some of the detail to smaller bones.

13.1.3 Three-Dimensional Skull Models from Limited Two-Dimensional Data

When access to the original specimen is not possible, either directly or via three-dimensional clinical imaging, methods of three-dimensional model production from two-dimensional data (such as radiographs, photographs, and craniometrics) may be utilized.

Radiographs and/or photographs are used as templates, and multiple views are aligned using cranial points as registration marks. Computer modeling software is then employed to create a three-dimensional model (Wilkinson 2005) or distort a template mesh (Davy et al. 2005) to reproduce the skull morphology. Extrapolation of surface morphology between the views is inevitable, and the more views that are available, the more accurate the resulting three-dimensional model of the skull will be (see Figure 13.7).

As these methods include a certain degree of estimation and loss of detail on the surface of the bone, any resulting facial reconstruction or approximation would require photographic records of the skull and an appreciation of the decrease in accuracy of any resulting face. Care must be taken when establishing anatomical landmarks.

13.1.4 Two-Dimensional Images

In certain circumstances, photographs or x-rays of the skull may be the only available information, and access to the original specimen may be restricted due to legal matters,

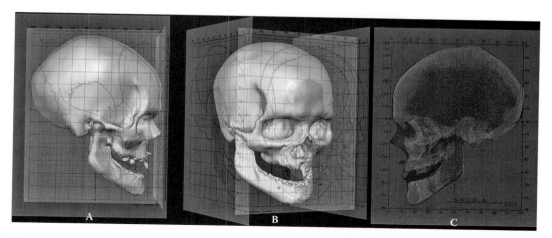

Figure 13.7 Production of a three-dimensional skull model from two-dimensional data. The skull was modeled utilizing the radiographs and scaled drawings as templates, whereas numerous craniometrics and photographs were used to provide the detail and enable accuracy. A = side view of skull model with scaled drawing as template; B = three-quarter view of skull model with all template images visible; C = side view of transparent skull model with radiograph as template. Courtesy of Caroline Wilkinson and Chris Rynn.

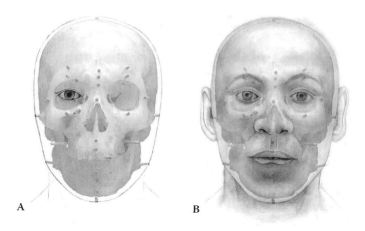

Figure 13.8 Two-dimensional facial reconstruction from a photograph of the skull. Reconstruction by Caroline Needham.

inaccessibility, destruction, or damage. Where images of the skull are considered adequate, two-dimensional facial reconstruction can be performed (see Figure 13.8). Ideally, the skull should be in the Frankfurt Horizontal Plane (FHP), and for 35mm photography, a lens with a focal length of 100–200mm and a camera position of no less than 12 ft/3 m from the skull will avoid distortion. When there is access to the original specimen, the facial anthropologist should take scaling measurements or include a visual scale in the foreground of the images.

If possible, tissue depth markers should be attached to the skull prior to production of the images to provide the maximum number of tissue indications. When this is not possible, but a scale has been included, some of the tissue depth markers can be indicated on overlays superimposed onto the images of the skull.

13.2 Soft Tissue Remains

Frequently, a body may present surviving soft tissue. It may be partially decomposed, affected by fire, water submergence, natural or artificial mummification, or burial distortion (see Figure 13.9). All available soft tissue information should be documented photographically. Where possible, the facial anthropologist should produce multiple images of the soft tissue morphology and status prior to any further examination.

Following death there are numerous soft tissue changes associated with decomposition, putrefaction, rigor mortis, bloating, etc., and many of these changes will affect the facial appearance of a cadaver.

There are a series of postmortem stages relating to human bodies, but there is a high variability to the timing of these stages, dependent upon the climate and conditions of the body. Some climates may lead to rapid deterioration of the body, so that the individual is unrecognizable in a matter of days, whereas other climates and soils will preserve a body for many centuries (e.g., peat bogs). The signs of death are usually noted as algor mortis, rigor mortis, livor mortis, and decomposition (Freedman 1996, Gordon and Shapiro 1975, Polson et al. 1985).

Algor mortis is the natural cooling in body temperature following death (latin *algor* meaning coolness and *mortis* meaning death). Circulation cessation due to cardiac inactivity and loss of skin elasticity will create early postmortem signs of flaccidity and pallor. A steady decline of body temperature will then occur to match the ambient temperature, although external factors will have a significant influence on the speed of this cooling. Body temperature will decrease faster in a cool, humid environment with air movement than a warm, dry one, and increased body exposure will lead to increased temperature decline. Thin bodies and juveniles will cool rapidly due to the surface area to body mass ratio. Furthermore, an obese body will take longer to cool because of the insulation provided by subcutaneous fat. Clothing and covers will also insulate against cooling. In addition, infections may slow the cooling process and may even cause the temperature of the body to rise for several hours after death.

Rigor mortis is described as when the limbs of the body become stiff (*rigor*) and impossible to move or manipulate. This is caused by a chemical change in the muscles and typically sets in several hours postmortem, subsiding spontaneously after several days. The time of rigor onset and duration depends on the ambient temperature, onset on average being 3 to 4 hours postmortem, with full rigor at approximately 12 hours, subsiding to relaxation at approximately 36 hours. ATP in the muscle tissue is the chemical energy source required for movement, and hydrolysis of ATP creates myosin molecules permanently attached to actin filaments, causing rigidity. The onset of rigor mortis does not follow a predictable order; however, the muscles of the face are frequently some of the first to become affected.

Livor mortis is the accumulation of blood in the capillaries of the skin due to the effects of gravity. Noncirculating blood will tend to flow downwards and consequently will accumulate in capillaries and small vessels in the lower positions of the body. Blood pooling is manifest as a purple or reddish-purple skin discoloration known as *lividity*. The torso, limbs, and earlobes of a corpse that has been laid on its back will exhibit lividity as early patchy mottling and, eventually, as extensive discoloration. Often distended blood vessels may rupture to produce a scatter of purple-black hemorrhages. Any pressure exerted upon areas of the body will prevent blood pooling at these areas and create patches of pale, bloodless skin. Livor mortis is usually apparent within 30 minutes to 2 hours postmortem, fully developing within 12 hours.

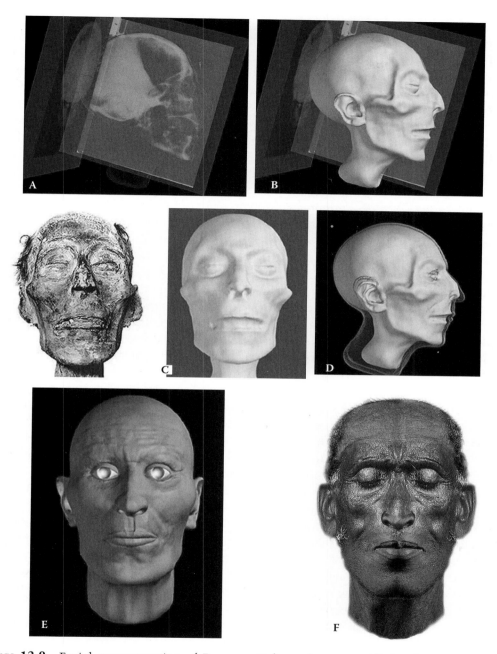

Figure 13.9 Facial reconstruction of Rameses II from the mummified soft tissue. Radiographs showing the soft tissue outlines (A) were employed as templates to create a three-dimensional model (B) of the mummified face, and the photographs (C) were used as reference for detail and accuracy. The soft tissues in life were produced by rehydrating the mummified remains (D) to establish facial appearance prior to mummification (E). Rameses II was between 87–93 years of age at death. Skin tone and texture were estimated (F). Reconstruction by Caroline Wilkinson.

Decomposition or putrefaction is the final sign of death, and is the gradual deterioration of the tissues due to bacterial and enzymatic activity. The onset of decomposition is affected by a variety of factors including environmental temperature, humidity, age, and preexisting infection. Bacteria housed in the respiratory and gastrointestinal systems and microorganisms from the environment rapidly invade and disintegrate the tissues. The first visible sign of decomposition is a green or greenish-red discoloration of the skin, where hemoglobin, from burst red blood cells, stains the surrounding tissues as it undergoes chemical breakdown. The discoloration usually begins at the skin of the abdomen and spreads to the chest, limbs, and face in a marble vein-like pattern. The skin surface becomes translucent and shiny and is a dusky reddish-green to purple-black color.

Fermentation within the body cavities also occurs due to hypoxia, and gases including methane, carbon dioxide, ammonia, and hydrogen are released. Skin blisters form filled with dark fluids and putrid gases, and the gas production will bloat the body and cause abdominal distension. The eyelids and lips become closed and swollen; the cheeks puff out, and the distended tongue may protrude between the lips. Hair, fingernails, and toenails become loose at the roots, and the abdominal cavity may burst open as the gas pressure within the body increases. Eventually, following soft tissue degradation, the connective tissue and cartilage will disintegrate, leaving only the skeleton.

When the environment is warm and moist and conditions are too acidic for bacterial activity, decomposition may not lead to skeletonization. On these rare occasions the body fat remains as adipocere, a yellow/white, waxy material, especially at the cheeks, breasts, and buttocks. The adipocere can combine with mummification to form a naturally preserved body with preserved facial features. This may take upwards of 6 months postmortem, and the body may endure for years in this condition. This process is known as *saponification*.

In conditions of dry heat with air movement, desiccation, or shriveling, of the soft tissues after death may occur. The skin around the groin, neck, and armpits will sometimes split due to shrinkage. The timescale for total *mummification* is variable, but in desert countries mummification may be complete within several weeks.

All these postmortem stages must be considered during analysis of the soft tissues. Skin color may be unreliable due to livor mortis, decomposition, or epidermal sloughing; eye color may be unreliable as putrefaction of the eyeballs will be almost immediate, and hair pattern may be unreliable due to hair loss at the roots or tissue shrinkage. In addition, insect, fish, and animal activity may cause feature distortion, facial distension, or surface marks. The jaw of the cadaver may become slack due to the relaxation of the masseter and temporalis and orbicularis oris muscles, and this may require repositioning to more realistically depict the appearance in life.

The forensic artist Karen Taylor also notes a change to the outer canthal angle following death, giving the appearance of upturned corners to the eyes (Taylor 2001). She describes this phenomenon and suggests that it may be due to a combination of the effects of gravity, position, and rigor mortis of the lateral palpebral ligaments.

Often soft tissue assessment will reveal details of facial morphology that cannot, as yet, be accurately determined from the skeleton alone (see Figure 13.10). Frequently, the ears will be preserved, with varying degrees of deterioration, and it may be possible to determine ear shape, size, protrusion, and detail. Similarly, the nasal tip, the vermillion line on the border of the lip, and facial wrinkle patterns may be visible. As bloating, shrinkage, and distortion may affect the facial appearance, the skeletal detail should also be assessed where possible to more reliably establish feature morphology.

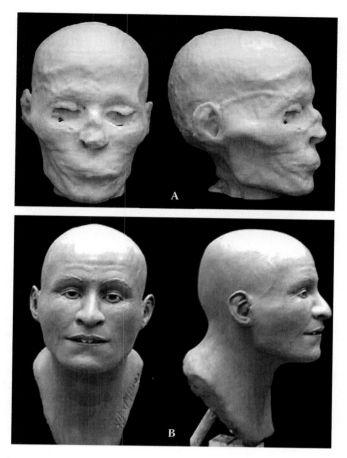

Figure 13.10   The preserved remains of an ancient Egyptian priest (A) and facial reconstruction. (B) The replica of the mummified face was produced from CT scan data using stereolithography. (Courtesy of the National Museum of Scotland and the National Centre for Product Design and Development Research (PDR) in Cardiff, Wales; facial reconstruction produced by Caroline Wilkinson).

13.3   Methods of Facial Reconstruction

Several facial reconstruction schools have developed from roots in Germany and Switzerland in the late 19th century. Early facial reconstruction techniques were pioneered by His (1895), Stadtmuller (1922), and Von Eggeling (1913), and facial tissue depth research was produced from cadavers using needle penetration (Welcker 1883, His 1895, Kollman 1898). Currently, we can divide the facial reconstruction methods into two basic groups, two-dimensional and three-dimensional techniques, and there are a variety of different methods within those groups.

13.3.1   Two-Dimensional Facial Reconstruction

Manual. Drawings and paintings of the face can be produced on overlays superimposed onto images of the skull (see Figure 13.11). Frontal and profile views are often produced using this technique. There are a number of publications outlining the methodology

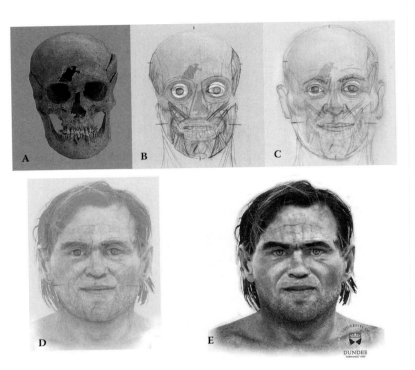

Figure 13.11 Manual two-dimensional facial reconstruction. Tissue depth measurements and anatomical structures (B) are drawn over a photograph of the skull (A). The facial features are then drawn over the muscle structure (C), and these facial proportions and morphology used as a template (D) to create a realistic face (E). (Facial reconstruction by Caroline Wilkinson.) (See color insert following page 362.)

(Taylor 2001, Krogman and Iscan 1986, Iscan and Helmer 1993). Some practitioners prefer to draw the facial musculature onto an initial overlay before attempting the finished facial morphology[*] (Needham et al. 2003), whereas others draw the finished face directly over the skull images (George 1993, Taylor 2001). A great deal of artistic ability and portraiture skill are necessary to produce a realistic facial likeness using the two-dimensional method.

Computerized. A facial composite using photographic or sketched features can be produced over an image of the skull using computer software designed specifically for the reconstruction of facial appearance from skeletal remains. Facial outlines and features are chosen from a database dependant upon the skeletal structure, and the proportions of the skull determine the overall face shape and appearance (see Figure 13.12). A variety of software exists, which create facial images similar to those of Efit, Identikit, or Profit composite systems. Usually frontal view images only are produced (Stratomeier et al. 2005, Evenhouse et al. 1992, Ubelaker and O'Donnell 1992, Miyasaka et al. 1995).

13.3.2 Three-Dimensional Facial Reconstruction

Manual. Facial sculptures are produced on the skull or skull replica (see Figure 13.13). Some practitioners favor an anatomical approach (Gerasimov 1955, Prag and Neave 1997, Wilkinson 2004), modeling the facial musculature before applying a skin layer to depict the facial appearance, whereas others favor a morphometric approach, using mean tissue

---

[*] Jay Matternes described in Taylor (2001).

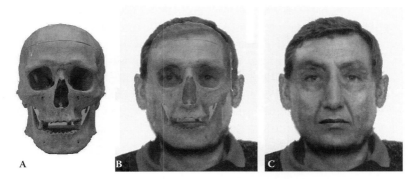

Figure 13.12 Computerized two-dimensional facial reconstruction. A = photograph of the unidentified skull, B = photograph of the skull with superimposed facial reconstruction. C = facial reconstruction produced from a photographic database of facial features. (Courtesy of Ursula Wittwer-Backofen, Institut für Humangenetik und Anthropologie, Freiburg, Germany.)

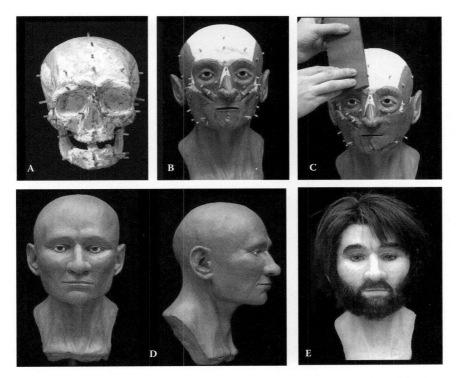

Figure 13.13 Manual three-dimensional facial reconstruction. The muscles of the face are modeled onto the skull replica (A), one-by-one in clay (B) and a skin layer (C) placed over the musculature to produce the finished face (D). The resulting head may be cast in wax or acrylic in order to paint skin color and attach hair, eyes, and facial hair to create a realistic model (E). (Facial reconstruction of Worsley Man by Caroline Wilkinson, courtesy of The Manchester Museum.)

depth data to create a contour map of the facial surface into which the facial features are modeled (Gatliff and Snow 1979, Krogman and Iscan 1986, Iscan and Helmer 1993). Current practitioners of the anatomical approach will also employ mean tissue depth data as guides, and practitioners of the morphometric approach will also apply some anatomical guidelines. There are a number of publications outlining these methodologies (Krogman and Iscan 1986, Iscan and Helmer 1993, Prag and Neave 1997, Clement and Ranson 1998, Taylor 2001, Wilkinson 2004).

Computerized. Over the last decade numerous systems have been developed to produce facial reconstruction, using computer software, with the aim of increasing the levels of flexibility, efficiency, and speed. The first computer technique to be developed for forensic purposes was produced by Moss and his colleagues at University College, London, and was based upon a system used for cranial reconstructive surgery (Moss et al. 1987). Currently, computerized facial reconstruction systems can be divided into two groups: automated systems and three-dimensional modeling systems.

Automated systems are based on anthropometrical data and/or templates of skeletal and facial morphology. Tissue data from clinical images are included, and facial templates (dependent upon the sex, age, and ethnic group of the skull) are "morphed" to fit the skull. Additional manual intervention may also be possible to apply external facial details. These systems create multiple variations for each skull and impose a very specific set of facial characteristics onto the facial reconstruction, in that the resulting face will ultimately resemble the sample face (Evison 1996, Michael and Chen 1996, Quatrehomme et al. 1997, Nelson and Michael 1998, Jones 2001).

Three-dimensional modeling systems have also been utilized to mimic the manual methods of facial reconstruction. Some modeling systems employ three-dimensional animation software (Buhmann et al. 2003, Eliasova et al. 2003, Kindermann 2003, Kahler et al. 2003, Evison et al. 2003) to model the face onto the skull, whereas other systems employ virtual sculpture systems with haptic feedback (Wilkinson 2003, Subke and Wittke 2005). The systems with haptic feedback have the advantage of being able to feel the surface of the skull during analysis, which will provide some important skeletal details for facial reconstruction such as determination of the malar tubercle or muscle attachment strength. Three-dimensional modeling systems may follow either the anatomical or morphometric approaches (see Figure 13.14).

One of the problems with computer-based facial reconstruction systems is that many of the systems have not been tested for accuracy or reliability before they are utilized in forensic investigations.

13.4   Presentation of the Facial Reconstruction to the General Public

Forensic facial reconstructions may be presented to the general public in a variety of ways. The degree of facial aging, clothing, hair, eye, and skin color detail that is necessary, and how many views of the head and in what format the head should be presented have been widely discussed issues.

The amount of extraneous information regarding the identity of the individual will be different for each investigation. Although most cases that involve facial reconstruction work offer very little information other than skeletal material, some scenes will reveal extra details regarding the appearance of the deceased, such as facial hair, skin color, eye color, hair, or clothing. In these cases, this information must be relayed to the public as part of the reconstruction as it may be important for recognition. However, the issue of whether to estimate appearance details without any certainty is controversial. Some practitioners (Prag and Neave 1997, Wilkinson 2004) prefer to include only appearance details that have been ascertained directly from scene evidence and not estimate any unknowns (see Figure 13.15).

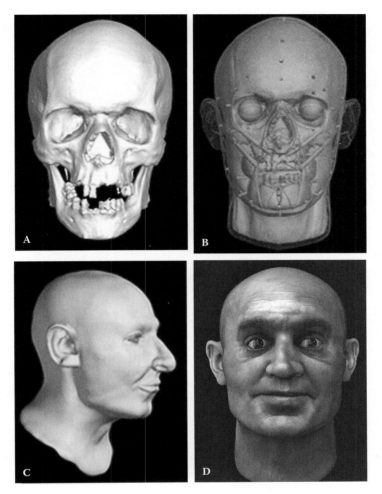

Figure 13.14 Computerized three-dimensional facial reconstruction. A digital model of the skull is produced from CT or laser scan data (A) and the facial musculature attached using three-dimensional modeling software (B). The facial reconstruction can be visualized as a "virtual" clay head (C) or skin, hair, and eye textures and colors can be added to create a more realistic three-dimensional model (D). (Facial reconstructions by Caroline Wilkinson; image [D] courtesy of Image Foundry Ltd.)

The theory behind this approach is that details which are wrongly estimated may confuse any viewer who may know the individual, and may discourage recognition and identification. In addition, it is believed that the viewer will be able to imagine extra appearance details, as long as vague or nondescriptive options are presented. Such practitioners will be disinclined to suggest even skin color as this may vary enormously within the same ethnic group. For example, some white Europeans will have very pale skin with ruddy tones, whereas others may be olive-skinned. Where two-dimensional reconstruction work has been carried out, pencil-drawn images or black-and-white computer images can eliminate any color estimation, and vague or unspecific hairstyles will not confuse the viewer with erroneous information (see Figure 13.5). Some two-dimensional practitioners (Clauwaert 2005) have produced facial reconstructions that do not include the top of the head at all, so as not to suggest any hairstyle. This is a very inventive way of allowing the viewer to add

Figure 13.15 Variation in facial reconstruction depiction. (A) = two-dimensional facial reconstruction without estimated surface details (courtesy of Peter Clauwaert); (B) = three-dimensional manual facial reconstruction without estimated surface details (courtesy of Chris Rynn); (C) = three-dimensional computerized facial reconstruction without estimated surface details (courtesy of Caroline Wilkinson); (D) = two-dimensional facial reconstruction with estimated surface detail (courtesy of Karen Taylor); (E) = three-dimensional manual facial reconstruction with estimated hairstyle and eye/skin color (courtesy of Caroline Wilkinson); (F) = three-dimensional computerized facial reconstruction with estimated hairstyle and eye/skin color. (Courtesy of Caroline Wilkinson and Image Foundry Ltd.). (See color insert following page 362.)

this information in their imagination. Where manual three-dimensional facial reconstructions are produced, the default option has traditionally been to present a head in organic clay color with absent or nonspecific hairstyles and sculptural eyeballs (with holes to represent the iris rather than painted false eyeballs) (Prag and Neave 1997), and a similar result has often been attempted with computer-generated facial reconstructions (see Figure 13.5).

However, there are many practitioners who will estimate facial appearance details such as skin color, eye color, hair style, etc., using the ethnicity, culture, period of time, and geographical factors likely to apply (see Figure 13.5). For example, if the remains are of a 6-year-old white European girl, the facial reconstruction will be produced with hazel eyes, pink skin, and long, fair hair in a ponytail, as these will be the most likely or closest descriptions for this ethnicity, age group, and sex from that particular part of the world.

Where manual three-dimensional facial reconstructions are produced, wigs may be attached, false eyes inserted, colored clay or paint or cosmetics employed to represent skin color, and clothing given to the sculpture (Iscan and Helmer 1993, Taylor and Angel 1998, Stratomeier et al. 2005). Two-dimensional manual practitioners will utilize colored media and add hairstyles, clothing, or accessories, and computer-generated work can include color images of these appearance details (Taylor 2001). Computer-generated three-dimensional facial reconstructions employ varying degrees of realism to the finished face, using simple manual coloration or complex texture wrapping (Lorenzi 2004).

It is unclear whether photographic realism will increase face recognition. Indeed, there is evidence to suggest that we recognize familiar faces more readily from caricatures than from accurate drawings (Bruce and Young 1998).

The manner in which a facial reconstruction is presented to the public varies, depending upon the country, media interest, and time of year. In the U.K., the police often attempt to show the face from multiple views in order to provide the maximum amount of facial morphology information. Consequently, three-dimensional work, both manual and computer-based, is more popular and, typically, a video of a full head rotation will be produced. In the U.S., where greater numbers of investigations will utilize facial reconstruction work, the media interest is lower than in the U.K. Websites are frequently employed to publicize the investigations and, therefore, two-dimensional reconstructions are preferred, and single views are presented. It is unclear whether multiple views produce higher recognition levels than single views, but where single views are utilized, the frontal view is the most reliable.

References

Auslebrook, W.A., Becker, P.J., and Iscan, M.Y., Facial soft tissue thicknesses in the adult male Zulu, *Forensic Science International* 79, 83–102, 1996.

Bibb, R., Freeman, P., Brown, R., Sugar, A., Evans, P., and Bocca, A., An investigation of three-dimensional scanning of human body parts and its use in the design and manufacture of prostheses, *Proceedings of the Institution of Mechanical Engineers* [H] 214, 589–594, 2000.

Bongartz, J., Giel, D., and Hering, P., Living human face measurements using pulse holography, *SPIE* 4149, 303–309, 2000.

Bruce, V. and Young, A., *In the Eye of the Beholder*, Oxford University Press, Oxford, 1998, pp. 165–176.

Buhmann, D., Bellman, D., Kahler, K., Haber, J., Seidel, H.P., and Wilske, J., Computer-aided soft tissue reconstruction on the skeletonised skull, *Proceedings of the 1st International Conference on Reconstruction of Soft Facial Parts (RSFP)*, Potsdam, Germany, 2003, pp. 37–39.

Bush, K. and Antonyshyn, O., Three-dimensional facial anthropometry using a laser surface scanner; validation of the technique, *Plast Reconstr Surg* 98(2), 226–235, 1996.

Caldwell, M.C., The Relationship of Details of the Human Face to the Skull and Its Application in Forensic Anthropology, Masters thesis, Arizona State University, 1981.

Clauwaert, P., Facial reconstruction exhibited as part of the comparative study, *2nd International Conference on Reconstruction of Soft Facial Parts (RSFP)*, Remagen, Germany, 2005.

Clement, J.G. and Ranson, D.L., *Craniofacial Identification in Forensic Medicine*, Arnold Publishers, Sydney, Australia, 1998.

Colledge, H., Loss of Face? The Effect on the Outcome of Craniofacial Reconstruction When Part of the Skull is Missing, M.Sc. thesis, University of Manchester, 1996.

Curry, S., Baumrind, S., Carlson, S., Beers, A., and Boyd, R., Integrated three-dimensional craniofacial mapping at the Craniofacial Research Instrumentation Laboratory, *Seminars in Orthodontics* 7, 258–265, 2001.

Davy, S.L., Schofield, D., and Evison, M.P., Creating a three-dimensional skull model from two-dimensional images: problems and practicalities in computerized facial reconstruction, *Proceedings of the 2nd International Conference on Reconstruction of Soft Facial Parts*, Remagen, Germany, 2005.

Eliasova, H., Dvorak, D., and Prochazka, I.O., Facial three-dimensional reconstruction, *Proceedings of the 1st International Conference on Reconstruction of Soft Facial Parts (RSFP)*, Potsdam, Germany, 2003, pp. 45–48.

El-Mehallawi, I.H. and Soliman, E.M., Ultrasonic assessment of facial soft tissue thicknesses in adult Egyptians, *Forensic Science International* 117, 99–107, 2001.

Evenhouse, R.M., Rasmussen, M., and Sadler, L., Computer-aided forensic facial reconstruction, *J Biol Chem* 19, 22–28, 1992.

Evison, M.P., Computerised Three-Dimensional Facial Reconstruction, www.shef.ac.uk/assem/1/evison.html, 1996.

Evison, M.P., The body in the bag, Presented at the 2nd British Association of Human Identification (BAHID) conference, Bradford, U.K., 2002.

Evison, M.P., Finegan, O.M., and Blythe, T.C., Computerized 3-D facial reconstruction: research update. assemblage.group.shef.ac.uk/4, 1999.

Evison, M.P., Davy, S.L., March, J., and Schofield, D., Computational forensic facial reconstruction, *Proceedings of the 1st International Conference on Reconstruction of Soft Facial Parts (RSFP)*, Potsdam, Germany; 2003, pp. 29–34.

Fedosyutkin, B.A. and Nainys, J.V., The relationship of skull morphology to facial features, in *Forensic Analysis of the Skull*, Iscan, M.Y. and Helmer, R.P., Eds., Wiley-Liss, New York, 1993, pp. 199–213.

Freedman, A.D., *Death and Dying*, The 1996 Grolier Multimedia Encyclopedia, 1996.

Gatliff, B.P. and Snow, C.C., From skull to visage, *Journal Biocommunication* 6(2), 27–30, 1979.

George, R.M., Anatomical and artistic guidelines for forensic facial reconstruction, in *Forensic Analysis of the Skull*, Iscan, M.Y. and Helmer, R.P., Eds., Wiley-Liss, New York, 1993, pp. 215–227.

Gerasimov, M.M., *The Face Finder*, Lippincott, New York, 1971.

Gerasimov, M.M., *The Reconstruction of the Face from the Basic Structure of the Skull*, trans. W. Tshernezky, Publishers unknown, Russia, 1955.

Giel, D., Frey, S., Thelen, A., Bongartz, J., Hering, P., Nuchter, A., Surmann, H., Lingemann, K., and Hertzberg, J., Ultra-Fast Holographic Recording and Automatic Three-Dimensional Scan Matching of Living Human Faces, http://citeseer.ist.psu.edu/719490.html, 2004.

Gordon, I. and Shapiro, H.A., *Forensic Medicine: A Guide to the Principles*, Churchill Livingstone, Edinburgh, 1975.

Haglund, W.D. and Raey, D.T., Use of facial approximation in identification of Green River serial murder victims, *American Journal of Forensic Medicine and Pathology* 12, 2, 132–142, 1991.

Helmer, R., *Schädelidentifizierung durch elektronische Bildmischung*, Kriminalistik-Verlag, Heidelberg, 1984.

Helmer, R., Rohricht, S., Petersen, D., and Moer, F., Plastische Gesichtsrekonstruktion als Möglichkeit der Identifizierung unbekannter Schädel (II), *Archives Kriminology* 184, 5–6, 142–160, 1989.

His, W., Anatomische forschungen ueber Johan Sebastian Bach's gebeine und antlitz'nesbst bemerkungen ueber dessen bilder, *Abhandlungen der Mathematisch-Physikalischen Klasse der Konigl. Sachsischen Gesellschaft der Wissenschaften* 22, 379–420, 1895.

Hjalgrim, H., Lynnerup, N., Liversage, M., and Rosenklint, A., Stereolithography: potential applications in anthropological studies, *American Journal of Physical Anthropology* 97, 329–333, 1995.

Iscan, M.Y. and Helmer, R.P., Eds., *Forensic Analysis of the Skull*, Wiley-Liss, New York, 1993.

Jones, M.W., Facial reconstruction using volumetric data, presented at: Vision, Modeling and Visualization conference, Stuttgart, Germany, 2001.

Kahler, K., Haber, J., and Seidel, H.P., Reanimating the dead: reconstruction of expressive faces from skull data, *ACM/SIGGRAPH Computer Graphics Proceedings* 22(3), 554–567, 2003.

Kau, C.H., Zhurov, A., Bibb, R., Hunter, L., and Richmond, S., The investigation of the changing facial appearance of identical twins employing a three-dimensional laser imaging system, *Orthodontics and Craniofacial Research* 8, 85–90, 2005.

Kindermann, K., Innovative approaches to facial reconstruction using digital technology, *Proceedings of the 1st International Conference on Reconstruction of Soft Facial Parts (RSFP)*, Potsdam, Germany, 127-132, 2003.

Knott, S., Reconstruction of skeletal remains — a new technique, presented at the *10th Biennial Scientific Meeting of the International Association for Craniofacial Identification*, Bari, Italy, 2002.

Kollman, J., Die weichteile des gesichts und die persistenz der rassen, *Anatomisch anzeiger* 15, 165–177, 1898.

Krogman, W.M. and Iscan, M.Y., *The Human Skeleton in Forensic Medicine*, 2nd ed., C.C. Thomas Publishers, Springfield, IL, 1986.

Lebedinskaya, G.U., Balueva, T.S., and Veselovskaya, E.B., Development of methodological principles for reconstruction of the face on the basis of skull material, in Iscan, *Forensic Analysis of the Skull*, M.Y. and Helmer, R.P., Eds., Wiley-Liss, New York, 1993, pp. 183–198.

Lorenzi, R., Santa Claus' face reconstructed, *Discovery News*, December 17, 2004.

Manhein, M.H., Barsley, R.E., Listi, G.A., Musselman, R., Barrow, N.E., and Ubelaker, D.H., In vivo facial tissue depth measurements for children and adults, *Journal of Forensic Science* 45, 1, 48–60, 2000.

Michael, S.D. and Chen, M., The 3-D reconstruction of facial features using volume distortion, *Proceedings of 14th Annual Conference of Eurographics U.K.*, 1996, pp. 297–305.

Miyasaka, S., Yoshino, M., Imaizumi, K., and Seta, S., The computer-aided facial reconstruction system, *Forensic Science International* 74, 155–165, 1995.

Moss, J.P., Linney, A.D., Grindrod, S.R., Arridge, S.R., and Clifton, J.S., 3-dimensional visualization of the face and skull using computerized tomography and laser scanning techniques, *European Journal of Orthodontics* 9, 247–253, 1987.

Moss, J.P., Linney, A.D., Grinrod, S.R., and Mosse, C.A., A laser scanning system for the measurement of facial surface morphology, *Optics and Lasers in Engineering* 10, 179–190, 1989.

Motoyoshi, M., Namara, S., Arai, H.Y., A three-dimensional measuring system for the human face using three-directional photography, *American Journal of Orthodontics and Dentofacial Orthopedics* 101, 431–440, 1992.

Needham, C., Wilkinson, C.M., and Knusel, C.J., Reconstructing visual manifestations of disease and trauma from archaeological human remains. In Collett, L.R., Ed., *Graphic Archaeology — The Journal of the Association of Archaeological Illustrators and Surveyors*, Short Run Press Ltd., Exeter, U.K. 2003, 15–20.

Nelson, L.A. and Michael, S.D., The application of volume deformation to 3-D facial reconstruction: a comparison with previous techniques, *Forensic Science International* 94, 167–181, 1998.

Phillips, V.M. and Smuts, N.A., Facial reconstruction; utilization of computerized tomography to measure facial tissue thickness in a mixed population, *Forensic Science International* 83, 51–59, 1996.

Polson, C.J., Gee, D.J., and Knight, B., *The Essentials of Forensic Medicine*, 4th ed., Pergamon Press, New York, 1985.

Prag, J. and Neave, R.A.H., *Making Faces*, British Museum Press, London, 1997.

Quatrehomme, G., Cotin, S., Subsol, G., Delingette, H., Garidel, Y., Grevin, G., Fidrich, M., Bailet, P., and Ollier, A., A fully three-dimensional method for facial reconstruction based on deformable models, *Journal of Forensic Science* 42(4), 649–652, 1997.

Rhine, S., Tissue Thickness for South-Western Indians, Ph.D. thesis, Physical Anthropology Laboratories, Maxwell Museum, University of New Mexico, 1983.

Sahni, D., Preliminary study on facial soft tissue thickness by magnetic resonance imaging in Northwest Indians, *Forensic Science Communications* 4, 1, 2002.

Sanghera, B., Amis, A., and McGurk, M., Preliminary study of potential for rapid prototype and surface scanned radiotherapy facemask production technique, *Journal of Medical Engineering and Technology* 26, 16–21, 2002.

Siebert, J.P. and Marshall, S., Human body three-dimensional imaging by speckle texture projection photogrammetry, *Sensor Review* 20, 218–226, 2000.

Seitz, H., Tille, C., Rieder, W., Irsen, S.H., and Bermes, G., Rapid prototyping models for facial reconstruction, Presented at *RSFP 2005: 2nd International Conference on Reconstruction of Soft Facial Parts*, Remagen, Germany, 2005.

Snow, C.C., Gatliff, B.P., and McWilliams, K.R., Reconstruction of facial features from the skull: an evaluation of its usefulness in forensic anthropology, *American Journal of Physical Anthropology* 33, 221–228, 1970.

Spoor, F., Jeffery, N., and Zonneveld, F., Imaging skeletal growth and evolution, in *Development, Growth and Evolution: Implications for the Study of the Hominid Skeleton*, O'Higgins, P. and Cohen, M., Eds., Academic Press, San Diego, 2000.

Stadtmuller, F., Zur beurteilung der plastischen rekonstruktionsmethode der physiognomie auf dem scadel, *Journal Morphologie und Anthropologie* 22, 337–372, 1922.

Stephan, C., Facial approximation: globe projection guideline falsified by exophthalmometry literature, *Journal of Forensic Science* 47, 4, 730–735, 2002.

Stephan, C., Facial approximation: an evaluation of mouth width determination, *American Journal of Physical Anthropology* 121, 48–57, 2003a.

Stephan, C., Predicting nose projection and pronasale position in facial approximation, *American Journal of Physical Anthropology* 122, 240–250, 2003b.

Stephan, C., Anthropological facial "reconstruction" — recognizing the fallacies, unembracing the errors and realizing method limitations, *Science and Justice* 43(4), 193–200, 2004.

Stephan, C. and Henneberg, M., Building faces from dry skulls: are they recognized above chance rates? *Journal of Forensic Science* 46(3), 432–440, 2001.

Stratomeier, H., Spee, J., Wittwer-Backofen, U., and Bakker R., Methods of forensic facial reconstruction, presented at the *2nd International Conference on Reconstruction of Soft Facial Parts (RSFP)*, Remagen, Germany, 2005.

Subke J. and Wittke M., CAD enhanced soft-tissue reconstruction in forensics with phantom- three-dimensional touch — an electronic modeling tool with hap tic feedback, presented at the *2nd International Conference on Reconstruction of Soft Facial Parts (RSFP)*, Remagen, Germany, 2005.

Suzuki, K., On the thickness of the soft parts of the Japanese face, *Journal Anthropology of Society of the Nippon* 60, 7–11, 1948.

Taylor, R.G. and Angel, C., Facial reconstruction and approximation, in *Craniofacial Identification in Forensic Medicine*, Clement, J.G. and Ranson, D.L., Eds., Arnold Publishers, Sydney, 1998, pp. 178–181, chap. 14.

Taylor, K., *Forensic Art and Illustration*, CRC Press, Boca Raton, FL, 2001, pp. 311–312.

Techalertpaisarn, R. and Kuroda, T., Three-dimensional computer-graphic demonstration of facial soft tissue changes in mandibular patients after mandibular sagittal ramus osteotomy, *International Journal of Adult Orthodontics and Orthognathic Surgery* 13, 217–225, 1998.

Ubelaker, D.H. and O'Donnell, G., Computer assisted facial reproduction, *Journal of Forensic Science* 37, 155–162, 1992.

Vanezis, P., Vanezis, M., McCombe, G., and Niblett, T., Facial reconstruction using 3-D computer graphics, *Forensic Science International* 108, 2, 81–95, 2000.

Van Rensburg, M.S.J., Accuracy of recognition of 3-D plastic reconstruction of faces from skulls (abstract), *Proceedings of the Anatomical Society of South Africa 23rd Annual Congress* 20, 1993.

Von Eggeling, H., Die leistungsfahigkeit physiognomischer rekonstruktionsversuche auf grundlage des schadels, *Archives Anthropology* 12, 44–47, 1913.

Welcker, H., Schiller's scadel und todenmaske nebst mittheilungen uber schadel und todenmaske Kants, *Vieweg und Sohn, Brauanschwei* 1–160, 1883.

Wilkinson, C.M., In vivo facial tissue depth measurements for White British children, *Journal of Forensic Science* 47, 3, 459–465, 2002.

Wilkinson, C.M., "Virtual" sculpture as a method of computerised facial reconstruction, *Proceedings of the 1st International Conference on Reconstruction of Soft Facial Parts (RSFP)*, Potsdam, Germany, 2003, pp. 59–63.

Wilkinson, C.M., *Forensic Facial Reconstruction*, Cambridge University Press, Cambridge, 2004.

Wilkinson, C.M., The Real Face of Santa, BBC2/Discovery Channel, 2005.

Wilkinson, C.M. and Neave, R.A.H., Skull reassembly and the implications for forensic facial reconstruction, *Science and Justice* 41, 3, 5–6, 2001.

Wilkinson, C.M. and Whittaker, D.K., Juvenile forensic facial reconstruction — a detailed accuracy study, *Proceedings of the 10th Meeting of the International Association of Craniofacial Identification*, Bari, Italy, 2002, pp. 98–110.

Wilkinson, C.M. and Mautner, S.A., Measurement of eyeball protrusion and its application in facial reconstruction, *Journal of Forensic Science* 48(1), 12–16, 2003.

Wilkinson, C.M., Motwani, M., and Chiang, E., The relationship between the soft tissues and the skeletal detail of the mouth, *Journal of Forensic Science* 48(4), 1–5, 2003.

Yamada, T., Mori, Y., Minami, K., Mishima, K., Sugahra, T., and Sakuda, M., Computer aided three-dimensional analysis of nostril forms, *Journal of Cranio-Maxillofacial Surgery* 27, 345–353, 1999.

Facial Recognition and Imagery Analysis

14

GEOFFREY OXLEE

Contents

14.1   Introduction 257
14.2   Imagery Analysis 258
14.3   Imagery Quality and Enhancement...259
14.4   Criteria for Court Work 261
14.5   The Techniques 262
14.6   Facial Morphology...262
14.7   Photogrammetry..264
14.8   Superimposition of Tracing 267
14.9   Conclusion...269
14.10 Forensic Imagery Analysis Group..269
References 270

14.1   Introduction

This chapter discusses practical methods of facial recognition and imagery analysis used in support of the judicial system. "Imagery" is a generic term for pictures. It comprises wave fronts of reflected or emitted energy captured by a camera system and recorded by film, magnetic media, optical disk, and other media. Therefore, it embraces photographs, television, and infrared pictures, as well as radar photography.

Recently, the use of CCTV for security purposes has led to a substantial increase in the use of imagery in support of the investigation of crime and the prosecution of criminals, and from this stems the need for expert imagery analysis; such analysis is essential for, among other uses, facial recognition and identification. Recognition or identification (see below) is most often achieved by facial comparison when the imagery of an offender is compared systematically with that of a person suspected of an offense.

Facial comparison from imagery is often called *facial mapping*. This name is, perhaps, a little misleading, and *facial comparison* is probably more apt. However, facial mapping has now become an accepted term for the processes used by imagery analysts who compare faces captured on imagery and comment on their similarity or dissimilarity. As mentioned above, imagery analysts are normally asked to compare imagery of an offender or offenders with imagery of the person or persons committing an offense, although this may not be confined to imagery of the face alone.

Even though they are the most important elements in recognition and identification, facial features are not the only factor. Height, build, posture, and gait are also features that the human mind will seek out when attempting to distinguish another person.

Many imagery analysts differentiate between *recognition* and *identification* in their work. *Identification* occurs when there is no doubt that Person A is one and the same as Person B. Such positive identification is only achieved if there is a unique identification mark (e.g., a scar or mole) or if the similarities are sufficiently numerous to be overwhelming. *Recognition* occurs when there are similarities to the extent that someone who knows a person well or has studied imagery of that person in detail believes it is possible that the subjects under comparison are one and the same. Recognition might have some probative value but normally only as support to other evidence. Identification, on the other hand, might stand as proof in its own right.

The need for *properly trained and experienced* forensic imagery analysts is underlined by the phenomenon which is sometimes called *cognitive preconception.*

An untrained eye will anticipate that an accused individual and the offender are likely to be the same person and hence subconsciously form the impression that this is a fact. Few people like to be wrong, and thus their minds have a tendency to look for features on the imagery to prove that they were correct and to discount clues that suggest otherwise. In other words, they make the facts fit the case.

14.2   Imagery Analysis

Imagery is the only permanent record of what actually happened during an event, and therefore it is very important that imagery evidence, where possible, is made available to the court. The camera never lies; it merely records what it sees, but this is only useful if the imagery recorded is properly and correctly interpreted. There have been several studies made to determine the capability of persons to correctly identify subjects on imagery. All have concluded that it is not a simple matter, and errors are common, but none have been able to produce reliable statistics on the percentage of errors made. So far there have been no tests using trained and experienced imagery analysts, and as their numbers are few, such a test would be statistically insignificant.

What is indisputable is that lay observers can easily be misled. For example, a professional cameraman using a combination of unusual angles or harsh lighting could record a photograph of a man in such a way that even his next of kin would fail to recognize him; nonetheless, the photograph is still a true image of that man. Properly qualified and experienced imagery analysts are able to understand how such a picture is recorded and therefore are able to interpret the imagery correctly. They take into account the specifications of the recording system, the nature of the lighting, the angular field of view of the camera, and the impact of shape, shadow, size, tone, and associated features. Thus, it is important that courts of law insist that the evidence be presented by expert imagery analysts in order to minimize the risk of incorrect interpretation leading to an unsafe conclusion.

Forensic imagery analysis, like all forensic work, needs to be completed with the utmost care for detail as the penalty for not doing so is severe. To understand the amount of detail to be considered, it is important that forensic imagery analysts have knowledge of the key subjects listed in Table 14.1 below. The topics in italics require a detailed understanding and are known as the base subjects. The others listed are nonetheless important, and they are matters about which all forensic imagery analysis practitioners require at least a rudimentary knowledge.

Table 14.1   Forensic Imagery Analyst — Knowledge Base

Images and Information

1. Imagery
   a. Characteristics of images
      i. The basic physical properties (physics of imagery)
   b. The history of imagery recording
   c. The physics and chemistry of imagery recording
2. Photography
   a. Analog systems
   b. Digital systems
   c. Storage and retrieval
3. Photogrammetry
   a. Scaling
   b. Alignment
   c. Measurement
4. Multisensor studies
   a. Multispectral imagery
   b. Infrared
   c. False color
   d. Microwave
   e. Ultraviolet
5. Video, CCTV, and television
   a. Fundamentals
   b. Transmission
6. Advanced concepts
   a. Holography
   b. Virtual reality
   c. Imagery enhancement
7. Imagery interpretation and analysis
   a. Theory of imagery analysis
   b. Basic identification studies
   c. Natural objects and systems
   d. Cultural objects and systems
8. Forensic imagery analysis
   a. Basic studies
   b. Forensic science
   c. Human morphology
      i. Facial landmarks and facial muscles
      ii. Gait
      iii. Posture
      iv. Human behavior (mannerisms)

14.3   Imagery Quality and Enhancement

A great deal of imagery made available in forensic work is of medium to poor quality. Surprisingly, this has little to do with the quality of the cameras. Most CCTV monitors show pictures that are mainly clear and unambiguous. Why then is the quality of the imagery recorded onto tapes so different? The answer lies in a combination of poor recording systems and the management of these systems. The situation is improving as more and more digital systems replace older VHS recorders.

CCTV systems are costly, and most users will weigh the cost outlay against the cost of offenses. Thus, there is a drive to reduce the costs, and hence a single recorder will be used to service several cameras. This leads to time-lapse imagery where only fields rather than whole frames are recorded and then as little as 6 fields a second (or use less when additional multiplexing is used) from each camera instead of the potential 50. Frequently, VHS tapes are used, wiped, and then used again many times with consequent progressive loss of magnetic material. Many users place the video cameras too far away from the likely human targets to obtain sufficient facial detail. Moreover, advertising boards and other obstructions are frequently placed in front of the camera blocking its view. All these aspects, plus the incorrect positioning of the titling data on the imagery frame, lead to reductions in the usefulness of the imagery and difficulties for imagery analysts.

The advent of digital recording systems has alleviated some but not all of the problems. However, these have their own problems in terms of evidential acceptability (see later text). Because of the quality of many tapes, specific image processing systems are used by imagery analysts to provide improved interpretability. However, they can only enhance what is already present on the tape and cannot introduce fresh data. Nevertheless, they have proved to be useful tools for the analyst.

If the data is on the imagery, why enhance it? This is a question sometimes posed in court. The answer lies in the comparatively poor performance of the human eye when compared with an electronic machine. For example, a monochromatic (black and white) picture can contain up to 256 gray scales (shades of gray between black at one end and white at the other); however, the average human eyes can only differentiate a small percentage (around 10%) of these. Nonetheless, the gray-scale data is, indeed, in the picture and could provide better discrimination for the analyst between an object and its background. Imagery processing software is able to stretch the contrast of the picture to bring many more of the subtle gray shades into the range of the human eye. Another way would be to turn the black-and-white picture into false color. This is achieved by the processor allocating a color to each gray shade. The advantage of this is that the human eye is infinitely superior in color perception and can see a significantly larger number of color shades.

There are many other useful enhancement processes too lengthy to discuss here. However, it is important that enhancements are presented to courts with great care not to go into unnecessary detail. One such method is stereoscopy. This technique has been used since before the First World War to provide extra perception and depth analysis (see Estes 1983). Successive frames of imagery show a change in angle of view to simulate the different angles viewed by each of our eyes. The use of special glasses, called *stereoscopes*, focus the right eye to view only the right-hand picture and the left eye the left picture. A three-dimensional view is obtained when the brain fuses the two images. Not everyone is able to accomplish stereo vision, however, and these people will invariably be cut from imagery analysis training courses if they fail this aptitude test. Stereo pictures are obtained by using a special stereo camera with twin lenses (unusual) or by moving a single lens camera further to one side of the subject. When the recording is from a single, static CCTV camera, the angle remains the same. However, if a subject of interest moves slightly during the event, the angle changes at which the camera sees it, and stereo vision of the moving part may then be achieved by viewing successive frames.

It would be appropriate to issue a warning here. Stereovision of CCTV is merely an aid to perception and must not be used for depth analysis or mensuration. Furthermore, it is important for imagery analysts to be properly trained in stereoscopy in order to

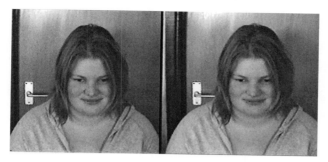

Figure 14.1   Stereo from video (view with stereoscopes).

comprehend the impact of stereo exaggeration and so on (see Ministry of Defence 2005). Stereoscopic methods can be effective for depth and shape studies but only when the imagery is obtained in specific circumstances. In these cases, precise calibration data on the camera system is known, and accurate stereo comparator equipment is used. Figure 14.1 shows a stereo pair recorded by a CCTV system.

14.4   Criteria for Court Work

Although APCO has provided guidelines, there are no definitive court rules that provide criteria for facial mapping, and its impact as evidence depends on the detail that an expert can observe and analyze. Results will vary between analysts because of visual acuity differences, but a sound principle for experts is to use as many of the techniques mentioned below before coming to any conclusions.

Lawyers and courts rather too often fall into the trap of trying to place imagery analysis precisely as either an art or a science because, as with much forensic work, it combines both. To make imagery analysis wholly objective is desirable but unobtainable, and indeed few sciences exist where it is possible. At the end of most experiments it is necessary to ask the question "So what?" and to realize that the results require interpretive judgments based on experience and probability.

Forensic recognition of persons embraces the factors of shape, shadow, size, tone, and associated features because they are all essential components, but as every picture is unique and these are all variables, the spatial resolution required to provide proof beyond reasonable doubt will also vary.

Most imagery from CCTV systems is unable to provide positive proof of *identification* which, as mentioned before, would require identification of unique features such as scars or moles, or a large number of clear similarities that, together, are overwhelming, in the opinion of the expert. Thus, imagery evidence is more often used to provide support to other evidence in order to make a case secure and, in this, imagery analysis differs little from most forensic disciplines.

The task of an expert performing facial or feature comparisons is to look first for significant differences between the faces under comparison. It takes only one clear difference to enable the analyst to conclude that the persons are not the same; however, several clear similarities do not prove they are the same, as many others may share these similarities. If no significant differences are found, similarities must be listed and presented to the court in a simple but concise way.

Imagery can be divided into three categories:

Category 1: Objective evidence. Objective evidence is independently measurable and verifiable and thus suitable for scientific comparison. Superimpositions and photogrammetric measurement come into this category.

Category 2: Subjective evidence. Subjective evidence is personally observable and demonstrable but not necessarily independently measurable.

Category 3: No credible evidence. Of no safe evidential value.

The Police Scientific and Technical Development Branch (PSDB) criteria of 12.8 TV lines as the minimum required to subtend a face for identification is useful in planning a CCTV security system. The number of TV lines is dictated by the distance of the subject from the camera. Thus, the design of the area captured by the system should be such that human subjects for surveillance must pass close enough to the camera for their faces to be covered by 12.8 lines; only then is Category 1 imagery the likely outcome. In most cases, however, this criterion is not achieved. This does not mean that imagery below this level is unsafe or unusable, but it does mean that facial data will need to be supplemented by other evidence to achieve identification.

14.5   The Techniques

Many techniques have been developed during the drive to achieve safe and reliable facial mapping. They have a variety of names but all are covered by the general headings used in the following paragraphs. These techniques are designed to accomplish the same thing — namely, to try to eliminate the suspect and, hence, they are focused on looking for the significant differences required.

The order in which the techniques are applied varies. Some analysts prefer to use photogrammetry or superimposition in a first attempt to eliminate the suspect. The basis for their method is that a clear difference in size is sufficient. For example, if the distances between the exocanthions on the left eye and the exocanthions on the right eye (see Figure 14.2) are significantly different, then they are not the same person. However, care must be exercised; normally, pictures of the accused and the offender are derived from different cameras, using different recording media. Consequently, there is a distinct requirement for accurate photogrammetry before a safe result can be achieved. Further details relating to photogrammetry are contained in paragraphs below.

In this chapter, facial morphology is first described, because the initial action by forensic imagery analysts is to assess in general terms the images of the faces being compared. This initial morphology study is not designed to come to any immediate conclusions, as this might result in cognitive preconception as mentioned earlier, but it provides an overall impression of the two faces and enables analysts to note any clear and possibly unique blemishes (e.g., moles or scars).

14.6   Facial Morphology

As with any comparison, it is necessary to compare like with like. Thus, it is essential to identify images of the accused and of the offender that are the same in terms of the angular field of view.

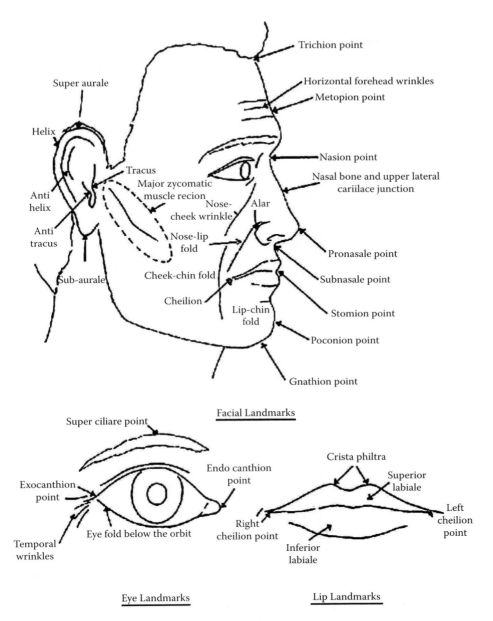

Figure 14.2 Some relevant facial landmarks.

The first action is to study carefully the facial features to see if there is an obvious difference. These must be profound, like a marked difference in the shape of the nose, the eyes, or the ears, and should be verifiable, if possible, in all of the comparison images. It is insufficient to accept that the persons under comparison simply look different, because differences may be caused by aging, lighting, clever disguise, or makeup, as well as transitory differences such as changes in hairstyle.

If no clear and obvious differences are identified, the next stage is to compare carefully each visible facial landmark on as many images as possible. Figure 14.2 shows the main facial landmarks used in this process. In conjunction with the observation of landmarks,

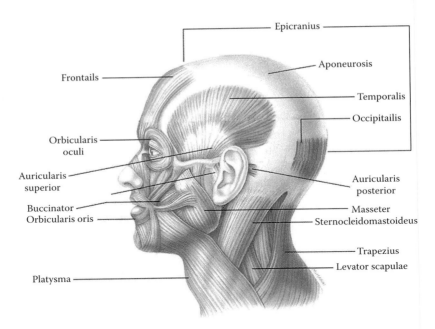

Figure 14.3   Some relevant facial muscles.

the imagery analyst must consider the underlying muscles of the face, which are foremost in determining expression. Further information can be obtained from books such as *The Anthropometry of the Head and Face* written by Farkas, and others (See Farkas 1994). This study is one of several standards for forensic imagery analysts.

Morphological examination is performed carefully from, for example, the apex of the head down to the neck. The landmarks serve as a guide to look in detail at all major features and in turn are considered from every angle provided by the imagery of the offender and the accused. The shape of the feature, the shadow cast, and the size in proportion to other features are noted and a conclusion drawn as to whether or not there are significant differences. If there are no significant differences, the similarity is noted and will be subjected to subsequent photogrammetric testing.

Figure 14.3 shows some of the underlying muscles. In addition to contributing strongly to expressiveness, some of these may be more developed in some faces than in others, giving rise to an alteration in the facial shape at particular points. These muscles can change size with age, adding, in some cases, another complicating variable.

14.7   Photogrammetry

Photogrammetry is defined as the use of photographic (imagery) records for precise measurement of distances or dimensions. Its effective use demands a detailed knowledge of the geometry and metrics associated with camera systems and recording media. Once the camera data is known and calibrated, trigonometric values can be calculated along the horizontal plane (the *x* axis), the plane from the foreground to the apparent horizon (the *y* axis), and the vertical plane (the *z* axis). It is too complex a subject for detailed explanations here but an excursion into the *Manual of Photogrammetry* (see ASP 1996) or similar publications will satisfy any requirement for further knowledge.

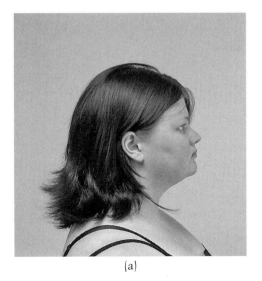
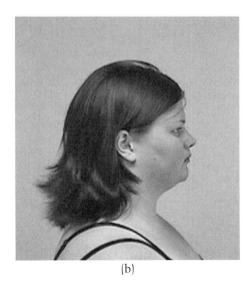

(a)   (b)

Figure 14.4 (a) Woman A photo; (b) Woman B video.

Table 14.2   Ratios between Facial Landmarks

Feature	Woman A	Percentage	Woman B	Percentage
Glabella	0 mm	0	0 mm	0
Nasion	1.5 mm	11.54	1.76 mm	11.5
Pronasale	4.5 mm	34.61	5.3 mm	34.64
Stomion	8.0 mm	61.54	9.4 mm	61.44
Gnathion	13 mm	100	15.3 mm	100

It is always preferable to use original imagery, particularly when dealing with analog recordings. Any reproductions will almost invariably have lost resolution and, thus, detail. Moreover, there is a chance that both lens aberrations and nonuniform enlargement will distort the geometry of the picture. These problems are not normally found in digital copies as they are replications, digit by digit, and not duplications. However, digital copies, too, have their problems, and the acceptability of evidence from digital systems must be subject to certain safeguards as the House of Lords Select Committee on Science and Technology recommended in their report entitled "Digital Images as Evidence" (see TSO 1998) — for example, that a warning should be given by judges to juries in cases of uncertainty and that authentication techniques should be used to verify image originality.

Measurement. As, in the main, the originals of images under comparison are different in scale, any photogrammetric comparison must be based on actual measurement after the correct scales have been established. However, as explained above, this demands detailed knowledge of the recording camera, which is not generally available to the analyst. Nevertheless, accurate work can be achieved on the original imagery by calculating the ratios between facial landmarks (see Figure 14.4a and 14.4b and Table 14.2).

In Figures 14.4a and 14.4b, the originals are of different scales but measurements of actual photo distances between facial landmarks can be made. In this case, the distance between the glabella and the gnathion was 13mm on the original of Woman A and, as this was the longest distance between two measure points, it is allocated the value of 100%. All the other distances were then measured and the distances stated as a proportion of the

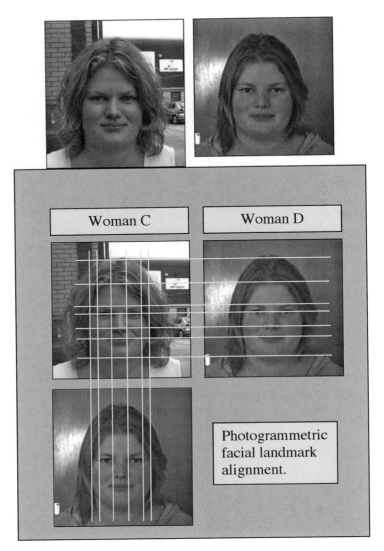

Figure 14.5 Photogrammetric facial landmark alignment.

total; hence, the distance between the glabella and the pronasale was 34.61% of the total and so on, for as many measurements as possible. The same process was completed on the video still of Woman B and the proportionalities compared. In this case, the proportional (percentage) distances were similar and thus unable to eliminate Woman B from being one and the same as Woman A. However, it is important to note that from this evidence alone the analyst could not say that the two were the same, because these ratios may be shared by many in the population.

When using techniques like the one illustrated in Figure 14.4, analysts must ensure that identical points are selected and measured using precision measuring magnifiers. Each measurement (or pointing) should be made at least ten times to minimize human error and the average used as the most accurate figure.

Facial alignment. Another technique used is facial alignment. In Figure 14.5, the pictures of Woman C and Woman D have been carefully scaled using the distances between two

Figure 14.6   Superimposition of tracing outline.

landmarks in the vertical plane and two in the horizontal plane. These are then equally carefully aligned and lines drawn through as many landmarks as possible. Once again, the exercise is to try to eliminate the person. Here, however, it can be seen that the lines pass accurately through the same landmarks on each picture and, again, elimination was not possible.

Superimposition. Superimposition of one picture upon another is a further method of testing the reliability of morphological analysis. Here, there are several methodologies. The first is to utilize tracings of one of the images and superimpose it upon the other. As with any work of this kind, great care must be taken with both the scaling and enlargement, particularly when the differences in geometry of the two pictures under comparison are marked. No attempt should be made to rectify the geometry as this is fraught with danger, and the results are, in effect, attempting to make one picture fit into another or vice versa.

14.8   Superimposition of Tracing

In Figure 14.6, a tracing of Woman D has been progressively (in percentage terms) super-imposed on the photograph of Woman C. As can be seen, there is no evidence to suggest elimination is possible. The tracings can be made by a qualified artist or created by a computer using standard line-detection algorithms.

Superimposition of imagery. In Figure 14.7, the face of Woman D has been super-imposed progressively on Woman C. As can be seen there is little difference between the two and, again, elimination would not be possible. However, there are some differences, such as the line of the hair, but these are termed *transitory differences* and would not be seen as significant.

Flicker and change detection. To identify differences, analysts use computer systems to alternate between the two pictures. If this is done rapidly, the differences flash (flicker) to the observer (first they are there, then they are not, then they are, then they are not, and so on). Another method to pinpoint differences is to use software to reveal differences (known as change detection). In this method, the computer will only show differences between the two pictures and can, for example, paint these differences in a contrasting color. Differences highlighted in this way can be studied in detail to determine if they are significant or not.

Wiping. Image technology is developing rapidly to allow useful techniques to enhance the interpretability of imagery. For example one of the two pictures shown above could

Figure 14.7   Superimposition of Woman D on Woman C.

Figure 14.8   Matching Woman C and Woman D.

be "wiped" electronically across the other, showing slowly, line by line, the similarities or, importantly, the differences between them. This is, of course, impossible to illustrate in an unanimated way. The wipes can be horizontal, vertical, or even diagonal across the pictures and are useful to analysts, but care must be taken before they are accepted as evidence before a jury as, like all such animation, they are powerful, and it is easy for the mind to be fooled. A moving video picture is more easily interpreted than a selection of single stills taken from it. The stills reveal all of the distortions and aberrations, whereas the brain discounts this detail when it watches the moving picture.

Matching. It is sometimes useful for analysts to place the right half of a face against the left half of the face under comparison or vice versa to determine if they match within reason. Once again, care must be taken in drawing conclusions. Human faces are seldom completely symmetrical and, hence, the geometric center is difficult to identify, but it is a technique which draws attention to anomalies, particularly on poor pictures, and may help to detect a meaningful difference between the two persons. Figure 14.8 shows Woman C and Woman D compared by using matching techniques. It also demonstrates how difficult it is to obtain exact scaling and alignment between two images.

Table 14.3   Level of Support for a Contention (Agreed upon by the FIAG — October 2003)

Level	Description
0	Lends no support
1	Lends limited support
2	Lends moderate support
3	Lends support
4	Lends strong support
5	Lends powerful support

Other features. As has been already mentioned, facial features are not the only factors that can help determine identification. There may be many other factors, including comparisons of height, build, gait, posture, and mannerisms, as well as matching clothing or accoutrements seized on arrest with articles worn or used by the offender. Only when all the factors are noted and taken into account should any conclusion be reached.

14.9   Conclusion

It is seldom that a forensic imagery analyst will be able to provide a positive identification that would stand in its own right as proof in court, but the importance of imagery evidence should not be underestimated. It is, above all, a permanent record of an event. The camera does not lie, although it might mislead lay persons into incorrect interpretations. Hence, qualified and experienced imagery analysts are needed for forensic purposes to aid the court in its deliberations.

Forensic imagery analysts have been reluctant to commit to defining in mathematical terms the strength of their conclusions. This is not from doubt about their own judgments but to ensure that the court is not misled. For example, a sureness of, say, 75% is very positive to some but not to others who would see it as 25% doubt. Many analysts feel that it is up to the jury to take their evidence and place upon it what reliance they judge to be correct when balanced against all the evidence they have heard. However, many courts require some understanding of the strength of the imagery evidence opinion and to this end a table has been agreed upon by the Forensic Imagery Analysis Group (FIAG) (Table 14.3).

A number of individuals and groups have become practitioners in this field in the past decade to satisfy the demand for imagery analysis and facial mapping, but the standard has been seen by the courts as variable, and hence the reliability of forensic imagery analysis, in general, has been subject to criticism.

14.10   Forensic Imagery Analysis Group

To provide consistency and high standards of imagery analysis and facial recognition, a group has been formed under the umbrella of the British Association for Human Identification (BAHID). This group is the FIAG and is currently working with the Council for the Registration of Forensic Practitioners (CRFP) to set standards of entry into the specialization.

Among other goals, the FIAG will be seeking research programs that can be introduced to provide more statistical data by which the courts can judge the impact of imagery identification evidence. Each human face is unique (even identical twins), but the differences are often subtle, and many shapes and sizes of individual features will be shared by many others. The exact occurrence of certain shapes and sizes in any one group or race in the population has not yet been determined, and the magnitude of such a project may be prohibitively costly. However, FIAG members are sharing data and experiences to refine both the techniques and the understanding.

There will inevitably be subjective judgments made by forensic imagery analysis practitioners (as with almost every science), but the aim is to base these judgments on as many objective facts as possible.

References

Colwell, R.N., Ed., *Manual of Remote Sensing*, 2nd ed., American Society of Photogrammetry, Falls Church, VA, 1983.

Ministry of Defence, Joint School of Photographic Interpretation — Notes on Stereoscopy, MOD, U.K., 2005.

Farkas, L.G., Ed., *Anthropometry of the Head and Face*, Raven Press, New York, 1994.

Manual of Photogrammetry, 4th ed., American Society of Photogrammetry, 1980.

The Stationary Office, House of Lords Select Committee on Science and Technology Report 64: Digital Images as Evidence, The Stationary Office, U.K., 1998.

Identifying Persons by Their Iris Patterns

15

JOHN DAUGMAN

Contents

15.1 Introduction 271
15.2 Anatomy, Physiology, and Development of the Iris..............................272
15.3 Iris Feature Extraction and Encoding 274
15.4 Matching Algorithm for Iris Comparisons...276
15.5 Results from 200 Billion Cross-Comparisons 277
    15.5.1 Database 277
    15.5.2 Comparisons of Different Irides without Rotations.................278
    15.5.3 Comparisons of Genetically Identical Irides 279
    15.5.4 Distribution of Best Matches after Multiple Rotations 279
15.6 Observed False Match Rates 281
15.7 Decidability of Iris Recognition 282
References 284

15.1 Introduction

Biometric identification of persons depends on variation among persons. The more complex and random the variation, the better, because this increases uniqueness and enables greater discriminating power. However, although maximal between-person variability is desirable, it is also desirable to have minimal within-person variability in the chosen biometric features, over time and across changing conditions of capture. If the first variability (between-person) is too small, the likelihood of false matches between different persons is increased. If the second variability (within-person) is too large, then the likelihood of false nonmatches is increased. In a sense, the entire mathematical and statistical science of pattern recognition can be reduced to questions about the relationship between these two variabilities. Classification is only reliable if the diameters of the clusters of data corresponding to the different classes are smaller than the distances between the clusters.

In the case of face recognition, for example, the within-person variability can be larger than the between-person variability. Difficulties for computer algorithms arise from the fact that faces are changeable social organs displaying a variety of expressions, as well as being active three-dimensional objects whose projected images vary with pose and viewing angle, illumination, accoutrements, and age.[1] Against this within-person (same face) variability, between-person variability is limited, because different faces possess the same canonical set of features, nearly always in the same general canonical geometry.

For all of these reasons, iris patterns become interesting as an alternative means of reliable visual recognition of living persons, especially if imaging can be done at distances of about a meter or less. Some new cameras for iris image acquisition have been demonstrated at distances of about 3 m and for subjects walking at a speed of about 1 m/sec, yielding successful recognition, but most current deployments require looking into a camera within arm's length. Iris recognition has limited forensic value, because (unlike fingerprints or DNA, for example) iris patterns are not left behind at crime scenes, and in death the pupil usually dilates significantly, the cornea clouds, and the iris tissue degrades relatively rapidly. Moreover, currently available iris databases are quite small (only a few million digitized samples of iris patterns exist today), and because of the novelty of this biometric, such data currently has no legal or established forensic status as admissible evidence.

Perhaps the most promising aspect of iris recognition is its extraordinary robustness against making false matches. This chapter will present data from 200 billion ($2 \cdot 10^{11}$) iris cross-comparisons with no false matches, a number that is larger than the estimated number of stars in our galaxy and larger than the estimated number of neurons in the human brain. Every day some 7 billion iris comparisons are performed in a national security deployment covering all 27 border crossings and air- and seaports of entry into the United Arab Emirates (U.A.E.), comparing arriving passengers against a central database of iris patterns. (About 9,000 daily arrivals are each compared by real-time exhaustive search against an enrolled database of 800,000 iris patterns, making 7.2 billion iris comparisons per day.) According to the U.A.E. Ministry of Interior, over the past 4.5 years this system has caught some 50,000 persons trying to enter or reenter the U.A.E. under false travel documents. The origin of such resilient performance is both the intrinsic uniqueness of iris patterns and also the mathematical principle of binomial combinatorics that is embedded into the iris recognition algorithms. All current public deployments of iris recognition use algorithms developed by the author, and these will be described in this chapter. We begin first by briefly reviewing the anatomy, genetics, physiology, and embryological development of the iris.

15.2   Anatomy, Physiology, and Development of the Iris

The iris is an internal effector organ of the eye, located behind the cornea and the aqueous humor but in front of the lens. Its function is to control the amount of light entering the pupil, by dilation and constriction under brainstem control (pretectal nucleus) via the parasympathetic nervous system. Although small (11 mm diameter) and sometimes problematic to image, the iris displays a textured pattern with great variability among different persons. The visible features of an iris arise in the trabeculum, a meshwork of connective tissue that displays arching ligaments, ridges, crypts, contraction furrows, a corona and pupillary frill, coloration, and sometimes freckles. The striated anterior layer covering the trabecular meshwork creates the predominant texture seen with visible light, but all of these sources of radial and angular variation taken together constitute a distinctive "fingerprint" that can be acquired from some distance, as illustrated by the two iris images in Figure 15.1.

As an externally visible but internal organ of the eye, the iris is well protected from the environment and is stable over time. As a quasiplanar object, its image is relatively insensitive to angle of illumination. For automatic systems of iris capture and recognition, further advantages include the fact that changes in viewing angle cause only reversible affine transformations of the pattern, and even the nonaffine pattern distortion caused by pupillary dilation is mathematically fairly well reversible. Finally, the ease of localizing eyes

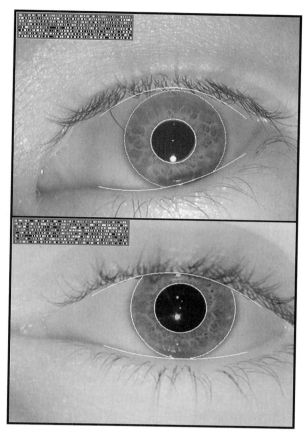

Figure 15.1 Examples of iris patterns, imaged monochromatically with NIR illumination in the 700 nm–900 nm band at distances of about 35 cm. The outline overlays show results of the iris and pupil localization and eyelid detection steps. The bit streams are the results of demodulation with complex-valued 2D Gabor wavelets to encode iris patterns as a sequence of phasor quadrants.

in faces, and the distinctive annular shape of the iris, facilitate reliable and precise isolation of this feature and the creation of a size-invariant representation of its pattern.

A property the iris shares with fingerprints is the random morphogenesis of its minutiae. Because there is no genetic penetrance in the expression of this organ beyond its anatomical form, physiology, color, and general appearance, the iris texture itself is stochastic and possibly chaotic. As its detailed morphogenesis depends on initial conditions in the embryonic mesoderm from which it develops, the phenotypic expression even of two irides with the same genotype (as in identical twins or the pair of eyes possessed by one individual) have uncorrelated minutiae,[2] as will be demonstrated later in this chapter. In these respects the uniqueness of iris patterns parallels the uniqueness of fingerprints, common genotype or not. In contrast, the heritability of iris color and its ethnological variations in man are well-documented (e.g., Davenport and Davenport).[3]

The iris begins to form in the third month of gestation,[4] and the structures creating its pattern are largely complete by the eighth month, although pigment accretion can continue into the first postnatal years. The layers of the iris have both ectodermal and mesodermal embryological origin, consisting of (from back to front): a darkly pigmented epithelium;

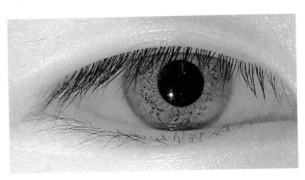

Figure 15.2 Even dark brown eyes reveal rich iris texture when illuminated with near-infrared light. The randomness of this texture across individuals and its complexity, spanning at least three octaves in useful scales of analysis, enables the discriminating power of the IrisCode.

pupillary dilator and sphincter muscles; heavily vascularized stroma (connective tissue of interlacing ligaments containing melanocytes); and an anterior layer of chromataphores and melanocytes with a genetically determined density of melanin pigment granules. Apparent iris color is determined mainly by the density of melanin[5] in the anterior layer, with blue irides resulting from an absence of pigment: longer wavelengths differentially penetrate, whereas shorter wavelengths are reflected and scattered, a phenomenon similar to that which makes the sky appear blue. In the near-infrared (NIR) wavelengths that are used for illumination in deployed iris recognition cameras, the melanin pigment no longer absorbs;[6] thus, even very darkly pigmented irides reveal rich and complex features as illustrated in Figure 15.2, which was acquired from a dark-eyed person using illumination in the NIR band.

15.3 Iris Feature Extraction and Encoding

To capture the rich details of iris patterns, an imaging system should resolve a minimum of 50 pixels in iris radius. In most current deployments of this technology, a resolved iris radius of 100–140 pixels is typical. Monochrome CCD cameras (480 × 640) are used with NIR illumination in the 700 nm–900 nm band, which is invisible to humans and thus not aversive. Some imaging platforms use a wide-angle camera for coarse localization of eyes in faces to steer the optics of a narrow-angle pan/tilt camera that acquires higher resolution images of the eyes; most cameras, however, do not incorporate active pan/tilt platforms. Instead they exploit visual feedback via a mirror or video image to guide cooperative subjects to position their own eyes within the field of view of a single narrow-angle lens. Examples of such resulting images acquired in NIR illumination are seen in Figure 15.1 and Figure 15.2. New systems for active eye-finding have been demonstrated at distances of 3 m or more and with briskly walking subjects.

Algorithms for automatic, real-time, iris recognition have been described extensively in Daugman,[7–9] and only an overview will be given here. The first steps involve localization of the iris from within the larger image. This requires detection of the inner and outer boundaries of the iris (which cannot be assumed to be either circular or concentric), and detection of both the upper and lower eyelid boundaries, so that the eyelids can be excluded from the encoding if they cover parts of the iris. Localization of such

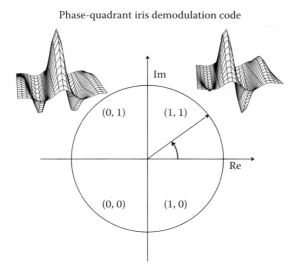

Figure 15.3 Extracting phase sequences to encode iris patterns. Local regions of an iris are projected onto quadrature two-dimensional Gabor wavelets, generating complex-valued coefficients whose real and imaginary parts specify the coordinates of a phasor in the complex plane.

boundaries is achieved by computer vision methods known as "active contours," which are flexible parameterized detectors that fit themselves to curvilinear edge structure in images. The white overlaid graphics shown at these iris boundaries in Figure 15.1 illustrate their behavior.

Once the boundaries are localized ("segmentation"), the iris portion can be encoded in a dimensionless representation that does not depend either upon the position of the iris within the image nor upon the size of the iris in the image (hence, not upon the distance to the subject nor the optical magnification factor), nor upon the dilation of the pupil, which can range from 0.1 to 0.8 of the iris diameter. A dimensionless coordinate system is established in which the image data is mapped as $I(\rho, \phi)$ where ρ ranges over the unit interval $(0, 1)$ between the inner and outer boundaries of the iris, thus achieving invariance to pupillary dilation, and ϕ ranges in angular coordinate from 0 to 2π around the iris.

Each isolated iris pattern is then "demodulated" to extract its phase information using quadrature two-dimensional Gabor wavelets.[7-9] This encoding process is illustrated in Figure 15.3. It amounts to a patchwise phase quantization of the iris pattern by identifying in which quadrant of the complex plane each resultant phasor lies when a given area of the iris is projected onto complex-valued two-dimensional Gabor wavelets. The encoding of the iris pattern into a sequence of any of four states superficially resembles the genetic code. Each bit h in an iris code can be regarded as a coordinate of one of the four vertices of a logical unit square in the complex plane. It is computed by evaluating, at a given scale of analysis, the sign of both the real and imaginary parts of the quadrature image projections from a local region of the iris image $I(\rho, \phi)$ onto a particular complex two-dimensional Gabor filter:

$$h_{Re} = 1 \text{ if } Re \int_{\rho} \int_{\phi} e^{-i\omega(\theta_0 - \phi)} e^{-(r_0 - \rho)^2/\alpha^2} e^{-(\theta_0 - \phi)^2/\beta^2} I(\rho, \phi) \rho \, d\rho \, d\phi \geq 0 \qquad (1)$$

$$h_{\mathrm{Re}} = 0 \text{ if } \mathrm{Re} \int_\rho \int_\phi e^{-i\omega(\theta_0-\phi)} e^{-(r_0-\rho)^2/\alpha^2} e^{-(\theta_0-\phi)^2/\beta^2} I(\rho,\phi)\rho \, d\rho \, d\phi < 0 \qquad (2)$$

$$h_{\mathrm{Im}} = 1 \text{ if } \mathrm{Im} \int_\rho \int_\phi e^{-i\omega(\theta_0-\phi)} e^{-(r_0-\rho)^2/\alpha^2} e^{-(\theta_0-\phi)^2/\beta^2} I(\rho,\phi)\rho \, d\rho \, d\phi \geq 0 \qquad (3)$$

$$h_{\mathrm{Im}} = 0 \text{ if } \mathrm{Im} \int_\rho \int_\phi e^{-i\omega(\theta_0-\phi)} e^{-(r_0-\rho)^2/\alpha^2} e^{-(\theta_0-\phi)^2/\beta^2} I(\rho,\phi)\rho \, d\rho \, d\phi < 0 \qquad (4)$$

Thus, a single complex two-dimensional Gabor filter, having a particular set of size and position parameters (r_0, θ_0; α, β, ω) in the dimensionless iris domain (ρ, ϕ), performs a coarse phase quantization of the local texture signal. By this means an iris pattern is encoded into 2,048 bits (or 256 bytes) of phase information called an *IrisCode*.

15.4 Matching Algorithm for Iris Comparisons

Comparing the IrisCodes from different images of eyes requires a metric of similarity. A simple but mathematically powerful and suitable one is Hamming distance, which is simply the fraction of bits that disagree between the two computed IrisCodes. This metric can be very efficiently computed by the Exclusive-OR (XOR) boolean operator $\otimes$, whose truth table for the four possible bit combinations (00, 01, 10, 11) is, respectively, (0, 1, 1, 0); in other words, the $\otimes$ of two bits is 1 if they disagree and 0 if they agree. Standard computer programming languages allow entire strings of bits (in length up to the word length of the machine, today normally 32 bits or 64 bits) to be XORed at once, in a single machine instruction. Thus, for example, on a standard 32-bit PC, it is possible in just a few machine clock cycles to tally the total number of bits that disagreed between two different strings of 32 bits, which in the present application would be chunks from two different IrisCodes. This operation can be repeated at nearly the clock frequency of the computer, for example, at typically 3 gigahertz today. This highly efficient method of measuring the degree of dissimilarity between the IrisCodes from two different eye images is the basis for the extremely rapid exhaustive search capability of this biometric technology. On a single CPU of that speed, it is possible to calculate the similarities between different pairings of iris images (over a wide range of relative rotations because the absolution orientation of a given iris image is unknown and depends on camera tilt, head tilt, and cyclotorsion of the eye) at the speed of roughly a million full comparisons of irides per second.

In addition to the 2,048 data bits (256 bytes) of phase information encoding each iris, an equal number of masking bits are also computed to signify whether any iris region is obscured by eyelids, contains any eyelash occlusions, specular reflections, boundary artifacts of hard contact lenses, or poor signal-to-noise ratio, and thus should be ignored as artifact. The masking bits from the two irides are ANDed (as in Eq. 5) with each other and also ANDed with the XORed data bits, in order to control whether or not any pair of corresponding data bits can influence the calculated similarity. The resultant number of set bits, or norm ($\| \, \|$), is then calculated in order to derive the raw Hamming distance HD_{raw}, which is the fraction of bits (deemed significant) that disagree between two irides. For any two different irides, statistical independence creates the expectation of a value of $HD_{raw} = 0.5$ for this score. If we denote the two iris phase data vectors as {$codeA$, $codeB$} and their associated mask vectors as {$maskA$, $maskB$}, then their raw dissimilarity score is:

$$HD_{raw} = \frac{\left\|(codeA \otimes codeB) \cap maskA \cap maskB\right\|}{\left\|maskA \cap maskB\right\|}$$ (5)

As different people expose different amounts of iris between their eyelids, and the amount visible depends also on occluding eyelashes, reflections, and other circumstances, the number of bits available for comparison between two different IrisCodes is quite variable. A close match (say a Hamming distance of $HD_{raw} = 0.100$) based on only few compared bits is much less indicative of identity than an apparently poorer match (say $HD_{raw} = 0.200$) based on a large number of compared bits. This requires a renormalization of any observed raw Hamming distance score HD_{raw} into one HD_{norm} whose deviation from statistical independence ($HD_{raw} = 0.500$) has been rescaled for statistical significance, based on the number of bits n that were actually compared between the two IrisCodes:

$$HD_{norm} = 0.5 - (0.5 - HD_{raw})\sqrt{\frac{n}{911}}$$ (6)

The parameters in the above equation influence the standard deviation of the distribution of normalized Hamming distance scores, and they give the distribution a stable form which permits a stable decision rule to be used whether much or little iris data is actually available.

15.5 Results from 200 Billion Cross-Comparisons

15.5.1 Database

In 2001 the U.A.E. launched a national border-crossing security system that is today deployed at all 27 of the Emirates' border entry points and air- and seaports. All foreign nationals who possess a visa to enter the U.A.E. must look at an iris camera installed at immigration desks. Algorithms developed by the author locate the eyes and compute their IrisCodes, as described above, from live video images acquired using infrared illumination in the NIR band (700 nm–900 nm). The database against which the visitors are checked is a "negative watch list" of persons deemed untrustworthy or who have been denied entry for a variety of reasons, including security concerns, past violations, previous imprisonment, travelling under false documents, or work permit violations. Most persons who reside and work in the U.A.E. are not U.A.E. nationals but foreign nationals. Many who had overstayed their work permits or committed other violations were expelled, under an amnesty program in lieu of other sanctions. The total number of persons on the watch list was about 316,250, spanning 152 nationalities. Both irides of each person were enrolled in the database, which thus consisted of about 632,500 different iris patterns. In live operation, each presenting iris is compared exhaustively against all in the watch-list database in less than 2 seconds. The U.A.E. Minister of the Interior, H.R.H. Sheikh Saif Bin Zayyed, made the enrollment database available to the University of Cambridge for detailed

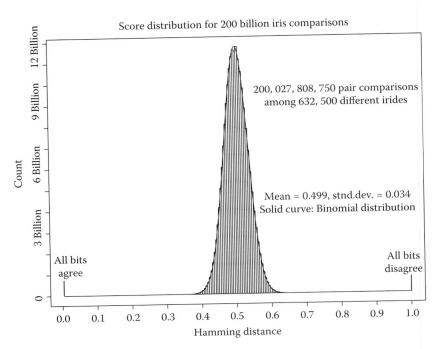

Score distribution for 200 billion iris comparisons

200, 027, 808, 750 pair comparisons
among 632, 500 different irides

Mean = 0.499, stnd.dev. = 0.034
Solid curve: Binomial distribution

All bits
agree

All bits
disagree

Hamming distance

Figure 15.4 Distribution of HD_{norm} Hamming distance scores for 200 billion different pairings of iris patterns, without relative rotations. The solid curve fitting the histogram is a binomial distribution, Equation 7.

analysis and dissemination of results. As N different objects can generate a total of $N \cdot (N - 1)/2$ different pairings, the total number of different pairings of irides that can be made in this database of $N = 632,500$ is more than 200 billion: 200,027,808,750.

15.5.2 Comparisons of Different Irides without Rotations

Figure 15.4 shows all the cross-comparison similarity scores HD_{norm} from the 200 billion different iris pairings. The vast majority of IrisCodes from different eyes disagreed in roughly 50% of their bits, as expected as the bits are equiprobable and uncorrelated between different eyes. Very few pairings of IrisCodes could disagree in fewer than 35% or more than 65% of their bits, as is evident from the distribution in Figure 15.4. The smallest and largest Hamming distances found in this set of 200 billion simple comparisons of different IrisCodes were 0.265 and 0.750, respectively.

The solid curve that fits the data very closely in Figure 15.4 is a binomial probability density function. This theoretical form was chosen because comparisons between bits from different IrisCodes are Bernoulli trials, or conceptually "coin tosses," and Bernoulli trials generate binomial distributions. If one tossed a coin whose probability of "heads" is p in a series of N independent tosses and counted the number m of "heads" outcomes, and if one tallied this fraction $x = m/N$ in a large number of such repeated runs of N tosses, then the expected distribution of x would be as per the solid curve in Figure 15.4:

$$f(x) = \frac{N!}{m!(N-m)!} p^m (1-p)^{(N-m)} \tag{7}$$

The analogy between tossing coins and comparing bits between different IrisCodes is deep but imperfect, because any given IrisCode has internal correlations arising from iris features, especially in the radial direction. Further correlations are introduced by the two-dimensional Gabor wavelet filters: their lowpass aspect introduces correlations in amplitude, and their bandpass aspect introduces correlations in phase, both of which linger to an extent that is inversely proportional to the filter bandwidth. The effect of these correlations[10] is to reduce the value of the distribution parameter N to a number significantly smaller than the number of bits that are actually compared between two IrisCodes; N becomes the number of effectively independent bit comparisons. The value of p is very close to 0.5 (empirically 0.499 for the U.A.E. database), because the states of each bit are equiprobable *a priori*, and so any pair of bits from different IrisCodes are equally likely to agree or disagree.

The binomial functional form that describes the distribution of dissimilarity scores for comparisons between different iris patterns is key to the robustness of this technology in large-scale search applications. The tails of the binomial attenuate extremely rapidly because of the dominating central tendency caused by the factorial terms in Equation 7. Rapidly attenuating tails are critical for a biometric to survive the vast numbers of opportunities to make false matches without, in fact, making any, when applied in an "all-against-all" mode of searching for matching identities, as is contemplated in some national projects.

15.5.3 Comparisons of Genetically Identical Irides

Genetically identical eyes were also compared in the same manner in order to discover the degree to which their textural patterns were correlated and hence genetically determined. A convenient source of genetically identical irides are the right and left pair from any given person; such pairs have essentially the same genetic relationship as have the four irides of monozygotic twins or, indeed, the prospective 2N irides of N clones. Although eye color is, of course, strongly determined genetically, as is overall iris appearance, the detailed patterns of genetically identical irides appear to be as uncorrelated as they are among unrelated eyes. Using the same methods as described above, 648 right/left iris pairs from 324 persons were compared pairwise. Their mean HD was 0.497 with standard deviation 0.031, and their distribution (Figure 15.5) was statistically indistinguishable from the distribution for unrelated eyes (Figure 15.4). A set of 6 pairwise comparisons among the eyes of actual monozygotic twins also yielded a result (mean HD = 0.507) expected for unrelated eyes. It appears that the phenotypic random patterns visible in the human iris are almost entirely epigenetic. The lack of genetic penetrance in the detailed iris texture indicates that the identification performance of this biometric is not impaired (as would be the case for face recognition or DNA) in circumstances of genetically identical or closely related persons.

15.5.4 Distribution of Best Matches after Multiple Rotations

When IrisCodes are compared in a search for a match, it cannot be known precisely what was the amount of head tilt, camera tilt, or eye rotation when the IrisCodes were obtained. Therefore, it is necessary to make comparisons over a reasonable range of relative tilts (rotations) between every pair of IrisCodes, keeping the best match as their similarity score. This generates an *extreme value distribution* that is skewed toward lower Hamming distances, even between unrelated irides, because of the increased number of opportunities to get a closer match just by chance.

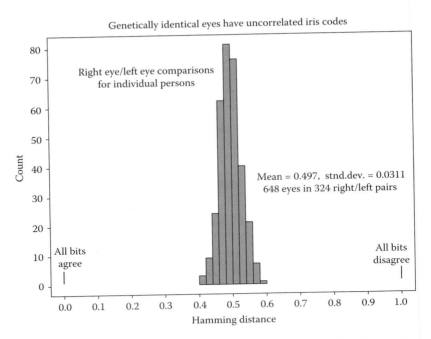

Figure 15.5   Distribution of Hamming distances between genetically identical irides, in 648 paired eyes from 324 persons. The data are statistically indistinguishable from that shown in Figure 15.4 comparing unrelated irides. Unlike eye color, the phase structure of iris patterns, therefore, appears to be epigenetic, arising from random events and circumstances in the morphogenesis of this tissue.

The new distribution after k rotations of IrisCodes in the search process still has a simple analytic form that can be derived theoretically. Let $f_0(x)$ be the raw density distribution obtained for the HD_{norm} scores between different irides after comparing them in only a single relative orientation; for example, $f_0(x)$ might be the binomial defined in Equation 7. Then $F_0(x)$, the cumulative of $f_0(x)$ from 0 to x becomes the probability of getting a false match in such a test when using an HD_{norm} acceptance criterion at x:

$$F_0(x) = \int_0^x f_0(x)dx \tag{8}$$

or, equivalently,

$$f_0(x) = \frac{d}{dx} F_0(x) \tag{9}$$

Clearly, then, the probability of not making a false match when using decision criterion x is $1 - F_0(x)$ after a single test, and it is $[1 - F_0(x)]^k$ after carrying out k such tests independently at k different relative orientations. It follows that the probability of a false match after a "best of k" test of agreement, when using HD_{norm} criterion x, regardless of the actual form of the raw unrotated distribution $f_0(x)$, is:

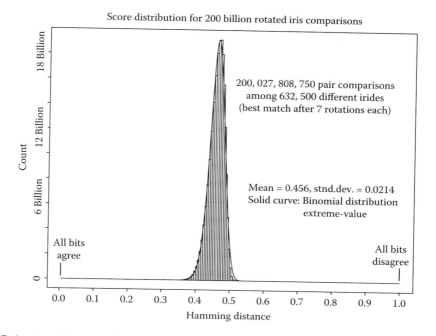

Figure 15.6 Distribution of dissimilarity scores between the same 200 billion iris pair comparisons as given in Figure 15.4, but showing only the best match after 7 relative rotations of each pair because of uncertainty about actual iris orientation. The solid curve is the extreme value of the binomial distribution, Equation 11.

$$F_k(x) = 1 - [1 - F_0(x)]^k \qquad (10)$$

and the expected density $f_k(x)$ associated with this cumulative is:

$$f_k(x) = \frac{d}{dx} F_k(x)$$
$$= k f_0(x)[1 - F_0(x)]^{k-1} \qquad (11)$$

Equation 11 for the extreme value distribution is the solid curve in Figure 15.6, fitting the distribution of the 200 billion IrisCode comparisons after $k = 7$ relative rotations of each pair.

15.6 Observed False Match Rates

The cumulative scores under the left tail of the distribution shown in Figure 15.6, up to various Hamming distance thresholds, reveal the false match rates among the 200 billion iris comparisons if the identification decision policy used those thresholds. These rates are provided in the following Table 15.1. No such matches were found with Hamming distances below about 0.262; but the table has been extended down to 0.220 using Equation 7 to Equation 11 for the theoretical cumulative of the extreme value distribution of multiple

Table 15.1   False Match Rates

HD Criterion	Observed False Match Rate
0.220	0 (theor: 1 in 5×10^{15})
0.225	0 (theor: 1 in 1×10^{15})
0.230	0 (theor: 1 in 3×10^{14})
0.235	0 (theor: 1 in 9×10^{13})
0.240	0 (theor: 1 in 3×10^{13})
0.245	0 (theor: 1 in 8×10^{12})
0.250	0 (theor: 1 in 2×10^{12})
0.255	0 (theor: 1 in 7×10^{11})
0.262	1 in 200 billion
0.267	1 in 50 billion
0.272	1 in 13 billion
0.277	1 in 2.7 billion
0.282	1 in 284 million
0.287	1 in 96 million
0.292	1 in 40 million
0.297	1 in 18 million
0.302	1 in 8 million
0.307	1 in 4 million
0.312	1 in 2 million
0.317	1 in 1 million

Note: False match rates either observed in the distribution of scores or predicted theoretically, tabulated as a function of possible decision policy match criteria imposed on the normalized Hamming distance scores HD_{norm}.

samples from the binomial (plotted as the solid curve in Figure 15.6), in order to extrapolate the theoretically expected false match rates for such decision policies. These false match rates, whether observed or theoretical, also serve as the confidence levels that can be associated with a given quality of match.

The U.S. Department of Homeland Security (DHS) in 2005 sponsored independent testing of the same Daugman algorithms as reported here for the U.A.E. database. In a total of 1,707,061,393 (1.7 billion) cross-comparisons between different irides, the smallest Hamming distance observed in the DHS test was in the range of 0.280, consistent with Table 15.1 for such a number of comparisons.[11]

15.7 Decidability of Iris Recognition

The overall "decidability" of the task of recognizing persons by their iris patterns is revealed by comparing the Hamming distance distributions for same vs. different irides. The left distribution in Figure 15.7 shows the HD_{norm} similarity scores computed between 7,070 different pairs of same-eye images acquired on different occasions, under different conditions, and usually with different cameras. The right distribution shows the results of comparisons among different eyes; this database is different from the large U.A.E. database presented earlier, but the distribution is indistinguishable in shape from that one in Figure 15.6. To the degree that one can confidently decide whether an observed sample belongs to the left or the right distribution in Figure 15.7, iris recognition can be successfully performed. Such a dual distribution representation of the decision problem may be called the "decision environment," because it reveals the extent to which the two cases

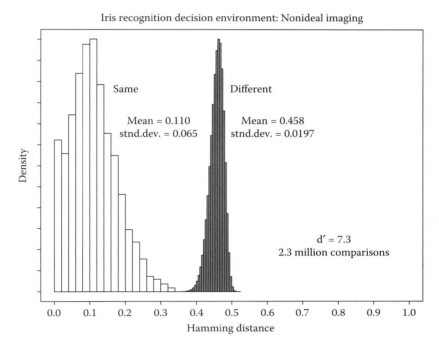

Figure 15.7 The decision environment for iris recognition under relatively unfavorable conditions, using images acquired at different distances, and by different optical platforms with somewhat different wavelengths of illumination within the near-infrared band.

(same vs. different) are separable and thus how reliably decisions can be made, as the overlap between the two distributions determines the error rates.

Whereas Figure 15.7 shows the decision environment under less favorable conditions (images acquired by different camera platforms), Figure 15.8 shows the decision environment under ideal (indeed, almost artificial) conditions. Subjects' eyes were imaged in a laboratory setting using always the same camera with fixed zoom factor and at fixed distance, and with fixed illumination. Not surprisingly, more than half of such image comparisons achieved an HD_{norm} of 0.00, and the average HD_{norm} was a mere 0.019. It is clear from comparing Figure 15.7 and Figure 15.8 that the "authentics" distribution for iris recognition (the similarity between different images of the same eye, as shown in the left-side distributions), depends very strongly upon the image acquisition conditions. However, the measured similarity for "imposters" (the right-side distribution, which in every case in this chapter derives from a different database) is apparently almost completely independent of imaging factors. Instead, it mainly reflects just the combinatorics of Bernoulli trials, as bits from independent binary sources (the phase codes for different irides) are compared.

For two-choice decision tasks (e.g., same vs. different), the decidability index d' is one useful measure of how well separated the two distributions are, as recognition errors would be caused by their overlap. If their two means are μ_1 and μ_2, and their two standard deviations are σ_1 and σ_2, then d' is defined as

$$d' = \frac{|\mu_1 - \mu_2|}{\sqrt{(\sigma_1^2 + \sigma_2^2)/2}} \qquad (12)$$

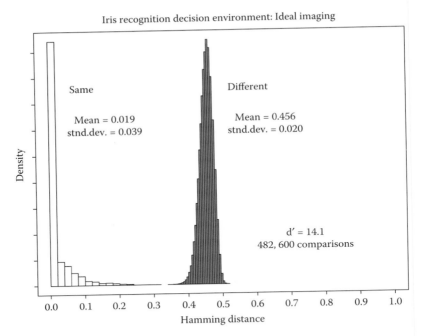

Iris recognition decision environment: Ideal imaging

Figure 15.8   The decision environment for iris recognition under very favorable conditions, using always the same camera, distance, and lighting, in a laboratory setting.

This measure of decidability is independent of how liberal or conservative is the acceptance threshold used. Rather, by measuring separation, it reflects the degree to which any improvement in (say) the false match error rate must be paid for by a worsening of the false nonmatch (failure-to-match) error rate. The measured decidability for iris recognition is $d' = 7.3$ for the nonideal (crossed platform) conditions presented in Figure 15.7, and it is $d' = 14.1$ for the ideal imaging conditions presented in Figure 15.8.

Although it is clear that image acquisition factors play a significant role in the ability of iris recognition to make matches, it is also noteworthy that this technology tolerates well such large amounts of poor or missing data. As illustrated by Figure 15.4 to Figure 15.8, up to about 30% of the bits in two IrisCodes can disagree (yielding a Hamming distance of about 0.30), whereas still the probability of error in accepting them as a match remains minuscule. This property reveals the power of a simple test of statistical independence having a high intrinsic number of degrees of freedom, generated by large random variation among individuals, when this feature is used for biological human identification.

References

1. Adini, Y., Moses, Y., and Ullman, S., Face recognition: the problem of compensating for changes in illumination direction, *IEEE Transactions on Pattern Analysis and Machine Intelligence* 19(7), 721–732, 1997.

2. Daugman, J. and Downing, C., Epigenetic randomness, complexity, and singularity of human iris patterns, *Proceedings of the Royal Society, B. Biological Sciences* 268, 1737–1740, 2001.

3. Davenport, G. and Davenport, C., Heredity of eye-color in man, *Science* 26, 589–592, 1907.

4. Kronfeld, P., Gross anatomy and embryology of the eye, in *The Eye*, H. Davson, Ed., Academic Press, London, 1962.

5. Imesch, P.D., Wallow, I., and Albert, D.M., The color of the human eye: a review of morphologic correlates and of some conditions that affect iridial pigmentation, *Surv Ophthalmol* 41(Suppl. 2), 117–123, 1997.

6. Kollias, N., The spectroscopy of human melanin pigmentation, in *Melanin: Its Role in Human Photoprotection*, Zeise, L., Chedekel, M., Fitzpatrick, T., Eds., Valdenmar Publishing Co., Overland Park, KS, 1995, pp. 31–38.

7. Daugman, J., High confidence visual recognition of persons by a test of statistical independence, *IEEE Transactions on Pattern Analysis and Machine Intelligence* 15(11), 1148–1161, 1993.

8. Daugman, J., The importance of being random: statistical principles of iris recognition, *Pattern Recognition* 36(2), 279–291, 2003.

9. Daugman, J., How iris recognition works, *IEEE Transactions on Circuits and Systems for Video Technology* 14(1), 21–30, 2004.

10. Viveros, R., Balasubramanian, K., and Balakrishnan, N., Binomial and negative binomial analogues under correlated Bernoulli trials, *The American Statistician* 48(3), 243–247, 1994.

11. The International Biometric Group, Independent Testing of Iris Recognition Technology, May 2005, sponsored by the U.S. Department of Homeland Security, 2005.

Section 6

**Identification from
Methods of Communication**

Handwriting 16

IAIN HENRY STEWART

Contents

16.1 Introduction 289
16.2 Handwriting and Identification of Handwriting 290
    16.2.1 Teaching, Identification, and Variation 290
    16.2.2 Signatures 294
    16.2.3 Handwriting Instruments 296
16.3 The Analysis of Inks 298
16.4 The Future of Handwriting Analysis..299
References 300

16.1   Introduction

Handwriting, whether pictographic or character based, has existed as a means of communi-cation since civilization began. The earliest records of writing come from China where it is thought it was used as far back as 5500 B.C. (*International Journal of Document Examiners* 1995). The Chinese also made great advances over 2000 years ago when they devised the first inks and papers, which facilitated record keeping for themselves and for posterity. These early writings, and all subsequent writings, had to resemble some sort of standard model that was used at the time of the writing, and it is these necessary similarities and unavoidable differences of which the document examiner must take cognizance.

The examination of documents is a very far-reaching discipline. A document is "any material containing marks, symbols, or signs that convey meaning or a message to someone" (Hilton 1982). This encapsulates a wide range of media including more obvious examples such as handwriting, typewriting and printing, and more obscure methods of documen-tation such as rubber stamps, graffiti, and passports.

In order to necessitate an examination, a document must somehow become a ques-tioned document. This implies that the document is suspected of being fraudulent (e.g., a forged tax disc), has an unknown origin (e.g., a malicious letter), or has a disputed background (e.g., an altered will).

The task of performing these examinations falls to the questioned-document examiner, although other terms such as handwriting analyst, handwriting expert, or document expert may be applied. Whatever title is used, forensic handwriting examination should not, however, be misconstrued as being involved with graphology. The graphologist seeks to discern personal characteristics from one's handwriting and pays no heed to the remainder of a document or, indeed, to anything other than any handwriting present. However, this is insufficient for document examiners; they must scrutinize closely all aspects of a questioned document, e.g., the handwriting, the ink, and the paper, as well as

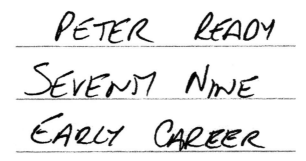

Figure 16.1   Natural variation in handwriting.

look for any evidence of forgery or different authors. Documents consisting of typewritten or printed text are examined using similar methods as those employed for examining handwriting, and each document is inspected extensively, for any signs of alteration, erasure, or addition.

The analysis of handwriting can seek to link various documents to one another through evidence of common authorship. To go one step further than this is to identify this author by comparison of the questioned documents with samples of known authorship. There exist two types of samples: "request" samples and "course of business" samples. Request samples are samples of writing of a specific nature, usually the text that is under question, whereas course of business samples consist of writings originating from day-to-day occurrences. Similar samples are sought when a typewriter or printer has been used in the creation of the questioned document.

These samples are then compared with the questioned documents. Comparison can only take place on a like-for-like basis, i.e., cursive (joined-up) writing is compared with cursive, script with script, block capitals with block capitals, etc. This is an important point, as is the number of samples that should be obtained. During the examination, the examiner attempts to identify distinguishing personal characteristics of the author of both the samples and the questioned documents. These distinguishing features are introduced or assimilated during the writing lifetime of an author. However, deliberate misconstructions aimed at disguising writing or accidental alteration possibly due to use of a poor-quality pen must also be recognized. These latter aspects must not be mistaken for part of the natural variation that occurs within every author's handwriting. All aspects of one's handwriting are subject to natural variation; this is inevitable due to our inability to exactly reproduce any physical movement. However, the range of natural variation can be gauged by the examination of sufficient sample material (Figure 16.1). The comparison of samples and questioned documents consists of finding not only similarities but also observing differences and diligently assessing the significance of each similarity and difference. Examiners then draw on their background knowledge and experience to eventually form their opinions.

16.2   Handwriting and Identification of Handwriting

16.2.1   Teaching, Identification, and Variation

The task of handwriting begins as a very conscious act, usually in infancy. The effort required to translate one's thoughts into a series of meaningful symbols is often underestimated.

However, as an author grows older and matures in innumerable ways, handwriting becomes less of a conscious act and increasingly semiconscious as the strokes made and rhythms employed begin to lose significance through frequent repetition.

Handwriting is usually taught at a rudimentary level in primary school and sometimes slightly before that in nursery school or at home. A fact that should be borne in mind when discussing handwriting is that none of the skills required are in any way innate; the whole method of handwriting must be taught. Most pupils are taught using a basic handwriting system, which can vary from region to region, school to school, teacher to teacher, etc. Some definite systems have been in use in recent years, e.g., the ball-and-stick method, the Fairbank system, or the Briem system (Sassoon 1990). The teaching generally begins in school where a particular system is used, and each pupil tries to learn constructions and apply methods and teachings to their own writing. Some pupils are more naturally adept at copying these methods, whereas some aspects of writing are more difficult to learn. These differences lead to personal alterations to various letters, which are subsequently influenced throughout the pupil's formative years by teachers, friends, and family. Eventually, usually at some time around the late teens, through experimentation, each author arrives at a style with which they feel most comfortable, and this style is then adopted for general use. However, it may alter in later years due to personal injury, nature of work, periods of inactivity, etc.

The letters and numerals that will be learned in most Western schools are derived from an alphabet that descends from Roman antiquity. As such, they were kept as simple as possible, i.e., the figures are almost entirely constructed from straight lines, thus enabling them to be easily carved into stone. This basic simplicity has been retained with some additions made in the form of arches and troughs to give the current alphabet that is employed in our handwriting. Owing to this common origin, most of the systems taught today have somewhat similar basic patterns. The differences that are apparent in the systems are termed *class* or *style characteristics*, which "derive from the general style to which the handwriting conforms" (Harrison 1966). This implies that any child within a certain era will have handwriting based on the same or similar styles. This may sound ominous for identification purposes but, for the expert, it is not the style characteristics that are looked for when examining handwriting; it is the personal or individual characteristics. These characteristics "which have been introduced into the handwriting, whether consciously or unconsciously, by the writer" (Harrison 1966) are of far greater evidential value to the examiner. They can manifest themselves as an infinite number of permutations, e.g., using the Greek "ε," forming any letter unconventionally, joining of words by initial and terminal strokes, and a clockwise pen direction for "o," etc. (see Figure 16.2 and Figure 16.3 for examples). Due to the large number of permutations, which can be introduced either deliberately to affect the appearance or unknowingly, perhaps, to compensate for, say, an unconventional pen grip, personal characteristics go a long way to offset the broad similarities due to style characteristics.

The reason for examining handwriting is, ultimately, to identify the author. This identification relies not only on the previously mentioned class and personal characteristics but also on the quality of one's handwriting. This is made up of a variety of factors that immediately affect the pen movement and, then, when taken as a whole, determine the handwriting line quality. The fluency and rhythm of movement contribute greatly to line quality; the more fluent and rhythmic a pen is in motion, the more smooth, continuous, and rapidly executed is the writing. This can be seen in the presence of a smooth ink line

Figure 16.2 Handwriting differing from conventional formation.

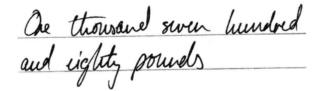

Figure 16.3 Handwriting differing from conventional formation.

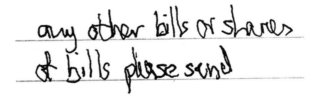

Figure 16.4 Fluent pen movement.

Figure 16.5 Nonfluent pen movement.

with few hesitations, pen lifts, or tremors; these three features of handwriting apply to a more labored and slow-moving writing motion, thereby producing a hesitant pen movement (Figure 16.4 and Figure 16.5). The line quality is also affected by the method of moving the pen. When writing, the fingers, hand, arm, or a combination of any of these three can move the pen. The fine muscular control required to manipulate the advancement of a pen across paper can be a deciding factor in the appearance of one's handwriting; those authors with less capability with regard to this control tend to be poorer writers. The general appearance of handwriting is governed by the preceding factors, i.e., class and personal characteristics and line quality, plus a few more, such as slope, shading, size, and spacing.

If one considers the multitude of factors affecting handwriting, it should come as no surprise to discover that each individual author displays a degree of natural variation. This is the term used to describe the fluctuations of letter formation and rhythm that randomly appear in the writing of one person. This does not indicate that an entirely new formation is applied, unlike in disguise, or that a whole new rhythm is discovered, rather that subtle "variations on a theme" are evident. For example, the letter "h" might normally be written with a curved arch approximately halfway up the upright whereas in a few examples the author places an angular arch low to the baseline or at three-quarters the height of the upright. This natural variation occurs because the human mind and body cannot combine to produce an exact replica of any motion undertaken a great number of times; not even signatures are ever exactly the same. It is because of this variation that numerous samples are required for proper identification, as will be seen later. Natural variation can also be exacerbated by a number of unavoidable or intentional circumstances, such as lack of space available, speed of writing, injuries, illness, medication, drug or alcohol use, stress, writing instrument, writing surface, or writing position.

A second type of variation is a much more deliberate method: that of disguise. Many people think that to disguise their handwriting is not an onerous task. However, they do not consider that to completely disguise their own handwriting it is necessary to do two difficult things. Firstly, the author must have a thorough knowledge of the identifying features of his or her own writing and the significance of each trait and, secondly, he or she must discard these identifying traits and adopt a wholly original set. Without having a full knowledge of these factors it would prove exceedingly difficult for authors to disguise their handwriting over any reasonable length of writing, although if the questioned writing is merely one or two sentences, there is always a chance that the pretense can be upheld long enough to effect a plausible disguise. The majority of attempts at disguise tend to eliminate the obvious, prominent features from the writing but leave a variety of personal characteristics that are useful for identification purposes. Disguised writing tends to show evidence of a conflict between the personal characteristics the author is trying to conceal and his attempts at disguise. The result is handwriting that is less skillfully executed than the usual writing of the author with many irregularities and inconsistencies appearing. These can be present as hesitation, variations in slant, strange and unnecessarily extravagant formations, retracing or touching up of strokes, and slowly executed and trembling lines. A study from 1997 (Keckler 1997) showed that among convicted criminals in America the most frequently altered aspects of handwriting were slope, size, speed, interchanging block capitals for small letters and vice versa, in addition to alterations to the upper and lower portions of letters.

Unlike some other forensic disciplines, e.g., blood typing or DNA, handwriting identification is not based upon statistical means or probabilities. Due to the varying nature of handwriting and the almost impossible task of determining the relationship between formations of different letters, and even the relationship between parts of a single letter, this avenue is closed to handwriting experts. Instead, identification is based on the rigorous study of similarities and differences and on the previous experience of the examiner. There are many aspects of handwriting that an examiner will analyze during his or her work, such as line quality, fluency, letter formation, slope of writing, positioning on the page, relative position to the margins, spacing, ratio of letter heights, positioning of dot on "i" or "j" or the bar on "t," presence of initial or terminal strokes and their length and angle, joining of letters, pen lifts, etc. Each of these aspects is compared between the questioned writing and the samples provided, usually by direct comparison between individual letters, e.g. "a" with "a," "b" with "b," "E," with "E," etc. For each letter examined the expert is trying "to determine its method of construction and proportions, or shape" (Ellen 1997), and hence to assess the extent of natural variation within the samples, and then to compare the questioned writing in order to determine if this writing fits into the range observed. When this process has been implemented for every letter in the questioned writing and all the writing has been examined, the other factors mentioned previously, e.g., fluency, slope, and proportions, are then considered *en masse*. If these are found to be similar, then the examiner must consult his or her knowledge and experience of handwriting and assess the significance of each similarity.

At the same time, however, the possibilities of chance match or simulation — the attempt of an author to disguise the identifying features of his or her own handwriting and adopt those of another author — must be considered. A chance match may occur a small number of times — i.e., once or twice, literally as if by chance — but it is extremely unlikely that the variation of each letter in the alphabet (or all those present in a questioned document) and the myriad parameters, e.g., fluency, slope, proportions, etc., would match consistently and without any significant differences between two or more authors. Simulation can be looked for by observing some of the features mentioned previously concerning disguise, e.g., inaccuracy in letter formation that is close to the imitated style but consistently different, line quality, hesitancy, and also indentations or remnants of pencil in the environs of the writing, which are indicative of copying or tracing. The presence of differences must also be noted and assessed by the examiner.

16.2.2   Signatures

In addition to handwriting comparisons, one of the more common examples of handwriting a questioned-document examiner looks at is signatures. These are probably the most frequently written pieces of information used by any author. In a similar fashion to handwriting, signatures evolve over a period of time. The early extravagance of youth gives way to a more practical and readily executed signature that will be used in various situations as a unique identifier of the author. In a hypothetical situation any questioned signature should be confidently attributed to the real author. Signatures can be a simple extension of an author's everyday handwriting or can depart significantly from the normal writing to become highly stylized. Due to the increased amount of stylization ordinarily present in signatures, they are not normally compared to samples of general handwriting. Irrespective of this, the same methods of identification are used as those previously discussed in relation to handwriting.

The identification of signatures can be hindered by a number of types of disguise or simulation. There are a number of scenarios when it could be claimed a signature is simulated:

1. An author signs a document unknowingly, e.g., some method of transfer is used (e.g., carbon paper) or the real content of the document is somehow hidden.
2. An author signs a document and knowingly refuses to admit to authorship.
3. An author signs a document but disguises his handwriting, usually by altering certain aspects of the signature.
4. An unknown author effects a simulation.

The first scenario is legally difficult to deal with because, as far as the document examiner is concerned, the signature is genuine, whereas the legality of this signature is dubious. The second scenario is easily resolved if the signature resembles all other natural examples of the author's signature. The third scenario can be more complicated, depending on the ability of the author to conceal or alter his or her personal characteristics. In the case of an author who is poor at disguise this may lead to identification, or in the case of an author who is competent at disguise, this may lead to an inconclusive result. The fourth scenario is much more complex because there are a number of methods of producing a simulated signature. The first two methods involve tracing a genuine signature. By placing the document bearing the genuine signature on a light box and then placing the other document on top of this, it is readily possible to lightly trace the silhouetted shape in pencil and then subsequently ink this outline. Alternatively, something like a piece of carbon paper can be placed between the document bearing the genuine signature and the second document, with the genuine document on top and the signature traced over, using a dry pen or pointed instrument with the resulting carbon image on the underlying document being overwritten with ink. This second method can leave traces of carbon or indentations around the simulated signature, whereas the first method can leave pencil or charcoal traces. The third method of simulation is freehand copying, which can potentially produce the most skillful imitations, although it is also the most difficult. Again, similar to hand-writing, authors must suppress their own tendencies to sign the name in their own style and also recognize all the salient features of the copied signature, incorporating them appropriately. These simulations should all contain evidence of their nongenuineness to differing degrees depending on the skill of the forger.

One class of signatures that can sometimes be mistaken for simulations is guided hand or assisted signatures. These are usually made by people who are very ill or, in some cases, on their deathbeds. Due to the fragility of these people, writing can prove an extremely difficult task owing partly to the fine muscular control that is required when writing. These signatures can appear jerky and hesitant as the hand is either gently supported as the author signs in his own manner, or the hand of the author is basically taken through the motions of signing and so the resultant signature bears the characteristics of the helper more than of the author. However, unlike simulations there are usually reliable witnesses and exten-uating circumstances surrounding these types of signature.

Line quality is one of the most important aspects of signature examination, i.e., whether the line wavers, whether it has any unusual pen lifts, retouching, or extra strokes (in comparison to any samples provided), or whether it has a trembling and hesitant appearance as opposed to the firmness of stroke or rhythm, continuity, freedom of movement, and smoothness that characterize genuine signatures. By using any of the three methods of simulation mentioned earlier, the forger is necessarily required to use one signature as the basis of his attempts. This can be of use to the examiner if the model signature is available, as invariably a copied/traced signature will share a common pen-path with the model signature when overlaid. Additionally, if a series of signatures have been simulated then they may all be shown to share a common origin, i.e., one genuine signature has been used for them all, and hence the simulations show a distinct lack of natural variation. Having identified the signature as a simulation, it is sometimes expected that the document examiner can then identify the perpetrator. Unfortunately, due to the nature of simulations this generally proves impossible. Although identification of the perpetrator is not possible, identifying the signature as a simulation is usually sufficient to prevent the document bearing the questioned signature from being acted upon.

16.2.3 Handwriting Instruments

One of the most basic types of writing instruments, and one that has been around for a long time, is the pencil. It consists of a "lead" center encased in wood, although it was not always as sophisticated as the present-day pencil. The lead consists of a mixture of graphite and clay, and it is the ratio of the mixture that endows the pencil lead with its hardness; the greater the proportion of graphite, the darker the stroke left by the pencil, whereas harder lead tends to leave light strokes. As a pencil is drawn across a surface, small particles of lead are continuously being dislodged from the lead shaft becoming entrenched in the uneven surface of the paper. It is because the lead sits on the surface of the paper unbound by any glues, etc., that it only requires the application of a rubber eraser to remove the stroke. Chemical eradicators used to remove ink are useless for the removal of pencil, whereas accidental rubbing or friction applied to the surface, insignificant to ink marks, can be enough to smudge the pencil deposits. The addition of colored pigments enabled the manufacture of colored pencils and crayons, although these usually prove harder to remove due to the presence of wax in their composition.

In modern times, there have been a number of additions to the family of writing instruments, most famously the ballpoint pen, the roller ball, and felt or fiber-tipped pens. The ballpoint pen was first introduced in America in 1945, although it was originally sold in Europe in 1935 where only approximately 25,000 pens were sold. Ladislo Biro first manufactured them in Argentina in the early 1940s leading to mass production of the ballpoint by Reynolds, which were purchased by millions in America. The pen seems quite simple in its design; it consists of a steel ball (approximately 1 mm in diameter) held in a housing that keeps it from falling out and yet allows it complete freedom of rotation. This ball is in contact with a reservoir of ink that is housed above it in the shaft of the pen, and the free rotation of the ball allows it to be coated in ink that is then transferred to the writing surface. Contrasted against the relative simplicity of the pen itself was the monumental task of creating ink that satisfied a long list of required properties to ensure correct functioning of the pen. The ink had to have the correct viscosity and adhesion to the ball to allow it to flow freely when required and to allow easy deposition onto the writing surface. The carrier solvent had to have the correct vapor pressure to prevent clogging, yet be rapidly drying once dispensed. It could not contain any particulate matter, as this would affect the free rotation of the ball in the housing. It also had to be nonhygroscopic and noncorrosive, and have high stability to light, oxidation, and polymerization. Finally, as with all inks, it had to have good adherence to paper and be highly resistant to solvents and bleaching agents. The resulting ink was a paste-like substance, oily in nature (based on olein); indeed, this oily nature very much restricted the types of dye that were available for use in the ink. However, this obstacle was overcome in the early 1950s when inks based on polyethylene glycols were introduced, the polar nature of which allowed a much wider range of dyes to be used. These inks were found to "adhere very firmly to the cellulose fibers so that writing can neither be smudged or transferred" (Harrison 1966).

Following the development of the ballpoint pen was the roller ball (1960s) and the felt and fiber-tip pens (at the end of the 1960s into the 1970s). The roller ball is very similar in its operation to the ballpoint pen, although the ink is aqueous based — a liquid ink like that of fountain pens. The felt- and fiber-tipped pens are similar to each other in that their tips consist of densely packed fibers through which the liquid ink is drawn by capillary action. Felt tips tend to be less densely packed and thus produce a thicker writing line than fiber tips, which are often manufactured in a variety of tip widths.

The nature of each type of pen dictates the type of stroke it is capable of producing and hence contributes to its identification. Fountain pen strokes tend to be variable in width, giving rise to shading in the stroke, and there can also be tramlines present caused by the pressure exerted on the nib. The flexibility of the nibs can affect the indentations left by a fountain pen; individual pen indentations can vary along the length of a stroke, whereas the depth of penetration of the ink into the fibers of the paper is similar among all fountain pens, being quite deep. The width of the nibs can vary between pens, a trait that is readily identifiable under microscopic examination and that can be used to distinguish between different pens used to write on the same piece of paper.

In comparison, the ballpoint pen gives a stroke that has a uniform distribution of ink along its length and, with the exception of the initial and terminal strokes, has a uniform stroke width because of the fixed diameter of the steel ball. Due to the nature of the ink and the pen itself, there are a number of interesting aspects to the writing line. As the ball of these pens rotates along a stroke, a build-up of unused ink can form at the junction of the ball and housing at a point diametrically opposite from the leading edge of the stroke. This build-up is the source of "glooping," where the build-up is deposited after a change in direction of the pen, i.e., the ball rotates in a different direction and, as such, can and usually will, pick up this build-up of ink and deposit it soon after the change in direction. Another evidentially important aspect of the operation of the ballpoint is the "inkless start." This occurs on the completion of a stroke where the tip of the ball has just ceased being in contact with the paper. At this point the tip is almost devoid of ink because it has been deposited on the paper. As ballpoint ink is so viscous, there is no possibility of the ink flowing onto the tip of the ball. This means that on commencement of a new stroke there will probably be some manifestation of this "inkless start," which can be a complete absence of ink at the very start of the stroke or it can be a smaller isolated island in the middle of a start. This characteristic of the ballpoint pen can be used to identify the movement or direction associated with the writing of a stroke.

The housing of the ball is involved again in the next feature of ballpoint pens called *burr striations* and an extension of these phenomena, which are called *memory effects*. Burr striations are formed when the ink that is collected on the ball from the internal reservoir is rotated past the housing; faults in or damage to the housing give rise to striations in the ink that is about to be deposited onto the paper (Figure 16.6). These are very helpful in identifying the direction of curved strokes, as it has been shown that a unique relationship exists between the orientation of burr striations and the direction of the pen movement

Figure 16.6 Striation in handwriting.

that produced the striations; the striations run toward the outside edge of the curve in the same general direction as that in which the pen has moved (Snape 1980). As the striations are formed between the ball and the housing, it will take a short period of time before they are deposited as part of the actual stroke, i.e., they will appear after the writing movement that has produced them. This delay is explained when the mechanics of the creation of the striations are considered. Firstly, the ink is deposited from the reservoir onto the ball, which then passes the housing and is endowed with striations. This ink then sits on the surface of the ball until the ball has traveled approximately one quarter of its diameter, and then this ink is at the writing tip where it is deposited onto the writing surface where the striations can be seen. It is because of this time lag that the striations present in a curved stroke run toward the outside edge of the curve in the same general direction as that in which the pen has moved (Snape 1980).

An extension of this effect occurs when the pen is lifted at the end of a stroke, where the ball will retain the striations that were generated by the completion of the last stroke, as if "memorized." When a subsequent stroke is executed, these "stored" striations corresponding to the direction of the final movement of the previous stroke will be deposited at the very beginning of this new stroke. This is a useful tool in sequencing strokes, e.g., discovering which strokes were written first in the construction of capital letters, or in following the direction of angled strokes, as the effect is regarded as still being reliable where the angle of the strokes lies between 30° and 160° (Hung and Leung 1995). The evidential value of these characteristics of ballpoint-pen writing is very high, indeed; they allow detailed examination of how an author constructs letters in his writing and, as mentioned, it allows some attempt at sequencing of strokes.

The strokes that are made by fiber or felt-tip pens are similar to each other. They consist of a continuous distribution of ink on the writing surface with some diffusion at the edges of the stroke. There are sometimes hairlines at the edges which would be caused by a number of the tightly packed fibers randomly protruding from the bulk of the tip through wear or damage and depositing some of the ink as a separate, though very light, stroke. The fiber tip leaves a heavier indent than the felt, as the felt tip is generally broader at the tip and so generates less pressure. These types of pens probably leave the least amount of handwriting line-quality information that could be of evidential value.

16.3 The Analysis of Inks

It is not only the mechanics of the writing instrument that can afford identification, but also the inks themselves, and their chemical composition can be exploited for identification purposes. Although two inks may be visually indistinguishable, their respective chemical contents can be very different. The ingredients of ink will have been recorded by the manufacturers and kept in a database by them. These databases may be acquired by other agencies such as the Laboratory of Alcohol, Tobacco, and Firearms (ATF) of the U.S. Treasury. This detailed knowledge of the content of the ink can help discriminate between questioned ink entries that look very similar to our unaided eye. This discrimination can be achieved using a variety of techniques, some nondestructive whereas some are destructive. The simplest is a nondestructive technique involving a piece of apparatus called a *video spectral comparator* (VSC). This equipment uses a combination of UV, visible light, and IR radiation in conjunction with various filters to exploit any differences in fluorescence, luminescence, or absorbance of the inks. This technique is generally readily available and is simple to use, however, the discriminatory power is quite poor. Recent improvements in technology have resulted in modern VSC machines that allow basic spectra to be obtained. Should VSC examination prove nondiscriminating, then destructive techniques may be employed. However, the use of destructive techniques would be dependent on the type and seriousness of the crime involved.

One such technique, thin layer chromatography (TLC), requires the removal of a small portion of the ink line, which is then dissolved in a suitable solvent. Different sections of the ink line, as required by the nature of the investigation, are removed and dissolved. A portion of the document containing no ink is also removed and used as a negative control. Very small volumes of these solutions are then placed on a stationary phase, i.e., a chromatographic plate, and the mobile phase, i.e., a liquid that separates different components of the ink, based on their affinity coefficient between the stationary phase and the mobile phase, carries the sample solutions up the plate. The mobile phase moves up the plate by capillary action, and as it rises it elutes each of the ink components as its affinity for the stationary phase overwhelms its affinity for the mobile phase. This offers a rapid and inexpensive method for discriminating between inks; however, it has limited resolving power between similar components. A more powerful method is high performance liquid chromatography (HPLC), which has much greater resolution and reproducibility, although it is considerably more expensive.

Spectrometry, a technique that depends on the individual absorptivities of dye molecules in the ink, can be used to obtain absorption spectra of the inks. When used over a wide range of wavelengths, this technique offers good discrimination. Some spectrometers require significant sample sizes to ensure quality spectra; however, this may not be compatible with the needs of the investigative body. Ideally, it would be best to use a microspectrophotometer, although this is extremely expensive and so for most agencies will be unobtainable.

Raman spectroscopy and x-ray fluorescence (XRF) can be used to examine dye molecules in inks, whereas scanning electron microscopy (SEM) and neutron activation analysis (NAA) can be used to examine metal content of inks. SEM and x-ray diffraction (XRD) can also be used to examine the elemental composition of papers. All of these techniques offer very powerful means of discrimination and identification. The main drawbacks of these techniques for investigative agencies are cost implications and training issues.

16.4   The Future of Handwriting Analysis

Although forensic handwriting analysis has been used for over 100 years, it is a discipline that does not normally require complex apparatus. For basic handwriting analysis, the most useful tools are a good method of magnification and good illumination. Computer handwriting databases are in existence that provide the basis for computer-aided searches; however, the results require human verification. Work continues on refining technology for computerized handwriting searching, although attuning the initial parameters of the algorithm to give output similar to the human assessment of the material is proving difficult.

The advance of technology in general has affected the traditional casework of forensic document examiners, e.g., proliferation of computers has led to less handwritten anonymous mail and "Chip and PIN" bank cards often remove the need for a signature. These examples could be seen to point toward the end of forensic handwriting analysis, yet it seems that often the most convenient and widespread means of human identification still remain intimately entwined with a handwritten signature.

References

Ellen, D., *The Scientific Examination of Documents Methods and Techniques*, 2nd ed., Taylor and Francis, London, 1997.

Harrison, W.R., *Suspect Documents: Their Scientific Examination*, 2nd impression with supplement, Sweet and Maxwell, London, 1996.

Hilton, O., *Scientific Examination of Questioned Documents* (revised edition), Elsevier, New York, 1982.

Hung, P.S. and Leung, S.C., Some observations on the morphology of a ballpoint pen stroke, *International Journal of Forensic Document Examiners* 1(1), 18, 1995.

International Journal of Document Examiners 1(1), 92, 1995.

Keckler, J. A., Felonious disguise — a study of the most commonly used modes of disguise adopted by convicted felons, *International Journal of Document Examiners* 3(2), 154, 1997.

Sassoon, R., *Handwriting: A New Perspective*, Stanley Thorne Ltd., Cheltenham, 1990, p. 8.

Snape, K.W., Detection of the direction of ballpoint pen motion from the orientation of burr striations in curved pen strokes, *Journal of Forensic Science* 25(2), 386–390, 1980.

Section 7

Identification from Podiatry and Walking

The Foot 17

WESLEY VERNON

Contents

17.1   Introduction 303
17.2   Identification of the Foot Using Podiatry Treatment Records 305
17.3   Identification from Marks of the Foot on the Surrounding Environment..........306
17.4   Direct Comparison 307
17.5   Measurement and Comparison Method 1 — The Gunn Method 307
17.6   Measurement and Comparison Method 2 — The Optical Center Approach 308
17.7   Measurement and Comparison Method 3 — The Overlay Method 309
17.8   Measurement and Comparison Method 4 — The Robbins Method 310
17.9   Measurement and Comparison Method 5 — Rossi's Podometric System 310
17.10 Comparison of All Methods — Which Is the Preferred Approach?....................311
17.11 How Should These Methods Be Used in Practice? 312
17.12 Additional Factors When Considering Identifications Involving Footwear 312
17.13 Interpretation of Footprints and Shoe Wear 313
        17.13.1 Toe Box Variables 314
        17.13.2 Excessive Footwear Length 315
        17.13.3 Inadequate Footwear Length...316
        17.13.4 Inadequate Footwear Width 317
        17.13.5 The Confounding Effects of Foot Function......................................317
        17.13.6 Additional Considerations in Footwear Identification......................318
17.14 Potential Future Developments in Identification from the Foot 318
References 319

17.1   Introduction

The foot is an anatomical region that may demonstrate a high degree of individuality. As recognized by Defoe (1719), the human foot is also distinctive from the foot of nonhumans. The divergent first ray in the ape foot, with accompanying opposing first digit position, is not present in humans (Kidd 1998), and suggestions have also been made that the individual foot is unique when compared to that of other humans (Robbins 1985, Kennedy 1996). To date, however, this belief has yet to be satisfactorily proved, although a significant study in Canada has attempted to illustrate this point statistically (Kennedy et al. 2003). In using the foot in identification, there are currently two main forms of approach — identification from the records kept by podiatrists on feet that they have examined and treated, and identification from marks left by feet on objects with which they have been in contact, especially on footwear and ground surfaces (e.g., stepping in soil, in blood on a hard surface, etc.).

There have been a number of past influences on making person identifications by foot, footprint, or shoe examination, beginning inauspiciously when Gerard (1920) published his thoughts about footprints. Notable beliefs expressed by Gerard included "determination is indicated by feet kept in a parallel position, a calculating and curious person toes out considerably, knock-kneed individuals are frequently found to be cranky, and people who lean to the right are alleged cynics and sarcastic in their mode of speech." This was followed several years later, when Muir (1935) published a paper in which he considered a case involving human footprints. Here, the perpetrator of a crime whose footprints had been found at the scene exhibited double ainhum, and the fifth toe of each foot had autoamputated, thereby presenting links to that individual. Although the paper was published after the arrest and conviction of the criminal, Muir presented clear and logical thinking of the type required in consideration of the foot in human identification.

In 1959, Sir Sidney Smith, a forensic pathologist, detailed a case in Falkirk, U.K., in which, by considering the foot impressions and the wear of the footwear found at a crime scene, he successfully predicted that the owner of the shoes would be short, have a short left leg, left pelvic drop, scoliosis, left foot drop, and would have a missing or deformed left lesser toe, possibly due to poliomyelitis (Smith 1959). The suspect when arrested matched this description, suggesting, although presumptively, that the foot did have potential in the identification process.

Later, Lucock, an English chiropodist and member of the Shoe and Allied Trades Research Association (SATRA), further considered identification from marks left by the foot upon worn footwear (Lucock 1967, 1979, 1980). In Lucock's first paper (1967) on identification from footwear, his personal theories relating to identification from shoe wear patterns and elimination of possible shoe owners through shoe sizing considerations were stated. There was, however, no evidence of supporting research or published records of actual case studies undertaken by Lucock to demonstrate the efficacy of his work.

In 1972, Dr. Norman Gunn, a Canadian podiatrist, began to undertake case work, pioneering many of the forensic techniques practiced today that involve considerations of the foot. Dr. Gunn's first reported case involved identification from a footprint found on the shore of a Canadian lake, and a method of comparison was devised by Dr. Gunn to demonstrate points of individuality of which he was aware as a podiatric physician. The success in this case led to Dr. Gunn's further involvement in identification procedures involving the human foot, some of which have been reported in the literature (Koehler 1986, Gunn 1991a, 1991b).

Later, however, some problems were experienced with the presentation of foot-related evidence. In 1981, podiatry professors Valmassey and Smith publicly challenged anomalous footwear evidence presented to an American court by Dr. Louise Robbins, an anthropologist (Valmassey 1982), suggesting that this area of practice in human identification was less than robust. The report of this case noted that Dr. Robbins' premise "that shoe prints are as individual as fingerprints is not sufficiently scientific for a court of law" (Valmassey 1982). Further errors in Robbins' position came to light during the reported trial and included a failure to appreciate the influence of the functional effects of the foot on shoe wear patterns and basic misconceptions of the anatomical makeup of the foot. Later challenges to Dr. Robbins' evidence led to the exposure of questionable practice in this area, and subsequent skepticism impeded further development of foot-related evidence in the U.S. Outside the U.S., however, consideration of the foot in human identification has continued to develop, albeit slowly.

In the U.K., a mainly research-based approach has been taken in this work to further test and enhance knowledge used in this field. In 1984 a suggestion was made by Dr. Ivor Doney, a police surgeon, that podiatry records could have value in identification (Doney and Harris 1984). Research was later undertaken to further demonstrate this potential by podiatrist Wesley Vernon (Vernon 1994, Sanger and Vernon 1997). Later, forensic scientist Owen Facey considered whether shoe outsole wear patterns could be related to the functioning foot as an identification factor (Facey et al. 1992a, 1992b, 1993), and this potential was later followed up by Wesley Vernon (2000) in his Ph.D. thesis. As Dr. Vernon's work dispelled a number of myths surrounding identification of the foot through shoe outsole wear pattern form, it did provide a baseline of understanding from which future developments could take place.

Interest from the podiatry profession in the U.K. subsequently led to a number of unpublished undergraduate projects considering various aspects of forensic podiatry (Doxford 1997, Thomas 1997) and one recently completed Master's level study (Pavey 2004). Although not complete at the time of writing, another Ph.D. study in forensic podiatry is taking place in Scotland. Here, the relationship between footprints and the stature of the owner are being reconsidered (Kerr 2004).

Developments have also been taking place in other countries, notably in Canada and the Australasian countries. The Royal Canadian Mounted Police (RCMP) have developed a research database of 24,000 human footprints in an attempt to demonstrate the uniqueness of the human foot (Kennedy 2005), whereas in Australia and New Zealand, there have been reports of the involvement of podiatrists in criminal case work (Kippen 1996). One podiatrist with such experience was subsequently awarded a Churchill Scholarship to study the development of practical forensic podiatry skills to assist criminal investigations in other countries (Churchill Trust 1995).

17.2   Identification of the Foot Using Podiatry Treatment Records

Podiatry is a relatively new profession in the U.K. that is not widely understood, and there is some confusion as to what podiatry is (Vernon 2004). Two definitions are offered: firstly, an American definition, which states that podiatrists are "foot specialists who study foot pathology from a structural and functional standpoint, and who treat medical problems dealing with the foot" (DiMaggio 1995). Secondly, in the U.K., the National Health Service states that podiatrists "diagnose and treat abnormalities of the lower limb. They give professional advice on the prevention of foot problems and on proper care of the foot" (NHS Careers 2005). Podiatry practice itself is based on core areas of knowledge including:

- Lower limb anatomy and physiology
- The structural pathologies of the foot
- The recognition and care of the at-risk foot (e.g., the diabetic foot and the ischemic foot)
- Podiatric biomechanics
- The relationship between footwear and the functioning foot

During the course of their practice, podiatrists keep records of the feet that they have treated, and these records cover the initial assessment of the feet, diagnosis of foot conditions present, and details of the treatments provided (Merriman and Tollafield 1999). It was these records that Dr. Ivor Doney suggested could be used to assist with the identification of deceased persons (Doney and Harris 1984). It was believed that this approach to identification could be especially useful in disaster situations where the foot is at an advantage through the protection offered by the encasing shoe. This belief was later reiterated by other authors who noted the additional degree of protection provided in traumatic situations by the architecture of the metatarsals and the cancellous nature of the calcaneum, all of which may allow better preservation than other anatomical regions (Smith 1997, Introna et al. 1997, Robling and Ubelaker 1997).

This detail recorded in podiatry records could, for example, classify the treated foot as being of a particular type, note that specific minor toe deformities were present at stated sites, list specific sites of nail thickening or deformities where present, and note defined forms of soft tissue lesions present at specific sites on the foot, sometimes with the exact size of these lesions being stated. Where those records have included foot and ankle radiographs, this provides an additional source of data that could be used to establish presumptive and positive identification (Brogdon 2005) and to relate visual osseous pathology to potential effects on footwear (DiMaggio 2005).

Vernon (1990) later tested Doney's theory. In this study, it was initially estimated that 7.25% of the U.K.-based population should have a podiatry record. The project continued by recruiting teams of podiatrists who compared known detail on podiatry records with the feet of unidentified subjects point by point and then concluded as to whether the records related to that subject or not. At this stage of the work, 97% of the record card identifications undertaken by the participating podiatrists were found to be correct (Vernon 1994). Later, a strength scale was incorporated into the technique allowing podiatrists levels of certainty in their judgments. When using a strength scale, 100% of judgments made with absolute certainty were found to be correct, with 56% of all judgments made being done so with absolute certainty (Sanger and Vernon 1997).

Although podiatry record card identification has proven potential in the field of identification, there are some limitations associated with the approach. Firstly, only two studies have been published to date to test the theory that identification from podiatry records is possible, with both these studies being small scale in nature. The work also relied on the subjective judgments of participating podiatrists, as incidence databases were not available to quantify the individuality of each feature or combination of features present. Whereas some features used by podiatrists in this identification process are demonstrably permanent (e.g., hammer toes and thickened nails), others are not (e.g., the presence of corns and callus, etc., in defined sites). Whereas record cards may show that such lesions have been constantly present for many years, their potential impermanence means that their stability may not achieve the requirements of true scientific identifiers, as suggested by Bernstein (1997). There is the potential for further research into the possibility of microscopic changes to areas of skin that have previously exhibited lesions of this nature; however, until such work has been undertaken, the value of podiatry record card identification remains below its optimum.

17.3 Identification from Marks of the Foot on the Surrounding Environment

In addition to individualization from podiatry records, identification of the foot can also be made from considering marks left by the foot on its surrounding environment. In this, prints and impressions formed by the foot on the ground, on any other surface, or within the shoe are considered. Unknown or questioned foot marks at such sites would be compared directly with the footprints of a known individual and a conclusion reached as to whether these marks shared common ownership. Plantar prints or impressions are fundamental to this process, although where a footwear item is involved, marks from the borders of the forefoot and the dorsum of the toes are also considered. There are two elements to this identification process — direct comparison and, under certain circumstances, interpretation.

17.4   Direct Comparison

In the examination of plantar prints and impressions of the foot, various anatomical measurements are considered to "describe" the footprint or impression. Several methods have been devised, but many initially consider heel-to-toe measurements, the angles between these measurements, and across-foot distances. These measurements can then be compared with other footwear or with casts or footprints of the feet of a potential shoe owner.

17.5   Measurement and Comparison Method 1 — The Gunn Method

The first method used in the assessment, comparison, and evaluation of plantar prints was one that was devised by Canadian forensic podiatrist Norman Gunn. Dr. Gunn advocated a method of footprint evaluation in which a series of five lines are initially drawn from the rearmost aspect of the heel print to the tip of each toe print (Figure 17.1). A further line is then taken across the widest aspect of the ball of the foot area. These lines are then measured, with each measurement being used in the comparison process between two separate footprints. In addition to allowing measurement comparisons, angles between the lines drawn from point to point can also be used as points of comparison. The basic measurements and angles that can be used in this approach are listed in Table 17.1. It is also possible to add many additional measurements between the various morphological landmarks involved as shown in Figure 17.2, this being of particular value when dealing with partial footprints only.

Figure 17.1   The Gunn method.

Table 17.1   The Basic Measurements and Angles Used in the Gunn Method

Measurement
Heel to first toe
Heel to second toe
Heel to third toe
Heel to fourth toe
Heel to fifth toe
Heel to first toe line — intersection with cross ball line
Heel to second toe line — intersection with cross ball line
Heel to third toe line — intersection with cross ball line
Heel to fourth toe line — intersection with cross ball line
Heel to fifth toe line — intersection with cross ball line
Angle between heel to first toe and heel to second toe lines
Angle between heel to first toe and heel to third toe lines
Angle between heel to first toe and heel to fourth toe lines
Angle between heel to first toe and heel to fifth toe lines

Figure 17.2   Development of the Gunn method.

17.6   Measurement and Comparison Method 2 — The Optical Center Approach

The optical center method is an evolution of the Gunn approach to footprint evaluation and was developed by the Royal Canadian Mounted Police in a long-term project to demonstrate the individuality of a human footprint (Kennedy 1996, Kennedy et al. 2003). In this major study, a computer database has been created of 24,000 human footprints (Kennedy 2005). In order to evaluate and compare the footprints on that database, the optical center approach was used. The optical center is a central point of a morphological feature as defined by the center of a circle when placed in a position of best fit (Figure 17.3).

Figure 17.3   The optical center method.

The Canadian database defines this position using computer software, although the optical center can also be shown manually using a device in which a series of concentric circles with a marked central position are present on a clear background. In use, this device would be placed over the feature to be examined (e.g., a toe print), the best fit of the concentric circles matched with the print, and the central position then pinpointed and marked.

The basic lines used in the optical center method commence from the defined center of the heel print to the optical centers of each toe print, and as in the Gunn method, a further line is then taken across the widest aspect of the ball of the foot area. Measurements are again taken from point to point for comparison between different footprints, with the angles between these lines also being available for comparison. Again, additional measurements between the morphological landmarks involved are possible, with a total of 38 variable measurements having been defined using this approach (Kennedy et al. 2003).

17.7   Measurement and Comparison Method 3 — The Overlay Method

The overlay method has been developed and used by the Forensic Science Service in the U.K. (Facey 2005) and represents a radically different approach to footprint comparison than those methods developed in Canada. Here, an outline of a known footprint is placed onto a clear acetate sheet, and this image is laid over a questioned print (Figure 17.4). The comparison detail used is not that of point to point measurements as in the previously described approaches but, instead, relies on morphological outlines. In this, the outline shape of a feature of the footprint being analyzed is considered and compared with that of a second footprint. This is a qualitative assessment process as the feature itself cannot be quantified; however, the work of Kennedy and others has suggested that these features may represent high degrees of individuality (Kennedy 1996, Kennedy et al. 2003).

Whereas this technique was developed using tracing of the footprint outline onto clear acetate sheets, with the development of digital camera systems, improved and more accurate comparison techniques have evolved. In the current approach, lifesize digital photographs are created of the known and unknown footprints. These images can then be enhanced as required to clearly demonstrate the footprint borders, and the known image can be laid over the questioned print for comparison, in exactly the same way as the tracing approach of the past.

Figure 17.4   The overlay method.

Figure 17.5   The Robbins method.

17.8   Measurement and Comparison Method 4 — The Robbins Method

As in the Gunn and Optical Center methods, an additional quantifiable measurement system was devised in the 1980s by a forensic anthropologist Louise Robbins (1985). This approach uses visual anthropological measurements, some of which have similarities to those used in the Gunn method. Other measurements are involved, however, that use right-angled lines drawn from a theoretical base line across the rear of the heel to the tips of each toe and an angle of declination drawn between the tips of the first toe to the fifth toe (Figure 17.5).

17.9   Measurement and Comparison Method 5 — Rossi's Podometric System

William Rossi, an American podiatrist, devised an alternative method of considering and categorizing landmarks of the foot, which he referred to as a *system of podometrics*, a new methodology for foot typing (Rossi 1992). Rossi's method was based on a system of triangular lines drawn longitudinally and transversely across the footprint and from which the foot could be categorized. An initial line is drawn to connect the outermost lateral aspect of the heel print with the lateral aspect of the ball of foot area, followed by a second line drawn to connect the innermost medial aspect of the heel with the medial aspect of the ball of foot area. A third line is then drawn central to these and a fourth and a fifth line added in the same manner. A similar approach is taken to the placing of five laterally placed lines (Figure 17.6). Angles and distances can then be recorded to quantify these dimensions for comparison purposes.

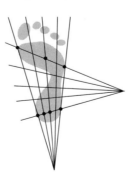

Figure 17.6   Rossi's system of podometrics.

17.10   Comparison of All Methods — Which Is the Preferred Approach?

The five approaches have all been variously advocated, considered, or used in the human identification process. There are strengths and weaknesses, however, to each method. Gunn's approach was the first to be used. It is simple to operate, allows a multitude of quantitative measurements to be taken, and considers the footprint as a whole. Because of its simplicity in use, it has also been one of the methods more frequently used by podiatrists. As a method in its own right, however, it does not allow comparison of the detail to be found in human footprints and has limited value when dealing with partial prints only. Whereas the creator of this method undertook private trials with the approach, to date, the repeatability of this method has not yet been validated in the public domain. This work must be undertaken in order to strengthen this novel approach to footprint identification.

The optical center method has the main advantage of being the only approach to footprint comparison, to date, to have been openly validated for repeatability. This validation work also offers some implied validity to the Gunn method upon which this approach is based. Being undertaken directly on the optical center method, however, suggests that this currently remains the more demonstrably robust approach. As in the Gunn method, objective quantifiable measurements are involved, and the footprint as a whole is considered. Through supportive research, related publications, and educational initiatives that have followed the optical center research, this is also one of the more commonly performed approaches to footprint identification, especially in Canada, the U.S., and Europe. As in the Gunn method, the optical centers do not allow comparison of the detail to be found in human footprints on their own and, again, there is limited value when dealing with partial prints only. The approach is also somewhat more complex in use, and repeatability has been demonstrated when using computer software. Because of potential difficulties in locating the best fit of the circle within the morphological feature of the footprint, there may be a greater margin of error when adopting a manual approach to this technique.

The optical center approach, therefore, has the strong advantage of having been validated for repeatability, although it may have more limited value when the required software is not available. Additional complexities of use and a greater margin of error occur where manual assessment is required.

In practice, the overlay method has the greatest value when considering discrete aspects of the total print. Movement of the foot can alter the position of these peripheral morphological features and, therefore, can prevent their consideration from one fixed overlaid position. The particular strength of this technique is that it allows the consideration of single aspects of the footprint under consideration and so can be used in the assessment of partial prints in the identification process (Figure 17.7).

Robbins' method is similar in approach to that of Gunn and, as such, does not retain any additional advantages or disadvantages over Gunn's original method. Robbins' method has not been as widely used, possibly due to past controversy surrounding Robbins' identification work in the U.S., which, although not related to this technique, did lead to questioning of her methods in general. For this reason, caution should be exercised when considering adopting Robbins' approach as opposed to any other in plantar print evaluation.

Rossi's approach, though novel, was not devised for identification of the foot, but instead as a means of classification. As such, this approach has potential in identification, although it has not yet been evaluated or tested in this field.

Figure 17.7 Dealing with a partial print with the overlay method.

Table 17.2 Comparison of Footprint Evaluation Methods

	Gunn	Optical Center	Overlay	Robbins	Rossi
Allows quantitative measurement	✔	✔	×	✔	✔
Allows detail comparison	×	×	✔	×	×
Repeatability validated	×	✔	×	×	✔
Ease of use	✔	×	×	✔	✔
Considers footprint as a whole	✔	✔	×	✔	✔
Frequency of use in footprint identification	✔	✔	✔	×	×
Use in dealing with partial footprints	×	×	✔	×	×

17.11 How Should These Methods Be Used in Practice?

Each method considered has its own strengths and weaknesses (Table 17.2), and these should dictate which would be the most appropriate under the circumstances of a particular case. Additionally, there is usually merit in using two different methods in the examination process as this may give more points of comparison than could be obtained when using one method in isolation. In this respect, using either the Gunn or optical center method in combination with the overlay method has particular advantages. Here, either of the first two approaches gives quantifiable detail of distances between landmarks of the footprint (e.g., heel to the first toe measurement and cross-ball measurement), whereas the overlay method would provide useful additional comparative detail such as the morphological outline of the anterior ball of the foot and the outline shapes of the toes.

17.12 Additional Factors When Considering Identifications Involving Footwear

The approach to examining the wear and impressions caused by feet within footwear is similar to that of barefoot analysis. The impressions caused by the plantar surface of the foot on the shoe insole, sock liner, or sock lining provide the strongest evidence of individuality in a worn shoe. Often, the insole of sports footwear (trainers) or of a shoe can be removed, facilitating the assessment of wear features present on that insole. Where the insole cannot be removed, after photographing and evaluating the shoe upper, the shoe is usually cut open as part of the examination process. The cut is positioned at the site where the upper joins the outsole unit, with enough material being left intact on the outer aspect of the shoe to allow the upper to be hinged open for assessment purposes. Once the insole has been made accessible in this way, the examination of any impressions apparent on that insole can be made using the same approaches as those involved in the analysis and comparison of barefoot impressions. Digital photography–based methods of capturing these marks for comparison are again useful in this task, and various texts are available to assist with the general forensic photography approaches required (Hilderbrand 1999, Bodziak 2000, Redsicker 2004).

The foot can also leave additional marks of wear on the shoe, which contribute toward individualization. When the shoe has been cut open, the internal lining of the shoe upper can also be examined. Here, the foot can leave wear marks at sites where the toes and medial and lateral aspects of the ball of foot areas have impinged against the shoe upper. These marks can then be compared with the outline of a foot and the toe joint positioning in order to determine compatibility. To assist with this task, an accurate foot outline can be created by impressing the foot under consideration into a biofoam material, then taking a scale digital photograph of that outline image (Figure 17.8). When printed lifesize and cut out, the peripheral aspects of that outline can then be compared with marks, creases, and impressions in the shoe upper, providing further points of comparison where a match is apparent.

It is important to note, however, that this is an area currently without a strongly researched evidence base. Such features should, therefore, be treated as an additional guide to ownership and not as a strong identification feature in themselves. Their value will increase in the presence of a foot with specific deformities such as a hammer toe or a bunion feature, where correlations will be apparent between wear of the shoe and the pathological feature present. These still, however, should be treated as class characteristics demonstrating compatibility and not as unique identification–features in themselves.

In addition to being compared with the foot, the wear features caused by the presence of a foot within a shoe can also be compared with the wear of other shoes as part of the identification process. Here, like-with-like footwear styles should be ideally compared to reduce the number of variables introduced through style differences. In this respect, where possible, training shoes should ideally be compared with training shoes, slip-on shoes with other slip-on shoes, and boots with boots, etc. Where such like-with-like comparisons are possible, these can provide more accurate comparative data than in the comparison of barefeet with questioned shoes. This is because such like-with-like comparisons provide a greater degree of standardization than that offered in the comparison of barefoot prints with those found inside a shoe.

17.13 Interpretation of Footprints and Shoe Wear

Various methods have been presented that allow the comparison of footprints and impressions for identification purposes. The process of comparison may not be straightforward; however, because of the variable effects of foot function and the relationship between the foot and the shoe may cause the marks of the footprint to be amended. Some interpretation may be required under these circumstances, especially when dealing with the shod foot, which can have many variables that affect the functioning and positioning of the foot and, in turn, the form of the plantar footprint pattern. Some of the more usual variables and their treatment are considered in the following sections.

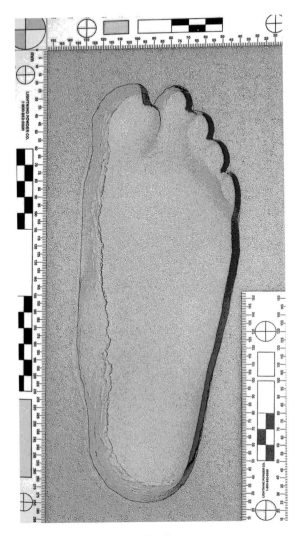

Figure 17.8   Foot outline preparation using biofoam.

17.13.1   Toe Box Variables

The toe box is the foremost aspect of footwear, the area of the shoe that contains the wearer's toes. The design of the toe box reflects the fashion-based or functional design of the shoe, and therefore it will vary in shape from a broad to pointed outline. This outline can impinge on the contained foot and in doing so, alter the toe positions inside the shoe. Figure 17.9 shows the effect of a pointed toe box on the foot structure. In human identification from footwear, this effect must be considered when using any of the comparative tools described earlier, as the toe impressions on the shoe insole may be forced inwards, away from their natural position, potentially confounding the process of comparison. The potential for such changes must be taken into account by the footwear examiner and whereas they may reduce the level of certainty that a known footprint matches that inside such a shoe, the recognition of these confounding factors may also negate the possibility of false elimination when such differences can be explained.

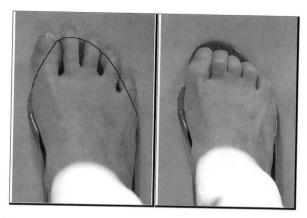

Figure 17.9 The effect of a tight shoe box on foot structure.

Table 17.3 Examples of Size Variations among Shoe Manufacturers

Make	Actual Length in cm for Marked U.K. Footwear Size (Men's)						
	6	7	8	9	10	11	12
Adidas	24.5	25.5	26.5	27.5	28.5	29.5	30.5
Fila	25	26	27	28	29	30	31
Merrell	—	25.5	26.5	27.5	28.5	29.5	30.5
Mizuno	25	26	27	28	29	30	31
Reebok	25	26	27	28	29	30	31
Teva	24.1	25	25.8	26.7	27.5	28.4	29.2
Timberland	24.5	25.5	26.5	27.5	28.5	29.5	—

Source: Sports Authority, www.sportsauthority.com. Accessed April 23, 2005.

17.13.2 Excessive Footwear Length

The fit of footwear in terms of length can also change the plantar print of the foot that has been contained inside. Foot- and shoe- length discrepancies are a common factor among the general public, with clinical observations and short research surveys suggesting that around 85% of the population wears shoes of incorrect length (Bestick 2004). This is compounded by a problem of standardization across the footwear industry, with footwear sizes varying between style and manufacturer (Rossi and Tennant 1984) (see Table 17.3). The choice of a shoe size is no indication of correct shoe fit, as sizing is just a general shoe-fitting guide and not a definitive gauge of fit. In shoe fitting, although the foot has been measured to indicate the required shoe size, this does not automatically guarantee that a shoe of a particular size will fit appropriately. Additionally, footwear is often purchased subjectively, so footwear marked or measured as being of a certain size is sometimes wishfully assumed to correlate with the buyer's required shoe size. At best, shoe sizing is only a general guide as the marked length can differ from the best fit and many other fitting variables are present to compound the problem of obtaining a correct size.

In human identification, this situation can cause a disagreement between the length of an exemplar footprint taken from a known individual and the print within a questioned shoe that has been subject to examination. If a shoe is too long, the foot can slide forward and create an impression that the foot is longer than it actually is. (Figure 17.10). In the footwear examination process, it is therefore important for all shoes to be internally sized,

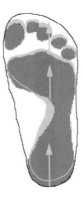

Figure 17.10   The apparent lengthening of a foot impression in an excessively long shoe.

and the feet of the individual with which the footprints are being compared to be measured, when possible. Differences noted between these measurements can be accounted for in the examination process and an opinion reached as to whether ownership can still be attributed, given the difference observed. As $^1/_3$ inch represents the difference between each footwear size, it can often be seen that wearing shoes one size too large will lead to uniform length differences in the order of $^1/_3$ inch for every toe position examined, suggesting that a length discrepancy has been a factor in the shoe being examined.

17.13.3   Inadequate Footwear Length

Conversely, where a shoe is too short for the owner, the foot will be unable to slide forward to any extent within the shoe, leading to a plantar impression apparently shorter than that of the owner's foot. Where this is especially pronounced, restriction from the tip of the shoe can push the toes into a position farther back than they would lie naturally, giving the impression that a foot smaller than the owner's has been contained within that shoe. When examining such a shoe, other wear features may also be present, strengthening this possibility. The first of these features may be an excessive wear of the outsole at the most distal aspect of the tip of the shoe, where the toe-off phase of walking has been more anteriorly situated in relation to the shoe than when the toes are correctly positioned. Impressions from the toes may also be positioned very close to the front edge of the shoe insole and even impinge on the shoe upper. Excessive wear within the shoe may also occur, corresponding with the apices and dorsum of the toes, when the toes have been forced backward by the shortness of the shoe (Figure 17.11). Here, restrictions within the toe box forcing

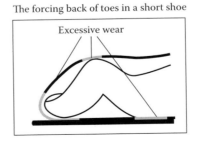

Figure 17.11   The forcing back of toes in a short shoe.

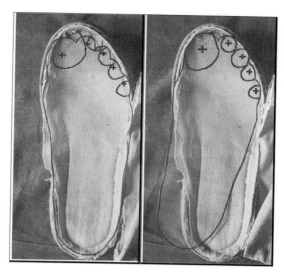

Figure 17.12   The effects of abductory twist.

the toe backward would, in turn, force the proximal interphalangeal joint of the toe upwards into greater contact with the shoe upper, causing accentuated wear at that site.

17.13.4   Inadequate Footwear Width

Wrong shoe width is a problem commonly encountered by podiatrists, especially when an individual has purchased footwear not available in different width sizes, yet has feet wider than standard. This may result in a plantar pattern of an apparently lesser width than the foot that actually made the impression. Indications would be present within the shoe upper, however, suggesting this possibility and would include bulging of the upper, corresponding with the inner and outer ball of foot areas and excessive wear of the shoe lining at these sites.

17.13.5   The Confounding Effects of Foot Function

In addition to the effects of footwear on the plantar print, foot function can also result in a misleading print form. The most commonly observed functional effect may be that of an abductory twist. Here, during the stance phase of walking, the heel may twist inwards excessively, as weight-bearing is transferred to the ball of the foot. This adaptation can be associated with pathological states of the foot, typically when hyperpronation occurs during the gait. The possible effects that this may have on the plantar print and other wear features are as follows:

- Alteration of the placing of the lateral toes, giving the impression that the lesser toes are more posteriorly positioned when compared to a standing print taken from the same individual (Figure 17.12)
- Accentuated wear of the ball of foot area of the plantar impression inside the shoe, corresponding to the pivotal position of the abductory twist
- Medial deviation of the heel counter of the footwear, relating to the inward movement of the heel as the abductory twist takes place
- A circular wear pattern apparent on the outsole, corresponding to the pivotal site of the ball of foot area

17.13.6 Additional Considerations in Footwear Identification

A number of additional considerations can be weighed in the assessment of shoe wear and its relationship to the contained foot.

The issue of shoe size compatibility in identification has been raised previously (Lucock 1967, 1979, 1980). Shoe fitting is not an exact science (Rossi and Tenant 1984), and variations of scale used within the industry, compounded by the subjective purchasing practice, creates a scenario in which the length size of a shoe is only a guideline to fit and does not correspond to an absolute measurement. The resultant wide variations of shoe size being worn by people with similar-length feet means that the use of shoe size as an identification guideline is limited. Some correlations do, however, exist (Cassidy 1987, Bodziak 2000), only in the sense, for example, that it is highly inprobable that an individual would wear shoes one-and-a-half marked sizes different from any other shoe in his or her possession (Lucock 1967, 1979, 1980). In person identification, shoe size can again be used indicatively, but such use should be undertaken with caution.

Previous work has also been undertaken to seek correlations between the dimensions of a human footprint and the height and weight of the owner (Robbins 1986, Giles and Vallandigham 1991, Gordon and Buikstra 1992, Ozden et al. 2005). These studies have had varying degrees of success and in Robbins' case, the work was controversial. Although some correlations have become apparent, the data produced, again, can be used only as an approximate guideline, with wide variations being possible. A study is, however, being undertaken in Scotland, in which new appreciations are anecdotally being produced, although the work has not been published to date and still requires validation (Kerr 2004).

17.14 Potential Future Developments in Identification from the Foot

There are many possibilities to further develop human identification techniques involving the foot. More research into the individuality of the foot will strengthen the value of this form of evidence and linked to this is the need to research and demonstrate the effects of the variables that can potentially influence the form of the plantar print. Here, it may be possible to determine a range of parameters within which it could be stated that an individual foot could have made an examined print despite differences observed or, alternately, that the foot could not have been responsible for a print's being outside that proven range. Further study of such variables would enable greater understanding of their effects to be made, thereby enhancing the strength of footprint evidence.

There is also potential for automated comparisons of footprints with relevance in the field of biometrics. Scanning technology already available could be adapted to the task of comparing footprints and impressions with scanned images of known feet, simplifying the process of footwear comparison, improving the accuracy of the techniques by eliminating human error, and reducing associated costs through improved efficiency.

Despite the long history of the foot's being considered an identification factor, there has been little research development in this field until recent times. The research undertaken to date has indicated that there is much potential for the use of the human foot in identification. Increasing interest and use of the foot in this arena are catalyzing further developments, which should, in turn, stimulate even greater interest in the not-too-distant future.

References

Bernstein, M., Forensic odontology, in *Introduction to Forensic Sciences*, 2nd ed., Eckert, W.G., Ed., CRC Press, London, 1997.

Bestick, L., Try This for Size — Are Your Shoes the Wrong Size? *The Times* April 21, 2004.

Bodziak, W.J., *Footwear Impression Evidence: Detection, Recovery and Examination*, 2nd ed., CRC Press, Boca Raton, 2000.

Brogdon, B.G., Radiology of the lower extremity, in *Forensic Medicine of the Lower Extremity*, Rich, J., Dean, D.E., Powers, R.H., Eds., Humana Press, Totowa, NJ, 2005.

Cassidy, M.J., *Footwear Identification*, RCMP, Ottawa, 1987.

Churchill Trust, Fellows Reports, 1995, www.churchilltrust.com, sampled April 16, 2005.

Defoe, D., *Robinson Crusoe*, 1719, prepared for the University of Virginia Library Electronic Text Center, 2000, chap. IX.

DiMaggio, J., Forensic podiatry — an emerging new field, *Journal of Forensic Identification* 45(5), 495–497, 1995.

Dimaggio, J.A., The role of feet and footwear in medicolegal investigations, in *Forensic Medicine of the Lower Extremity*, Rich, J., Dean, D.E., Powers, R.H., Eds., Humana Press, Totowa, 2005.

Doney, I.E. and Harris P.H.G., Mass disaster identification: can chiropodists help?, *The Police Surgeon* 25, 14–20, 1984.

Doxford, M., Techniques in Forensic Podiatry: A Comparison of Two Foot Casting Methods, B.Sc. (Hons.) project, University of Salford, U.K., April 1997 (unpublished).

Facey, O.E., Hannah, I.D., and Rosen, D., Shoe wear patterns and pressure distribution under feet and shoes, determined by image analysis, *Journal of the Forensic Science Society* 32(1), 15–25, 1992a.

Facey, O.E., Hannah, I.D., and Rosen, D., Analysis of low-pass filtered shoeprints and pedobarograph images, *Pattern Recognition* 25(6), 647–654, 1992b.

Facey, O.E., Hannah, I.D., and Rosen, D., Analysis of the reproducibility and individuality of dynamic pedobarograph images, *Medical Engineering and Technology* 17(1), 9–15, 1993.

Facey, O.E., personal communication, 2005.

Gerard, W.V.M., Foot and fingerprints, *The Pedic Items* 10(3), 5–8, 1920.

Giles, E. and Vallandigham, P.H., Height estimation from foot and shoeprint length, *Journal of Forensic Sciences* 36(4), 1134–1151, 1991.

Gordon C.C. and Buikstra J.E., Linear models for the prediction of stature from foot and boot dimensions, *Journal of Forensic Sciences* 37(3), 771–782, 1992.

Gunn, N., New methods of evaluating footprint impressions, *R.C.M.P. Gazette* 53(9), 1–3, 1991a.

Gunn, N., New and old methods of evaluating footprint impressions by a forensic podiatrist, *British Journal of Podiatric Medicine and Surgery* 3(3), 8–11, 1991b.

Hilderbrand, D.S., *Footwear, the Missed Evidence: A Field Guide to the Collection and Preservation of Forensic Footwear Impression Evidence*, Staggs, Temecula, CA, 1999.

Introna, F., Jr., Di Vella, G., Campobasso, C.P., and Dragone, M., Sex determination by discriminant analysis of calcanei measurements, *Journal of Forensic Sciences* 42(4), 725–728, 1997.

Kennedy, R.B., Uniqueness of barefeet and its use as a possible means of identification, *Forensic Science International* 82, 81–87, 1996.

Kennedy, R.B., Pressman, I.S., Chen, S., Peterson, P.H., and Pressman, A.E., Statistical analysis of barefoot impressions, *Journal of Forensic Sciences* 48(1), 55–63, 2003.

Kennedy, R.B., personal communication, 2005.

Kerr, W., personal communication, 2004.

Kidd, R., The past is the key to the present: thoughts on the origins of human foot structure, function and dysfunction as seen from the fossil record, *The Foot* 8(2), 75–84, 1998.

Kippen, K., Australia News, Society News: Newspaper of the Society of Chiropodists and Podiatrists, Vol. 8, No. 5, May 1996, p. ii.

Koehler J.R.G., Footwear evidence, *R.C.M.P. Gazette* (48)9, 17–21, 1986.

Lucock, L.J., Identifying the wearer of worn footwear, *Journal of the Forensic Science Society* 7(2), 62–70, 1967.

Lucock, L.J., Identification from footwear, *Medicine, Science and the Law* 19(4), 225–230, 1979.

Lucock, L.J., Identification from footwear, *The Chiropodist* 35(9), 343–350, 1980.

Merriman, L.M. and Tollafield, D., *Assessment of the Lower Limb* Churchill Livingstone, London, 1999.

Muir, E., Chiropody in crime detection, *The Chiropodist* 22, 165–166, 1935.

NHS Careers, What Does A Chiropodist/Podiatrist Do?, www.nhscareers.nhs.uk, Sampled March 7, 2005.

Ozden, H., Balci, Y., Demirustu, C., Turgut, A., and Ertugrul, M., Stature and sex estimate using foot and shoe dimensions, *Forensic Science International* 147, 181–184, 2005.

Pavey C., A Delphi Study of Forensic Podiatry Practice, M.Sc. project, University of Brighton, U.K., 2004 (unpublished).

Redsicker, D.R., *The Practical Methodology of Forensic Photography*, 2nd ed., CRC Press, New York, 2004.

Robbins, L.M., *Footprints: Collection, Analysis and Interpretation*, Charles C. Thomas, Springfield, IL, 1985.

Robbins, L.M., Estimating height and weight from size of footprints, *Journal of Forensic Sciences* 31(1), 143–152, 1986.

Robling, A.G. and Ubelaker D.H., Sex discrimination from the metatarsals, *Journal of Forensic Sciences* 42(6), 1062–1069, 1997.

Rossi W.A., Tennant R., *Professional Shoe Fitting*, Pedorthic Footwear Association, New York, 1984.

Rossi, W.A., Podometrics: a new methodology for foot typing, *Contemporary Podiatric Physician*, Nov. 1992, p. 28–38.

Sanger, D. and Vernon, W., The value of a strength scale in identification from podiatry records, *Journal of Forensic Identification* 47(2), 162–170, 1997.

Smith, S., *Mostly Murder*, Companion Book Club, London, 1959.

Smith, S.L., Attribution of foot bones to sex and population groups, *Journal of Forensic Sciences* 42(2), 186–195, 1997.

Thomas, D., The Role of the Podiatrist in Forensic Medicine: A Literature Review, B.Sc. (Hons.) project, Durham School of Podiatric Medicine, U.K., April 1997 (unpublished).

Valmassey, R.L., A Podiatrist in Court, *Pacesetter* 2(4), 1982.

Vernon, W., The Potential of Chiropody Records in Forensic and Mass Disaster Identification, B.Sc. (Hons.) project, University of Brighton, U.K., October 1990 (unpublished).

Vernon W., The use of podiatry records in forensic and mass disaster identification, *Journal of Forensic Identification* 44(1), 26–40, 1994.

Vernon, W., The Functional Analysis of Shoe Wear Patterns: Theory and Application, Ph.D. thesis, Sheffield Hallam University, U.K., October 2000.

Vernon, W., A workforce planning and development strategy for podiatry, South Yorkshire Workforce Development Confederation, 2004.

Footwear Marks

18

TERRY NAPIER

Contents

18.1 Introduction 322
18.2 Footwear Marks at the Crime Scene 322
    18.2.1 How Marks Are Made 322
        18.2.1.1 Transfer 322
        18.2.1.2 Compression 322
        18.2.1.3 Surface Changes 322
18.3 Locating Marks 323
18.4 Recovery and Enhancement of Footwear Marks...323
    18.4.1 Footwear Marks in Blood 324
18.5 Selection of Methods for Enhancement and Recovery................................324
    18.5.1 Photography and Illumination...324
        18.5.1.1 Distortion-Free Photographs 324
        18.5.1.2 Contrast and Illumination 324
        18.5.1.3 Definition 324
    18.5.2 Physical Methods 325
        18.5.2.1 Electrostatic Lifting..325
        18.5.2.2 Gelatin Lifting 325
        18.5.2.3 Casting...325
        18.5.2.4 Chemical Methods..326
    18.5.3 Information from Footwear Marks 327
        18.5.3.1 Pattern 327
        18.5.3.2 Size..330
        18.5.3.3 Degree of Wear 331
        18.5.3.4 Characteristic Features of the Tread....................................332
    18.5.4 Footwear Mark Intelligence Indices 335
        18.5.4.1 Tread Most Easy to Recognize of Marks............................335
        18.5.4.2 Patterns Allowing Fixed-Value Classification 336
        18.5.4.3 Passage of Time Alters Values..336
        18.5.4.4 Good Discrimination 336
    18.5.5 Using a Footwear Marks Index..336
    18.5.6 Other Aspects of Footwear Databases...338
    18.5.7 The Comparison of Marks And Footwear Items..............................338
        18.5.7.1 Is the Exact Pattern the Same or Different? 338
        18.5.7.2 Is the Pattern Size the Same or Different?..........................338
        18.5.7.3 Is the Degree and Distribution of Wear Observed
                on the Tread and That Indicated in the Mark the Same? 338

18.5.7.4 Are There Any Features in Marks That Correspond to
          Random Specific Wear or Damage Features to the Tread? 340
Further Reading...341

18.1 Introduction

Marks left by footwear are routinely used in the investigation of crimes. In most but not all cases, footwear is personal only to one owner, but it is also an artifact easily subject to replacement or change. Therefore, there can be time considerations affecting the use of footwear mark evidence in most investigations. This, in turn, has implications for the way this evidence and intelligence is used and presented in court. The time element, as much as the fact that footwear has a peripheral association with an individual and is not a body part, is what separates footwear marks from finger and other friction-ridge marks, forms of evidence considered to be the nearest evidential analog. These differences, as well as a number of less immediately obvious disparities, make footwear mark investigation a quite distinct discipline with a number of quite different, and in some cases, unique considerations.

18.2 Footwear Marks at the Crime Scene

18.2.1 How Marks Are Made

The method of scene examination or examination of items removed from the scene containing footwear marks needs to include consideration of the nature of the marks. Marks are made in quite distinct ways. These are described in the following subsections.

18.2.1.1 Transfer

First, we examine the transfer of material to or from footwear that has come into contact with a surface. If there is a net transfer from the footwear to the surface, the resulting marks are referred to as *deposited* or *positive* marks. If there is a net transfer from the surface to the footwear, the mark is referred to as *lifted* or *negative*. The techniques used will be the same for both.

18.2.1.2 Compression

Compression results in three-dimensional marks which, by definition, have a perceptible depth. As the materials in which such marks are made can vary considerably in consistency and other physical properties, the persistence and the detail of such marks can also vary considerably. This type of mark will require very specific recovery methods.

18.2.1.3 Surface Changes

On occasion, the interaction between footwear and a surface will result in a mark that does not involve transfer of material or appreciable compression. The most obvious example of this in crime investigation is bruising in cases of murder or assault. Less obvious but occasionally encountered in casework are marks on materials such as fabrics where the direction of fibers is changed relative to the background. These do not lend themselves to any particular recovery method other than illumination as there is no material to transfer and no impression to cast.

It is quite possible, and in practice quite likely, that more than one of these mechanisms occurs when any mark is made. It is also possible that two marks may be made by different mechanisms at the same time by the same action. Victims of assault may be wearing clothing on which a mark has been produced by transfer, but it will often be the case that associated bruising will occur on the skin immediately beneath the clothing.

18.3 Locating Marks

The distinctions between footwear marks and finger and palm marks become apparent even at the crime-scene stage. The scene examiners' first task in relation to marks is their discovery. The appearance of fingerprints is quite predictable, and even the average person would recognize, with a reasonable degree of confidence, an area of friction-ridge detail associated with a finger- or palm print, particularly if the shape of the hand is apparent. Footwear marks often have a general outline that suggest a foot or have a pattern that is recognizable to the examiner. It may even be the case that a mark is considered a footwear mark just because it consists of a material such as mud in the wrong place. The classic example of this is the muddy smudge in the middle of an otherwise clean floor or kitchen worktop. The fact remains that there are probably a large number of footwear marks that do not get recovered, not because they are not seen but because they are not recognized. Given the diversity of patterns that is discussed later, this is unlikely to change and is an inherent feature of footwear marks at the crime scene.

18.4 Recovery and Enhancement of Footwear Marks

The area where fingerprints and footwear marks show a greater degree of common process is the enhancement and recovery of the marks. Enhancement in relation to marks simply refers to improving their visibility. Recovery is the process of removing them, or the item on which they were made, from the scene.

Enhancement generally entails the application of a technique based on illumination or a physical or chemical process that will improve the visibility of the marks. There are a range of techniques available to do this, and some of these also serve to recover the mark as part of the process. The most commonly used in examination of footwear marks are electrostatic and gelatin lifting. These are well established techniques and are commonly used at crime scenes in routine cases — particularly gelatin lifting.

The main consideration in the enhancement and recovery process is obtaining the maximum amount of visual information in the mark without adversely affecting part, or even all, of the mark. For this reason, footwear mark examination, like finger marks, involves the application of techniques in a sequence. The least destructive are used first, usually visual examination with different light sources, some of which can be highly specialized. Application of the physical and chemical techniques will have no set sequence as this will depend on the nature of the surface as well as the material in which the mark is made. A sequence will be selected based on the combination of these two factors. There may also be further considerations such as the presence of other evidence types. The most obvious example of this is a footwear mark in blood.

18.4.1 Footwear Marks in Blood

It may well be that a sample of blood from the mark is required for analysis. There is no set procedure to deal with this scenario as the context of each case is different. If there is no contention about the origin of the blood, and the mark is considered as crucial evidence in relation to the case, it may be that the optimum development route for the footwear mark takes precedence. It is normally the case that a strategy can be developed without adversely compromising either evidence type. The main issue is usually the sampling procedure of the blood specialist. Swabs are normally taken, and this may damage crucial visual information in the mark. At the very least, the sampled area should be indicated in any photographs of marks presented to the footwear mark examiner, particularly if they were not present during the scene examination. The problem becomes more acute with fragments of marks that may contain just enough blood to satisfy the blood specialist. The obvious implication is that, by sampling, there is little mark left for the footwear examiner afterward. Consideration must also be given to invisible or latent parts of the mark, which could later be developed.

18.5 Selection of Methods for Enhancement and Recovery

18.5.1 Photography and Illumination

Good photography is critical in footwear mark work, and footwear marks demand more from the photographer than just about any other evidence type. As with finger marks, most enhancements by illumination or physical and chemical methods will result in recoding by photography. The main requirements in footwear photography are discussed in the following subsections.

18.5.1.1 Distortion-Free Photographs

Marks photographed from a nonperpendicular viewpoint will inevitably be distorted with regard to their dimensions. Given that size and dimensional relationships between the pattern elements in a mark are a crucial part of the examination, the fewer distortions present in a photograph, the greater the degree of confidence in dimensional and spatial aspects of the tread design of the shoe that made the mark.

18.5.1.2 Contrast and Illumination

The photographer has the opportunity to apply the first stage of enhancement, using illumination. This may involve lighting from different angles or using different light sources, different wavelengths and filters, and different films. All of these affect the contrast of the mark to a greater or lesser degree, and the application will depend on the mark in question. The relatively recent advent of specialist dyes in anticrime measures has resulted in marks being made in these dyes that are revealed using special light sources.

18.5.1.3 Definition

The definition of a mark is affected by a number of considerations. Definition is critical to the footwear mark examiner, as the detail used in conclusively matching a given mark to a given item of footwear is sometimes smaller than finger mark ridge detail. Given the relative sizes of finger marks and footwear marks, the photographer has a real problem in recording the same level of detail in a footwear mark. A finger mark can be recorded at actual- or life-size on the negative itself. Unless the footwear mark is a very small fragment, the photographic film or digital chip has to capture an area often 20–30 times larger. Optimizing the resolution is therefore essential.

Other less obvious causes of loss of definition are practical and can be solved by simple practice. The most obvious is poor focusing, as this is often difficult to achieve in low light levels. This is particularly true of marks in soil or other three-dimensional marks where the camera's depth of field may only keep certain parts of the mark in sharp focus, especially when the camera cannot be positioned perpendicular to the mark. Camera shake will also reduce definition and is caused when marks are photographed with a handheld camera using relatively low shutter speeds. Where possible, a tripod and flash should be used to minimize these problems.

18.5.2   Physical Methods

There are a number of physical methods deployed in the enhancement and recovery of footwear marks. The most familiar is the application of powder followed by photography or lifting onto a film. This is a standard recovery method for finger marks, and it is not uncommon for both types of marks to appear in the same lift. There are three other physical techniques used to enhance or recover footwear marks, which are almost exclusively associated with footwear marks, although they can be applied to tire impressions in the same way. These techniques are discussed in the following subsections.

18.5.2.1   Electrostatic Lifting

Electrostatic lifting involves applying a laminated plastic and metal film to a surface to be examined. The film is then charged, and a portion of the dust on the surface below the film is attracted onto the surface and held by static charge. The black glossy plastic surface then acts as an ideal photographic background, allowing the marks to be easily visualized by oblique illumination.

This technique is particularly useful for searching large areas such as floors for latent marks in dust.

18.5.2.2   Gelatin Lifting

This technique involves the application of a sheet of clear or pigmented gelatin to a surface. The freshly exposed gelatin surface is slightly tacky and elastic, and is particularly effective at lifting marks in dust, often those revealed by electrostatic lifting. Consequently, it is often used in sequence afterward. Its elastic properties make it useful for slightly uneven or textured surfaces. As it is particularly useful for marks in dust, the most commonly encountered color for gelatin lifts is black, again, to optimize photographic contrast. Gel lifts that contain white pigment or no pigment are available. These can be used when the mark has been developed with aluminum or carbon powder but result in very poor contrast with latent dust marks. Figure 18.1 shows the improvement of the visibility of a mark obtained using a gelatin lifter.

18.5.2.3   Casting

Casting is not exclusive to footwear marks but is strongly associated with it. The materials used for footwear mark casting often originate in the dental profession and would be more

Figure 18.1 Improvement of the visibility of a mark obtained using a gelatin lifter.

familiar to odontologists than finger mark examiners. Casting is a very specific method and, by definition, is not used in a sequence other than after photography. It is applied to three-dimensional impressions caused by the footwear compressing a deformable material that holds its shape after the footwear is removed. It is possible that in certain materials a three-dimensional mark may have a latent impression associated with it but, as the mark is always recessed, applying the other methods is impractical.

There are other physical methods used occasionally in the development of footwear marks mainly originating from finger mark development work. These are not used as matter of routine, and some are completely laboratory-based and would not normally be available to the scene examiner.

18.5.2.4 *Chemical Methods*

There are a large number of chemical methods associated with the development of finger marks. Some of these have become routinely used in footwear mark examination at scenes. Chemical methods rely, to a large degree, on predicting the composition of a mark as there is little purpose in applying a reagent to a material that is inert to the reagent. As the material in which footwear marks are made is usually indeterminate, in most cases chemical methods are rarely used. Finger marks, despite their often complex biological content, tend to be more predictable in their composition, and some of the chemically based finger mark techniques are well established and routine. The material most commonly subject to chemical development in footwear mark examination is blood. Stains and reagents such as Amido Black™ and Luminol™ are often applied to footwear marks at crime scenes.

It is quite apparent, even at the scene examination stage, that finger marks and footwear marks need to considered from slightly different perspectives and that footwear marks have requirements that are quite different from finger marks. These differences become more pronounced when the actual marks are processed for intelligence and evidential purposes.

18.5.3 Information from Footwear Marks

It is possible, prior to the arrest of a given individual and the seizure of footwear, that the footwear mark examiner might be able to provide information about the footwear that made the marks. This is where footwear marks have an advantage over finger marks. The finger mark examiner can provide a name for the person leaving a mark, using computerized or manual indices. The footwear mark examiner cannot hope to provide such individual identification. If the finger mark has no match on an index, however, from an intelligence point of view it can provide no predictive information associated with the person that left it. Footwear marks have the advantage that they can give some useful pointers about what the person committing the offense may be wearing on their feet or at least what kind of footwear they may have in their possession. Each aspect of the shoe may be considered useful. It is not difficult to envisage a situation where investigators would greatly appreciate being told they are looking for a Nike™ XXX (model), size 10.5, very worn with a large cut in the toe. In practice the reality is somewhat different to this, and there are problems of a greater or lesser magnitude associated with providing this type of information. Each attribute of the mark should, in principle, reflect that of the footwear tread that made it, but this is not as simple a process as might be imagined. Limitations apply to each of the attributes in the degree of confidence that can be attached to any information that results from them. These limitations are considered in the following subsections.

18.5.3.1 *Pattern*

A pattern is the first and usually most obvious attribute of a mark and is often the reason it is recognized as a potential footwear mark. Assuming the pattern could be associated with a particular make and model, it would be useful to inform the investigator that they are looking for an Adidas™ XXX or a Nike XXX. The current footwear market does, however, contain many patterns that can be considered as generics, copies, or variants. Generics are patterns that are essentially the same on a number of different brands with no one brand being particularly associated with the pattern. Copies will look identical to what should, in principle, be an exclusive or protected design (see Figure 18.2 and Figure 18.3). Variants have parts of the tread pattern that are common to more than one overall design, which often occurs on different models within the same brand.

The only way to establish the make of shoe with absolute confidence is to identify a make-specific feature such as a name or logo associated with a brand. This could be graphic such as the Adidas "Trefoil," Nike "Swoosh," or a written name. It may also be the case that a mark contains brand-associated technical terms such as Duralon,™ BRS1000 (Nike), Adiprene and Torsion® (Adidas), or Hexalite (Reebok). If such information is not present in the mark, at best it can only be assumed that a pattern is exclusive to a given brand, and in some cases this will not necessarily be true. It is generally the case that, if the mark is of a pattern that corresponds to a current and recently introduced model, it would have originated from that model.

Variants can be one of two types. One type has a part of the tread that is identical to the corresponding part of the tread of a different overall tread pattern. Partial marks left by the corresponding area of the respective tread pattern variants will effectively appear identical, and the marks could be attributed to either model (see Figure 18.4). Both possibilities could be presented to the investigator, if known. The other type of variant is

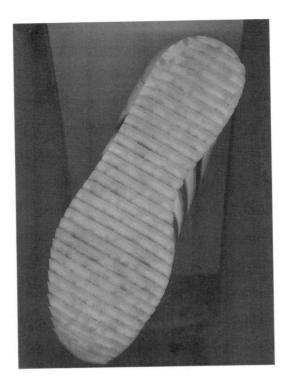

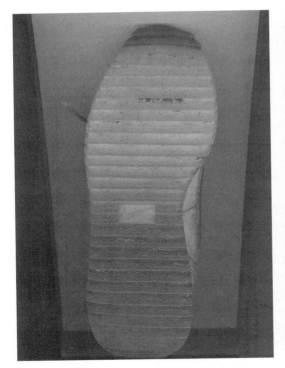

Figure 18.2 The ripple pattern which is essentially the same on all three major brands. These can often be distinguished in scene marks using minor differences in pattern detail.

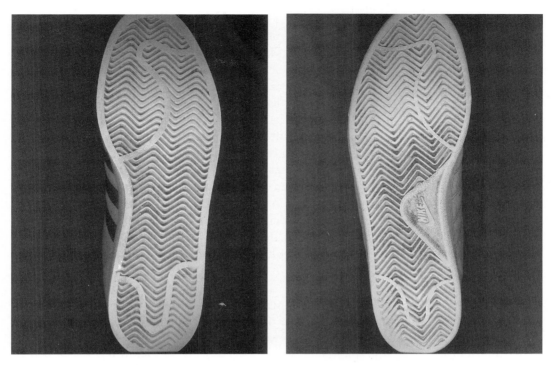

Figure 18.3 The pattern used by both Nike and Adidas, again with minor variations.

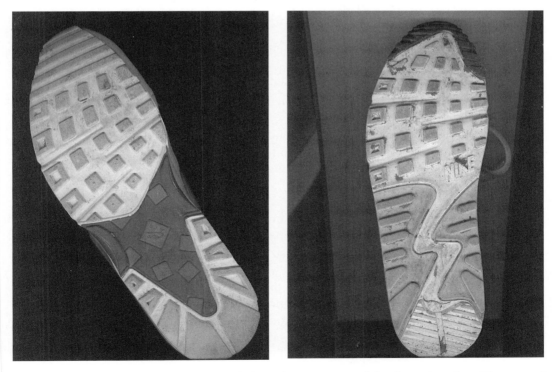

Figure 18.4 The Nike Max Classic and the Nike Max 90 models of training shoe. The central sole is almost identical. Marks left by this area of the tread could be attributed to either model.

where components are common, but their arrangement is slightly different. Again, in a series of partial marks where no overall structure is apparent, it may not be possible to determine which variant made the marks. The investigator would need to be advised of the known possibilities. It is quite possible in these cases that the origin of the marks is yet another variant unknown to the marks examiner. This typically happens where a given brand has a range of shoes that have similar technical features and pattern elements. A familiarity with these possibilities on the part of the examiner is most useful even when extensive image databases are available, as often pattern element size and spatial arrangements are as important as the basic pattern components.

Generic patterns tend to be industry standards and are featured more on boots and casual and formal shoes than sports footwear, where technical function as well as aesthetics and marketing play a greater role. Patterns in the generic category can show a number of variations, but these are not necessarily associated with any given brand and, indeed, may even appear on unbranded shoes. The best the footwear mark examiner can provide for the investigator in these cases is an indication of the type rather than the make of shoe.

18.5.3.2   Size

Determining footwear size from marks seems like a classical piece of forensic science. In practice, studying the pattern has a number of important limitations.

Within the finite range of normal footwear sizes, whether using U.K. sizing or any other international scale, the difference between sizes in measurement terms tends to be very small. Consecutive U.K. sizes may vary by approximately 0.3 of an inch or approximately 8 mm over the whole length of the shoe. This raises the first problem. All of the following distinct factors can influence the physical measurements of a mark:

- Distortion of the footwear when moving
- Distortion of the surface when the mark is made
- Nonflat surface on which the impression is made
- Subsequent movement or environmental changes to the surface after the mark is made
- Foreshortening caused by nonperpendicular photography
- Stretching or movement of lifting films when marks recovered
- Environmental changes to some lifting films during storage

All of these can result in a mark that is considerably more or less than the actual dimensions of the footwear. The variation can easily be greater than consecutive footwear sizes and, when based on physical dimensions, an allowance of at least two consecutive U.K. sizes could be typically applied to a sizing. Some assessment of the nature of the mark and the surface and recovery method would be made in determining limits for the allowance. Given this, a typical range in the uncertainty of size could be up to five consecutive sizes. If the adult male population was considered and the estimated range was, for example sizes 6–11, this would include approximately 90% of all footwear in this population (see Figure 18.5). The discrimination between sizes in given population is at best limited, but when the uncertainty of measurement in marks is introduced, the potential usefulness of size information is limited.

There is, however, an opportunity for the footwear examiner to estimate size using more specific manufacturing detail found in the treads of certain types of footwear. The

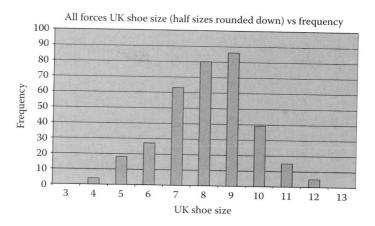

Figure 18.5 Distribution of footwear sizes in footwear examined in casework.

most obvious pattern detail is a number that corresponds to a known size. Care must be applied in determining whether such a feature in a mark is genuine. It may be the case that the pattern is familiar to the examiner, the size marking is in a location where it would be expected, and the number corresponds to a known sizing system. It is also possible that two sizes are apparent that are known to be consistent with each other, e.g., 8/42, which correspond to U.K. size 8 and the continental equivalent. Some allowances must be made when single numbers are apparent on unfamiliar patterns, as numbers often appear in logos and trademarks.

In the absence of specific numbering, other manufacturing detail may be used if the manufacturer of the tread is known. The footwear mark examiner has two options. If the manufacturer is known, it should be possible to collate a full series of size examples or, in some laboratories previously examined, examples of known size could be used. Taking these, a reductive method could be applied to eliminate certain sizes from having made the mark. If the quality of the mark and the type of manufacturing detail allows, it may be possible to associate the mark with a specific mold. If the manufacturer is able to confirm the size or sizes associated with a given mold, this establishes either a single size or range of sizes as being able to produce a given mark. This process can be time consuming and in most cases is impractical as it requires the following:

- A suitably detailed mark
- Knowledge of the manufacturer
- A tread type that shows discernable variation between sizes

This may be considered in certain serious cases where the size of the footwear that made the given marks becomes a critical issue.

18.5.3.3 Degree of Wear

Wear patterns on treads depend on a number of factors. Where most pressure is applied to the tread is determined by the mechanics of anatomy and individual styles of movement. The style of the footwear may make some parts of the tread more prone to wear than others, and the construction may compound this if it results in weak points in the tread design. Again, consideration must be given to how wear translates into the appearance of marks left by a tread. Fine tread detail, such as textures introduced during manufacture, will be lost quickly, and their presence across most of the tread would indicate a relatively new or, at least, little-worn footwear item. Fine pattern elements also wear quickly, and on very uniform patterns the wear pattern left in a mark is a very good indicator of the age of the footwear. Some pattern elements are relatively unchanged throughout the life-time of the tread until the end of its useful life when the whole tread begins to break up. By this time the tread will have very little original pattern left, and determining whether a given mark has been made by a very worn tread of a given pattern or a different pattern altogether is not always possible.

The relationship between tread pattern detail, which is often related to the size, and wear, which often manifests itself in marks as a change in shape and size of pattern detail, creates more uncertainty in assignment of these attributes to a footwear item from a mark. When considering size the footwear examiner will often use the size and spatial arrangement of certain pattern elements in including or excluding certain molds or sizes from having made a mark. If the size or shape of the pattern elements is modified by wear (Figure 18.6) and the size and shape of the pattern elements is critical in determining the size of footwear that made the mark, even more caution is needed in completely excluding the possibility that treads from footwear of a given size would not produce a given mark.

A good working knowledge of the pattern in question, or examples of previously examined footwear of the same pattern showing the effects of wear to the particular tread, would be needed to predict the degree of wear to a tread that had made the impression under examination. Allowances would also have to be made for the time elapsed between the recovery of the mark and any potential search for footwear. If the time was substantial, the treads may show the same degree of wear they did when the mark was left. If used regularly in the intervening period, however, a greater degree of wear would be expected; the difference would be difficult to predict as the degree of use would be unknown.

18.5.3.4 *Characteristic Features of the Tread*

Tread characteristics mainly originate from damage but can include random manufactur-ing defects or objects foreign to the tread. These features are often represented in marks left by a tread and give it a "signature" that allows conclusive associations to be made between a tread and a mark in a typical comparison. Predicting the presence of these features on a tread before the footwear is recovered is in most cases impossible. Empirical evidence from casework in most laboratories shows that a large proportion of marks contain little or no characteristic detail. This type of detail is the most easily lost when the mark is made and is unlikely to be visible in marks of limited definition. It is also the case that there is very little significant characteristic detail on some treads or at least very little that is likely to be reproduced, even in a mark of relatively good definition.

The second, and equally important limitation in predicting characteristic detail in a tread is recognition. Even when a mark is of good definition, assigning certain features as damage with any degree of confidence is risky, given that a large proportion of marks will be of a pattern unfamiliar to the examiner. Even when the pattern is familiar, features that could be taken for damage to the tread may in fact originate from other sources such as imperfections in the surface, uneven distribution of contaminant on the tread or surface, and in some cases worn or modified pattern detail.

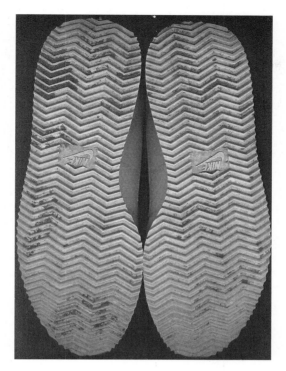

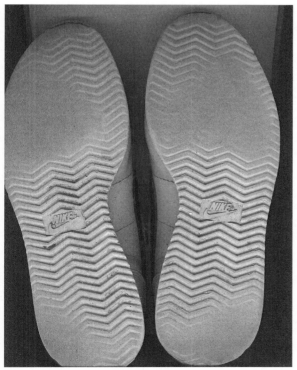

Figure 18.6 The effect of wear on two common patterns, mainly modification or removal of the tread surface.

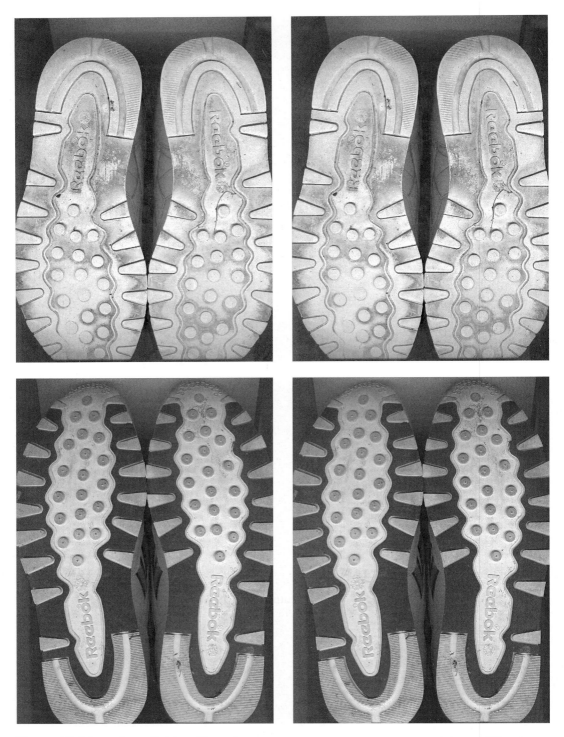

Figure 18.6 (continued) The effect of wear on two common patterns, mainly modification or removal of the tread surface.

The final limitation is the transitory nature of damage or manufacturing defects. These will be subject to change as the tread wears, and if there is a substantial period of time between the mark being left and the recovery of the footwear, it is likely that there will be considerable differences in the appearance of characteristic features in the tread. Obviously, once acquired they will change relatively slowly and eventually be lost, but acquisition is instantaneous, and one incidence of heavy stresses or exposure to sharp objects to the tread, such as climbing or walking on broken glass, can result in very marked changes in the degree and nature of the characteristic features on the tread.

In practice, correctly assigning features as characteristic, even if this were routinely possible, does not translate into information that would be useful to the investigator, as it is not possible to represent this in a form that would be unequivocal. Patterns or shoe models are easy to represent visually. Size is simply a number or range of numbers that may be present on the footwear in question. Even the suggestion or indication that the footwear is quite new or very worn would mean something to investigators, but characteristic features do not lend themselves to such descriptions.

In summary, it is apparent that predicting the attributes of a footwear item before its recovery is rather precarious, but within practical limits, useful information can be provided to the investigator when the case demands it.

The limitations of the information available from the tread that is apparent in footwear marks impose some constraints on the way footwear mark intelligence indices can be effectively structured.

18.5.4   Footwear Mark Intelligence Indices

We have just considered the single-case scenario in which a mark or marks have been recovered from a crime scene, and the information from these marks, as well as its limitations, can be usefully applied to a particular investigation. The possibility also exists that footwear marks from other crime scenes can be considered collectively to provide intelligence to the investigation of the crime, particularly burglary, as a whole.

If one offender is responsible for a number of offenses while wearing the same footwear and leaves marks which are subsequently recovered, the marks from each crime scene should share the same attributes. Collation of the marks in terms of these attributes, particularly using computerized databases, should allow investigators to identify potential areas of activity related to a single or restricted number of offenders.

For marks to be collated effectively, the attributes of the treads that could potentially be represented in the marks need to fulfill certain requirements, particularly for computerized indices. These are described in the following subsections.

18.5.4.1   *Tread Most Easy to Recognize of Marks*

Given the limitations of marks as described previously, only certain attributes can be determined with confidence from these marks. The most obvious is the tread pattern. To even consider determination of the size and wear in the absence of any specific information, the pattern would have to be known as a starting point. Assuming this could be done with a reasonable degree of confidence for some marks, it is a relatively small proportion, and is unlikely to be possible for most and certainly not practical.

18.5.4.2   *Patterns Allowing Fixed-Value Classification*

Any record retrieval system, including manual or computerized footwear mark indices, will work most efficiently when working with preset values. For patterns, this might translate into specific names such as Nike "Cortez" or Nike XXX or Pattern XXX but may also include descriptive values such as "straight bars," "circles," etc. Patterns lend themselves to this approach as, if the pattern is evident, it can either be recognized as a set pattern or at the very least be given a preset description. If the size could be determined for each mark, the most obvious value is the numerical value of the size, e.g., U.K. 8 or Euro 42.

Wear and characteristic damage do not allow this, even when they can be recognized with confidence. Wear could be divided into categories based on subjective descriptions such as "new," "medium wear," and "heavy wear."

18.5.4.3   *Passage of Time Alters Values*

Any attributes that change relatively quickly or even progressively do not lend themselves to classification on an index. Marks left by the same treads over extended periods would be given different values. If the values associated with an attribute change with time, the marks will belong to different groups according to the structure of the values.

18.5.4.4   *Good Discrimination*

If an index is to be useful it needs to have variables that separate marks effectively into certain groups. If the value of parameter or attribute is too broad, the group will include too many marks to be useful and, in practice, may include marks that on simple inspection are actually quite different. In the current footwear market there are some fairly broad pattern groups that would apply to a large number of footwear models. It stands to reason that the more specific a pattern description is, the fewer patterns there are that would comprise this group. When analyzing crime patterns using a footwear mark index, only marks that are the same specific pattern are linked using this approach. This greatly improves the quality of information. If a search against a prisoner's footwear is made against marks on the index, it makes sense to only consider marks left by the same shoe type or at least that are with the same specific pattern.

Characteristic damage could be considered the ultimate discriminator between two items of footwear of the same general attributes. This in practice is not used on an index as it is difficult to "describe" as a fixed value, it is prone to relatively rapid change, and prior to the examination of the shoe that made a mark, it is not possible to assign certain features in a mark as being characteristic damage on the tread that made it.

General wear and size are actually relatively poor discriminators when applied to the relatively large number of marks recovered in crime scene examination.

18.5.5   Using a Footwear Marks Index

In practice, pattern is the only attribute of the tread that can realistically satisfy all the requirements of a searchable marks index or database but even this needs some consideration, particularly in relation to discrimination. How a pattern is classified is critical to the efficiency and effectiveness of the marks index. As an example, consider patterns that consist of mainly or exclusively four-sided or rectangular blocks. This would consist of hundreds of different patterns in the current footwear market. If, however, there was sufficient information in the mark to assign it a specific pattern name, discrimination would improve considerably. Marks left by a Nike Max XX, Nike Max Classic, and Nike Max Ltd. would all be treated by the index or database as quite distinct patterns, even though they share the same broad description. Given that the purpose of the index is to provide the investigator with the best information about what make and model of footwear made a particular mark on a scene-by-scene basis, it makes perfect sense to consider classifying all marks along these lines where possible. This allows the marks index to perform its key functions more efficiently. These are:

- Link crime scene marks to other crime scene marks
- Link prisoners' footwear to marks they have left during previous criminal activity

If all marks are classified as specific patterns, e.g., Pattern A, Nike XXX, and Nike Max Ltd., it is very straightforward to use standard computer queries to allow analysis of such an index. The query could be of the following types:

- Collate a list of all scenes where the footwear mark pattern and division is the same (scene linking).
- Show all marks that are the same pattern as the suspect's footwear.

As both of these are based on the pattern, the strength of the potential links generated will depend on the frequency of the occurrence of the pattern in question. Obviously, the more common a pattern is, the more likely it will occur in a given area at a given time, and the converse will apply if the pattern is relatively rare. The quality of the intelligence provided from scene linking and footwear checking on an index will require current information in relation to the patterns. A frequency report for the marks from a typical police force is shown in Table 18.1.

The discrimination is, in practice, not so much limited by the number of different patterns, of which there are thousands, but by their relative popularity. The marks index will be self-analyzing in this respect as looking for clusters of multiple occurrences of a pattern will also indicate how many occurrences there have been as a whole over a much wider area. The analyst can readily assess the weight that should be given to the strength of pattern-based links. The same process can be applied to the search of a prisoner's footwear pattern. If the index yields a number of occurrences in relation to the pattern, and these are all in the suspected area of activity and nowhere else in a whole police force catchment region, there would be a significant possibility that the prisoner's footwear had made the marks, assuming the information about the suspected area of activity is well founded. Once the scene marks of interest are selected, it may be that the footwear can be conclusively linked to the marks or eliminated from having made them. This requires examination and comparison of the footwear with the marks by the footwear mark examiner.

Table 18.1 Percentage Pattern Frequencies for Most Common Patterns in a Typical Force Area

Pattern	Percentage of Total
Generic ripple soles	9
Reebok Classic 1	9
Nike Cortez	4
Reebok Workout	4
Reebok Workout SE	3

18.5.6   Other Aspects of Footwear Databases

In crime investigation the most obvious point of focus is the marks database, as without a mark from a scene, other databases are not particularly useful. Assuming a well-ordered marks database is held, two other databases could also be developed. The first and most obvious is a reference database of footwear pattern images. This assists greatly in the ordered classification of the scene marks. The other is records of the footwear from previously arrested offenders. These are relatively easy to deal with, as the make of shoe is known and model identification would be relatively straightforward. Some indices consist of records of all three sources.

18.5.7   The Comparison of Marks And Footwear Items

When a footwear item is recovered, and a comparison with marks from the crime scene is required, this situation is analogous to the fingerprint and finger mark process, but footwear mark examination and comparison requires a distinctly different method. This procedure has more in common with trace evidence in the approach taken. Each attribute of the tread of the footwear must be investigated for significant differences with the corresponding attributes in the mark, which could be considered as a series of questions.

18.5.7.1   Is the Exact Pattern the Same or Different?

If the pattern is deemed to be partly or completely different, the mark could not have been made by the footwear in question. If the pattern is the same, this might be considered a significant match, depending on how common the pattern is. Data collected from a marks index or casework, and even national sales figures, can be used to assess this significance

18.5.7.2   Is the Pattern Size the Same or Different?

More care is needed with this attribute of the tread, as the exact detail within the pattern can vary between treads and also between marks made by the same tread, depending on the pressure exerted, movement, or changes to the surface during and after the marks were made. If there are differences that cannot be reasonably explained, it would be logical to suggest the mark has not been made by the footwear examined. If the pattern detail is the same, the significance of the match would be enhanced, depending on the construction of the tread and how peculiar its pattern detail is. Some treads are made in such a way that some individualization of the tread occurs in respect of the pattern detail during manufacture (Figure 18.7). The effect of wear must also be considered, as the shape and size of some pattern components will almost certainly be influenced by wear as well as manufacture.

18.5.7.3   Is the Degree and Distribution of Wear Observed on the Tread and That Indicated in the Mark the Same?

Degree and distribution of wear on tread is more complex as wear assessment is strongly influenced by time considerations. The shorter the time between the recovery of the footwear and the recovery, or more strictly speaking, the deposition of the mark, the closer should be the correlation between the wear to the tread and that indicated in the mark. If the mark indicated more wear than that present on the tread, it would be reasonable to assume that the footwear item did not make the mark. Again, careful assessment of the indicated wear is needed. This would require some knowledge of the pattern and construction of the tread to assess the likely appearance of marks left at the various stages of wear.

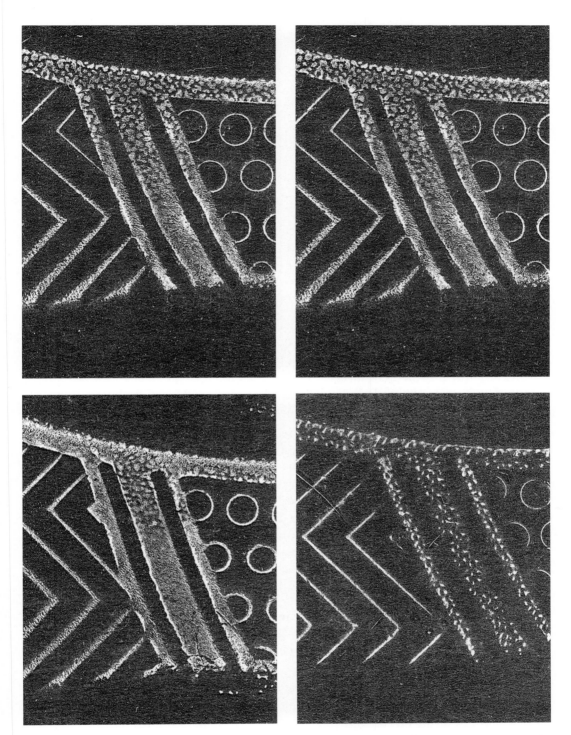

Figure 18.7 Part of a Reebok pattern that is known to vary according to pattern. Note the differences in the positions of the zigzag bars relative to the boundaries. It is apparent that the images from the size 5 shoes are also different from each other in respect to the exact pattern detail. The images have actually originated from a nonsymmetrical pair. This shows that the detail of this pattern is not completely dependent on the marked size.

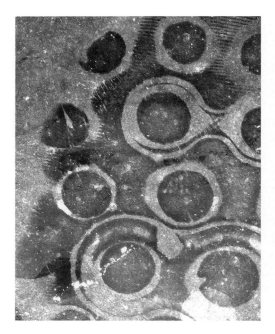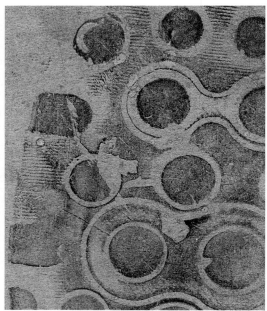

Figure 18.8 Matching damage. Note, also, how there are features in the tread that do not appear in the mark. Given the conclusive association between the mark and shoe, this damage must be acquired between the shoe depositing the mark and the one being seized for examination. Given the quality of the mark and the magnitude of the damage, it is unlikely it has been obscured when the mark was made.

Pattern features that are cut perpendicular to the tread base will tend to remain the same shape and size until they reach a fairly advanced degree of wear. Pattern elements that are concave, convex, or are of an angled or tapered cut will tend to change shape and size progressively and predictably with increasing wear. The finer the pattern elements that are worn, the more precisely the degree of wear can be determined. If a footwear item is recovered relatively quickly after a mark is deposited, and there is a very close or exact match in the degree of wear to both gross and fine pattern elements, the match would be considered highly significant. This is particularly true if the precise degree of wear matches in various parts of the tread and suggests the same distribution of wear. The distribution of wear will, to some degree, be influenced by the wearer and will tend to increase the degree of individualization.

18.5.7.4 Are There Any Features in Marks That Correspond to Random Specific Wear or Damage Features to the Tread?

Specific damage can occur to the tread in a number of ways. Some of these are very obvious such as cuts and nicks but there are others, such as the distortion by foreign objects or embedded objects and fine abrasion patterns, that are less so. The presence of features in a mark that can be aligned and attributed to features on an examined footwear item can form the basis for a conclusive link (Figure 18.8).

The absence of such features in the mark, however, does not in itself constitute a reason to exclude the possibility of the footwear's making the mark. Again, time is an important factor. If the marks and footwear are recovered within a relatively short time frame, it may be reasonable to expect features in the mark that correspond to damage on the tread. It is a fact of mark examination, however, that damage is often in the form of relatively fine features, and these are easily obscured in marks of poor definition. Marks made with liquid contaminants such as blood, water, or mud often show very little, if any, fine detail. This is due to the obvious property of the contaminant to flow and fill in fine damage features, which are most often areas where the tread material has been removed, leaving hollows, channels, or holes. These readily fill with liquid materials when pressure is applied to the tread. Fine dust marks are not prone to this problem, but poor contrast and heavily textured surfaces or substrates can all easily obscure detail of the dimensions commonly encountered in damage features to footwear treads.

Possibly the biggest deviation between the footwear mark comparison and the finger mark comparison is the level of matching detail required to make a conclusive association. The match of the footwear and mark may yield a high level of significance simply on the basis of the general attributes of the tread, and only a limited number of damage features are required to satisfy the footwear examiner that there is no practical prospect of another footwear item matching to the same degree. Some individual features can in themselves be highly characteristic, and this will be a matter for assessment by the examiner. For this reason, footwear mark matches do not have an equivalent to the fingerprint identification standard, as the match is made on a number of attributes in combination rather than on a set quantity of features. As a combination of attributes is used in the footwear match, and as these have varying degrees of discrimination, it is possible for the conclusions drawn in footwear cases to vary from weak corroboration to a conclusive match. One aspect of the footwear comparison that is often overlooked is the possibility of finding matches in other footwear items a suspect owns. The more shoes they have, the more likely it is to find a match of certain attributes in the patterns. An individual only has one set of fingerprints and one DNA profile, so with these such further matching is unnecessary. Some consideration must also be given to comparisons resulting from database searches where crime scene marks will be selected on the basis that they are of the same pattern as the suspect footwear. It is important to the footwear examiner, therefore, that the background of a comparison request is known before reaching conclusions for comparisons where the match is not conclusive.

Further Reading

Bodziak, W.J., *Footwear Impression Evidence: Detection, Recovery, and Examination (Practical Aspects of Criminal and Forensic Investigation)*, CRC Press, Boca Raton, FL, 1999.

Cassidy, M.J., Footwear Identification, Royal Canadian Mounted Police, Ottawa, Canada, 1980.

Gait

19

MICHAEL G. GRANT

Contents

19.1 Introduction 343
   19.1.1 Motivation and Feasibility 344
   19.1.2 What Is Gait? 344
      19.1.2.1 Features and Measurements of Gait 344
   19.1.3 Early Approaches and Proof of Concept 345
   19.1.4 Gait as a Biometric 346
19.2 Available Databases 347
   19.2.1 The Gait Challenge Dataset 347
   19.2.2 The Southampton Gait Database 349
19.3 Progress in Gait Recognition 349
   19.3.1 The Human ID Program 349
      19.3.1.1 Baseline Algorithm University 351
      19.3.1.2 Carnegie Mellon University 351
      19.3.1.3 Georgia Tech 352
      19.3.1.4 Maryland 352
      19.3.1.5 MIT 353
      19.3.1.6 Southampton 353
   19.3.2 Other Contemporary Work 354
   19.3.3 Summary and Future Directions 358
19.4 Acknowledgments 359
References 359

19.1 Introduction

Gait recognition is the process of identifying people by the unique characteristics of their manner of walking. Many people have had the experience of recognizing a friend from a distance despite being too far away to actually see their face, and this is often attributed to their unique way of walking. Literature has many references to this phenomenon. Converting such everyday experience into a useful technique for recognizing people raises two major research questions: Which features should be extracted from a person's gait in order to recognize them, and how well do these features generalize to a large population?

This chapter reviews the existing work on these questions in the context of biometrics by computer vision.

19.1.1   Motivation and Feasibility

Studies of human motion have existed for centuries, with perhaps some of the earliest applications of the principles of mechanics to anatomy stretching back as far as Leonardo Da Vinci in the Renaissance. Motion analysis appeared shortly after the development of cinematography in the latter half of the 19th century, first deployed scientifically by Etienne Marey in Paris (Braun 1992), using techniques that have considerable similarities with modern methods. At the same time, Muybridge in California was taking stop-motion photographs of animals (famously, a horse's gallop) and men in motion (Braun 1992). Medical studies expanded into increasingly detailed gait analysis, particularly for the correction of pathological gait. Studies of normal gait patterns, such as Murray's work on the walking patterns of normal men (Murray 1967), suggested that gait is unique to the individual. Matching work in the field of psychology demonstrated that gait as a movement was recognizable even with minimal information (Johannson 1972). Further work showed recognition of generic attributes such as gender (Mather and Murdock 1994) and, later, of individuals known to the observer (Cutting and Kozlowski 1977, Cutting et al. 1978, Stevenage et al. 1999).

19.1.2   What Is Gait?

Often gait analysis has been primarily restricted to the motion of the legs, but it is equally valid to consider the full dynamics of the body, as walking is a process that engages the entire body. In a dictionary, gait is defined as "a manner of walking," one's bearing or carriage as one walks (Tulloch 1997), which lends support to a more holistic view of the body.

Gait is a cyclic motion with three key stages of relevance here. These are: the heel strike (when the foot first meets the ground), the double support phase where weight is transferred to the leading foot, and the propulsive push-off from the back foot leading to the midstance position where weight is only on one foot and the legs are at their closest (see Figure 19.6). Locomotion is periodic and bodywide; as the legs swing, the body twists and the arms counterswing to support the movement. Even the head moves a little to stay level. The forward motion varies, accelerating from the push-off to the next heel strike, then decelerating as weight shifts to the leading foot.

Considerable individual variation exists within all this movement, which gait recognition techniques attempt to capture, as stated above. The challenge is to find the combination of features that provides an accessible and identifiable metric characteristic of an individual in a general population.

19.1.2.1   Features and Measurements of Gait

At this point, it is useful to consider the variety of features in the human gait and how they may be measured from image sequences. Nonvisual measures, such as mechanical joint measurement or impact sensors, require specialized environments and don't offer the biometric benefits (particularly, noninvasiveness) of a vision-based technique. Therefore, they are not discussed here.

Static measures are those that can be derived from a single (possibly posed) picture, as in face recognition. Some examples are the basic physical measurements (e.g., length of limbs, proportions of various body parts in relation to others, etc.), appearance measures (e.g., color, texture, reflectivity, etc.), and physical interrelationship (e.g., angle and position of the limbs in a standard pose).

Dynamic features are derived from data that include an element of time. Some examples include changes of appearance measures (variations in reflectivity or shading from changes in limb angle), speed and direction of motion, changes of position and interrelationship of body parts (particularly movement from one stance phase to another), and changes in shape (either deformation or to shape perceived at the sensor). As measurements of walking are affected by many factors other than individual variation, a prospective gait recognition technique must be evaluated for how well its results can be generalized. Existing databases have captured sequences that make it possible to examine some of these factors (especially circumstances affecting normal gait, e.g., kinds of clothing, different shoes, or loads being carried) (see section titled "Available Databases"). Studies of exceptional vs. population variation are also important as individual distinctiveness is key to successful recognition. The effects of age and health on gait over time also require study but are harder to capture. The longest time frame studied so far in this regard is approximately 1 year.

19.1.3 Early Approaches and Proof of Concept

Work on gait recognition via computer vision can be roughly categorized as holistic or model based. Holistic measures examine the dataset as a whole, with no interpretation of the structure of the body dynamics. Model-based approaches attempt to fit a structural model to the data and then examine the parameters of the model. Considerable blurring and combination of the two approaches occur, but the distinction can be useful. Due to the computational cost of the large search-space dimensionality of a person model, many initial approaches used the cheaper holistic measures. The main advantage of a model-based approach is the clear and direct linkage to the body and its dynamics.

The measurements mentioned above are normally processed for features that are more invariant to changes in the environment or other factors, such as attire of the subject, or to extract particularly informative components from the raw data. Typically, these features will be normalized in some fashion (e.g., using ratios of limb lengths instead of raw lengths) and often will apply dimensionality-compression and feature-significance methods (e.g., principal components analysis). In the case of the measures relating to movement, frequency space is often examined using Fourier or wavelet transforms. Biometric techniques using a model take a different approach, and either search for the model most closely matching the measurements (a recognition task) or fit the model to the measurements, then examine the model parameters to derive a signature.

Early holistic approaches included analyzing trajectories of key body parts in XT space (Niyogi and Adelson 1994a) (where a slice is taken through the horizontal rows of the images over time; see Figure 19.1) and later in XYT space (Niyogi and Adelson 1994b), Murase and Sakai's parametric eigenspace decomposition of gait patterns (Murase and Sakai 1996), recognition by phase components of periodic moments (of optical flow) (Little and Boyd 1998), temporal integration with Fourier analysis, and a combination of principal components analysis (PCA) and canonical analysis (Huang et al. 1999), extending Murase's work. All of these techniques operated on silhouettes (or optical flow of silhouettes as in the case of Little and Boyd).

Whereas a number of model-based techniques for motion analysis and classification exist (e.g., Meyer et al. 1998, Rohr 1994), perhaps the earliest that directly-yielded a gait signature used for recognition was Cunado's Hough transform (HT) modification (Cunado et al. 1997).

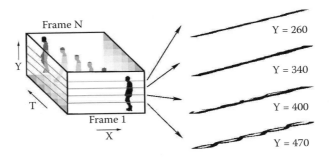

Figure 19.1   An example of XT plots at various heights (Y constants).

The thigh is modeled as a pendulum (or, later, as a dual pendulum [Cunado et al. 2003]) and evidence-gathering finds the parameters governing the movement of the thigh, with phase-weighted magnitude spectra from a Fourier analysis forming the gait signature.

These approaches were applied to databases of the order of five to ten people with several sequences for each, often using approximately ten features to characterize a person's gait. Although the database sizes were small, recognition results were generally high and encouraged the development of larger and more detailed datasets.

19.1.4   Gait as a Biometric

As a biometric, gait has some unique advantages; in particular, it is possible to acquire data remotely and noninvasively, and it is difficult to disguise. Acquisition of data is often restrictive for many biometrics, possibly requiring specialized environments for data capture or intrusive measures such as attaching markers, which may also require a cooperative subject. Gait has the potential to be usable from a greater distance than other biometrics due to the simple fact that the motion of the body is physically larger than, for example, the details of the face. As a result, it may be usable in situations where resolution of the sensors is inadequate for other biometrics or at greater distances for the same class of sensor. Intuitively, it seems that disguising one's gait by attempting to alter one's natural pattern of walking would be awkward to maintain and likely to attract attention. The *Monty Python* TV sketch, "Ministry of Silly Walks" (Python n.d.), is often jokingly referred to in this context. However, the degree to which it is possible to generate a gait signature that is invariant to common or small-scale alterations, such as clothing and natural variation over time, is still a subject of continuing research.

As a practical matter, there are several independent stages in the process of identifying someone by his/her gait. First, the human figure must be isolated and extracted from the data. Second, a set of measures of the person are made. Third, features are extracted from the measures and processed into a signature. Finally, this signature is compared with a database to find a match and thus identify the person.

The first stage, finding and extracting the figure, is perhaps the most vigorous area of research owing to the enormous range of applications for techniques that extract human figures from images. Consequently, the field is too large to encompass in this chapter, but several excellent surveys exist. Of particular relevance are three surveys (Gavrila 1999, Aggarwal and Cai 1999, Wang and Singh 2003). Generally, extraction for gait recognition (Grant et al. 2004) uses a side-on (fronto-parallel) camera view to capture the most movement. Then, simple binary silhouettes are extracted with a background subtraction process. The silhouettes are filtered to remove noise and then normalized, using the silhouettes as the basis for further processing.

Like the basic extraction techniques, a huge base of work exists on abstracting important characteristics from large feature spaces, e.g., PCA, on distance metrics for comparison of signatures (e.g., Euclidean or Mahanalobis) and on clustering methodologies (e.g., k-nearest-neighbor or Gaussian clustering). Again, these are outside the scope of this chapter and may be found in textbooks on statistical data analysis (Jobson 1999), although Veres et al. (2004) give a brief coverage of several statistical techniques in the context of gait recognition.

The parts of approaches covering the remaining stages, the measurements made, and the features extracted are reviewed here. For biometric techniques that seek to calculate a signature directly from image sequence, measurements are limited in accuracy and are often processed for features that are unaffected by common variations such as attire, load, time and health. As stated above, the challenge is to find which features provide an identifiable metric characteristic of a single person in a general population.

19.2   Available Databases

A number of gait databases of varying degrees of sophistication have been developed from the initial small databases. Two large databases are currently publicly available, both created as part of the Human ID program (see subsection titled "The Human ID Program") and will be briefly described here. Others exist, and it is likely that access would be granted by contacting the relevant authors.

19.2.1   The Gait Challenge Dataset

One aim of the recently established Human ID Program in the U.K. is to facilitate comparisons between techniques by the provision of a standard dataset and a baseline algorithm. The Gait Challenge Problem, set by Sarkar and Phillips et al. (Phillips et al. 2002a,b; Sarkar et al. 2005), describes these. The dataset selected is described briefly here and was a collaboration mainly between the University of South Florida (USF), the National Institute of Standards and Technology (NIST), and the University of Notre Dame.

The full dataset amounts to 1.2 TB of data, with 122 subjects and 1870 sequences in total. Subjects walk in an ellipse in front of two cameras, once on a grass surface and once on a concrete surface. They are also recorded with two different shoe types and with or without a briefcase on both surfaces (see Figure 19.2 for example frames). The sequences were filmed in two periods, 6 months apart (May and November, so seasonal clothing changes may have occurred) with 33 of the subjects appearing in both the earlier and later periods, giving a time covariate. USF offers for downloading the precomputed silhouettes (Figure 19.3) generated by the baseline algorithm and, by physical distribution, the full color dataset.

In addition, a set of standard experiments exists, forming the challenge problem (Table 19.1). The experiments are of different difficulty levels, mainly related to the number of different covariates. The baseline algorithm results for the challenge problem are in Table 19.2.

Information on acquiring the Gait Challenge dataset and baseline algorithm is available from http://www.GaitChallenge.org.

(a) Grass, no briefcase, left view, subject 02463   (b) Concrete, with briefcase, right view, subject 02463

Figure 19.2   Example images from the Gait Challenge dataset.

(a) Silhouette of Figure 19.2(a)   (b) Silhouette of Figure 19.2(b)

Figure 19.3   Gait Challenge precomputed silhouettes.

Table 19.1   Gait Challenge Experiment Precis

Experiment	Subjects	Covariates
A	122	View
B	54	Shoe
C	54	View, shoe
D	121	Surface
E	60	Surface, shoe
F	121	Surface, view
G	60	Surface, shoe, view
H	120	Briefcase
I	60	Shoe, briefcase
J	120	View, briefcase
K	33	Time (+ shoe, clothing)
L	33	Surface, time

Table 19.2   Gait Challenge Baseline Algorithm Results

Experiment	Recognition Rate (%, rank 1)	Recognition Rate (%, rank 5)
A	73	88
B	78	93
C	48	78
D	32	66
E	22	55
F	17	42
G	17	38
H	61	85
I	57	78
J	36	62
K	3	12
L	3	15

19.2.2   The Southampton Gait Database

Southampton produced a gait database partitioned into two major sections, with a total size of approximately 500 GB. A large-population section (approximately 115 subjects) captures between-subject variation, and a small-population section (10 subjects, all in the large-population database and taken 6 months earlier) captures within-subject variation. The large-population dataset has multiple sequences from two viewpoints (fronto-parallel and 20° oblique) of subjects walking in a laboratory environment, on a treadmill, and outdoors. The small-population dataset has sequences of the subjects in the laboratory environment, wearing a variety of footwear and clothes, carrying various bags, and walking at different speeds, all viewed from four angles (fronto-parallel, 20° oblique, elevated, and front-on). Figure 19.4 shows examples.

The laboratory environment was filmed with green backdrops, allowing very clean extraction of silhouettes by chroma-keying techniques (Figure 19.5). The database is documented with still photographs and measurements of subjects, and has some additional metadata (such as the occurrence of heel strikes) available for some views. Descriptions of the database may also be found in the literature (Shutler et al. 2002, Nixon et al. 2003).

Information on acquiring the Southampton database is available from http://www.gait.ecs.soton.ac.uk/.

19.3   Progress in Gait Recognition

Continuing the brief retrospective in the Section "Early Approaches and Proof of Concept," this section reviews recent work, though space limitations constrain the scope to techniques embodying particular approaches.

19.3.1   The Human ID Program

The Human ID Program was established by the Defense Advanced Research Projects Agency (DARPA), aiming to investigate and improve existing and potential biometrics. Gait recognition was targeted as a potential biometric. There were several goals for the gait recognition

(a) Large-population, normal view, indoor track   (b) Large-population, normal view, indoor treadmill

(c) Large-population, normal view, outdoors   (d) Small-population, high view, barrel bag

Figure 19.4   Sample frames of the Southampton database.

Figure 19.5   Sample silhouette of Figure 19.4(a) from the Southampton database (clean chroma-key extraction).

effort: to increase database sizes, availability, and quality; to establish baseline performance and enable comparisons of techniques; and to develop new and existing techniques. The earlier Face Recognition Technology (FERET) Program (Phillips et al. 2000) had the same aims and brought standardized databases and procedures to evaluate systems to that community. A number of teams worked on gait recognition as part of this project and have published novel techniques and databases as part of it. The project was a major contribution to gait research, and the following subsections describe the approaches it developed to give an overview of contemporary gait recognition techniques.

19.3.1.1 Baseline Algorithm University

A companion to the standardized Gait Challenge dataset described in the subsection titled "The Gait Challenge Dataset" was a baseline algorithm providing a benchmark to measure improvement against Sarkar et al. (2005). It was created at the University of South Florida, NIST, and Notre Dame. The baseline algorithm has two major phases: extraction and similarity computation. Silhouettes are extracted using a background model generated from the whole sequence but excluding the area containing the subject, using predefined bounding boxes (manually initialized, then interpolated, and part of the Gait Challenge dataset). Foreground pixels are detected by thresholding the Mahanalobis distance between it and the estimated mean background. Smoothing reduces boundary noise. Small areas of noise are deleted by connected component labelling and removal of small blobs. Finally, the silhouette is normalized to 128 × 88 pixels.

To compute a similarity measure, a probe sequence of silhouettes is split into sub-sequences approximately the length of a single stride (manually set at 30 frames). Each sub-sequence is compared to the target sequence, using a correlation measure formed by summing frame similarities. The frame similarity measure is simply the ratio of pixels in the intersection of the two frames to their union. Maximum correlation is sought by shifting the probe sub-sequence with respect to the target to get the highest match. The median value of the maximum correlations for each sub-sequence yields the final similarity measure.

A later modification removed the three manual parameters; expectation maximization estimates the silhouette from the Mahanalobis distances, only the largest connected component is kept, and a period detection scheme replaces the stride length parameter.

19.3.1.2 Carnegie Mellon University

Collins et al. developed a simple but effective method (Collins et al. 2002) with similarities to the later version of the Gait Challenge baseline algorithm. A silhouette sequence is analyzed by simple periodicity measures of silhouette height and width to find particular keyframes, the mid-stance or double-support phases of the gait cycle (Figure 19.6). Only these keyframes are normalized and retained, ensuring that later stages operate on matching frames regardless of speed differences. A similarity score between probe and gallery keyframes of the same stance uses a Fourier transform cross correlation to test all displacements for the best match.

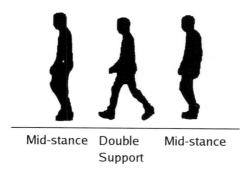

Figure 19.6 The gait cycle (showing double support and midstance phases).

Classification returns the gallery subject with the best match to four adjacent keyframes (a complete gait cycle). Testing on multiple databases gave good results (76–100%), even on different walk speeds due to the removal of time information by keyframing. Like all silhouette approaches, viewpoint changes cause difficulties as a new aspect of the subject is presented and training on multiple viewpoints is suggested. A drop of approximately 40% occurred when sequences of the same subject across different days were compared, possibly due to appearance changes.

Liu et al. examined "frieze patterns" (Liu et al. 2002), which are formed by compressing a silhouette frame in the vertical or horizontal direction (summing rows or columns) into a one-dimensional line, then concatenating each into a two-dimensional pattern. Using artificial walker sequences, they measured the effect of viewing angle changes and were able to compensate for smaller viewpoint variations in real sequences. Although not extensively applied to gait recognition, a demonstration on the CMU Motion of Body (MoBo) Database scored 80–100% recognition rates when aligned frieze patterns were correlated.

19.3.1.3   Georgia Tech

Johnson and Bobick extract static body parameters from a sequence (Johnson and Bobick 2001), reasoning that they are less subject to extraction problems owing to appearance changes (e.g., viewpoint). They segment a silhouette into head, pelvis, and foot regions, using predefined body ratios. Refinement of position uses the centroid of the head and pelvis regions to define head and pelvis points. The foot region is split into two, locating each foot as the furthest point from the head centroid (distinction of left and right foot is irrelevant). Pixel distances between regions are converted to centimeters via a calibration with a known-height subject. Four pieces of information are recorded for each stride at the double-support stance: height of the bounding box around the subject, distance between head and pelvis centers, the longer of the distances between pelvis center and each foot, and distance between the feet. Averaging over multiple strides refines a sequence vector. Perspective errors were compensated for using conversion factors derived from motion capture of a single subject at known viewpoints. On a dataset of 18 subjects with multiple viewpoints, the technique achieved 90–100% recognition rates (classifying by a maximal likelihood method matching sequences to Gaussian models of individuals).

19.3.1.4   Maryland

Kale et al. used continuous Hidden Markov Models (HMMs) on key stances (Kale et al. 2002, 2004). They measure body contour widths at each row of each frame. This feature vector is reduced by measuring the distances from five exemplar stances for each individual in the training set, a model suitable for HMM state transitions. The HMM is trained on test sets and, together with the individual exemplar stances, represents a subject's gait. This allows computation of the likelihood that an observation sequence was generated by an individual. By examining all individuals in a database and selecting the best match, recognition is achieved. A Maryland database, the CMU MoBo database, and the Gait Challenge dataset all gave good results of 60–100%. The Gait Challenge results paralleled the trend of the baseline algorithm (though generally higher), with weaker recognition as more covariates were introduced.

BenAbdelkader et al. used similarity plots (BenAbdelkader et al. 2002) to produce a signature in a space they termed *eigengait*. A self-similarity plot is computed from a silhouette sequence by correlating blobs from all consecutive pairs of frames. The periodicity of gait is

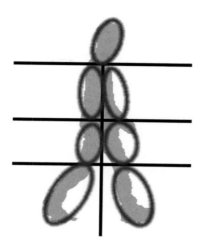

Figure 19.7 Impression of Lee and Grimson's (2002) silhouette regioning with ellipses.

exploited by tiling the plots (with normalization) into a representation containing self-similarities for all pairs of images in the sequence. Treated in the same way as a face image is in the eigenface algorithm (Turk and Pentland 1991), PCA reduces the tiled representation's dimensionality (retaining eigenvectors capturing 95% of the variation). Classification uses k-nearest-neighbor and gave 90% on Little and Boyd's 6-subject dataset, whereas on the larger UMD2 dataset (44 people), performance dropped to approximately 75%. Increasing k caused a small drop, perhaps indicating clusters overlapping in eigengait space.

19.3.1.5 MIT

Lee and Grimson divided a silhouette into seven regions (approximately both lower legs, both thighs, front and back of the torso, including arms, and the head) using standardized body proportions (Lee and Grimson 2002). The parameters of an ellipse are fitted to each region, and the normalized height of the silhouette centroid makes a frame-feature vector, describing the body shape and position (Figure 19.7). A 57-dimensional gait-appearance vector is calculated from frame vectors by taking the mean and standard deviation of the ellipse parameters and averaging the height measure, thus encoding the subject's average shape and motion. A 56-dimensional gait spectral vector combines the dominant walking frequency with phases and magnitudes of a Fourier transform of per-frame ellipse parameters, thus encoding a characteristic of the motion. Analysis of Variance (ANOVA) is used to discard components that have low distinctiveness. A MIT database of 24 subjects with an average of 8 sequences per subject over 4 separate days (a total of 194 sequences) was analyzed. Sequences taken on the same day gave perfect recognition, but comparing across longer time periods (e.g., a day 1 probe and day 4 gallery), performance dropped significantly to approximately 70%. As the measure is appearance based, the authors postulated that different clothing on different days reduced performance, and they suggested multiple representations of a subject or additional modalities might circumvent the problem.

19.3.1.6 Southampton

The University of Southampton's team had already developed some of the earlier techniques (Huang et al. 1999, Cunado et al. 1997) and continued exploring both model-based and holistic solutions.

Shutler et al. modified both Cartesian and Zernike moments to include a time dimension, terming the result *velocity moments* (Shutler and Nixon 2001). By extending the calculation of moment values over a silhouette or optic-flow sequence, these generate holistic representations of subjects that retain a significant degree of physical interpretation, allowing one to identify the general motion that a particular moment was detecting (e.g., rate of change of centroid shift). Discriminative velocity moments were selected by ANOVA and achieved 100% recognition on a small dataset. Shutler's thesis (Shutler 2002) describes extensive testing on a number of databases, all yielding results of 80–100% and using 6–13 moments. Combining velocity moments derived from spatial (binary silhouettes) and temporal (optic-flow images) gave the best result on the largest dataset (96% on 50 subjects).

Hayfron-Acquah et al. analyzed symmetry in walkers, motivated by psychological studies on the symmetricity and periodicity of gait (Hayfron-Acquah et al. 2001, 2003). A slight modification of the discrete symmetry operator is applied to an edge-detected, centralized, and normalized silhouette sequence, giving a skeleton-like image that detects reflectional symmetry. Each symmetry image is summed and averaged to generate a single temporally-accumulated image capturing a complete gait cycle (normalizing speed to some extent). A Fourier transform of this image is low-pass filtered to remove some noisier frequency components, keeping 4096 magnitude components as the gait signature. On a database of 28 subjects, the algorithm scored 97% correct classification (using the Euclidean distance to compare gait descriptions). In a later paper (Nixon et al. 2003), the technique achieved 94% on the large-population Southampton database, making it the most potent of Southampton's holistic techniques.

A model-based approach extended Cunado's work (Cunado et al. 2003), where the thigh was described by a single oscillating pendulum and extracted by evidence gathering. Yam's extension (Yam et al. 2002, 2004) improved the leg model to include lower leg motion. Two models were proposed: a bilateral symmetric model, where the lower leg angle is a function of thigh angle, and a forced-coupled-oscillator model, where the leg is modelled by a joined pair of pendulums with the thigh motion driving the lower leg. The models are used to extract the position of legs in edge-detected sequences by a template matching process. Per-frame position estimates are refined by local fitting, capturing individual variation. A Fourier transform of a single cycle of leg rotations is taken, following alignment to remove phase distortions. Phase components then weight the magnitudes to merge the extent and timing of motions. Five harmonics (excluding DC) are retained for the gait signature (a medical study showing a maximum gait frequency content of 5 Hz is quoted). Performance analysis on a 20-subject database, including running and walking, gave 80% CCR (walking) and 90% (running) using the forced-coupled-oscillator model, implying running is more distinctive than walking. The bilateral symmetric model results were approximately 20% lower. No general mapping between walking and running feature spaces was found, though individual mapping appeared possible.

19.3.2 Other Contemporary Work

Both outside of and continuing from the human ID project, there has been a considerable amount of research interest in gait. Some of the more significant or illustrative work is described here.

Wagg and Nixon adopted a hierarchical approach to deriving walker signature (Wagg and Nixon 2004a, b), breaking the problem down into a series of computable phases. They begin by estimating horizontal motion using a motion-compensated temporal accumulation of edge images, then refine with a coarse person-shaped template. Estimates of gait period (derived from area variation around the lower legs) further improve the accumulation, and the model is refined to an ellipse each for head and torso. Using the period estimate together with a leg model derived from medical studies, articulated legs scaled to the subject's height are added. Adaptation to individual gait is accomplished in two ways: by improving the leg shape model using line HTs to determine widths at hip, ankle, and knee (both upper and lower leg at the knee to allow for discontinuity in width from clothing) and by repeatedly refining joint rotation models until convergence occurs (using template matching to measure quality of fit). The joint models are iteratively improved by adding Gaussians (thus enforcing smoothness) at sample points, adapting hip and knee rotations first, then ankle rotations. Samples from the joint rotation models (15 each from hip, knee, and ankle) and 18 parameters describing speed, gait frequency, and body shape make a feature vector. Features are weighted by their discriminatory power (using ANOVA). The top five were four shape measures and gait frequency. Testing on the large-population Southampton database gave rates of 84% (laboratory) and 64% (outdoors).

A contrasting algorithm by Mowbray and Nixon (Mowbray and Nixon 2004) uses spatio-temporal Fourier descriptors (FDs) to represent a deforming contour, deriving from the four-dimensional boundary. Selecting 20 features from the FDs by their ability to separate classes, a k-nearest-neighbor classifier gave 84.5% ($k = 1$) on the Southampton large-population database. Somewhat unusually, at $k = 3$ recognition was 86.2%, implying better feature-space clustering than most techniques described here, perhaps owing to the access to scale and frequency from the hierarchical nature of FDs of boundary shape and motion.

Han and Bhanu attacked the view-dependence problem of two-dimensional silhouettes with a three-dimensional model formed of spheres (joints) connected by cones (limbs), which they fit to silhouettes (Han and Bhanu 2005, Bhanu and Han 2002a, b). By using a full three-dimensional kinematic body model, they eliminate the common requirement for fronto-parallel view. A few basic assumptions regarding camera position and distance, and assuming natural walking, allow their model to have 33 parameters — 20 stationary (describing radii and length of various body parts) and 13 kinematic (angles of joints). Selecting several key frames of silhouettes with high reliability and quality, a least-squares matching procedure (using a genetic algorithm for speed) estimates the parameters. These kinematically predict parameters in other subsequent frames. Many parameters are discarded as unreliable for recognition, retaining torso, upper arm, lower arm, thigh, calf, and foot lengths. Recognition rates were 40–60%, but they include an interesting analysis allowing them to predict performance of their features at various resolutions and for different database sizes. Optimal performance on their data was 95%, with the difference attributed mainly to extraction and matching errors, and model-fitting ambiguities arising from self-occlusion of the subject.

The Chinese Academy of Sciences has investigated gait biometrics with a focus on two methods. Wang et al. began with a silhouette boundary approach (Wang et al. 2002, Wang et al. 2003), where a one-dimensional signal is formed by measuring distance from a silhouette centroid to the boundary of the body and tracing out the full contour. The set of these signals over the full sequence is compressed by PCA (keeping the first 15 eigenvectors) and a form of dynamic time warping (DTW) used to normalize for comparison. Testing on the 20-person NLPR database and on the Gait Challenge dataset gave favorable results, with some difficulties attributed to extraction problems.

In a considerable extension to this work (Wang et al. 2004), the boundary model of the silhouette (now using Procrustes shape analysis for comparison) was complemented with a body dynamics model. A Gaussian-based motion model for each joint (with constraints describing dependency relations between body parts) can be derived from exemplar sequences and, within the conditional density propagation (CONDENSATION) framework, used to predict the position of the body in the following frames. Predicted positions are hierarchically refined using a pose evaluation function balancing boundary adhesion with area coverage. The motion model is described in detail in Ning et al. (2004a) and an alternative kinematics-based model appears in Ning et al. (2004b). After convergence, joint angles are extracted, and DTW and normalization are applied to align the signals to a reference phase for comparisons. Applied to the NLPR database, the body shape measures evaluated at 84%, whereas the motion measures achieved 87%, with fusion raising results to 97%.

Shakhnarovich et al. approached the viewpoint problem by using image-based visual hulls to generate novel views (Shakhnarovich et al. 2001). The visual hull (VH) is the maximal volume that creates all the perceived views, with a set of cameras around a walker, and virtual views can be rendered from any point in three-dimensional space. The degree of error is dependent on the object and the spread of the cameras. The VH is used to generate a fronto-parallel view and input to Lee's recognition algorithm from the subsection "MIT." Recognition from the generated views was 87% vs. 52% from raw views (12 subjects).

Liu et al. published an excellent study on silhouette quality and the effect it has on gait recognition (Liu et al. 2004). Many papers have speculated that errors in silhouette extraction reduce recognition rates. Although clearly true for extreme errors, this was not established for more minor noise. A subset of the Gait Challenge silhouettes were manually segmented, ensuring clean silhouettes and providing a unique ground truth set covering a single gait cycle of 71 subjects across the experiments A (view), B (shoe), D (surface), and K (time). In addition to manual extraction, an automatic silhouette reconstruction method based on HMMs and eigenstances is presented that, by virtue of being trained on the ground-truth silhouettes, is able to remove shadows and other common extraction errors. Using the manual silhouettes and a slightly modified baseline algorithm (compensating for only having a single gait cycle), they found a small but statistically significant drop in performance while retaining the same trend. They conclude that the low performance of experiments, varying surface, and time thus cannot be attributed to silhouette quality. Furthermore, using the HMM-cleaned silhouettes to allow bulk testing, they achieved results that were similar. They also found that error pixels corrected by the algorithm appeared to contribute to distinguishing people, implying that erroneous correlations may actually improve recognition. A similar effect was noted by Shutler (2002) where adding noise or random holes to silhouettes actually improved recognition, with the supposition that the holes added internal detail and allowed higher-order statistical descriptors to become effective.

Liu and Sarkar also presented an extremely simple but effective gait representation (Liu and Sarkar 2004). They simply normalize, align, and average silhouettes for one gait cycle (Figure 19.8), then use the average silhouette directly as a feature vector. The time spent at each point in the cycle is proportional to the intensity. Comparing representations for similarity uses a direct Euclidean distance measure, taking the median of multiple probes. Performance on the Gait Challenge dataset is equivalent to the baseline algorithm, but significantly faster. In an experiment to determine which parts of the silhouette had most influence, they found that both upper and lower body appeared to contribute equally. The

Figure 19.8   Averaged and aligned silhouette sequence.

manual silhouettes described above were also used but did not affect the results significantly, perhaps because random errors in the original silhouettes will be averaged away.

Veres et al. found which information was important in silhouette representations (Veres et al. 2004), applying statistical techniques to isolate areas of high relevance. They used an aligned and averaged silhouette representation (identical to Liu and Sarkar's (Liu and Sarkar 2004)) that emphasizes nonmoving areas and also a differential representation (differencing instead of summing silhouettes) that emphasizes areas of high motion. These representations were generated from the Southampton databases, and ANOVA and PCA determined which features captured high variation between subjects. Using the averaged representation, they could reduce the feature space from 4096 features to 237 (large-population database), 1006 (temporal database), or 218 (small-population database) while retaining 100% recognition. Of these reduced features, 65 were in common across all databases, and these alone gave 60% recognition on the complete dataset (vs. 62% for all features). Features with high variation, necessary for recognition, were found to be concentrated around head and body boundaries but very little around the legs, implying static shape of the head and body is important for recognition with averaged silhouettes. Using differential silhouettes, 115 features in common gave 46% recognition (vs. 56% for all 4096 features) with important features again being concentrated mainly in the body and head contour, though with more in the legs and arm contour. They conclude that body shape is the most important recognition factor in representations involving silhouette averaging.

In recent work, Veres et al. examined recognition of gait over time using the Southampton databases (a time difference of 6 months) (Veres et al. 2005). Two feature sets were used: the average silhouette algorithm (mainly capturing static shape) and Wagg's algorithm described above (capturing dynamic aspects). Using the small-population database as a probe into the full (6 months earlier) large-population gallery, the static technique achieved approximately 40% recognition whereas the dynamic technique achieved 20%. A prediction model was proposed to counter the time effect, using a training set of old and new silhouettes of a subject to establish per-feature changes. When a corresponding new silhouette does not exist for a subject in the (larger) gallery, the most similar subject is substituted. Using this prediction model to "age" the gallery, recognition rates increased dramatically (96% for static, 88% for dynamic). A further test used probes with the full range of covariates (clothing, shoes, luggage, etc.), in addition to time, and achieved 65% (static) and 50% (dynamic) vs. uncorrected performance of 20% and 13%. This work shows that the deleterious effects of time difference can be compensated for, to a considerable degree.

19.3.3   Summary and Future Directions

Looking over the body of work in the field, some conclusions may be tentatively drawn and some future directions of research inferred. In 5 years, gait databases have expanded by an order of magnitude (from approximately 10 subjects to approximately 100), and performance has held steady, with promisingly high recognition rates. Considerable understanding has been gained in the acquisition of databases, in large scale testing on those databases, and in ways to analyze performance. The difficulty of comparing recognition techniques due to testing on different datasets and in different conditions continues to some extent. The creation of the Gait Challenge problem with standard datasets, well-defined experiments, and a standard baseline offers hope on this front and, increasingly, recent work has used this dataset.

Of the two general approaches to gait recognition, the holistic or statistical approach largely achieves higher recognition rates for less computational effort (although continuing improvements in computation power mitigate this). The more complex model-based solutions often produce a smaller feature vector than the holistic approaches, raising the question as to whether generating a larger feature space (with a small number of subjects sampling the space) increases discrimination without providing real insight. By their nature, model-based approaches frequently concentrate on analyzing the positions and angles of components of the body: the dynamics of the physical measurements. In contrast, many of the holistic measures are more concerned with the appearance parameters of silhouettes, mostly body shape and changes in body shape. These measurements are frequently complementary and uncorrelated with a potential for fusion to improve classification, as shown in some approaches above.

The majority of approaches produce meaningful representations in feature space as a whole, although it is often difficult to understand why particular aspects of that space are important. A deeper understanding of the feature spaces seems necessary, particularly in terms of which characteristics are significant for recognition, encompassing the range of variation that a single subject has vs. the population and thus the quality of clustering. As the field matures, this type of analysis has progressed with the more recent work on covariates and on silhouettes (Veres et al. 2004, 2005; Liu et al. 2004).

The work on silhouette quality suggests that extraction is not the core problem to overcome, though the results on clean indoor silhouettes vs. noisier outdoor silhouettes indicate that improvements in extraction will benefit outdoor scenarios. The limit on the discrimination available from simple measures on binary silhouettes has not yet been reached, but with clean, manually segmented silhouettes giving poorer results than the noisier automatic results, it may be reached with the next iteration of databases. The general trend seems to show a slow progression toward more complex measures, although ones that are more fundamental and essential to the nature of gait. It intuitively seems that a discriminative measure of gait must be more than just the easily altered shape of the body silhouette. The work on viewpoint-invariant body modelling holds promise, as does the holistic-style approach of examining characteristics of body flow between stances. Similarly, the difficulties that all techniques have had with probes across long time periods indicate that simple shape measures, although potent in fixed circumstances, may not suffice for a complete solution.

Further expansion of gait databases, both in numbers of subjects and internal variation, will enable more exploration of these issues of generalization and quality of measures. The next order of magnitude increase in number of subjects presents considerable logistical difficulties and may require more automation of the capture process (at human and computing levels) to make it practical. A possible alternative to expansion of databases might be to advance the current work on prediction of performance, using a smaller dataset and some understanding of the measurements taken to extrapolate recognition rates for larger datasets. Increasing the number of subjects will allow for improved determination of population variance, but enlarging the within-subject variation in the databases is equally important. Changes of clothing, multiple viewpoints (perhaps even leading to three-dimensional spatial descriptions), and measurements taken over long time periods seem especially significant, as they are currently among the most problematic covariants.

Gait recognition is now a biometric with recognized potential. Although not fully developed for applications, the field has matured considerably with recent large-scale projects and has many promising avenues of research awaiting investigation.

19.4   Acknowledgments

Thanks are owed to Sudeep Sarkar of the University of South Florida for kind permission to reproduce samples of the Gait Challenge database and to Mark Nixon of the University of Southampton for comments and permission to reproduce samples of the Southampton database.

References

Aggarwal, J.K. and Cai, Q., Human motion analysis: a review, *Computer Vision and Image Understanding* 73(3), 428–440, 1999.

BenAbdelkader, C., Cutler, R., Nanda, H., and Davis, L., Motion-based recognition of people in eigengait space, in *Proceedings of the Fifth IEEE International Conference on Automatic Face and Gesture Recognition*, 2002, pp. 267–272.

Bhanu, B. and Han, J., Bayesian-based performance prediction for gait recognition, in *Proceedings of the Workshop on Motion and Video Computing*, 2002a, pp. 145–150.

Bhanu, B. and Han, J., Individual recognition by kinematic-based gait analysis, in *Proceedings of the 16th International Conference on Pattern Recognition*, 2002b, pp. 343–346.

Braun, M., *Picturing Time: The Work of Etienne-Jules Marey (1830–1904)*, University of Chicago Press, Chicago, 1992.

Collins, R.T., Gross, R., and Shi, J., Silhouette-based human identification from body shape and gait, in *Proceedings of the Fifth IEEE International Conference on Automatic Face and Gesture Recognition*, 2002, pp. 366–371.

Cunado, D.C., Nixon, M.S., and Carter, J.N., Automatic extraction and description of human gait models for recognition purposes, *Computer Vision and Image Understanding* 90(1), 1–41, 2003.

Cunado, D.C., Nixon, M.S., and Carter, J.N., Using gait as a biometric, via phase-weighted magnitude spectra, *Lecture notes in Computer Science 1206 (Proceedings of the 1st International Conference on Audio- and Video-Based Biometric Person Authentication)*, 1997, pp. 95–102.

Cutting, J.E. and Kozlowski, L.T., Recognizing friends by their walk: gait perception without familiarity cues, *Bulletin of the Psychonomic Society* 9, 353–356, 1977.

Cutting, J.E., Proffitt, D.R., and Kozlowski, L.T., A biomechanical invariant for gait perception, *Journal of Experimental Psychology* 4(3), 357–372, 1978.

Gavrila, D.M., The visual analysis of human movement: a survey, *Computer Vision and Image Understanding* 71(1), 89–98, 1999.

Grant, M.G., Shutler, J.D., Nixon, M.S., and Carter, J.N., Analysis of a human extraction system for deploying gait biometrics, in *Proceedings of the IEEE Southwest Symposium on Image Analysis and Interpretation*, 2004, pp. 46–50.

Han, J. and Bhanu, B., Performance prediction for individual recognition by gait, *Pattern Recognition Letters* 26(5), 615–624, 2005.

Hayfron-Acquah, J.B., Nixon, M.S., and Carter, J.N., Automatic gait recognition by symmetry analysis, in *Proceedings of the 3rd International Conference on Audio- and Video-based Biometric Person Authentication*, 2001, pp. 272–277.

Hayfron-Acquah, J.B., Nixon, M.S., and Carter, J.N., Automatic gait recognition by symmetry analysis, *Pattern Recognition Letters* 24(13), 2175–2183, 2003.

Huang, P.S., Harris, C.J., and Nixon, M.S., Human gait recognition in canonical space using temporal templates, in *IEE Proceedings on Vision and Image Signal Processing*, Vol. 146, IEE, 1999, pp. 93–100.

Jobson, J.D., *Applied Multivariate Data Analysis: Regression and Experimental Design*, Vol. 1, Springer-Verlag, New York, 1999.

Johannson, G., Visual perception of biological motion and a model for its analysis, *Perception and Psychophysics* 14, 201–211, 1972.

Johnson, A.Y. and Bobick, A.F., A multi-view method for gait recognition using static body parameters, in *Proceedings of the Third International Conference on Audio- and Video-based Biometric Person Authentication*, 2001, pp. 301–311.

Kale, A., Rajagopalan, N., Cuntoor, N., and Kruger, V., Gait-based recognition of humans using continuous hmms, in *Proceedings of the Fifth IEEE International Conference on Automatic Face and Gesture Recognition*, 2002, pp. 336–341.

Kale, A., Sundaresan, A., Rajagopalan, A., Cuntoor, N., Roy-Chowdhury, A., Kruger, V., and Chellappa, R., Identification of humans using gait, *IEEE Transactions on Image Processing* 13(9), 1163–1173, 2004.

Lee, L. and Grimson, W., Gait analysis for recognition and classification, in *Proceedings of the Fifth IEEE International Conference on Automatic Face and Gesture Recognition*, 2002, pp. 155–162.

Little, J.J. and Boyd, J.E., Recognizing people by their gait: the shape of motion, *Videre* 1(2), 2–32, 1998.

Liu, Y., Collins, R., and Tsin, Y., Gait sequence analysis using frieze patterns, in *Proceedings of the European Conference on Computer Vision*, 2002.

Liu, Z. and Sarkar, S., Simplest representation yet for gait recognition: averaged silhouette, in *Proceedings of the International Conference on Pattern Recognition*, Vol. 4, 2004, pp. 211–214.

Liu, Z., Malave, L., and Sarkar, S., Studies on silhouette quality and gait recognition, in *Proceedings of IEEE Conference on Computer Vision and Pattern Recognition*, Vol. 2, 2004, pp. II-704–II-711.

Mather, G. and Murdock, L., Gender discrimination in biological motion displays based on dynamic cues, *Proceedings of the Royal Society of London* B: 258, 273–279, 1994.

Meyer, D., Posl, J., and Niemann, H., Gait classification with HMM's for trajectories of body parts extracted by mixture densities, in *Proceedings of British Machine Vision Conference*, Vol. 2, 1998, pp. 459–468.

Mowbray, S.D. and Nixon, M.S., Extraction and recognition of periodically deforming objects by continuous, spatio-temporal shape description, in *Proceedings of IEEE Conference on Computer Vision and Pattern Recognition*, Vol. 2, 2004, pp. 895–901.

Murase, H. and Sakai, R., Moving object recognition in eigenspace representation: gait analysis and lip reading, *Pattern Recognition Letters* 17, 155–162, 1996.

Murray, M.P., Gait as a total pattern of movement, *American Journal of Physical Medicine* 46(1), 290–332, 1967.

Ning, H., Tan, T., Wang, L., and Hu, W., People tracking based on motion model and motion constraints with automatic initialization, *Pattern Recognition* 37(7), 1423–1440, 2004a.

Ning, H., Tan, T., Wang, L., and Hu, W., People tracking based on motion model and motion constraints with automatic initialization, *Image and Vision Computing* 22(5), 429–441, 2004b.

Nixon, M.S., Carter, J.N., Shutler, J.D., and Grant, M.G., Automatic recognition by gait: progress and prospects, *Sensor Review* 23(4), 323–331, 2003.

Niyogi, S.A. and Adelson, E.H., Analyzing and recognizing walking figures in XYT, in *Proceedings of IEEE Conference on Computer Vision and Pattern Recognition*, IEEE Computer Society, 1994a, pp. 469–474.

Niyogi, S.A. and Adelson, E.H., Analyzing gait with spatiotemporal surfaces, in *Proceedings of IEEE Workshop on Nonrigid Motion*, IEEE Computer Society, 1194b, pp. 64–69.

Phillips, P.J., Moon, H., Rizvi, S.A., and Rauss, P.J., The FERET evaluation methodology for face-recognition algorithms, *IEEE Transactions on Pattern Analysis and Machine Intelligence* 22(10), 1090–1104, 2000.

Phillips, P.J., Sarkar, S., Robledo, I., Grother, P., and Bowyer, K., Baseline results for the challenge problem of human ID using gait analysis, in *Proceedings of the Fifth IEEE International Conference on Automatic Face and Gesture Recognition*, 2002a, pp. 137–142.

Phillips, P.J., Sarkar, S., Robledo, I., Grother, P., and Bowyer, K., The gait identification challenge problem: data sets and baseline algorithm, in *Proceedings of the International Conference on Pattern Recognition*, 2002b, pp. 385–389.

Python, M., Ministry of silly walks, http://guardian.curtin.edu.au/cga/art/tv.html (accessed Jan. 25, 2006), n.d.

Rohr, K., Towards model-based recognition of human movement in image sequences, *CVGIP Image Understanding* 59(1), 94–115, 1994.

Sarkar, S., Phillips, P.J., Liu, Z., Vega, I.R., Grother, P., and Bowyer, K.W., The humanid gait challenge problem: data sets, performance, and analysis, *IEEE Transactions on Pattern Analysis and Machine Intelligence* 27(2), 162–177, 2005.

Shakhnarovich, G., Lee, L., and Darrell, T., Integrated face and gait recognition from multiple views, in *Proceedings of IEEE Conference on Computer Vision and Pattern Recognition*, Vol. 1, 2001, pp. I-439–I-446.

Shutler, J.D., Velocity Moments for Holistic Shape Description of Temporal Features, Ph.D. thesis, University of Southampton, U.K., 2002.

Shutler, J.D. and Nixon, M.S., Zernike velocity moments for the description and recognition of moving shapes, in *Proceedings of the British Machine Vision Conference*, Manchester, U.K., Vol. 2, 2001, pp. 705–714.

Shutler, J.D., Grant, M.G., Nixon, M.S., and Carter, J.N., On a large sequence-based human gait database, in *Proceedings of the 4th International Conference on Recent Advances in Soft Computing*, 2002, Nottingham, U.K., pp. 66–71.

Stevenage, S.V., Nixon, M.S., and Vince, K., Visual analysis of gait as a cue to identity, *Applied Cognitive Psychology* 13, 513–526, 1999.

Tulloch, S., Ed., *The Oxford Dictionary and Thesaurus*, Oxford University Press, Oxford, 1997.

Turk, M. and Pentland, A., Face recognition using eigenfaces, in *Proceedings of IEEE Conference on Computer Vision and Pattern Recognition*, Maui, HI, 586–591, 1991.

Veres, G., Gordon, L., Carter, J.N., and Nixon, M.S., What image information is important in silhouette-based gait recognition?, in *Proceedings of the International Conference on Pattern Recognition*, Vol. 2, 2004, pp. 776–782.

Veres, G.V., Nixon, M.S., and Carter, J.N., Modeling the time-variant covariates for gait recognition, in *Proceedings of Audio- and Video-based Biometric Person Authentication*, Rye Brook, NY, 597–606, 2005.

Wagg, D.K. and Nixon, M.S., Automated markerless extraction of walking people using deformable contour models, *Computer Animation and Virtual Worlds* 15(3–4), 399–406, 2004a.

Wagg, D.K. and Nixon, M.S., On automated model-based extraction and analysis of gait, in *Proceedings of the Sixth IEEE International Conference on Automatic Face and Gesture Recognition*, pp. 11–16, Seoul, Korea, 2004b.

Wang, J.J. and Singh, S., Video analysis of human dynamics — a survey, *Real-Time Imaging* 9(5), 321–346, 2003.

Wang, L., Hu, W., and Tan, T., A new attempt to gait-based human identification, in *Proceedings of the Sixteenth International Conference on Pattern Recognition*, Quebec, PQ, IEEE, pp. 115–119, 2002.

Wang, L., Ning, H., Tan, T., and Hu, W., Fusion of static and dynamic body biometrics for gait recognition, *IEEE Transactions on Circuits and Systems for Video Technology* 14(2), 149–158, 2004.

Wang, L., Tan, T., Ning, H., and Hu, W., Silhouette analysis-based gait recognition for human identification, *IEEE Transactions on Pattern Analysis and Machine Intelligence* 25(12), 1505–1515, 2003.

Yam, C.Y., Nixon, M.S., and Carter, J.N., Gait recognition by walking and running: a model-based approach, in *Proceedings of the Asian Conference on Computer Vision*, Melbourne, Australia, Vol. 1, pp. 1–6, 2002.

Yam, C.Y., Nixon, M.S., and Carter, J.N., Automated person recognition by walking and running via model-based approaches, *Pattern Recognition* 37(5), 1057–1072, 2004.

Color Figure 6.1

Color Figure 6.2

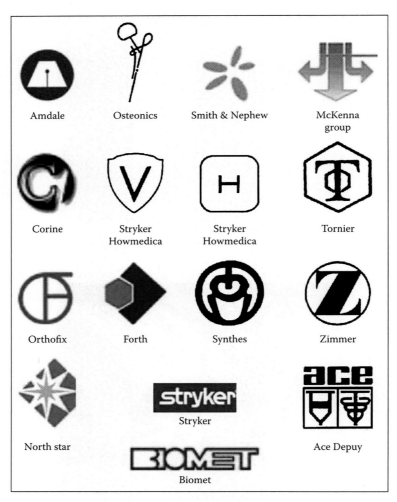

Color Figure 8.9

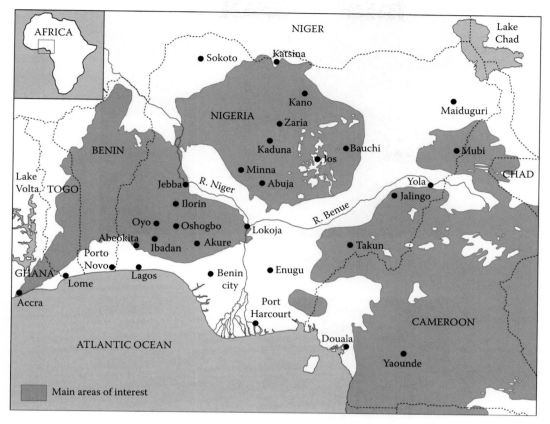

Color Figure 27.2

Color Figure 28.3

Color Figure 28.4

Color Figure 28.7

Color Figure 28.8

Section 8

Identification from Personal Effects

Personal Effects

20

TIM THOMPSON
ALAN PUXLEY

Contents

20.1 The Significance of Personal Effects..365
    20.1.1 Significance within Identification Contexts.................................365
    20.1.2 Significance to the Individual...367
    20.1.3 Significance to Others, Including Family Members and Next of Kin 368
20.2 Identification Using Personal Effects...369
    20.2.1 Personal Effects Management...369
        20.2.1.1 The Starting Point 369
        20.2.1.2 On-Site Collection 369
        20.2.1.3 The Processing Point 369
        20.2.1.4 The Care of the Bereaved...372
    20.2.2 The Direct Comparison of Personal Effects................................372
    20.2.3 The Comparison of Antemortem Records and Postmortem
        Personal Effects...373
    20.2.4 Personal Effects and DNA..373
20.3 Problems with Using Personal Effects for Identification.......................374
20.4 Conclusion 375
References 375

20.1 The Significance of Personal Effects

20.1.1 Significance within Identification Contexts

Personal effects can be defined as those items that belong to an individual, although they do not necessarily have to be found on the individual. A significant number of personal effects during our life will be "at rest" in storage such as wardrobes (Cwerner 2001). Personal effects can be items relevant to both the personal, social, and business life of the individual, and they can be found at the incident site, scattered over many kilometers in the vicinity of the incident, left in a work locker, desk, or recovered from a separate location, e.g., the site of disposal of the deceased in the case of illegal burials and cremations.

The identification of incident location could be on land or under water, and the personal effects will often have considerable damage due to water, fire, impact, corrosion, or contamination. An important significance of personal effects is that they often survive decompositional and taphonomic processes better than the traditional focus of identification — human bodies. Personal effects, principally composed of synthetic materials in particular, are resistant to degradation beyond forensic timescales (Janaway 2002, Rowe 1997) and as such are a potentially powerful identification tool. In addition, not all human remains will be suitable for the traditional means of biological human identification (Budowle et al. 2005), for example, due to postmortem degradation.

A significant problem associated with the use of comparative methods of identification (that is, those that require the comparison of ante- and postmortem records, such as with forensic odontology) is the requirement for current, accurate, and reliable antemortem information. Such records are often not available in key identification contexts such as those associated with the acts of genocide in the Balkans (Djuric 2004, Komar 2003) or the loss of medical infrastructure following Hurricane Katrina whereby many doctors, dentists, and other antemortem agencies had their records destroyed by the subsequent floods. Here, it was reported that when the police entered those homes affected by the floods, they found bodies lying in their own clothes with handwritten notes stating who they were and their realization that they would not be rescued in time. Therefore, although the medical information was lost, and in some cases other family members dispersed to unknown locations, the clothing, personal effects, and handwritten notes gave strong indicators to the identity of the deceased. Furthermore, because biological profiles of the deceased created in these key identification contexts are often very similar (adult males with the same ethnic affinity and cause of death) (Komar 2003), personal effects can be vital in distinguishing separate identities.

There is also concern regarding the ability of lay people to accurately describe medical and dental conditions and features to the practitioners collecting antemortem information. Indeed, Komar (2003) demonstrated this in her study of Srebrenica and expanded the potential problem to include the provision of antemortem information of a nonmedical nature such as stature. The use of personal effects for identification still requires the comparison of antemortem information to postmortem evidence; however, this may be more reliable as descriptions may be easier to provide and more readily available. DNA, though providing excellent opportunities for confirming identity, is not always appropriate or possible, and again personal effects can be of use in these situations, as is illustrated by Kringsholm et al. (2001).

The use of personal effects is also desirable when trying to gather information from the public to assist with criminal investigations. The personal effects may be displayed to act as a trigger as to the identity or movements of the deceased or possible origin or identity of the perpetrator of a criminal act. Unlike with images of decomposing bodies, it is entirely appropriate to display images of personal effects in advertisements and in the media.

It is important to bear in mind that personal effects are usually used in conjunction with other methods of identification. They can provide another degree of certainty to support the conclusions reached by soft- or hard-tissue identification. Table 20.1 highlights the position that personal effects hold in relation to other methods of confirming identity.

The examination of personal effects can also provide information surrounding the context of identification. Perhaps the most useful is to indicate whether a death was the result of an accident, suicide, or homicide. For example, the removal and careful placement of key effects at the scene of a drowning may indicate premeditation and suicidal intent, whereas finding the effects in the water is more suggestive of nonsuicidal drowning (Davis 1999). Furthermore, the position of cut marks through the clothing of a stabbing victim is a fundamental principle of determining homicide or suicide (Dettling et al. 2003). In other contexts, the condition of personal effects on a victim can indicate whether a death was homicide — for example, whether the articles are damaged or soiled (Komar and Beattie 1998). This can further inform investigators of the nature of the attack — for

Table 20.1 The Levels of Identification and the Location of Personal Effects within Them

Level	Techniques for Identification		
	Primary	Secondary	Tertiary
Definition	Sufficient on their own for confirmation	Not sufficient on their own but could be, in combination	Not sufficient on their own but may support primary and secondary
Methods of identification	DNA Fingerprints Odontology Unique medical features (visual, radiography)	Unique personal effects (e.g., jewelry) Visual inspection Blood group Nonunique medical features (visual, radiography)	Photographs Description Body location Personal effects (e.g., clothing)

Source: Adapted from Dorries, C., *Coroner's Courts: A Guide to Law and Practice*, John Wiley & Sons, U.K., 1999, p. 271.

example, exposure of the genitals and breasts being traditionally indicative of a sexual nature to the attack (Komar and Beattie 1998). Campobasso et al. (2003) state that the nature of the personal effects with the body can indicate the speed with which an incident occurred — whether there was time to state that the relation of the personal effects with the body can suggest the speed with which an incident occurred — for example, whether there was time to dress at night. Finally, Janaway (2002) notes that in war zone contexts personal effects can be crucial in distinguishing between military personnel and civilians. This, in turn, can be imperative in determining crimes against humanity and breaches of the Geneva Convention. In cases such as these, information gleaned from the nature of personal effects can be just as important to the investigation as the autopsy (Davis 1999). It is acknowledged, however, that attempts to disguise crimes against humanity by swapping clothing of the deceased have been seen in the field.

The distribution of personal effects at a crime scene may give additional information about the nature of the scene and the fate of the individual. Movement of the remains and secondary burials can all be suggested by the personal effects. Skinner and Sterenberg (2005) note this significance with regard to mass graves whereas Webster (1998) reports the use of the presence, location, and dispersal of personal effects to ascertain crash sites of American fighter jets in Vietnam. Recovery and subsequent identification of the crew was possible due to the use of personal effects. Campobasso et al. (2003) record how the dispersal of personal effects after the collapse of a residential apartment block was used to retrospectively place the victims at the time of the incident.

As well as providing a means of identification, it must not be forgotten that personal effects can be evidence, too, whether implicated directly in a crime — for example, household or other types of knives in stabbings — or as a conduit for trace evidence (for example, Lindsay et al. 1987, Rowe 1997).

20.1.2 Significance to the Individual

Personal effects are an aspect of a person's appearance and identity that varies to a great extent (Seitz 2003). The relationship of personal effects to their owner can be complicated, yet it is this that is fundamental to the process of identification. An item of personal effect can be a visual badge of social identity, an expression of political allegiance, and a symbol of communal value (Kelly 2003). They are the convergence of the social, the aesthetic, and the self (Johnson 2001). It is this significance that determines which personal effect individuals will associate with themselves. Indeed, the multiple aspects and fluid nature of our identity demand a pool of identity tokens, some of which will be stored until required, and personal effects constitute the focus of these tokens (Cwerner 2001).

The reaction of individuals to their effects is also of interest and, as discussed previously, can intimate the context of the identification scenario. For example, items, when left near a scene of water-oriented death, seem to be important enough not to have been associated with the very act of death itself, and their placement at a waterside can strongly suggest suicide over accidental death. Davis (1999) states that such items can include folded clothes, watches, hearing aids, glasses, and shoes.

20.1.3 Significance to Others, Including Family Members and Next of Kin

The monetary value of an item of personal effect is often immaterial; it is the emotional value that it holds for the family and loved ones of the deceased that is most significant. The item may be a reminder of special times and occasions spent together or, indeed, a gift from a child to a loved parent or relation. Therefore, it becomes essential to be nonjudgmental regarding what should or should not be detailed as a personal effect. To a family or loved one, a simple item such as a paper napkin imprinted with a restaurant's name may be the memory of the last meal they and the deceased had shared, a precious last moment of happiness together, and in value terms may to them have no equal. To the families and loved ones of the deceased, these items represent a final link between them and the deceased at the time of death. Their ultimate significance lies in the reality that the personal effects may well be their only positive proof that the deceased really died. For some cultures, the return of personal effects is more conclusive of the death of a loved one than photographic evidence (Koff 2004).

Acknowledging this value to the families and loved ones should be done by whatever agency has custody of the items of personal effects. It is important that agency personnel remember, at all stages, to keep the legal next of kin, if known, informed of the processes involved in the retention, care, and return of these precious items.

There is a need to be especially mindful of the significance of personal effects when those items are required to be retained, for sometimes considerable lengths of time, as evidence or exhibits in investigations. When all actions are completed, the chances are that loving relatives or friends eagerly await the return of their personal link with the deceased.

Personal effects will have a different meaning and significance to different peoples, depending on their cultures and associations with the identification incident. The grieving process may have universally agreed stages, but people will reach these stages at varying paces, and therefore the significance of the personal effects may also come to the fore at different times for different individuals involved in the same incident. Furthermore, the context surrounding the identification effort may well be too significant to ignore or forget (Holland et al. 1997), and thus personal effects associated with that event adopt a special significance. An example would be the personal effects recovered from crashed American planes that were then kept and subsequently displayed by local Vietnamese villagers during the war. Here, the context surrounding the identification incident (a plane crashing onto their land) was more significant to them than the actual identification procedure (Holland et al. 1997, Webster 1998).

20.2   Identification Using Personal Effects

20.2.1   Personal Effects Management

Regardless of the size of the identification problem, whether it be for an individual or hundreds of individuals who died as a result of a mass fatality incident, the management of the personal effects is, at its core, essentially the same.

A large part of the use of personal effects for identification involves the gathering, collating, checking, curation, and storage of effects (Budowle et al. 2005). As such, the processing of personal effects requires much planning. The management of personal effects in a high-stress context is a great deal more efficient if much of this planning has been preemptive.

From the outset, the collection of personal effects needs to be performed carefully. The following guidelines may be of assistance.

20.2.1.1   The Starting Point

- What does the law of the country involved in the process require to be done?
- What, culturally, can be deemed as personal effects? (Many Middle Eastern countries would not deem shoes or underwear as personal effects and would certainly not permit photographs of such items in any catalogs.)
- What is to be deemed as evidence or exhibits, particularly in cases where the death is being investigated as an unlawful act or subject to litigation?
- Create a protocol to cover those items that will receive special treatment, e.g., illegal goods and substances, pornography, dangerous goods, and sensitive items (e.g., condoms in certain countries).

20.2.1.2   On-Site Collection

- A detailed risk assessment of the recovery environment must be prepared for explosive hazards, likely contamination, local wildlife problems, the creation of chain of command and agreed protocols, and universal agreement on the type of protective clothing to be worn and used by all.
- Ensure exact gridding of the incident area or the ability to record, by a global positioning system, the location of items found.
- Ensure the ability to photograph each item found and subsequently issue with a unique reference number. The maintenance of an accurate log of those same numbers is essential.
- The ability to store and transport the personal effects without increasing the rate of deterioration is important (e.g., putting clothes into cardboard wardrobe boxes as opposed to plastic bags that would increase the growth of mildew and hasten the decomposition of the item).

20.2.1.3   The Processing Point

Often this will be the mortuary, but in the case of a mass fatality incident this may well need to be a large warehouse with sufficient floor space to both set up lines of drying racks and to store the processed items, possibly for years. In these situations, one should not

Figure 20.1 The cleaning and drying area for the personal effects, Kosovo 2000.

Figure 20.2 Personal effects drying after cleaning, Kosovo 2000. They will then be used for identification purposes.

underestimate the sheer volume of personal effects that will be recovered. If the personal effects are to be used for identification, they may need to be cleaned in order to allow examination. Figure 20.1 and Figure 20.2 show this process in Kosovo, following recovery from a mass grave.

It is also essential to have good air extraction facilities as the smell from personal effects contaminated by aviation fuel or human remains is particularly potent. This may also need to include lines of chest freezers to store contaminated items and reduce the odor coming from them. Such a processing facility, as well as being secure, will also need administration, photography, storage, inventory, and meeting rooms in addition to staff rooms, toilets, and shower facilities.

Preparation of confidentiality agreements are an important consideration, as in many large incidents, the handling of the personal effects may be outsourced or in the control of a nongovernmental agency. Therefore, it is important that all workers understand the sensitivity of entering the private lives of the deceased. Contractors, process team members,

Table 20.2   Transcription Problems When Using Personal Effects for Identification

Example Item	Correct Description	Explanation
Gold wedding ring	Ring, yellow metal	Yellow — The item may look gold but this cannot be determined visually
		Ring — Postmortem, it cannot be known whether the ring was associated with a marriage, regardless of the finger it is on
Reading glasses	Spectacles	Glasses — "Spectacles" remove ambiguity with regard to the type of glass
		Reading — Postmortem, this is supposition, and again the term *spectacles* refines the definition more appropriately

Table 20.3   Definitions of Personal Effects

Associated Items	Items Immediately Identifiable as Belonging to an Individual
Unassociated items	Personal effects that cannot, after examination, be associated to a named individual
Wreckage	Items which on closer examination prove to be from the incident site, e.g., wiring, metal fixtures, building material, etc.
Company property	Items which belong to a company involved in the incident, e.g., in an air crash this could be duty-free products, uniforms, etc.
Mail in transit	Mail being carried by the national postal authority
Foreign items	Items that were either already at the site prior to the incident or items that did not come from the individuals involved, e.g., medical kit from emergency services
Cargo/luggage	Items in transit and therefore not directly belonging to individuals involved in the incident

and service providers, i.e., launderers and jewelry repairers, should all be briefed in the requirements of their role and obliged to sign a confidentiality agreement before they commence work.

Although it is likely that personal effects can be described with greater ease than medical conditions, transcription of the details must avoid assumptions and subjective conclusions. Table 20.2 illustrates this further and also highlights the importance of standardization of the personal effects descriptions, especially when processing large quantities of items, where the need to use effective database entry techniques becomes paramount. For example, should an entry be "2 shoes" or "pair of shoes," or "pr of shoes," or, in another case, "10 × $5 dollar bills," "$5 bills × 10," "$50," or "10 5-dollar notes"?

Standardization can also be a problem when practitioners or interviewees originate from different countries. This is significant for two reasons. First, the fact that one item may have different names in different countries (such as "trousers" in the U.K. being "pants" in the U.S. and "pants" in the U.K. being underwear). Second, different cultures may be uncomfortable with discussing certain personal effects such as underwear or contraceptives. However, arbitrarily removing such items may cause unnecessary distress; for example, removing condoms may cause someone to think that a partner has been unfaithful.

Therefore, having agreed upon the protocols for processing, it is important that the legal next of kin are aware of these. This will assist when explaining, for example, that loose cash cannot be easily associated with any particular individual and therefore will not be included in any catalogs. It may also be worth stating the eventual disposal of such items, e.g., donation to charity.

The initial gathering of personal effects from identification contexts may also have to be scrutinized in order to be subdivided. This is detailed in Table 20.3.

20.2.1.4 The Care of the Bereaved

Many identification contexts will require continued contact with the families and loved ones of the deceased, and with many of the incidents that occur this will mean having an understanding of different cultures.

In the current global environment, it is not uncommon to have 20 different nationalities involved in a single air crash. Such incidents require an understanding of many issues. The following list is not exhaustive:

- In the deceased's country, who is defined as the legal next of kin?
- What are the appropriate words to write concerning the explanation of this process? Some cultures prefer long, flowing expressions of condolence whereas others require just the details of the personal-effects process that is to take place.
- The importance of treating all equally so that no group perceives others as having preferential treatment.
- The recognition that many cultures have various milestones in their grieving that may cause delays in responses. Agree on the flow of the process and agree on landmark points within that process that can be communicated to the next of kin.
- Issue invitations to next of kin to participate in the personal effects process, but stress it is an elective process and that they can participate in all, part, or none of it.
- If items that are unassociated (see Table 20.3) are being put into a catalog, do they wish to have the opportunity to view this catalog? If so, do they wish to see all or only limited sections?
- Agree on a final date for replies to be received and the process to start.
- If returning associated items (see Table 20.3), issue a list of these items and seek next of kin's instruction as to what condition they wish to have the items returned, e.g., clean, uncleaned, restored, or repaired.
- Distribution process: Bearing in mind the sensitivity of the items being returned and the nature of the incident, training may well have to be given to personnel delivering and handing over the personal effects.
- Create an arbitration process for disputed claims.

20.2.2 The Direct Comparison of Personal Effects

The comparison of personal effects for identification purposes is complicated because, unlike biometric analysis of bodily features, personal effects are "unstable" and change frequently during the life-course of an individual (Seitz 2003). Indeed, it has long been acknowledged that changes of personal effects constitute one of the most significant problems of eyewitness testimony (Seitz 2003). Seitz's study (2003) found this to be true for both adults and children. This is unfortunate, as it has also been shown that a significant number of eyewitness identifications are based solely upon clothing (Lindsay et al. 1987). A potential solution to this might be to ask eyewitnesses to identify suspects from both their clothing and from their physical features (Lindsay et al. 1987).

The standard use of personal effects for human identification is to ask next of kin or family and friends if they recognize the personal effects of a deceased individual. Unfortunately, this has been employed with only limited success in, for example, Rwanda and the former Yugoslavia (Komar 2003). However, the collection of antemortem personal effects information allowed Brannon and Morlang (2002) to identify 19% of their victims and Kringsholm et al. (2001) to identify 58% of their deceased.

Finally, an advantage of comparing one personal effect directly with a picture of the same personal effect, for example, via CCTV or photographic images, is that the comparison is made between actual features in the present before deterioration or any other change can happen. The comparison of dentition with antemortem dental records is the comparison of current teeth with a historical record of the dental arcade. Much could have happened and, significantly, been unrecorded between the recording of the antemortem record and the current dentition. This is not the case when comparing personal effects in the current time period.

20.2.3 The Comparison of Antemortem Records and Postmortem Personal Effects

Identification using personal effects is also possible when the comparison is made from personal effects collected postmortem and noneffects in antemortem records. This would include the comparison of spectacles collected from a deceased individual with the optician's records in an attempt to match the prescription. This may also be possible for contact lenses. Inscriptions observed on rings and other jewelry may need to be compared to the records maintained by the jeweler who did the engraving or to the original receipt for the work. This approach was used by the New York Police Department Crime Scene Unit for its work after the World Trade Center incident. The use of a macro lens and high magnification allowed for the recording of information and engravings not clearly visible with the naked eye (Bush 2005).

20.2.4 Personal Effects and DNA

Identification of an individual using DNA collected from personal effects can be an extremely significant technique. Collection of DNA samples from cadavers or biopsy material associated with stored medical records is often not possible (Tanaka et al. 2000). In addition, the comparison of DNA collected from human remains to siblings and family members may be inconclusive (Sasaki et al. 1997) or may not be possible — for example, if relatives are unknown or nonexistent (Tanaka et al. 2000). A further complication with the use of family members is the variety of genetic combinations possible at each locus of analysis (Sasaki et al. 1997). In these situations, identification through the use of DNA is only possible by comparison with DNA collected from personal effects of the individual. Examples of personal effects regularly laden with useful DNA include toothbrushes (Staiti et al. 2004, Tanaka et al. 2000), lipsticks, and lip balms (Webb et al. 2001), and unlaundered clothing (Budowle et al. 2005, Sasaki et al. 1997). Toothbrushes in particular are extremely useful as these items tend not to be shared, therefore reducing the complications associated with contamination (Tanaka et al. 2000). Determination of identity using DNA extracted from personal effects also has the advantage of not increasing stress on the next of kin and family members of the deceased (Budowle et al. 2005).

It is important to bear in mind that personal effects can also be used to identify individuals who do not own the articles in question. For example, the personal effects of an attacker may subsequently contain the soft or hard tissue, DNA, or personal effects (such as jewelry) of his victim.

20.3   Problems with Using Personal Effects for Identification

There are a number of fundamental problems with the use of personal effects as a means of individual identification. Primarily, these refer to the fact that personal effects are neither unique nor restricted to the body of one individual.

Personal effects, by their very nature, tend not to be unique. With the widespread availability and low cost of clothing and accessories, combined with the presence of the same chain stores in most cities and towns, individuals across the country have the option of purchasing and wearing the same items of clothes. This is compounded by the increase in consumer and retail globalization and the increase in the efficiency of Internet shopping to provide access to a greater number of people. This means that it is not possible to use certain personal effects as a means of identification verification — for example, on CCTV images. This is not to say that mass-produced clothing and the like cannot be modified by an individual to make it unique (such as through accessorization of an item, by mending damage, adding inscriptions, etc.), but this will only be useful if these modifications are known to others during the collection of antemortem information.

Personal effects also tend to be removable, and this creates additional problems for identification. This may mean that the personal effects of one individual may be on the person of another. This was a problem experienced by Kringsholm et al. (2001) when they attempted to identify bodies found in the waters around Denmark. This may occur for a number of reasons including one or a combination of legitimate borrowing (for example, of a coat), theft (for example, of a wallet), scene-specific factors (for example, the forces associated with a mass fatality incident can cause personal effects to become associated with others), and intentional attempts to hamper the identification process (for example, the forced swapping of clothes of victims in the Balkans).

As with many forms of identification that rely on antemortem and postmortem comparisons, the lack of a personal effect associated with the deceased does not mean that this individual did not own that item. This again reflects the removable and transferable nature of personal effects.

Accurate identification using personal effects can also suffer because the articles can be damaged peri- and postmortem. This makes comparison with antemortem information difficult. As with human remains, the willful or accidental postmortem damage of personal effects can have a significant effect on attempts at human identification (Holland et al. 1997).

If associated with buried human remains (as they are in many forensic investigations), fabric personal effects will undergo a deleterious degradation process (Janaway 2002). Soil, in particular, has been acknowledged as being a particularly aggressive environment for personal effects (Janaway 2002). It must be remembered, however, that personal effects of a metallic origin will also degrade, and thus their use will be limited as an identificative tool. The complexity surrounding the decomposition of personal effects is brought about by many factors, including material composition, dyes, surface finishes, wear patterns, laundering, and treatments, as well as the actual depositional milieu (Janaway 2002). This is further complicated by the generally unknown relationship between the chemistry of body decomposition and degradation of associated personal effects (Janaway 2002, Rowe 1997). Natural fibers will suffer biodegradation over a short period of time unless the deposition environmental conditions inhibit microbial action, as would dessicated, frozen, or high metal-ion conditions (Janaway 2002, Rowe 1997). However, studies show that personal effects composed of proteinic natural fibers will survive better than those of a cellulose composition (Janaway 2002). Furthermore, the presence of certain personal effects can increase the preservation of other types of effects — for example, through the mineralization of fibers by metal corrosion deposition (Janaway 2002). Other significant taphonomic events that can negate the use of recovered personal effects as a tool for identification include animal scavenging and insect activity (Komar and Beattie 1998).

The collection of antemortem personal effects information can also cause problems for subsequent identification. Kringsholm et al. (2001) demonstrate the restriction placed on successful identification as a direct result of this problem. As has been discussed, it is likely that personal effects can be described with greater ease than medical conditions; transcription of the details must avoid assumptions and subjective conclusions. Table 20.2 illustrates this further.

The collection of DNA from personal effects is also problematic. Whereas certain items may have restricted exposure to DNA from the population (such as toothbrushes) (Tanaka et al., 2000), other effects (such as clothing) will suffer cross-contamination from individuals as diverse as family members to random strangers. Additional contextual information regarding the personal effects used for direct DNA comparison will increase one's confidence in their use as a reference sample (Budowle et al. 2005). If concerns are still present with these reference samples, then additional kinship analysis might be necessary to increase overall confidence in the final identification (Budowle et al. 2005). This will clearly add to the financial, emotional, and psychological expense of the identification.

20.4 Conclusion

It is important to appreciate, when using personal effects to confirm identity, that different effects will hold different weights of importance. For example, a passport with a photograph and fingerprint is more useful to identification scientists than a coat. Ultimately however, it is desirable to use as many techniques and personal effects as possible when attempting to establish identity, thereby increasing the validity of that identification (Brannon and Morlang 2002, Budowle et al. 2005). However, in the field there are frequently taphonomic, political, and logistical restrictions placed upon the practitioner that negate this ideal (Brannon and Morlang 2002, Djuric 2004, Holland et al. 1997, Komar 2003). In these situations the use of personal effects can provide a relatively straightforward starting point or, as is more common, further support to another identification technique.

However, once personal effects are used in an identification context, this will inevitably lead to an end point that, so often, will be a time of closure for families and loved ones of the deceased or the victims of crimes.

If we are using personal effects to investigate terrorist events, tragic events, or crimes against humanity, we must take care ourselves, for we will be entering into the very private lives of others.

References

Brannon, R.B. and Morlang, W.M., The crash of LOT Flight 007: dental identification, *Journal of Forensic Sciences* 47(6), 1–3, 2002.

Budowle, B., Bieber, F.R., and Eisenberg, A.J., Forensic aspects of mass disasters: strategic considerations for DNA-based human identification, *Legal Medicine* 7(4), 230–243, 2005.

Bush, D., NYPD Crime Unit Case Study, 2005, downloaded from http://www.polaroid.com/global/printer_friendly.jsp;jsessionid=DwrDsU2UJHUmSVgjFBcF1De6aQ16WdUyTJ1JMESm5vTEtnKiqcgk!-763122065!-1979950386!7005!8005!-20220595!-1979950377!7005!8005?PRODUCT%3C%3Eprd_id=845524441760368&FOLDER%3C%3Efolder_id=282574488338439&bmUID=1131457411240&bmLocale=en_US.

Campobasso, C.P., Falamingo, R., and Vinci, F., Investigation of Italy's deadliest building collapse: forensic aspects of a mass disaster, *Journal of Forensic Sciences* 48(3), 1–5, 2003.

Cwerner, S.B., Clothes at rest: Elements for a sociology of the wardrobe, *Fashion Theory* 5(1), 79–92, 2001.

Davis, L.G., Suicidal drowning in South Florida, *Journal of Forensic Sciences* 44(5), 902–905, 1999.

Dettling, A., Althaus, L., and Haffner, H-Th., Criteria for homicide and suicide on victims of extended suicide due to sharp force injury, *Forensic Science International* 134, 142–146, 2003.

Djuric, M.P., Anthropological data in individualization of skeletal remains from a forensic context in Kosovo — a case history, *Journal of Forensic Sciences* 49(3), 1–5, 2004.

Dorries, C., *Coroner's Courts: A Guide to Law and Practice*, John Wiley & Sons: U.K., 1999.

Holland, T.D., Anderson, B.E., and Mann, R.W., Human variables in the postmortem alteration of human bone: examples from U.S. war casualties, in *Forensic Taphonomy: The Postmortem Fate of Human Remains*, Haglund, W. and Sorg, M., Eds., CRC Press, Boca Raton, FL, 1997, pp. 263–274.

Janaway, R.C., Degradation of clothing and other dress materials associated with buried bodies of archaeological and forensic interest, in *Advances in Forensic Taphonomy: Method, Theory, and Archaeological Perspectives*, Haglund, W. and Sorg, M., Eds., CRC Press, Boca Raton, FL, 2002, pp. 379–402.

Johnson, R., The anthropological study of body decoration as art: collective representations and the somatization of affect, *Fashion Theory* 5(4), 417–434, 2001.

Kelly, M., Projecting an image and expressing identity: T-shirts in Hawaii, *Fashion Theory* 7(2), 191–212, 2003.

Koff, C., *The Bone Woman: A Forensic Anthropologist's Search for Truth in the Mass Graves of Rwanda, Bosnia, Croatia, and Kosovo*, Random House, New York, 2004.

Komar, D., Lessons from Srebrenica: the contributions and limitations of physical anthropology in identifying victims of war crimes, *Journal of Forensic Sciences* 48(4), 1–4, 2003.

Komar, D. and Beattie, O., Postmortem insect activity may mimic perimortem sexual assault clothing patterns, *Journal of Forensic Sciences* 43(4), 792–796, 1998.

Kringsholm, B., Jakobsen, J., Sejrsen, B., and Gregersen, M., Unidentified bodies/skulls found in Danish waters in the period 1992–1996, *Forensic Science International* 123, 150–158, 2001.

Lindsay, R.C.L., Wallbridge, H., and Drennan, D., Do the clothes make the man?: an exploration of the effects of lineup attire on eyewitness identification accuracy, *Canadian Journal of Behavioural Science* 19(4), 463–478, 1987.

Rowe, W.F., Biodegradation of hairs and fibers, in *Forensic Taphonomy: The Postmortem Fate of Human Remains*, Haglund, W. and Sorg, M., Eds., CRC Press, Boca Raton, FL, 1997, pp. 337–351.

Sasaki, M., Shiono, H., Fukushima, T., and Shimizu, K., Human identification by genotyping of personal articles, *Forensic Science International* 90, 65–75. 1997.

Seitz, K., The effects of changes in posture and clothing on the development of unfamiliar person recognition, *Applied Cognitive Psychology* 17, 819–832, 2003.

Skinner, M. and Sterenberg, J., Turf wars: authority and responsibility for the investigation of mass graves, *Forensic Science International* 151(2–3), 221–232, 2005.

Staiti, N., Spitaleri, S., Vecchio, C., and Saravo, L., Identification of a carbonized body by DNA profiling, *International Congress Series* 1261, 494–496, 2004.

Tanaka, M., Yoshimoto, T., Nozawa, H., Ohtaki, H., Kato, Y., Sato, K., Yamamoto, T., Tamaki, K., and Katsumata, Y., Usefulness of a toothbrush as a source of evidential DNA for typing, *Journal of Forensic Sciences* 45(3), 674–676, 2000.

Webb, L.G., Egan, S.E., and Turbett, G.R., Recovery of DNA for forensic analysis from lip cosmetics, *Journal of Forensic Sciences* 46(6), 1474–1479, 2001.

Webster, A.D., Excavation of a Vietnam-era aircraft crash site: use of cross-cultural understanding and dual forensic recovery methods, *Journal of Forensic Sciences* 43(2), 277–283, 1998.

Body Modification 21

SUE BLACK
TIM THOMPSON

Contents

21.1 Introduction to Body Modification...379
21.2 Dermal Modification 382
    21.2.1 Permanent Tattoos...382
        21.2.1.1 Introduction 382
        21.2.1.2 Procedure...385
        21.2.1.3 Removal 386
    21.2.2 Temporary Tattoos...387
21.3 Scarification...388
    21.3.1 Branding...389
    21.3.2 Cutting..389
    21.3.3 Body Etching..390
    21.3.4 Other Forms of Scarification 390
21.4 Subdermal Implants 391
    21.4.1 Beading...391
    21.4.2 3D Body Art 391
21.5 Transdermal Modification...392
    21.5.1 Introduction 392
    21.5.2 Procedure..394
    21.5.3 Anatomical Locations..395
21.6 Conclusions..397
21.7 Acknowledgments...398
References 398

21.1 Introduction to Body Modification

The definition of "body modification" is very wide and covers a variety of practices —
temporally, geographically, and anatomically. It is necessary to define body modification
with regard to the aims of this chapter and in relation to human biological identification
in general. We regard it here as the intentional alteration of the human phenotype.
However, there are a number of caveats surrounding this definition with regard to this
chapter. First, the definition between surgical intervention and body modification initially
seems to be clear. However, as the more extreme forms of alteration are considered, the
line becomes less distinct. Extreme modifications (tongue splitting, penile glans splitting,
penilectomy, etc.) may involve anaesthetics and may utilize the services of a trained
surgeon. Therefore, this chapter does not attempt to address the issues of extreme body
modification but is restricted to those practices that are performed by nonmedically

trained artists or practitioners who frequently do not retain detailed patient records. We are, therefore, focusing on the more common forms of body modification undertaken in a nonmedical environment. Thus, we also exclude plastic and cosmetic surgery and orthodontic treatment from our definition and subsequent discussion (however, see Chapter 8 for further discussion of this). Second, while we acknowledge that body modification has been an important sociological factor for thousands of years, for identification purposes we restrict our definition to what is current in Western society today, acknowledging that concepts alter with the passage of time, the popularity of different procedures, and the introduction of new trends.

Body modifications are potentially an important aspect of human identification because of their increasing prevalence and their impact on other methods of human identification (such as visual, pathological, or trauma-based identification); they may have value as jewelry and associated artifacts within the identification context and can be potentially unique identifiers. Their use as identifiers requires a method that is as applicable to the identification of the living as it is to the dead.

The reasons that individuals decide to obtain body modifications are many and sometimes difficult to ascertain. This is partly due to the interconnectivity of these reasons. The most fundamental cause, however, will either be positive self-expression or negative self-mutilation (Braithwaite et al. 2001, Brooks et al. 2003, Quint and Breech 2005). Beyond this, surveys have shown that reasons include making a fashion statement (Brooks et al. 2003), sensation seeking, exposure to psychosocial stressors and subsequent coping strategies, increasing attractiveness and sexual appeal, commemorating a significant event, increasing self-esteem (Johnson 2001, Moser et al. 1993, Myers 1992, Quint and Breech 2005, Roberti et al. 2004, Seiter and Hatch 2005), increasing sexual arousal (Millner et al. 2005, Myers 1992) and seeking individualization or, conversely, to declare allegiance to a specific group (Braithwaite et al. 2001, Brooks et al. 2003).

Of particular relevance to the issue of identification is the fact that body modifications are almost exclusively self-directed. That is, the individual chooses which modifications to undergo, where they will occur topographically, and when they will be undertaken. Furthermore, body adornment or modification of this sort is rarely just utilitarian (Johnson 2001). Modification of the body, therefore, is the intentional incorporation of the cultural world into the biological (Johnson 2001, Myers 1992). As such, body modification is often a strong reflection of an individual's perception of his or her own identity or the identity he or she wishes to portray. In addition, there is an important aspect concerning taking control of one's own body (Johnson 2001). Indeed, it has even been argued that the impulse to "retouch" the body is what distinguishes humans from other animals (Myers 1992). Practitioners of Western body modification are a select demographic of the population, although many studies (Gold et al. 2005, Nicoletti 2004, Roberti et al. 2004) show that this demographic is expanding both horizontally and vertically (i.e., in the volume and disparate variety of participants). Although body modification practices can vary (and are discussed further below), there appear to be three main motives for modification. The first is decoration, whether the aim is for an attractive, aggressive, or alternative appearance. This will often involve regions of the body that are visibly exposed and will vary depending on the nature of the modification. For example, tattoos may be located on the arms or lower back, whereas piercings may be found in the ears, face, or navel. The second motive is sensation, where traditional foci are the genitals and nipples. The third main motive is for spiritual or religious reasons, although these may indirectly incorporate aspects of the first two motives. It is also important to note that whereas body modification is a self-directed act on the external body, it affects the perception of the internal characteristics of the modified (Seiter and Hatch 2005).

It has also been argued that there is an element of addictive progression with the acquisition of body modifications, perhaps through the influence of endorphin release attributed to the stimulation associated with modification (Roberti et al. 2004). It is also argued that, following modification, there is a process of reconceptualization that decrees that further and progressive body modification is now entirely acceptable (Vail 1999). It has been argued that there is often a relationship between body modification and other perceived nonmainstream behavior, such as drug and excessive alcohol consumption (Brooks et al. 2003, Braithwaite et al. 2001), violence, and unprotected sexual activity (Roberti et al. 2004). Perhaps this comes as no surprise and is indeed to be expected as those who overcome the stigma of one form of unconventional behavior may be the ones who are more likely to sample other forms of unorthodox behavior (Moser et al. 1993); however, this must be borne in context, and inferences must reflect realistic evidence-based information. It is very easy to jump to incorrect conclusions about categorization of an individual, as our Western community willfully attaches labels and stigmas to those that they may not understand or who do not conform to their perception of mainstream society. The study of body modification, therefore, is intensely complicated due to this interaction between the self and the social (Johnson 2001).

The health and safety implications of body modification are extremely significant, and because they are held to be of the utmost importance by professional artists, they are unfortunately, and perhaps imprudently, overlooked by many less reputable practitioners (Strang et al. 2000) and recipients. These issues generally concern either the quality of the equipment or the jewelry and the skill of the practitioner, all of which will have a bearing on any ensuing physical injuries (López Jornet et al. 2004). Reported complications for body modifications include pain, hemorrhaging, and hematoma formation, cyst formation, allergic reactions, and scarring (Braithwaite et al. 2001, Gold et al. 2005, Koenig and Carnes 1999, Moser et al. 1993, Whittle and Lamden 2004). Associated infections can range from mild local-site occurrences to osteomyelitis and toxic shock syndrome (Fisher et al. 2005, Gold et al. 2005). Indeed, a modification-induced *Mycobacterium fortuitum* infection can resemble a carcinoma (Lewis et al. 2004). Complications associated with oral modifications include fractures of the teeth, gum recession, speech impediment, and airway obstruction (Brooks et al. 2003, Gold et al. 2005, Kieser et al. 2005, Whittle and Lamden 2004). The transmission of viral hepatitis and human immunodeficiency virus infection are also real possibilities (Braithwaite et al. 2001, Brooks et al. 2003, Gold et al. 2005). An important consideration is that these risks are increased greatly if the body modification is performed by oneself or a nonprofessional (Brooks et al. 2003). For teenagers, Brooks et al. (2003) found this to be true for 22% of piercings and 18% of tattoos. Many of the consequential pathologies mentioned above may in themselves be useful for identification purposes (see Chapter 6 for greater discussion on the use of pathology for identification). The rise in popularity and associated acceptability of body modification consequently demands an improvement in health and safety awareness within the health care provision community (Brooks et al. 2003, Gold et al. 2005). Finally, it is worth noting that even pseudo-modifications can be problematic. Karkos et al. (2003) record that the use of magnetic piercings in the nose in place of the transdermal variety can still lead to severe pain, bleeding, and septal perforation. As a point of interest, body modifications have also been used for medicinal purposes, such as clitoral hood piercings to relieve anorgasmia (Millner et al. 2005).

There are also legal considerations surrounding body modification. On the whole, there is a lack of legislation governing the act of body modification, although some restrictions are in place through other acts — for example, female clitoral piercing is technically illegal under the Prohibition of Female Circumcision Act, 1985 (Swift 2004). The lack of a standard for obtaining informed consent is perhaps the greatest cause of uneasiness (Koenig and Carnes 1999). In addition, concerns have been raised over the lack of legislation regarding standard hygiene practices in establishments in many states of America (Braithwaite et al. 2001, Fisher et al. 2005). A U.K. parliamentary debate in 2003, following the death of a teenager as a consequence of a lip piercing, revealed that only in London do the local authorities have the power to license body piercing (under the London Local Authorities Act, 1991), whereas local authorities elsewhere in the country do not (Whittle and Lamden 2004). However, it should be noted that many piercing facilities are associated with tattooists, who are regulated by local government (Whittle and Lamden 2004). Tattooing facilities are currently regulated under the Tattooing of Minors Act (1969) and the Health and Safety at Work Act (1974) (Walters 2001). The main inadequacies of this legislation, however, center on the lack of an agreed standard for good practice and on the lack of coverage of those modifying at home (Walters 2001). Many practitioners are acutely aware of this situation and have adopted a policy of self-regulation through various associations (Koenig and Carnes 1999). Unfortunately, the practitioners likely to self-regulate are also those most likely to be responsible in their work. It is the irresponsible workers who are of greatest concern. As a consequence, a recent Scottish Executive Consultation suggested a revision of the law to demand licensing of facilities, accreditation of practitioners, and stricter controls on the modification of minors (Walters 2001).

With regard to the identification of the deceased, body modifications are, to a greater or lesser extent, only as useful as the degree of preservation of the skin. The skin is the primary contact barrier between the external environment and the rest of the corpse, offering a large surface area for taphonomic alterations that manifest as decomposition. Therefore, for the examination of body modifications to be of greatest value as an identification tool, they are most effective in the analysis of the recently deceased or well-preserved corpse. However, when a foreign body is involved in the modification, e.g., piercings or subdermal implants, these may in themselves provide some opportunity for confirmation of identity. In a similar way to personal effects (see Chapter 20), body modifications can also be used to identify living individuals via CCTV images or witness statements. One of the main complications with using body modification as a means of identification of the living is the temporary nature of many of the modifications, in that they can be removed, and evidence for them can heal. Therefore, they may be of value as confirmation of identity rather than as a primary determinant in their own right, unless they are specifically personal and unique in nature (see Chapter 14 for a greater discussion of these issues in identification from imagery).

21.2 Dermal Modification

21.2.1 Permanent Tattoos

21.2.1.1 Introduction

Tattooing is one of the most ancient forms of body modification with origins that trace back through modern times to the ancient Egyptians and beyond to Neolithic humans

(Caplan 2000, Green 2003). There seems to be little debate that the word is derived from the Polynesian "tatau" although its exact definition remains in some doubt. Varying opinions state that it means "appropriate" or "balanced," others that it means an "open wound," "mark" or "strike," and others still that it means "repetitive tapping." The finding of 15 groups of simple geometric tattoos on the back, knee, calf, foot, and ankle of the Copper Age iceman from the Alps caused a tremendous furor. Much speculation arose as to their origins, ranging from ritualistic tribal markings to the stimulation of body energy lines that would alleviate arthritic suffering. There can be a tendency to overanalyze tattoos, and we need to appreciate that our interpretation may be more speculative than etiological.

Much has been made of tattooing in human history, usually as a branding to identify specific cultures (for example, sailors, war veterans, and bikers) and the socially disenfranchised such as psychiatric patients, prostitutes, and criminals. In more recent years there has been an attempt to reclaim the tattoo by the so-called "urban primitive" as a mark of some inner expression or group belonging. This has led to many purists claiming that the value and power of the tattoo is being violated by insecure and thrill-seeking consumer hordes who demote the practice to little more than "a permanent reminder of a temporary emotion." This opinion has been greatly bolstered by the perceived "frivolous" use of tattooing in permanent make-up, which involves introducing pigmentation to the face, usually on the eyebrows, eyelids, and lips.

There is no doubt that the popularity of tattooing in our modern culture is on the increase. A recent paper surveying the undergraduate students in an American university found that 22% of males and 26% of females sported at least one tattoo (Mayers et al. 2002). Another survey showed that 23% of the German population aged between 15 and 29 has at least one tattoo (Adatto 2004). Tattooing has been reported as the sixth fastest growing retail business in the U.S. (Seiter and Hatch 2005). This increase in popularity raises the importance of body art in the process of identification as it provides a potentially readily recognizable, verifiable, and describable (potentially assisted by photography) set of variables for comparison. However, it should be borne in mind that for comparative purposes it is essential that information is derived from someone with an intimate recent knowledge of the individual, as parents and family members are often unaware of the more personal nature of body adornment. In addition, tattoos are not always readily visible, and some ingenuity and perseverance may be required to locate them, e.g., genital labia, scrotum, anus, perineum, eyelids, fingertips, scalp, and inside the mouth. Equally, although tattoos are generally perceived as being permanent, there are effective methods to facilitate their removal or alteration and so their "absence" in a suspected identification must be considered carefully. Finally, it is worth noting that although tattooing seems to be on the increase, this will not be the case in all demographics. For example, traditional Jewish law forbids the acquisition of tattoos (Lapidoth and Aharonowitz 2004), and this in itself might be a useable form of negative evidence.

The application of a tattoo can also be used as a means of concealment. This may be to mask perceived unsightly skin anomalies such as moles, birthmarks, or skin conditions, or indeed to disguise scars or cover up preexisting tattoos. The identification practitioner needs to consider all of these factors.

Tattoos are mainly located on externally visible skin, which is, after all, the largest organ of the human body with a surface area of between 1.5 and 2 square meters. This offers a rather conveniently large area on which one can be creative and personal with intimate artwork. While body decomposition seems an obvious limiting factor to tattoo

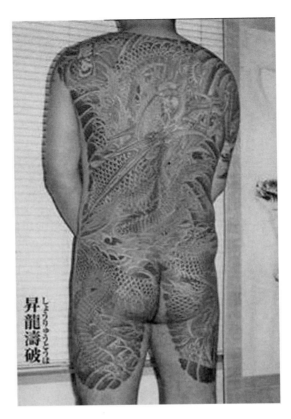

Figure 21.1 Japanese body suit.

identification, it is not so in the early stages when skin slippage (sloughing of the epidermal layer) can actually result in a clearer image of the tattoo. However, once the tissues become green/brown in advanced decomposition, then the modification is progressively obscured (Saukko and Knight 2004).

There seem to be no limits to the size or complexity of the tattoo, ranging from a dainty outline of a butterfly on the shoulder to a full Japanese body suit (Figure 21.1), and from the monochrome anchor on Popeye's forearm to the polychromatic body work of the "Lizard Man" or the "Leopard Man" of Skye (see individualistvoice.com/leopardman.html). The limits seem to exist only in the imaginations of the artist and the willingness of the client, although recent fluorescent dyes, favored by the club scene, have raised health and safety issues that may ultimately secure statutory limitations. It should be appreciated that in the U.K., as in many other countries, tattooists, their facilities, and the pigments they use are generally not regulated by any standards agency and are left only to the discretion of local authorities. Equally, this means that record keeping is generally nonexistent.

It is usually very obvious when a tattoo has been applied by an experienced professional rather than more crudely crafted at home. Home tattoos are more likely to be monochromatic, and retention of definition tends to be poor due to the nature and inconsistency of the impregnation of the pigment. Older military tattoos or those performed in correctional establishments tend to fall into the latter category. For example, the most frequently identified British prison tattoo is the letters "ACAB" across the four fingers of the hand. These letters may sometimes be substituted by single dots on each finger but are taken to

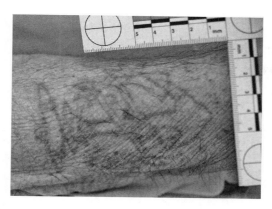

Figure 21.2   Faded skin tattoo.

mean "All coppers are bastards" or "Always carry a Bible," depending upon who asks the question. However, the presence of a group-specific tattoo does not necessarily confirm a legitimate involvement or alliance with a particular group but, on occasion, it can prove useful. Therefore, it is important to understand the "potential" significance of particular symbols, bearing in mind that the actual significance may vary geographically and that there may of course be no significance involved, other than personal choice.

21.2.1.2   Procedure

The tattoo is formed by the injection, deposition, and retention of insoluble pigmented macromolecules into the upper dermal layer of the skin. A tattoo can be made by penetration of the skin using any sharp object but is usually performed by an electric tattoo machine that pierces the skin at a rate of between 50 and 3000 strikes per minute, rather like a sewing machine, and penetrates to a depth of between 0.1–1.6 mm. The outline of the tattoo is generally traced by a single needle, and then the image is filled in using a bar containing multiple needles.

The dermal deposition of the pigment ensures that, as the epidermis is sloughed away, the tattoo remains more or less permanent, although it does fade with time (Figure 21.2). Most tattoo inks are not in fact ink, but rather suspensions of mineral salts, plastics, or occasionally vegetable dyes in a carrier solution, or even just simple charcoal impregnation (Lapidoth and Aharonowitz 2004). The pigments in a tattoo range from 2–400 nm in diameter with the most common particle size being approximately 40 nm. Very shortly after the tattoo has occurred, "ink" can be detected within large phagosomes in the cytoplasm of keratinocytes and phagocytic cells. Around 1 month after the application of the tattoo, the ink accumulates within the basal cells of the basement membrane. By 2–3 months, ink is only found in dermal fibroblasts where the remaining pigment molecules remain as they are too large to pass into the lymphatic system (Fujita et al. 1988). There is some debate as to whether free tissue deposits may also exist. A prominent network of connective tissue surrounds each of the fibroblasts, effectively trapping and immobilizing that cell — often for the lifetime of the individual. Random biopsies of older tattoos show a translocation of ink to deeper layers of the dermis partially explaining the loss of definition and color in the older tattoo. Eventually, tattoo pigments will be detected in the regional lymph nodes (Figure 21.3), making them a particularly useful indicator of the presence of tattoos in a dismembered body.

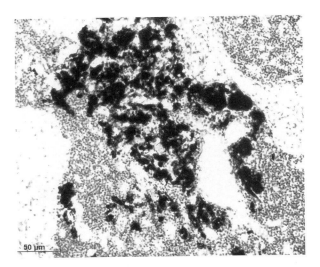

Figure 21.3 Ink trapped in an apical lymph node.

21.2.1.3   *Removal*

The expansion of tattoos from communicating status or messages into the realm of the purely decorative has become gradually more socially acceptable in contemporary society. With an estimated 20 million tattooed Americans, and a widening diversity of clients, it is only natural that removal becomes a pertinent issue. The main disadvantage with amateur and earlier methods of tattoo removal is the high risk of scarring. A number of the methods of tattoo removal will leave behind some form of evidence of the original tattoo. This itself can be useful for identification purposes.

Salabrasion is the oldest method and simply involves physical tissue destruction by abrading the superficial dermis with coarse grains of salt. Dermabrasion was the earlier method of mechanical removal whereby a rapidly spinning diamond fraise wheel or wire brush abraded the skin. The skin was usually frozen by a proprietary chemical to ensure a hard surface for abrasion. The procedure was bloody, painful, and often led to infection and extensive scarring. Surgical excision was also relatively common although again this involved scarring and all the inherent clinical problems associated with large wounds. The chemical (tannic acid, silver nitrate, etc.) or thermal (hot coals, cigarettes, etc.) approaches are crude, unpredictable, and unreliable and always result in unsightly scarring.

Quality switched (Q-switched) lasers were identified in the 1960s as being of possible value in the removal of tattoos, but it was not until the 1980s that Anderson and Parrish (1983) proposed a theory of selective light absorbtion in the skin (Reid et al. 1983). The tattoo pigment must be able to absorb light pulses or there can be no chemical interaction initiated. The absorption of the short laser pulses causes a conversion of the light into heat, which fragments the cell containing the pigment and also breaks the chemical bonds within the pigment, leading to fragmentation. Several treatments may be required, and although the pigments may appear to be removed they can be translocated to deeper layers in the dermis and still be present but just not visible to the naked eye. However, it should be borne in mind that the macromolecules will always be retained in the appropriate lymph node pathways. Unfortunately, this technique does suffer difficulties when removing tattoos from darker skin (Lapidoth and Aharonowitz 2004).

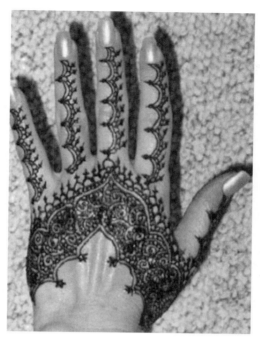

Figure 21.4 Henna art.

Some tattoo artists will cover an existing tattoo with a new image (retattooing), and removal of this is much more complicated as there are multiple layers of pigments to be removed. The absorption of laser energy is so intense that it can produce extensive heat-related dermal damage. In particular, yellow pigments can be particularly difficult to remove so that a "shadow" of the tattoo may still be evident on the skin even after several attempts at laser removal (Adatto 2004).

21.2.2 Temporary Tattoos

Not all body art is permanent. The ancient practice of *mendhi* (henna art), which dates back to ancient Egypt, is widespread throughout South Asia, the Middle East, and North Africa. The dried leaves of the henna plant (*Lawsonia inermis*) are crushed into a powder, formed into a paste (often with hot tea), and applied to the body in elaborate patterns and designs, traditionally on hands and feet (Figure 21.4). This is most frequently carried out on women for ceremonial purposes, e.g., a wedding or the birth of a child. After several hours the paste is scraped off, leaving a brown/reddish trace behind that can last for 2–4 weeks. Some henna products can leave a stain that will last longer, suggesting an active uptake into the deeper layers of the skin. Henna naturally occurs in red, brown, or orange. The black variety has been shown to contain harmful chemicals and has been classified as a mutagen as it contains PPD (para-phenylenediamine), which is known to be the main cause of contact dermatitis and other allergic cross-reactions due to such tattooing (Martin et al. 2005, Van den Keybus et al. 2005).

Other mass-produced, decal-type forms of temporary body art were favored in the past by teenagers and children but are now gaining more widespread acceptance as they have become more sophisticated. These involve the application of a transfer that exists between a plastic cover and a paper backing. When water is applied to the plastic cover, the image is transferred onto the skin and adheres, using safe-backing glue. These images are essentially waterproof and will last only 2–7 days, leaving no permanent mark. It should be appreciated that these temporary tattoos can be quite convincing, and transfers of very realistic bruises are on the market. Impregnation of decal transfers by illegal substances, including narcotic drugs, effectively use the process as a pharmaceutical "patch" to facilitate slow absorption from the skin into the blood system.

The practice of air-brush body art is also on the increase, adapting the traditional home improvement technique of stenciling. This involves placing a stencil over the skin and spraying with special air brush inks to transfer a temporary image onto the skin. These stencils tend to last for only a week or so and will eventually wash away to leave no permanent image. The use of nonpermanent pigments allows a greater range of spectral colors and increased vibrancies to be used.

21.3 Scarification

Scarification involves making marks on the skin that will result in raised scarring or keloids (fibrous scars). Although tattooing is the favored body art for lighter skins, scarification is favored for darker skins where the relief caused by scarring leads to striking images (Figure 21.5). There are several types of scarification, depending upon the method of production.

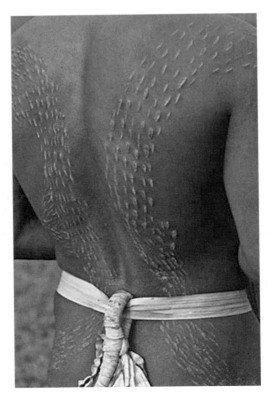

Figure 21.5   Keloid scarring.

Figure 21.6 Heat branding with subsequent tattooing.

21.3.1 Branding

A pattern is produced on the skin by the application of either a hot or cold metal, or ceramic implement placed on the skin for long enough to burn through to deeper layers and leave a permanent scar. Removal of heat-branded scars can only be done through surgical means and frequently requires a skin graft. When the scar has healed sufficiently, it is possible to tattoo over the scar to introduce color and attempt to disguise the scar, but often the uptake of pigment is not very satisfactory.

Hot branding is not a new phenomenon and has been used for many centuries as a method of identifying the socially unacceptable (e.g., a *fleur-de-lis* on the shoulder or an "S" branded onto the cheek of a slave). Strike branding occurs when a heated metal or ceramic implement is repeatedly applied to the skin to build up the desired pattern (Figure 21.6). Cautery branding uses a specific tool such as a soldering iron, whereas laser branding uses a piece of equipment similar to an arc welder.

Cold branding works on the same principle as hot strike branding but uses an implement that is first dipped into liquid nitrogen before being applied to the skin.

Large flat areas of skin function best for successful branding, such as the chest, back, and thighs (Myers 1992). These, therefore, are the most likely locations to find such modifications when performing a visual inspection of a body.

21.3.2 Cutting

This involves making marks on the skin with a sharp implement (usually a scalpel). This can be done to induce scars as with branding, and it is quite common for pigments to be rubbed into the newly formed cuts to result in colored scars (Figure 21.7). Cutting like this allows for the creation of any shape, and it is possible that the individual artist can be identified from the cutting, in much the same way as with a painting (Myers 1992).

Alternatively, large areas of skin may be removed (skinning) to produce a different type of pattern. A procedure referred to as "braiding" has appeared in recent literature, although no credible verification of this procedure has been forthcoming. This modification allegedly

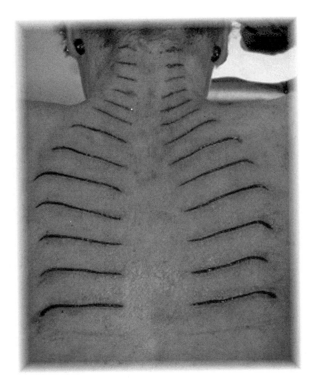

Figure 21.7 Cutting.

involves the cutting of three strips of skin (leaving them attached at a base line) and then braiding the strips across the open wound. As with branding, fleshy areas of the body are the most appropriate for cutting-based modifications and are the most likely locations for noting them.

It is also important to note here that practitioners will need to be able to differentiate aesthetic cutting from self-harm. Cutting as a form of self-harm is increasing within the same demographic that often undertakes body modification. Key differences may include pattern of cuts, location, and depth.

21.3.3 Body Etching

This is essentially a "white tattoo," where a traditional electrical tattoo machine is utilized to transfer the image onto the skin. No dye is included in the operation, and therefore scarring occurs but with no coloration (Figure 21.8).

21.3.4 Other Forms of Scarification

These include chemical scarification that usually occurs through the application of strong acids or alkalis. Injection scarification arises through the injection of noxious chemicals to cause a blister, which in turn leaves pockmarks similar to the scars left by inoculations. Abrasive scarification is caused by friction burning and can arise through the application of mechanical devices, sandpaper, or any abrasive substance including scouring pads and cleaning solutions.

Figure 21.8   Etching. A tattoo with no pigment.

21.4   Subdermal Implants

There are many forms of subdermal implants, ranging from soft tissue augmentation (breasts, buttocks, gastrocnemius, etc.), hormonal pellets (contraceptive, etc.), cosmetic (extraocular and dental) to microchip and radio frequency identification inserts. Here we will only consider subdermal implants undertaken for aesthetic reasons to sculpt body appearance and alter surface topography. In this situation, inert foreign bodies are surgically placed deep in the skin to alter the contours of the normal body form. In addition to the aesthetical reasons for implantation, insertion of these objects into regions of the genitalia are said to heighten sexual stimulation.

21.4.1   Beading

This involves the insertion of inert metal (titanium or Teflon®), bone, pearl, or plastic (nylon) beads under the skin (Figure 21.9). These beads are generally no larger than 1 cm in diameter. The desired position of the bead or series of beads are first ascertained (perhaps on a limb, sternum, face, scrotum, or shaft of the penis) and skin incisions (entrance and exit) are made some distance from the desired implant position. Using a dermal separator, a small subdermal pocket is created, and the bead is deposited between the skin and the superficial fascia.

21.4.2   3D Body Art

In addition to beads, many other shapes can be inserted under the skin to radically alter body shape. The insertion of the nonreactive shape is placed into a dermal pocket so that the outline remains visible but is fully encapsulated. Alterations to the face, anterior chest wall, and the limbs are most commonly effected by this process (Figure 21.10). There is also a recent trend to utilize magnetic implants.

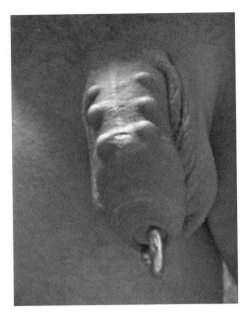

Figure 21.9   Beading in the shaft of the penis. The incision scar is evident on the upper surface.

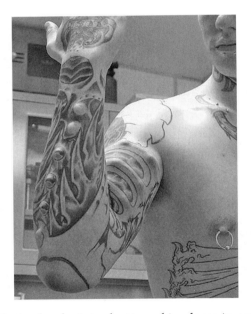

Figure 21.10   Body sculpting by the introduction of implants in association with tattooing.

21.5   Transdermal Modification

21.5.1   Introduction

Transdermal modification can be considered to be a modification that involves inserting an object through a part of the body so that, in most circumstances, it comes out the other side. Gold et al. stated that this practice could be defined as "putting holes in your body

Table 21.1 Glossary of Key Transdermal Modification Terms

	Term	Definition
Artifact	Ball-closure ring	Circular ring, inserted through the hole and closed with a small ball
	Bar	Inserted through the hole and closed with two end pieces
	Labret	Similar to the bar, but with one permanently fixed end and the other closed with a screwed piece
	Stud	Similar to the bar, but closed with a butterfly piece
Ear piercing	Industrial	A bar that goes through the anterior and posterior aspects of the helix, the bar of which lies superficial to the ear morphology
	Inner Helical	Through the anterior portion of the helix
	Helix	Through the helix of the ear
	Outer Conch	Through the outer conch, often inferior to the auricular tubercle
	Rook	Through the anterior crus of the anti helix
	Inner Conch	Through the inner conch of the ear
	Antitragus	Through the antitragus of the ear
	Local spool	Artifact placed in the lobule in order to create a large hole
	Tragus	Through the tragus of the ear
Male genitals	Prince Albert	Through the end of the urethra meatus and out of the ventral aspect of the penis
	Ampallang	Transervesly through the end of the penis
	Trans-scrotal	Through the scrotal skin
	Guiche	Transversely through the perineum
Female genitals	Hood	Anterior to the clitoris
	Clitoral	Through the clitoris
	Inner labial	Through the inner labia
	Outer labial	Through the outer labia
	Fourchette	Anterior to the anus

Source: Adapted from Swift, B., in *Essentials of Autopsy Practice: Recent Advances, Topics and Developments*, Rutty, G.N., Ed., Springer-Verlag London, 2004, pp. 159–186.

that were not there before" (2005, p. 19). This definition is inadequate in this context; however, the function of body modification is more than just the creation of holes (whether this is for display, sensation, etc.). Brooks et al. (2003) argue that body modification is the permanent alteration of one's appearance. Again, this is inadequate, as piercings can be a temporary feature (as, indeed, certain dermal modifications can be; see above). Perhaps a suitable definition is simply the intentional insertion of an artifact through the skin. Certain body piercing is now considered a mainstream activity in Western society (Gold et al. 2005, Whittle and Lamden 2004) with more procedures becoming gradually socially acceptable. This increase in social acceptance and the associated increase in modifications acquisition demand that the forensic identification community become more aware of the potential of this as a viable method of identification. Table 21.1 and Figure 21.11 contain glossaries of terms for specific locations and styles of piercing. It is no longer acceptable to merely state whether a piercing is present or absent, especially when greater specificity can be achieved through the use of such terms.

Although Gold et al. (2005) state a total of 11 reasons for obtaining a transdermal modification, the 5 most popular reasons are associated with appearance, the next 2 concern rebellion, and then 3 of the final 4 reasons are associated with acceptance. With so few of those pierced (5%, according to Gold et al. 2005) admitting that no one knew about their piercing, this suggests an important aspect of this form of body modification: it is as a statement to be seen and acknowledged.

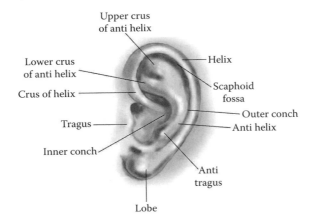

Figure 21.11 Location of key transdermal ear modification.

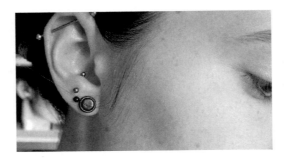

Figure 21.12 Varied ear piercings.

Although it has been found that many people find at least one piercing site to be acceptable, there is a variety of opinion as to the location of "best" sites (Gold et al. 2005). In Western society the earlobe is by far the most conventional location for a piercing (Figure 21.12), particularly in females. In the U.K. there is no age restriction on this modification, with ear piercing being offered in jewelry shops of many shopping centers. With the increasing adoption of transdermal modification, it can be argued that other sites are slowly becoming more acceptable and therefore mainstream, such as the upper ear (Figure 21.12), nose, eyebrow, and navel. Among those with piercings, it is not surprising to discover that individuals tend to view the site of their own piercing as being the most socially tolerable location (Gold et al. 2005). It has been reported that up to 75% of adolescents liked body piercings on others (Gold et al. 2005), and this may be significant in both the proliferation of piercings on an individual and the adoption of piercings by others.

21.5.2 Procedure

Regardless of the location, the basic procedure for inserting a transdermal modification is very similar. First, an area is chosen. It is important that this location avoids the major cardiovascular bundles, although this is not always the case (such as with subclavicle piercings, which carries severe risk of puncture of the subclavian vessels). A small mark is made with ink at the point of the insertion and, on occasion, the exit to assist with guiding the initial

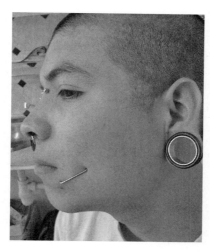

Figure 21.13 Ear stretching and pocketing of the cheek.

needle. If a thick or particularly sensitive area of the body is to be pierced, for example, the penis, then a local anesthetic may be applied. The area surrounding the piercing site is secured to limit movement, and the initial perforation is caused by either manual puncture (needle) or a piercing gun. The manual piercing equipment should be single-use, whereas the piercing gun should have disposable or autoclavable parts (Koenig and Carnes 1999). An inert, sterile piece of "jewelry" is then placed through the hole. It is entirely possible for the transdermal piercing to heal if jewelry is not inserted for a prolonged period of time.

Of note here is the practice of stretching. Following the creation of a piercing, progressively larger artifacts can be placed within the hole to increase its size, thereby "stretching" the initial modification. Common sites of stretching include the ear lobes and nostril (Figure 21.13) but can also include nipples, penis, scrotum, and labia.

The mechanics of piercing the tongue (Figure 21.14) are slightly different, in that it involves the implantation of a barbell through the tongue with two screw-on balls on the ends (López Jornet et al. 2004). A longer bar than ultimately desired is inserted initially until the swelling of the tongue reduces. The original barbell can then be replaced. The tongue is particularly susceptible to complications following transdermal modification due to its highly vascular nature (López Jornet et al. 2004).

A feature particular to transdermal modifications that should be visible histologically is the presence of necrotic tissue surrounding the transdermal passage. This has been attributed to repetitive epithelia necrosis as a result of continuous mechanical pressure from the implant (López Jornet et al. 2004). One might even be able to use the degree of healing to estimate the time since the modification.

Stapling or "pocketing" is also a form of transdermal modification. Instead of a single piercing being created in order to hold, for example, an item of jewelry, staples are inserted into the skin (Figure 21.13). In this way, the skin can also be folded to form pockets that are held in place by the staples.

21.5.3 Anatomical Locations

Table 21.2 shows the relative popularity of the common anatomical locations for piercings, with the ear being the most common site. Of note is the fact that the more popular sites

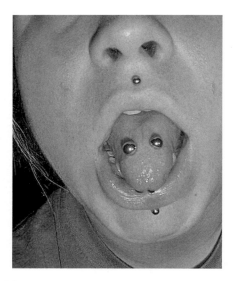

Figure 21.14   Tongue and lip piercings.

are those that are visible when wearing standard clothing, although Whittle and Lamden's (2004) survey found that the tongue was a more popular piercing site than the lip (Figure 21.14). However, their survey has many problems, and they neglect to say why this is so. One feasible explanation could be the ability to conceal a tongue piercing over that of a lip piercing, although it is interesting to note that the procedure of piercing a tongue is much more complicated and dangerous than that of the lip.

There are clear age and gender differences with regard to the location and number of transdermal modifications. Studies have demonstrated that, unlike dermal modification, a greater number of females undertake transdermal modifications (Braithwaite et al. 2001, Roberti et al. 2004, Kieser et al. 2005). In addition, the average age for obtaining a body modification is lower with piercings than with tattoos (Roberti et al. 2004). This age is also lower in females than males (Roberti et al. 2004). These findings may suggest that if evidence of a transdermal modification is found on, for example, a young male, it may inherently carry more identification significance.

As with all body modifications there is a wide spectrum of piercing locations. Whereas the more common are listed in Table 21.2, it should be recognized for identification purposes that piercings can occur in many other anatomical locations, e.g., penis, scrotum, perineum, genital labia, toes, webs of fingers, frenula in the mouth, eyelids, etc.

Temporary piercings also occur in association with increasingly popular procedures such as body suspension (Figure 21.15). It is likely that this process has its origin in: (1) the

Table 21.2   Anatomical Location of Mainstream Piercings

| Study | Demographic | N | Location of Piercing (%) | | | | | | |
			Earlobe	Upper Ear	Eyebrow	Nose	Tongue	Navel	Nipples
Brooks et al., 2003	Adolescents	210	94	34	3	26	4	8	1
Gold et al., 2005	Adolescents	225	74	—	15	34	30	27	3
Moser et al., 1993	Adults with piercings	362	45	10	—	17	—	15	100

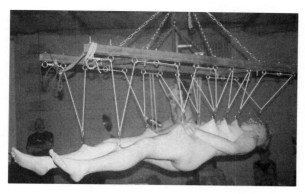

Figure 21.15 Whole body suspension.

ritualistic piercings associated with the Tamil Kavadi festival of penance (originating in South India), where multiple piercings are intended to bring the bearer to spiritual heights by inducing a trance-like and pain-free exhilaration and (2) in the North American Indian ritual of *o-kee-pa*, which was designed to produce a near-death experience and bring the warrior closer to his gods.

21.6 Conclusions

Much research has been conducted into the body modification arena, but this has originated from sociological or medical perspectives. The forensic and identification communities are yet to appreciate fully the sheer volume and variety of modifications present in current Western society. By discussing the reasons behind, and methods of, modern body modification, this chapter aims to go some way toward highlighting this potential. Once the mechanics and frequency of these modifications are appreciated, their contribution to human body identification can be discussed. As a result, it may be possible to change practices to maintain useful antemortem records for potential comparison. The lack of such details in records has already been highlighted as contributing to public health risks following outbreaks of modification-induced infections (Fisher et al. 2005).

Although this chapter has focused on the more common forms of body modification that are most likely to be found in identification contexts, it should be noted that other more extreme forms exist. The splitting of the tongue, the remodelling of the upper ear, the insertion of hooks into the skin for body suspension, and the amputation of digits, for example, can all be witnessed, though in very small numbers. It would be advisable for the forensic practitioner to be open-minded when examining a corpse for body modifications. This is also true when assuming the intention of such body modifications. For example, an amputation seen during a visual examination of a body may not be an enforced medical occurrence but rather a voluntary personal choice.

In addition, the forensic practitioner must become familiar with the hardware associated with body modifications and the likely anatomical locations where these modifications can be found. For example, the barbells that are inserted through the tongue, ear, and penis all differ in shape and size, and for recovered barbells to be of use in identifying an individual, we must be able to state in which of these locations they would be found when the individual was alive. Some hardware will be highly indicative of a select community, e.g., scrotal weights, or of a personal condition, e.g., a "sleeper" navel piercing, which would indicate pregnancy.

Body modifications are rapidly becoming a symbol of modern times, and their uniquely personal implications are important for the practitioner of human identification. In the words of H.D. Thoreau (1854) "Every man is the builder of a temple, called his body, to the god he worships, after a style purely his own, nor can he get off by hammering marble instead. We are all sculptors and painters, and our material is our own flesh and blood and bones. Any nobleness begins at once to refine a man's features, any meanness or sensuality to imbrute them."

21.7   Acknowledgments

We are indebted to the editors (particularly Shannon Larratt) and members of the BMEzine for their support with the writing and editing of this chapter, and for providing many of the images used here. We advise that practitioners involved in forensic identification would do well to familiarize themselves with the vast wealth of information available on this site: http://www.bmezine.com.

References

Adatto, M.A., Laser tattoo removal: benefits and caveats, *Medical Laser Application* 19, 175–185, 2004.

Anderson, R.R. and Parrish, J.A., Selective photothermolysis: precise microsurgery by selective absorption of pulsed radiation, *Science* 220, 524–527, 1983.

Brooks, T.L., Woods, E.R., Knight, J.R., and Shrier, LA., Body modification and substance use in adolescents: is there a link? *Journal of Adolescent Health* 32, 44–49, 2003.

Braithwaite, R., Robillard, A., Woodring, T., Stephens, T., and Arriola, K.J., Tattooing and body piercing amongst adolescent detainees: relationship to alcohol and other drug use, *Journal of Substance Abuse* 13, 5–16, 2001.

Caplan, J., *Written on the Body*, Reaktion Books, London, 2000.

Fisher, C.G., Kacica, M.A., and Bennett, N.M., Risk factors for cartilage infections of the ear, *American Journal of Preventative Medicine* 29(3), 204–209, 2005.

Fujita, H., Yamshita, K., Kawamata, S., and Yoshikawa, K., The uptake and long-term storage of India ink particles and latex beads by fibroblasts in the dermis and subcutis of mice, with special regard to the non-inflammatory defense reaction fibroblasts, *Archives of Histology and Cytology* 51(3), 285–294, 1988.

Gold, M.A., Schorzman, C.M., Murray, P.J., Downs, J., and Tolentino, G., Body piercing practices and attitudes among urban adolescents, *Journal of Adolescent Health* 36, 17–24, 2005.

Green, T., *The Tattoo Encyclopedia*, Simon and Schuster, London, 2003.

Johnson, R., The anthropological study of body decoration as art: collective representations and the somatozation of affect, *Fashion Theory* 5(4), 417–434, 2001.

Karkos, P.D., Karagama, Y.G., Manivasagam, A., and Reda El Badawey, M., Magnetic nasal foreign bodies: a result of fashion mania, *International Journal of Pediatric Otorhinolaryngology* 67, 1343–1345, 2003.

Kieser, J.A., Thomson, W.M., Koopu, P., and Quick, A.N., Oral piercing and oral trauma in a New Zealand sample, *Dental Traumatology* 21, 254–257, 2005.

Koenig, L.M. and Carnes, M., Body piercing: medical concerns with cutting-edge fashion, *Journal of General Internal Medicine* 14, 379–385, 1999.

Lapidoth, M. and Aharonowitz, G., Tattoo removal among Ethiopian Jews in Israel: tradition faces technology, *Journal of the American Academy of Dermatology* 51(6), 906–909, 2004.

Lewis, C.G., Wells, M.K., and Jennings, W.C., *Mycobacterium fortuitum* breast infection following nipple-piercing, mimicking carcinoma, *The Breast Journal* 10(4), 363–365, 2004.

López Jornet, P., Vicente Ortega, V., Yánez Gascón, J., Cozar Hidalgo, A., Pérez Lajarín, L., García Ballesta, C., and Alcaraz Banos, M., Clinicopathological characteristics of tongue piercing: an experimental study, *Journal of Oral Pathology and Medicine* 33, 340–345, 2004.

Martin, J.A., Hughes, T.M., and Stone, N.M., Black henna tattoos: an occult source of natural rubber latex allergy, *Contact Dermatitis* 52, 145–146, 2005.

Mayers, L.B., Judelson, D.A., Moriarty, B.W., and Rundell, K.W., Prevalence of body art (body piercing and tattooing) in university undergraduates and incidence of medical complications, *Mayo Clinic Proceedings* 77, 29–34, 2002.

Millner, V.S., Eichold, BH., II, Sharpe, T.H., and Lynn, S.C., Jr., First glimpse of the functional benefits of clitoral hood piercings, *American Journal of Obstetrics and Gynecology* 193, 675–676, 2005.

Moser, C., Lee, J., and Christensen, P., Nipple piercing: an exploratory-descriptive study, *Journal of Psychology and Human Sexuality* 6(2), 51–61, 1993.

Myers, J., Nonmainstream body modification: genital piercing, branding, burning and cutting, *Journal of Contemporary Ethnography* 21(3), 267–306, 1992.

Nicoletti, A. Teens, tattoos and body piercing, *Journal of Adolescent Gynecology* 17, 215–216, 2004.

Quint, E. and Breech, L., Tattoos: beautification or something else? *Journal of Pediatric and Adolescent Gynecology* 18, 129–131, 2005.

Reid, W.H., McLeod, P.J., Ritchie, A., and Ferguson-Pell, M., Q-switched ruby laser treatment of black tattoos, *British Journal of Plastic Surgery* 36, 455–459, 1983.

Roberti, J.W., Storch, E.A., and Bravata, E.A., Sensation seeking, exposure to psychological stressors, and body modifications in a college population, *Personality and Individual Differences* 37, 1167–1177, 2004.

Saukko, P. and Knight, B., *Knight's Forensic Pathology,* 3rd ed., Arnold, London, 2004.

Seiter, J.S. and Hatch, S., Effect of tattoos on perceptions of credibility and attractiveness. *Psychological Reports* 96, 1113–1120, 2005.

Strang, J., Heuston, J., Whiteley, C., Bacchus, L., Maden, T., Gossop, M., and Green J., Is prison tattooing a risk behaviour for HIV and other viruses? Results from a national survey of prisoners in England and Wales, *Criminal Behavior and Mental Health* 10, 60–65, 2000.

Swift, B., Body art and modification, in *Essentials of Autopsy Practice: Recent Advances, Topics and Developments,* Rutty, G.N., Ed., Springer-Verlag London Ltd., 2004, pp. 159–186.

Vail, D.A., Tattoos are like potato chips … you can't have just one: the process of becoming and being a collector, *Deviant Behaviour: An Interdisciplinary Journal* 20, 253–273, 1999.

Van den Keybus, C., Morren, M.-A., and Goossens, A., Walking difficulties due to an allergic reaction to a temporary tattoo, *Contact Dermatitis* 53, 180–181, 2005.

Walters, R., Regulation of Skin and Body Piercing Analysis of Written Submissions to Consultation, Scottish Executive Central Research Unit, Edinburgh, 2001.

Whittle, J.G. and Lamden, K.H., Lip and tongue piercing: experiences and views of general dental practitioners in South Lancashire, *Primary Dental Care* 11(3), 92–96, 2004.

Part B

The Context and Significance of Forensic Human Identification

Section 9

The Context of Forensic Human Identification

Identity Fraud and Theft

22

NATASHA SEMMENS

Contents

22.1 Introduction 405
22.2 What Is Identity Theft? 406
    22.2.1 What Are Personal Data? 406
    22.2.2 The Process of Identification 407
    22.2.3 Types of Identity Theft and Fraud 408
    22.2.4 Identity Fraud 408
    22.2.5 Identity Theft 409
22.3 The Victims of Identity Theft and Fraud 410
22.4 Responding to Britain's Fastest Growing Crime 411
22.5 Conclusion 413
References 413

22.1 Introduction

In this chapter we consider how different elements of an individual's identity have become attractive commodities in the criminal world. Through analysis of the emergent phenomenon of identity theft, we will come to appreciate how the changing value of personal data in modern society has impacted on the nature of crime. We will explore the different methods employed to identity thieves, which may vary according to different motivations, and highlight the complexities underlying the concept of "identity theft." In addition, we will examine the phenomenon from the victim's perspective, taking into account both financial harm and the impact on the victim's sense of identity. Finally, the chapter concludes with a brief overview of the various responses to the growing problem of identity theft, with particular emphasis on the U.K. experience. It is hoped that the overall discussion will be of interest to anyone with an interest in data crimes.

It is important to preface the discussion with a brief consideration of the social and temporal contexts in which identity theft is evolving. Although identity theft is often heralded as a new crime threat, the phenomenon itself is by no means unique to the modern world or, indeed, to the Information Age. Throughout history, criminals have used false identities to commit their crimes, and their motivations have ranged from social control to commercial exploitation, financial gain, voyeurism, political protest, stalking, and harassment (Grabosky et al. 2001, Garfinkel 2001). However, as identity theft emerges as a growing crime problem in the 21st century, it has new features that are closely linked with changes in modern society. Globalization has brought with it a faster, more mobile way of life with increasing opportunities for travel and business, and this has brought significant new opportunities for the criminal. Technological advances, including the advent of the Internet, email, and mobile phone technology, have transformed the way in which we live our everyday lives and, in many ways, have facilitated criminal enterprise. With all of these changes come new risks and, with them, new challenges. Whom can we trust? Where is it safe? Who is vulnerable? As a result we are increasingly required to prove our identity as we interact with other individuals in both real and virtual environments, and the identification process is more important now than it has ever been.

22.2 What Is Identity Theft?

Although not a clearly defined legal term, the concept of identity theft has been absorbed into the consciousness of the British public with some ease. The terms *identity theft* and *identity fraud* are used interchangeably by government agencies, the media, and marketing personnel, and most of us have a broad understanding of what they are talking about. For many people, identity theft invokes ideas of credit card fraud and benefit cheats; for others, it is more associated with illegal immigration and organized crime. However, although a broad understanding may be sufficient to raise public awareness of the risks associated with identity theft, the lack of conceptual certainty has proved to be more problematic for those involved in policy and prevention. Indeed, when we begin to unravel the different methods of identity theft and explore the motivations of its perpetrators, it becomes apparent that it is a complex, multidimensional concept.

From the outset, it is important to distinguish identity thefts from other data crimes (Semmens 2004). There are essentially two defining features of identity theft. First, there must be an appropriation of another individual's personal data and, second, an act of impersonation in which the perpetrator masquerades as that individual in order to commit another crime. We must, therefore, discount cases of fraudulent misrepresentation in which dishonest individuals lie about some of their own circumstances (for example, by giving a false address to commit a benefit fraud). Before we move on to examine the different methods of, and motivations behind, identity theft in more detail, it is necessary to first consider the nature of personal data and to understand how it is used in the process of identification. Only then can we truly appreciate the skills and knowledge required to commit these offenses.

22.2.1 What Are Personal Data?

The term *personal data* is commonly defined as data relating to an identified or identifiable individual (Booth et al. 2004). It does not necessarily have to identify the individual, but in cases of identity theft, it is identifying data that is targeted by the criminal. There are three types of personal data that may be used for identification purposes: attributed identifiers, biographical identifiers, and biometric identifiers (Jones and Levi 2000, Cabinet Office 2002). Attributed data are the components of an individual's identity, which are established or assigned at birth. These include name, date and place of birth, and parents' names, and are permanently associated with the individual. Biographical identifiers are the elements of identity that are accumulated after birth, as an individual progresses through life. They include educational achievements and qualifications, financial records, property ownership, marriage, and employment history, thus representing an individual's interactions with public and private institutions. Biometric identifiers are biological characteristics which relate to an individual's physical make up. These may then relate to the physical appearance (e.g., fingerprints or facial structure) or the biomolecular profile (e.g., DNA) of an individual. Some will be permanent characteristics, and some will change as an individual ages.

A portfolio of information, then, is collected throughout an individual's life, and different pieces of personal data serve different functions. As a result, personal data can have intrinsic value or instrumental value, and that value can be attached to information by ourselves and by other people. For the criminal, it is the instrumental or commercial value of personal data that is attractive. Most personal information has commercial value in the sense that it can be exchanged (Grabosky et al. 2001). It may be exchanged for goods and services or for more information; thus it is described by Jones and Levi (2001) as *persuasive data*. In practice, different pieces of information have different levels of exchange value. A passport, for example, will open the doors to more facilities than a membership card for the local video store. Personal data is the key to the identification process.

22.2.2 The Process of Identification

Clarke's (1994) theory of identification firmly establishes human identification as a process of association of data with a particular human being. More specifically, the identifier is attempting to establish that a person who is the subject of one observation is also the subject of a previous observation (LoPucki 2001). Thus, identification is a layered process that always must refer back to a *base layer* in which the identifying characteristics were originally recorded as belonging to a specific individual. Accordingly, in order to commit an act of identity theft, the criminal must either intercept the relevant identifying characteristics present in the base layer or establish a new base layer.

The purpose and nature of the identification process reflect the needs of the identifier. When an individual interacts with a state agency or public institution, for example, the purpose of the identification process is to enable the state to monitor and control entitlement to public services and contribution to societal structures. Identification, then, is required when an individual wishes to enter or leave the country (temporarily or permanently), access state benefits, use healthcare services, and enter the employment system. This is most likely to require an individual to provide knowledge and evidence of attributed information. In contrast, for private sector institutions, the process of identification is less about control of citizens and more about protecting the interests of the business or service provider. Put simply, private sector institutions need to ensure the identity of an individual before entering into a contract or financial relationship in order to reduce the risk of nonpayment or fulfillment of some other contractual obligation. Thus, an individual probably will need to produce evidence of biographical information, in addition to attributed information.

Evidence of identity may take one of three forms: token-based identification (where documents or other tokens are used to prove identity), knowledge-based identification (information only the individual would know), and biometric identification (where physical characteristics are used to identify an individual) (Clarke 1994). In order for an identifier to be effective, it must fulfill a number of different requirements. These include universality of coverage (all individuals must possess the identifier), uniqueness, permanence, precision, and acceptability (socially and ethically). The problem is that no single identifier can be said to satisfy all requirements. Although physiological identifiers are universal and usually indispensable, they are not necessarily unique or permanent. Yet, nonphysiological identifiers are equally problematic, because they are unlikely to be unique, permanent, or universal. We must conclude that an effective system of identification must combine different types of identifiers (Clarke 1994). In practice, attributed data are often used as *primary identifiers* in a variety of contexts, in both the public or private spheres. Data may be used in token form (the birth certificate) or in knowledge form (date and place of birth, parents' names, etc.). However, because attributed data are not unique, it is usual for *secondary/confirmatory identifiers* to be used in conjunction with attributed data. Secondary identifiers are likely to be derived from biographical personal data; for example, a credit history or current address.

Importantly, this analysis gives us a clear insight into the territory of the identity thief. According to a recent study by the U.K. Cabinet Office (2002), fraud using attributed information is the greatest cause for concern. Evidential documentation can be forged, stolen, or acquired via a false application. Biographical information is harder to acquire as it usually requires the criminal to actually "live as the victim" for a period of time, appearing on public and private databases. Although difficult to achieve, it is possible with time and careful planning. In contrast, biometric information, in theory at least, is less vulnerable to criminal manipulation, and it may be deemed easier to tamper with the central system holding the data than it is to forge biometric features. The criminal may employ one or more different methods of identity theft, each characterized by different levels of immersion, the duration of the offense, and the motivations of the offender. We now move on to explore the different types of identity theft in more detail.

22.2.3   Types of Identity Theft and Fraud

Finch (2002) identifies two types of identity theft: *total* and *partial*. Total identity theft involves the permanent adoption of all the victim's details in order for the criminals to start a new life. In contrast, partial identity theft is the temporary use of some of the victim's details to facilitate the commission of a criminal offense. Jones and Levi (2000) adopt a similar approach, distinguishing between cases where elements of another individual's identity are "borrowed" and those in which an entire identity is "developed." For the purposes of this discussion it may be helpful to combine these approaches and distinguish between those temporary offenses in which personal data are borrowed in order to commit a fraudulent offense (*identity fraud*), and those cases in which the victim's entire identity is permanently appropriated (*identity theft*).

22.2.4   Identity Fraud

In cases of identity fraud, the identifying information serves merely as a tool for the criminal to use in order to commit another offense. The motivation of these offenses tends to be financial, either to obtain goods or services, or to establish credit or a loan, and the impersonation is temporary.

Perhaps the most straightforward and, indeed, most common offenses for the criminal to commit are those where purchases are made using another person's financial details. The targeted personal data in most cases are credit and debit card details, which will usually be used in the short term until the credit limit is reached or the card is reported lost or stolen. In face-to-face transactions, the criminal will need to be in possession of the card itself and, in most cases, the PIN. There will usually be no need for the criminal to verify any further personal details at the point of sale. However, in the online environment, the situation is slightly different in that the criminal will need to supply further details such as the billing address, the start/end dates of the card, and the security code. In these cases, the criminal will benefit from having access to some of the victim's receipts or card statements, which will allow the criminal to break through the security barriers.

Banks and credit card companies have become increasingly aware of the vulnerabilities of their customers and have introduced measures to combat these kinds of frauds. The "Chip and PIN" system, for example, has been introduced to stem fraud in face-to-face transactions. The security code (a three- or four-digit code that is printed on the card) has been introduced to make online purchases more secure. The effect of these innovations has been that criminals now need to steal more information in order to commit these frauds, therefore they are being pushed to adapt their methods. So, we now see cases where criminals are inventing methods of duping the victim into handing over their details voluntarily, rather than stealing them or "dumpster diving" (cases in which criminals rifle through trash containers to find items containing personal data that can be used to commit thefts or frauds). This is commonly done by sending an email to the genuine customer requiring them to enter their details onto a website that is a "copycat website," a method known as *phishing*. These methods create more complex cases of identity fraud as it affects both the individual and the financial institution having their identities abused.

In cases of application fraud, where the criminal uses another individual's information to set up a credit agreement or loan, the need for a portfolio of personal data is much greater. Typically, these offenses will require the criminal to acquire a combination of attributed and biographical data: proof of name and address (3-year history), a sound credit history, date of birth, proof of income, and employment details. Therefore, for most applications it will be necessary for criminals to produce documentary evidence in the form of a passport/birth certificate, utility bills, bank statements, and pay slips in order to establish their identity. These documents will then need to be acquired from the victim (through loss or theft) or acquired via "address impersonation" (Jones and Levi 2000). Fraudsters may achieve this by a number of routes, depending on their individual situation. First, it may be possible for a fraudster living in rented property to intercept the mail of either the current owner of the property (the landlord) or other current occupants of the house (where it is a shared tenancy or multiple-occupant household). Second, the fraudster might target previous occupants of the property, usually by taking receipt of mail that has been sent to the old address by mistake. Finally, it may be possible for the fraudster to adopt the name and current address of another individual and then register his or her own address as if that individual has moved. Once the fraudsters have managed to collect a series of documents (utility bills, bank or card statements, or junk mail (loan applications)) they can go on to apply for loans or, where necessary, acquire further documentary evidence (for a detailed discussion of these methods see Jones and Levi 2000).

22.2.5 Identity Theft

In cases of identity theft, the identity of another individual is "hijacked" by the fraudster with the aim of a permanent appropriation. These cases are rare as the new identity will need to be meticulously developed over time and requires considerable effort on the part of the fraudster. As noted by Jones and Levi (2000), the motivations for a permanent change of identity may be legitimate (for example, change of name in the U.K. by deed poll following gender reassignment or victim/witness protection schemes) but may also be criminal in nature — for example, to remain unlawfully in the country or to conceal a criminal record. Identity theft is most easily achieved where the victim is deceased, especially where the victim died in infancy and has not already built a portfolio of biographical data (Jones and Levi 2000). In such a case, fraudsters may find the details of a deceased child in a graveyard, selecting one with a partial date of birth close to their own (Cabinet Office 2002). From this point, it is relatively easy to obtain a birth certificate, which then becomes an important "breeder document."

22.3   The Victims of Identity Theft and Fraud

Having explored the nature and characteristics of identity theft and fraud, we turn now to consider how these crimes can impact the lives of the victims. The victims of identity theft/fraud are exposed to several different forms of harm, and these may be experienced in various combinations. Although the immediate loss of large sums of money is a commonly held fear, it is actually quite unlikely for the individual victim to be held liable for hefty debts incurred where an identity theft/fraud has taken place. More likely is the damage caused to the victim's credit history, which will have a negative impact on future financial autonomy. One of the major problems faced by the victims of identity theft/fraud is the subsequent time and effort needed to remedy the situation. The U.K. Cabinet Office (2002) has estimated that in the U.K., the average time spent restoring a reputation is 60 hours. We can see, then, that by assuming control of the victim's personal data, the perpetrator is taking full advantage of the instrumental value of that data. Accordingly, the victim loses control of that instrumental function. In short, although the criminal act is often simply the theft of identifying information, the victim suffers theft of identity.

Exactly how serious an impact the identity theft/fraud will have on the victim's sense of identity will depend upon the individual's wider value system. The value attached to personal data will determine the individual's desire for control of that data. It is argued that to lose control of one's personal information is potentially damaging to quality of life. Grabosky et al. (2001) allude to a deep psychological harm: "the loss of one's private life is often accompanied by a decline in spontaneity, creativity, and a diminished sense of self" (p. 176).

This reference to the sense of self is important. According to Goffman (1971, 1990, 1991), one forms a sense of self by negotiating the different social roles that are required by different social situations. By understanding the value of personal information within a context of social interaction, we appreciate the wider-reaching effect of what might initially be viewed as simply a "one-off loss" for the victim. The perpetrators in this kind of crime take over the identity of the victims, leaving them less able to control their identifiers in social situations. Thus, a victim may feel vulnerable or, in more extreme cases of identity theft, powerless, in the course of everyday life. Moreover, victimization of this type of crime may carry with it a distinct kind of stigma. The fact that one has been a victim of information theft may suggest that one is more stupid, negligent, or weaker than one's peers. Indeed, this type of reaction would echo the findings of previous studies on the victims of fraud (Levi and Pithouse 1992).

22.4   Responding to Britain's Fastest Growing Crime

We have now established that identity theft and fraud is a significant crime problem that has a serious impact on its victims. But how big is the problem and what can be done to prevent it? The phenomenon was first formally recognized as a new crime threat in the U.S. in the mid-1990s (Brin 1998). Since then, it has swiftly emerged as a key issue on the crime agendas of governments across the Western world. The U.S. was the first country to take significant legislative action and has been providing a national integrated support system for the victims of identity theft since 1999. The Identity Theft and Assumption Deterrence Act was enacted in 1998, establishing identity theft as a criminal offense and requiring the Federal Trade Commission (FTC) to set up a central repository for identity theft complaints (Federal Trade Commission 2003a). In 2003, the Federal Trade Commission (FTC) reported that in the period 1999–2002 customer complaints had more than doubled each year to a 2002 total of 161,896 complaints (Federal Trade Commission 2003). In 2004, that figure had risen to 246,570 (Federal Trade Commission 2005).

In the U.K., the response to the threat of identity theft/fraud has been slower, and we are still some way from being able to provide realistic estimates as to the extent of the problem this side of the Atlantic. As there is not yet a national, integrated method of data collection in this area, we must base our estimates on the figures provided by a range of government agencies and regulatory authorities (including the DVLA, Passport Authority, Home Office, APACS, CIFAS, and DWP). In a recent report, the Cabinet Office estimated the cost of identity theft/fraud to be in excess of £1.3 billion per annum (the total cost of all theft/fraud was estimated to be in excess of £13.8 billion per annum). However, it is suggested that these are likely to be underestimates due to the problems of underreporting, low detection rates, and offense classification (Cabinet Office 2002).

As the problems associated with identity theft/fraud have become more widespread and publicized, businesses, the finance industry, and government have been placed under increasing pressure to respond. Not only is it necessary for these groups to work together to reduce the incidence of identity thefts/frauds but also to provide better support for the victims. As the need to bring cases of identity theft/fraud and fraud to courts rises, it has become apparent that existing legislation, which exists mostly within the Theft Act of 1968, is inadequate. The Law Commission is currently exploring reform to the law relating to theft/fraud. It is hoped that eventual reforms will establish identity theft/fraud as a criminal offense. It has also been suggested that both businesses and individuals are encouraged to pursue civil actions against fraudsters to prevent them from keeping the proceeds of their crimes (Fraud Advisory Panel 2003).

To date, however, the responses have been mostly aimed toward prevention, with very little in the way of change to the processes of detection, prosecution, and victim support. Preventive responses have fallen into two main categories: developments in identification procedures and education strategies. As a sizeable proportion of identity theft/fraud cases involve the misuse of a credit or debit card, significant investments have been made by the financial industry to make improvements to card security and to create a secure environment online. In 2004/5, the Chip and PIN system was rolled out in the U.K., replacing the magnetic strip and signature panel, which have long been recognized as ineffective security features (Levi et al. 1991). The latest fraud figures show a reduction in counterfeit cards (produced by skimming or cloning existing cards) but a growth in fraudulent applications and cards being intercepted in the mail (APACS 2005). Although it is too early to draw conclusions on the impact of Chip and PIN, the initial trends would seem to suggest that criminals are already managing to circumnavigate the new security features. Furthermore, there is little evidence to suggest that Chip and PIN will do anything to prevent online identity thefts/frauds. It is not surprising, then, that banks and credit card companies are now seeking alternative cost solutions by marketing identity theft/fraud insurance schemes.

In the U.K., the problem of identity theft has become more associated with illegal immigration and the threat of terrorism than it is with fraud. This is mainly because awareness of the problem of identity theft/fraud escalated in the wake of 9/11. In countries where the problem had been recognized earlier, such as the U.S. and Australia, identity theft/fraud is more firmly associated with fraud and organized crime. The result is that the British debate surrounding identity theft/fraud has become entwined with government proposals to introduce a national identity card. Following a consultation exercise in 2003, and despite vociferous objections from civil liberties groups and agencies in both the public and private sectors, the Labour government has been keen to push through proposals to introduce a compulsory identity card scheme. One of the most controversial proposals is the use of biometric identifiers, criticized mostly because the technology is presently unreliable and expensive. Indeed, the results of the first biometric trial for identity cards in the U.K. revealed some highly significant flaws in iris scanning and facial recognition technology in particular, calling into question the use of biometric indicators for identity verification in the near future (U.K. Passport Office 2005).

Both the government and the finance industry have been particularly keen to emphasize the importance of education and guidance in the fight against identity theft and fraud. Increasingly, individuals are being encouraged to develop a more responsible attitude toward their personal data. Credit card holders, for example, are repeatedly told to keep their card details and PIN confidential and to shred or burn their statements and receipts. Businesses, too, are being encouraged to think more seriously about the threat of identity theft and the safety of their customers. In a recent report by the Fraud Advisory Panel (2003), a number of recommendations were made aimed at improving business practices to prevent identity thefts and frauds. Businesses were criticized for failing to monitor employees, to store and dispose of customers' personal data responsibly, and to share important information relating to frauds with market competitors. They called for improvements in personnel management, data storage practices (both off- and online), and data sharing practices (within both the public and private sectors), and recommended the establishment of a national fraud database together with a register of stolen identities.

Together, these responses to the growing problem of identity theft should be welcomed, but it is clear that a more proactive and coordinated response strategy is needed if the problem is to be effectively reduced. For the government, this means an overhaul of the public records system (to include the registering of births and deaths, the electoral system, and the issuing of passports), reform of the law relating to theft and fraud, and the adequate provision of resources to fund specialist training for the police. Businesses and government agencies should be held more accountable for their data storage and data sharing practices, and should be actively developing new schemes of personnel management. Individual consumers and citizens have an equally important role to play by learning to control their personal data responsibly. Crucially, all of these responses need to be carried out collectively and systematically. The million dollar question, quite literally, is who should ultimately be responsible? Until that question is addressed, it seems more likely that efforts will continue to lack the necessary force.

22.5 Conclusion

Urbanization, increased anonymity and mobility in everyday life, and new instruments of data surveillance are all features of globalization that can be seen working against the individual and against the achievement of privacy. Thus, the significance of privacy issues in the context of crime and crime control are more significant now than they have ever been. Developments in technology are challenging the relationship between privacy and the criminal law. In short, the threat of identity theft represents a shift in the nature of crime.

We have seen in this chapter that, although the value of personal data is certainly not a new realization to the criminal, it has become a more accessible tool in the modern world. Not only is there an increase in the amount of information available, but there is also an increase in the number of uses and, importantly, misuses for that information. For the potential victim, then, the control of personal information is fast becoming a primary concern, and there is now a growing demand for action. As we have seen, this action must ideally be driven by a joint strategy between government agencies and business and industry. To conclude, it is hoped that this chapter has enlightened the reader as to the risks associated with the identification process and will encourage those involved in the future development of biological identification technologies to take these risks into account.

References

APACS, U.K. Car Fraud Losses Reach £504.8M: Criminals Increase Their Efforts as Chip and PIN Starts To Make Its Mark, press release available at http://www.apacs.org.uk/, 2005.

Booth, S., Jenkins, R., Moxon, D., Semmens, N., Spencer, C., Taylor, M., and Townend, D., What Are Personal Data? A Study Conducted for the U.K. Information Commissioner, available at http://www.informationcommissioner.gov.uk/cms/DocumentUploads/what%20are%20personal%20data%20research.pdf, 2004.

Brin, D., *The Transparent Society: Will Technology Force Us to Choose Between Privacy and Freedom?* Perseus Books, 1998.

Cabinet Office, Identity Fraud: A Study, HMSO, London, 2002, also available online at http://www.homeoffice.gov.uk/.

Clarke, R., Human identification in information systems: management challenges and public policy issues, *Information, Technology and People* 7(4), 6–37, 1994.

Federal Trade Commission, National and State Trends in Fraud and Identity Theft (January–December 2004), available at http://www.consumer.gov/sentinel/pubs/Top10Fraud2004.pdf, 2005.

Federal Trade Commission, Federal Trade Commission Overview of the Identity Theft Program, available at http://www.ftc.gov/os/2003/09/timelinereport.pdf, 2003.

Finch, What a tangled web we weave: identity theft and the Internet, in *Dot.cons: Crime, Deviance and Identity on the Internet*, Jewkes, Y., Ed., Willan Publishing, Cullompton, U.K., 2002, pp. 86–104.

Fraud Advisory Panel, Identity Theft: Do You Know the Signs?, available at http://www.fraudadvisory-panel.org/newsite/PDFs/advice/Identity%20Theft%20Final%20Proof%2011-7-03.pdf, 2003.

Garfinkel, S., *Database Nation: The Death of Privacy in the 21st Century*, O'Reilly and Associates Inc., Cambridge, MA, 2001.

Goffman, E., *The Presentation of Self in Everyday Life*, Harmondsworth: Penguin Books.

Goffman, E., *Stigma: Notes on the Management of Spoiled Identity*, Penguin Books, Harmondsworth, U.K., 1990.

Goffman, E., *Asylums: Essays on the Social Situation of Mental Patients and Other Inmates*, Penguin Books, Harmondsworth, U.K., 1991.

Grabosky, P., Smith, R.G., and Dempsey, G., *Electronic Theft: Unlawful Acquisition in Cyberspace*, Cambridge University Press, Cambridge, 2001.

Jones, G. and Levi, M., The Value of Identity and the Need for Authenticity, DTI Office of Science and Technology Crime Foresight Panel Essay for Turning the Corner, 2000.

Levi, M., Bissell, P., and Richardson, T., The Prevention of Cheque and Credit Card Fraud, Crime Prevention Unit Paper 26, Home Office, London, 1991.

Levi, M. and Handley, J., The Prevention of Plastic and Cheque Fraud Revisited, HORS 182, Home Office, London, 1998.

Levi, M. and Pithouse, A. The victims of fraud, in Downes, D. Ed., in Unravelling Criminal Justice, London: Macmillan Press Ltd., pp. 229–246, 1992

LoPucki, L., Human identification theory and the identity theft problem, 80 *Texas Law Review*, 89–136, 2001.

Semmens, N., Plastic card fraud and identity theft: implications of data crimes for the future of society, business and crime control, *Contemporary Issues in Law* 7(2), 121–139, 2004.

U.K. Passport Office and Atos Origin, Biometrics Enrolment Trial Report, available at http://www.homeoffice.gov.uk/downloads/UKPS_Biometrics_Enrolment_Trial_Report.pdf, 2005.

Biometric Identity Cards

23

TIM THOMPSON

Contents

23.1 Biometric Identification 415
23.2 Identity Cards and Their Biometric Identifiers.....................................416
23.3 Existing Biometric Identity Card Schemes 418
23.4 Biometric Identity Cards in the U.K...419
23.5 The Identity Cards Bill..419
23.6 Legal, Ethical, and Social Issues Concerning Biometric Identity Cards.................420
23.7 Conclusions...422
References 422

23.1 Biometric Identification

For thousands of years, people have sought to restrict others from having access to certain locations, objects, and information they either own or hold. The traditional means of gaining access to these restricted articles have been the presentation of a password or a key. Little has changed over the years, and although modern passwords may be encrypted or the keys may have become more complicated, the same basic techniques of access are used (Rejman-Greene 2002). Recent advances in computer software and technologies have allowed a new method of identity confirmation and verification to be explored — that of biometric identifiers. Thus, we have moved away from using as a key something that we have acquired to an inborn characteristic of our bodies (Furnell and Clarke 2005).

"Biometric" stems from the Greek *bio* — "life" — and *metric* — "measure." Thus, biometric identification is concerned with the identification of individuals from the measurement of their biological and behavioral features (Furnell and Clarke 2005, Ma et al. 2004, Sanchez-Avila and Sanchez-Reillo 2005, Soutar 2003). Regardless of the surrounding controversy, biometric identifiers are merely measurements of the human body (Mathieson 2005). Indeed, it is the method by which we humans are able to identify ourselves in the everyday world (Furnell and Clarke 2005).

Rejman-Green (2002) summarized the three significant circumstances necessary for the implementation of such identification schemes: (1) the identities of individuals must be fixed, (2) a distinctive and stable physical feature or action that can also distinguish between individuals can now be coded, and (3) automated processes have become available to allow for the comparison of this coded feature or action with a version obtained at the point of registration or enrollment. Crudely put, this process of biometric identification relies on scanning, pattern recognition, and pattern matching (Kemp 2005).

Further developments that have allowed for the advancement and adoption of biometric identification include the increase in accuracy of the technology and the decline of financial costs (Takahashi et al. 2004). In essence, there are three stages to the successful use of modern technology and biometric identifiers to confirm identity: the initial registration and association of a given feature with an identity, the verification of that identity, and the subsequent identification of an identity (Furnell and Clarke 2005, Rejman-Greene 2002, Soutar 2003).

There are a number of distinct advantages to using biometric forms of identification. One of these is that the technique places fewer demands on the users, because they are no longer required to memorize passwords or carry tokens (Furnell and Clarke 2005). Importantly, biometric identifiers also greatly reduce the risk of a compromise of security as a result of lost, stolen, forgotten, or shared passwords, tokens, or keys (Furnell and Clarke 2005, Schuckers 2002, Takahashi et al. 2004). Biometric identifiers also allow for authentication of an individual to go beyond the initial point of entry and provide continuous and dynamic assessment of that individual (Crosby and Ikehara 2004, Furnell and Clarke 2005) — for example, with the use of a computer after initially logging on. Finally, of particular significance is that biometric methods authenticate the individual directly — they are not a proxy for that identity in the way that keys and tokens are (Rejman-Greene 2002).

Unfortunately, there are also some distinct disadvantages to the use of biometric identifiers. For example, whereas a password or token can be right or wrong, present or absent, biometric identification relies on the comparison of an existing template to a captured sample, both of which may be variable to some degree (Furnell and Clarke 2005). An exact match is therefore extremely unlikely (Furnell and Clarke 2005). Conceptually, if this is so, then boundaries of acceptability are necessarily introduced, which in turn allow for the occurrence of false positive and negative matches. Trials have already shown that it is impossible to eliminate these (Hunter 2005). Indeed, these are so universal that they are now used as a measure of accuracy for biometric verification systems (Takahashi et al. 2004).

23.2 Identity Cards and Their Biometric Identifiers

It is important to appreciate that the biometric identity card can only compare presented biometric information with information stored within an existing database, thus taking for granted the identity suggested by the accompanying identifying personal data (Grijpink 2005, Soutar 2003). True identity is established at the moment of registration (Barnes 2004), and this may well depend upon key "breeder documents" such as birth certificates (Soutar 2003), themselves the primary focus of identity fraudsters and the very weak link that these identity cards are trying to remove.

The first question faced when deciding upon the implementation of such a scheme is whether to store the biometric information template in a portable device such as on a smart card or in a centralized database (Mayes et al. 2005). The latter is clearly more useful if the information is to be accessed by third parties (for example, banks or credit agencies) such as with the proposed U.K. scheme (discussed later). Associated with this is the mechanism of comparison for verification purposes. This could be either a one-to-one check, comparing the details of an individual with his recorded details on file, or a one-to-many check, comparing the details of an individual with the entire database in order to ascertain identity (Furnell and Clarke 2005, Mathieson 2005). The former is likely to be the most reliable, whereas the latter is argued to be statistically doomed from the outset (Mathieson 2005).

Identification using the fingerprints, face, and the iris — the key biometric identifiers — are discussed in great detail elsewhere (see Chapters 3, 14, and 15 of this book) and so will not be covered in detail here. Suffice to say, facial images will clearly require frequent updating, whereas fingerprints and iris patterns have been shown to be stable over time (Rejman-Green 2002).

Iris recognition is thought to be one of the most promising areas of biological human identification (Ma et al. 2004, Sanchez-Avila and Sanchez-Reillo 2005). The iris is the region of the eye between the pupil and the white sclera. It has a remarkable structure of minute characteristics, such as freckles, coronas, stripes, furrows, etc. (Ma et al. 2004). These visible characteristics are referred to as the texture of the iris; they are unique to an individual and are thus the subject of identification research (Ma et al. 2004). Methods of identification that focus on the iris can be highly noninvasive (Ma et al. 2004), which, as a consequence, makes it an attractive biometric identifier to users. Although the iris has been shown to be stable throughout life (Ma et al. 2004), the reliability and accuracy of its use as a biometric identifier are greatly improved if the verification equipment has a human operator (Mathieson 2005). This makes it useful for immigration controls but less efficient for lower-value transactions (Mathieson 2005). This is an important consideration for all methods of biometric identification.

Other potential identifiers that could be used in conjunction with biometric identity cards include hand geometry and voice recognition. Hand geometry is similar to fingerprint comparison but is also useful for those who might be unable to provide fingerprints such as manual workers (fingerprints can temporarily wear away), those groups with weaker prints, or those born without prints (Furnell and Clarke 2005, Mathieson 2005, Takahashi et al. 2004). Voice recognition, which uses the rich spectral signal produced by the modulation of airflow by the vocal cords and then filtered by the vocal tract (Trevisan et al. 2005), could also be useful because it is relatively inexpensive and the appropriate hardware already exists (Mathieson 2005). Currently, less feasible modes of biometric identification include the use of facial thermograms and vascular patterning of the palm of the hand (Furnell and Clarke 2005).

The future of biometric identifiers may, of course, lie with DNA. DNA has the potential to revolutionize the use of biometric identification because it is inherently unchangeable, is valid during both life and death, and is intrinsically digital (Hashiyada 2004). Furthermore, the level of discriminatory power can be modified by simply increasing or decreasing the number of short tandem repeat (STR) loci analyzed (Hashiyada 2004). Unfortunately, DNA has not been developed for the identity card application as yet (Schuckers 2002), and currently the main problem with using DNA as a biometric identifier is the length of time required to analyze the samples (Hashiyada 2004). It has also been shown that DNA could be used to identify nonhuman objects, including manuscripts, through the incorporation of encoded DNA in ink (Hashiyada 2004).

Regardless of the biometric identifier used, any combination in a multimodal system will clearly increase the accuracy of any biometric verification undertaken (Takahashi et al. 2004).

Table 23.1 Examples of Identity Card Schemes around the World

Country	Status
Belgium	Compulsory
Greece	Compulsory
Luxembourg	Compulsory
Portugal	Compulsory
Spain	Compulsory
France	Voluntary
Germany	Compulsory
Italy	Compulsory
Austria	Voluntary
Finland	Voluntary
The Netherlands	Voluntary
Switzerland	Voluntary
U.S.	None
Canada	None
Australia	None
New Zealand	None
Haiti	Compulsory

23.3 Existing Biometric Identity Card Schemes

Although the debate surrounding the implementation of biometric identity cards is new and ferocious in the U.K., similar card-based schemes are already widely used elsewhere. Table 23.1 provides examples of countries that use such schemes. It is interesting to note that the U.S. introduced the Enhanced Border Security and Visa Entry Reform Act of 2002 to demand biometric passports for visitors to the country (Mathieson 2005), whereas simultaneously refusing to introduce a biometric-based identity scheme for its own citizens. It is also worth noting, however, that the introduction of these biometric passports will potentially be delayed due to the unconvincing results of trials of biometric identification (Hunter 2002).

The EU has recently agreed that member states will add digitized fingerprints as well as photos to all passports by the end of 2007 (Mathieson 2005). To this roster, the U.K. government wants to add iris scans (Mathieson 2005). The EU presents an interesting social case, because for a number of countries (such as The Netherlands), national identity cards are still associated with wartime Nazi occupation and are thus frequently resisted (Institute for Public Policy Research [IPPR] 1995).

The International Civil Aviation Organization has selected the three more popular forms of biometric identifiers — the face, fingerprints, and the iris — for use within biometric passports (Furnell and Clarke 2005). The problem here is that only the facial identifier is mandatory and, statistically, this is the weakest discriminator of the three, with a 1 in 1,000 false match rate compared to 1 in 100,000 or 1 in 1,000,000 for fingerprints and irises, respectively (Furnell and Clarke 2005). The more accurate fingerprint identifier was trialed in The Netherlands for frequent travelers but was unfortunately abandoned because it was impeding travel too much (IPPR 1995). This, however, may be less of a concern today when compared to the perceived threat of terrorism during travel.

23.4   Biometric Identity Cards in the U.K.

It is interesting to note during the heated debate surrounding the implementation of this scheme in the U.K. that the passports issued in 1915 contained more biometric identifiers than the currently planned identity card database (Mathieson 2005). Those identifiers were far less sophisticated, however, and included measures such as "nose: large" and "eyes: small" (Mathieson 2005). Furthermore, identity cards were issued throughout the U.K. from 1939 until 1953, when the National Registration Act was finally repealed (IPPR 1995). Regardless, the introduction of a universal system of individual identification in today's society would be a profound shift in economic, legal, and cultural terms (IPPR 1995; London School of Economics [LSE] 2005).

Reasons proposed to justify the introduction of biometric identity cards in the U.K. include the reduction of crime, the fight against terrorism, the combating of fraud, and the control and regulation of immigration (IPPR 1995, LSE 2005). Skepticism remains regarding the effectiveness of national biometric identity cards to tackle all of these proposed justifications. For example, the Madrid train bombers carried national identity cards whereas the U.K. government admitted that such a scheme would not have prevented the July 7th, 2005 London bombings (Hunter 2005, Jones 2005). Skepticism also derives from the fact that little research has been conducted into the benefits of identity cards in the countries where they are either compulsory or voluntary (IPPR 1995), see Table 23.1. The London School of Economics adds in their report (2005) that attempts to address multiple, divergent goals such as proposed for the U.K. will never be as successful as a scheme that addresses a clear and focused purpose. For example, the goal of crime prevention may involve applications and functions that may not be appropriate for an identity system that seeks to achieve the goal of the efficient delivery of public services (LSE 2005).

It is important to bear in mind that, by and large, the technology associated with this proposed scheme is largely untested and unreliable (LSE 2005). However, between April and December 2004, the U.K. Passport Service, together with the Home Office and the Driver and Vehicle Licensing Agency trialed the use of biometric identification with 10,000 volunteers. Although this was stressed as a trial of the technology, it could not help but also trial the concept of biometric identification as well. The biometric identifiers used were facial images, fingerprints, and iris scans. An electronic signature was also taken. The trial highlighted some very real problems with the technology, which were the result of positioning, behavioral, and medical problems of the trialists, among other factors. The test also showed that about 90% of individuals were able to register using all three biometric identifiers, this was vastly reduced to 61% for disabled individuals. There were also clear sex- (females verified less successfully), age- (increased age decreased the chances of verification), and ethnicity-related problems (specifically, with the use of facial biometrics; see also Lu and Jain [2004] for a discussion and potential mathematical solution to this very issue). It is acknowledged that many of the limiting factors could well be rectified in the future; nonetheless, the use of biometric identifiers in this large U.K. study stumbled when applied in the real world.

23.5   The Identity Cards Bill

The new Identity Cards Bill proposes a number of changes that would affect the way people currently live their lives in the U.K. Central to the issue of the cards themselves, which under certain conditions can be compulsory under the act, is the establishment of an associated database of personal information. This database would be accessible by state departments and also by certain commercial and industrial bodies for a fee. This is to allow for more secure sales and credit transactions.

A new agency would be established whose responsibility would be to issue the identity cards. It will also incorporate some current functions of the U.K. Passport Service. The plan to combine the new identity cards with driving licenses has been dropped from this current version of the bill. Although the cards would not necessarily be compulsory, it is expected that this will change with time. The cards would store standard information, such as name, address, date of birth, and gender, but also biometric information, such as facial information, fingerprints, and likely iris scans. A national database will be created to store all of this information on U.K. citizens, and a new independent watchdog will be charged with overseeing the whole operation.

The cost of this scheme has been a cause of some consternation; however, the government estimates that the cost to the country will be £93 for a combined identity card and passport. The fee that a member of the public would have to pay for this document is not yet set. It is expected that children under 16 and retired individuals over the age of 75 years will not have to pay anything, whereas discounts are to be offered to low-income families. The report by the London School of Economics (2005) disputes the practicality of these proposals, estimating that costs could escalate up to £19.2 billion, substantially higher than governmental projections.

23.6 Legal, Ethical, and Social Issues Concerning Biometric Identity Cards

What should not be forgotten in this strive for biometric identity cards is that it is the general population that must use them. The potential success of this is currently open to debate. Of note is the recent implementation of "Chip and PIN" in the U.K. Here, it was decided that the next generation of credit and debit card security would be password based, as there was not enough consumer or industry confidence in biometric identification (Furnell and Clarke 2005). This lack of consumer confidence will, no doubt, be related partly to an observed ignorance (Furnell and Clarke 2005) of the techniques and principles of biometric identification and partly to the lack of notably successful examples of biometric identification (Hunter 2005). This lack of public understanding could be problematic because the most effective method of introducing the scheme would be upon a foundation of public trust (LSE 2005). The alternative approach of enforcement through criminal and civil penalties, the stick instead of the carrot, is argued as being far less effective (LSE 2005) and may even introduce an element of resentment from the public.

The general public is also somewhat suspicious of the reasons for the introduction of biometric identity cards, and this is likely due to an unclear and unconvincing argument presented in their defense. There is a great worry that once introduced, an element of "function creep" would occur, thus expanding the purpose of the cards from those initially proposed. Indeed, this perceived function creep was an important contributing factor to the eradication of the previous U.K. identity card scheme in 1953 and the abandonment of a similar scheme in Australia (IPPR 1995). One must not forget that identity cards, and their associated records, are a natural and intrinsic instrument of state control and are thus open to this form of abuse (IPPR 1995); the public is aware of this. Lack of clarity has been a constant problem with governmental arguments for the cards. For example, the U.K.'s Green Paper of 1995 did not describe a purpose for identity cards, and it was left to the reader to assume this from the text presented (IPPR 1995).

There is also some evidence to show that there is a general unwillingness of the public to use certain key biometric identifiers — for example, fingerprint identifiers, due to their association with identifying and arresting criminals, and print sensors due to hygiene concerns (Kemp 2005, Rejman-Greene 2002), or the fear of damage to the eyes from constant iris scanning.

A number of the concerns besetting the introduction of biometric identity cards surrounds not the cards themselves but the associated database, which may pose a greater risk to the security and safety of the population than the problems it is attempting to combat (IPPR 1995, LSE 2005). One of the major concerns that the public has regarding the implementation of such a scheme is the fear surrounding the information that is held by the government about an individual. It will be interesting to see the effect of the new U.K. Freedom of Information Act in this context. Here, the legislation demands increased transparency at all levels of decision-making (Turle and Hordern 2005). Although there are exemptions to the scheme, this nonetheless could assuage some of the initial concerns. This general concern is also very applicable to other countries too. There are real concerns that these cards could be a means of marking and tracking those perceived to be undermining the government. Such an example may be with the recent introduction of biometric identity cards in politically repressed Haiti. Rejman-Greene (2002) even argues that because a biometric template can be traced back to a specific individual, it could be classed as personal data and therefore subject to the provisions of the European Directive on Personal Data Protection of 1995. Further protection for the individual could be offered by Article 8 of the European Convention on Human Rights, which guarantees rights regarding the respect of private and family lives. Soutar (2003) is keen to point out that the privacy issue concerns both the use of biometric identifiers and the potential cross-referencing of the associated database. Hunter's (2005) concern is broader, arguing that the focus of privacy concerns should not be the biometric identity cards themselves, but the overarching privacy framework associated with new and developing technology.

Furthermore, it is possible for these cards to become a means of institutionalizing stratifications and discrimination within a society. For example, in developing countries it may be very difficult for those in remote or poorer regions to travel to the centers of registration of the scheme. If biometric identity cards are needed for key state services, those poorer demographics may again find themselves with restricted access. Efforts must be maintained to ensure equality of access, particularly for compulsory schemes.

Unfortunately, with specific regard to the U.K. scheme, the current proposed legislation may be unsafe in law (LSE 2005). For example, there could be conflict and compromise with Articles 8 (privacy) and 14 (discrimination) of the European Convention on Human Rights, the Disability Discrimination Act, the Race Relations Act, the Data Protection Act, the Immigration Act, and EU Directive 68/360 governing the rights of entry and residence of EU workers (LSE 2005). This is contrary to the statement from the Home Office at the beginning of the Identity Card Bill.

23.7   Conclusions

Currently, biometric identity cards remain one of the most expensive forms of authentication available (Kemp 2005), especially when compared to the perceived "zero cost" of passwords (Furnell and Clarke 2005). A number of key questions also still remain regarding their application. For example, if multiple biometric identifiers are used, as is recommended to increase verification accuracy (Takahashi et al. 2004), what would happen if the biometric identifiers concluded different identities were being offered (Mathieson 2005), and what are the best methods, such as pupil size, blood flow, or electrodermal measures, for confirming liveness in the subject being verified (Crosby and Ikehara 2004)? The introduction of biometric identity cards can only be viewed as a long-term strategy against crime and terrorism; to rush the process will only result in failure (Hunter, 2005). Indeed, current U.K. proposals are far from ready for a swift introduction (LSE 2005). Their introduction may be expedited if they could be linked to uses for the individual other than just state functions (Jones 2005). This, in turn, has further issues, as discussed previously.

No biometric identification process will work effectively across all user demographics (Barnes 2004, Furnell and Clarke 2005). In addition, identity card checks will never be foolproof (Barnes 2004, Grijpink 2005, Schuckers 2002). The main problem here is that one's biometric measurements are permanently compromised if they are compromised at all (Furnell and Clarke 2005, Mathieson 2005); one cannot change them as one would a password. Possible methods of improving the security of such schemes include deritualizing the identity checking process and increasing the variety of biometric identifiers selected for verification (Barnes 2004, Grijpink 2005). It is also important to appreciate that a biometric identity card will verify that someone is the correct person but that this process does not necessarily require knowledge of who they are (Grijpink 2005). Furthermore, it is not the identity card itself that conducts the fraud, but the individual (Grijpink 2005). Arguably, we must focus here if we are to successfully reduce identity fraud. As a final consideration, the system may be flawed, but as Schuckers (2002) argues, normal keys are not discredited simply because they can be stolen or copied.

Despite the current problems, this is an exciting area of research leading to a better understanding of identity, both anatomically and psychologically. It is also worth remembering in conclusion that, unlike other forms of authentication, biometric methods are anything but discreet (Kemp 2005). One's biometric identifier is there for all to see.

References

Barnes, R., The HazMat credential, *Biometric Technology Today* 12(6), 7–8, 2004.

Crosby, M.E. and Ikehara, C.S., Continuous identity authentication using multi-modal physiological sensors, in *Biometric Technology for Human Identification*, Jain, A.K. and Ratha, N.K., Eds., *Proceedings of SPIE — The International Society for Optical Engineering*, The International Society for Optical Engineering, Bellingham, WA, 2004.

Furnell, S. and Clarke, N., Biometrics: no silver bullets, *Computer Fraud and Security* 8, 9–14, 2005.

Grijpink, J., Biometrics and identity fraud protection: two barriers to realizing the benefits of biometrics — a chain perspective on biometrics, and identity fraud: part II, *Computer Law and Security Report* 21, 249–256, 2005.

Hashiyada, M., Development of biometric DNA ink for authentication security, *Tohoku Journal of Experimental Medicine* 204, 109–117, 2004.

Hunter, P., London terrorist attaches heat up identity card debate and highlight uncertainties over their efficacy, *Computer Fraud and Security* 7, 4–5, 2005.

Institute for Public Policy Research, Identity Cards Revisited, IPPR, London, U.K., 1995.

Jones, D., Viewpoint — a tale of two cards, *Card Technology Today* 17(9), 16, 2005.

Kemp, M., Biometrics: the eye of the storm, *Network Security* 4, 11–13, 2005.

London School of Economics, The LSE Identity Project Report, LSE, London, 2005.

Lu, X. and Jain, A.K., Ethnicity identification from face images, in *Biometric Technology for Human Identification*, Jain, A.K. and Ratha, N.K., Eds., *Proceedings of SPIE — The International Society for Optical Engineering*, The International Society for Optical Engineering, Bellingham, WA, 2004.

Ma, L., Tan, T., Wang, Y., and Zhang, D., Local intensity variation for iris recognition, *Pattern Recognition* 37, 1287–1298, 2004.

Mathieson, S., Biometrics: what are they good for? *Infosecurity Today* 2(1), 24–28, 2005.

Mayes, K., Markantonakis, K., and Piper, F., Smart card based authentication — any future? *Computers and Security* 24, 188–191, 2005.

Rejman-Greene, M., Secure authentication using biometric methods, *Information Security Technical Report* 7(3), 30–40. 2002.

Sanchez-Avila, C. and Sanchez-Reillo, R., Two different approaches for iris recognition using Gabor filters and multiscale zero-crossing representation, *Pattern Recognition* 38, 231–240, 2005.

Schuckers, S.A.C., Spoofing and anti-spoofing measures, *Information Security Technical Report* 7(4), 56–62, 2002.

Soutar, C., Recognition versus identity — the role of biometrics. *Biometric Technology Today* 11(6), 7–8, 2003.

Takahashi, K., Mimura, M., Isobe, Y., and Seto, Y., A secure and user-friendly multi-modal biometric system, in *Biometric Technology for Human Identification*, Jain, A.K. and Ratha, N.K., Eds., *Proceedings of SPIE — The International Society for Optical Engineering*, The International Society for Optical Engineering, Bellingham, WA, 2004.

Trevisan, M.A., Eguia, M.C., and Mindlin, G.B., Topological voiceprints for speaker identification, *Physica D* 200, 75–80, 2005.

Turle, M. and Hordern, V., Introduction to freedom of information act, *Computer Law and Security Report* 21, 415–419, 2005.

Missing Persons in the United Kingdom

24

TERI BLYTHE
SOPHIE WOODFORDE

Contents

24.1   Introduction 425
24.2   The Scale of the Missing Problem...426
24.3   Who Goes Missing? 427
     24.3.1   Young People...427
     24.3.2   Abductions 427
     24.3.3   Missing Adults...428
24.4   Why People Go Missing 428
24.5   Police Procedures for Missing Persons..428
24.6   Role of the National Missing Persons Helpline..429
24.7   A Coordinated Response to Missing Persons 431
24.8   Identification within the Context of Missing Persons 432
24.9   Long-Term Unidentified..432
24.10 Who Are the Unidentified? 433
24.11 Standard Procedures for Identification 434
     24.11.1 Case Study 1 435
24.12 Identification and Reconstruction Department of NMPH 435
24.13 NMPH's National Database 435
     24.13.1 Case Study 2 436
     24.13.2 Case Study 3 436
24.14 Forensic Artwork..436
     24.14.1 Age Progression, Image Enhancement, and Long-Term
             Missing Persons...437
     24.14.2 Unidentified Individuals...437
     24.14.3 Postmortem Composites 439
     24.14.4 Facial Reconstruction 439
24.15 Other Identification Techniques 440
     24.15.1 Facial Recognition Software...440
     24.15.2 DNA 441
24.16 Conclusion...442
References 442
Appendix 24.1..443

24.1   Introduction

An unidentified person is most likely to be a missing person.

The Association of Chief Police Officers (ACPO) defines a missing person as "anyone whose whereabouts is unknown whatever the circumstances of disappearance. They will be considered missing until located and their well-being or otherwise established" (ACPO Guidance to Missing Persons, 2005). This broad definition hints at the scale of the problem and the diverse nature of the subjects involved. Many different types of people of all ages go missing in a variety of different circumstances and for a range of different reasons.

In the past, unless the disappearance was suspicious or involved a young child, such an incident was commonly viewed as a private matter and often not considered a serious issue for the police to investigate. According to research carried out by the Home Office in 1999 (Newiss 1999), many police officers indicated that they viewed a missing report as an administrative exercise, especially when the report involved a repeat runaway. However, over the last 15 years, particularly in the U.K. in the light of several high profile missing persons' cases, such as Suzy Lamplugh, Milly Dowler, Ben Needham, and the victims of Fred and Rosemary West, police procedures concerning the recording and response to all missing persons' cases have greatly changed and improved. There is now a heightened awareness among police forces that not only could a missing person's case turn into a homicide investigation but also that missing persons could be vulnerable in other ways and warrant proper assessment and investigation. There is also now a greater understanding of the needs of the families of missing persons, with recognition that they require support and help. It should also be noted that police procedure has been greatly influenced by pressure from the only nongovernmental organization (NGO) dedicated to working in this area, the National Missing Persons Helpline (NMPH).

24.2   The Scale of the Missing Problem

There are no accurate national numbers of missing persons reported in the U.K. Local police forces compile their own figures, and all unresolved reports of missing persons are passed to the Police National Missing Persons Bureau (PNMPB) at New Scotland Yard after 14 days. The PNMPB, however, cannot provide a national figure as the information it holds only relates to cases outstanding for more than 2 weeks. The key organizations involved in missing persons' cases (the Home Office, police, and NMPH) generally agree on the estimate that over 200,000 people are reported missing in the U.K. each year; it is also estimated that nearly half of the reported incidents relate to young people under 18. Although the vast majority of all missing persons return safe and unharmed within 72 hours, a small percentage will have come to harm or will have been victims of crime. It must not be overlooked that the missing person report could be the start of a major crime enquiry.

Of the resolved cases registered each year as "missing" by the NMPH, around 10% are eventually found to have died, and whereas most of these will be identified quickly, some will not. For these cases, every effort needs to be taken to ensure their identity is established and their next of kin informed as soon as possible. As a matter of procedure in any unidentified person's case, an initial enquiry should be the checking of all missing persons' databases for a possible match, e.g., neighboring forces, NMPH, and PNMPB.

It should be noted that not all missing persons are reported to the police. There are a variety of reasons for this. For example, there may be reluctance on the part of family or friends to approach the police; some missing people have no family to report them missing, whereas others may be considered to have drifted out of contact so long ago that it is not appropriate to contact the police. Of further concern, some missing persons' cases may not be registered because they do not fall into the criteria dictated by local police procedures and policies. The assessment of risk directed by these procedures considers issues such as potential for self-harm or suicide, the possibility of the missing being a victim of crime, vulnerability due to age, medical needs, out-of-character behavior, drug or alcohol dependency, etc. This, however, is a dynamic process with further assessments being made as the investigation progresses and as new information and evidence come to light.

As the police tend not to actively look for people except in cases of high risk or crime, they regularly refer "nonvulnerable" cases to NMPH. Other specialized agencies, official and voluntary (for example, the Salvation Army Family Tracing Service), deal with various aspects of the missing persons phenomenon, and although there are a number of statutory organizations and NGOs that play a role in the prevention and management of missing persons' cases (see Appendix 24.1), there is currently no central or single source of general or statistical information on this social problem.

24.3 Who Goes Missing?

Missing people come from all age groups, racial backgrounds, differing social and income groups, and from all geographical areas. They disappear for a variety of reasons and in a range of different circumstances. NMPH considers a missing person to be anyone whose whereabouts are unknown and who is missed.

24.3.1 Young People

According to the Children's Society (Children's Society 1999), each year 100,000 young people run away or are forced to leave home to escape problems. Missing young people face many dangers, e.g., around 40% of young runways sleep "rough" while they are missing and almost one third stay with a stranger. Research has shown that one in eight young runaways has been physically hurt, and one in nine has been sexually assaulted while away (Beihal et al. 2002).

24.3.2 Abductions

Some young people disappear as a result of abduction. Many incidents of abduction (23%) involve the child being taken by one of their parents due to a custody dispute, with slightly more males than females being taken (56%). Successful abduction (rather than attempts) by a stranger or nonfamily member is rare (9% of all police-recorded abductions) with slightly more females than males being taken (54%) (Newiss and Fairbrother 2004). Table 24.1 provides some data concerning the number of recorded offenses of child abduction in England and Wales.

Home Office figures (2002) show that the number of homicides by strangers involving children under 16 has remained constant over the last 20 years, with about 7 occurring each year.

Table 24.1   Child Abduction Definition: Abduction of a Child by Parent/Abduction of Child by Other Persons

Police-Recorded Offenses	2000/01	2001/02	2002/03
Child abductions	546	583	846

Source: Home Office (July 2003), Crime in England and Wales 2002/2003.

24.3.3   Missing Adults

Very little general information exists on missing adults. NMPH commissioned research in this area for two main reasons: there is a dearth of statistical information and analysis on missing persons, and NMPH itself possesses more general information on its unique database than any other organization. The findings of the research, undertaken by the University of York, culminated in the "Lost from View" report, 2002 (Beihal et al. 2002) and included information such as:

- Males in their late 20s are more likely to disappear than any other group of adults.
- Among those aged 60 years or over, the most common reason for going missing is dementia or mental health problems.
- Of adults who go missing, 28% sleep "rough," as do 40% of young runaways.
- Of resolved cases registered with NMPH, 10% are eventually found dead.

24.4   Why People Go Missing

Reasons for going missing vary widely. A large body of empirical information gives some clear causes:

- Family conflict and relationship problems
- Stress, anxiety, depression, or other mental illness
- Amnesia, senile dementia, or Alzheimer's disease
- Alcohol, drug, or solvent misuse
- Illness or accident
- Debt
- Abduction and foul play
- Abuse, sexual exploitation, and trafficking
- Forced marriage
- Some adults simply drift out of contact with their families

There are, of course, some people who make a conscious and rational decision to disappear from the lives of their families and do not want to maintain contact. The right of individuals to go missing is respected and acknowledged by the key agencies involved in the issue of missing persons.

24.5   Police Procedures for Missing Persons

Although individual police forces may have their own procedures, details of all missing persons are generally recorded on the Police National Computer (PNC) within 48 hours of their disappearance. After or within 14 days, police forces are obliged to send notification of all outstanding missing persons to the PNMPB at New Scotland Yard. However, most missing persons are found locally within this period. If there is particular concern for a missing person's case, police forces are encouraged to forward information to the PNMPB in a shorter time period. Additionally, the police should agree on the appropriate level of assistance from the services provided by NMPH (Centrex 2005).

24.6 Role of the National Missing Persons Helpline

Established as a charity in 1992, the National Missing Persons Helpline (NMPH) was set up to support and help the families of missing persons and the missing themselves. As such, NMPH complements and supplements the work of the police, though still protecting confidentiality and independence. NMPH is often approached by the police to publicize cases of vulnerable missing people, help support their families, and cross-match their database for serious crime inquiries.

NMPH helps to make contact with missing people, particularly those who are vulnerable, reuniting them with family members if that is their wish. NMPH respects the confidentiality of all parties and the right of people to go missing; the concern in all cases is for the vulnerable missing person's well-being and safety. NMPH is a unique charity that also assists cases of British nationals thought to be missing abroad and people from abroad missing in the U.K., and is a valuable resource to families, the police, social services, coroners, and hospitals.

A national database of runaway cases, missing persons, and unidentified persons is held by NMPH. This extensive database is maintained, updated, and searched daily both for finding missing persons and for establishing matches with unidentified persons. Due to the high numbers of persons who return safe and well soon after their disappearance, only a small proportion of the total missing persons' reports are made and actively managed cases by NMPH. This figure is likely to rise significantly over the next few years due to implementation of the National Police Protocol (see later in this chapter).

A key method of finding missing persons and identifying unknown people is to publicize the case in the hope that someone may see the publicity and provide information as to the whereabouts or identity of an individual. NMPH works with police press offices and has many media outlets to publicize cases including the local and national newspapers or magazines, television news and documentaries, the sides of trucks (as can be seen in Figure 24.1 and Figure 24.2), the *Big Issue* magazine in the U.K., TV screens on some bus routes, and the NMPH website (www.missingpersons.org). Posters are a regular feature in generating publicity for a case and are an immediate source of publicity that can target specific areas where a person is thought to be from or was last seen in. Two days of the year are now assigned to help highlight the issue of missing: in the U.K. the 15th of May is National Missing Persons Day and the 25th of May is marked as International Missing Children's Day.

In many instances where publicity is sought, a photo or image will help gain interest. In this way NMPH's Identification and Reconstruction Department regularly becomes involved and can produce image enhancements, postmortem composites, and age progressions as described in more detail in the following pages.

In December 2003, NMPH launched the U.K.'s first national database of unidentified persons, available to the public. This is featured on the NMPH website (www.missing-persons.org/unidentified.asp) and contains information and pictures, where appropriate,

Figure 24.1   Together with newspapers, magazines, and posters, other media outlets, such as information printed on the sides of trucks and on milk cartons, can help to publicize a case.

Figure 24.2   Information printed on milk cartons can help to publicize a case.

of unidentified persons (see Figure 24.3). The information includes where a person or body was found and when, a detailed description of that person, and any possessions found near them thought to belong to that individual. Postmortem photos are not shown on the site as it is a publicly accessible site, but when an artist's impression or reconstruction is available, this image is shown. Photos of possessions may also be shown in the hope that they may spark recognition. The aim is to obtain more information that may establish an individual's identity.

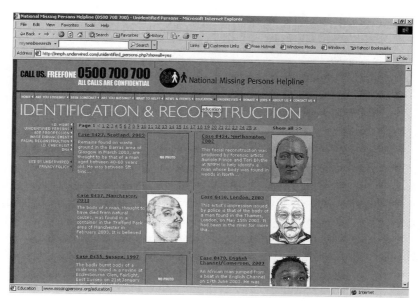

Figure 24.3 The NMPH website includes, within the unidentified section, a list of individuals whose identities have yet to be established. The information given includes where and when they were found, a physical description, and an artist's impression, reconstruction or similar, where appropriate. (See color insert following page 362.)

24.7 A Coordinated Response to Missing Persons

The working partnership between the U.K. police and NMPH came about during a famous investigation, the Cromwell Street enquiry in Gloucestershire. The need for a more comprehensive register of missing people was highlighted after NMPH helped to identify several victims who were not registered with the police. In 1998, NMPH and the Gloucestershire police signed a formal protocol that inspired others, including the National Crime Faculty, to look at their policies and sign up with NMPH.

Commissioned by the U.K. Home Office in 2000, the Compass Report (internal publication) recommended a joint national agreement between NMPH and the U.K. police service. The National Police Protocol was formally approved by ACPO and the Association of Chief Police Officers, Scotland (ACPOS), in January 2005 and is "an agreement between the U.K. police service and the NMPH, to exchange, handle, and respond to issues surrounding missing persons, thereby improving the accuracy of information on all missing persons, furthering public protection and enhancing community safety." The agreement should enhance information sharing and identify similarities and trends to improve coordination of statistics. Part of the exchange of information includes details of unidentified persons (alive or dead) being passed to NMPH for cross-referencing against their database of missing persons.

Although currently there is no obligation for the police forces to contact NMPH, more and more forces are learning about it and its services, and are approaching NMPH for help with identification. The recently published ACPO manual, *The Management, Recording, and Investigation of Missing Persons* (Centrex 2005) encourages police officers to make use of the services NMPH can provide.

24.8   Identification within the Context of Missing Persons

Over 200 cases of unidentified bodies or persons are reported each year. These cases range from scant skeletal remains, such as a foot washed up on a beach, decomposed bodies found in woods, and bodies pulled from rivers to living people brought to the attention of hospitals or social services. The available information about each individual varies enormously and has obvious implications for the speed of establishing identity.

Although the number of cases where an individual is found but cannot be identified is very small, these people have a big impact on the work of the police and those trying to identify them, but more importantly, on the families who may never discover the fate of their relative. It is generally acknowledged by NMPH that the worst part for the families of missing people is not knowing what has become of their relative. This stops families from being able to come to terms with the fact that their relative may have died and from being able to grieve for that person.

In cases of murder or suspicious death, it also proves much more difficult for the police to solve a crime if the individual remains unidentified. Thus, in a murder case it is imperative that the identity of the victim is discovered in order to enable the investigation to move forward.

24.9   Long-Term Unidentified

In many cases, the identity of an unknown person is established within days; however, others may remain unidentified for years. At any one time, there may be as many as 300 cases of unidentified persons within the U.K. that remain unresolved.

Perhaps the best-known example of a long-term unidentified case is "Body 115," the man from the Kings Cross fire of 1987, who remained unidentified for over 16 years. Eventually, he was identified as 72-year-old Scotsman Alexander Fallon who had been living on the streets in London since leaving Falkirk in the mid-1980s and was considered missing by his family.

In cases of this nature, people are often not reported missing until many years after they may have died, if, indeed, they are ever reported. It is not uncommon to receive a report of an unidentified individual thought to have been "living rough" for many years, about whom very little is known. As people with such transient lifestyles may literally have come from anywhere, they may not have been reported missing and may not have a criminal record (and, thus, no fingerprints or DNA on file); it is often almost impossible to identify them. Publicity for these cases does not have a possible geographical target, and even an image of the person may be of little use due to the slim chances of someone recognizing an individual whose appearance may undoubtedly have changed considerably during many years of living rough.

In certain cases, people may not want their body or their identity to be found and may take measures to this effect. For example, the case of the suicide victim whose body was eventually found, almost by accident, in a very isolated and hidden spot in the mountains of Scotland, hundreds of miles from his missing address. No form of identification was found with the body, and even any identifying features of his clothing had been removed. He was eventually identified following publicity of a facial reconstruction produced from his skull.

A further example is the case of a man thought to have mental health problems who was found by police lying in the rain in London. He was taken to a hospital for treatment and attempts were made to establish his identity. Communication with him was very limited, but after many enquiries and database searches of missing persons, and after several months of treatment and care in the hospital, he was identified. It became apparent, however, that rather than being a vulnerable missing person he was actually wanted by the police for criminal damage and domestic violence. By his identity remaining unknown for so long, he had avoided arrest.

24.10 Who Are the Unidentified?

Only a small proportion of bodies found each year remain unidentified for any length of time. Although many are matched to missing persons' cases, a number of the unidentified cases reported to NMPH are later identified as people who have never been reported missing.

Perhaps surprisingly, approximately one third of the unidentified cases reported to NMPH are cases of living individuals such as the "Piano Man" in April 2005 who gained intense media interest. These may be people suffering from amnesia, mental health problems, or people who are unconscious due to an accident or illness.

Figures 24.4 to 24.6 show the demographics of sex, age, and ethnic appearance of unidentified cases held at NMPH. As can be seen, more males than females, a greater

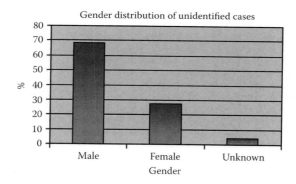

Figure 24.4 The gender distribution of unidentified cases.

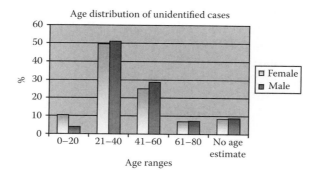

Figure 24.5 Only an indication of age distribution can be given as each individual's age had to be calculated based on the average of the estimated age range given.

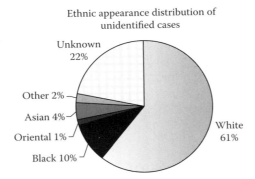

Ethnic appearance distribution of
unidentified cases

Unknown
22%

Other 2%

Asian 4%

Oriental 1%

Black 10%

White
61%

Figure 24.6 Ethnic appearance distribution of unidentified cases.

number of 21–40-year-olds in both sexes, and a higher proportion of people of white ethnic appearance become unidentified persons. This corresponds closely with the reported statistics for missing persons' cases.

24.11 Standard Procedures for Identification

In England and Wales the coroner usually has overall responsibility for the identification of the deceased; however, in most circumstances the police start the initial processes of identification.

Usually, when a body has been found it can be identified almost immediately. This may be due to identification found on the body, location of the body, an address, or witnesses. In cases where an identification is not established immediately, it may only be a short time before the case is confirmed to match a missing person reported to the same local force. If an identification is still not forthcoming, fingerprints or DNA may establish a match, but this can still take time and will only be successful if prints or DNA are held in a relevant database.

The relative rarity of unidentified cases may lead to variations in how they are handled; however, the police guidelines (Centrex 2005) state that in the event of an unidentified person, body, or body part being found, full descriptive details must be entered into the PNC as soon as possible. The local coroner should be informed, and details should be sent to both the PNMPB and NMPH (as their database includes missing persons who are not reported to the police) within 48 hours. It is also usual for forces to circulate details of unidentified bodies or persons to other forces during the early stages of an enquiry. If no identification is made in the U.K., consideration should also be given to circulating details abroad via Interpol.

Once an unidentified case has been reported, the PNMPB and NMPH can compare details of the unidentified body with records held in their respective databases to search for possible matches. Information that is particularly useful in identifying a possible match includes scars, tattoos, jewelry, piercings, clothing, dental details, and photographs of the individual.

Ideally, a full and accurate description of an individual or body is necessary due to the large numbers of missing persons' records with which it will be compared. However, the amount of description available for a body and the comparable information available for missing persons' cases can vary enormously and can have obvious implications for the success of identification.

The factors affecting the amount of description available include how much of a body is found, the degree of decomposition that has occurred, and the presence or absence of clothing or possessions. In cases of living people who do not wish to, or are unable to, identify themselves, their aliases, unusual behavior, local accents, and other distinguishing features may all assist with their identification.

Once a possible match is established for an unidentified body, confirmation may be achieved by comparisons of dental records, fingerprints, and DNA profiling. With the unidentified cases of living people, it is often considered sufficient by the police for relatives to confirm their identity.

24.11.1   Case Study 1

In November 2001, a woman's body was found off the coast of Germany, was estimated to be between 20–40 years of age, and was thought to have been in the water between several months and a year. It was believed that she might have been British due to the manufacturers' names on some of her clothing, and so missing persons' records were checked, but no match was found. Later, photos of the woman's clothing were seen on a poster, recognized by a relative, and her identity was established. Although reported missing, she had initially been ruled out as a possible match due to her actually being in her mid-50s and the fact that she had only been missing 3 weeks when her body had been found.

24.12   Identification and Reconstruction Department of NMPH

Due to the various types of unidentified cases and their circumstances, many and different organizations may be involved in trying to establish someone's identity. The identification and reconstruction department of NMPH regularly liaises with other organizations or individuals when involved in such a case. These include the police, coroners and coroner's officers, social services, hospitals, the PNMPB, scene of crime officers, pathologists, the forensic science service, other forensic specialists and NGOs, and, of course, may include the families of missing persons. The department is routinely asked for help or may have cases referred to it from other sources. It feels that it is not important who determines a person's identity but rather that the identification is made as quickly as possible, both for the family to learn what has happened and to minimize time and expense for those investigating the case.

The department is unique in being able to provide many services to the police and other organizations. These include cross-checking and searching the NMPH national database for both matches against unidentified persons and for extensive police inquiries, such as nonbody murders. The department can also provide various forms of forensic artwork, produce and gain publicity for cases including the unidentified list found on the website, and use up-to-date facial recognition software. These include postmortem composites, image enhancement, facial reconstruction, and specialist child and adult age progressions for long-term missing persons as detailed in the following pages. The staff in the department are ACPO-accredited and trained in forensic art.

24.13   NMPH's National Database

NMPH's database is used to register information on all missing persons and unidentified cases that come to its attention. The database contains powerful searching functionality, allowing users to perform extensive cross-matching searches. As a result of all NMPH enquiry calls being registered and all missing persons' cases being held on a national database, NMPH can provide an additional service to the police through database searches for a variety of enquiries. These are wide ranging but include searches for possible unidentified body matches in nonbody suspected murders, a possible link with a missing person for unidentified possessions, and a possible match in identity fraud cases, etc.

Other cases that should be registered with NMPH and recorded on the PNC are details of identified persons and bodies when the next of kin are either unknown or uninformed. This is important to match cases with families especially if they are reported missing later or if reported missing in another area.

24.13.1 Case Study 2

In February 1994, a man in his early 20s committed suicide by jumping from a bridge. The police were unable to identify his body. When the unidentified body came to the attention of NMPH in May 1997 (having remained unidentified for over 3 years), post-mortem photos were requested and a case file was opened. Upon receipt of the photos, the staff at NMPH immediately recognized the man in the photos as a long-term missing case held on the database. The details of both cases were compared, and his identity was confirmed. The interesting, yet worrying, aspect to this story is that the man had gone missing only a few miles away from the neighboring county where his body was found, and his body was discovered on the same day he went missing. Although this is an extreme example of how an ID can be missed, and cases such as these are becoming much rarer as guidelines have existed for the police, this problem can and does still occur. A similar case was highlighted in October 2005 when a missing man had died less than a few weeks after his disappearance in June 2003, yet his body had remained unidentified and had been held for over 2 years in a different county than where he was reported missing. Unfortunately, although the man was registered with NMPH as a missing person, it had not been informed of the unidentified body so its database had not been searched for a possible match.

24.13.2 Case Study 3

In April 2003 a man's body was found in the sea a few miles off the south coast of the U.K. NMPH took a call from the police requesting forensic artwork of the man to help identify him as the police had no initial idea of his identity. As with all cases of unidentified bodies, the ID department did a database search of all registered missing persons for a possible match before commencing with potentially lengthy artwork. Within minutes a good possible match was suggested, and the missing person's details were forwarded to the police who were then able to confirm the man's identity. NMPH was later informed that although fingerprints from the body had already been checked, they had not returned a match even though his prints were held on file. Only by running a second check based on the possible match were they able to identify the man. The speed in which this individual was identified enabled the police to proceed with the murder investigation much faster.

24.14 Forensic Artwork

Various forms of forensic artwork may help in either seeking the identity of an unknown individual or finding a missing person, as publicizing images of individuals may lead to recognition and, thus, more information about their whereabouts or possible identity.

The success of any forensic artwork is very difficult to quantify. Not only is it largely subjective as to whether an image resembles an individual, but also if the publicity of the image is not seen by anyone who would have recognized the person, a resulting match is unlikely. However, there are many reported cases where forensic art has proved invaluable to an investigation.

24.14.1 Age Progression, Image Enhancement, and Long-Term Missing Persons

The majority of seemingly long-term cases are lost-contact cases, but there are many among them where the circumstances of the disappearance of the individual can either not be explained or their possible whereabouts ever determined. In these cases, using publicity to try to find them may be difficult as their appearance may have altered substantially, particularly in cases of missing children.

For this reason, the techniques of image enhancement and age progression can be used when a more recent image of an individual is required as a method of obtaining up-to-date information as to their whereabouts. Usually, this involves computer-generated manipulation of a photograph to make an individual's appearance change or to make them appear several years older. The resultant images are then used in publicity alongside an original image of the individual to highlight the differences.

Age progression as we know it was developed in the early 1990s at the National Center for Missing and Exploited Children (NCMEC) in the U.S., specifically to aid in the recovery of children who have been missing for more than 2 years. It is also a technique that has been used by the police to aid in the investigation of disappearances of convicted criminals, fugitives, etc., and, more recently, to "age regress" by the undercover police officers working to combat child victimization on the Internet. Age progression also has the added value of offering support to families when it may be felt that very little else can be done on a case.

The availability of good quality photographs is the most important part of the technique and ideally a large portrait-type photo is used. Reference photos of the missing person's parents (in particular, at the age to which the missing person is being progressed) are also essential when age progressing a child and can be very helpful in discerning aging patterns in adults. Most importantly, however, the individual's unique likeness is maintained by keeping his or her facial features key to the image.

Although currently it is a specialized and often time-consuming skill, research is ongoing into more accurate and automated systems of age progression. The current technique has, however, been proven to be effective, and although very difficult to quantify, NCMEC reports that it plays an important role in the recovery of one of every seven children reported missing to them. Figure 24.7 to Figure 24.11 show examples where age progressions have been produced for missing persons' cases.

24.14.2 Unidentified Individuals

Generally, it is considered inappropriate to publicize an image of a deceased individual, not only due to the potential upset caused but also as the individual may not be recognized due to alterations in appearance after death. Forensic artwork is, therefore, a valuable way of creating much-needed publicity and thus increasing the chances of establishing an identity. The aim, as with all forms of forensic artwork, is not necessarily to produce an exact photo of the individual, as this may be extremely difficult, but to produce a likeness that will spark recognition. Used as a tool for recognition rather than proof of identity, forensic artwork can be the key to identification by providing the opportunity for possible matches to be suggested.

Figure 24.7 and Figure 24.8   These children, Ali and Aqsa Mohammed, were the subjects of an alleged parental abduction. Age progressions were produced to use in general publicity and, specifically, in areas where the children were thought to have possibly been taken. Aged 3 in the original photo, the boy has been age progressed to age 8. Aged 2 in the original photo, the girl has been age progressed to age 7. Both age progressions take into account and show the effect of skull growth and development. Original photo reproduced with kind permission from the children's mother.

Figure 24.9   This teenage boy, Kevin Hicks, went missing aged 16 in 1986. Aged 15 in the original photo, he has been age progressed to his early 30s. Although his face had grown to near adult size, the age progression illustrates the more adult, masculine features he is likely to have developed. The original photo of Kevin has been reproduced with kind permission of Kevin's sister. Kevin's parents have both died since his disappearance.

Figure 24.10 This young woman, aged 18 in the original photo, went missing in 1988 and has been age progressed to her early to mid-30s. Photos of her sister were useful reference photos to help give her an up-to-date appearance. Original photo reproduced with kind permission from the family.

Figure 24.11 Aged 17 in the original photo, this man, Jeffrey Allen, who has been missing over 20 years, has been age progressed to age 40. Although he already has a very adult appearance in the original photo, the alteration of hair and clothing (alongside the detail of facial features) has a dramatic effect on his appearance. Original photo reproduced with kind permission from the family.

24.14.3 Postmortem Composites

The amount of artwork required for each postmortem case varies due to the condition of the body. Photos can be altered to show eyes open and remove evidence of pre- or postmortem injuries, and changes can be made to clothing and backgrounds in order to produce a more sanitized image. In cases where injuries are more severe or greater amounts of decomposition have taken place, more work may be needed to "recreate" facial tissues, etc., but the relative proportions of the facial features can be retained from an original postmortem photo. Alternative views or additional images may highlight distinguishing features. Figures 24.12 to 24.14 show examples where forensic artwork has been used to produce postmortem composites.

24.14.4 Facial Reconstruction

In some cases where very badly decomposed or skeletal remains have been found but no identity has been established, a facial reconstruction of the individual may be created to gain publicity (more information on these techniques can be found in Chapter 13 of

Figure 24.12 This man had been severely beaten and stabbed, and had a distinctive scar across his left cheek. The postmortem photo composite provides a sanitized image and the sketch enables his scar to be highlighted, also giving the impression of an alternative possible hairstyle. These pictures enabled police to gain suggestions from the public about this man's identity and more information surrounding the case. The original photo of the deceased male is reproduced with kind permission of Sussex police.

Figure 24.13 Once this man, who was found on a beach on the north coast of Scotland, had been identified (as a man missing from Wales) a photo became available for comparison. It was valuable for future work to note that details such as his broken nose and distinctive lip shape, suggested to have been the result of postmortem damage, were in fact distinctive features of this man. Postmortem photo reproduced with kind permission from the procurator fiscal, Wick. Antemortem photo reproduced with kind permission of the *Western Mail and Echo* (South Wales) and the man's family.

this book). As with other forensic art techniques, the success of facial reconstruction is very difficult to quantify, but many cases have been solved due to the information gained by the publicity of such an image. Figure 24.15 illustrates the three-dimensional facial reconstruction process.

24.15 Other Identification Techniques

24.15.1 Facial Recognition Software

An additional tool for potentially cross-matching unidentified individuals with missing persons is facial recognition software. Advanced biometric software measures for facial proportions, allowing an immediate comparison of a photo or an artist's impression, etc., of an unidentified person to be made against all photos within the database of missing

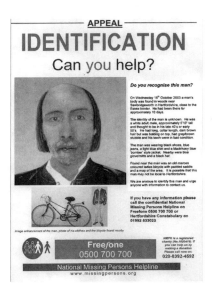

Figure 24.14 After several months of enquiries had failed to identify a man found in Hertfordshire, a postmortem composite was produced and shown in local papers and posters with the hope of gaining more information as to his identity. He was identified immediately by a neighbor, who recognized him from the image. (See color insert following page 362.)

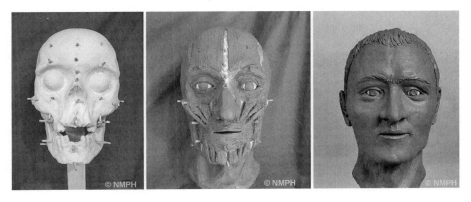

Figure 24.15 The skeletonized remains of an adult male were found in woods in Northampton in 2002. Police investigations, unfortunately, did not succeed in establishing the identity of this man, so a three-dimensional facial reconstruction was produced from the skull, the process of which is illustrated in three stages. It is thought he was "living rough" and his identity has yet to be established. (See color insert following page 362.)

persons. The search can be filtered by such criteria as gender, ethnicity, or age, and the results are presented in order of those people who most closely resemble the "target image." A manual visual cross-check of the closest matches may then highlight cases that should be investigated further. Ideally, a "face-on, head and shoulders" photo would be used; however, positive results are possible with snapshots, CCTV footage, etc.

24.15.2 DNA

As mentioned earlier, once a possible identity has been established for an unknown body, this can be confirmed by the use of DNA, fingerprints, and dental records (more information can be found on each of these subjects in Chapters 1, 3, and 10 of this book). DNA is considered one of the most effective ways of confirming a match, and where two comparable samples are available, this is often the preferred method. Unfortunately, however, although DNA can be taken from unidentified bodies and a search against samples on the National DNA Database (NDNAD) can be carried out, this will only find a match if the individual's DNA is already held in the database — for example, if he or she has been arrested and has had DNA taken by the police.

In certain cases of long-term missing persons, particularly if there is suspicion of their being involved in a crime, e.g., victims of a murder, it may be possible to collect a DNA profile from articles likely to yield such a profile, e.g., an old toothbrush, hairbrush, etc. The sample may then be submitted to the NDNAD as a crime stain against elimination in the future. For this to be applicable, the missing person must be considered to be a suspect in, or to have committed, a crime (Centrex 2005). Unfortunately, for the majority of missing persons' cases this does not happen; however, it is hoped that in the future more matches will be made in this way and a "noncriminal" database will be available for such missing persons' cases.

24.16   Conclusion

It is inevitable in today's society that the "missing phenomenon" will continue. Many different types of people of all ages go missing in a variety of different circumstances and for a range of different reasons, and may even go to extreme lengths to remain missing or anonymous. Some unidentified cases are, however, later identified as people who have never been reported missing at all. What is clear is that with any unidentified person's case, alive or dead, it should be considered early on that they may be a missing person, officially reported or otherwise. Although it is recognized that every adult, unless subject to a section under the mental health act, has a right to "go missing," it is crucial for the sake of the families of missing persons that the identity of every unidentified individual is established as soon as possible. It is also vital to enable an investigation to move forward in cases where foul play is suspected.

As it is often a difficult task to determine someone's identity, multiple organizations may be involved. Although the key investigators in each case are often the police, guidelines now exist that recommend that the NMPH should also be involved in all cases of unidentified individuals, as not all missing persons are reported to the police. In this manner, both databases of missing persons can be checked for any possible matches. If a match is not established immediately, extra services (such as the provision of forensic artwork and help with media coverage) on offer to the police, hospitals, etc., may help lead to an identity.

There are currently no accurate national statistics of missing persons reported in the U.K. It is hoped that, by working toward a more efficient multiagency approach and using all the services available, a greater understanding of why people go missing, and why a proportion of these individuals remain unidentified, will be gained. Eventually, this may help to lessen the number and proportion of individuals to whom this happens.

References

ACPO, Guidance on the Management Recording and Investigation of Missing Persons, Centrex, UK, 2005

Beihal, N., Mitchell, F., and Wade, J., NMPH Report: Lost from View, University of York, York, 2002.

Children's Society, Children's Society Report: Still Running, Children's Society, U.K., 1999.

Home Office, Crime in England and Wales 2002/2003, 2003.

Compass Report 2000 Compass Report, Home Office, Internal publication.

Newiss, G., Police Research Series Paper 114, 1999.

Newiss, G. and Fairbrother, L., Child abduction: understanding police recorded crime statistics, Findings 225. Research, Development and Statistics Directorate, Home Office. Home Office: London, U.K., 2004.

Appendix 24.1

National Organization for the Counseling of Adoptees and Parents (NORCAP)
International Social Services
Reunite
British Red Cross
Salvation Army
Child Focus
British Association for Adopting & Fostering (BAAF)
Centerpoint
Childline
The Children's Society
Crimestoppers
Crisis
The National Center for Missing and Exploited Children (NCMEC)
The Nation's Missing Children Organization & Center for Missing Adults (NMCO)
National Society for the Prevention of Cruelty to Children (NSPCC)
Parents & Abducted Children Together (PACT)
Shelter

Crimes against Humanity and Other War Crimes

25

HELENA RANTA
KARI T. TAKAMAA

Contents

25.1 Introduction 445
25.2 Types of Crimes 447
25.3 Forensic Investigations 449
25.4 Legal Proceedings..450
25.5 Future Developments 451
    25.5.1 Universality of Human Rights and Dignified Handling of
        Human Remains 451
    25.5.2 Harmonization of Investigative Procedures and Training the
        Forensic Experts...452
    25.5.3 The Role of Forensic and Identification Evidence in
        International Legal Proceedings 452
25.6 Conclusion 453
Further Reading...453
End Notes 454

Don't forget, when the killing stops, the genocide is not over ...

Don't forget the survivors ... don't condemn them to a second death ... support them, listen to them; they are our teachers ...

Don't forget the forgotten ... they have no face, no name, no intellect, power, or portfolio ... they were raped in the streets, thrown in the gutter, beaten, hacked ... shot, gassed, burned ... and they only have us ...

And if you must remember anything ... remember for the future.

Stephen D. Smith
"Preventing Genocide — Threats and Responsibilities"
Stockholm International Forum, 2004

25.1   Introduction

During the last 20 years, independent forensic investigations of alleged violations of human rights and breaches of international humanitarian law in international and internal armed conflicts have become more frequent. In many cases, the findings and conclusions of these investigations have also been submitted as evidence in international and national legal

Figure 25.1   The massacre in Katyn, Poland (1940). Photograph #36 in *Amtliches Material zum Massenmord von Katyn*, Deutschen Verlag, Berlin, 1943.

Figure 25.2   Surveying and metal detection in November 1999 at Racak, Kosovo. The site of recovery of 23 victims in January 1999. European Union Forensic Expert Team, Department of Forensic Medicine, University of Helsinki, Finland.

proceedings. Historically, forensic fact-finding has been implemented at sites of recovered human remains, e.g., in Katyn (Poland; see Figure 25.1), in the Ukraine, in Nanking (China), Vilnius (Lithuania), and the former Soviet Union during or after the Second World War. The most extensive of these reports was the German report published in 1943 on the massacre of Polish officers in Katyn, which also named the Soviet Army as a perpetrator.[1] Later examples include exhumations and subsequent investigations by the Argentine National Commission on the Disappeared, the Finnish Forensic Expert Team in Bosnia-Herzegovina (BiH) and Kosovo (see Figure 25.2), the Physicians for Human Rights, *inter alia*, in BiH, Croatia, El Salvador, Guatemala, Iraq, and Turkey, and the International Commission of Missing Persons (ICMP) in BiH and Serbia and Montenegro. In addition, several national forensic teams have worked in Croatia and BiH. The International Criminal Tribunals for the Former Yugoslavia (ICTY) and Rwanda (ICTR) have conducted exhumations and subsequent investigations assisted by international forensic experts. In some instances, the corresponding competent court has evaluated the results, and some earlier cases may still lead to legal proceedings. Some of the cases raised have been set aside because of humanitarian concerns or issues of internal politics involving the accused. Regrettably, due to the nature of the incident, postconflict chaos, or reluctance from the international community, many findings have often been forgotten, and some of them have only recently reemerged and been given some scholarly attention.

The establishment of the International Criminal Court (ICC) as a permanent and independent legal institution in 2002 can be seen as a major achievement in attempts to end the culture of impunity. Recently, the U.N. Security Council (UNSC) has referred the situation in Darfur to the prosecutor of the ICC[2] and the court, and the court has begun proceedings in the case.[3] It has published a list of over 50 Sudanese nationals to be investigated in relation to the situation. The Sudanese government has announced the establishment of a national special tribunal and refused to extradite its own citizens to be tried at the ICC. Moreover, during the last 20 years, several other *ad hoc* tribunals and mixed criminal courts have also been established to investigate and judge in specific areas that have enacted violations against human rights and humanitarian law. They have developed and clarified the applicable international law in their judgments, which form an impressive case law on these matters.

25.2 Types of Crimes

The crimes addressed in this section are principally crimes based on international law. Most of them are stated in international treaties, which have required them to be incorporated also in national legislation of states partied to these treaties. Therefore, some crimes may be found in international law and national law, which results in the situation that the violators of these crimes may be prosecuted in international criminal tribunals or in national criminal courts. Some of the crimes (war crimes) can only be enacted in the time of internal or international armed conflicts (times of "war"), whereas some can also be enacted in times of peace (e.g., crimes against humanity, genocide). The crimes, which are only crimes in the time of peace, are always homicides under national law, but depending upon their (political) context they may be characterized from the point of human rights as, for example, enforced disappearances, arbitrary executions, etc.

The law relating to an armed conflict is currently referred to as international humanitarian law, and its main treaties are the four Geneva Conventions of August 12, 1949 and their two Additional Protocols, which bind the majority of member states. Moreover, several of their rules bind also as rules of international customary law, which means that they bind every state, whether they are parties to these conventions or not. These legal rules governing the conduct of armed conflict between the states are detailed and well developed, covering nearly all the possible situations occurring during an armed conflict. However, there are problems in their enforcement at the areas of conflict, situations which may relate to, for example, the lack of education of their context, lack of discipline of the fighting groups of persons, lack of knowledge of their context or, if intentional, criminal conduct. The legal rules relating to the armed conduct in internal armed conflicts are less developed and also, due to the nature of many conflicts, more frequently violated.

The term *crimes against humanity* is sometimes erroneously used in a moral sense in political discussion. However, from a legal point of view, that use refers to different categories of crime, which are war crimes, crimes against humanity, and genocide. These categories of crime (together with the crime of aggression) are also the categories of crime which fall within the jurisdiction of the International Criminal Court according to its statute (the ICC Statute).[4]

The category of war crimes is extensive and includes (a) grave breaches of the four Geneva Conventions of August 12, 1949;[5] (b) other serious violations of the laws and customs applicable in international armed conflict; (c) serious violations of Article 3 common to the four Geneva Conventions of August 12, 1949, concerning other than international armed conflicts; and (d) other serious violations of the laws and customs applicable in internal armed conflicts. The acts referred to at (c) and (d) do not concern situations of internal disturbances and tensions, such as riots, isolated and sporadic acts of violence, or other acts of a similar nature. As the attention of forensic expert teams is usually focused on the remains of deceased humans, therefore, from the numerous different serious crimes included in the mentioned categories, the most meaningful are the acts of willful killing, directing attacks against a civilian population or protected persons, killing of surrendered combatants, physical mutilations and medical experiments, intentional starvation, and extrajudicial executions, etc.

The category of crimes against humanity in the ICC Statute means any of the following acts when committed as part of a widespread or systematic attack directed against any civilian population, with knowledge of the attack: (a) murder; (b) extermination; (c) enslavement; (d) deportation or forcible transfer of population; (e) imprisonment or other severe deprivation of physical liberty in violation of fundamental rules of international law; (f) torture; (g) rape, sexual slavery, enforced prostitution, forced pregnancy, enforced sterilization, or any other form of sexual violence of comparable gravity; (h) persecution against any identifiable group or collectivity on political, racial, national, ethnic, cultural, religious, gender, or other grounds that are universally recognized as impermissible under international law, in connection with any act referred to in this paragraph or any crime within the jurisdiction of the Court; (i) enforced disappearance of persons; (j) the crime of apartheid; and (k) other inhumane acts of a similar character intentionally causing great suffering or serious injury to body or to mental or physical health.

If these acts are not committed as part of a widespread or systematic attack directed against civilian population, they probably fall within the category of war crimes.

The most serious form of these crimes is genocide, which in the ICC's statute means any of the following acts committed with intent to destroy, in whole or in part, a national, ethnical, racial, or religious group, as such: (a) killing members of the group; (b) causing serious bodily or mental harm to members of the group; (c) deliberately inflicting on the group conditions of life calculated to bring about its physical destruction in whole or in part; (d) imposing measures intended to prevent births within the group; (e) forcibly transferring children of the group to another group.

The legal context and the aims set forth for the investigations may affect the methods chosen and applied in the investigations. Medicolegal investigations of violent death naturally have to follow the best practices in the forensic science for every investigated case. However, the impact of the conflict and aims may affect these investigations at least in a few ways: (1) For example, it may be that the already autopsied bodies by other forensic "actors" may be reautopsied to ensure that the evidence found can be verified;[6] (2) if the aim is not to identify the remains found at the mass graves, but instead, to concentrate to establish evidence on the nature and scale of these atrocities, the type and amount of samples taken may be smaller than in the situations in which there is also an aim to create basis for later identification of the remains of each individual body; and (3) relating to the previous example, it may also be necessary to establish the minimum number of individuals in a given mass grave and through different sampling techniques to investigate only portions of each mass grave.[7]

25.3   Forensic Investigations

In addition to the categories of crime and bases for action for the law enforcement and courts, the law also provides the context in which the forensic investigations are to be enacted. The different types of forensic teams may include professional high-profile teams that may serve the interests of international or intergovernmental organizations and low-profile voluntary groups working under human rights and nongovernmental organizations. This chapter will concentrate mostly on the former kind of teams.

In cases where the team's mandate is given by an international or intergovernmental organization, experiences achieved through functioning in conflict areas highlight the crucial importance of clearly and sufficiently defining the mandate for the team (and the aims and the tasks following from it). The mandate and the aims set forth for the project, and means given to meet these aims, are crucial for the planning of the team's formation and activities. On their basis, the project plan is prepared for the team, and this plan guides the team's work during the project. It is an internal team document, which may contain, for example, lists of experts and equipment needed, the logistical support arrangements, general plans for investigations at different sites, etc. Moreover, there are several other legal issues relating to the establishment of a team, which require the numerous agreements of different kinds to be concluded with several contract parties. For these arrangements sufficient attention is recommended to avoid unnecessary surprises later.

Among the most important issues relating to the establishment of a team are the agreements and arrangements to be concluded with the host state. The term *host state* refers to the state in whose territorial area investigations are to be conducted. These documents usually may govern and affect the actual functioning of teams and experts in the target areas of the host state. At negotiations, strict impartiality and independence must be maintained. The host state must guarantee unhindered access to any sites and freedom to investigate any alleged atrocity enacted against individuals of parties to the conflict; give the right to exhume the alleged mass graves and to investigate the alleged sites of atrocities; and grant the right to perform the forensic investigations, including full-scale autopsies, and to take appropriate samples for further examination. Moreover, the host state bears also the responsibility for the security arrangements and the immunity of the experts. Naturally, this does not exclude the possibility of making arrangements on security, logistics, transportation, etc., with the operating peacekeeping units or representatives of the international community present in the area.[8]

Security risks are always present in this kind of work. In some instances, the importance of a forensic team may not be fully recognized by parties of the conflict or even by international entities searching for a settlement in the conflict. The work may also involve strong political and publicity pressures. However, for the accomplishment of its duties, a forensic team can only act by maintaining the highest professional standards and relevant ethical codes of the scientific community concerned, and restricts its conclusions solely to its area of expertise,[9] trying to avoid the unnecessary publicity relating to its work.

Forensic experts may also be asked to be a part of an international fact-finding team whose task may be to gather factual information on a certain incident or issue for further political decision-making and to offer a basis for reaction to it. These teams have a different task, which is naturally reflected in their structure and working methods, in the expertise required of them, and in the nature of the final report on the designated tasks.[10]

Not all forensic teams are professional high-profile teams. Despite of the nature of a team, the basic working principles are nearly identical at sites of investigation. While creating these teams, the persons in charge have to be careful. It has sometimes occurred that the rights of these teams to function have (for several reasons) not been arranged sufficiently. There have also been a few rare cases in which they have not been formed from forensic experts, which in some cases may have endangered the use of their results in legal proceedings. These missions, usually organized by nongovernmental organizations and private organizations, are important tools that may also be used to disclose hidden atrocities. These "clandestine" investigations may be helpful, especially in revealing human rights violations, but they can also, in some instances, be counterproductive.[11] However, when conducted under an international criminal tribunal or established professional organizations like the International Committee of the Red Cross (ICRC) and Physicians for Human Rights (PHR), and under strict observance of professional competence and applicable best practices of forensic conduct, their results have been of great value for international criminal tribunals.

Even if the team's mandate does not necessarily always involve the aim to provide evidence for later criminal proceedings, it is advisable to plan and exercise the team's activities in such a manner that the facts found and the materials produced could be used in court proceedings, if that becomes possible. Therefore, it is advisable to take into consideration different requirements that follow from these aims, like ensuring the admissibility of the teams' work and findings, for example, by maintaining the strict chain-of-custody procedures at every stage of the investigation.

Moreover, before the team begins its work at the sites, the handling of human remains and their burial after the investigations has to be generally planned and arranged with the local authorities.

25.4   Legal Proceedings

It is probable that the findings and results of the forensic expert team are at some point of time used as part of the legal proceedings in international or national courts. Therefore, as this phase may happen several years after the investigations are completed, it is important to make sufficient preparations for possible later legal proceedings before the team concludes its functions. These preparations may make it easier to return to the material several years after the conclusion of the work, if necessary.

The procedural rules applied in international proceedings are quite often a mixture of rules from different legal traditions, and they may vary slightly from one tribunal to other. Therefore, forensic experts testifying in these proceedings may consider the rules governing their conduct, while submitting evidence and giving the testimony that is partially familiar and partially new or different. Before submitting materials or giving evidence, the expert should become thoroughly acquainted with it.

The task of the forensic odontologist, forensic pathologist, forensic anthropologist, and identification scientist at the international criminal proceedings is usually to act as an expert witness.[12] This means that they are to give factual information on the investigations enacted at the site or sites relevant to the court proceedings. All the conclusions and comments are therefore to be limited strictly to the professional sphere and competence of the expert witness. All comments going beyond that sphere are "layman comments" and do not fall within the role of an expert witness, even if the defense counsel or the prosecutor may propose or encourage this kind of conclusion to be made. The situation does not change even if experts are invited to testify for the prosecution or defense team as long as they are heard as expert witnesses. It is not the task of expert witnesses to build the case or fill the gaps in the evidence for the defense or the prosecution; instead, they are expected to provide facts and scientific conclusions solely based on these facts. It is the role of the defense and prosecution teams to connect those materials to other available evidence, and the task of the judges of the court or tribunal concerned to decide what legal conclusions the presented forensic material might support or what possible circumstances they may exclude in the possible scenarios of chain-of-actions.

The situation may be different if the experts have, during their activities in the host state, seen some circumstance relevant to the proceedings that does not relate to their professional work but may be important for the criminal court or tribunal. On those matters they should be heard separately as normal witnesses. For these situations, if necessary, international experts have also developed effective witness protection measures that may protect the identity of the witness whose security may be endangered by testimony. Naturally, these measures do not concern the expert witnesses, as their role is different in the proceedings.

25.5 Future Developments

25.5.1 Universality of Human Rights and Dignified Handling of Human Remains

The evolving concept of the universality of human rights is in development to include the view that these rights be extended to the deceased in the form of dignified handling of human remains and burial. This view is also becoming widely accepted within the forensic science community. The interpretation has its roots in the ethical code of forensic science and is, in addition, partially based in the legal framework of international human-itarian law.[13] This necessary code of conduct is also emphasized in the recently published recommendations (best practices) of the International Commission of the Red Cross.[14] Moreover, the recent resolution of the U.N. Commission on Human Rights 2006, on "Human Rights and Forensic Science"[15] explicitly addresses the dignified handling, proper management, and disposal of human remains, in addition to respect for the needs of families. These developments should ensure that samples taken from the human remains are removed solely for investigation of the manner and cause of death and for the identification of the deceased.

These codes of conduct also imply that the possibilities for identification of recovered human remains should be ensured, for example, by preserving data and possible samples for later identification, wherever possible, when forensic investigations are conducted. The identification procedures may include different methods. Basically, it is important to gather extensive postmortem data. This includes all forensic information available from human remains and the site of recovery. The collection of antemortem data for comparison is frequently organized by international and national nongovernmental humanitarian and human rights organizations. Their role can be supplementary and often crucial in provid-ing data of individuals unaccounted for. Today, different DNA methods can be used in identification. Therefore, after completion of the pedigree, DNA samples from selected potential family members should be collected for identification.

Figure 25.3 Temporary graveyard at Gornje Obrinje, Kosovo, in December 1998. European Union Forensic Expert Team, Department of Forensic Medicine, University of Helsinki, Finland.

Besides the connected implications of human rights, the remains of the victims deserve the last rites of their own traditions and religion and are to be buried in proper graves with their own and true names identifying each grave (see Figure 25.3). This conduct is also an important part of the reconciliation process and, therefore, the costs of identification procedures should be made available during the early stages of reconstruction and normalization of any broken society.

25.5.2 Harmonization of Investigative Procedures and Training the Forensic Experts

The experiences of different teams conducting forensic investigations in conflict areas have established that the procedures followed in these operations should be harmonized as much as possible to ensure that the work done meets the required professional standards of the work. In cases of inadequate investigative procedures due to insufficient expertise or suspected bias, an independent commission should undertake the investigations. Moreover, the differences in national procedures and legislations, and the level of forensic sciences in different nations, are also reflected in the work done in the international sphere. The most basic requirement is that the persons doing that work should be properly educated experts of forensic sciences. Naturally, a number of persons training in these fields can also be included in the work as supporting roles.

25.5.3 The Role of Forensic and Identification Evidence in International Legal Proceedings

The forensic investigations of crimes against humanity and other war crimes could be more clearly incorporated into the doctrines regarding legal means of settling international and national disputes or internal crises. The investigations have become one of the tools for producing factual information on the treatment of civilian populations in conflict and crisis areas. In addition to their possible role as a basis for policy-making decisions at the international level, such investigations may also have an impact on issues of responsibility and criminal liability for acts committed. In connection with other supporting and incriminating evidence and other materials, the results of properly conducted forensic investigations may offer a solid basis for a prosecutor to establish a case. This kind of forensic evidence, which in practice is unchallengeable, also has certain limitations. However, it can be used, for example, in valuing the circumstantial or other evidence, and to exclude alternative explanations that, when plausible, are not supported by it. However, mere forensic evidence can never establish issues of liability and guilt. These decisions are to be left to the appropriate legal institutions to emerge through fair and impartial legal proceedings after criminal investigations are completed.

This fact has to be acknowledged by the public, the media, the international community, politicians and diplomats, the lawyers, and, most important, by the forensic experts involved. As moral and political judgements are not based on scientific expertise, they are private opinions and should be understood as such. Thus, experts following the highest scientific standards of their profession cannot be expected to comment on their investigations or derive political implications from their results. All parties should honor this view, based on a clear principle of code of conduct, which in many countries may also have been affirmed in the form of legal obligation. This principle also honors the privacy of the victims of the crimes and protects the emotions of the survivors and their relatives. No specific details of these investigations relating to individual persons should therefore be given out or publicized by the press. When they are addressed in legal proceedings, the issue is often regulated by the legislation on publicity of the official documents and the use of the public material is also regulated by courtesy and the ethical standards of the media.

25.6 Conclusion

Forensic investigations of crimes against humanity and other war crimes, including eventual identification of recovered human remains, are important not only from the legal point of view. For the survivors, having lost their family members and loved ones and possibly being subject to discrimination, sexual abuse, or other violence, it is imperative to learn of their fate and, in the worst cases, when there is no hope of finding them alive, whether their remains are among those recovered. They have the right to know in order to rebuild their lives, to look toward the future, and most importantly, to break the vicious circle of hatred and revenge which otherwise is so easily passed to future generations. Moreover, the demands of justice require that at least the major perpetrators, wherever possible, are to be punished for these atrocities. These legal consequences are also important both for preventive reasons and for establishing the proper historic record of these atrocities. Biological human identification forms an important component of this motion toward justice.

Further Reading

Bass, G.J., *Stay the Hand of Vengeance: The Politics of War Crime Tribunals*, Princeton University Press, Princeton, NJ, 2000.

Bassiouni, M.C., *Introduction to International Criminal Law*, Transnational Publishers, Ardsley, New York, 2003.

Cassese, A., *International Criminal Law*, Oxford University Press, Oxford, 2003.

Dörmann, K. et al., *Elements of War Crimes under the Rome Statute of the International Criminal Court*, Cambridge University Press, Cambridge, 2003.

Executive Summary on the Work of the European Union Forensic Expert Team in Kosovo, the Federal Republic of Yugoslavia in 1998–2000, Helsinki, 2000.

Gutman, R. and Rieff, D., Eds., *Crimes of War: What the Public Should Know*, W.W. Norton and Company, New York, 1999.

Hayner, P.B., *Unspeakable Truths: Confronting State Terror and Atrocity*, Routledge, New York, 2001.

Hedman, M.H., Identification of Finnish Soldiers Left to the Battlefield in the Soviet Territory during 1939–44 Wars Using Mitochondrial DNA-Sequence Analysis, M.Sc. thesis, Department of Forensic Medicine, University of Helsinki, Helsinki, 2002.

ICRC, Operational Best-Practices Regarding the Management of Human Remains and Information on the Dead by Non-Specialists: For All Armed Forces; For All Humanitarian Organizations, ICRC, Geneva, 2005.

Interpol, *Disaster Victim Identification Guide*, Interpol, Lyon, France, 2003.

Jurovics, Y., *Réflexions sur la spécifité du Crime contre L'Humanité*, L.G.D.J., Paris, 2002.

Kittichaisaree, K., *International Criminal Law*, Oxford University Press, Oxford, 2001.

May, L., *Crimes against Humanity: A Normative Account*, Cambridge University Press, Cambridge, U.K., 2005.

The Medical Profession and Human Rights: Handbook for a Changing Agenda, British Medical Association, London, 2001.

Ratner, S.R. and Abrams, J.S., *Accountability for Human Rights Atrocities in International Law*, 2nd ed., Oxford University Press, Oxford, 2001.

Schabas, W.A., *Genocide in International Law*, Cambridge University Press, Cambridge, 2000.

Takamaa, K.T., From Kradjik to Racak and Orahovac: Selected Legal and Practical Issues Relating to the Work of International Forensic Fact-Finding Teams [currently a classified document], Helsinki, 1999.

United Nations, Guidelines for the Conduct of United Nations Inquiries into Allegations of Massacres, United Nations, New York, 1995.

http://www.un.org/icty, International Criminal Tribunal for the Former Yugoslavia, accessed 8/19/06.

http://www.ictr.org, International Criminal Tribunal for Rwanda, accessed 8/19/06.

http://www.icrc.org, International Committee of the Red Cross, accessed 8/19/06.

http://www.sc-sl.org, The Special Court for Sierra Leone, accessed 8/19/06.

End Notes

1. See, *Amtliches Material zum Massenmord von Katyn*, Deutschen Verlag, Berlin, 1943.
2. Security Council Resolution 1593 (2005), March 31, 2005, SC/RES/1593.
3. ICC Doc. The Presidency. Decision assigning the situation in Darfur, Sudan to Pre-Trial Chamber 1, ICC 02/05.
4. Actually, this illegality of these crimes is derived from several international treaties, international customary law and case law of international tribunals. For the case of simplicity and available limited space, the authors have decided to limit the presentation to the Statute of the ICC. See the Rome Statute of the International Criminal Court, U.N. Doc. 2187 *UNTS* 90 et seq.
5. They are: Geneva Convention (I) for the Amelioration of the Condition of Wounded and Sick in armed Forces in the Field 1949, 75 UNTS (1950) 31-83, UKTS 39 (1958), Cmnd.

550; Geneva Convention (II) for the Amelioration of the Condition of Wounded, Sick and Shipwrecked members of Armed Forces at Sea, 75 UNTS (1950) 85-133, UKTS 39 (1958), Cmnd. 550; Geneva Convention (III) relative to the Treatment of Prisoners of War, 75 UNTS (1950) 135-285, UKTS 39 (1958), Cmnd. 550; and Geneva Convention (IV) relative to the Protection of Civilian Persons in the Time of War, 75 UNTS (1950) 287 et seq., UKTS 39 (1958), Cmnd. 550.

6. This is rare, but has happened, e.g., in investigations enacted by the International Criminal Tribunal for Former Yugoslavia at several situations. An example is the Finnish Expert Team Kosovo 2000, a different team from the Finnish/EU Forensic Expert Team, which has became famous in several contexts and has enacted autopsies under and for ICTY in 2000. Part of these autopsies were reautopsies done for already once autopsied human bodies, done for specific internal reasons of ICTY, not disclosed to the members of the Team.

7. This may be necessary, e.g., due to the security situation at the sites and/or the limited available resources for these activities. Then the aim is to provide basis for the possible legal proceedings to be conducted in the future. This does not exclude proper full-scale medicolegal investigations to be done later, when the security situation is different.

8. Unfortunately, in many cases, due to the nature of escalating crisis, it is not always possible to follow these necessary and crucial prerequisites. There have been situations in which the legal status of a particular team has remained unclear and in which some team may even have functioned without proper authorization and security guarantees. In these situations, the most vulnerable are the voluntary groups that may have easier access to the hidden sites but which may take risks of being arrested or even prosecuted for having conducted allegedly illegal exhumations. The official, high-profile teams' leaders, their country of origin, and the authorizing international organization can exert pressure on governments aiming to prevent their proper impartial functioning in the area.

9. Accordingly, drawing any political conclusions or suggesting any implications never belong to the professional sphere of the sole forensic team or expert. The nature of the task thus differs from the one of a politically designated entity, whose purpose and mandate under international law usually related to a specific dispute. If the team is required to make such conclusions, then this has to be stated in its mandate, and it has to affect its formation as then the team's task can include more elements from traditional fact-finding activities under international law. In those cases, the team has to comprise a mixture of professionals from different disciplines and may include forensic, legal, political, and other experts. A typical example of these activities is the U.N. Secretary-General's Expert Mission of Jenin, launched in 2002. See, for example, U.N. document report of the Secretary-General prepared pursuant to General Assembly resolution ES-10/10.

10. This difference is evident as it does not fall within the competence of a proper forensic team or an expert to comment on issues, e.g., on who the eventual perpetrators are, which party of the conflict they represent, or why certain victims are executed. The mere human remains and physical evidence, the focus of forensic investigations, can disclose only a limited number of facts. Observations of and conclusions on any possible chain of action should therefore always be based on other forms of evidence and facts.

11. Many jurisdictions may only allow registered medical practitioners in that country to conduct medico-legal autopsies. Therefore, failure to follow the national legislation of the host state, if the exhumations are not authorized, can be considered as an offense or used as an excuse to challenge the information provided.

12. The expert may be a witness for the tribunal, or a witness called by either the prosecution or the defence team. Whoever the requesting side is, that should not affect to her/his testimony as an expert witness in any manner.

13. See, e.g., Articles 32–34 of the I Additional Protocol to the Geneva Conventions of 12 August 1949, 1125 UNTS (1975) 3-608; UKTS 29 (1999), Cm. 4338.

14. See, e.g., ICRC, publication *Operational Best-Practices Regarding The Management of Human Remains And Information on the Dead by Non-Specialists: For All Armed Forces; For All Humanitarian Organizations*, ICRC, Geneva, 2005.

15. U.N. document, Office of the High Commissioner for Human Rights. Human Rights and Forensic Science. Human Rights Resolution 2005/26, 61 CHR, E/CN.4/RES/2005/26, 4/20/2005. This resolution was adopted without a vote at the 61st session of the U.N. Commission on Human Rights.

Section 10

**Forensic Human Identification
Case Studies**

The Rolex Murder, Southwest England

26

PHILIP SINCOCK

This case study concerns one of the most unusual murder investigations ever undertaken by the Devon and Cornwall police forces. The investigation hinged on a variety of identification techniques relating to both the victim and the perpetrator of this heinous crime. The case itself has been the subject of a number of books, documentaries, and television films.

At 3:30 p.m. on Sunday July 28, 1996, John Copik and his son Craig were fishing six miles off the south Devon coast in a trawler called the *Malkerry* (Figure 26.1). It was not a successful day, and the crew had caught few fish, despite trawling their nets twice along the seabed. Taking in the nets for a third time, however, they were excited to see the net was bulging with fish and seemed the best catch they had made in months. The net was lowered over the deck and emptied but, as the fish slid onto the boat, the fishermen made a gruesome discovery. Among the catch was the dead body of a man dressed in a blue checked shirt, green trousers, and brown shoes. He was about 40 to 50 years of age but facially unrecognizable due to decomposition.

The Coastguard was informed, and the body landed at Brixham Quay, where the local police officers would commence the investigation to identify the remains and ascertain the circumstances of death. A forensic pathologist conducted a full autopsy, and the cause of death was found to be drowning. The body showed two injuries, a large bruise on the left hip and a deep laceration to the back of the head. The head injury was severe enough to render a person temporarily unconscious but would not have proved fatal. In the opinion of the pathologist, the injuries could be consistent with a person slipping on the deck of a boat, striking his head, and falling into the sea, and drowning. Such boating accidents are not uncommon off the large expanse of coastline around the Devon and Cornwall area.

The police needed to identify the man, inform relatives of his demise, and, through lines of enquiry, ascertain how he came to be at sea, satisfying themselves that there was no question of "foul play." Unfortunately, nothing in the clothing assisted the identification process, and, perhaps unusually, there was nothing at all in his pockets. He did have a tattoo on the back of his right hand (Figure 26.2) that appeared to be groups of stars joined together to form a shape like a large leaf. He had a silver-colored Rolex Oyster selfwinding watch on his right wrist. The watch had stopped, showing a time of 11:35 and the calendar date 22.

There were no such persons reported missing locally; enquiries with cross-channel ferries, shipping lines, and fishing fleets were negative. No trace existed on the national database in respect to the man's fingerprints or DNA, indicating that he was unknown to the police. There was no match with any person listed on the Police National Computer (PNC), no one reported missing in the country, or any details held by the National Missing Persons Helpline. There was no trace against the index of tattoos held on the PNC in

Figure 26.1   The *Malkerry* fishing trawler.

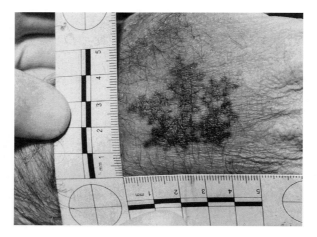

Figure 26.2   Tattoo on the back of the hand of the body recovered from the sea.

relation to persons known to the police nationwide. Media assistance was sought, and the story of the "mystery of the Rolex man" was widely circulated with pictures of the watch and his tattoo, but no one came forward with any suggestions as to the man's identity.

The weeks passed with no information coming to light that would suggest anything other than that the death was not suspicious, but probably a boating accident. The police had exhausted all conventional means of identification, but a mortuary technician suggested the Rolex watches had unique serial numbers, and this might well be an avenue of enquiry.

The Rolex manufacturers were contacted and stated that the serial number was engraved on the shoulder of the watch underneath the area where the bracelet joined the watch itself. They kept records in relation to all watches, including details of repairs and services. The watch was forwarded to Kent for examination and, in due course, Rolex confirmed that it had been serviced or repaired on three occasions in 1977, 1982, and, most recently, in 1986. On all occasions the owner was recorded as a "Mr. Platt" from various addresses in Harrogate, West Yorkshire (Figure 26.3). Investigations at these addresses revealed the man was Ronald Joseph Platt, born on March 22, 1945, his last known address being a rented property at 100 Beardsley Drive, Chelmsford, Essex.

Figure 26.3   Ronald Joseph Platt (left) and a National Service picture of Platt (right).

Platt left the Chelmsford address on June 21, 1996, some 5 weeks before his body was pulled from the sea in south Devon. He left no forwarding address, but a check of the renting agency file revealed that in order to obtain the accommodation, Platt had given the name and mobile telephone number of a reference. The reference was given by someone called David Davis but showed no current address. With no other obvious leads, a detective telephoned the mobile telephone number and spoke to David Walliss Davis.

David Wallliss Davis told the officer that Ronald Platt was a friend and business associate whom he had last seen in Chelmsford at the end of June that year. Platt had borrowed £2,000 from him to travel to France and start a business. The arrangement was that, when Platt had set himself up, he would contact Davis, advise him of his whereabouts, and arrange to repay the loan. He had not heard from Platt since that time. Davis was shocked that his friend had been discovered drowned off the Devon coast and could offer no explanation as to why he had been there. He volunteered to attend Chelmsford police station and give any detail to assist in his friend's identification.

By arrangement, David Walliss Davis visited the police station and was interviewed by a detective sergeant. Davis was a tall and smartly dressed man in his early 50s with a strong American accent. He was very concerned about the demise of Platt and very helpful, giving much detail, including the fact that Platt had recently returned from Canada, having tried to emigrate on a permanent basis. Platt had a tattoo of a maple leaf, the national emblem of Canada, on the back of his right hand, and, although Platt was not wealthy, his prized possession was an old Rolex Oyster watch. He had been brought up in Canada as a child and had always wanted to return. He had a long-term girlfriend called Elaine Boyes who had emigrated with him, but the relationship had failed in Canada, and they had separated. Platt had been in the Army in the 1960s on National Service (see Figure 26.3). Davis left, saying that if he could help further, he could be contacted at his home, Little London Farmhouse, Woodham Walter, near Chelmsford.

The service file of Ronald Platt was obtained from the Army and inside was his medical record, which detailed a maple leaf tattoo on the back of his right hand and also a dental chart from 1963 (Figure 26.4). Dr. Hugh Walters, a consulting oral and maxillofacial surgeon, confirmed the identity of the deceased as Ronald Joseph Platt by comparing the teeth of the deceased and the chart from these records (Figure 26.5).

Figure 26.4 Ronald Platt showing tattoo and wearing Rolex watch. (See color insert following page 362.)

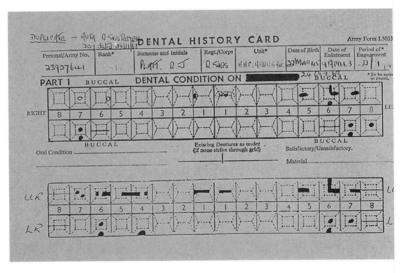

Figure 26.5 Dental chart.

One question remained before this case could be filed: Where was Platt between June 21, when he left the address in Chelmsford, and July 28, when his body was recovered from the sea? The detective who interviewed David Walliss Davis was asked to visit him and obtain more details, including a written statement for the subsequent coroner's inquest. The officer made an understandable, but in this case lucky, mistake by calling at the wrong house. Instead of Little London Farmhouse he called at the next-door property, Little London House. The elderly gentleman who answered the door pointed out the officer's mistake but asked who he wanted to see. The officer informed him that he wished to see David Davis. "There's no David Davis living next door," said the man. "I have known the people next door for 3 years. They are Mr. Ronald Platt and his young wife, Noel Platt. They live there with their two young children, Emily and Jane." "The Mr. Davis I want to see is a tall man with an American accent," said the detective. "That's right," said the neighbor, "Mr. Ronald Platt is tall and American, he's a businessman who deals in stocks and shares. He's obviously doing well for himself because he has a yacht down in south Devon." It seemed to the officer that the man he saw at the police station, David Walliss Davis, was using the identity of the dead person dragged from the seabed off south Devon and that he owned a yacht moored in the same area of the country. The officer persuaded the neighbor to remain silent concerning his visit and withdrew. He did not confront Davis but reported his findings back to colleagues in Devon.

Over the next few weeks, Devon detectives put David Walliss Davis "under the microscope." Discreet enquiries were made with passport authorities, the Inland Revenue, the U.K. Department of Social Services, utility companies, banks, and credit card companies, as well as immigration and the registrar of births, deaths, and marriages. The only record existing of David Walliss Davis was held by the immigration authority and related to a person of that name who was recorded as emigrating from the U.K. in 1945, destination unknown, and had never returned. Every other enquiry, however, confirmed that the man who had posed as Davis had been using the identity Ronald Joseph Platt for the past 3 years. The births of the children, Emily and Jane, had been registered with the father being Ronald Joseph Platt, and the mother listed as Noel Platt (also known as Elaine Boyes). During the 3 years concerned, the real Ronald Joseph Platt was living in Canada. Davis had obviously stolen the identity of his friend Platt.

The real Elaine Boyes, girlfriend of the deceased, was traced and interviewed by the police. She was shocked to hear of the death of her ex-boyfriend but was able to give some useful background information. She had a long-term relationship with Platt and in 1990 was working as an auctioneer's assistant at a gallery in Harrogate. She was asked to show some expensive paintings to an American called David Davis and, during this, he engaged her in a lengthy conversation. He was a charming man with whom she felt at ease, and he seemed very interested in her life history, her relationship with Platt, their wish to emigrate to Canada, her interests in photography, and foreign travel. At the end of their conversation he offered her a job working for his company, "The Cavendish Corporation." Her duties would involve traveling throughout Europe to inspect business opportunities such as investment properties and paintings. She would photograph these and bring them back to the U.K. for further consideration by Davis, who would pay her more than her current earnings at the auctioneer's, and in cash, as he had "issues" with the Inland Revenue.

Elaine Boyes considered Davis to be a charming American who might also be an eccentric millionaire and persuaded her boyfriend, Ronald Platt, that she should take the job. They met up with Davis and his attractive young wife, Noel, and Elaine started the duties as described, meeting the couple socially on a frequent basis. Boyes made many trips to European countries for Davis, with Platt sometimes accompanying her, and took photographs of business opportunities. On each trip she was also given packets of money, which were usually French or Swiss francs, and he asked her to deposit them in various bank accounts while she was in certain countries. It is clear that Davis was involving her in some form of money laundering operation, but she was either too naïve to realize this or put it down to his being an eccentric millionaire.

On December 25, 1992, Boyes and Platt spent the day with David and Noel Davis. During the celebrations, Davis handed them an envelope in which, he explained, was a Christmas present for his two good friends. Opening the envelope, Platt was excited to find two airline tickets to Canada. Davis explained that they could now start their new life together as they had always wanted, and he would settle all their debts, start them off with some working capital, and take care of their outstanding business in the U.K. They could emigrate to Canada fully equipped for their new life. Davis explained that in order to settle outstanding bank and credit card debts he would retain possession of Platt's driving license, checkbook, and credit cards.

In March 1993, Platt and Boyes used the tickets and flew to Calgary, Canada. As things did not go well and Platt could not get a job, their relationship suffered, and she returned to the U.K., leaving Platt on his own. She heard that Platt also returned later, having run out of money. She had not seen him, as their relationship was over, but she knew that he had renewed his contact with David Davis.

During the police interview with Elaine Boyes, she asked the officers whether David Davis was aware that Platt was dead. The officers told her that they had informed Davis some weeks earlier. She looked deeply shocked, "I spoke to David Davis on the phone just last week, and I asked him how Ronald was. He said that he hadn't seen him since the end of June." Davis had not mentioned the fact that Devon police officers had informed him that his friend had been dragged from the seabed. Davis had lied to Elaine Boyes, and a further revelation was about to occur.

As part of the discreet investigations into Davis, detectives had applied for the itemized billing accounts for his mobile telephone. These records arrived on the same day that officers were interviewing Elaine Boyes, and caused more suspicion about Davis and his account of events. Cell site analysis showed that all calls from Davis's mobile in July were made while the phone was in south Devon. Investigations into the subscriber details of telephone numbers called during this time led officers to discover that a man calling himself Ronald Platt, but described as a tall charming American (Davis), had stayed at a hotel in Totnes, south Devon, during July. He was accompanied by another man who had little to say but was remembered as having a tattoo on the back of his hand. Further enquiries revealed that Davis and his wife, Noel, together with the two children, had also stayed in a nearby rented cottage, leaving on July 23.

Detectives now knew that Davis had been using the identity of the dead man, he had lied to Elaine Boyes and the police about the last time he had seen the deceased, and he had been in the south Devon area in the days leading up to Platt's death. He also, on the account of a neighbor, had a yacht moored in south Devon and, therefore, the means to deposit Platt in the sea. There was good reason to suspect Davis had something to do with the death, but exactly what had happened? The cause of death was drowning, but if this occurred as murder, what was the motive? Davis had been using the identity of Ronald Platt, which was obviously false, but the identity of David Walliss Davis was also false. What was his real identity, and what reason did he have for hiding it?

At 10:30 a.m. on October 31, 1996, undercover detectives watching the home of David and Noel Davis in Woodham Walter saw a taxi arrive at the front door. Davis emerged from the house, got into the taxi, and directed it toward Chelmsford. Armed officers stopped the car and ordered Davis to get out. He stepped out with his hands over his head and said calmly, "Good morning, officers, can I help you?" He was arrested on suspicion of the murder of Ronald Platt, taken to the local police station, and searched. In his possession were credit cards, a checkbook, and other documents in the name of Ronald Joseph Platt, as well as a birth certificate and identity cards in the name of David Walliss Davis.

The officers returned to the house and arrested Noel Davis on suspicion of murder. She was also very calm but asked if she could take a bag for her baby whom she was still breastfeeding. They agreed, but were suspicious at the weight of the bag. On checking it, they found that under the baby clothes was £10,000 in cash and two ingots of solid gold. She was removed to the police station, and a team of officers commenced a painstaking search of the house.

The search proved to be time-consuming, as the house contained a wealth of documentation in the names of Ronald Platt, David Davis, Noel Davis, Elaine Boyes, and various other identities. The total number of documents seized was enough to fill the back of a transit van. The officers were amused to find a number of brown envelopes concealed around the house that were variously filled with £50 notes and French and Swiss francs, together with more gold ingots. The total value of cash and gold seized amounted to £250,000.

Davis, his wife, and the exhibits seized from the house were driven to south Devon so that detectives could question the couple about the death of Ronald Platt and find out their true identities. Noel Platt was evasive but stated that she met her much older husband while studying in the U.K. He had been a friend of her father's, and they got together. The reason for using Platt's identity was that Davis's ex-wife hired a private detective to find them to seek a large alimony settlement. She claimed that Davis was from the U.S., and his ex-wife was a famous gynecologist. Davis, on the advice of his solicitor, refused to answer questions on any subject put to him. The custody clock was ticking and, despite frantic investigations, no further evidence to implicate them in a murder was obtained.

In the U.K., the police may hold a suspect for a maximum of 36 hours before either charging them with an offense or releasing them. The magistrate's court can authorize a further 60 hours in the most serious cases where the suspects need to be detained for further questioning. The magistrates reluctantly agreed to the extra detention, despite the fact that the defense for Davis strongly claimed that there was insufficient evidence to prove that Davis had murdered Platt, and there was no evidence to say that Platt had been murdered in the first place.

During the period of extra detention, it was decided to release Noel Platt on police bail. She would be kept under observation, and she would find it difficult to abscond as she had a child and a young baby, her husband was in custody, the police had all their money, and she had no transport. This allowed officers to concentrate on David Davis and pursue enquiries to link him with the death.

Davis's yacht, the *Lady Jane,* was discovered in dry dock in Essex. It had been removed from its mooring on the River Dart in south Devon some weeks earlier on the instructions of Davis. Initial forensic examination of the yacht revealed not a single fingerprint, and it was ascertained that it had been steam cleaned on the instructions of Davis. The yacht was transported to the forensic science laboratory for detailed examination, but the results would not be available before the extended detention time for Davis had elapsed. Time was running out. If Davis were not charged, he would have to be released. Checks on his fingerprints and DNA were negative; his prints were forwarded to the U.S., but again the result was negative. Who was Davis? Why had he used the identity of Platt? Why and how had he killed Platt? What was behind the large amounts of cash, and where did the gold ingots come from?

Having reviewed the available evidence, it seemed to the Crown Prosecution Service that it could not be proved that Platt had been murdered. The only evidence to connect Davis was his use of Platt's identity, his lies to the police, the fact that he had a boat, his suspicious wealth, and his refusal to answer any questions. Under the circumstances, they recommended that he be released. Detectives investigating the case, however, had a "gut feeling" that there was something very sinister behind this case and that if Davis were released, they would never see him again. Despite legal advice and the protest of the defending solicitor, Davis was charged with murder and remanded in custody for a week. The Crown Prosecution Service was clearly uneasy with this decision and stated that if no further evidence was forthcoming by the following week, they would have no alternative than to withdraw the prosecution and have Davis freed.

The pressure was now back on the investigating officers. Where would they find the evidence and the answers to the many questions concerning Davis and his involvement with Platt? As with all good police work, the first step is to go right back to the start. The start of this investigation had been the trawler *Malkerry* and its skipper, John Copik, who had been interviewed by a junior officer at a time when the death was not thought to be suspicious. John Copik was reinterviewed in detail. He repeated how the body was trawled from the seabed at the same time as a "bonanza" catch of fish and spoke of the debate that occurred on deck before the Coastguard was radioed. (Under regulations a body recovered in this fashion would mean that the fish must be discarded.) "We decided to do the right thing because it was suspicious," said Copik. "He had a nasty injury on the back of his head, and his trouser pockets were turned inside out." This was the first time the officers were aware of the pockets being turned out; it clearly supported a theory of foul play in terms of someone removing items from the body and, to Copik's amusement, they became quite excited. "If you are excited about that wait until I tell you about the other thing that was in the net when we dragged the body up!" said Copik. "What other thing?" asked the detective.

"There was a small plough anchor stuck in the net, the sort you would use on a small boat or yacht," replied John Copik. "Why on earth didn't you tell us about this at the time?" the officer demanded, as this was clear evidence of foul play in terms of the body's being weighed down. Back came the answer, an object lesson in police work: "You didn't ask, boy."

The anchor was recovered from a friend of Copik who was intending to sell it at a "car boot" sale, and it was forwarded to the forensic science laboratory. It was a 10-lb So'wester plough anchor suitable for use with a small boat such as a dinghy or speedboat but not suitable for a yacht the size of the *Lady Jane*.

At about this time, the defense, with the smell of victory in their nostrils, demanded a second autopsy on Ronald Platt, who was removed from cold storage for that purpose. On examination, it was discovered that, as often happens, another injury had become visible since the first autopsy. In addition to the bruise on the left hip, there was also a bruise just above the left knee. When the plough anchor was placed against the two bruises, the length of the anchor corresponded exactly with them. It seemed clear that the anchor had been slipped inside Platt's trouser belt so that it was worn like a sword, and this was evidence that the death was definitely murder. Forensic scientists later found deposits of zinc similar to the coating on the anchor on the inside of the left-hand side of the belt recovered from the body, and fibrous material similar to the belt on the shank of the anchor. There was now conclusive proof that Platt had been murdered; the next stage was to prove by whom.

Officers in the investigation incident room had been tasked to sift through all the documentation seized from the house in Woodham Walter, a long and painstaking undertaking, but a vital one in the search for evidence and identification. They found a small duplicate cash register receipt relating to a purchase made on the July 8, 1996, at a shop called *Sport Nautique* in Dartmouth, south Devon. The purchase was made with a Master Card in the name of R.J. Platt and related to seven items of yachting equipment, including a 10-lb So'wester plough anchor. Detectives visited the shop and the owner remembered the transaction. The man had been a tall, charming American who wanted the anchor for his yacht, but the staff were confused because it was the wrong weight for his type of craft, which required a 20-lb anchor and, also, that he did not want any chain to go with it. These types of anchor would not function unless a length of chain was attached prior to its being fixed to the rope. What could he possibly want this anchor for?

A search of the *Lady Jane* yacht revealed that all other six items from the sales receipt, complete with their Sport Nautique bar-coded price labels, were in the cabin. The only item missing was the 10-lb plough anchor. Police could now prove that Davis had purchased an identical anchor to the one used to weigh down the body of Platt in the days leading up to his death, but when did Platt die exactly?

The Rolex watch that had been instrumental in identifying the body was bench tested by the company. It would be remembered that the watch was self-winding and would, therefore, wind down and eventually stop sometime after the death of the wearer. When the body was recovered the watch read 11:35 with the date 22 in the calendar window, and the body was estimated by the pathologist to have been in the water for between 1 and 2 weeks, having been recovered on July 28. Testing showed that the watch took 44 hours to wind down, which proved that Ronald Platt entered the water and drowned at some time on July 20, 1996.

Meanwhile, the officers searching through the documents back at the incident room had discovered another interesting piece of paper; a receipt for a storage container issued to "R. Platt" in September 1996 by a company in Northampton. Detectives traveled to Northampton, obtained a search warrant from magistrates, and looked in the container. Inside were some furniture, paintings, £10,000 cash, more gold ingots, and an Apelco GXL 1100 Global Positioning System (GPS) display unit. A GPS is an incredibly accurate navigational device used on vessels that works by triangulating its position on the globe, using radio waves transmitted by U.S. space satellites. It had been noticed that the GPS handset was missing from the *Lady Jane* yacht, so this handset was taken to the manufacturers to see if any information useful to the investigation could be obtained from it.

The handset retains in its memory the coordinates of its position at the time it was last switched off; these coordinates were downloaded from the handset and plotted on a nautical chart. The officers were excited to see that the coordinates related to a place six miles off the south Devon coast in exactly the same area as where the body of Ronald Platt had been recovered. This showed that Davis's yacht, the *Lady Jane*, had been in the exact area where Platt met his death. The officers could not retain their excitement any longer

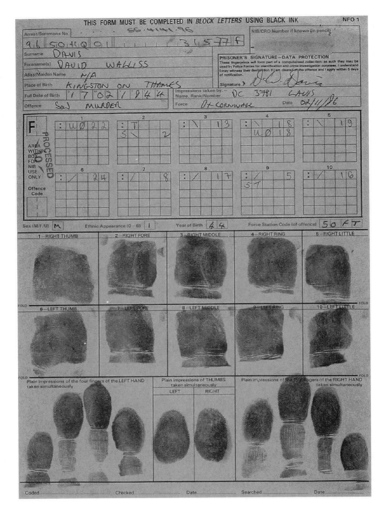

Figure 26.6 Fingerprints taken of Davis.

when they were told that details of time and date were also included in the retained data within the device. This was downloaded to show that the yacht was in that location at 8:59 p.m. on July 20, 1996. The police could now prove that Davis's yacht was at the murder scene on July 20, which was the day the murder, as evidenced by the Rolex watch examination, had occurred. The evidence against Davis was building, but why had he killed Platt? How could officers prove he was on the yacht on the day of the murder, and who was he? Was the true identity of Davis the key that would unlock the answers to all these questions?

Detectives were dismayed that the fingerprints of Davis (Figure 26.6) were not on record, but they widened their search by sending a copy of the prints to all countries that had been mentioned for any reason in the whole of the investigation to date.

Meanwhile, more good news arrived from the forensic laboratory in relation to their painstaking search of the *Lady Jane* yacht. Inside the cabin, a crumpled plastic carrier bag marked "Sport Nautique" had been examined, and the fingerprints of the victim, Ronald Platt, had been found on the bag. Furthermore, three head hairs attached to a piece of

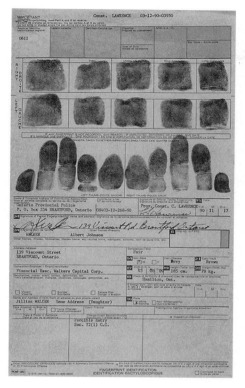

Figure 26.7 Fingerprints taken of Walker.

cellular material had been discovered on a cushion inside the cabin of the yacht. These were the subject of DNA comparison and were a virtually identical match with the deceased. Experts could give evidence that these head hairs had been removed from the head of Ronald Platt as a result of some form of trauma, such as a blow to the head, rather than the normal process of hair being naturally shed.

Telephone calls from Interpol and the Royal Canadian Mounted Police provided the final piece of the jigsaw in this case and answered the many questions that had perplexed the investigators. The fingerprints of Davis (Figure 26.6) forwarded to Switzerland, as one of the countries mentioned during the enquiry, had been identified as Albert Johnson Walker, born on March 22, 1945 (Figure 26.7). He was wanted in Canada on an international arrest warrant for numerous offenses of multimillion-dollar fraud, was fourth on the list of Interpol's most wanted fugitives worldwide, and was Canada's "Most Wanted Man." Walker had defrauded elderly investors of their life savings in Canada and absconded from that country 6 years earlier in 1990, taking with him his 15-year-old daughter, Sheena Walker. Despite investigations for over 6 years by Interpol, the Royal Canadian Mounted Police, Ontario Provincial Police, and private detectives hired by Mrs. Walker to locate her missing daughter, Albert Walker and Sheena disappeared without a trace.

Now that they knew the true identity of Davis, detectives visited his young wife, who had returned to Chelmsford with their two children. They had barely noticed the uncanny resemblance between the photograph of the missing 15-year-old Sheena Walker and the 21-year-old Noel Davis, but another revelation in this case seemed inevitable. She told the officers that she was, indeed, Sheena and that she had been on the run with her father for the past 6 years, using the name "Davis" from a birth certificate that her father had stolen from a financial client in Canada. They had survived under this flimsy false identity for over 2 years but were looking for a more tangible identity when Ronald Platt came on the scene and was persuaded to emigrate to Canada, leaving behind his driving license, birth certificate, checkbook, and credit cards. On his departure, they had become "Mr. and Mrs. Ronald Platt." She had two children but would not speak about the parentage. Her father's money and gold could be laundered through the Platt bank account and the company he started, the Cavendish Corporation.

When asked about Ronald Platt's return to the U.K., she told the officers that he had returned without money and, homeless from Canada, had looked to his old friend, David Davis (now also called Ronald Platt) to help him. They had gone to south Devon on holiday in July and, once there, her father had been with her all the time, except for one day. On this day, he told her that he was going sailing on the *Lady Jane* alone. He was gone all day and came back very late at night, at which time she noticed that he was disheveled and nervous about something. She did not know what day this was, but remembered that she had spent the evening watching the opening ceremony of the Atlanta Olympic games. Detectives found the final piece of the evidential jigsaw; when checking the television schedules they discovered that the date was July 20, 1996 — the same day, from the examination of the Rolex watch, that Platt met his death and the same day, from the examination of the GPS, that the *Lady Jane* was at sea in exactly the same place as Platt was dispatched to his watery grave. With Sheena Walker's evidence, they could now put Albert Walker on the yacht at that time. The puzzle was complete.

Albert Johnson Walker, an accomplished fraudster wanted for multimillion-dollar theft, absconded from Canada with his 15-year-old daughter and lived on the stolen money, using a birth certificate in the name of David Walliss Davis to evade capture. He met the gullible Ronald Joseph Platt through Platt's girlfriend, Elaine Boyes, befriended them, and assisted them to achieve their dream of emigrating to Canada. Using Platt's identity documents and bank cards, they were now safe with a tangible identity as "Mr. and Mrs. Platt." Walker could launder the stolen money through the Platt accounts, set up a company, buy a yacht, and live the good life with a beautiful young wife and children. But the plan went wrong when the real Ronald Platt returned like the proverbial "bad penny." There were now two Ronald Platts and that was one too many. The whole façade that Walker had constructed to prevent capture was under threat. One of the Platts had to disappear — and it was not going to be Walker.

Walker invited his friend Ronald Platt for a holiday in south Devon where they could go sailing together on his yacht, the *Lady Jane.* Once 6 miles out to sea, he struck Platt a heavy blow to the back of the head, rendering him unconscious. He removed everything from Platt's body that might identify him in the unlikely event that the body was ever found — everything, that is, except the Rolex watch. He slipped the 10-lb anchor he had bought from Sport Nautique some 12 days earlier down the trouser belt of Platt and placed him over the side, where he sank slowly to the seabed and drowned.

Albert Johnson Walker was tried at Exeter Crown Court in 1998 and convicted of the planned and callous murder of Ronald Joseph Platt. He was sentenced to life imprisonment because he made one mistake. Leaving the Rolex watch on the wrist of his victim had provided the police with the means of identifying the body, which, in a one-in-a-million chance, had been dragged up in the nets of the *Malkerry*. Platt rose from his watery grave and pointed the finger of his tattooed hand at his killer, not his good friend David Walliss Davis, but the thief and accomplished con man Albert Johnson Walker. This started the whole chain of events that hinged on the work of identification scientists employing discovery methods involving property, documents, fingerprints, DNA, dental examination, and personal witness accounts. This led to the collapse of Walker's house of cards and brought him to justice for the murder of a gullible but innocent man.

The "Adam" Case, London

27

WILL O'REILLY

Contents

27.1 The Finding of the Body...473
27.2 The Postmortem 474
27.3 Initial Forensic Examinations 475
27.4 Advanced Forensic Investigations...476
27.5 The History of the Red/Orange Shorts...................................483
27.6 The Enquiries in Nigeria 483
27.7 Conclusion 484

Once or perhaps twice in their careers, detectives may come across a case so challenging that it has a lasting impact not only on the way they investigate crimes in the future, but it also influences how policing in general approaches specific major investigations. Such an investigation started in 2001 and is still ongoing.

27.1 The Finding of the Body

The body was first spotted by a London commuter as he walked across Tower Bridge from north to south just after 4 p.m. on Friday, September 21, 2001. At first, he thought that the object moving fast on the incoming tide was a wooden beer barrel but, as he looked closer, he realized that it was, in fact, a small human torso dressed just in a pair of bright red-orange shorts. He called for the police on his mobile phone. September 2001 was a significant time for London. Just after the terrorist outrages in America (see Chapter 28), the city was at a high level of alert, and his call was answered by one of the patrolling police boats. The crew police constables, Mark Rigby and Gregor Watson, commenced a search and eventually recovered the body some 20 minutes later near the Globe Theatre on the South Bank. In those 20 minutes, the torso had traveled approximately a mile on the strong upstream tide.

Both officers are experienced in dealing with human remains found in the river, but this was different, as the head, arms, and legs were missing (Figure 27.1). The torso was placed in a body bag and taken to Wapping Police Station. A forensic medical examiner was called and at 6:22 p.m. officially confirmed life extinct.

I was the on-call senior investigating officer for the Serious Crime Group South. This is a group of experienced detectives whose role is to investigate all homicides and unexplained deaths south of the River Thames. Two similar units cover the larger northern area. It had been a long week already when my pager went off around 6 p.m.; the only details given were that a male body had been recovered under suspicious circumstances. I turned the car around and headed for Wapping Police Station, ruing

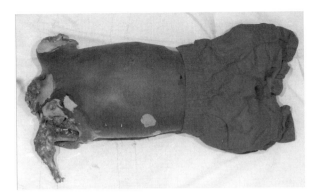

Figure 27.1 The torso removed from the Thames. (See color insert following page 362.)

the intricacies of the currents. Why wasn't it recovered on the northern side? After all, most are suicide jumpers. When I got there, my view changed quickly. This tiny torso had obviously been intentionally dismembered; this was not the result of a boating accident. A murder investigation was commenced, and the rest of the evening was taken up with organizing a river search and a review of the current missing persons reports. I expected to identify the child at a very early stage, the victim perhaps of a domestic murder. To show the child respect and personalize his remains, we decided some months later to name him "Adam."

27.2   The Postmortem

Often, the most significant clues in any investigation arise from the postmortem. This took place at Poplar Mortuary the following morning, Saturday, September 22, 2001. It was conducted by Dr. Michael Heath. The examination itself was lengthy, taking some 5 to 6 hours. Dr. Heath concluded that the body was of a well-nourished male with amputations of the head, neck, and upper and lower limbs. He gave an estimation of age from bone measurements as 5 to 7 years and an estimation of height as just under 4 feet. This height estimation is the same as the size of the shorts worn and consistent with an age of the wearer between 6 and 7 years old. Dr. Heath gave the cause of death as an incised wound to the neck and went on further to describe a "sticking" action with the sharp edge of the knife facing away from the spine. In his opinion, the amputations were made after death in a very skilled manner with knives kept sharp and a heavier instrument such as a cleaver to cut through the bones. There was no sign of sexual interference, and the child had a full, well-healed circumcision. There was nothing of substance in the child's stomach.

Dr. Heath, in a debriefing after the examination, went on further to describe the cutting motion to the neck as similar to a ritual animal slaughter, death ensuing very quickly from massive and violent blood loss. There was no blood left in the child, raising the possibility that "Adam" was held either upside down or at least horizontally at the time of his death. The pathologist gave an estimated time in the water of between 2 to 5 days. The upper epidermis skin layer had started to peel off. Taking into account that the river is at its warmest in September, Dr. Heath, who has examined many bodies recovered from the Thames, stated that at 10 days he would expect to see no sign of this layer. He also adduced that the shorts were placed on the child after death and after dismemberment. It was the pathologist at this meeting who first raised the possibility that the child may have been the subject of a ritual murder.

Many motives were considered for the murder of Adam in those early days: domestic, mercy, stranger, sexual, and others more obscure. However, in considering these, it became increasingly difficult to give any adequate explanation as to why the child had not been reported missing. Other unanswered questions were: Why was the child dressed in bright fluorescent shorts after death and dismemberment, and why were the body parts not hidden in the normal way in bags before disposal? In seeking answers to these questions and others, the National CATCHEM database was consulted. CATCHEM is a database of all child murders in the U.K. over the past 40 years. The search found that a six-part dismemberment of a child under the age of 7 years is unique. The reasons given are that a child of this age is so small that a complete body can be hidden easily for disposal and that weight is not an issue. The other reason for partial dismemberment is to hide identity, but there is no benefit to the removal of the arms and limbs in a young victim.

Other than those initial remarks by Dr. Heath, our attention was first drawn to the possibility of a ritual murder or human sacrifice by callers to the very first *Crimewatch* program. A number of callers suggested that the murder was similar to *muti* murders in South Africa. A little research found that these murders are not uncommon in that country. *Muti* is the Zulu word for "medicine." Human body parts are taken normally while the victim is alive. (It is believed that their cries awake the ancestors.) The parts are then given to a *sangoma* or witchdoctor who mixes these with various herbs and animal parts, depending on the requirements of the customer.

Enquiries with the South African police revealed that a specialist police squad had been set up just to deal with those murders involving a ritual element. An exact figure is not known, but hundreds come to the attention of the police each year. This liaison identified a pathologist, Prof. Hendrick Scholtz, head of the Department of Forensic Medicine, University of Witwatersrand, Johannesburg.

Prof. Scholtz accepted an invitation to come to the U.K. to complete a second postmortem on Adam. Scholtz agreed in all areas with Heath and added that the incised wound is in keeping with the bleeding of the body prior to death. Importantly, he concluded that the wounds, clothing, and mechanism of death are consistent with those of ritual murder as practiced in Africa. Since the initial examination by Prof. Sholtz, there have been four subsequent examinations, mainly for the removal of organs for forensic examination.

27.3 Initial Forensic Examinations

John Birkett is a forensic scientist specializing in implement marks. At the first postmortem, a decision was made to dissect the stump bones on the amputated limbs. Once these were defleshed, they were examined by Birkett, who concluded that all the bones bore the marks of a heavy blow by a knife or machete in an attempt to sever the limbs. The ends of the bones were fractured rather than cut through. On both humeri he found evidence of score marks around the circumference of both ends, suggesting that a sharp knife had been used to cut through the flesh and expose the bone prior to being chopped.

Andrew McKinnon is a forensic scientist specializing in toxicology. He screened samples for drugs. The only unexplained substance he detected was Pholcodine. This is a pharmaceutical opiate-type drug normally in the form of a medicine used to treat coughs.

The presence of the drug was found in small quantities in muscle tissue and at a very low level in the stomach contents. Pholcodine is used widely in the U.K. and elsewhere as a constituent part of proprietary, over-the-counter cough medicines. The presence of the drug in the child is somewhat puzzling; it either shows a period of caring before death or perhaps use as a lubricant to assist consumption of a ritual-type potion later found in the intestines of Adam. Another explanation offered by cultural advisors is the belief in the need for a perfect specimen in human sacrifice for best possible results. There was only a very small amount of fluid found in his stomach, which suggests a period of fasting or starving before death.

Geoffrey Roe is a forensic scientist specializing in biology. He was able to obtain a full DNA profile of Adam from deep muscle tissue. He examined the various sexual swabs and confirmed that there was no evidence of any sexual interference. Some fibers were found from tapings, but these took us no further. The Thames is awash with all forms of detritus, and various types of fibers and hairs would adhere to a floating object. He found some discrete areas of bloodstaining that matched the profile of Adam. No other match was found.

27.4   Advanced Forensic Investigations

The position in January 2002 was that conventional forensics had been exhausted but had not taken us much further in establishing identity or the context of the crime. Various motives were still under consideration including, increasingly, that of a ritual, even a domestic murder carried out in a traditional, ritualistic way. Our main concern was that we had still been unable to identify the victim, despite national and international appeals. A large reward of £50,000 was on offer, to date the highest the Metropolitan Police has ever offered. We had ruled out all the missing persons reported in the U.K. and had extended our enquiries to include Europe and beyond. We had written to every doctor and school in the U.K. and followed up a large number of referrals. Unfortunately, we were still no nearer to identifying our victim and were therefore missing a vital area for investigative opportunities.

A meeting was then arranged at Bramshill, the National Police Training College of forensic scientists and senior detectives, posing the question, "Can advancements in science help us to discover Adam's background?" At that stage we knew the child had dark skin but we did not know whether the family origins were Asian, Caribbean, African, or, for that matter, from anywhere else. A forensic strategy was agreed upon that, to our knowledge, had not been used anywhere else in the world before. Various scientists at the forefront of their specialties were instructed in this strategy, and further samples were obtained from the body of the child and handed over.

As the first part of the strategy, the first area we looked at was the then-new idea of familial searches. Through Specialist Advisor Ray Fysh of the Forensic Science Service, a search was made of the National DNA Database for profiles that could represent individuals related to Adam. Such searches are now becoming commonplace in protracted investigations, but at the time the science was new and, in fact, this was the first investigation where it was tried out. We decided to do a parent–child search. A sibling search was considered but, bearing in mind the age of the child and the fact that he had not been reported missing, it was felt that such a search would be unrealistic. In the parent–child search we examined the National DNA Database that then stood at about 1.5 million and compared our reference sample (full SGM+ profile from Adam) against each of these nominals. We inherit one allele from each of our parents at each of the 10 loci in a STR profile; therefore, if the reference sample did not match one of the two alleles, it could be excluded.

The speculative search produced a large number of hits, which were reduced using both a geographic boundary around Greater London and the racial marker on the database. We ended up with 34 males and 11 females that shared 10 or more alleles. Each of these was researched, traced, and visited. We soon found this to be a resource-intensive task. Even with a willing and compliant individual we had to trace and obtain a DNA elimination swab from previous partners as well as complete family trees to similarly eliminate full siblings. The process contained a number of ethical issues, especially when enquiring about previous relationships, and in many cases proved to be confrontational. Eventually, the enquiry moved on in a different direction, but it would be fair to say that the majority of these matches were not fully eliminated.

What we learned on this familial search was invaluable when, on another enquiry, we went down a similar route, although this time on a sibling search. This form of search looks at the total number of shared alleles; the higher the number, the more likely the two profiles are from siblings as opposed to unrelated individuals. The average allele match between two unrelated individuals is in the region of 6 and between two full siblings, 13. Sometimes the data search provides the result very easily, with one high allele match say of 16 or 17. Such was the case in March of 2003 with the killer of trucker Michael Little, who was hit by a brick thrown through his cab window. In the main, however, a large number fall around the 13 or 14 match number. My most recent case involved 97 within such a range, even with a geographic boundary imposed and also using an ethnic marker. Recognizing the difficulties encountered in the Adam case and talking to colleagues around the country who were also going down the familial route, we were well aware that the task was massively resource-intensive. Working with Ray Fysh we devised a new way of approaching the problem. This involved obtaining a mitochondrial profile from the crime scene stain or unidentified body. Once this was successful, through the custodians of the National Database, the second or B swab of the 97 nominal hits (every person arrested has two mouth swabs taken) were removed from storage and a mitochondrial DNA (MtDNA) profile similarly obtained. As the basis of the sibling search is that they must share the same biological parents and therefore the same MtDNA, once the profiles were obtained it was simple to compare the 97 against the reference sample. MtDNA is less discriminating than second generation multiplex plus (SGM+), about 1 in 100, so, as expected, in the 97, we found one exact match in both regions of the mitochondria. We then proceeded to examine the Y-chromosome using the same principles. Unfortunately, in this case all 97 were eliminated but in a very cost-effective manner and with no intrusion into any individual's life.

Another area of interest was DNA research, especially ancestral backgrounds. The scientists consulted here were Andy Urguart and Penny Noake from the Forensic Science Service Research Unit at Birmingham, U.K. They looked at the MtDNA inherited down the maternal line and the Y-chromosome inherited down the paternal line. Again, at the time, this was a new area for law enforcement. The standard ethnic inference test had told us that Adam was very likely to be Afro-Caribbean or African. The FSS scientists analyzed two hypervariable areas of the mitochondrial sequence HVR1 and HVR2. Published or publicly available databases of these sequences exist for various human populations, those for HVR1 being far more extensive, though by no means comprehensive. They concluded that the mitochondrial type of Adam and those closely related to it is found most commonly in Northwest Africa, particularly Niger and Nigeria, but also in Senegal and in samples from Morocco. More importantly, no matches were made with sequences from South Africa or East Africa —thereby potentially excluding these areas.

Two types of analysis were performed on his Y-chromosome. Y-SNPs are indicative of ancient human origin. They split the ancestors of modern man into 18 ancestral groups. Adam fell into group E, found almost exclusively among Africans. Group E is found in 95% of West Africans compared with East Africans' 48%, Southern Africans' 42%, and Northern Africans' 50%. Y-STRs are more variable and show more recent mutations than SNPs. The results on Adam showed several variants that are much more common in Africa than elsewhere.

The scientists concluded that taking into account both the MtDNA and the Y chromosome analysis, Adam was more likely to come from Northwest Africa than anywhere else. This would tend to suggest a recent African, and specifically West African, origin for Adam. The main alternative, an ancestry via the New World with subsequent emigration to Britain, involves a far higher likelihood of contribution of non-African DNA.

As well as exploring new ancestral testing, we wanted to investigate his biological character, recent diet, environmental exposure, and movement history. In the first instance, the scientist we turned to was Ken Pye, a professor of environmental geology from the Royal Holloway University of London and also an independent geoscientist. He had offered his services at the Bramshill conference and, as did our other experts, contributed in answering the overall question, "Where was Adam from?" Each of these pieces of work in a way complemented each other. The first area he suggested to explore was isotopic trace element analysis. Pye explained this as, "Basically, you are what you eat. The chemical composition of an individual's bones and other tissue primarily reflects the diet. The bone chemistry reflects the surface geology, both soil and water, in the area where a person lives. Specific isotopic ratios of the elements of strontium and neodymium reflect both the rock composition and age, and therefore show a relatively large variation across the globe. These chemical elements exchange with calcium in bones, but it is a slow process, taking some 6 to 10 years. Technically, bone examination like this can reveal distinct periods of movement in a person's life." Although this was a first in a criminal investigation, we agreed to give it a try.

Pye's first results supported that of the DNA researchers. He was able to rule out vast areas of the globe. By comparison with verified data he was able to say that Adam spent all of his life other than the last few weeks on or close to three areas of Precambrian rock in West Africa (Figure 27.2). The first area stretched from north of Accra in Ghana in the west slicing through Togo and Benin and forming the Yoruba Plateau in Nigeria north of Lagos. The second was the Central or Jos Plateau, totally in Nigeria, and the third was the area bordering Cameroon in the east of Nigeria. Unfortunately, the geological data held was poor in comparison with that in the West, and Pye could not take his examinations much further. A decision was then made to obtain further samples. Initially, this was attempted through international requests, but as we were subsequently to learn, to get things done in Nigeria you have to be there yourself.

A request was made through the Foreign and Commonwealth Office to allow U.K. scientists to obtain further samples. Eventually, in November 2002, I traveled to Nigeria with Andy Urguart and Forensic Science Service Specialist Advisor Ray Fysh. In the space

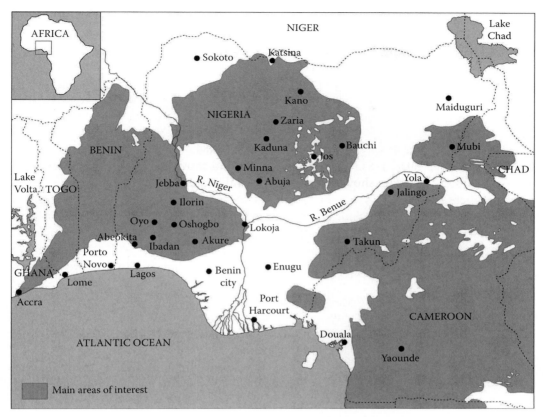

Figure 27.2 Three regions of Africa where the victim may have lived. (See color insert following page 362.)

of three weeks we crossed over 17,000 km, much on unimproved roads, obtaining soil and rock samples. These were normally taken north and south in the area of a town or city selected by Pye. The exact location was plotted using global satellite navigation systems. Also obtained were bone samples from wild animals being sold at the side of the road as bush meat, the underlying principle here being that the sample was born and bred locally. We visited many markets and purchased joints of domestic animal meat. Whenever possible, human postmortem bone samples were obtained from public mortuaries. In total, more than 150 such samples were gathered and plotted including bones from wild animals such as elephant that we could reasonably be sure had not been transported vast distances to market. We were accompanied on our travels by the Nigerian Police Force, who provided a needed armed escort, together with a detective superintendent and a state pathologist. Our escorts became very adept at defleshing delicacies such as grass cutter (a large rodent), monkey, and snake being cooked at the side of the road. In the markets the stallholders laughed in amazement when I ask for a joint of local goat but took only the bone and returned the meat.

All these samples were given to Pye on our return. After further examination he was able to conclude that Adam originated from an area stretching from south of Ibadan and North of Lagos in the west to Benin City in the east. This is a corridor of land of mainly tropical rainforest with small villages outside the cities. These villages consist of huts made of mud bricks and corrugated iron roofs, most with no water or electricity. This area measures approximately 100 mi by 50 mi at its widest. Pye was also able to say that the most similar matches came from the Benin City mortuary; he found this quietly striking. His conclusion was that Adam had spent much of his life in this area. Pinpointing any area from the entire world to such a precise and small area is a remarkable feat. Benin City has a population somewhere between 200,000 and 300,000 (there has not been an official census for some years in Nigeria). The city is also historically steeped in past occurrences of mass human sacrifices and is known for its fetish or *ju-ju* (the Nigerian word for *voodoo*) area.

Other isotopic work was conducted by a team led by Layla Renshaw from Oxford University. Their brief was to ascertain if Adam had spent any significant time in the U.K. before his death. There is a strong archaeological precedent for such work, but it has normally focused on teeth, hair, and nails, none of which were present. Renshaw worked on skin and fat samples provided. There is less scientific precedent for such examinations, but her conclusions are that Adam underwent a significant dietary change around four weeks prior to his death. This could be explained either by a move from West Africa to a more northwestern European diet or an *in situ* change in diet, for instance, to maintain health or weight.

Pye was also instructed to examine sedimentary particles from the body and shorts. His conclusions were that there was no evidence to suggest that the body of Adam had been exposed to any other area outside the tidal stretch of the River Thames where he was found.

A colleague of Pye's from Royal Holloway, Dr. Nick Branch, undertook the palynology work, or the study of pollen. The purpose of this examination was to discover if Adam was alive in the London area or whether he was killed elsewhere such as Africa and his dismembered body parts were disposed of in the River Thames. A further visit to the mortuary provided the lungs together with the contents of the small and large intestines; these together with the stomach contents were examined for traces of pollen. Surprisingly, the only sample that contained traces was the lower or large intestine. The assemblage consisted mainly of grasses and cultivated cereals of a type particularly found in northern and northwestern Europe in early September. Pollen from European trees was also found. The presence of such tree pollen is explained by its presence in household dust that is then ingested at a later date. Branch did much work in an attempt to explain these quantities of pollen in the large intestine. He tested a large number of food products and examined their pollen content, but, with the exception of honey, found none. To test the assumption that airborne pollen may be ingested in saliva, fecal samples of volunteers were examined. All contained pollen.

Branch's work also looked at London pollen samples from the September period and found a degree of matching. The importance of this work is that it is entirely consistent with the premise that Adam was killed in the London area and deposited in the river. In an attempt to narrow down the deposition site, an expert oceanographer, Dr. Michael Fennessy, was consulted. His view was that the downstream deposition limit irrespective of time in the water was a little below the Thames Barrier and, in particular, Barking Creek Tributary of the Thames. This tends to rule out the possibility that the torso floated in from the sea or estuary, therefore assisting the assumption of a London-based murder.

While Dr. Branch was examining the contents of the lower intestine, he discovered other foreign matter (Figure 27.3 to Figure 27.6). These were first sent to Pye. We soon

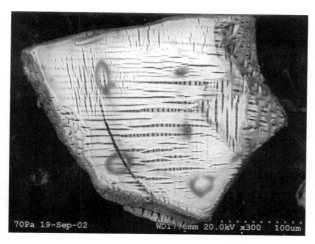

Figure 27.3 Bone-like material from stomach.

Figure 27.4 Clay particle from stomach.

discovered that this foreign matter had no nutritional value and formed part of a potion or traditional medicine taken 24 to 48 hr before his death.

All the fragments in the potion were small, less than 1 mm. Included were angular calcium phosphate particles of the appearance of ground-down bone (Figure 27.3). Pye could find no exact match. Samples of these particles have now been sent to the Office of the Chief Medical Examiner in New York. Scientists there have volunteered their services and have a newly acquired knowledge coming out of 9/11; they are examining degraded small bone fragments for DNA. Cultural advice suggests that if we were able to ascertain a species, this would help identify a purpose for the ritual and would paint a signature of the maker.

Quartz grains were also identified. Pye's opinion was that their appearance was similar to those found in a tropical or subtropical environment. Pellets of clay were found (Figure 27.4). His view was that these were probably derived from a riverbank, floodplain, or lake margin. Again, their composition suggested a tropical or subtropical origin. These pellets were high in minerals and metallic particles, particularly gold. Attempts to source the gold against known data failed.

Figure 27.5   Carbon particle from stomach.

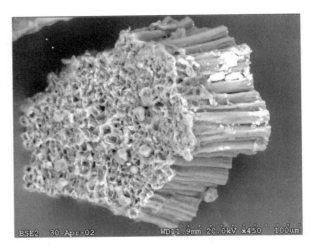

Figure 27.6   Cellulose material from stomach.

Carbon particles were also identified (Figure 27.5), but normal sources such as coal, charcoal, and carbon filters revealed no clear match. These contained traces of heavy metals and a possible suggestion is that these form the powdered remains from burnt residue in a cooking pot. Such a powder from burnt herbs is often used is West African witchcraft potions.

One other item that was puzzling us has now been identified. This is the recent discovery made at Kew Gardens of traces of a poisonous bean. SEM photographs of various items discovered in the concoction were shown on BBC Television's *Crimewatch* program. Following calls, botanists at Kew started to research items with a fibrous texture. The majority of the work was undertaken by Dr. Hazel Wilkinson. She has now identified the item as remnants of a Calabar bean. This is a highly poisonous bean indigenous to West Africa particularly around the area of Calabar in West Nigeria from where it gets its name. It is known as *essere* or the ordeal bean in Nigeria where it was fed to an accused person. If the accused was able to vomit, innocence was established; if not, guilt was proven and death would ensue, probably within the hour. Half a ripe bean can kill an adult, but in small quantities, it has a powerful sedative action on the spinal column that brings on paralysis. Adam clearly had been fed this bean some time before death, as it had made its way to the lower intestine. Its use in witchcraft is well known, and although the victim would remain conscious and feel pain, he would be unable to struggle against his killers.

The findings of all these items and the conclusions of the pathologists do, I suggest, prove conclusively that the murder of Adam was ritually motivated.

27.5   The History of the Red/Orange Shorts

The only visible clue to assist the investigation in the first few days was the pair of orange shorts. These were in relatively good condition, had pockets front and back, and bore the label "Kids and Company." Inside the shorts was a size label of 116 cms and washing instructions in German. These shorts were the main appeal point over the first few days; all possible permutations of similar-sounding U.K. manufactures were eliminated. Only two calls were received in the incident room identifying their origin. One was from a German now living in Essex who had purchased similarly labeled clothes recently from Woolworth's in Germany. The other was from a woman calling from Germany who had seen the appeal in that country and who also identified a German origin for the shorts.

Woolworth's in Germany split from the U.K. group of the same name many years ago and is a separate company. The buying director for Woolworth's was shown pictures of the shorts and positively identified them as being sold in the German stores. To be precise, he was able to say that the shorts were exclusively manufactured for Woolworth's. A total of 1000 pairs of these shorts in size 116 were imported into Germany and went on sale March 13, 2001, in the 336 stores in Germany and eight stores in Austria. By the time the body of Adam was found, 820 pairs of this size had been sold. The purchases were fairly even across all the stores with no bulk buyings identified. Importantly, these shorts were styled and sold as a garment for females and in the girl's area of the stores. It was impossible to follow up the sales further because the CCTV records are not kept, and most of the sales were in cash.

The company director of the suppliers "Happy Kids" verified that the consignment of shorts was made in China to Woolworth's instructions. They were shipped from China arriving in Rotterdam toward the end of January. They were transported in a sealed container and then, via the forwarding agents, to Woolworth's distribution center. There is no indication that anything other than the full consignment arrived.

27.6   The Enquiries in Nigeria

In February 2003 the investigating team had received the results of the forensic examinations on the samples brought back on the first visit. Pye's conclusions as to the area of the country where Adam was from was a vital breakthrough and supported the other scientific findings. This was a very small area where we could work. A decision was made to return to Nigeria in an attempt to find the family of Adam, who may or may not have been aware of his demise. To this end a separate reward was published, the equivalent of £2,500 sterling, to encourage anyone with information to come forward. For two weeks we called at villages, towns, and cities speaking to traditional leaders, village elders, and chiefs of police. We were told of some children going missing, but there were no records to view. Surprisingly, many knew of ritual murders taking place locally, and all agreed, when told the facts on Adam, that this was why he was killed. Taking into account the findings of Ken Pye, we felt our best chance of finding his family, and therefore discovering his identity, was looking in the area around Benin City. Unfortunately, the city is sprawling with a large population of children living and fending for themselves on the street.

We believed before setting off for Nigeria that we would be inundated with information, perhaps a large amount of it false but given in the hope of claiming the hefty reward, especially where a large percentage of the population live below the poverty line of a dollar a day. But that quantity of information just did not materialize; why we are not sure, although some suggested that this was a taboo subject surrounded by fear.

27.7 Conclusion

From finding a torso — with no identifying features that, literally, could have originated anywhere in the world — to narrowing this down to a relatively minuscule area is, I believe, a remarkable feat. The scientific developments pioneered in this case have served as a blueprint for investigations, and some of these areas have been expanded greatly, especially in the area of ancestral DNA. It is with deep regret that we have not as yet found the true identity of Adam and his family, and his body still lies in a mortuary freezer. However, I firmly believe we are closer than ever. Our investigation is still ongoing; in fact, it has now more momentum than ever. Only when we finally lay this small child's body to rest with a name on a headstone can we be sure that all our scientific endeavors were worthwhile.

The World Trade Center — September 11, 2001

28

GAILLE MACKINNON
AMY Z. MUNDORFF

Contents

28.1 Introduction 485
28.2 The Process of Identification 487
28.3 Considerations of Taphonomy 491
28.4 The Anthropological Verification Project and Final Anthropological Review 493
28.5 Conclusion 495
28.6 Acknowledgments..497
References 497

28.1   Introduction

The September 11, 2001 terrorist attacks on the World Trade Center in New York, the Pentagon in Washington, and the hijacking and subsequent crash of a commercial aircraft near Shanksville, PA, will remain — and be forever remembered — by the millions of people from the U.S. and around the world who bore witness to the extraordinary scenes and images of the aftermath of these terrible events.

The *9-11 Commission Report* was produced by the National Commission on Terrorist Attacks upon the United States, a bipartisan committee charged with investigating the events that occurred that day (GPO 2004). The report describes in detail how the hijackings unfolded and recounts the preparedness and response of the Office of Emergency Management and the various emergency services who handled the disaster in New York. The various eyewitness testimonies and 911 emergency calls made by individuals in and around the buildings of the World Trade Center on the morning of September 11, 2001 are also documented and provide a chilling narrative of the circumstances surrounding the day's events, a necessarily small number of which are reproduced below (GPO 2004).

At 7:59 on the morning of September 11, 2001, American Airlines Flight 11 departed Boston bound for Los Angeles, carrying 81 passengers, 2 pilots, and 9 flight attendants. Just 15 minutes later, United Airlines Flight 175 departed Boston *en route* to Los Angeles, with 56 passengers, 2 pilots, and 7 flight attendants on board. Both of these aircraft were hijacked shortly after their departure and subsequently diverted to New York City.

At 8:46 a.m., American Airlines Flight 11 was flown into the upper levels of the North Tower of the World Trade Center in downtown Manhattan. Thousands of people were already in the North Tower that morning, including approximately 80 catering and restaurant staff who worked in the Windows on the World restaurant on the 106th floor. Hundreds of people were killed immediately when the plane struck the building, and stairwells on the impacted floors quickly became impassable, trapping many individuals. From the 92nd floor up, hundreds more remained alive and trapped on many of the floors and elevators. The aircraft was also fully loaded with aviation fuel at the time of the crash, and the resultant impact into the building created a number of devastating fireballs. These are thought to have exploded onto numerous lower floors (including the West Street lobby and a basement level four floors below ground surface), causing thick, acrid, black smoke to envelope the upper floors and roof of the building. As the painfully poignant images that were subsequently broadcast around the world attest, many people were trapped in the building with no immediate prospect of relief and — faced with the increasingly insufferable heat, smoke, and fire — were pushed from the building to their deaths.

The *9-11 Report* notes that "in the 17-minute period between 8:46 and 9:03 a.m. on September 11, New York City and the Port Authority of New York and New Jersey had mobilized the largest rescue operation in the city's history. Well over 1000 first responders had been deployed, an evacuation had begun, and the critical decision that the fire could not be fought had been made. Then the second plane hit" (GPO 2004, p. 310).

At 9:03 a.m., United Airlines Flight 175 was flown into the South Tower of the World Trade Center, hitting the 77th to 85th floors. As the plane banked before impact, several areas of the impacted floors remained undamaged. It is believed that this allowed at least one stairwell to remain open and passable, possibly from the 91st floor down. Unfortunately, hundreds of people who had only minutes earlier witnessed the first aircraft's impact had evacuated their offices in the South Tower and were waiting for rescue on the sky-lobby level of the 72nd floor, when the second aircraft struck their own building. Similar to the situation that had just occurred in the North Tower, hundreds of people were killed instantly throughout the building, many hundreds more remained trapped, while others miraculously escaped unharmed. The United Airlines flight was also fully loaded with fuel, and so many floors and sections of the North Tower were also affected by the rapidly intensifying heat, smoke, and fire from the leaking fuel.

At 9:58 a.m., the South Tower collapsed in approximately 10 seconds, killing all remaining civilians, first responders, and emergency personnel who were still trapped inside. An unknown number of individuals on the World Trade Center concourse within the adjacent Marriott Hotel, and those unfortunate enough to have been on the surrounding streets, are also thought to have been killed at this time. Less than 30 minutes later, the North Tower also imploded, killing all remaining individuals in the building, apart from 12 firemen, one Port Authority police officer, and three civilians, who were descending Stairwell B of the tower and actually survived its collapse.

The area of devastation that later came to be known as "Ground Zero" covered approximately 16 acres and encompassed the land upon which the two towers, and five other commercial buildings that had also been destroyed, had been located. The building and other destruction debris rose 70 feet above the ground and extended to more than 70 feet below the original ground level surface (Langewiesche 2003). Subterranean fires in a number of "hot spots" within the debris were calculated to have burned at temperatures exceeding 1500°F (815.5°C) for more than 3 months after the incident, causing extremely hazardous working conditions for all those involved in the recovery operation. Approximately 1.7 million tons of debris were eventually excavated from the site at Ground Zero. Around 500,000 tons of steel were subsequently taken directly to scrapyards, and 1,200,000 tons of debris were transported to a New York City landfill site on Staten Island to be sifted for human remains (Hirsch 2005).

Immediately following the disaster, New York City officials began implementing plans for the process of identifying the victims. This would be a project of mammoth proportions and one in which both authors were involved. This chapter will outline the identification procedures and protocols adopted by the Office of Chief Medical Examiner (OCME), New York City, in handling the unprecedented severity and nature of the disaster and will also briefly discuss the various contributions made by the multidisciplinary victim identification team, with particular reference to those made by the attending anthropologists. A number of problems encountered during the identification process will then be examined and a description provided of how some of these were ultimately resolved. Finally, this chapter will conclude with a brief discussion on the importance of the Anthropological Verification Project and the Final Anthropological Review that were subsequently undertaken by the OCME. It will detail the success with which these programs were implemented, which ultimately led to additional identifications and the reassociation of body parts, a process that continues to this day.

28.2   The Process of Identification

Unlike airline disasters in which passenger manifests are used to determine the number and identity of the victims, the World Trade Center disaster had an "open population." Therefore, the true number of missing and presumed dead remained unknown for many months. This is not surprising, considering that approximately 50,000 people were known to have worked in the buildings of the World Trade Center. There were 430 businesses from 26 different countries that had offices in the complex, whereas victims of the disaster are estimated to have come from more than 30 countries around the world (Brondolo 2004).

From the very beginning, officials at the OCME recognized that the sheer scale and extraordinary severity of the disaster necessitated an innovative approach to the identification process. Chief Medical Examiner Dr. Charles Hirsch decided that the few intact bodies recovered from Ground Zero, together with any victims who subsequently died in the city's hospitals, would not be autopsied. The primary role of the Medical Examiner's Office was, therefore, to provide positive identification of the human remains, issue certifications of death, and facilitate the repatriation of the remains to the victim's families.

The New York City Police Department (NYPD), the Port Authority of New York and New Jersey Police Department (PAPD), the Fire Department of the City of New York (NYFD), the New York Department of Corrections (NYDC), the Federal Bureau of Investigation (FBI), the Disaster Mortuary Operation Response Team (DMORT), local medical students, and hundreds of other volunteers were needed to assist the OCME with the monumental task of identifying the victims of the disaster.

Anthropologists were assigned to work in three separate locations: a temporary body collection point erected adjacent to Ground Zero; the Freshkills landfill site on Staten Island, New York; and the temporary mortuary established at the OCME in New York City. The role of the anthropologists and attending pathologists who were initially mobilized at one of several body collection points adjacent to Ground Zero was to attempt to identify and separate possible "Members of Service" (that is, officers from the FDNY, PAPD, and NYPD) from those of civilian casualties. This was accomplished primarily by visual observation of clothing and uniform material still seen to be associated with the remains. However, as all of the identifications were ultimately to be made at the medical examiner's office, it quickly

Figure 28.1 Screening and sifting facility at Freshkills landfill site, Staten Island, New York City. (Photo by Richard Press, copyright © 2002.)

became apparent that the specific expertise of these specialists was not needed at this site. These duties were subsequently taken over by a number of medicolegal investigators from the OCME who manned this facility until the site at Ground Zero was finally shut down at the end of May 2002.

As previously stated, over 1.7 million tons of destruction debris from Ground Zero was taken to the Freshkills landfill site on Staten Island, New York, to be sifted for additional human remains that may have been missed during the initial recovery process at Ground Zero (Figure 28.1). The primary role of the anthropologists at this location was to distinguish human from nonhuman remains. Their expertise proved to be vitally important to the recovery process as many catering services and restaurants were destroyed when the buildings collapsed, leading to a greater than anticipated proportion of nonhuman remains within the destruction debris. According to the NYPD, approximately 4,200 remains were recovered from the landfill site, and of these approximately 2,411 were found to be human. There were 1,228 fragments that have since been positively identified and confirmed as representing the remains of 648 individuals (OCME 2005).

A temporary morgue was also rapidly established after the disaster at the Office of Chief Medical Examiner on First Avenue and 30th Street in Manhattan (Figure 28.2). This facility was staffed 24 hours a day, 7 days a week, by forensic specialists and practitioners, officers, and members of the various emergency response teams, together with personnel from the OCME. Every subspecialty of forensic science was employed in this multidisciplinary endeavor including, but not limited to, forensic pathologists, anthropologists, odontologists, radiologists, radiographers, fingerprint experts, DNA specialists, evidence technicians, medicolegal investigators, photographers, morgue technicians, medical scribes, computer and information technology specialists, records personnel, and ancillary office staff.

As previously stated, the primary purpose of the investigation was to identify the victims rather than, as is more traditionally the case, first establishing the cause and manner of death. For the World Trade Center disaster, neither cause nor manner was in question, with the vast majority of victims being signed out as "blunt force trauma, homicide." It was therefore decided that the rapid flow and processing of the human remains would best be facilitated by a number of receiving stations, forming an assembly line. This particular

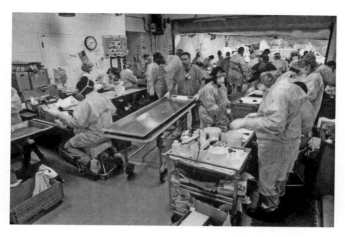

Figure 28.2 Temporary morgue at the Office of Chief Medical Examiner, New York City. (Photo by Richard Press, copyright © 2001.)

Figure 28.3 Sorting biohazard bags at triage table. (Photo by Richard Press, copyright © 2001.) (See color insert following page 362.)

methodology of human remains processing has been frequently adopted and utilized in numerous other mass disaster facility settings (Jensen 2000, Levinson and Granot 2002, Wagner and Froede 1993).

Human remains were transported multiple times a day to the Medical Examiner's Office from both Ground Zero and the landfill operation. These remains were held in a preprocessing refrigerated trailer outside the temporary morgue until they were to be analyzed. Once inside the mortuary, the remains were first taken to the triage station for initial assessment by the attending anthropologist, who was generally assisted by a number of officers of the NYPD, PAPD, and/or FBI (Figure 28.3). Anthropologists were asked to assess each incoming body bag in order to establish whether the contents were human or nonhuman and whether there was any evidence of commingling (and, if so, to split these remains into separate individual cases); and then attempt to reassociate or reconstruct remains that lacked soft tissue attachment but which appeared to be associated.

It had also been decided from the outset that every effort would be made to test every fragment of human tissue recovered for DNA. This was done with the knowledge that

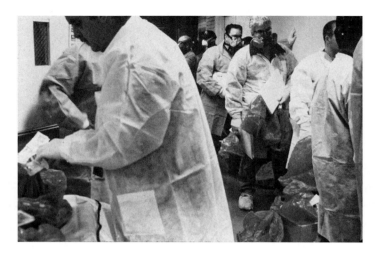

Figure 28.4 Escorting cases through the morgue. (Photo by Richard Press, copyright © 2001.) (See color insert following page 362.)

there would be victims who were only identified, in part, from a small shard of bone or piece of soft tissue. Therefore, every fragment larger than a thumbnail that was not attached by hard or soft tissue to another fragment was separated by the anthropologist, given its own case number, and individually sent through the identification process, in order to be tested for DNA. Often times, a single body bag received from Ground Zero would be separated into multiple different individual cases as it went through the rigorous triage process. As these cases were sorted out of the initial body bag, the accompanying site provenance information would then be transcribed onto the newly separated cases, together with a brief description of the human remains present. In addition to the tasks performed at the triage table, anthropologists also provided assistance to radiology and odontology in the identification of individualizing morphological skeletal features, anatomical landmarks, and antemortem trauma (Mundorff 2003).

From the triage station, the remains would then be placed on a holding table to await the medical examiner's examination, where the contents of each body bag were subsequently numbered, documented, photographed, and sampled for DNA analysis. Depending upon which parts of the body were present — and whether there were any identifying features, personal effects, or evidence associated with the remains — each case was then subsequently taken to the areas occupied by specialists in odontology, radiology, fingerprints, and evidence collection for further examination. The transfer of the remains from one specialist team to another was undertaken by individual escorts, who were usually either a Member of Service or a DMORT team member. Each escort remained with a single, assigned case and its paperwork at all times, thereby ensuring continuity and chain of custody (Figure 28.4).

Following these examinations, the remains were returned for storage to 1 of 16 refrigerated trailers situated in an area at the bottom of 30th Street, in order to await identification, release to funeral homes, and final repatriation to their families for burial. This area subsequently came to be known as "Memorial Park," and it is here that the victims' families came in order to pay their respects and leave flowers and personal tokens for the deceased. Indeed, many families who still await the identification of their loved ones' remains continue to be regular visitors to Memorial Park.

28.3   Considerations of Taphonomy

The nature and circumstances of the disaster subjected the recovered remains to a number of taphonomic variables, complicating the subsequent identification process. These included such factors as the force and velocity of the initial impact of the aircraft; the abnormally high temperatures generated by the aviation fuel explosions; and the extraordinary devastation wreaked by the subsequent destruction and collapse of the buildings. In addition, the recovery process took many months, leading to the prolonged exposure of the remains to differing weather conditions; subterranean fires (and the continual application of water to douse these fires); and the extremely deleterious effects caused by heavy machinery used in the excavation and recovery process. These factors caused extraordinarily high levels of fragmentation, commingling, and varying stages of decomposition, mummification, and cremation. Such conditions have been frequently recorded in the literature from other mass fatality disasters and are known to commonly and adversely affect human remains (Brannon and Morlang 2004, Brannon et al. 2003, Campobasso et al. 2003, Crane 2000, Eckert 1990, Meyer 2003, Soomer et al. 2001).

The observed taphonomic variables and their destructive effect on most of the recovered remains cannot be overstated. The role of the anthropologist, therefore, became very important within the identification process, as they often proved integral to the identification of cases involving fragmented and commingled individuals (Hinkes 1989, Kahana and Hiss 2000, Kahana et al. 1997, Sledzik 1998, Sledzik and Rodriguez 2003, Stewart 1970, Ubelaker et al. 1995). However, traditional anthropological methods normally utilized by the anthropologist in a mass disaster context, such as establishing individual biological profiles to determine age, sex, stature, and ancestry, were not generally possible due to the extreme fragmentation of the majority of the remains. Indeed, there was rarely a whole bone present for analysis. In addition, considering the nature of the sample (i.e., that of an "open population"), together with the fact that approximately 45% of the victims were males between 30–45 years old, such methods would have at best only provided presumptive data, as final identification was to be confirmed by DNA analysis (OCME 2005).

Other forensic specialists within the multidisciplinary team also faced similar problems during the identification process, as they responded to the unique nature of the disaster by radically adapting their standard disaster victim methodologies. As an anecdotal example, single teeth were found with great regularity embedded in muscle tissue or areas of the body that were anatomically impossible to reconcile (their presence in such areas overwhelmingly demonstrating the force and velocity that caused them to be removed from an individual and subsequently impacted into another). The vast majority of the dental identifications only occurred, however, when the dental arcade — or reasonably sized fragments thereof — were present. Single, isolated teeth rarely resulted in dental identifications but were, instead, identified through DNA analysis. This was unexpected and, as there were a multitude of isolated teeth found that ultimately could not be associated with other remains, unfortunately prolonged the process of final identification and repatriation.

However, not only isolated teeth were found within the remains of other victims. Many bone fragments were also discovered embedded into the extremities, body cavities, and clothing of other individuals (Brogdon 2003, Lichtenstein 1998). This radiograph (Figure 28.5) displays the upper limbs and torso of an individual and, as can be seen, both right and left arms, forearms, and hands remain attached to fragments of the upper torso. However, if one looks carefully in the area immediately above the mid-shaft region

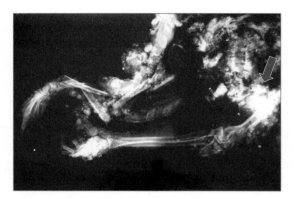

Figure 28.5 Radiograph of the remains of an upper torso with attached upper limbs. (From the Office of Chief Medical Examiner, New York City.)

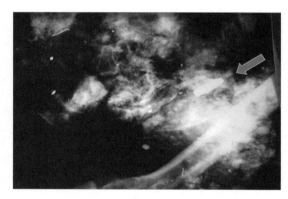

Figure 28.6 Radiograph of amputated hand and finger-ring in thoracic cavity. (From Office of Chief Medical Examiner, New York City.)

of the left humerus, a small, circular-shaped, radio-opaque area can be seen (Figure 28.6). Upon further investigation of the thoracic cavity, it was found that an isolated finger, together with an amputated hand wearing a metal ring on one finger, had become embedded in the chest of this individual. This is just one example of how stringent triage protocols implemented at the beginning of the temporary morgue process can rapidly identify and separate cases of extreme commingling.

As mentioned above, there were also a number of "hot spots" within the destruction debris at Ground Zero that continued to burn at temperatures approaching 1500°F for close to 3 months. When these areas were finally excavated, dozens of buckets of calcined, commingled human remains were recovered. Attempts were made to identify the cremated skeletal and dental elements (Figure 28.7), together with a determination of the minimum number of individuals present. However, this did not ultimately produce any identifications, as the burnt and calcined condition of the remains was such that it precluded the use of DNA. The calcined teeth that were recovered were cremated to such an extent that dental identification was impossible; likewise any accompanying dental restorations were reduced to amorphous concretions that were completely unidentifiable. In fact, the only positive identifications of cremated remains that occurred were in cases where prosthetic hardware was present (Figure 28.8), which could then be traced by their individual serial number back to a specific individual, surgical procedure, and/or antemortem radiographs.

Figure 28.7   Establishing a minimum number of individuals from calcined human remains. (From Office of Chief Medical Examiner, New York City.) (See color insert following page 362.)

Figure 28.8   Calcined proximal tibia with prosthetic device. (From Office of Chief Medical Examiner, New York City.) (See color insert following page 362.)

Whereas DNA analysis was the method by which positive victim identifications were ultimately established, this process was also beset with many difficulties. For example, in the early stages of the identification process, soft tissue samples were preferentially taken for DNA analysis, rather than skeletal or dental samples. (Budimlija et al. 2003a). However, the transfer of soft and hard tissues between individual victims often caused enormous contamination problems. This contamination was found to be particularly apparent in the muscle tissue samples, so that remains often had to be resampled for bone (if present) in order to achieve final positive identification (Budimlija et al. 2003b).

28.4   The Anthropological Verification Project and Final Anthropological Review

In May 2002, the OCME decided to implement an Anthropological Verification Project (AVP) (Wiersema et al. 2003). This was deemed necessary in order to address the enormous commingling and cross-contamination problems and to increase the accuracy of the documentation within the case files.

Three anthropologists (including one of the authors, GM) were hired to review each set of human remains to ensure that there was no evidence of commingling within each body bag. All existing paperwork associated with each case was reassessed, verified, and cross-checked with the physical remains. A detailed reinventory of the remains was then produced on a separate form which was added to the original case file. This process provided an opportunity to add any additional pertinent information and anatomical detail that may not have been recorded when the case was originally processed through the temporary morgue (Bartelink et al. 2003). For instance, if a file contained the description of a partial right humerus and, upon reviewing the remains during the AVP, it was determined that the humerus was specifically from the mid-shaft to the distal end, that additional detail was added to the supplemental form. Equally, if it was determined during this analysis that there were fragments associated with a case that were not contiguous or did not appear to belong, they were removed, new cases were created, and the remains were resampled for DNA. In addition, the AVP confirmed that the case numbers and associated tag and body bag numbers matched the accompanying paperwork. The AVP also verified the storage trailer manifests in order to ensure that the body parts were accurately logged and matched their recorded location in the database.

Of the 19,963 cases created during the World Trade Center investigation, 16,915 were processed through the AVP, resulting in multiple new identifications and links with previously unassociated remains (OCME 2005).

Although the role of the AVP was to review the unidentified remains, the Final Anthropological Review was established in order to provide one last opportunity to exercise quality assurance before the final release of identified remains. Therefore, before an identification was finally ratified and the family subsequently notified, every effort was made to ensure that the identification was scientifically secure and that there was no chance of misidentification.

A detailed review was instigated once the DNA laboratory had issued an identification sheet, which could list from one to over 100 pieces as being linked to a single individual (Holland et al. 2003). A medicolegal investigator then collected all of the files and biographical information from each "identified-as-linked" case, which was then compiled onto a single form to include the RM (Reported Missing) number, the decedent's name, and a numerically ordered list of all the case numbers linked by DNA to that particular individual. The form also contained information such as: the name of the medical examiner who processed the case; the date of identification; the type of sample taken for DNA (i.e., bone, soft tissue, or both); whether it was an "entire sample" (taken for DNA); a brief description of the remains; how other linked or associated fragments were identified (i.e., DNA, dental, fingerprint, etc.); and, finally, whether the remains were still curated at Memorial Park or had been released. Once this information had been correlated for each individual as being either a "new identification" or as an "additional links to an established identification," the anthropologist would then review all of the documents against the physical remains in order to identify any possible anthropological or documentary inconsistencies.

The following case is an example of remains that might have been linked to the wrong individual had they not gone through the Final Anthropological Review process, and been assessed and reevaluated for inconsistencies and duplication of body parts. This case had a number of remains that had been positively identified to Individual "A," which included:

1. Right pelvis (partial ilium/ischium)
2. Right proximal femur
3. Right proximal and distal tibia
4. Partial right foot
5. Left proximal and distal femur
6. Left distal tibia
7. Left calcaneus

DNA had subsequently linked extra remains to this particular case, which consisted of:

8. Complete left tibia (conflicts with [6])
9. Complete left fibula
10. Left foot (no calcaneus present)
11. Right proximal femur attached to fragment of pelvis (conflicts with [1])

The review of the documentation clearly indicated that multiple duplications were identified to the same individual. A further review of the remains was undertaken to ensure that the documentary information was correct and was not merely a data entry mistake, i.e., a right element mistakenly recorded as a left. This subsequently confirmed the presence of duplicate elements, and the remains and the identification were therefore put on hold and resampled for further DNA testing. The results of the DNA analysis confirmed that contamination of the samples had indeed occurred, with it being subsequently established that: (10) the left foot did indeed belong to individual A; whereas (8), (9), and (11) were the partial remains of another individual.

DNA-based identification programs achieve the highest level of positive identification of victims of mass disaster incidents. However, the success with which this is ultimately achieved is mediated by the contextual and taphonomic variables inherent within each mass disaster. The Final Anthropological Review allowed the OCME to resolve any final and outstanding issues of commingling and contamination, and ultimately provided the opportunity to reconfirm the correlation between the case files, the identification modalities, and the physical remains before final repatriation of the victim occurred. Both the Anthropological Verification Project and the Final Anthropological Review process clearly demonstrate the value of having such procedures and protocols in place, and emphasize the benefit of anthropological evaluation during the final identification, confirmation, and release phase of the investigation.

28.5   Conclusion

At the present time, 2,749 people are known to have been killed on September 11, 2001, at the World Trade Center. A total of 19,963 pieces of human remains were finally recovered from both the Ground Zero and Staten Island landfill sites (OCME 2005). Of these, 10,769 have since been positively identified as representing the remains of 1,591 (58%) of the

Table 28.1   Identification Achieved by Single Modality

Single Modality	Number	Percentage
DNA	849	87%
Dental	57	6%
Fingerprints	37	4%
Photograph	9	1%
Visual identification	12	1%
Personal effects	8	1%
Other	3	0%

Source: Office of Chief Medical Examiner, New York City.

Table 28.2   Identification Achieved through Multiple Modalities

Multiple Modalities	Number	Percentage
DNA	553	90%
Dental	470	76%
Fingerprints	269	44%
Photograph	16	3%
Visual identification	2	0%
Personal effects	69	11%
Body x-ray	3	0%
Tattoos	7	1%
Other	45	7%

Source: Office of Chief Medical Examiner, New York City.

victims (excluding the terrorists) (OCME 2005). There were 5,311 pieces labeled as "entire samples" and sent in their entirety for DNA analysis, from which 2,453 have since been identified and linked to multiple individuals (OCME 2005). The tables above (Table 28.1 and Table 28.2) indicate how many single and multiple modalities have so far yielded identifications and in what percentage this has occurred. Only 39 (2.5%) of these identifications were achieved through personal recognition, with the remaining 97.5% of victims rendered unrecognizable by the disaster (OCME 2005).

With regard to the statistics associated with identified individuals, 343 firemen from the Fire Department of New York, 37 policemen from the Port Authority of New York and New Jersey, and 23 policemen from the New York City Police Department are now known to have died in the disaster (OCME 2005). These figures represent the largest recorded loss of life of members of emergency response agencies in any mass disaster. From American Airlines Flight 11, 55 of the victims have been identified, whereas 32 remain unidentified. Similarly, 25 of the victims from United Airlines Flight 175 have been identified, leaving 35 unidentified (OCME 2005). The difference between the number of passengers listed on the official flight manifests and the OCME's missing persons list given above is due to the fact that the five terrorists who were onboard each aircraft have not been included in the official OCME record (although three of the ten terrorists have subsequently been identified by DNA).

The extraordinary events of September, 11, 2001, necessitated the development of an innovative approach and adaptation of methodologies by the OCME, New York City, to successfully implement the ongoing identification of the thousands of victims from the World Trade Center disaster (Budowle et al. in press, Cash et al. 2003, Mundorff and Steadman 2003).

It is not possible, however, to execute an identification project of this size and magnitude without mistakes inevitably being made. Therefore, the challenge lies in identifying, isolating, and rectifying problems as they occur, and adapting methodologies accordingly to facilitate best practice and achieve a scientifically robust victim identification program.

Additionally, the circumstances that initiated the AVP and the Final Anthropological Review may also be logically taken as lessons for the future, as it has been demonstrated that these processes can be vitally important to the identification of fragmented and commingled human remains (Mundorff and Steadman 2003).

Finally, the enormous problems faced during the World Trade Center victim identification process have accelerated the development of new methods and alternative approaches to DNA-based mass fatality victim identification programs (Cash et al. 2003, Budowle et al. in press). Hopefully, the advances that are currently being made in DNA technology, when used in conjunction with the expertise and experience of forensic practitioners, will ultimately result in the swifter identification and repatriation of victims of mass disaster incidents.

28.6 Acknowledgments

The authors would like to thank Dr. Charles Hirsch, Chief Medical Examiner, Office of Chief Medical Examiner, New York City; Richard Press, freelance photographer, who took so many extraordinary images of the aftermath of the disaster; and finally, the thousands of individuals who assisted in the World Trade Center recovery and identification process.

References

Bartelink, E.J., Wiersema, J.M., Parks, M., MacKinnon, G., and Mundorff, A.Z., Back to the basics: anatomical siding of fragmentary skeletal elements from victims of the World Trade Center disaster, in *Proceedings of the 55th Annual Meeting of American Academy of Forensic Sciences*, American Academy of Forensic Sciences, Colorado Springs, 2003, p. 243.

Brannon, R.B. and Morlang, W.M., The USS Iowa disaster: success of the forensic dental team, *J Forensic Sci* 49(5), 1067–1068, 2004.

Brannon, R.B., Morlang, W.M., and Smith, B.C., The Gander disaster: dental identification in a military tragedy, *J Forensic Sci* 48(6), 1331–1335, 2003.

Brogdon, B.G., Radiological identification of individual remains, in *Forensic Radiology*, Brogdon, B.G., Ed., CRC Press, Boca Raton, FL, 2003, pp. 149–187.

Brogdon, B.G., Vogel, H., and MacDowell, J.D., *A Radiologic Atlas of Abuse, Torture, Terrorism, and Inflicted Trauma*, CRC Press, Boca Raton, FL, 2003, pp. 255–279.

Brondolo, T., Resource requirements for Medical Examiner response to mass fatality incidents, *Medico-Legal J Ireland*, 10(2), 91–99, 2004.

Budimlija, Z.M., Nazaruollo, B., Estacio, S.M., Prinz, M.K., and Shaler, R.C., Bone extraction procedure for nuclear DNA analysis used in World Trade Center human identification project, in *Proceedings of the 55th Annual Meeting of American Academy of Forensic Sciences*, American Academy of Forensic Sciences, Colorado Springs, 2003a, p. 204.

Budimlija, Z.M., Prinz, M.K., Mundorff, A.Z., Wiersema, J.M., Bartelink, E.J., MacKinnon, G., Nazzaruolo, B.L., Estacio, S.M., Hennessy, M.J., and Shaler, R.C., World Trade Center human identification project: experiences with individual body identification cases, *Croatian Med J* 44(3), 259–263, 2003b.

Budowle, B., Bieber, F.R., and Eisenberg, A.J., Forensic aspects of mass disasters: strategic considerations for DNA-based human identification, *Legal Med* (in press).

Campobasso, C.P., Falamingo, R., and Vinci, F., Investigation of Italy's deadliest building collapse: forensic aspects of a mass disaster, *J Forensic Sci* 48(3), 635–639, 2003.

Cash, H.D., Hoyle, J.W., and Sutton, A.J., Development under extreme conditions: forensic bioinformatics in the wake of the World Trade Centre disaster, *Pac Symp Biocomput* 638–653, 2003.

Crane, J., Violence associated with civil disturbance, in *The Pathology of Trauma*, 3rd ed., Mason, J.K. and Purdue, B.N., Eds., Arnold, London, 2000, pp. 75–88.

Eckert, W.G., The Lockerbie disaster and other aircraft breakups in midair, *Am J Forensic Med Pathol* 11, 93–101, 1990.

GPO, The 911 Commission Report — Final Report of the National Commission on Terrorist Attacks upon the U.S., Official Government Edition, Government Printing Office, Washington, DC, 2004.

Hinkes, M.J., The role of forensic anthropology in mass disaster resolution, *Aviation, Space, and Environmental Medicine*, 60, (7, Suppl.), A18–25, 1989.

Hirsch, C.S., Foreword, in *Being There — Medical Student Morgue Volunteers Following 9-11*, Goldstein, B., Ed., Master Scholars Press, New York University School of Medicine, 2005, pp. 6–13.

Holland, M.M., Cave, C.A., Holland, C.A., and Bille, T.W., Development of a quality, high throughput DNA analysis procedure for skeletal samples to assist with the identification of victims from the World Trade Center attacks, *Croatian Med J* 44(3), 264–272, 2003.

Jensen, A.J., *Mass Fatality and Casualty Incidents: A Field Guide*, CRC Press, Boca Raton, FL, 2000.

Kahana, T. and Hiss J., Modern war wounds, in *The Pathology of Trauma*, 3rd ed., Mason, J.K. and Purdue, B.N., Eds., Arnold, London, 2000, pp. 89–102.

Kahana, T., Freund, M., and Hiss, J., Suicidal terrorist bombings in Israel — identification of human remains, *J Forensic Sci* 42, 259–263, 1997.

Langewiesche, W., *American Ground*, Scribner, New York, 2003.

Levinson, J. and Granot, H., *Transportation Disaster Response Handbook*, Academic Press, London, 2002.

Lichtenstein, J.E., Radiology in mass casualty incidents, in *Forensic Radiology*, Brogdon, B.G., Ed., CRC Press, Boca Raton, FL, 1998, pp. 189–205.

Meyer, H.J., The Kaprun cable car fire disaster — aspects of forensic organization following a mass fatality with 155 victims, *Forensic Sci Int* 138 (1–3), 1–7, 2003.

Mundorff, A.Z., The role of anthropology during the identification of victims from the World Trade Center disaster, in *Proceedings of the 55th Annual Meeting of American Academy of Forensic Sciences*, American Academy of Forensic Sciences, Colorado Springs, 2003, p. 277.

Mundorff, A.Z. and Steadman. D.W., Anthropological perspectives on the forensic response at the World Trade Center Disaster, *Gen Anthropol* 10(1), 2–5, 2003.

Office of Chief Medical Examiner, New York City, personal communication, 2005.

Sledzik, P.S., Anthropology and mass fatality response, in *Proceedings of the International Symposium on Family and Victim Assistance for Transportation Disasters*, National Transportation Safety Board, Arlington, VA, 1998, pp. 1–8.

Sledzik, P.S. and Rodriguez, W.C., Damnum fatale: the taphonomic fate of human remains in mass disasters, in *Advances in Forensic Taphonomy: Method, Theory and Archaeological Perspectives*, Haglund, W.D., and Sorg, M.H., Eds., CRC Press, Boca Raton, FL, 2003, pp. 321–330.

Soomer, H., Ranta, H., and Pettila, A., Identification of victims from the M/S Estonia, *Int J Legal Med* 114(4–5), 259–262, 2001.

Stewart, T.D., *Personal Identification in Mass Disasters*, Smithsonian Institution, Washington, DC, 1970.

Ubelaker, D.J., Owsley, D.W., Houck, M.M., Craig, E., Grant, W., Woltanski, T., Fram, R., Sandness, K., and Peerwani, N., The role of forensic anthropology in the recovery and analysis of Branch Davidian Compound victims: recovery procedures and characteristics of victims, *J Forensic Sci* 40, 335–340, 1995.

Wagner, G.N. and Froede, R.C., Medicolegal investigation of mass disasters, in *Spitz and Fisher's Medicolegal Investigation of Death: Guidelines for the Application of Pathology to Crime Investigation*, Fisher, W.U., Ed., Charles C. Thomas, Springfield, IL, 1993, pp. 567–584.

Wiersema, J.M., Bartelink, E.J., Budimlija, Z., Prinz, M., Shaler, R., Mundorff, A.Z., and MacKinnon, G., The importance of an interdisciplinary review process in the World Trade Center mass disaster investigation, in *Proceedings of the 55th Annual Meeting of American Academy of Forensic Sciences*, American Academy of Forensic Sciences, Colorado Springs, 2003, p. 194.

Index

A

AAS, *see* Atomic absorption spectroscopy
Abductions, 427
ABFO, *see* American Board of Forensic Odontology
ABO blood typing system, 8
Abrasion, 116
Accidents, 94, 122
ACE-V process, *see* Analysis, comparison, evaluation, and verification process
Acid Bath Murderer, 106
Acne vulgaris, 101
ACPO, *see* Association of Chief Police Officers
ACPOS, *see* Association of Chief Police Officers, Scotland
"Adam" case (London), 473–484
    advanced forensic investigations, 476–483
    DNA profile, 476
    enquiries in Nigeria, 483–484
    finding of body, 473–474
    history of red/orange shorts, 483
    initial forensic examinations, 475–476
    materials from stomach, 481, 482
    motives considered for, 475
    parent–child search, 476
    postmortem, 474–475
    regions of Africa where victim may have lived, 479
    Serious Crime Group South, 473
Address impersonation, 409
Adhesive tape, stable isotope signatures of, 39
Adipocere formation, 93
Adrenal gland tumors, 107
Adult dentition, possibilities in charting of, 178
AFIS, *see* Automated Fingerprint Identification System
Africoid-type hair, 150
Afro-Caribbean hair, 150
Age
    assessment, use of teeth in, 191
    changes in skin, 101
    determination
        bones, 224
        dental microstructure and, 208
        juvenile skeleton, 208

AIDS, 100
Air-brush body art, 388
Alcohol consumption
    body modification and, 381
    fatty change in liver and, 106
Algor mortis, 242
Alien food and drink, 48
Alleles, 21
Alzheimer's disease, 101, 178
American Board of Forensic Odontology (ABFO), 184
Amido Black™, 326
Amphetamine, detection of, 159
Analysis, comparison, evaluation, and verification (ACE-V) process, 65
Analysis of Variance (ANOVA), 353, 355
ANOVA, *see* Analysis of Variance
Antemortem records
    comparison of personal effects and, 373
    dental, 179, 180
Anthropological Verification Project (AVP), 493–494, 495
Anthrosilicotic nodules, 108
Application fraud, 409
Arms reattachment of, 135
Artificial devices, implanting of, 139
Artwork, forensic, 436
    age progression, 437
    facial reconstruction, 439
    image enhancement, 437
    long-term missing persons, 437
    postmortem composites, 439
    unidentified individuals, 437
Asbestos, workers exposed to, 108
Assaults, 122
Association of Chief Police Officers (ACPO), 64, 116, 426
Association of Chief Police Officers, Scotland (ACPOS), 431
Association of Forensic Radiographers, 222, 224
Asthma, 104, 105
Atherosclerosis, 102
Atomic absorption spectroscopy (AAS), 160
Atomic force microscopy, 150

Autolysis, 100
Automated Fingerprint Identification System (AFIS), 66, 67
AVP, *see* Anthropological Verification Project

B

BAHID, *see* British Association for Human Identification
Baker classification, breast capsule formation, 145
Bali bombing, dental identification and, 178
Ballpoint pen
    first use in America, 296
    inkless start, 297
    stroke of, 297
Bank cards, Chip and PIN, 300, 409, 411, 420
Basal cell carcinoma, 101
Basic periodontal examination (BPE), 186–187
Beading, 391
Benign nephrosclerosis, 106
Bernoulli trials, 278
Bertillon anthropometric system, 58–59
Big Issue, 429
Biographical identifiers, 406
Biological identification, sex determination and, 203
Biological identity, categories associated with, 203
Biometric data, global standard for, 70
Biometric identification, 407
    advantages of using, 416
    circumstances necessary for, 415
    disadvantages of using, 416
Biometric identifiers, 68, 406–407
Biometric identity cards, 415–423
    biometric identification, 415–416
    existing biometric identity card schemes, 418
    function creep and, 420
    Identity Cards Bill, 419–420
    identity cards and their biometric identifiers, 416–417
    legal, ethical, and social issues, 420–421
    U.K. biometric identity cards, 419
Birth defects, 208
Bitewing radiographs, 187, 188
Blood typing system, 8
Blueprint of life, DNA as, 7
Bluetooth technology, 120
Blunt trauma, 124
Body art
    air-brush, 388
    decal-type forms of, 387
    3D, 391
Body modification, 122, 379–399
    addictive progression with acquisition of, 381
    complications for, 381
    definition of, 379

dermal modification, 382–388
    permanent tattoos, 382–387
    temporary tattoos, 387–388
    extreme, 379
    health and safety implications, 381
    legal considerations surrounding, 382
    personal implications of, 398
    reasons for obtaining, 380
    scarification, 388–390
        body etching, 390
        branding, 389
        cutting, 389–390
        other forms, 390
    self-directed, 380
    subdermal implants, 391–392
        beading, 391
        3d body art, 391–392
    transdermal modification, 392–397
        anatomical locations, 395–397
        procedure, 394–395
Body parts, relative height of, 213
Body preservation, climate and, 242
Body recovery teams, welfare of, 114
Bomb spike carbon, 158
Bone(s)
    age determination, radiological standards for, 224
    cement, 139
    development, most useful phase of, 209
    DNA amplification from, 205
    identification of, 200
    immature, 203
    limb, ethnic identity from, 213
    loss, trabecular, 212
    mineral, 30, 43, 45
    Paget's disease of, 101
    pathological conditions of, 203
    posture and, 121
    remodeling, 156, 212
    trauma, 120
BPE, *see* Basic periodontal examination
Brain, age-replaced changes seen in, 101
Branding, 389
    cautery, 389
    cold, 389
    hot, 389
Breast
    augmentation, 137
    capsule formation, Baker classification of, 145
    implant, evolution of, 141
    reconstruction, 136
Breastfeeding, 157
Breeder documents, 416
Briem handwriting system, 291
British Association for Human Identification (BAHID), 269

Bruise, definition of, 117
Brush abrasion, 116
BSIA, *see* Bulk material stable isotope analysis
Bulk material stable isotope analysis (BSIA), 34
Burn(s), 118
   identification problems and, 125
   scars, 136
   surgery, 136
Burr striations, 297

C

^{13}C
   isotopic fractionation of, 32
   stable isotope analysis, 36
Calvin cycle, 32
Cambridge Reference Sequence, 23
CAM pathways, *see* Crassulacean acid metabolism
      pathways
Cannabis smoking, 109
Cañon Diablo troilite (CDT), 31
Capillary gas chromatography (cGC), 36
Cardiothoracic surgery, 128, 129
Carnegie Mellon University, Motion of Body database,
      352
Carpenters, injuries to, 121
Cartilage injuries, 121
Casting, 325
CATCHEM database, 475
Caucasoid-type hair, 150
Cautery branding, 389
CBRN event, *see* Chemical, biological, radiological, or
      nuclear event
CCTV
   image, comparison of personal effect with, 373
   monitors, picture quality of, 259
   security system, TV lines required to subtend face
      for identification, 262
   stereovision of, 260, 261
   systems
      cost of, 260
      proof of identification from, 261
   use for security purposes, 257
CDT, *see* Cañon Diablo troilite
CENP-B gene, 153
Central nervous system disease, muscle wasting and,
      107
Cerebral artery atheroma, 101
CF-IRMS, *see* Continuous-flow isotope-ratio mass
      spectrometry
cGC, *see* Capillary gas chromatography
Chain of evidence, identification and, 95
Change detection, 267
Charnley Hip prosthesis, 133

Chemical, biological, radiological, or nuclear (CBRN)
      event, 119
Child abduction definition, 428
Children, homicides by strangers involving, 427
Children's Society, runaways and, 427
Chip and PIN bank cards, 300, 409, 411, 420
Chronic obstructive pulmonary disease, 104, 108
Clavicle, medial epiphysis of, 210
Coal miners' tattoos, 121
Cocaine
   detection of, 159
   geographic origin of, 38
   result of snorting, 109
CODIS loci, 15
Cognitive preconception, 258
Coincidence, agreements occurring by, 75
Cold branding, 389
Combined DNA Index System, 15
Complex atheroma, 102
Compound specific isotope analysis (CSIA), 36
Computed tomography (CT), 223, 237
Conditional match probability, 18
Confidentiality agreements, personal effects and, 370
Conflict areas, forensic investigations in, 452
Contact evidence, hair as, 148
Continuous-flow isotope-ratio mass spectrometry
      (CF-IRMS), 34, 41
Contusion, 117
Copycat website, 409
Cosmetic dentistry, 180
Cosmetic surgery, 137
Costal cartilage calcification, 206, 212, 224
Council for the Registration of Forensic Practitioners
      (CRFP), 199, 269
Crack keratitis, 110
Cranial landmarks, common, 236–237
Cranial terms, common, 234
CRANID program, 213
Crassulacean acid metabolism (CAM) pathways, 33
Credit history, damaged to identity theft victim's, 410
CRFP, *see* Council for the Registration of Forensic
      Practitioners
Crimes against humanity and other war crimes,
      445–456
   attempts to disguise, 367
   forensic investigations, 449–450
   future developments, 451–453
      harmonization of investigative procedures and
         training of forensic experts, 452
      role of forensic and identification evidence in
         international legal proceedings, 452–453
      universality of human rights, 451–452
   international humanitarian law, 447
   legal proceedings, 450–451
   types of crimes, 447–448

Crimewatch, BBC's, 475, 482
Criminal investigations, use of personal effects in, 366
Crohn's disease, 105
CSIA, *see* Compound specific isotope analysis
CT, *see* Computed tomography
CT scanner software, 223
Cushing's disease, 107
Cutting, scarification and, 389, 390

D

DARPA, *see* Defense Advanced Research Projects
            Agency
Database(s)
    biometric information, 420
    CATCHEM, 475
    CMU Motion of Body, 352
    DNA, 19–21, 24, 214, 476
    fingerprint, 214
    footprints, 305
    footwear, 338
    gait, 347–349
    Gait Challenge dataset, 347, 348, 351
    Implantable Cardiac Defibrillator Database, 140,
    iris patterns, 277
    National Pacemaker Database, 140
    National Transplant Database, 132
    NMPH, 429, 435
    noncriminal, 442
    Operational Response Database, 67
    SIP and, 48
    Southampton gait database, 349, 350, 355
    walking factors, 345
Data Protection Act, 421
Date-rape drugs, 159
Daugman algorithms, testing of, 282
Decision environment, 282
Decomposition, 93
    onset of, 244
    soft tissue changes associated with, 242
Defense Advanced Research Projects Agency (DARPA),
            349
Degenerative joint disease, 212
Dental data recording, standard of, 185
Dental identification
    features examined during comparative, 181
    history of, 178
Dental microstructure, age determination and, 208
Dental profiling, 195
Dental radiograph(s), 187, 223
    information provided by, 189
    most common antemortem, 188
    plated fracture site shown on, 189
    poor quality, 188

Dental record(s)
    accuracy of, 180
    antemortem, 179, 180
    conclusions drawn about, 184
    human error and, 179
    Rolex murder, 462
Dental study casts, 190
Dental wax, gluing of skull fragments with, 235, 239
Denture(s), 89
    construction of, 190
    ID marking of, 193
    marking techniques, 193–195
    proving identity with, 192–193
    -wearing victims, 195
Deposited marks, 322
Dermal modification
    permanent tattoos, 382–387
    temporary tattoos, 387–388
DHS, *see* United States Department of Homeland
            Security
Digit, loss of, 120, 121
Digital medical imaging, 225
Digital recording systems, 260
Disability Discrimination Act, 421
Disaster victim identification (DVI), 186
    form used by odontologists, 186
    team, 114
Dismemberment, 125
Distortion-free photographs, 324
Diverticular disease, 105
DNA, 5–27, 119
    allelic dropout, 155
    amplification, 12, 205
    analysis of short tandem repeats, 10–18
        amplification of DNA, 12–14
        collection of biological evidence, 10–11
        detection of amplified PCR products, 15
        development of STR systems, 14–15
        extraction of DNA, 11
        quantification of DNA, 12
        statistical analysis of STR profiles, 16–18
    biometric identifiers and, 417
    databases, 19–21, 24, 476
    double-stranded, 12
    earmark, 73
    evidence
        comparative sample and, 29–30
        disadvantage of, 74
    extraction, 11
    fingerprint, 6
    flanking, 9
    forensic dentistry and, 190–191
    future developments, 23–24
    hair, 154
    heteroplasmy, 155

human genome, 7–8
lawful sampling of, 115
lineage markers, 22–23
mitochondrial, 22, 153, 477
molecule
    components of, 7
    nucleotides of, 8
nail, 155
nonhost sources of, 156
nuclear, 153
personal effects and, 373, 375
polymorphisms, 8–10
presentation of DNA evidence, 18–19
    defendant's fallacy, 19
    prosecutor's fallacy, 19
profiling, 6, 10, 435
quantification, 12
role of forensic geneticist, 6–7
single nucleotide polymorphisms, 21
SNPs and lineage markers, 21
structure, 7
target, 13
Documents, examination of, 289
Dog hair, 148
Drinking water, isotopic composition of, 42, 44
Drug(s)
analysis, soil burial and, 160
body modifications and, 381
isotope data, 37
misuse, 109
use, hair analysis for, 159
DTW, *see* Dynamic time warping
Dumpster diving, 409
DVI, *see* Disaster victim identification
Dynamic time warping (DTW), 355

E

EA, *see* Elemental analyzers
Ear
fidgeting of, 77
modification, transdermal, 394
piercings, varied, 394
stretching, 395
waxes present in, 77
Ear, nose, and throat surgery, 128, 129
Earprints, 73–84
automatic classification and matching, 78–82
digitization of, 78
earprints as identification tool, 73–75
evidence, process of creating, 75, 76
functional, 76, 78
identification system, computerized, 79
individualization, 79
intra-individual variation, 75–78

keypoint matching, 80, 81
limitations of, 74
Ecstasy, 38, 39
Efit composite system, 246
Eigengait, 352
Electron microscopy, hair examination using, 150
Electrostatic lifting, 325
Elemental analysis
IRMS, 32, 34, 35, 36
thermal conversion, 35
Elemental analyzers (EA), 34
Emphysema, 104
Enamel hypoplasia, 196
Endocrine surgeons, 132
Endorphin release, body modification and, 381
Enhanced Border Security and Visa Entry Reform Act
    of 2002, 418
Entomotoxicology, 111
Epidermolysis bullosa, 101
Ethnic identity, 213
European Convention on Human Rights, 421
European Directive on Personal Data Protection of
    1995, 421
European Visa System (E-VIS), 68
Evidence
foot-related, 304
guilt and, 453
imagery, 269
Evidential documentation, forged, 408
E-VIS, *see* European Visa System
Exclusion, identification by, 91, 92, 95
Exclusive-OR (XOR) boolean operator, 276
Explosives, 124, 153
Eyelid reduction, 138

F

Face lift, 138
Face recognition, within-person variability, 271
Face Recognition Technology (FERET) Program, 350
Facial anthropology and reconstruction, 231–255
methods of facial reconstruction, 245–248
    three-dimensional facial reconstruction,
        246–248
    two-dimensional facial reconstruction,
        245–246
presentation of facial reconstruction to general
    public, 248–251
skeletal remains, 233–241
    access to original specimen, 235–237
    three-dimensional skull models from clinical
        imaging, 237–240
    three-dimensional skull models from limited
        two-dimensional data, 240
    two-dimensional images, 240–241

soft tissue remains, 242–245
Facial anthropometry points, common, 238
Facial approximation, see Facial anthropology and
         reconstruction
Facial comparison, 257
Facial implants, 138
Facial landmarks, 263, 265
Facial mapping, 257
Facial morphology, imagery and, 262
Facial muscles, 264
Facial recognition and imagery analysis, 257–270
         criteria for court work, 261–262
         facial morphology, 262–264
         Forensic Imagery Analysis Group, 269–270
         imagery analysis, 258–259
         imagery quality and enhancement, 259–261
         photogrammetry, 264–267
         superimposition of tracing, 267–269
         techniques, 262
Facial recognition software, 435, 440
Facial reconstruction
         automated systems, 248
         depiction, variation in, 250
         forensic artwork and, 439
         photographic realism and, 251
         practitioners
                  background of, 231
                  studies of, 232
         success rates, 232
Fairbank handwriting system, 291
False identities, motivations for, 405
Familial searching, 20
Faraday cup (FC) detectors, 34
FAST, see Fully Automated Seamless Travel
FC detectors, see Faraday cup detectors
FDI system, see Fédération Dentaire International
         system
FDs, see Fourier descriptors
FearID, see Forensic Ear Identification
Federal Trade Commission (FTC), 411
Fédération Dentaire International (FDI) system, 185
FERET Program, see Face Recognition Technology
         Program
Fermentation, body cavity, 244
FHP, see Frankfurt horizontal plane
FIAG, see Forensic Imagery Analysis Group
Fingerprint(s), 57–72, 119
         age of modern fingerprinting, 61–62
         artifacts bearing, 58
         digitized, 418
         dummy, 69
         early beginnings, 57–58
         fingerprint patterns, 63
         fingerprint standard, 62

founders of modern fingerprinting, 58–61
         Galton and Bertillon, 59–60
         Henry and Vucetich, 60–61
         Herschel and Faulds, 58–59
         Henry classification method, 66
         identification process, 62–63
         major disasters, 70–71
         modern biometric identification, 66–70
         ridge characteristics, 64–66
                  analysis, 65
                  chart, 64
                  comparison, 65
                  evaluation, 65
                  verification, 65–66
         templates, 69
         worn-down, 69
Fingerprinting, 59
         burns and, 125
         earliest evidence of, 58
         history of, 57
Firearms, 124
Flanking DNA, 9
Fluoroscopy, 222, 226
Fluorosis, teeth, 196
Foot, 303–320
         additional factors when considering
                  identifications involving footwear,
                  312–313
         comparison of methods, 311
         direct comparison, 307
         how methods should be used in practice, 312
         hyperpronation, 317
         identification from marks of foot on surrounding
                  environment, 306–307
         identification using podiatry treatment records,
                  305–305
         individuality of, 303
         interpretation of footprints and shoe wear,
                  313–318
                  additional considerations in footwear
                           identification, 318
                  confounding effects of foot function, 317
                  excessive footwear length, 315–316
                  inadequate footwear length, 316–317
                  inadequate footwear width, 317
                  toe box variables, 314–315
         measurement and comparison method, 307–310
                  Gunn method, 307
                  optical center approach, 308–309
                  overlay method, 309
                  Robbins method, 310
                  Rossi's podometric system, 310
         outline preparation, 314
         potential future developments, 318
         -related evidence, problems with, 304

shoe wear patterns and, 304
Footprint(s)
    database, 305
    digital photography–based methods of capturing, 313
    evaluation methods, comparison of, 312
Footwear
    databases, 338
    identification, 312, 318
    items, comparison of marks and, 338
    length
        excessive, 315
        inadequate, 316
    photography, 324
    width, inadequate, 317
Footwear marks, 321–341
    casting of, 325
    chemical methods associated with development of, 326
    comparison, finger mark comparison and, 341
    definition of, 324
    footwear marks at crime scene, 322–323
        compression, 322
        surface changes, 322–323
        transfer, 322
    index, 336
    locating marks, 323
    pattern, 327
    recovery and enhancement of footwear marks, 323–324
    selection of methods for enhancement and recovery, 324–341
        comparison of marks and footwear items, 338–341
        footwear mark intelligence indices, 335–336
        information from footwear marks, 327–335
        other aspects of footwear databases, 338
        photography and illumination, 324–325
        physical methods, 325–326
        using footwear marks index, 336–337
    size of, 330, 331
Forced-coupled-oscillator model, 354
FORDISC2.0 system, 213
Forensic dentistry, definition of, 177
Forensic Ear Identification (FearID), 77, 79
Forensic geneticist, role of, 6
Forensic genetics, DNA polymorphisms used in, 8
Forensic Imagery Analysis Group (FIAG), 269
Forensic imagery analyst, knowledge base of, 259
Forensic investigations
    clandestine, 450
    legal context, 449
    security risks, 449
Forensic odontology, definition of, 177
Forgery, 408

Fourier descriptors (FDs), 355
Fourier transformed infrared spectroscopy (FTIR), 39
Frankfurt horizontal plane (FHP), 241
Fraud
    application, 409
    dental identification, 185
    identity, 408
    law relating to, 411
Fraud Advisory Panel, 412
Frequentist approach, DNA evidence and, 18
Friction skin, layers of, 63
Frieze patterns, 352
FTC, see Federal Trade Commission
FTIR, see Fourier transformed infrared spectroscopy
Fully Automated Seamless Travel (FAST), 68
Functional earprints, 76, 78
Function creep, biometric identity cards and, 420

G

Gabor filter, 275, 276
Gabor wavelets, 275
Gait, 343–362
    advantages as biometric, 346
    available databases, 347–349
        Gait Challenge Dataset, 347–349
        Southampton Gait Database, 349
    biometrics, 355
    databases, 359
    definition of, 344–345
    early approaches and proof of concept, 345–346
    features of, 344
    gait as biometric, 346–347
    motivation and feasibility, 344
    progress in gait recognition, 349–359
        future directions, 358–359
        Human ID Program, 349–354
        other contemporary work, 354–358
    recognition, definition of, 343
    signature, 346
    symmetricity of, 354
Gallstones, 106, 214Gait Challenge dataset, 347, 348, 351
Gas chromatography (GC), 34
    capillary, 36
    high-resolution capillary, 36
Gastroesophageal reflux (GOR), 195
Gastrointestinal tract, diseases in, 105
Gaussian-based motion model, 356
Gaussian clustering, 347
GC, see Gas chromatography
Gelatin lifting, 325, 326
General public, presentation of facial reconstructions to, 248

General surgery, 129, 131
Genes, 8
Geneticist, forensic, role of, 6
Genetics, forensic, DNA polymorphisms used in, 8
Geneva Convention
    breaches of, 367
    international humanitarian law and, 447
Genome
    definition of, 7
    mtDNA, 22
Genotype proportions, 17
Geographical information system (GIS) maps, 43
Geographic proxy data, 47
GHB, 159
GIS maps, *see* Geographical information system maps
Global Network for Isotopes in Precipitation (GNIP),
        45
Global terrorism, fears of, 68
GNIP, *see* Global Network for Isotopes in
        Precipitation
GOR, *see* Gastroesophageal reflux
Graffiti, 289
Green hair, 150–151
Guided hand signatures, 295
Guilt, evidence and, 453
Gunn foot measurement method, 307
Gunshot
    injuries, 124
    residues, presence of in hair, 153
    trauma, skull fragmentation and, 215

H

Hair
    growth, 148, 157
    light microscopy of, 150
    morphological traits, 150
    permanent curling of, 151
    peroxide bleaching, 155
    shaft, anatomy of, 149
    structural chemistry of, 150
    style, cultural practices and, 151
    types, 148
    weathering, 151
Hair and nail, 147–174
    biomolecular evidence from hair and nail, 153–156
        DNA from hair, 154–155
        DNA from nail, 155–156
        heteroplasmy and allelic dropout, 155
        nonhost sources of DNA from nail, 156
        what DNA can do, 153–154
    hair and nail growth as record of recent life history,
        156–160
        record of drug use or exposure to pollutants,
        159–160

            time-resolved information for diet and
                location, 157–158
        increasingly important resources to identification
            scientist, 147–148
        integrity of tissue samples, 160–161
        physical and chemical evidence, 150–153
            environmental evidence, 152
            explosives and gunshot residues, 153
            form, style, color, and other traits, 150–151
            hair and nails as source of residual information,
                151
            shampoos, conditioners, and other cosmetic
                products, 152
        structure of hair and nail, 148–150
Hamming distance, 276, 277, 281
Hand
    geometry, 417
    reattachment of, 135
    surgery, 134
Handwriting, 289–300
    analysis of inks, 298–299
    Briem system, 291
    differing from conventional formation, 292
    disguised, 293
    earlier records of, 289
    factors affecting, 293
    Fairbank system, 291
    future of handwriting analysis, 299–300
    handwriting and identification of handwriting,
        290–298
        handwriting instruments, 296–298
        signatures, 294–296
        teaching, identification, and variation, 290–294
    natural variation in, 290
    reason for examining, 291
    simulated, 294
    striation in, 297
    systems, style characteristics of, 291
    teaching of, 291
Haplotype frequencies, measurement of, 23
Hardy Weinberg equilibrium, 17, 18
Hatch-Slack cycle, 32, 33
Heart, brown atrophy, 104
Heat branding, 389
Heel-to-toe measurements, 307
Henna art, 387
Henry fingerprint classification method, 66
Hidden Markov Models (HMMs), 352, 356
High performance liquid chromatography (HPLC),
        299
High-resolution capillary gas chromatography
        (HRcGC), 36
Hip replacements, 144
Histoplasmosis, 100
HMMs, *see* Hidden Markov Models
Hobbies, localized abnormalities and, 122

HOCM, *see* Hypertrophic obstructive cardiomyopathy
Homicide, use of personal effects in investigation, 366
Horn of Africa, 47
Host state, 449
Hot branding, 389
Hough transform (HT) modification, 345
House of Lords Select Committee Report on Science and Technology, 216
HPLC, *see* High performance liquid chromatography
HRcGC, *see* High-resolution capillary gas chromatography
HT modification, *see* Hough transform modification
Human bone, identification of, 200
Human genome, 7
Human ID Program, 347, 349
Human motion, studies of, 344
Human rights, universality of, 451
Human sacrifices, mass, 480
Human tissue
    light element isotopes in, 42
    radiogenic trace element isotopes in, 47
Hurricane Katrina, loss of medical infrastructure following, 366
Hutchinson's incisors, 196
Hyaline cartilage ossification, 212
Hypertrophic obstructive cardiomyopathy (HOCM), 103–104
Hypervariable regions, 22
Hypostasis, 92

I

IAEA, *see* International Atomic Energy Agency
IBM, biometrics identifiers and, 68
ICAO, *see* International Civil Aviation Organization
ICC, *see* International Criminal Court
ICC Statute, category of crimes against humanity in, 448
ICMP, *see* International Commission of Missing Persons
ICP-MS, *see* Inductively coupled plasma–mass spectrometry
ICRC, *see* International Committee of the Red Cross
ICTY, *see* International Criminal Tribunals for the Former Yugoslavia
Identification
    biometric, 407, 415
    by exclusion, 91, 92, 95
    CCTV systems and, 261
    criteria, primary, 119
    footwear, 318
    knowledge-based, 407
    methods, soft tissues and, 222
    problems with using personal effects for, 374

theory of, 407
token-based, 407
trauma as aid to, 120
trauma as hindrance to, 123
Identikit composite system, 246
Identity cards, 416, 418
Identity Cards Bill, U.K., 419
Identity fraud and theft, 405–414
    definition of identity theft, 406–410
        identification, 407–408
        identity fraud, 408–409
        identity theft, 409–410
        personal data, 406–407
        types of identity theft and fraud, 408
    responding to Britain's fastest growing crime, 411–412
    victims of identity theft and fraud, 410
IIK, *see* Inkless impression kit
Ilizarov bone distraction, 133
Illegal immigration
    fears of, 68
    identity theft and, 406, 412
Illumination, photographic, 324
Imagery, 257
    analysis, 258, 259
    categories of, 262
    flicker, 267
    matching, 268
    recognition vs. identification, 258
    stereoscopy, 260
    superimposition of, 267, 268
    transitory differences, 267
    wiping, 267
Immigration Act, 421
Implantable Cardiac Defibrillator Database, 140
Implanted device, registries for, 140
Implant materials, 139
Incident location, identification of, 365
Incised wound, 118
Incisor teeth, 182
Individualization, definition of, 74
Inductively coupled plasma–mass spectrometry (ICP-MS), 39
Industrial disease, pathology of, 108
Information Age, identity theft in, 405
Information vacuum, 92
Injection scarification, 390
Ink(s)
    analysis of, 298
    glooping, 297
Inkless impression kit (IIK), 77
Inkless start, ballpoint pen, 297
Insulin-dependent diabetes, 106
International Atomic Energy Agency (IAEA), 31
International Civil Aviation Organization (ICAO), 70

International Commission of Missing Persons
    (ICMP), 446
International Committee of the Red Cross (ICRC),
    450, 451
International Criminal Court (ICC), 447
International Criminal Tribunals for the Former
    Yugoslavia (ICTY), 446
International humanitarian law, 447
    breaches of, 445
    Geneva Convention and, 447
International Missing Children's Day, 429
Internet
    child victimization on, 437
    criminal enterprise facilitated by, 406
Interpol DVI forms, 116, 186
Interventional cardiology, 139
Interventional radiology, 225
Intravenous drug misuse, endocarditis and, 109
Iris
    color, determination of, 274
    formation, 273
    recognition
        algorithms, 274
        decision environment for, 283, 284
        most promising aspect of, 272
    texture, 417
IrisCode(s)
    comparisons, distribution of, 281
    dissimilarity between, 276
    extreme value distribution, 279
Iris patterns, identifying persons by, 271–285
    anatomy, physiology, and development of iris,
        272–274
    database, 277
    decidability of iris recognition, 282–284
    encoding, 275
    examples, 273
    iris feature extraction and encoding, 274–276
    matching algorithm for iris comparisons, 276–277
    observed false match rates, 281–282
    results from 200 billion cross-comparisons,
        277–281
        comparisons of different irides without
            rotations, 278–279
        comparisons of genetically identical irides, 279
        database, 277–278
        distribution of best matches after multiple
            rotations, 279–281
IRMS, see Isotope ratio mass spectrometers
Isotope(s)
    abundances, 30
    analysis
        bulk material stable, 34
        compound specific, 36
    calibration, 35

effects, 31
    reference gas, 34
    stable, physical evidence and, 37
Isotope ratio mass spectrometers (IRMS), 33
    continuous flow, 41, 34
    elemental analysis, 32, 34, 35, 36
    instrumentation, sensitivity of, 33

J

Japanese body suit, 384
Joint replacement, 133, 135
Juvenile skeleton
    age determination, 208
    sexual dimorphism in, 205

K

Kaposi's sarcoma, 100
Keloid
    formation, 117
    scarring, 388
Keyhole surgery, 225
Keypoint matching, 80, 81
Kinetic isotope effect, most significant, 31
Kings Cross Underground fire, 94
Knowledge-based identification, 407
Kosovo
    recovery of victims, 446
    temporary graveyard at, 452

L

Laceration, 117
Laptop computers, fingerprint sensors and, 69
Laryngeal cartilage ossification, 212
Latent fingermarks, 66
Lawsonia inermis, 387
LCN, see Low copy number
Legal proceedings
    DNA evidence and, 19
    examination of skeletal remains and, 216
    international investigations, 450, 452
    silicone gel implants and, 142
Leisure activities, localized abnormalities and, 122
Liability, evidence and, 453
Lifted marks, 322
Lights out processing, 66, 67
Likelihood ratio, 18
Limb
    bones, ethnic identity from, 213
    loss of, 120
Lineage markers, SNPs and, 21
Liposuction, 137
Lip piercing, 396

Lividity, 242
Livor mortis, 242
Low copy number (LCN), 14
Luminol™, 326
Lung fibrosis, 109

M

Madrid train bombers, 419
Magnetic resonance imaging (MRI), 223
Major incidents
    categories of, 94
    fingerprints and, 70
Malpighian layer, 58
Manubriosternal joint, sclerotic fusion of, 212
Mass fatalities
    identification parameters, 114
    investigation, radiography imaging provision in, 222
    temporary mortuaries for, 116
Massive pulmonary fibrosis, 108
Mass spectrometers (MS), 33
Mastectomy scar, 136
Maxillofacial surgery, 129, 134, 138
MDMA, 38
Medical images, superimposed, 226
Members of Service, World Trade Center, 487
Memory
    effects, 297
    loss, 178
Mendelian genetics, second law of, 18
Mendhi, 387
Methamphetamine, detection of, 159
Microsoft, biometrics identifiers and, 68
Military tattoos, 384
Milk cartons, missing persons publicized on, 430
Minimum number of individuals (MNI), 203
Missing persons, see also United Kingdom, missing
        persons in
    adults, 428
    definition of, 426
    families of, 432
    long-term, forensic artwork and, 437
    nonvulnerable cases, 427
    publicized cases, 430
    reasons people go missing, 428
    unreported, 427
Missing phenomenon, 442
Mitochondrial DNA (mtDNA), 22, 153, 477
MNI, see Minimum number of individuals
Moor's Murders, 201
Mortuaries, visual identification of bodies in, 94
Motion
    analysis, 344
    model, Gaussian-based, 356

Mottling of the enamel, 196
MRI, see Magnetic resonance imaging
Mr. Punch-like appearance, 89
MS, see Mass spectrometers
mtDNA, see Mitochondrial DNA
Mulberry molars, 196
Multiplexing, 14
Mummification, 93, 244
Murder victims, stable isotope profiling of, 43, 45
Muscle
    tissue, ATP in, 242
    wasting, central nervous system disease and, 107
Muti murders, 475
Mycobacterium fortuitum infection, 381
Myocardial infarction, 103

N

NAA, see Neutron activation analysis
Nail(s), see also Hair and nail
    bed, anatomy of, 149
    decontamination protocols, 160
    DNA from, 155
    growth rates, 157
    structural chemistry of, 150
National Breast Implant Registry, 140
National Center for Missing and Exploited Children
        (NCMEC), 437
National Crime Faculty, 431
National DNA Database (NDNAD), 442, 476, 477
National Fingerprint Evidence Standard Project
        Board, 64
National Health Service (NHS), 133, 180–184
    defrauding of, 185
    dentistry, under-funding of, 180–184
    hip replacements performed by, 133
National Institute of Standards and Technology
        (NIST), 347
National Joint Registry, 140
National Missing Persons Day, 429
National Missing Persons Helpline (NMPH), 426
    database, 429, 435
    identification and reconstruction department of,
        435
    missing adults, 428
    role of, 429
    website, 429, 431
National Pacemaker Database, 140
National Police Protocol, 429
National Transplant Database, 132
Navel piercing, 398
NCMEC, see National Center for Missing and
        Exploited Children
NDNAD, see National DNA Database
Negative marks, 322

Negative watch list, 277
Neonatal sternum, ossification in, 209
Neurosurgery, 129, 132
Neutron activation analysis (NAA), 160, 299
New Scotland Yard, Police National Missing Persons
        Bureau, 426
NGO, *see* Nongovernmental organization
NHS, *see* National Health Service
9-11 Commission Report, 485, 486
NIST, *see* National Institute of Standards and
        Technology
NMPH, *see* National Missing Persons Helpline
Noncriminal database, 442
Nongovernmental organization (NGO), 426, 427, 435
Nonsurgical specialties, 130
North West Arthroplasty Register, 140
Nose job, 137
Nuclear DNA (nuDNA), 153, 154
nuDNA, *see* Nuclear DNA

O

Obstetrics and gynecology, 129, 132
Occupational disorders, 108
Occupational trauma, 120
OCME, *see* Office of Chief Medical Examiner
Odontology, 119, 177–198
    age assessment using teeth, 191–192
    dental charts and charting systems, 184–185
    dental profiling, 195–196
    dental radiographs, 187–190
    dentures and denture marking, 192–193
    example of best practice, 185–187
    inclusion marking technique, 194–195
    other problems encountered with dental
        identification, 185
    problems encountered when using teeth for
        postmortem identification purposes,
        179–184
    surface marking techniques, 193–194
    use of DNA in forensic dentistry, 190–191
    use of study casts to aid postmortem
        identification, 190
Office of Chief Medical Examiner (OCME), 487
Onychomycosis, 151
Operational Response Database (ORD), 67
Ophthalmic surgery, 129, 133
Opiates, detection of, 159
OPTs, *see* Orthopantomograms
ORD, *see* Operational Response Database
Organ decomposition, 100
Organic compound, retention index, 37
Organized crime, identity theft and, 406
Orthognathic surgery, 138
Orthopantomograms (OPTs), 189, 190

Orthopedic companies, logos for, 142
Orthopedic implants, 133
Orthopedic manufacturers, U.K., 141
Orthopedic surgery, 129, 133
Osseous integration, 144
Osteology, 199–219
    age at death, 205–212
        adults, 210–212
        juveniles, 207–210
        young adults, 210
    biological identity, 202
    determination of sex, 203–205
        adults, 203–205
        juveniles, 205
    ethnic identity, 213–214
    positive identification of personal identity,
        214–216
    stature, 212–213
Osteomyelitis, 381
Otolaryngology, 128

P

Pacemaker, 214
Paint, testing of, 38
Pancreas, autolysis of, 106
Pancreatitis, 106
Paper exercise, 90, 91
Partial identity theft, 408
Passwords, 415, 422
Paternity testing, DNA profiling and, 6
Pathologist, role in identification, 114
PCA, *see* Principal components analysis
PCR, *see* Polymerase chain reaction
PDB standard, *see* Pee Dee Belemnite standard
PECAM-1 gene, 153
Pediatric surgery, 129, 132
Pee Dee Belemnite (PDB) standard, 30
Pen movement, 292
Periodic Table of Elements, 30
Perpetrator height, earprint location and, 73
Personal data, definition of, 406
Personal effects, 365–377
    cleaning and drying area for, 370
    confidentiality agreements and, 370
    cross-contamination of, 375
    damage to, 374
    definition of, 365, 371
    emotional values of, 368
    identification using personal effects, 369–373
        comparison of antemortem records and
            postmortem personal effects, 373
        direct comparison of personal effects, 372–373
        personal effects and DNA, 373
        personal effects management, 369–372

management
  care of bereaved, 372
  on-site collection, 369
  processing point, 369
  starting point, 369
  problems with using personal effects for
    identification, 374–375
  significance of, 365–368
    family members and next of kin, 368
    identification contexts, 365–367
    individual, 367–368
  transcription problems, 371
Personal identity, forensic osteologist and, 214
Persuasive data, 407
3-PGA, see 3-Phosphoglycerate
Phishing, 409
Pholcodine, 475, 476
3-Phosphoglycerate (3-PGA), 32
Photogrammetric facial landmark alignment, 266
Photogrammetry, definition of, 264
Photographs, distortion-free, 324
Photography, footwear, 324
PHR, see Physicians for Human Rights
Physical appearance, 87–97
  collection of information, 89–90
  discussion, 93–96
  elements composing, 88, 89
  lack of specificity of, 87
  making identification, 90–92
  nature of physical appearances, 87–89
  postmortem changes, 92–93
Physicians for Human Rights (PHR), 450
Piano Man, 433
Piercing(s), 122
  anatomical locations, 395
  ear, varied, 394
  equipment, manual, 395
  lip, 396
  navel, 398
PIT, see Principle of identical treatment
Plain film radiography, 223
Plantar prints, 307
Plastic surgery, 129, 134, 137
PNC, see Police National Computer
Pneumoconiosis, 108
PNMPB, see Police National Missing Persons Bureau
Podiatry treatment records, foot identification using,
  305
Police National Computer (PNC), 428, 459
Police National Missing Persons Bureau (PNMPB),
  426
Police procedures, missing persons, 428
Police Service Northern Ireland (PSNI), 43
Polymerase chain reaction (PCR), 12, 13, 153
  products

  amplified, 15
  labeled, 16
  real-time, 12
Positive marks, 322
Postmortem dental identification, 178
Posture, bones and, 121
Pre-existing medical condition, identification of, 214
Primary identification criteria, 119
Primary identifiers, 408
Primary isotope effect, 31
Principal components analysis (PCA), 345, 347, 353
Principle of identical treatment (PIT), 40
Privacy, globalization and, 413
Profit composite system, 246
Prohibition of Female Circumcision Act, 382
Prostatic carcinoma, 106
PSNI, see Police Service Northern Ireland
Psychological stress, 114
Ptosis, 137
Putrefaction, 151, 244
PyGC, see Pyrolysis-gas chromatography
Pyrolysis-gas chromatography (PyGC), 39, 152

Q

QC, see Quality controls
QUAD, 14
Quality controls (QC), 35
Quality switched lasers, tattoo removal using, 386

R

Race Relations Act, 421
Radiography, 221–228
  dental, 223
    human profiling and radiography, 224
    plain film, 223
    radiography procedures in identification of
      human remains, 222–223
    role of radiographer in identification of human
      remains, 224
Raman spectroscopy, 39, 299
Rameses II, facial reconstruction of, 243
RCMP, see Royal Canadian Mounted Police
Real-time PCR, 12
Recent life history, hair and nail growth as record of,
  156
Recreational drugs, 109
Renal carcinoma, 106
Repetitive strain injuries, 121
Retention index, organic compound, 37
Rheumatic heart disease, 104
Rhinoplasty, 137
Ribs, methods for aging, 211

Rigor mortis, 242
Ritual tooth mutilation, 183
Robbins foot measurement method, 310
Rolex murder (southwest England), 459–471
    arrest, 465
    cell site analysis, 463
    Crown Prosecution Service, 466
    dental chart, 462
    documentation seized, 467
    enquiries made, 463
    Exeter Crown Court, 470
    fingerprints taken, 468, 469
    fraud, 470
    GPS, 467
    Malkerry fishing trawler, 460, 466
    media assistance, 460
    Rolex manufacturers, 460
    Ronald Joseph Platt, 461, 462
    Royal Canadian Mounted Police, 469
Roller ball pen, development of, 296
Rossi's podometric system, 310
Royal Canadian Mounted Police (RCMP), 305
Runaways, 427, 429

S

Sacroiliac joint, changes in appearance of, 211
Safety matches, SIP and, 39
Salabrasion, 386
Saponification, 244
SATRA, *see* Shoe and Allied Trades Research
    Association
Scanning electron microscopy (SEM), 299
Scar(s)
    assessment, 143
    burn, 136
    surgery and, 128
    variables, laboratory-based, 144
Scarification, 388
    body etching, 390
    branding, 389
    cutting, 389
    injection, 390
Scene of crime (SOC), 19
Scotland Yard, Fingerprint Department at, 62
Sebaceous cysts, 101
Seborrhoeic keratosis, 101
Secondary/confirmatory identifiers, 408
Second Generation Multiplex (SGM), 14
Selected ion monitoring (SIM), 33
Self-harm, 427
Self-inflicted injury, 122
SEM, *see* Scanning electron microscopy
Senile dementia, commonest type of, 101

September 11 (2001), *see* World Trade Center
    (September 11, 2001)
Serious Crime Group South, 473
Sex
    determination, 203
    identity, soft tissue pathology and, 111
SGM, *see* Second Generation Multiplex
SGM Plus kit, 15, 16, 21
Shampoos, additives to, 152
Shoe(s)
    degrees of wear, 331, 333–334, 338
    establishment of make of, 327
    footwear marks and, 327
    manufacturers, size variations among, 315
        generic patterns on, 330
    manufacturing defects, 335
    tread damage, 340
    tread pattern of, 327, 328, 329, 332, 335
    wear, interpretation of, 313
Shoe and Allied Trades Research Association
    (SATRA), 304
Short tandem repeats (STRs), 9
    amplification of DNA
    collection of biological evidence, 10
    detection of amplified PCR products, 15
    development of STR systems, 14
    extraction of DNA, 11
    loci, analysis of, 417
    profiles
        allelic frequencies, 17
        Hardy Weinberg equilibrium, 17, 18
        product rule, 17
    quantification of DNA, 12
    statistical analysis of STR profiles, 16
SIA, *see* Stable isotope analysis
Signature(s)
    examination, line quality and, 295
    guided hand, 295
    identification of, 294
Silhouette
    quality, 358
    sequence, 357
Silicone gel implants, legal hysteria surrounding, 142
SIM, *see* Selected ion monitoring
Single nucleotide polymorphisms (SNPs), 10, 21
Sinus patterns, human variation in, 222
SIP, *see* Stable isotope profiling
Skeletal remains, facial reconstruction and, 233
Skeleton
    age-related changes in, 205
    juvenile
        age determination, 208
        sexual dimorphism in, 205
        sex determination in, 205

Skin
    age-related changes in, 101
    color, change of, 96
    grafting sites, 118
Skull(s)
    assessment guidelines, 233
    bones of, 234
    differences between male and female, 204
    fragmentation, gunshot trauma ad, 215
    models
        three-dimensional, 237, 241
        two-dimensional data and, 240
    reassembly
        computerized, 240
        manual, 235
    replication, mold-making and, 237
    symmetry, 235
    visualization, methods of, 233–234
Sleeper navel piercing, 398
Smartcards, 68
SMOW standard, see Standard Mean Ocean Water
        standard
SNPs, see Single nucleotide polymorphisms
SOC, see Scene of crime
Soccer players, cartilage injuries to, 121
Soft tissue pathology, 99–111
    age-related changes and, 101–107
        biliary system, 105–106
        cardiovascular system, 102–104
        central nervous system, 101–102
        endocrine system, 107
        gastrointestinal system, 105
        genitourinary system, 106
        lymphoreticular system, 107
        musculoskeletal system, 107
        respiratory system, 104
        skin, 101
    occupational disorders, 108–111
        drug misuse, 109–110
        pathology of industrial disease, 108–109
        sex identity and soft tissue pathology, 111
        toxicology, 110–111
    usefulness in biological human identification, 100
Soft tissue trauma, 113–126
    identification criteria and documentation, 118–120
    role of pathologist in identification, 114–116
    trauma as aid to identification, 120–123
        accidents and assaults, 122
        body modifications, 122
        hobbies and leisure activities, 122
        medical intervention, 122–123
        occupational trauma, 120–121
        posture, 121
        self-inflicted injury, 122

    trauma as hindrance to identification, 123–125
        blunt trauma, 124
        burns, 125
        dismemberment, 125
        explosives, 124
        firearms, 124
        transportation, 124
    types of trauma, 116–118
        abrasion, 116–117
        bruise, 117
        burn, 118
        incised wound, 118
        laceration, 117
Soil, SIP and, 41
South Africa, muti murders in, 475
Southampton gait database, 349, 350, 355
Southeast Asia tsunami, 120, 214
    dental identification and, 178
    fingerprints and, 70
Spleen, diseased, 107
Spot welders, trauma to, 121
Squamous cell carcinoma, 101
Stable isotope analysis (SIA), 34
Stable isotope fingerprinting, 29–53
    analysis at natural abundance level, 33–37
        instrumentation, 34–37
        principal considerations, 33–34
    background on stable isotopes, 30–31
    caveats, 48
    forensic applications of stable isotope profiling,
        37–47
        human identification, 41–47
        physical evidence, 37–41
    isotope effects, mass discrimination, and isotopic
        fractionation, 31–33
Stable isotope profiling (SIP), 30, 37
    adhesive tape, 39
    global databases and, 48
    human identification and, 41
    murder victims, 43, 45
    paint, 38
    physical evidence and, 38
    safety matches, 39
    soil, 41
Standard Mean Ocean Water (SMOW) standard, 31
Stature, estimation of, 213
Stereoscopes, 260
Steroid use, long-term, 107
STRs, see Short tandem repeats
Subdermal implants
    beading, 391
    3D body art, 391
Sudden infant death syndrome, 208
Suicide, 366, 427
Superimposition, imagery, 267, 268

Supernumerary tooth, 182, 183
Surgical intervention, 127–146
    biological changes, 143–144
    implant material, 139–142
    scars associated with, 130, 131, 133, 135, 138
    surgical specialties, 128–139
        cardiothoracic surgery, 128
        ear, nose, and throat surgery, 128–131
        general surgery, 131–132
        neurosurgery, 132
        nonsurgical specialties that operate, 139
        obstetrics and gynecology, 132
        ophthalmology, 133
        orthopedic surgery, 133–134
        pediatric surgery, 132
        plastic surgery and maxillofacial surgery,
            134–138
        urology, 138–139
Surgical prostheses, 123
Survivors, rights of, 453
Swanson's arthroplasty implants, 135
System of podometrics, foot as, 310

T

Tamil Kavadi festival of penance, 396–397
Taphonomy, 160, 201, 491–493
Target DNA, 13
Tattoo(s)
    faded, 385
    Japanese body suit, 384
    military, 384
    permanent, 382–387
    procedure, 385
    removal, 386
    temporary, 387–388
    value and power of, 383
    white, 390
TC/EA, *see* Thermal conversion EA
TDI, *see* Time since death interval
Terrorism, identity theft and, 412
Terrorist events, use of personal effects to investigate,
    375
Tetracycline staining, 182, 196
Theft Act of 1968, 411
Therapeutic drugs, presence of in hair, 159
Thermal conversion EA (TC/EA), 35
Thermodynamic isotope effects, 31
Thin layer chromatography (TLC), 299
Three-dimensional facial reconstruction
    computerized, 248, 249, 251
    manual, 246–248
Thumb stool, 66
Time since death interval (TDI), 201, 202
Tissue grafting, 134

TLC, *see* Thin layer chromatography
Token-based identification, 407
Tongue piercing, 395, 396
Tooth (teeth)
    age assessment using, 191
    DNA amplification from 205
    doctors, unqualified, 180
    eruption, 192, 207
    fluorosis of, 196
    incisor, 182
    jewelry, 183
    mineral material in, 43
    mottling of enamel, 196
    mutilation, ritual, 183
    notations, worldwide, 179
    replacement, 89
    supernumerary, 182, 183
    surface loss (TSL), 183
    tetracycline staining of, 182
Total identity theft, 408
Toxic shock syndrome, 381
Trabecular bone loss, 212
Transdermal modification, 392
    ear, 394
    key terms, 393
    procedure, 394
Transposing the conditional, 19
Trauma
    abrasion, 116
    blunt, 124
    bruise, 117
    burn, 118
    incised wound, 118
    laceration, 117
    occupational, 120
Trephination, 132
TSL, *see* Tooth surface loss
Tuberculosis, 100, 104
Two-dimensional facial reconstruction
    computerized, 246
    manual, 245, 246

U

Unidentified cases
    DNA profiling of, 435, 441
    ethnic appearance distribution of, 434
    gender distribution of, 433
    long-term, 432
    procedures for identification, 434
United Kingdom
    armed forces dental service, dental chart used by,
        187
    biometric identity cards in, 419
    Defence Dental Services, 185

Freedom of Information Act, 421
Heart Valve Registry, 140
Hydrocephalus Shunt Registry, 140
Identity Cards Bill, 419
Ionisation Radiations Regulations, 224
missing persons, high-profile cases, 426
National Transplant Database, 132
orthopedic manufacturers in, 141
Passport Service, 420
paternity testing, 6
regulation of immigration in, 419
STR systems, 14
United Kingdom, missing persons in, 425–443
appendix, 443
coordinated response to missing persons, 431
forensic artwork, 436–440
age progression, image enhancement, and
long-term missing persons, 437
facial reconstruction, 439–440
postmortem composites, 439
unidentified individuals, 437
identification and reconstruction department of
NMPH, 435
identification within context of missing persons,
432
long-term unidentified, 432–433
NMPH's national database, 435–436
other identification techniques, 440–442
DNA, 441–442
facial recognition software, 440–441
police procedures for missing persons, 428–429
role of National Missing Persons Helpline,
429–431
scale of missing problem, 426–427
standard procedures for identification, 434–435
who goes missing, 427–428
abductions, 427–428
missing adults, 428
young people, 427
who the unidentified are, 433–434
why people go missing, 428
United Nations
Commission on Human Rights 2006, 451
Security Council (UNSC), 447
United States Department of Homeland Security
(DHS), 282
Universality of human rights, 451
UNSC, see United Nations Security Council
Unterzaucher reaction, 34–35
Urban primitive, 383
Urology, 129, 138

V

Valvular heart disease, 104

Vancouver Scale, 143
Variable number tandem repeats (VNTRs), 9
Vascular surgeons, 132
Vector template matching, 79
Velocity moments, 354
VH, see Visual hull
Video, stereo from, 261
Video spectral comparator (VSC), 298
Vienna PDB (VPDB) standard, 30
Vienna-SMOW (VSMOW) standard, 31
Viewpoint-invariant body modelling, 359
Visual hull (VH), 356
Visual identification, use as confirmatory process, 90
VNTRs, see Variable number tandem repeats
VPDB standard, see Vienna PDB standard
VSC, see Video spectral comparator
VSMOW standard, see Vienna-SMOW standard

W

Walker signature, 354
Walking, unique way of, 343
War crimes, see Crimes against humanity and other
war crimes
War zone, personal effects in, 367
Website
copycat, 409
NMPH, 429, 431
Wefts, 151
White tattoo, 390
Whole body suspension, 397
Womb stones, 106
World Trade Center (September 11, 2001), 485–499
Anthropological Verification Project and final
anthropological review, 493–495
considerations of taphonomy, 491–493
DNA analysis, 21, 490, 493
documentation, 495
Final Anthropological Review, 495, 497
Freshkills landfill site, 487, 488
Ground Zero, 486, 487, 488
hot spots, 492
human remains processing, 488–489
identified-as-linked cases, 494
Memorial Park, 490
9-11 Commission Report, 485, 486
number of cases created, 494
number of people killed, 495
Office of Chief Medical Examiner, 487
open population at, 487
personal effects, 373
process of identification, 487–490
separation of Members of Service, 487
South Tower collapse, 486
subterranean fires, 486

temporary body collection point, 487
    temporary mortuary, 487
Wound healing, effect on soft tissues, 128
Writing, *see* Handwriting
Writing instrument, basic, 296

X

X chromosome, 8
XOR boolean operator, *see* Exclusive-OR boolean
    operator

X-ray, *see also* Radiography
    diffraction (XRD), 299
    fluorescence (XRF), 299
    imaging, principles of, 221
XRD, *see* X-ray diffraction
XRF, *see* X-ray fluorescence
XT plots, 346

Y

Y chromosome, 8, 23, 477, 478